Marketing Management
Text and Cases

Wiley/Hamilton Series In Marketing
David A. Aaker, Advisor Editor

MARKETING MANAGEMENT
Text and Cases

Douglas J. Dalrymple
Indiana University
Leonard J. Parsons
Georgia Institute of Technology

A Wiley/Hamilton Publication

JOHN WILEY & SONS, INC.
Santa Barbara · New York · London · Sydney · Toronto

Library of Congress Cataloging in Publication Data:

Dalrymple, Douglas J.
  Marketing management.

  (Wiley marketing series)
  Includes bibliographical references and indexes.
  1. Marketing management. 2. Marketing management—Case studies. I. Parsons, Leonard J., joint
author. II. Title.
HF5415.13.D32   658.8   75-35760
ISBN 0-471-19130-2

10 9 8 7 6 5

Preface

This book is intended for use in marketing management courses at both the under-graduate and graduate levels. We believe that a combination of text and cases provides an ideal mixture to help students improve their decisions on product development, pricing, promotion, and physical distribution. The text furnishes the background and tools necessary to attack marketing problems, and the cases supply practical experience in analyzing and making decisions in real business situations. There is no better way to learn how to make marketing decisions than to have students work out solutions to actual marketing problems. Combination text and casebooks have been pioneered in the marketing field by Hansen and by Davis, and our book follows in this tradition.

Perhaps the most distinctive feature of our book is the emphasis on data-based decision making. We want to show how marketing information can be manipulated to gain insight for the control of marketing programs. To do this, we have included some concepts that help define the operation of various market processes. Our discussion is straightforward and emphasizes practical applications rather than abstract theory. We also show how marketing programs are integrated with the central planning activities that are being developed to guide business organizations.

The text discusses the role of marketing in business and society and then reviews the types of activities performed by marketing executives. Next we consider social responsi-bility and how businessmen are expected to relate to stockholders, employees, the environment, and customers. Chapter Two discusses the decision-making process and the gathering of data within a marketing environment. Chapter Three examines a variety of approaches to demand forecasting and analysis. In Chapter Four we introduce the concept of segmentation and explain why businessmen divide customers into subgroups so that they can be approached separately. Business success depends on attracting customers and understanding how and why they make purchases. Chapter Five reviews the theory of buyer behavior and shows how these ideas can be used to plan marketing programs. Chapters Six and Seven are concerned with the product decisions made by the firm with emphasis on how new products are developed and how they are controlled after they have been introduced. Chapter Eight introduces a variety of pricing strategies to provide the student with background for making decisions in this area. Chapter Nine focuses on the problem of creating efficient distribution systems for different types of products and organizations. The accent is on selecting channels and physical handling procedures that maximize sales and minimize cost. In Chapter Ten we cover the subject of advertising. The major concern is with the size of budgets and the allocation of funds among different promotional activities and advertising media. In Chapter Eleven we deal with the problems of organizing and controlling sales personnel. Finally, Chapter Twelve brings together all of the elements of the marketing mix and integrates them with the objectives of the firm. The stress is on using information systems and decision models to help plan and control marketing activities. Our discussion of legal constraints on marketing programs has been integrated with the material on pricing, advertising, social responsibility, and other areas instead of being covered as a separate chapter.

Cases appear at the end of each chapter to stimulate interest and to add realism to the marketing curriculum. Our experience has shown that cases force students to analyze data and make decisions. This gives them an opportunity to apply some of the concepts and techniques that they have learned from the text and their instructor. Also, the presentation and discussion of cases help students improve their skills in oral and written expression. A most important and lasting benefit of the case approach is the experience that it provides in thinking logically about different sets of data.

The thirty-five cases selected for the book cover a wide range of products and organizations. Sixteen cases deal with consumer products, fifteen are concerned with industrial goods, and four cases deal with the marketing of services. Seven of the cases are set in foreign countries to add an international dimension, and two of the cases are built around data banks that encourage the use of computer programs for analysis. Also two of the forecasting cases are designed so that students can make use of the computer. The last case in the book (Hahn, Inc.) has a supplementary computer decision simulation that allows students to evaluate the effects of alternative marketing strategies. The two data banks and the simulation program are available on computer cards from us for a nominal cost.

All of the materials in this book have been tested in one-semester undergraduate and graduate marketing management courses. The text portion of the book has been kept relatively short to allow for the inclusion of a variety of cases. We feel that the book offers instructors the flexibility to emphasize text or case material as they prefer and to employ different methods of instruction. Some instructors may want to supplement the text with specialized readings or add some of their own cases. Others may want to delete technical discussions that are not required for some students. We have included ''how to do it'' material to provide students with the tools that they will need to work with the cases (this material may not be necessary for some graduate students and advanced undergraduates). The book has worked well for us, and we hope that others will find this combination of text and cases useful in their marketing management courses.

This task was made possible through the cooperation and contributions of many friends and colleagues. We especially thank Dave MacKay, Hal Kassarjian, Dave Aaker, Winston Stahlecker, and other reviewers who read the entire manuscript and provided many valuable comments and suggestions. We appreciate the help of George Haines, Fred Kraft, Jim Utterback, Dan DeHayes, and Dave MacKay in preparing original case materials for use here. We also thank Jim Patterson, Hans Thorelli, Don Granbois, and several groups of students who helped to review parts of the manuscript. In addition, we would like to thank our secretaries, Candy, Sarah, Pat, Donna, and Gail for typing countless drafts and revisions. Finally we thank our wives Nancy and Julie for their help and encouragement.

Douglas J. Dalrymple
Leonard J. Parsons

Table of Contents

Marketing Management
Text and Cases

One

Marketing: The Firm and Society

Before you can score you must first have a goal.
Greek Proverb

Marketing activities occur in business and nonprofit organizations and in the social environment that surrounds them. In this chapter we first define marketing and explain how it is used by businessmen and other organizations to sell goods and services. Then we show how marketing activities interact with government agencies and other social institutions.

MARKETING AND THE FIRM

Marketing is one of the essential ingredients employed by businessmen in their never-ending search for survival, growth, and profits. Success in achieving business goals depends on the skills that a firm commands in marketing, production, finance, and other areas and on their ability to combine these functions into a smoothly running organization. We view marketing as a system of interrelated activities designed to develop, price, promote, and distribute goods and services to groups of customers.[1] These activities operate within an environment bounded by the resources of the firm, the laws of the land, and the social conscience of the business community. In most cases marketing attempts to generate profits from the sale of goods and services created to fill customer needs. However, marketing is also used to develop, promote, and distribute programs and services (i.e., Planned Parenthood, the U.S. Navy, energy conservation) sponsored by nonprofit organizations. Thus the job of the marketing manager is to select and implement a set of marketing activities that will help achieve the goals of the organization.

The Marketing Mix

The specific collection of marketing activities employed by the firm to stimulate sales of its products and services is known as the *marketing mix*.[2] The basic functions included

[1] Adapted from a definition by William J. Stanton in *Fundamentals of Marketing* (New York: McGraw-Hill Book Company, 1975), p. 5.

[2] The phrase "marketing mix" was first used by Neil Borden in 1950 and is explained in detail in his article "The Concept of the Marketing Mix," George Schwartz, ed., *Science in Marketing* (New York: Wiley, 1965), pp. 386-397.

in the mix are product development, packaging, pricing, promotion, advertising, selection of channels, physical handling, and personal selling. Chapters Six to Eleven explain how these marketing variables are manipulated to achieve the goals of the firm. Organizations must not only select the right marketing mix for their product lines, but they must coordinate the various elements of the mix so that they function as an effective marketing program.

Product development is clearly essential to the long-run survival of business firms, and companies must have systems to develop, screen, and evaluate new items. They are also obliged to make decisions on what brands and price levels to adopt to generate desired levels of sales and profits. Advertising and promotion are basic competitive tools in business and the firm has to decide how much to spend and where to spend it. Marketing executives not only must choose among newspaper, radio, television and magazine media, but they must determine budgets for displays, contests, and other promotional activities. Personal selling is required for many products and marketing managers have the job of hiring, training, and deploying the right number of salesmen to meet the needs of potential buyers. Marketing also has the task of organizing brokers, wholesalers, and retailers into channels of distribution so that merchandise and services will be available at the point of final consumption. In addition, the optimum number and location of distribution facilities must be determined so that products can be moved quickly to customers at the lowest possible cost.

Marketing is much more, however, than a list of jobs to be performed; it resembles a sporting event where marketing programs fight it out against the products and policies of other companies. Marketing personnel can be viewed as ball players who attempt to score by locating customers and convincing them to buy goods and services. As a result, marketing is a dynamic, reactive, multidimensional relationship among firms and the buyers of their products. In short, marketing is the process of competing both in finding customers and in designing products and strategies to tap these opportunities.

Marketing Strategy

Marketing strategy can be described as a grand design to promote the distribution of goods, services, or programs. The idea is to identify target groups of potential customers and attempt to sell them on the goods or services of the sponsoring organization. Successful marketing strategies are often built around one or more of the marketing mix factors. Firms may develop separate product, price, promotion, or distribution strategies or combine several of these variables into an overall strategic plan. For example, Figure 1-1 presents a variety of product-oriented marketing strategies. With a market penetration strategy (1), the firm attempts to fill the needs of an existing market with current products. This is the most difficult of all marketing strategies because you must attack your competitors head-on. One effective way to penetrate current markets is by offering consistently lower prices. Other approaches include distinctive advertising programs such as the Avis "We Try Harder" campaign for rental cars and the improved distribution efficiency offered by direct air-freight shipments of merchandise.

Current markets can also be assaulted by reformulating existing products (2) to improve their appeal. Examples of this strategy include the pull-top beer can and sugar coatings for cereals. Replacement strategies (3) try to expand sales in current markets by offering customers new products with better performance characteristics. Gillette, for example, introduced the continuous band razor and the two-bladed razor to compete directly with its established safety razor. The idea of product line extensions (4,5) is to exploit traditional distribution channels by offering consumers a broader

Products / Markets	Present Products	Improvements In Present Products	New Products with Related Technology		New Products With Unrelated Technology
			Assortment Manipulation	Expansion of the Variety of the Product Line	
Same Markets	(1) Market penetration strategies	(2) Reformulation strategies	(3) Replacement Strategies	(4) Product-Line extension strategies	(5) Horizontal diversification strategies
New Markets	(6) Market development stragies	(7) Market extension strategies	(8) Market segmentation product-differentation strategies	(9) Concentric diversification strategies	(10) Conglomerate diversification strategies
Resource and/or Distribution Markets	(11) Forward and/or backward integration strategies				

Figure 1-1 Product-Market Growth Strategies.
Source. From *Stategic Marketing* by David T. Kollat, Roger D. Blackwell, and James F. Robeson. Copyright © 1972 by Holt, Rinehart and Winston, Publishers. Reprinted by permission of the Dryden Press.

choice of merchandise. Thus, although Campbell is world famous for its soups, it has grown by expanding its line to include TV frozen dinners and Pepperidge Farm bread.

The second group of strategies described in Figure 1-1 is concerned with expanding sales in new markets. The simplest approach (6) is to find new customers for present products. For example, Knox gelatin has been successfully sold to strengthen fingernails as well as for its traditional uses in cooking. Market extension strategies (7) modify present products to appeal to new groups of customers. DuPont has had a great deal of luck selling nylon for stockings and has since developed new forms of nylon for use in sweaters and carpeting. Product differentiation strategies (8) attempt to reach new customers by enlarging assortments. Thus, Breck has been able to attract more customers by marketing one shampoo formulation for people with oily hair and a second for individuals with dry hair. Diversification strategies (9,10) attract new groups of customers by striking out into entirely new lines of business. Philip Morris, for example, once relied entirely on cigarettes, but has grown rapidly by expanding into razor blades, deodorants, chewing gum, beer, packaging materials, and industrial adhesives.[3]

Although the critical marketing functions and competitive strategies are fairly easy to list, the firm still needs a unifying force to tie the factors together and provide leadership for the marketing program. For the past twenty years, this organizational theme has been known as the *marketing concept.*

[3]Ross R. Millhiser and S. Harrison Poole, "Diversification as a Marketing Strategy," F. E. Webster, ed., *New Directions in Marketing* (Chicago: American Marketing Association, 1965), pp. 108-121.

The Marketing Concept

The basic philosophy of the marketing concept is that the customers' wants and needs should be the rallying point for all activities of the firm. Under the marketing concept, research, engineering, finance, personnel, and other business functions all concentrate on satisfying customers' needs. Although this customer orientation is constrained by profit and growth objectives, the concept is appealing because it can increase sales by creating products that are easy to use, easy to buy, and easy to repair. The application of the marketing concept seems to offer great potential to firms that are not presently organized or operated with customer satisfaction as a guiding principle.

There is more to the marketing concept, however, than simply increasing the businessman's concern for the needs and problems of customers. The concept also states that marketing activities should be closely coordinated with each other and the various functional areas of the firm. To accomplish this objective, marketing activities are usually grouped under a chief marketing officer who reports directly to the president of the firm. The chief marketing officer coordinates activities so that marketing research is conducted before funds are committed to the development of new products. He makes sure that marketing works with production in scheduling product introductions and promotional programs. Simply stated, marketing decisions cannot be isolated from each other and the other areas of the firm.

In the past, marketing has emphasized sales goals, production has attempted to minimize costs, and research and development has been concerned with unique ways to apply technology. Although these objectives may be useful performance standards in individual areas, they are not compatible with the marketing concept and it is unlikely that the profits of the firm will be maximized when they are pursued separately. The objective of the firm should be to operate each part of the company so that the overall goals are achieved. The marketing concept has been a useful vehicle for helping to unify the independent functional areas to increase customer satisfaction and improve profits for the firm.

However, by 1970 many firms had adopted customer orientations and had integrated marketing decisions with other functional areas of the firm. For these companies, a new "call to arms" was needed to help raise efficiency in the decades ahead.

SYSTEMS PLANNING

We believe that the future holds a much greater integration of business functions than has been achieved in the past. This new doctrine can be described as systems planning. The systems concept goes one step beyond the marketing concept and constructs comprehensive decision models that can be used to operate the entire firm. The trend is toward more centralized planning where maketing, production, and financial goals become secondary to the maximization of profits for the whole company. The rapid growth of centralized business planning has been faciliated by the increased capacity and availability of computer services. Boulden and Buffa, for example, describe several systems models[4] that have proved effective in the day-to-day management of business firms. These models were designed to allow businessmen to ask a variety of "what if" questions and to find out immediately the effects of changes in sales on profits, cash

---

[4]James B. Boulden and Elwood S. Buffa, "Corporate Models: On-Line, Real-Time Systems," *Harvard Business Review,* Vol. 48, No. 4 (July-August 1970), pp. 68-85.

flows, break-even points, production scheduling, and other variables. The corporate systems models have also been used to analyze sales data, make forecasts, study the effects of price changes, and to estimate market penetration rates. The models described by Boulden and Buffa were constructed by adapting a general system program to the needs and data files of individual firms. This modular approach can reduce the costs of centralized planning and one large firm was able to develop a set of simple models to describe its various operations at a cost of only $25,000.[5]

The specific capabilities and limitations of systems planning models are not an issue at this point, but we want to point out that these models are operational and will grow in popularity and sophistication.[6] If systems planning does become the new path to corporate salvation, what will become of the functional areas within the firm? We believe that marketing, production, and financial decision making will always be a major part of business management although the growth of central planning may change the job titles of some executives. It seems likely that in the future many of the routine jobs will be handled by the computer, and marketing executives will have more time for making innovations in methods and procedures.

One of the functions of this book is to explain how these new approaches are being applied in specific problem areas. However, before we get to these issues you must understand the organizational arrangements used to build and control marketing programs.

Marketing Organization

The optimal structure for marketing activities is one that works best for any given firm and it tends to vary with the size of the company and the complexity of the markets to be served. The typical arrangement has a strong historical base that has been modified to fit a changing environment.

A Structure For Today. A representative arrangement for marketing activities is shown in Figure 1-2. The diagram has the chief executives from six main functional areas on the same level and reporting directly to the president. This balanced approach keeps marketing, production, finance, research, personnel, and consumer affairs on equal terms. The particular activities placed under the marketing vice-president vary and the arrangement shown in Figure 1-2 is only one of many possibilities. The plan described is representative of current practice, however, and indicates how the elements of the marketing mix are controlled.

Product managers are given responsibility for the everyday management of the marketing programs in the organization described in Figure 1-2. A new products department has been included in the diagram to coordinate the activities needed to originate and produce new items. Note that the sales manager is given complete control over the field salemen, warehousing, transportation, and inventories needed to move the product to the customers (Figure 1-2). Data-gathering activities for new and existing products are concentrated in the marketing information systems department. This includes both field marketing research activities and the analysis of the internally generated data. Also, the service function is placed under the consumer affairs vice-president to assure this area receives proper attention by top level executives.

---

[5]The company referred to was Potlatch Corporation, which has annual sales of about $335 million and operates 44 plants, ibid., p. 77.

[6]See Philip Kotler, "Corporate Models: Better Marketing Plans," *Harvard Business Review,* Vol. 48, No. 4 (July-August, 1970), pp. 135-149 and Philip Kotler and Randall L. Schultz, "Marketing Simulations: Review and Prospects," *The Journal of Business,* Vol. 43, No. 3 (July 1970), pp. 237-295.

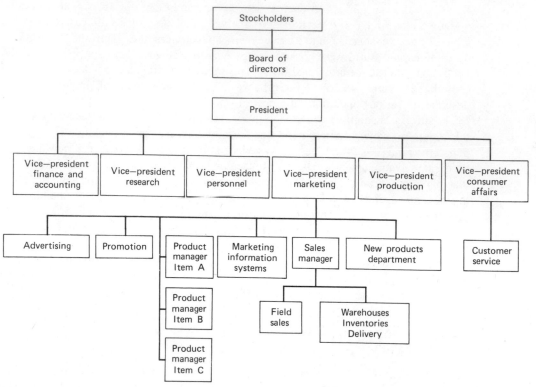

Figure 1-2 An Organizational Plan For Today.

The methods used to control price are not shown in the diagram and this factor is usually monitored at several levels in the organization. Price is such a powerful demand creation device that the chief marketing officer, the financial vice-president, and the president of the company usually work together to determine overall pricing strategies. In terms of specific pricing tactics for particular items, perhaps the most logical approach is to give this responsibility to the product managers who monitor the day-to-day activities of individual brands. In the long run, of course, the issue is not what activities report to the chief marketing executive, but how to organize the firm so that the whole business functions effectively.

Product-oriented marketing organizations such as the one described in Figure 1-2 can provide flexibility and employee incentives that may be absent in other plans. Assigning products to individual brand managers promotes competition among marketing staff members and assures that new items will receive adequate supervision. An alternative to the product orientation is to structure activities around groups of customers. Under this plan *market* managers would replace the product managers shown in Figure 1-2. Still another possibility (and one that tends to be expensive) is to divide the firm into separate product divisions and create a separate marketing staff for each division. Because of the widespread use of product managers in consumer and industrial firms, we will examine some of the duties performed by these unique staff specialists.

Brand and Product Managers. Product managers operate as independent entre-preneurs with responsibility for generating profits on the merchandise under their supervision. They create marketing programs designed to attract customers and function as the key decision makers in the day-to-day management of groups of products. Brand and product managers coordinate all of the pricing, promotion, distribution, and research activities employed by the firm to make money satisfying customer needs for goods and services. Thus, it is the brand manager who has the primary responsibility to see that the philosophy of the marketing concept is applied in the day-to-day management of the product line. Some of the duties assigned to product managers are listed in Table 1-1. The job of a brand and product manager covers almost all the elements of the marketing mix and is one the most important and challenging occupations in the business world.

Although brand managers are expected to plan and coordinate a vast array of activities related to their assigned products, they rarely have line authority over workers who make the product or salesmen who sell it. The job becomes even more difficult when you realize that many product managers have no staff other than a secretary. Thus, to accomplish their goals, product managers must establish and maintain communication lines with many individuals and departments inside and outside the firm. Success depends on their ability to work with the people who provide needed services and who implement the brand managers' plans. Thus, product managers must have the skill to cross organizational lines and know how to persuade others to support their programs.

Product/brand managers have not worked for every company and some like Kodak and Pepsico have switched to functional- and channel-oriented systems.[7] Other firms have broadened the concept of brand manager and introduced more flexibility to allow increased attention to problems of market segmentation. Part of the trouble with brand managers is that although they must be generalists, there is frequently a need for decisions to be made by specialists. Also, rising concerns for consumerism and ecology tend to require more centralized decision making rather than the decentralized control that occurs with the use of brand managers.

Perhaps the best description of the product manager system is to call it an experiment in decentralization. Responsibility for individual products is delegated to energetic

Table 1-1
Primary Activities of Product Managers

1. Forecast sales and set sales quotas with sales manager.

2. Prepare marketing plans for the following year including merchandising, advertising, and selling activities to reach sales and profit goals.

3. Recommend prices, discounts, and allowances.

4. Analyze sales results, share of market, competitive activity, and brand profits and adjust plans where necessary.

5. Initiate market research when necessary.

6. Initiate product improvements as dictated by changes in customer requirements and competitive action.

7. Continually appraise product performance, quality, and package design.

8. Recommend products to be eliminated.

[7]"The Brand Manager: No Longer King," *Business Week* (June 9, 1973), pp. 58-66.

entrepreneurs who coordinate marketing activities, but do not have the line authority over the areas they work with. As sales volume increases, however, separate profit centers may be established and, at this point, the brand manager becomes a division manager with the unqualified responsibility and authority to produce profits on a line of products.

The Marketing Plan

The most important job performed by product managers is the preparation of detailed marketing plans for each item under their supervision. The marketing plan is a comprehensive statement of what management expects from each product in the future. It is prepared on an annual basis and includes both historical data and recommendations on how to improve performance. The plan combines a set of marketing strategies with a timetable for action so that specific financial goals can be achieved.

A Planning Model. An example of a simple planning model[8] that can be used to build marketing programs is described in Figure 1-3. The model is designed to create programs that will achieve overall company objectives for growth, profits, and stability. The planning process begins with a review of existing or proposed products or services. Customers are essential in sales planning and product managers must analyze data on current and potential buyers to find what product attributes, price ranges, and distribution systems meet customer needs. Data for this activity can be obtained from company records, private research firms,[9] trade associations, and government publications. Customer wants must also be balanced against the capabilities of the firm and the possible reactions of competitors. In addition, the firm must determine whether marketing of the product or service will violate any existing laws or be detrimental to the interests of consumers, workers, or the environment. Raw material availability has become an important consideration in this era of shortages, and businessmen must also think about substitute ingredients and long-run supply contracts when they are preparing marketing plans.

Once a decision is made on the basic dimensions of the product or service, the next step is to pin down the most lucrative target market segments. Segmentation of potential customers into homogeneous groups in terms of preference or response makes it easier to reach these people with advertising, direct mail, or personal contact by salesmen. Perhaps the most creative step in marketing planning is devising detailed strategies to tap the target markets. Specific plans can be built around one or a combination of the marketing mix factors (Figure 1-3). For example, a firm might decide to expand market coverage by adding ten salesmen, six new distributors, and $300,000 in advertising funds while leaving product lines, price, and physical handling alone.

After appropriate strategies have been selected, the firm is able to predict how sales volume will react to the marketing program (Figure 1-3). If projected sales do not agree with stated objectives, the company can make adjustments in its marketing strategies. The success of marketing programs often depends on the personal efforts of salesmen and dealers, so the firm must take steps to inform and train these individuals on the details of

---

[8]The model was developed from discussions in Ernest C. Miller, *Marketing Planning* (New York: American Management Association, Research Study No. 81, 1967), John M. Brion, *Corporate Marketing Planning* (New York: Wiley, 1967), and Harper W. Boyd, Jr. and William F. Massy, *Marketing Management* (New York: Harcourt Brace Jovanovich, 1972).

[9]The A. C. Nielsen Company provides store sales and market share data for products from its audits of 1600 grocery stores and the Market Research Corporation of America provides similar figures from purchase diaries maintained by a national sample of customers.

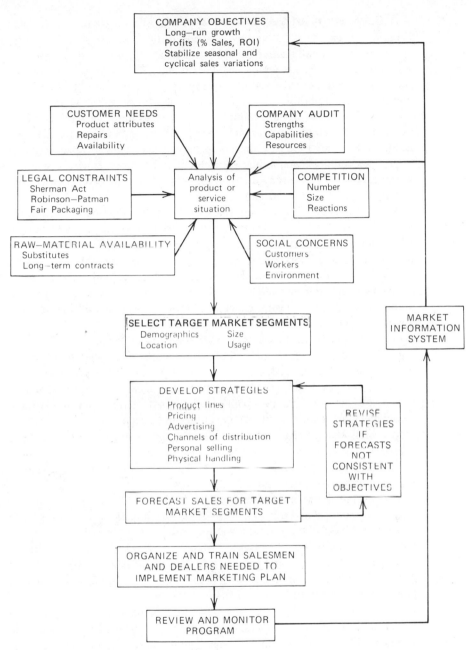

Figure 1-3 Marketing Planning Model.

the marketing plan. Responsibility for implementing marketing plans rests with product managers, and they must continually monitor results and make recommendations for changes in the plan. The last phase of the planning process (Figure 1-3) is a feedback loop that sends data on performance and market conditions back to the starting point so that programs can be adjusted for the next planning period.

A Case Study of Marketing Planning. The utilization of the planning model (Figure 1-3) can be illustrated by referring to the case of Metal Products, Inc.[10] This company was a small (sales of $4.2 million) manufacturer of quality sliding glass doors for residential and commercial installation and of "window-wall" prefabricated wall sections for commercial construction. Figure 1-4 shows how the planning process was applied by the authors to a series of events that occurred at Metal Products.

The objectives of Metal Products, Inc., were to increase sales 20 percent per year, achieve a 20 percent return on net worth, and strengthen their position in the building field. At the time of the case, the company was operating at capacity with 90 percent of their sales coming from sliding glass doors and 6.6 percent from window-wall units. Metal products had a strong distribution network and was well known for the superior design and construction of their doors.

Metal Products believed their goals could be achieved by either introducing a new *low-priced* door to compete in the mass market or by expanding their efforts to sell "Window Wall" panels. Low-priced doors looked particularly attractive because industry sales of sliding doors were expected to grow 50 percent in the next three years and 80 percent of this volume fell into the low-priced category. Wall panels, on the other hand, were made to order and required extensive direct selling and advertising to convert architects to the new design concept. Although the potential market for wall panels appeared large, there was some doubt whether sales of this item could be developed fast enough to meet Metal Products' growth objectives.

Competition in the low-priced sliding door market consisted of 300 smaller manufacturers who sold direct to local contractors at prices 40 percent below Metal Products (Figure 1-4). The door market was easy to enter because the aluminum extrusions were simple to work with and the smaller firms copied designs from larger companies. The wall panel market had few direct competitors and each product was sold on the basis of its own design characteristics. There were no significant legal, raw material, or social problems associated with either of the product alternatives under consideration. This preliminary review prompted Metal Products to look further into the economics of manufacturing low-priced doors.

The most attractive market segment for low-priced doors appeared to be the 5 percent of the contractors who built 70 percent of the new homes. Since the contractors selected doors on the basis of bid prices, it was important to be able to deliver the new door to the distributor at $45 or less. At this price, Metal Products would have very little promotional money available and would have to add several distributors who specialized in low-priced doors. Metal Products estimated that sales of 3000 units per month would allow them to break-even within two years at a selling price of $45. This appeared to be a reasonable sales goal since it only represented 4 percent of the low-priced door market.

The addition of the new doors seemed to be a logical product-line extension for Metal Products. Money invested in the project would be returned in two years and the larger facilities would allow expanded production of "Window Wall" units. Metal Products decided to go after the low-priced door market and they invested $210,000 in new facilities, equipment, and inventory.

The move into low-priced doors turned out to be hasty and ill advised. Local competitors, operating with almost no overhead, immediately began to cut prices to keep their share of the business. Since Metal Products was the high-cost manufacturer, they could not compete on price and were stuck with a large inventory of unsold merchandise.

[10]Harper W. Boyd and Robert T. Davis, *Marketing Management Casebook* (Homewood, Ill., Richard D. Irwin, 1971), pp. 307-324.

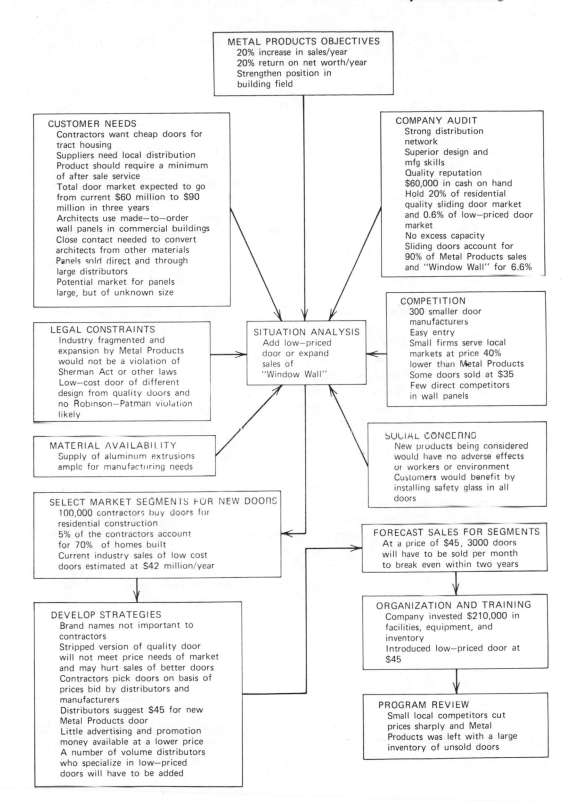

Figure 1-4 Marketing Planning For Metal Products, Inc.

The resulting financial strain was so severe that Metal Products was forced to sell out to a larger firm.

What went wrong? Why didn't Metal Products anticipate the reactions of the smaller firms? Part of the problem was that Metal Products was production oriented and lacked a planning model and marketing sophistication. Metal Products was so eager to reach their unrealistic sales goals, that they ignored the factor of risk. They completely misjudged the response of their smaller competitors and failed to see that the new product would put a strain on working capital. Metal Products should have realized that although "Window Wall" offered lower immediate sales, it fit in well with the *quality* image of the firm and represented substantially lower risk. Even after they decided to go into low-priced doors, they could have saved the company if they had tried to sell a few doors in a limited geographical area before going into national distribution. This test market could have shown the price cutting reaction of competitors in time to kill the project before any damage was done.

Although this illustration of the use of the planning model shows how to build marketing programs, it does not combine the various components into a single working document.

Organizing the Marketing Plan. Many firms require product managers to write up their annual plans using a standard format to simplify comparisons and discussion. A representative outline for a marketing plan is shown in Table 1-2. Marketing plans often begin by reviewing historical data accumulated for each product. This includes information on sales, earnings, markets, packaging, advertising, and product quality. Next the plan lists the problems, opportunities and objectives derived from the analysis of the historical data. This is followed by the general strategies to be employed to overcome the problems and take advantage of the opportunities. Then the product manager spells out the exact procedures that will be used to sell the product during the coming year. These recommendations are quite specific with regard to advertising themes, copy, media schedules, timing, and costs. The product manager will also indicate the responsibilities of different personnel and the procedures to be used to review the program during the year. A complete marketing plan usually includes a discussion of the marketing research that is needed to provide data to improve future decision making. The concluding sections of the plan present a tabulation of the anticipated costs of implementing the marketing program and a detailed income statement showing the expected results for different products, departments, and time periods. Thus the preparation of a formal planning document forces the product manager to think about all aspects of his marketing program and provides a set of standards that can be compared later with actual performance.

Our discussion of planning models and applications has attempted to show that effective planning requires an understanding of the marketing environment, imagination, and—perhaps most important—a detailed knowledge of how and where the product is used. Marketing planning is a creative activity where the elements of the marketing mix are manipulated for specific products and services with the intent of maximizing sales and profits.

In spite of the contributions made by marketing activities, the general public has become concerned with preserving natural and human resources and the marketing concept has been criticized as too self serving to guide future business activities.[11]

---

[11]Leslie M. Dawson, "The Human Concept: New Philosophy for Business," *Business Horizons,* Vol. 12, No. 6 (December 1969), pp. 29-38.

Table 1-2
Suggested Outline for a Marketing Plan

1. Current Market Situation
   Potential, sales position, consumption habits, product performance
2. Problems, Opportunities, and Objectives
   Goals for profit, growth, and related assumptions
3. Strategies to Meet Problems and Objectives
   Market development, reformulation, penetration, extension, diversification
4. Recommended Sales Tactics
   Pricing, promotion, distribution, personnel responsibilities, completion times, and review procedures
5. Marginal Income Statement
   Detailed breakdown of costs and revenues for marketing plan year by product and
   quarter

Businessmen are being asked more and more to take a broader, long-run view of their role in our society.

SOCIAL RESPONSIBILITY

Historically, businessmen have concentrated their attention on creating profits for their stockholders and have not paid much attention to events outside their gates. Hackett suggests that the heavy emphasis on short-run profits comes from a failure to build social, cultural, and humanitarian values into business investment decisions.[12] Businessmen have been reluctant to spend corporate profits to fight such things as malnutrition and they wonder about their proper role in combating social problems traditionally handled by government agencies. However, since the business community has accumulated large reserves of capital, leadership, and initiative, businessmen are being called on to assume a greater social responsibility to go along with this power.[13]

Dimensions of Responsibility

Businessmen operate in a variety of settings that have social implications. The businessman's first responsibility, of course, is to make a profit so his organization can survive. Without profits, business firms cannot continue to provide jobs for workers or goods and services to meet society's needs. Profits are a rightful reward for stockholders who risk their capital to start businesses and they are a driving force in a free enterprise society. Although profits are necessary, they are not the only obligation of businessmen in a modern civilization.

Businessmen also have a responsibility to take care of their employees. This means that companies are expected to provide workers with fair wages, safe working conditions,[14] and the right to union representation. In addition, the courts in recent years have

[12]J. T. Hackett, "Corporate Citizenship," *Business Horizons,* Vol. 12, No. 5 (October 1969), p. 72.
[13]Keith Davis, "Understanding the Social Responsibility Puzzle," *Business Horizons,* Vol. 10 (Winter 1967), pp. 45-50.
[14]In 1973, McGraw-Hill estimated businessmen devoted 3 percent of all capital expenditures to comply with the 1970 Occupational Health & Safety Act. See "The High Price of Job Safety," *Business Week* (May 26, 1973), p. 27.

ruled that business must offer equal opportunities in hiring, pay, and promotions to women, blacks, and other minority groups.[15] When employees are being exploited, common decency suggests that adjustments should be made regardless of the depressing affect this may have on the profits of the firm. Indeed, some companies believe that generous pay and fringe benefits for all workers lead to greater productivity.

A third area of social responsibility for businessmen is concerned with the physical environment that surrounds company plants and offices. Society no longer tolerates pollution of its air and water resources and a variety of federal and state laws have been enacted to curb the discharge of harmful industrial wastes. Businessmen who fail to clean up their plants are subject to fines and unfavorable publicity that can reduce sales. The public has become quite sensitive to pollution problems and businessmen are being asked to install expensive control procedures even if it means higher prices and lower profits.

Another environmental field where businessmen are being asked to assume greater responsibility is in the communities that surround company plants and offices. These areas are often older neighborhoods that suffer from deteriorating housing, lack of recreational facilities, unemployment, and despair. This is an explosive mixture and businessmen should not have to experience a riot to realize that good community relations is good business. The Eli Lilly Company, for example, has extensive facilities in the center of Indianapolis and has expanded its programs to help stabilize this environment and enhance its human resources.[16] In 1971, Lilly community relations activities including a remedial reading program, construction of four neighborhood playgrounds, loan of an executive to the city, a neighborhood scout troop, big brother and sister programs, an industrial training program, Junior Achievement, and a high school auditorium series.

Consumerism

Perhaps the most important dimension of social responsibility, from a marketing point of view, is the relationship between a firm and its customers. Since the middle 1950s the marketing concept has been promoted as a way for businessmen to improve their profits by emphasizing customer wants and designing products to fill these needs. Despite the widespread adoption of this philosophy, the 1960s saw an explosive growth of consumer dissatisfaction. The increase in consumer discontent was fostered, in part, by a failure of business to deliver the quality merchandise demanded by an increasingly affluent society, by shortages of reliable product information, and by the growing complexity and impersonal nature of the marketplace.

The consumer movement was given an added boost by Senate investigations of the drug industry, Ralph Nader's crusade against automobile manufacturers,[17] and the publication of a report by President Kennedy's Consumer Advisory Council.[18] This document was the first presidential endorsement of consumer affairs and included a "Bill of Rights" for consumers. The federal government committed itself to make sure consumers had:

---

[15]See Griggs v. Duke Power 401 U.S. 424 (1971) and Bowe v. Colgate Palmolive 416 F. 2d 711 (7th Cir. 1969).

[16]John T. Moore and James B. Spalding, Jr., *Eli Lilly and Company: Social Responsibility* (Boston: Intercollegiate Case Clearing House, Case No. 9-573-691, 1972), pp. 6-7.

[17]Ralph Nader, *Unsafe at Any Speed* (New York: Grossman Publishing Co., 1965).

[18]*First Report of the Consumer Advisory Council* (Washington: United States Government Printing Office, 1963), pp. 23-27.

Consumer bill of Rights

1. **The right to safety.** By stopping the marketing of products hazardous to health or life.
2. **The right to be informed.** By protecting against fraudulent, deceitful, or misleading information, advertising or labeling.
3. **The right to choose.** By assuring that competition was maintained in the marketplace.
4. **The right to be heard.** By assuring that consumer interests would receive full and sympathetic consideration by governmental agencies.

The net result of this activity was the passage of more consumer protection laws[19] and the birth of the consumerism movement.

For our purposes consumerism can be defined as a "social force within the environment designed to aid and protect the consumer by exerting legal, moral and economic pressure on business."[20] The fact that consumers banded together to protect their own interests while businessmen were applying the marketing concept has been a source of embarrassment to some marketing professionals. *Business Week* said it rather strongly when they described consumerism as the "bankruptcy of . . . the marketing concept.[21] Others would say that the marketing concept has *not* been implemented correctly and often focuses on short-term and exploitive gains. Thus although the marketing concept has helped tie the activities of the businessman to the interests of consumers, companies are still faced with hoards of customers demanding refunds, suing for damages, and supporting restrictive legislation. The problem is that the marketing concept does not distinguish between satisfying consumers wants in the short run (for big cars and detergents) and the need for consumer welfare in the long run (i.e., clean water, conservation of energy). By catering too closely to short-run demands, the long-run welfare of consumers has been overlooked. Instead of replacing the time-tested marketing concept with new dogma, Kotler suggests revising the marketing concept to read:

> The *societal marketing* concept is a *customer orientation* backed by *integrated marketing* aimed at generating *customer satisfaction* and *long-run consumer welfare* as the key to satisfying organizational goals.[22]

This new charge asks the marketing manager to include long-run societal values in his product and marketing decisions. If marketing executives fail to implement a societal view of the marketing concept, they can expect increased governmental regulation of their activities.

Reactions by Businessmen. The first reaction of businessmen to the consumer movement was a series of denials that any problems existed. This was followed by attempts to discredit the critics, the hiring of public relations firms, and strenuous efforts to cripple impending consumer legislation.[23] Aaker and Day suggest that defensive

---

[19]For example, Kefauver-Harris Drug Amendments, 1962; Fair Packaging and Labeling Act, 1965; National Traffic and Motor Vehicle Safety Act, 1966; Consumer Credit Protecting Act, 1968; Child Protection and Toy Safety Act, 1969; Federal Boat Safety Act, 1971. For a more complete list see Ralph M. Gaedeke and Warren W. Etcheson, *Consumerism* (San Francisco: Canfield Press, 1972), pp. 373-374.

[20]David W. Cravens and Gerald E. Hills, "Consumerism: A Perspective for Business," *Business Horizons*, Vol. 13, No. 4 (August, 1970), p. 24.

[21]"How Business Responds to Consumerism," *Business Week* (September 6, 1969), p. 96.

[22]Philip Kotler, *Marketing Management: Analysis, Planning and Control,* (Englewood Cliffs, N.J.: Prentice-Hall, 1972), p. 27.

[23]The most notable examples are General Motors' efforts to pry into the personal affairs of Ralph Nader and the success of industry lobbyists to water down the Fair Packaging and Labeling Act.

responses of this type avoid the basic consumer problems that cause complaints and are apt to lead to greater governmental control.[24] What is needed is better information on consumer needs, formation of independent consumer interest groups within organizations, and carefully designed programs to improve customer relations.

For example, vice-presidents of consumer affairs have been recently appointed at RCA, Chrysler, and other firms and these firms have begun to install toll-free telephone lines so consumers can complain directly to headquarters about their problems.[25] At Whirlpool the connections are called "cool lines" and are used to tell customers the location of the nearest appliance service center, provide technical information, or arrange for visits by field representative in the case of serious service problems. Whirlpool has also simplified their warranty certificates and converted them to a friendly letter format. In addition, Whirlpool has expanded their field service staff and accepted full responsibility for dealer service labor during the life of the warranty contract. They have also initiated a program to identify their best service outlets so they can be awarded special *Tech Care* designations.[26] As a direct result of these actions, Whirlpool has reduced their complaint/sales ratio to a relatively low 20 percent over a seven-year period.[27]

At the Ford Motor Company, the consumer movement has helped upgrade the service department so that it is on a par with the sales division and the goal is "no unhappy owners." Ford has also extended its warranty coverage and now guarantees dealer service work for 90 days or 4,000 miles. This means that if any additional repairs are needed during that period, they will be fixed free of any charge for parts or labor. Ford also attaches report cards to service bills so that customers can comment on dealer service and mail the reports directly to headquarters. In addition, Ford has a 24-hour toll-free number to help customers who break down on the road find repair centers, tow trucks, and motel accommodations.[28]

Consumerism has also helped eliminate abuses among the fast-talking representatives of door-to-door sales organizations. At Grolier, Inc., for example, every order for reference books is double checked with the purchaser before it is shipped. The idea is to catch misrepresentations by overzealous salesmen so that orders can be canceled and refunds made to unhappy buyers. As a result of this new policy, several hundred salesmen quit or were fired and Grolier suffered a 16 percent decline in quarterly sales and a $800,000 drop in profits.[29]

Agitation by consumer advocates has lead to increases in the amount of information businesses print on product labels. Magtag and Whirlpool, for example, now attach tags to appliances that specify product features, the amount of electricity used, installation requirements, special safety requirements, and warranty terms. CPC International has begun to print the nutritional content of Skippy peanut butter on the jars and the Jewel grocery chain now marks its private-label foods with the dates they are to be removed from sale.

[24]David A. Aaker and George S. Day, "Corporate Responses to Consumerism Pressures," *Harvard Business Review*, Vol. 50, No. 6 (November-December 1972) pp. 114-124.

[25]John A. Prestbo, "Seller Beware-Consumer Proposals Bring Changes in American Business," *Wall Street Journal* (June 21, 1971), p. 1.

[26]Stephen E. Upton, "The Use of Product Warranties and Guarantees as a Marketing Tool," *Consumerism*, David A. Aaker and George S. Day, eds., (New York: The Free Press, 1971), pp. 277-282.

[27]George Fisk, "Guidelines for Warranty Service After Sale," *Journal of Marketing*, Vol. 34 (January 1970), p. 64.

[28]*The Wall Street Journal* (May 22, 1973), p. 7.

[29]John A. Prestbo, op. cit. p. 1.

Planned Obsolescence. Some consumer advocates believe that businessmen deliberately design products so that they will quickly wear out and allow companies to make money in selling replacements. As evidence of this planned obsolescence they point to annual model changes in appliances and automobiles and the frequent changes in clothing fashions. Although businessmen often restyle products to renew customer interest, most businessmen depend on *repeat buyers* and they honestly try to build as reliable a product as possible. This was shown recently in a study of washers, dryers, refrigerators, and television sets sponsored by the National Science Foundation.[30] The results showed that today's appliances are substantially more reliable than their predecessors. For example, over the past eight years there has been a 50 percent decline in first-year service on color TV sets and a similar drop has occurred in first-year refrigerator repairs over the past fourteen years. This suggests that it is easier for manufacturers to design and build reliable products at the factory than to have large groups of disgruntled customers trying to get 30,000 service centers to improve product performance.

All of the consumer affairs activities enacted by businessmen are designed to enhance long-run consumer welfare and at the same time boost company revenues. Although consumer programs cost money in the short run, they pay their way over the long haul by improving goodwill, avoiding embarrassing disclosures, and by helping to diffuse expensive and less effective legislative solutions. The consumer movement has lobbied effectively for increased regulation of business practices and politicians have responded with a variety of new laws on product safety, warranties, and buyer information. If businessmen expect to avoid further restrictions on their activities, they will have to demonstrate that customer satisfaction and environmental protection are just as important as profit maximization. One of the classic examples of a collision between business profit objectives and social responsibility has occurred in the area of packaging.

Container Pollution

Marketing executives have the responsibility for designing packages that protect products and help increase sales. Frequently this can be accomplished by creating containers that make it easier for the customer to use the product. For example, for many years beer and soft drinks were only available in heavy glass bottles and customers were required to make a deposit when the beverages were purchased. This encouraged the consumer to return the empty containers to the store so they could be refilled by the bottler. To help build sales and increase customer convenience, some manufacturers started packaging drinks in throwaway steel cans. The glass companies responded to this threat to their business by designing lighter, more compact, one-way bottles. Multiple purchases were encouraged by overwrapping the containers with paper or plastic so customers could carry home six, eight, or twelve cans or bottles at a time. Since the glass and steel containers required special tools for opening, some creative marketing manager designed twist-off caps and pull-tabs that allowed the consumer to open the packages with his hands. Another innovation was to make beer cans out of aluminum to prevent corrosion and allow faster cooling of the product.

Although these packaging developments helped increase the per capita consumption of beer and soft drinks, environmentalists have begun to complain about the high social costs of the new containers.[31] In the old days, scavengers would collect empty beverage

---

[30]*The Wall Street Journal* (June 19, 1974), p. 14.

[31]Arsen J. Darnay, Jr., "Throwaway Packages—A Mixed Blessing," *Environmental Science and Technology*, Vol. 3 (April 1969), pp. 328-333.

bottles and return them to stores to obtain the deposits. Today with the development of one-way packages we find our forests, parks, highways, and beaches littered with millions of discarded beverage containers. A survey of a one-mile stretch of Kansas highway for example, turned up 590 beer cans, 130 soft drink bottles, 120 beer bottles, and 90 beer cartons.[32] Even when beverage cans are disposed of properly, the ground is frequently covered with the aluminum pull-tabs used to open the containers. Not only are the tabs sharp edged and unsightly, but they cannot be picked up by magnetic collection devices. The pull-tabs were not a problem with the old-fashioned beer can that had to be punctured with a special opener. Also the steel cans eventually rusted away whereas the new aluminum cans last virtually forever.

Since businessmen helped create the problem of container pollution, they are now being asked to find ways of disposing of the empty packages. One approach employed by beverage manufacturers has been the use of advertising campaigns to remind consumers to pick up litter and the printing of slogans—such as "Dispose of Properly"— on the tops of beer cans. Another method employed by the aluminum industry has been the expansion of efforts to recycle beverage containers. For example, the aluminum industry was able to reclaim 16 percent of all cans produced in 1972 by offering one-half cent bounties at 1200 redemption centers located in 39 states.[33]

Litter can also be reduced by careful package design. American Can Company, for example, has developed a new way of opening beverage cans that eliminates the pull-tabs entirely.[34] With the new container, two buttons are pushed down to allow pouring and they stay inside the can for disposal. Scientists are also working on plastic containers that decompose after extended exposure to sunlight.

The concern of businessmen for packaging pollution has been increased by the efforts of environmental lobbyists to ban the use of one-way beverage containers. Oregon and Vermont have already passed laws that require deposits on beer and soft-drink containers and they have reduced roadside litter.[35] The new laws call for 5¢ deposits on all beverage packages and as a result returnable bottles have replaced cans in these states.

If these laws become popular in the thirty other states where they are being considered, the beverage industry will have problems filling enough returnable bottles to meet the demand created by earlier packaging innovations. These examples suggest that businessmen can no longer make marketing decisions without considering long-term social implications.

Marketing in an Era of Shortages

Shortages of raw materials and energy have produced situations where some firms face greater demand for their products than they are able to supply. This has forced companies to allocate limited output among their customers and raises questions as to the proper role and utility of marketing activities during times of scarcity. One approach that has been suggested to help resolve the problem of shortages is known as *demarketing*.[36] Demarketing is the manipulation of the marketing mix to discourage customers from buying on a

---

[32]"Why the U.S. Is in Danger of Being Engulfed by Its Trash," *U.S. News & World Report (September 1969), Vol. 67, pp. 64-66.*

[33]*"Cans and Kilowatts," The Wall Street Journal,* (June 4, 1973), p. 26.

[34]*The Wall Street Journal* (May 23, 1973), p. 19.

[35]"Industry Battles to Keep Oregon Law from Spreading," *Consumer Reports* (June 1973), p. 370.

[36]Philip Kotler and Sidney J. Levy, "Demarketing, Yes, Demarketing," *Harvard Business Review,* Vol. 49 (November-December 1971), pp. 74-80.

temporary or permanent basis. The gas and electric companies, for example, now advertise how to cut energy consumption by turning off lights and installing insulation instead of their usual endorsement of more and bigger appliances.

Demarketing can be described as normal marketing in reverse. Thus to cut demand, prices are raised, product selection and availability reduced, promotions dropped, advertising eliminated or directed towards substitute products. During the 1974 gasoline shortage, for example, service stations cut their hours of operation, discontinued trading stamps, raised prices, and the oil companies began to advertise gas stations as your friendly tire store. The main problem with demarketing is knowing where to stop so that promotional skills and customers are not permanently lost when shortages ease.

Several strategy alternatives[37] available to marketing managers who face shortages are described in Table 1-3. The most desirable situation occurs when the firm faces a growing demand and has adequate resources and capacity (cell A). These conditions were common for most firms until recently and companies could follow a normal growth strategy.

When demand is growing and capacity and resources are inadequate, firms should pursue a strategy of market retention (B, Table 1-3). The idea is to keep the most desirable portions of the market until the firm is in a position to expand production to meet demand. Industries that have experienced this problem include synthetic fibers, molded plastics, and aluminum. Businessmen who want to retain markets must be able to forecast environmental changes that promise to ease resource constraints. They also need to identify the market segments that offer the best long-run sales potential. In times of shortages, there is a temptation to sell to the most profitable markets, instead of taking care of customers who can be retained when supplies are more abundant. Firms that cut back on their sales staffs when supplies are limited will not be in a position to expand sales efforts rapidly when shortages ease. Research suggests that material shortages have caused many firms to expand their sales forces and spend additional time on prospecting and customer education.[38]

Table 1-3
Alternative Marketing Strategies

Market Demand	Resources and Productive Capacity	
	Adequate	Inadequate
Increasing	A. Growth strategy	B. Market retention strategy
Decreasing	C. Market building and/or diversification	D. Balancing and realignment strategies

Source. David W. Cravens, "Marketing Management in an Era of Shortages," *Business Horizons* (February, 1974), p. 80.

[37]David W. Craven, "Marketing Management in an Era of Shortages," *Business Horizons* (February 1974), pp. 79-85.
[38]*Business Week* (March 9, 1974), p. 122.

A more difficult situation occurs when demand is reduced by environmental factors and companies have adequate capacity and raw materials. The gasoline shortage of 1974, for example, caused a sharp decline in the sales of recreational vehicles. Under conditions of declining demand, businessmen should follow a market building and/or diversification strategy. The objective is to search out new market segments (perhaps overseas) that are not being served. If market declines are projected to be permanent then the company should attempt to diversify into other fields. During the gasoline shortage, for example, manufacturers of recreation vehicles converted their campers into small buses.

Perhaps the most unusual strategy position (D, Table 1-3) occurs when a firm faces declining demand with inadequate resources and productive capacity. This situation calls for a strategy designed to realign supply with demand. Normally, price increases are used to achieve the desired balance. For example, in 1973 a shortage of feed grains reduced the supply of beef and chickens in the United States. Prices rose dramatically and demand declined to balance supply with demand. These equilibrium positions tend to be unstable so businessmen must be able to estimate the duration of the supply shortages. In time, demand or production will improve and the firm can move to one of the three other positions in Table 1-3.

Shortages disrupt normal marketing activities and managers must be able to find new opportunities and correctly assess the affects of environmental changes. After all a shortage for one company is in reality an opening for another company. We believe that periods when firms are unable to fill customers orders should not be the time to slash marketing staffs but, instead, a time to redirect energy toward new products and new markets that are not as dependent on critical materials. In the long run the key to success is the ability to adapt to the changing environment by working to satisfy the additional needs of target customers.[39]

Summary

The chapter has explained the role of marketing in our society and its place in business and nonprofit organizations. The basic functions of marketing have been described as planning, pricing, promoting, and distributing goods and services to customers. The *marketing concept* helps organizations achieve their goals by emphasizing customer satisfaction and long-run consumer welfare through close coordination of marketing and environmental factors with the other operating areas of the institution. The desired coordination is also enhanced by organizational structures designed to promote cooperation and the free exchange of ideas and data. A major integrating theme that helps synchronize marketing with production, finance, and other areas is the emerging concept of systems management. The systems approach encourages the development of corporate planning models so that executives can make better decisions for the day-to-day operation of the firm.

We are concerned with showing how product managers develop marketing plans and manipulate marketing variables to fill long-run customer needs and protect environmental and human resources. We believe product managers are the driving entrepreneurial force that allow organizations to compete successfully in the race for customer acceptance. Every organization should understand why product managers are needed and how they function to build sales for the firm. The materials in this chapter were designed to

---

[39]Philip Kotler, "Marketing During Periods of Shortage," *Journal of Marketing,* Vol. 38 (July 1974), pp. 20-29.

introduce the reader to the world of marketing and to stimulate a thirst for additional information. The next chapter is organized around marketing decision making.

Questions

1. Describe your concept of the marketing mix and a marketing strategy.
2. Do you agree with current thoughts that businessmen and women have a social responsibility to the world in which they live? Explain your answer and cite examples of where you think business should be exercising greater social awareness and/or where business is involved in areas where it should not be.
3. Is consumerism a permanent force to be considered or is it a here-today gone-tomorrow fad? Cite examples of where you have experienced or observed changes in a company's attitude concerning consumerism.
4. Is marketing really the champion of consumerism or is it merely a force used by firms for appearance while they are merely complying with legal requirements?
5. Why is systematic marketing planning important for business organizations? Who usually performs this work?
6. Marketing's role in the organization has changed dramatically from twenty years ago. What role do you see it playing in the future in an era of increasing shortages and pollution?
7. Define marketing as it relates to the Greek proverb quoted at the beginning of the chapter.
8. Pick any product of your choice and develop a *new* product-market growth strategy for it. Identify the strategy used as shown in Figure 1-1.
9. Is the idea of the marketing concept relevant or appropriate for all firms? All industries? Why?
10. Do you agree with Hackett's assessment that "the heavy emphasis on short-run profits comes from a failure to build social, cultural, and humanitarian values into business investment decisions"? Explain your answer.

Case 1-1
The Case Method

One of the basic objectives of the case method is to introduce a measure of realism to business education. The case method forces students to deal with problems as they actually occur in a business environment. Each case is simply a written description of the facts surrounding a particular business situation. With the case approach, it is the students' responsibility to develop solutions to the problems while the instructor plays several supporting roles. The instructor, for example, may set the stage for the case discussion by providing background material or by helping the students gain insight into the problem. He may also act as devil's advocate and critic to test the arguments and proposals put forth by the students. Finally, the instructor must evaluate the students' performance, assign grades, and make suggestions for improvement.

BENEFITS AND LIMITATIONS

The case method becomes an effective teaching device when students are encouraged to analyze the data presented and to formulate their own set of recommendations. Since each case is different, the solution that is developed for one case cannot be randomly applied to other problems. This raises a question of what students actually learn by working with business cases. One obvious benefit is that the preparation and discussion of case studies helps students improve their skills at oral and written expression. In addition, the case method provides an easy way for students to learn about current business practices and methods. Perhaps the most important advantage of the case method is the experience it provides in thinking logically about different sets of data. It seems clear that the development of the student's analytical ability and judgment is the most valuable and lasting benefit derived from the case method.

Most cases, including those in this book, are drawn from the experience of real firms. Typically, the names and locations are disguised to protect the interest of the companies involved. In addition, final decisions are usually omitted to enhance the problem-solving orientation of the cases, thus permitting students to reach their own conclusions without being forced to criticize the actions taken by others. The case approach departs from the typical business situation in that the businessman normally does not have the facts presented as clearly and neatly as they are in casebooks. Problem solving in business usually involves extensive data collection, something that has been essentially completed for students who work with the cases in this book.

A FRAMEWORK FOR ANALYSIS

There are many ways for students to approach the analysis of business cases. Each instructor has his own ideas on the number and nature of the steps that are involved. We believe that the following four-step procedure is a logical and practical way to begin.

1. Define the problem.
2. Formulate the alternatives.
3. Analyze the alternatives.
4. Recommend a solution.

Defining the Problem

Once the student is familiar with the facts of the case, it is important that he isolate the central problem. Until this is done, it is usually impossible to proceed with an effective analysis. The questions at the ends of the cases do not always focus directly on the principal issue. They are designed to help the student start his analysis. Students should look on the questions as guides for action rather than as

specific issues to be resolved. In no way are the questions designed to limit the scope or breadth of the discussion. All cases should be considered as problems in the management of the marketing mix, not as specific issues concerned only with some narrow phase of management.

Selecting the Alternatives

The second step is the definition of possible alternatives available to resolve the problem around which the case is organized. Some of these may be obvious from the materials supplied in the case and from the statement of the main issue. Others may have to be supplied by the student. One alternative that should always be considered is the maintenance of the status quo. Sometimes doing nothing is the best course of action to follow.

The Analysis

The most crucial aspect of the case method is the analysis of alternatives. To analyze is to separate into parts so as to find out the nature, proportion, function, and underlying relationship among a set of variables. Thus, to analyze is to dig into and work with the facts to uncover associations that may be used to evaluate possible courses of action. The student's analysis should begin with a careful evaluation of the facts presented in the case. He should be sensitive to the problem of sorting relevant material from that which is peripheral or irrelevant. In some cases, information designed to distract and confuse the imperceptive reader has been included. In reviewing a case, the student must be very careful to distinguish between fact and opinion. It is also the student's responsibility to make sure that the facts are consistent and reliable. Sometimes cases contain errors (either by accident or by design), and the instructor may prefer to remain silent.

Sometimes the most important facts in a case are obscurely buried in some chance remark or seemingly minor statistical exhibit. It is the responsibility of the student to carefully sift through the data to uncover all of the relationships that apply to the alternatives being considered. This usually means that the quantitative information must be examined, using a variety of ratios, graphs, tables, or other forms of analysis. It is rare that the data supplied in a case are presented in the form most appropriate to finding a solution, and instructors expect students to work out the numbers.

Frequently, students will find gaps in the data provided in the cases. This means that assumptions must be made if the analysis is to continue. Students should be aware of and able to defend the assumptions they make. It is also important to realize that a complete analysis is not one sided. A review of a business situation is not sound unless both sides of important issues are examined. This does not mean that every point must be mentioned, but major opposing arguments should be refuted where possible.

Students sometimes review the facts and decide that they do not have enough information to reach a decision. They recommend that the decision be postponed pending the results of further research. Normally, "get more information" is not an acceptable solution in a business case. Decisions often cannot wait the length of time necessary to conduct good research. In addition, it is unlikely that we can ever expect to have all the information that we think we need. Because of the cost of research and the penalties of delay, business decisions are almost always made under conditions of uncertainty. When a student says that he needs more information, the instructor may be tempted to conclude that he does not know how to analyze the facts available or is too lazy to collect more information.

Students are expected to base their analysis on the evidence presented in the case, but this does not mean that other information cannot be used. Students should utilize facts that are available to the trade, and information that is general or public knowledge. It is also appropriate to incorporate relevant concepts from other disciplines, such as accounting, statistics, economics, psychology, and sociology. The criterion in using "outside" material is that it must be appropriate to the particular situation. It would be unfair, for example, to use census data published in 1976 to make decisions in a case dated 1970. For this book we have attempted to select cases that provide students with enough information to complete the analysis. In some situations, however, the student may wish to collect additional materials.

Recommendations

After the student has carefully analyzed the data and alternatives, he is in a position to make his recommendations. It is quite possible that more than one course of action will look attractive. This is not an unusual situation, as most cases do not have a single "right" solution. Still, the student must come up with a set of specific recommendations. To arrive at a solution, the student must judge the relative risks and opportunities offered by the various alternatives. The optimum choice is the one that provides the best balance between profit opportunities and the risks and costs of failure. Students should make

a clear-cut decision and avoid qualifications and other obvious hedges. Instructors are much more concerned with the way a particular decision was reached than they are with the individual alternative selected.

If a student feels that the collection of additional information is the only feasible solution to a case, he must provide support for this decision. First, he should state exactly what the research will show and how this information will be used. In addition, he should indicate the research methodology to be followed and the anticipated cost of the study. After he has completed these tasks, he will be in a position to decide whether additional research is needed.

WRITING THE REPORT

We believe that students who prepare written reports do a better job of analyzing business problems. Writing a good report takes a certain skill, however, and we would like to suggest a few ideas that may be of help.

When instructors read reports, they look to see whether the student fully understands the situation and whether his interpretation of the facts is reasonable. They also like to see papers that are objective, balanced, consistent, and decisive. Perhaps the most common error made by students in writing case reports is to repeat the facts that have been provided. Instead of analyzing the data in light of the alternatives, students frequently repeat statements that appear in the cases, with no clear objective in mind. Nothing upsets an instructor more than reading a paper that devotes several pages to telling him what he already knows about the case.

Another deficiency often observed in written reports is a lack of adequate organization. Students who have this fault will begin with the first thought that comes into their heads and continue, in almost random fashion, until they run out of ideas. The end result is a paper that has no beginning, and no end, and often consists of one long paragraph. To avoid this problem, some instructors require reports to be presented in outline form. The condensed nature of such reports sometimes makes them hard to follow, and we prefer the more readable narrative approach.

In one system of organization that has proved effective, the report is divided into three sections. The sections are designated by Roman numerals and arranged in the following order:

I. Problem statement
II. Analysis
    A. Subheadings
III. Recommendations

The problem statement is brief: it rarely runs to more than one or two sentences. The analysis section makes up the bulk of the report and should include a number of subheadings. The first subheading might be a statement of the possible alternatives. Other subheadings might include evaluations of the data or discussions of the influence of the data on the various alternatives. Some of the topics that might be considered in the analysis section include:

1. Customer demand.
2. Competition, types and possible reactions.
3. Distribution channels.
4. Product characteristics.
5. Advertising and promotion.
6. Price.
7. Effects on company sales, costs, and profits.

The recommendations section should be relatively short and concise. This is not the place to evaluate the facts or to hedge your position.

There is no optimum length for a written case analysis. It all depends on the amount of data provided in the cases, the preferences of the instructor, and the number of cases turned in by the student during the course. The report should be long enough to adequately cover the subject but not so long as to bore the instructor and the class. It is fairly obvious that written reports must be neat, legible, and free of errors in grammar and spelling. Business professors are not hired to teach English composition, but they do expect certain minimum standards of performance in written expression. Their standards for written work are reflections of what the business community expects from college graduates.

SUMMARY

Case analysis is designed to give the student an opportunity to develop a productive and meaningful way of thinking and expressing himself about business problems. It must be remembered, however, that solutions to problems are worthless unless they can be sold to those in a position to act on the recommendations. The case approach provides students with practical experience in convincing others of the soundness of their reasoning.

The case method also helps train students to use logic to solve realistic business issues. In addition, the case method requires student involvement and brings a little excitement to what might otherwise be a dull subject. The case approach is not a panacea for business education, however, and we have found that a combination of lecture, discussion, and casework provides the greatest rewards for students and faculty.

Case 1-2
Dura-Medical Company[1]

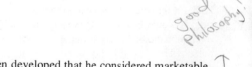
good Philosophy!

Dura-Medical was incorporated in Texas with the objective of manufacturing and selling products to the medical supply field. Dura-Medical subsequently acquired the assets of Dura-Medical Scientific Corporation, a nonaffiliated company, and Mr. Gerald Malone was named president of the company.

New Products

The principal activity of Dura-Medical Scientific Corporation had been research and new product development. At the time Mr. Malone assumed leadership of the company, it was producing several industrial moisture sensing devices, but no new items

[1]This case was written by Professors Larry Gene Pointer and Charles E. Yeager of Texas A. & M. University under the auspices of the Southern Case Writers Association. Used by permission of the Association.

had been developed that he considered marketable. Mr. Malone was particularly interested in developing products for use in hospitals and operating rooms where, he believed, the high cost of labor was causing an increasing demand for labor saving devices. Mr. Malone thought the company's engineering abilities might be used to devise unique approaches to the resolution of new and existing problems in the biomedical market.

Sponge Handling System. The company had two practicing surgeons on its board of directors and one suggested that the company develop a sponge-counting device. Every operating sponge must be accounted for to avoid delaying the surgeon or increasing the time the patient must be under anesthesia. The procedure is simple, yet it can be agonizing when a sponge is missing from the final count.

A survey conducted through the insurance program of the California Medical Association revealed that in spite of correct counts at time of dispensing, some sponges were still being lost. An incorrect count requires an immediate search of the operating field and if the missing sponge is not found, the patient is usually X-rayed before leaving the operating room.

To help with the problems of counting sponges, Dura-Medical developed an electro-optical device. The Sponge-Handling System (SHS) featured:

1. A light source and electronic logic capability to distinguish between two different sizes of sponges and provide a digital readout that allows continuous monitoring of the sponge count.
2. A scale system for continuous monitoring of blood loss.
3. A disposable plastic bag that containerizes the sponges giving a more accurate blood loss determination and prevents used sponges from contaminating the operating room.
4. A removable funnel that can be easily sterilized.
5. Disposable sterile drapes so that the unit can be placed in the sterile field.

To determine the market for the SHS, Mr. Malone hired Mr. Lewis Hall to serve as vice-president of marketing. A prototype of the SHS was developed by the company's engineering department for Mr. Hall's use. Feedback on the feasibility of the new product was obtained through conversations with local surgeons and operating room nurses, and at regional conventions of the medical profession. Mr. Hall reported that the idea was always well received. He estimated that it would be possible to sell as many as 8000 SHS units per year.

Based on the number of operating rooms in the United States Mr. Hall estimated that SHS had a total market potential of 15,000 to 18,000 units. The projected manufacturing costs of each SHS unit was estimated at $250 to $260 per unit. It was expected that a unit could be marketed at retail for $850. Mr. Malone believed the company had funds adequate for developing and producing the SHS (working capital in excess of $250,000).

If Dura-Medical marketed the sponge counter, salesmen would have only one item to sell and there would be very little repeat business. To make a sale, a salesmen would have to call on the chief surgeon, head operating room nurse, and the administrators at each hospital to convince them that the SHS worked and the machine would improve efficiency. Mr. Hall planned to display a prototype of the SHS unit in the spring at the national conventions of the medical professions. At the convention the company was contacted by several medical instrument companies who were interested in marketing the SHS when it went into production. Mr. Hall was particularly impressed with the American Sterilized Company (AMSCO). After seeing the SHS demonstrated, the director of product marketing for AMSCO suggested a meeting between the two companies.

The AMSCO manager of surgical equipment, Mr. Robert Carlson, and Mr. Hall held a meeting and discussed the following points.

1. Product identity—Dura-Medical wants their name on SHS.
2. Ability to recall the product if minimum sales not met.
3. Development costs—Dura-Medical wants to recover its developmental costs on the first 200 units sold. It does not want this reflected in the retail price. Thus the purchase price to AMSCO would decrease after the first 200 units were sold. Dura-Medical wants AMSCO to take less profit off the first 200 units and rely on the volume from a lower retail sales price, Mr. Carlson said he felt an arrangement could be worked out at a later date.
4. Exposure at conventions—Dura-Medical desires as wide an exposure as possible. Mr. Carlson said that with AMSCO's strong position in operating room marketing, they would be able to give the SHS excellent exposure. He suggested that AMSCO plan now to expand their booth facilities for this purpose at the four major conventions: American College of Surgery, American College of Anesthesiology, American Hospital Association, and the Association of Operating Room Nurses.
5. Sales volume—Mr. Carlson would be product manager for the SHS and he agreed that a sales volume of 1000 units for the first year and 1500 units per year thereafter would not be out of the question.
6. Marketing cost—AMSCO generally requires 50 percent of the retail selling price to market a piece of equipment. This includes all marketing costs (including all data sheets), advertising costs, and sales costs.
7. Advertising budget—AMSCO will submit an initial advertising budget and an advertising budget based on a percentage of sales at the next meeting.
8. Warehousing—Mr. Carlson said that AMSCO would warehouse the SHS inventory rather than have them drop shipped.

During this same period, Mr. Hall also held meetings with representatives of several other companies that were interested in a SHS marketing agreement. The analysis shown in Exhibit 1 was based on what he was able to learn from this series of meetings. Mr. Hall saw some advantage in Dura-Medical developing and controlling the marketing activities, but he felt it would be preferable if someone (like AMSCO) with an established and qualified sales force would undertake the SHS marketing job.

Catheters. The following spring Mr. Malone became interested in the possibility that the company could broaden its product line by entering the cardiovascular catheter[2] market. Mr. Hall estimated that the potential cardiovascular catheter market amounted to $11 million annually in the United States, and $4 million in foreign countries. He estimated that a hospital of 400 to 700 beds would spend $6000 to $10,000 annually for cardiovascular catheters. Some of the larger institutions, such as the National Institute of Health and Mount Sinai of Miami, Florida, spend approximately $30,000 annually on cardiovascular catheters. The catheters are used by radiologists, doctors, and surgeons specializing in the diagnosis and treatment of heart disease and related problems. Usually the catheters are purchased in small quantities and it is essential that salesmen maintain close contacts with users so that requests for special purpose catheters can be accommodated.

There are many different types and styles of cardiovascular catheters. Mr. Hall pointed out that only one company was supplying more than two types of catheters, and no company provided a presterilized line of disposable catheters. Mr. Hall described the competition as follows:

1. Cook, Inc., Bloomington, Indiana; one to two salesmen; very little journal advertising; exhibit at most major conventions; direct mail effort, mostly catalogues.
2. Cordis, Florida; three to four salesmen, expanding their sales efforts; very little journal advertising; exhibit at most major conventions; moderate direct mail effort, mostly catalogues.
3. Elecath Corp., New Jersey; one to two salesmen; some dealers; very little journal advertising; exhibit at most major conventions; some direct mail effort, mainly catalogues.
4. U.S. Catheter and Instrument Corp., (USCI), New York; ten to twelve salesmen; moderate journal advertising; exhibit at all major and some

regional conventions; limited direct mail effort; new catalogue annually; USCI is considered to be the pioneer of commercial cardiovascular catheters; they have been in operation for approximately twenty-five years and are operating today much as they were at their inception.
5. Westport, a division of Brunswick, Missouri; dealer sales only, very little journal advertising; exhibit at very few, if any, major conventions; some direct mail effort, mainly catalogues.

Mr. Hall pointed out that hospitals have begun to use large amounts of disposable products. He also noted that regular catheters are very difficult to clean and resterilize. In addition, the physical characteristics of reusable catheters often change with each sterilization. Thus a presterilized disposable catheter line appeared to have a promising market potential.

Mr. Malone formed a new subsidiary, Dura-Medical Catheter Corporation, to go after the disposable catheter market. John Nelson was placed in charge and Steve More was named director of research and development. Because of the technology involved in the cardiovascular field, Mr. Nelson believed the company should try to build a high level of confidence between the using physician and the manufacturer. To this end it was decided that the cardiovascular catheters should be sold by the company's own sales force.

Mr. More pointed out that specifications that were important to physicians using catheters had not been standardized in the industry. Parameters such as hardness, elongation, flexibility, pressure capacity, torque, and the toxicity of the product varied among manufacturers, even between successive shipments. He particularly stressed that no other manufacturer had quality control standards that included chemical and biological testing for toxicity to insure against adverse effects when used in the body.

Dura-Medical Catheter Corporation adopted a marketing program that stressed the image of high quality, presterile, disposable cardiovascular catheters. After contacting potential suppliers, Mr. Nelson began to make plans to produce prototypes by the middle of the summer. The following list of catheter products, the estimated market, and the timetable for Dura-Medical catheter production were included in this report.

I. Presterile disposable polymer catheter, estimated current annual market $2.5 million
   A. Cook, Inc.; Line of polymer catheters supplied nonsterile; limited variety; $5.95 to $10.20
   B. Elecath Corp.

---

[2]A cardiovascular catheter is a diagnostic device used in taking blood samples, recording pressures, and injecting radiopaque material into specific areas of the heart or circulatory system.

1. Corolan II, line of polymer catheters supplied nonsterile; $7.20 to $18.00
2. Rothene and Rothene II, nonsterile at $47.40/doz. and sterile at $54.00/doz.; very long delivery time for sterile catheters; four sizes and four tip configurations

C. USCI Corp.
   1. Swiss-made catheter; nonsterile; suggested for disposable use; $5.75 to $6.50
   2. Also sells a kit for making your own catheters; raw material cost approximately $2.50 per catheter

D. Westport; line of disposable, presterile catheters; limited variety, $4.75 each; four sizes and four tip configurations

E. Dura-Medical; the initial entry will be with a line of presterile, disposable, cardiovascular catheters, selling at a projected price of $54.00/doz. It is planned that the Dura-Medical catheter line will consist of fourteen sizes and eleven tip configurations for a total of 154 combinations of varying lengths.

II. Spring guides[3], estimated annual market $2.5 million
   A. Cook, Inc.; non-Teflon coated, $3.35; Teflon coated, $7; soldered tip; nonsterile; rumored to be the largest supplier because of Teflon coating
   B. Elecath Corp.; non-Teflon coated, $4.00; soldered tip imported from England; nonsterile
   C. USCI Corp.; non-Teflon coated, $5.00 to $6.00 depending on size; good quality welded tip
   D. Dura-Medical; Teflon coated, projected at $84.00/doz.; sterile; welded tip; will also offer a non-Teflon coated for projected $50.00/doz.; it is projected that Dura-Medical will sell 40,000 spring guides in the next calendar year

III. Disposable presterile polymer catheter with wire mesh between coating, estimated current annual market $1 million
   A. Cordis; $9.50 each or $78.50/ten currently the only company supplying this type of catheter and have been very successful

with it; the major advantage of wire mesh is additional torque control
   B. Dura-Medical; in development; planned to be in the market about the first of the year, at approximately the same price as Cordis

IV. Woven Dacron-base plastic-coated catheter, estimated current annual market $2 million
   A. WSCI Corp., $18.00 to $25.00; currently the only company with this line of cardiovascular catheters; used for many years on the theory that the woven base gives superior torque control, even though it can be demonstrated that this is not true
   B. Dura-Medical, in development; projected to be in the market about the first of the year at prices competitive with USCI; because of the high price and resterilization cost, this type seems to be decreasing in popularity; enough people will continue to request this type of cardiovascular catheter to justify producing it and Dura-Medical will become the only company with a complete catheter line.

V. Electrode catheter,[4] estimated current annual market $5 million
   A. Elecath and USCI Corp., currently the only manufacturers supplying this type of catheter; the available units are reusable and retail at $43.00 to $50.00 each
   B. Dura-Medical, in the development stage; presterile, disposable; projected to sell at approximately $15.00 each; expected marketing date: December

VI. Embolectomy catheters,[5] estimated current annual market $1.75 million
   A. Edwards Laboratory, $18.00 each; supplied sterile; currently the only company supplying an embolectomy catheter; it has been very successful in the market; the major problem with this catheter is that the balloon, in many cases, does not inflate symmetrically
   B. Dura-Medical, projected $10.00 to $12.00; supplies sterile and recommended disposable; Dura-Medical has this type of catheter in development and initial engineering studies indicate that the problem of symmetrical inflation has been solved;

---

[3]A spring guide is a tightly wound spring with a core wire that goes inside some catheters for guidance purposes. Spring guides come either soldered, which has limited shelf life, or welded, which is considerably stronger and has extended shelf life.

[4]These catheters are used primarily to regulate the heart rate of patients with an electrical abnormality of the heart.
[5]This catheter has a balloon on the distal tip that can be inflated. It is used to remove known emboli or for general cleaning of the vasculature.

it is projected that Dura-Medical will be in the market with this catheter by December

VII. Ureteral catheter,[6] the total current market is very difficult to estimate, but it appears that Dura-Medical's share of the market would be in excess of $100,000 per year; there are several companies producing this type of catheter, including C. R. Bard, Inc. and American Cystoscope, Inc.; Dura-Medical may be able to market these catheters through selected dealers nationally and supply private-label catheters for other manufacturers

Officers' Meeting

At the June officers' meeting, Mr. Hall reported that he had been able to turn up some outstanding prospects for the Dura-Medical Catheter sales force. He recommended that the new men, one each for Chicago, Los Angeles, Atlanta, and New York, join the company in August for a two-week sales training program. Charts, forms, and a list of procedures to be used in the training program were displayed for Mr. Malone.

Mr. Hall reported that plans called for ureteral catheters to be placed initially with dealers in four cities: Atlanta, Dallas, Houston, and New Orleans. He and Mr. Nelson had planned to begin setting up these dealer arrangements in about three weeks. A formal statement of the catheter marketing plan is shown in Exhibit 2.

The development of the sponge handling system had involved a process of trial and error. When the unit was demonstrated in the operating rooms, it was found that the nurses felt uneasy about using it. At the same time, the demonstrations revealed several minor problems that required modifications in the SHS.

Mr. Nelson reported that the following problems with the SHS had arisen:

1. The blocking circuit had not been functioning as designed, occasionally causing extra counting of small sponges. Although the problem had not yet been resolved, the engineering department believed that the problem could be solved by not later than June 21st. It was also reported that the problem of an extra total count when the power cord was disconnected had been resolved.

2. Some difficulty had arisen in getting access to service the electronics of the system.

3. Marketing had suggested that the funnel height should be shortened and the bottom diameter of the SHS input funnel should be increased.

Mr. Nelson reported that a booth had been reserved at the Palmer House in Chicago for a convention the second week in July. At this convention, Dura-Medical would display the cardiovascular catheter, the ureteral catheters and their accessories. Advertising for Dura-Medical Catheter Corporation had been placed to appear in the July and August issues of the *Journal of the American College of Radiology,* the *Journal of the American College of Cardiology,* and the *Journal of the American College of Thoracic Cardiovascular Surgery*. He also noted that the art work for the preliminary catalogue had been approved.

Mr. Hall recommended that the sales force receive salaries of $8000 to $10,000 plus commissions; with a first-year guarantee of $12,000. Mr. Malone requested that Mr. Hall make a careful review of all marketing programs in view of the May 31 financial statements (Exhibits 3 and 4).

Questions

1. Should Dura-Medical sell its sponge counter through AMSCO?
2. What price and promotional arrangements should be used to market the sponge counter?
3. Are the differences between the sponge counter and the catheter markets important enough to warrant separate selling and distribution programs?
4. Should Dura-Medical enter the catheter market? If so, what products should they sell?
5. Develop a marketing plan for Dura-Medical Company based on the suggested format discussed in Chapter One.

[6]These are specialty catheters used by urologists in diagnostic work involving the ureters and kidneys.

Exhibit 1

An Analysis of Methods of Marketing the Sponge Counter

Method	Advantages	Disadvantages
AMSCO and other representatives	Large sales force; large service force; immediate personal coverage; advertising their responsibility; large sales for their inventory stock; they have sales and marketing experience	Loss of sales for our salesmen; possible long term contract, possible loss of product identity; lose complete control if not handled adequately
Dealers (a) Independent, house directed (b) National (c) Intermediary	Wide coverage; they have sales and marketing experience; large sales for their inventory stock	Advertising would be our responsibility; extremely difficult to organize; if exclusives are granted, bad relations may result with other dealers.
Dura-Medical sales force	Possibility of sales force expansion; product and company identity	Require service capabilities; lack necessary sales and marketing experience; require large cash outlays for advertising and hiring new men

Exhibit 2

Dura-Medical Catheter Marketing Plan

Our marketing program will include a direct sales force of five regional salesmen. Initially, we plan to have offices in Dallas, Atlanta, New York City, and Los Angeles with an office in Chicago as soon as a man is hired. Additional offices in Northern California and Washington, D.C. are also planned. We not only expect to market our present and future products but also to act as the marketing arm for other companies.

Although we are aware of the advantages of using dealers to market our products, we chose to sell our products direct for the following reasons:

1. By having Dura-Medical people handle our products we know that our items will be given maximum attention.
2. A direct sales force can be better trained and the overall quality of the sales force controlled.
3. Physicians prefer to talk to a salesman connected with the company he represents, since their time is valuable and his knowledge is important in helping them to acquire products to best do their job.
4. A sales force well trained in the specialized cardiovascular area of medicine offers an

excellent sales arm to other companies with products in this area.

In addition to a direct sales force, other marketing tools used by Dura-Medical Catheter are:

1. *Direct mail advertising.* We have found this to be a successful media. Our first direct mail brochure for Dura-Medical Catheter was sent to 15,600 cardiologists, cardiovascular surgeons and radiologists, of which only a fraction actually do cardiovascular catheterizations. We received over 1000 business reply cards requesting additional literature. We are now compiling a mailing list of physicians interested in catheterization work for future direct mail advertising.
2. *Convention exhibits.* The cost of a sales call and demonstration is less from a convention booth than any other method of personal contact. It also gives a company the opportunity to exhibit products that might not otherwise be shown to physicians.
3. *Professional journal advertising.* We use journal advertising in introducing both the company and specific Dura-Medical products. Journals in which we have advertised

or are planning to advertise are the following:
Circulation
Cardiology
Radiology
Association of Operating Room Nurses
J.A.A.M.I.
Anesthesiology

Surgery Digest
Survey of Anesthesiology
4. *Film presentation of new products.* We plan to make a film of the Sponge-Handling System to use as an aid for sales representatives. A training film for purchasers is also planned.

Exhibit 3
Dura-Medical Consolidated Balance Sheet

May 31

ASSETS

Cash	$ 10,054
Certificates of deposit	150,000
Accounts receivable-trade (less allowance for doubtful accounts—$2,500)	35,600
Inventories	54,992
Prepaid expenses	6,694
	$257,340
Research and development costs	$ 48,771
Excess of investment over equity in net assets acquired	20,528
Other	4,158
	$ 73,457
Machinery and equipment	$102,987
Furniture and fixtures	15,762
Vehicles	24,245
Leasehold improvements	14,008
	$157,002
Less accumulated depreciation	30,142
	$126,860
	$457,657

old method

LIABILITIES AND STOCKHOLDERS' EQUITY

Notes payable	
Banks	$ 59,205
Other	48,698
Accounts payable	50,512
Accrued expenses	12,051
Federal income taxes	4,100
	$ 174,566
Interest	$ 2,231
Common stock, $.25 par value, authorized 5,000,000 shares, issued 673,734 shares including 93,001 shares in the treasury	$ 168,434
Additional paid-in capital	390,224
Retained earnings (deficit)	(139,316)
	$ 420,362
Less treasury stock, at cost, 93,001 shares	139,502
	$280,860
	$457,657

Exhibit 4
Consolidated statement of operations

(Five Months Ended May 31)

Revenues	
Net sales	$ 12,502
Interest income	4,992
	$ 17,494
Cost and Expenses	
Cost of goods sold	$ 20,550
Selling, general, and administrative expenses	110,031
Research and development costs	96,972
Finance and interest expense	6,500
	$ 234,053
Loss before federal income taxes, minority interest, and extraordinary item	$ 216,559
Federal income taxes	—
Loss before minority interest and extraordinary item	$ 216,559
Minority stockholders' interest	28,197
Loss before extraordinary item	$ 188,362
Extraordinary item—gain on discontinuance of oil and gas operations	43,754
Net loss	($ 144,608)

Case 1-3
Cigarette Industry[1]

In 1969, the Federal Communications Commission ruled that all advertising of cigarettes on radio and television was to be eliminated as of January 1, 1971. The action was expected to have a significant effect on advertising practices and on the relationship between advertising and government. The issues involved were complex, and a substantial amount of controversy existed prior to and after the decision was made. The significance of the debate and of subsequent actions can be better understood by reviewing the events which took place prior to 1970.

In 1964, "Smoking and Health," a Public Health Service report, condemned the use of cigarettes, but not cigars or pipes. The action initiated a bitter controversy over the effects of cigarette smoking on an individuals's health. The federal government,

[1]Steven J. Shaw, John F. Willenborg, and Richard E. Stanley, *Marketing Management Strategy: Cases and Problems,* copyright © 1971. Reprinted by permission of Prentice-Hall, Inc., Englewood Cliffs, N.J.

through its various agencies, took the position that a relationship existed between cigarette smoking and lung cancer, heart disease, emphysema, and numerous other diseases. The cigarette industry, which is by far the major purchaser of the nation's tobacco crop, maintained that there was no conclusive proof of a positive relationship between cigarette smoking and poor health.

Opposition to Cigarette Smoking

Among the anticigarette sources, the Department of Health, Education and Welfare, the Public Health Service, the Federal Trade Commission, and the Federal Communications Commission took the lead in making the public aware of the dangers of cigarette smoking. Studies that were undertaken by HEW officials indicated that cigarette smoking was associated with an increase in overall mortality and morbidity. Public Health Service reports suggested that cigarette smoking was the main cause of 50,000 deaths that occurred annually from lung cancer and 25,000 deaths from emphysema and chronic bronchitis. According to this source, one-third of all deaths of men between the ages of 35 and 60 were related to cigarette smoking.

Few scientists doubted that a direct relationship existed between smoking and lung cancer. One cancer expert explained that although improved medicine, public health, and living standards added four years to the expected life of white males from 1919 to 1965, about 3.4 of those years were erased by cigarette smoking.

The advertising of cigarettes was the special target of the Federal Trade Commission and the Federal Communications Commission. The FTC repeatedly made its position clear on cigarette advertising. In the words of the Commission: "Cigarette advertising continues to depict smoking as an enjoyable activity while ignoring completely the health hazard."[2]

Cigarette advertising aimed at teenagers was particularly disturbing to the FTC. In its view: "Teenagers are exposed to an endless barrage of subtle messages that cigarette smoking increases popularity, makes one more masculine or attractive to the opposite sex, enhances one's social poise, etc."[3] The Commission believed that such commercials were successful in persuading teenagers to smoke in spite of the known health hazard.

The FTC recommended a three-step program to combat cigarette smoking:

1. Replacement of the warning on cigarette packages from "caution: cigarette smoking may be hazardous to your health," to "cigarette smoking is dangerous to health and may cause death from cancer and other diseases."
2. Termination or drastic alteration of cigarette advertising on radio and television.
3. Conducting a vast educational campaign to negate the image of cigarette smoking as harmless and satisfying.

The Federal Communications Commission joined the FTC in its fight against cigarette smoking. The "Fairness Doctrine," which was originally developed to give opposing political candidates equal time on the air, was expanded to state that broadcasting stations carrying cigarette advertising must also carry a significant amount of time for the other view. A ratio of one antismoking commercial to every three cigarette commercials was established. This was in keeping with the FCC's view that stations present cigarette advertising have the duty of informing their audiences that "however enjoyable, such smoking may be a hazard to the smoker's health."[4]

A broadcasting industry research organization reported that antismoking commercials on an annual basis numbered around 2000 on network television and 3150 on network radio in 1969. Some newspapers and magazines also carried antismoking advertisements. These anticigarette commercials received free air time, were expertly prepared, and were furnished by such private agencies as the American Cancer Society and the American Heart Association.

Cigarette Industry's Defense

The cigarette industry adopted the position that no published reports proved that cigarettes cause lung cancer or any other illnesses. The industry took the stand that cigarettes were a legitimate product and any prohibition of their advertising would be regarded as an unwarranted and punitive measure. Any specific measure to ban cigarette commercials from the broadcasting media would tread on the delicate ground of free speech and the First Amendment to the Constitution.

The broadcasting industry, faced with the loss of over $200 million in cigarette advertising revenue, joined cigarette manufacturers in opposing the banning of cigarette commercials from television and radio. The broadcast media believed that the loss of revenue from cigarette advertising would mean the difference between profit and loss for a number of broadcasters. Cigarette advertising, prior to 1971, accounted for approximately 7 percent of all national television revenue. Total expenditures on cigarette advertising from 1959 through 1967 are shown in Exhibit 1.

Cigarette Companies Diversify

The declining domestic consumption of cigarettes led cigarette manufacturers to diversify their product lines. Cigarette consumption from 1959 through 1968 is shown in Exhibit 2.

The domestic consumption of cigarettes declined sharply in 1968. This was the first year-to-year drop since 1964. Dr. Daniel Horn, director of the National Clearing House of Smoking and Health, said "there may be about 1.5 million fewer cigarette smokers now than there were a year ago although

[2]"It's War on Cigarette Advertising," *Broadcasting* (July 3, 1967), p. 9.

[3]"Can FTC Stunt Growth of Smokers?" *Business Week* (July 8, 1967), p. 34.

[4]Fairness Applied to Cigarettes," *Broadcasting* (June 5, 1967), p. 9.

Exhibit 1
Expenditures on Cigarette Advertising, 1959-1967[a]
(in Million of Dollars)

Year	Expenditures
1959	$138.2
1960	140.0
1961	141.9
1962	139.0
1963	174.6
1964	191.1
1965	188.7
1966	213.3
1967	265.2

Source. "Cost of Cigarette Advertising 1959-1967," *Advertising Age* (September 16, 1968), pp.103-104.

[a] Totals are only for cigarette brands whose 1967 sales exceeded one billion cigarettes. Expenditures represent dollars spent in general magazines, newspapers, network TV, spot TV, and outdoor advertising (from 1959 through 1962). Radio advertising expenditures, costs of point-of-purchase materials, and nonmeasured media expenditures are excluded.

Exhibit 2
Domestic Consumption of Cigarettes in the United States, 1959-1968

Year	Billions of Cigarettes	Per Capita Number of Cigarettes	Pounds
1959	454	4071	9.44
1960	470	4171	9.64
1961	488	4266	9.84
1962	494	4265	9.69
1963	510	4345	9.70
1964	497	4194	9.21
1965	511	4258	9.37
1966	522	4287	9.08
1967	528	4280	8.85
1968	523	4186	8.65

Source. Annual Reports on Tobacco Statistics, Statistical Bulletins No.'s 356, 372, 397, 424, 435 (Washington, D.C.: United States Department of Agriculture, Consumer and Marketing Service), April, 1964, 1965, 1966, 1967, 1969.

there are about 3 million more people in the United States."[5]

On a per capita basis, cigarette consumption in pounds turned downward in 1966. In 1967, the number of cigarettes consumed per capita also declined. In 1969, it was still too early to predict a declining future demand; however, indications of the development of such a trend were present. In

[5] "Cigarette Gains Go Up in Smoke," *Business Week* (December 21, 1968), p. 68.

light of these figures, cigarette manufacturers began to diversify.

By 1969, the American Tobacco Company owned Sunshine Biscuit and James B. Beam Distilling Company; Liggett & Myers had bought its way into the food and liquor fields; Philip Morris produced razors, blades, paper, packaging, textile chemicals, hospital products, and toiletries; R. J. Reynolds manufactured packaging and industrial corn products and operated a containerized freight and trucking system; and Lorillard intended for 40 to 50 percent of its sales to be of nontobacco products within a short period of time. This movement away from complete dependence on cigarettes and tobacco indicated that the cigarette companies were taking no chances on the outcome of the cigarette controversy.

Economic Importance of Tobacco

Since colonial times, tobacco has been considered the "golden" leaf in the major tobacco-raising states of the United States. European demand for this "cash" crop contributed greatly to the early economic development of Virginia, Maryland, and North Carolina. In 1969, tobacco was still the mainstay of the agricultural sectors of many Southern states and contributed to the economic welfare of the entire nation.

The billions of dollars spent on cigarettes each year created jobs for many people and provided income with which to purchase the other products of our economy. In 1965, United States cigarette manufacturers employed 35,924 people and paid an annual payroll of $199 million. Exhibit 3 shows the growth in dollar sales of cigarettes for the period 1959 to 1968. During 1968, cigarette sales accounted for approximately 1.7 percent of total personal consumption expenditures in the United States.

The federal government also has benefited from high taxes on cigarettes throughout much of the history of cigarette manufacturing. As shown in Exhibit 4, cigarette taxes have provided a stable source of revenue. If the federal government were successful in reducing or eliminating the sale of cigarettes in the United States, it would have to find other sources of tax revenue.

The Importance of Tobacco to a Southern State: South Carolina

South Carolina is one of the nation's leading tobacco-producing states, and most of its tobacco crop is used in the manufacture of cigarettes. Tobacco is an important cash crop for over 12,000 commercial farmers in the Palmetto State. Any severe drop in tobacco sales or prices will have an adverse economic effect on the entire state. Over one-fifth of total cash receipts from all farm commodities in South Carolina is derived from tobacco, as shown in Exhibit 5. Loss of any substantial portion of the revenue from this crop would place many South Carolina farmers in serious financial condition. Among all crops, tobacco has one of the highest cash yields per acre. It would be difficult for the farmer to find another crop as suitable for South Carolina soil and having an equally high return per acre.

A decline in tobacco consumption would affect seriously not only tobacco growers but also approximately 9,000 seasonal tobacco laborers who have an annual payroll of almost $8 million. Others, such as warehouse workers, employees of business establishments servicing tobacco growers, advertising personnel, wholesalers, and retailers would not escape the financial "pinch".

Moreover, a decline in the demand for tobacco

Exhibit 3

Estimated Cigarette Sales in the United States, 1959-1968
(in Millions of Dollars)

Year	Sales
1959	$5854
1960	6244
1961	6538
1962	6675
1963	7055
1964	7024
1965	7609
1966	7997
1967	8432
1968	8910

Source. Annual Report on Tobacco Statistics 1968, Statistical Bulletin No. 435 (Washington, D.C.: United States Department of Agriculture, Consumer and Marketing Service), April, 1969, p. 35.

Exhibit 4

Federal Tax Receipts from Cigarettes in the United States, 1959-1968 (in Millions of Dollars)

Fiscal Year	Cigarette Tax Receipts
1960	$1864
1961	1924
1962	1957
1963	2011
1964	1977
1965	2070
1966	2006
1967	2023
1968	2066

Source. Annual Report on Tobacco Statistics, Statistical Bulletins No.'s 343, 372, 435 (Washington, D.C.: United States Department of Agriculture, Consumer and Marketing Service), April 1964, 1965, 1969.

Exhibit 5

Cash Receipts from Tobacco Compared with Total Cash Receipts from all Farm Commodities, South Carolina, 1959-1968

Year	Tobacco Cash Receipts (in millions of dollars)	Tobacco Cash Receipts as a Percentage of Total Farm Commodity Receipts
1959	$ 00	24.9
1960	91	24.7
1961	100	26.2
1962	116	29.5
1963	97	24.6
1964	94	23.0
1965	88	22.0
1966	88	22.4
1967	107	25.1
1968	81	21.5

Source. Annual Reports on Tobacco Statistics, Statistical Bulletins No.'s 308, 330, 356, 372, 397, 424, 435 (Washington, D.C.: United States Department of Agriculture, Consumer and Marketing Service), April, 1962, 1963, 1964, 1965, 1966, 1967, 1968.

products would directly affect many public programs in South Carolina because the state also receives a considerable amount of revenue from taxes on tobacco products sold locally. Exhibit 6 presents the amount of tobacco tax revenue received by the state between fiscal years 1959 and 1968. The loss of any great portion of these funds would certainly be detrimental to state programs. In all likelihood, it would mean increasing the burden of existing taxes or perhaps adding new levies.

Questions

1. Should cigarette advertising have been banned from radio and television?
2. Should cigarette advertising be banned from all media?
3. Should consumers be protected against the promotion of products that health authorities consider dangerous to health?

Exhibit 6

Total State Receipts and Tax Receipts from Tobacco Products Sold in South Carolina, 1960-1968 (in Millions of Dollars)

Fiscal Year	Total State Tax Receipts	Tobacco Tax Receipts	Tobacco Tax Receipts as a Percentage of Total State Tax Receipts
1960	$214.1	$11.5	5.3
1961	215.5	11.9	5.5
1962	221.3	12.1	5.4
1963	240.0	12.0	5.0
1964	253.6	12.4	4.9
1965	281.9	12.9	4.5
1966	329.0	13.3	4.0
1967	362.9	13.7	3.7
1968	377.2	13.7	3.6

Sources. Annual Reports on Tobacco Statistics, Statistical Bulletins No.'s 343, 371, 424, 435 (Washington D.C.: United States Department of Agriculture, Consumer and Marketing Service), April, 1963, 1965, 1967, 1969. *Annual Reports of the South Carolina Tax Commission* 1959-1968 (Columbia, S.C.: State Budget and Control Board).

4. Since public health authorities were convinced that cigarette smoking contributed to lung cancer, emphysema and heart disease, why wasn't the sale of cigarettes made illegal?
5. What can cigarette manufacturers do to protect the sales of cigarettes if the advertising of cigarettes is banned completely?
6. What can major tobacco-raising states like South Carolina do to counteract a shrinking demand for cigarette tobacco?
7. Evaluate the recent removal of cigarette advertising from radio and television in terms of its effects on cigarette manufacturers and cigarette consumption.

Case 1-4
Standard Oil Company of Ohio[1]

In its 1972 annual report, The Standard Oil Company (Sohio) stated that, ''The energy shortage is not a distant problem. It is a fact of life today, and it will be a part of the operating climate for our Company and part of the lives of the people of this country for the foreseeable future.'' By the middle of 1973, Sohio was actively ''demarketing'' its petroleum products through a series of advertisements and promotional brochures designed to inform motorists about the more efficient consumption of gasoline.

[1]From *Contemporary Cases in Marketing* by W. Wayne Talarzyk. Copyright © 1974 by The Dryden Press. Reprinted by pemission of The Dryden Press.

OPERATING CHARACTERISTICS

Sohio is a diversified corporation that traces its history back to the original Standard Oil Company founded by John D. Rockefeller. The company currently markets petrolem products and services under the BP name in Eastern Seaboard states from Maine to Virginia, and the District of Columbia, under the Boron name in New York, Pennsylvania, West Virginia, Kentucky, and Indiana, as well as the Sohio name in Ohio.

A wholly owned subsidiary, Vistron Corporation, makes and markets many products including toothbrushes, chemicals, plastics, and fertilizers. Sohio also owns the Old Ben Coal Corporation and has interest in Hospitality Motor Inns, Dutch Pantry restaurants, and various vending and food service activities.

Total sales and operating revenues of Sohio increased about 4 percent in 1972 to $1447 million from $1394 million in 1971. Net income in 1972 of $57.5 million represent a 5 percent increase over the $54.7 million of 1971.

REASONS BEHIND THE GASOLINE SHORTAGES

Sohio is producing gasoline at record rates along with most other refiners. The demand for gasoline, however, is also growing at record rates. For the first time in the United States history, demand for gasoline threatens to exceed the supply. The two main reasons for the difference between demand and supply are changes in automobile characteristics and the lack of new refineries.

CHANGES IN AUTOMOBILES

There are an estimated 25 million more cars and trucks on the road today than just five years ago. Also, 1973 cars are being produced and purchased at all-time record levels. Sales of new cars in the United States increased by over 20 percent for the first three months of 1973, compared to the same period of 1972, with the added result of more two- and three-car families than ever before.

All cars since 1968 have been equipped with emission control devices, with the 1973 cars having more controls than any previous models. These devices are helping to clean up the air, but also are contributing to increased fuel consumption. According to figures from the U.S. goverment, standard-size 1973 cars use significantly more gasoline than previous models and deliver an average of only eleven miles per gallon.

Devices such as air conditioning, power brakes, power steering, and automatic transmissions have all grown more and more popular in the past five years. All of these conveniences also contribute to increased fuel consumption, especially air conditioning.

FEWER NEW REFINERIES CONSTRUCTED

Since late 1970, only three major new refineries have been built in the United States. Several important factors discouraged the construction of others, according to industry sources.

First, by 1970 environmentalism had become a major political force, and this made it difficult to find acceptable sites for new refinery construction. Second, the National Environmental Protection Act created some uncertainty on the regulations for antipollution engines of the future, so no one was sure of what plant design would be required to produce the needed gasoline. In addition, there was also uncertainty as to where the necessary crude oil was going to come from due to goverment restrictions on imports. Since domestic crude oil has a much different sulphur content than foreign crude oil, there was again the question of what type of refinery to design.

SOHIO'S MARKETING PROGRAM

In an attempt to communicate to the public about the energy crisis Sohio utilized a series of newspaper advertisements. A sample advertisement featuring a series of questions and answers about the gasoline shortages is shown in Exhibit 1.

Sohio also developed a program to suggest methods by which consumers might utilize gasoline more efficiently. Television commercials were prepared to support this program. The cover and inside of a brochure distributed through the company's service stations is given in Exhibit 2.

Questions

1. Evaluate Sohio's advertisement for informing the public of the nature of the gasoline shortage.
2. Discuss Sohio's strategy of reducing gasoline consumption through the suggestion of ways that consumers might use gasoline more wisely. What is the danger to Sohio with this approach?
3. What other alternatives are open to Sohio to temporarily reduce the demand for its gasoline? What strategy do you recommend?

Exhibit 1

Newspaper Advertisement on the Gasoline Shortage

Why it's important to conserve gasoline

Sohio is doing its best to produce gasoline at record rates. Most other refiners are doing the same. However, the *demand* for gasoline is also growing at record rates. For the first time in our nation's recent history, demand for gasoline threatens to exceed the supply. Here are some of the reasons for this unprecedented demand.

More cars than ever before

There are an estimated 25 million more cars and trucks on the road today than just five years ago. And 1973 cars are being produced and purchased at all-time record levels. U. S. new car sales increased by over 20% for the first 3 months of 1973, compared to the same period of 1972. And there are more 2- and even 3-car families than ever before.

Engine emission controls

All cars since 1968 have been equipped with emission control devices. The 1973 cars have more controls than any previous models. These devices are helping clean up our air. They are also contributing to increased fuel consumption. According to U. S. Government figures, standard-size 1973 cars use significantly more gasoline than previous models.

Air conditioning and power aids

Devices such as air conditioning, power brakes, power steering, and automatic transmissions have grown increasingly popular in the past 5 years. They all contribute to increased fuel consumption—especially air conditioning.

What is Sohio doing to help?

We're running our Ohio refineries at maximum capacities, and despite some problems we are trying to keep them running that way. We've also expanded these capacities in recent years: our Toledo refinery in 1966 and our Lima refinery in 1970. We're also buying more crude oil for these refineries than ever before, even though crude oil is harder to get. We're doing our very best to help. Won't you help, too?

We want you to use Sohio gasoline, but we want you to use it wisely.

You get more than great gasoline at Sohio.

Gasoline Saving Tips from Sohio

Exhibit 2
Cover and Inside of Promotional Brochure

Two

Decision Making in Marketing

The man who insists on seeing with perfect clearness before he decides, never decides.

Henri Frederick

Marketing managers must make decisions in a complex and uncertain environment. The manager has a degree of control over an array of marketing instruments. These managerial decision variables are primarily in the areas of pricing, promotion, product, and channels. However, the manager can only attempt to influence a number of other factors affecting most marketing decision situations. Environmental factors such as competitors' actions, government regulations, economic conditions, and, most importantly, buyer behavior are often decisive.

The environment is dynamic and, to a great extent, beyond the control of the manager. The impact of social change on one established product class—the shampoo market—illustrates this point. In breaking with the establishment, young people let their hair grow long. This long hair requires washing more frequently. Increased usage of strong shampoos means that the oils that are stripped away by shampooing do not have adequate time to build up again. Johnson & Johnson capitalized on this opportunity with their gentleness theme. If their shampoo is gentle enough for a baby, then it is gentle enough to use often. Johnson & Johnson and others such as Herbal Essence have made major gains at the expense of traditional brands. Head and Shoulders and Prell have seen their combined market share be eroded from over 50 percent to about 20 percent.

Marketing managers make decisions on the basis of insufficient information and the quality of these decisions can be improved by the application of a systematic process of problem solving. This chapter introduces the concepts of decision theory and discusses securing marketing information for making decisions. Expert opinion, experiments, surveys, and existing sources provide data inputs.

TRADITIONAL ANALYSIS

Rational decisions require a logically consistent decision process. A traditional method of analysis has evolved to help insure a reasoned approach. More recently, a more formal mathematical approach to decision analysis has appeared to supplement the traditional methods. The traditional method of analysis consists of a five-step sequence:

1. Define the central problem.
2. Formulate the alternatives.
3. Analyze the alternatives.
4. Recommend a solution.
5. Suggest a plan of action.

Each of these steps will be discussed in detail in the following sections.[1]

[1] The section is based on Thomas C. Raymond, *Problems in Business Administration* (New York: McGraw-Hill, 1964), pp. 2-10.

Define the Problem

The central problem is the fundamental issue in a situation. In order to proceed with an effective analysis, management must have the correct focus. Being able to assess the heart of a matter frequently simplifies what seems to be a complex situation.

Decision analysis concentrates on structuring and solving problems, but first the existence of a problem must be recognized.[2] A good manager has the ability to identify problems and opportunities early. One fundamental issue that continually must be addressed is the determination of what our business should be. Information bearing on this decision is obtained by monitoring who our customers are, who they should be, and what they value. Managers must first be concerned with doing the right things, then with doing things right.[3]

Sometimes managers look for situations in which there is a negative variance between an existing condition and desired results. Then the manager attempts to reduce this difference. Caution must be exercised so that symptoms are not mistaken for the problem. Profits or sales can decline but the real issue may be that we have not spent enough on advertising. Although often neglected, unusually good results should also be investigated to improve our understanding of market mechanisms. In one sense, the introduction of the highly successful Mustang was as big a managerial error as the Edsel. Both involved major errors in the estimation of demand.

The Alternatives

Managers must specify all possible solutions to the central problem. One alternative that is almost always included is the choice of doing nothing. This provides a baseline against which other alternatives can be measured. Alternatives can sometimes be clarified by considering what has failed to work in the past.

The Analysis

Facts needed to evaluate the alternatives must be collected and organized. Some facts will be impossible to procure and others will be unavailable because of costs or the pressure of time. In the absence of needed data, assumptions must be made and justified. Even when data are available, they may not be in the most useful form and often require additional manipulation. Some commonly used statistical tools are discussed at the end of this chapter and in Chapter Three.

In many problem situations, the facts can be usefully organized as pros and cons under each alternative. A one-sided analysis rarely leads to sound conclusions and the advantages and disadvantages of each alternative should be stated. These arguments should be weighted using managerial judgement to show their relative importance.

Solution and Plan of Action

With the factors ordered and weighted, the manager is able to recommend a logical solution. Since subjective assessment of opportunities and risks is inherent in the decision process, different managers can reach different conclusions from the same

[2]William F. Pounds, "The Process of Problem Finding," *Sloan Management Review,* Vol. 11 (Fall 1969), pp. 1-19 and John W. Bonge, "Problem Recognition and Diagnosis: Basic Inputs to Business Policy," *Journal of Business Policy,* Vol. 2 (Spring 1972), pp. 45-53.

[3]Peter F. Drucker, *Management: Tasks, Responsibilities, and Practices* (New York: Harper & Row, 1974).

facts. When making a decision, a plan of action for implementing the decision should be specified. In addition, objectives and measures of results should be made explicit. The plan of action may identify some important factors that were omitted from the analysis.

The traditional method of problem analysis that has been described provides an excellent approach to the solution of the case problems that have been included in this text. The five-step procedure gives students a method of attacking marketing problems and a way to organize their reports. Although the problems of tomorrow are sure to be different, students who develop effective methods of analysis will be better managers and decision makers.

Traditional analysis has been supplemented by decision theory known as personalist decision analysis. The approach requires that the manager stipulate the alternatives, supply probabilistic assessment of uncertainties, and quantify potential consequences of action.

THE FORMAL DECISION MODEL

Personalist decision theory insures that a good decision is made given the manager's knowledge and beliefs. Decision theory has a formal structure and often utilizes symbols.[4] Decisions involve a choice between two or more alternative courses of action. The set of n possible acts is

$$A = \{A_1, A_2, \ldots A_i, \ldots, A_n\} \tag{1}$$

Thus a product development manager may face the alternative courses of action A_1: introduce the new product or A_n: do not introduce the new product.

Environmental conditions beyond the manager's control are termed states of nature. Each state represents one possible environment that may be encountered during the planning horizon.[5] The set of m states is

$$S = \{S_1, S_2, \ldots, S_j \ldots, S_m\} \tag{2}$$

In the new product example, the states of nature are the various market shares that the product may capture. Three states might be: capture 10 percent of market (S_1), capture 3 percent of market (S_2), and capture 0 percent of market (S_3). The more realistic case in which market share would vary continuously between 0 and 100 percent could also be analyzed.

The consequences of adopting a particular alternative are a function of the state of nature that actually occurs. Thus, the values of the results of all combinations of the ith alternative action and the jth state of nature must be determined. The value of a specific combination may be written as

$$V_{ij} = f(A_i, S_j) \tag{3}$$

The values for all combinations can be represented as a payoff table as shown in Table 2-1. The values may be expressed either in monetary form such as discounted profit or nonmonetary terms.

[4]The theoretical discussion in this section relies heavily on Gerald J. Glasser, "Systematic Decision Making," *Preparing Tomorrow's Business Leaders Today,* Peter F. Drucker, ed. (Englewood Cliffs, N.J.: Prentice-Hall, 1969), pp. 137-157 and Ben M. Enis and Charles L. Broome, *Marketing Decisions: A Bayesian Approach* (Scranton: Intext Educational Publishers, 1971). The example is taken from Frank M. Bass, "Marketing Research Expenditures: A Decision Model," *Journal of Business,* Vol. 36 (January 1963), pp. 77-90.
[5]These states are assumed to be mutually exclusive and collectively exhaustive.

Table 2-1
Discounted Profits in New Product Example
(Million Dollars)

| Act | State | | |
	S_1 10 Percent of Market	S_2 3 Percent of Market	S_3 0 Percent of Market
A_1 Introduce	10	1	−5
A_2 Do not introduce	0	0	0

Subjective Probability

When the outcome of a decision is uncertain but the alternatives are known, the manager must specify the probabilities of the various states of nature. If the manager considers that future conditions will be similar to those that have held in the past and a historical record is available, then the long-run frequency for an event can be found. However, many business decision situations occur only once and so the relative frequency concept proposed by classical statisticians does not provide much assistance for the businessman.

If objective statistics are not available, then the manager assigns his own subjective probabilities. For instance, the manager appraising the new product situation assigns probabilities of .7, .1, and .2 to the three possible states of nature: 10 percent, 3 percent, and 0 percent of the market. These probabilities reflect the degree of belief that the manager has that a given outcome will happen. Managers usually have strong intuitive feelings about the likelihood of a particular outcome of a chance process and decision theory attempts to elicit and quantify these probabilities. A technique for obtaining these probabilities will be discussed later in this chapter.

Choice Criterion = expected monetary value

Although a number of choice criteria can be used in formal decision making,[6] only one—expected monetary value—is widely employed in marketing. Expected monetary value is the long-run "average" result that could be anticipated if the same marketing situation happened again and again a large number of times. Managers develop the monetary consequences for each combination of acts and states of nature and then assess the subjective probabilities that the various states of nature will occur. Then, the manager calculates the expected monetary value. This is the sum obtained by multiplying each monetary consequence by the corresponding probability:

$$\text{EMV}[A_i] = \sum_{j=1}^{m} P_j V_{ij} \tag{4}$$

[6]These include the game theoretic approaches: maximax, maximin, and minimax regret and the probabilistic approaches: the Laplace criterion, expected monetary value, and expected opportunity loss. The expected monetary value criterion presumes that the manager is risk neutral. The analysis can be elaborated in order to consider risk aversion or risk seeking.

Finally, the manager adopts the act with the largest expected monetary value. In the example of the new product introduction, the expected monetary value of the two acts would be:

$$EMV[A_1] = .7 \times \$10 \text{ million} + .1 \times \$1 \text{ million} + .2 \times \text{-}\$5 \text{ million}$$
$$= \$6.1 \text{ million}$$
$$EMV[A_2] = 1.0 \times \$0 = \$0$$

Thus in this case the manager should take the first action and introduce the product.

The choice criterion can be modified to take into account the possibility of ruin. Some alternative actions might involve threats to the survival of the firm. These alternatives will be ruled out when the probability of ruin is more than some specified limit, such as one chance in 10,000. For example, in Figure 2-1, the expected monetary value of Plan A is greater than Plan B. However, Plan A has a substantial ruin probability. Therefore, Plan B will be chosen. Each firm will have to determine its own ruin threshold.[7]

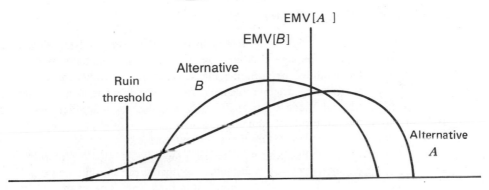

Figure 2-1 Threshold—Constrained Choice.
Source. Martin K. Starr, "Planning Models," *Management Science,* Vol. 13 (December 1966), p. 135.

Expected Value of Perfect Information

The manager may wonder if additional marketing research should be done before a decision is made. The amount by which this information could increase expected monetary value can be determined. Managers will not purchase additional research that costs more than this amount.

To calculate the expected value of perfect information, the expected monetary value under certainty must be defined. This is the amount that would be received if the best action is taken for each state of nature. The expected value under certainty is found by (1) finding the maximum payoff for each state of nature, (2) multiplying each maximum by the corresponding probability of that state, and (3) summing over all states. This procedure is written as

$$EVUC = \sum_{j=1}^{m} (\max_{i} V_{ij}) \times P_j \tag{5}$$

[7]Martin K. Starr, "Planning Models," *Management Science,* Vol. 13 (December 1966), pp. 115-141.

The expected value of perfect information is determined by subtracting the maximum expected monetary value from the expected value under certainty.

$$EVPI = EVUC - \max EMV \qquad (6)$$

The manager would not be willing to pay more than EVPI for additional information. In most situations, the information will not be entirely accurate and is worth less than the expected value of perfect information.

In the new product example, the expected value under certainty is

$$EVUC = .7 \times \$10 \text{ million} + .1 \times \$1 \text{ million} + .2 \times \$0 = \$7.1 \text{ million}$$

The manager would not be willing to pay more than EVPI for additional information. In product would be introduced, but if the manager knew the product would not sell at all, the product would not be introduced. Consequently, the value of perfect information is

$$EVPI = \$7.1 \text{ million} - \$6.1 \text{ million} = \$1 \text{ million}$$

This means $1 million is the most the manager would pay for market research.

Applications of Decision Theory

Implementation of decision theory in the real world has been slow and generally limited to middle managers. A number of large companies have used decision theory analysis: Du Pont for determining the scale of pilot production of a new product, Pillsbury for deciding whether to change from a box to a bag as a package for a grocery product, General Electric for analyzing a shortage of manufacturing capacity for a mature industrial product, Inmont for evaluating potential acquisition candidates, and General Foods for developing a new instant coffee.[8]

Esso Petroleum (London) uses decision theory to evaluate promotional activities.[9] Since a promotional war can substantially reduce profit margins, their policy is to run a promotion only if their major competitor runs one. For example, the Esso Tiger campaign involved point-of-purchase displays, gaily decorated pumps, tiger tails, as well as heavy media advertising. The profitability of a promotional campaign is indicated by the disguised figures shown in Table 2-2. The estimated added volume is ten million gallons and the retained volume is four million gallons. These sales generate an incremental profit of £350,000. The promotion costs £325,000 leaving a profit of £25,000. Suppose that the probability that the competitor will run a campaign is .9, should Esso prepare a promotion? The cost of preparing but not running a promotion is £50,000. The decision tree shown in Figure 2-2 indicates Esso should prepare a promotion. In fact, Esso should prepare a promotion as long as the probability that a competitor will run a promotion is greater than .3.[10]

Limitations of Decision Theory

Decision theory acts to make sure the decision-making process is good. However, it can not guarantee the outcome of the decision will be good. When the underlying market

[8]Rex V. Brown, "Do Managers Find Decision Theory Useful?" *Harvard Business Review,* Vol. 48 (May-June, 1970), pp. 78-89 and Joseph W. Newman, *Marketing Management and Information* (Homewood, Illinois: Richard D. Irwin, 1967), pp. 317-385.

[9]This example is drawn from D. Lowe Watson, "The Contribution of Research to the Planning, Budgeting, and Evaluation of Below-the-Line Activity," *Seminar on "Below-the-Line Activities"* (Noordwijk aan Zee, The Netherlands, May 1971), pp. 189-228.

[10]The breakeven probability, x, is found as follows:
$$x(25,000) + (1 - x)(-50,000) \equiv x(-100,000) + (1 - x)(0)$$
$$\text{and} \qquad x = 50,000/175,000 = .286.$$

Table 2-2
Promotion Evaluation

Sales effect		
Added volume	10,000,000	gallons
+ retained volume	4,000,000	gallons
Total volume effect	14,000,000	gallons
Marginal profit		
Net unit realization	£0.075	
Less marginal product cost	0.040	
Less marginal marketing cost	0.010	
Net marginal profit per unit	£0.025	
Incremental profit		
Incremental profit =		
Total volume effect × net marginal profit per unit		
14,000,000 × 0.025 =	350,000	
Costs		
Direct promotion cost	£200,000	
Media advertising support	100,000	
Point of sale advertising material	15,000	
Other costs	10,000	
Total cost of promotion	£325,000	
Profitability		
Incremental profit	£350,000	
Less cost of promotion	325,000	
Net profit or loss	£25,000	

£ – British pounds

Source. D. Lowe Watson, "The Contribution of Research to the Planning, Budgeting, and Evaluation of Below-the-Line Activity," *Seminar on "Below-The-Line Activities"* (Noordwijk aan Zee, The Netherlands: ESOMAR, May 1971), p. 223.

mechanism is probabilistic, unfavorable events can and will occur.

One of the problems in applying statistical decision models is that managers usually do not think in terms of probability distributions. Asked to estimate future sales, most managers will provide their best guess: a point estimate. Some will indicate a range, that is, plus or minus x per cent. Rarely will they visualize a probability distribution for sales.[11]

Moreover, many managers seek to reduce the uncertainty in their decision making rather than to improve their ability to deal with uncertain decisions. Harlan Meal of Arthur D. Little notes that "executives want to think of themselves as individuals whose greater grasp of the available information and whose greater insight remove the uncertainty from the situation."[12]

[11]David W. Conrath, "From Statistical Decision Theory to Practice: Some Problems with the Transition," *Management Science,* Vol. 19 (April 1973), pp. 873-883.

[12]Rex V. Brown, "Marketing Applications of Personalist Decision Analysis", (Cambridge, Mass.: Marketing Science Institute, July 1971).

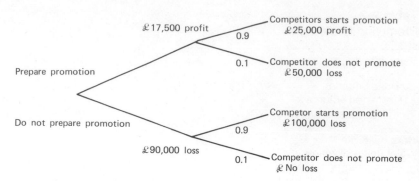

Figure 2-2 Promotional Decision Tree.
Source. D. Lowe Watson, "Contribution of Research to the Planning, Budgeting, and Evaluation of Below-the-Line Activity," *Seminar on "Below-the-line Activities"* (Noordwijk aan Zee, The Netherlands; ESOMAR, May 1971), p. 224.

SECURING MARKETING INFORMATION FOR DECISION MAKING

A marketing-oriented firm will constantly be trying to know its customers and their requirements better. This effort will reduce the chances that the firm might be surprised by market changes. These and other information needs can be met by information obtained from experts, through experimentation, through surveys, or from existing sources. The actual choice will involve a trade-off between desired accuracy and desired expenditures of money and time. The manager must weight the anticipated benefits of uncertainty reduction against the estimated cost of the information.

The quality of research information is judged by its validity and reliability. Validity indicates whether an investigation measures that which it intends to measure. The results should reflect true differences and not just random noise. Reliability, a component of validity, indicates the extent of random variation. Reliability guarantees only that the results of replications of the study will be consistent. It does not insure that the results are correct.[13]

Securing Information from Experts

Decision theory requires that individuals be able to express their beliefs as personal expectations about uncertain events. A method for eliciting personal probabilities is given in the Appendix. When more than one expert provides an opinion, their possible divergent views must be reconciled. The Delphi technique provides one approach to this problem. Eventually you as a manager must decide whether to rely on your own opinion, on that of a particular expert, on the average opinion of a group of experts, or on a composite of one or more experts and your own opinion.[14]

[13]See Julian L. Simon, *Basic Research Methods in Social Science: The Art of Empirical Investigation* (New York: Random House, 1969) or Claire Selltiz, Marie Jahoda, Morton Deutsch, and Stuart W. Cook, *Research Methods in Social Relations* (New York: Holt, Rinehart and Winston, 1959) for more detailed coverage of the research process.

[14]For a complete discussion, see L. J. Savage, "Elicitation of Personal Probabilities and Expectations," *Journal of the American Statistical Association,* Vol. 66 (December 1971), pp. 783-801.

Group Opinion Measurement. Often group judgement about subjective probabilities is used instead of individual judgement. The Delphi method is a technique for eliciting and reaching a group consensus. Individuals anonymously report their subjective probabilities. The median probability estimates of the group are reported back to the individuals.[15] Often a list of the explanations given by the individuals for their decisions is provided. The individuals submit revised subjective probabilities. The feedback and revision process continues until the responses converge.

The Evaluation of Assessors. The competence of individual managers in providing subjective probabilities will vary. Expertise in the technical aspects of probability assessment is a function of the manager's ability to adhere to the axioms of probability theory and to provide assessments that correspond to his or her judgements. Incentives to encourage quantification of judgements in accordance with beliefs are often necessary.[16]

The technical capability to express judgements in probability terms is insufficient if the judgements themselves are not good. Marketing expertise can be gauged by the length and breadth of the manager's experience and the scope of the analysis. Source evaluation questions such as the following might be asked:

1. How much experience have you had in the industry?
2. How much experience have you had in the following?
   (a) Technical design analysis.
   (b) Economic analysis, operations analysis.
   (c) Political evaluation.
   (d) Technical development forecasting.
3. Did you consider the following in your analysis?
   (a) Political position.
   (b) Competition from others.
   (c) Product restrictions trend.
   (d) Effect of advantages of new product on demand.
   (e) Effect of price on the demand.
4. Were the following market segments considered?
   (a) U.S. domestic.
   (b) U.S. international.
   (c) Remaining international.

Past judgements of an individual can be examined to see whether they are optimistic or pessimistic in any sense.

Securing Information Through Experimentation

Experimentation is a methodology in which one or more variables called the experimental variables are manipulated in such a way as to show their impact on some dependent variable while controlling for the contemporaneous impact of extraneous

---

[15]These estimates are normalized so that the probabilities sum to one. For an application of the method see Marvin A. Jolson and Gerald L. Rossow, "The Delphi Process in Marketing Decision Making," *Journal of Marketing Research,* Vol. 8 (November 1971), pp. 443-448. A formal mathematical method can be found in Morris H. DeGroat, "Reaching a Consensus," *Journal of the American Statistical Association,* Vol. 69 (March 1974), pp. 118-121.

[16]Robert L. Winkler, "The Quantification of Judgement: Some Methodological Suggestions," *Journal of the American Statistical Association,* Vol. 62 (December 1967), pp. 1105-1120.

[17]G. J. Brabb and E. D. Morrison, "The Evaluation of Subjective Information," *Journal of Marketing Research,* Vol. 1 (November 1964), pp. 40-48.

variables. Because the market place is a complex environment, the market researcher cannot hold these extraneous factors constant. This does not matter as long as marketing management is interested in a comparison between alternative courses of action, such as whether to distribute to customers through wholesalers or company-owned branches. Then the evaluation can be done on the basis of *relative* effectiveness.

Experimental Designs. There are a variety of experimental designs.[18] A very general design is the Solomon four-group design. This design is as follows:

	Experimental Group I	Experimental Group II	Control Group I	Control Group II
Before measurement	Yes	No	Yes	No
Experimental variable	Yes	Yes	No	No
After measurement	Yes	Yes	Yes	Yes

Individuals are randomly assigned to the four groups. Thus, there is no selection bias.

The purpose of a control group is to indicate the effect of confounding factors. Control group I is needed to assess the combined effects of history, maturation, mortality, and miscellaneous influences. History refers to those events occuring between the first and second measurement in addition to the experimental variable. The longer the time period between measurements, the greater the probability that history will jeopardize the results. Maturation refers to physiological or psychological processes within the subject that take place as a function of time alone. Mortality refers to the loss of respondents between measurements. Control group II serves to assess the effects of testing. Testing refers to the influence of the before measurement on the after measurement. The before measurement may cause the respondents to start thinking about the topic under study. Furthermore, the respondents might remember their answers to the first measurement.

The expense of the four-group design limits its use. In addition, the testing factor is important only when we are interested in individual internal processes such as awareness and attitude. When the dependent variable is an aggregate variable such as sales, both control group II and experimental group II can be eliminated. The resultant design is called the before-after control-group design.

A widely used example of the before-after control-group design is an experiment run by the National Broadcasting Company.[19] NBC interviewed 2441 household heads in a medium-size midwestern market twice three months apart. At each interview, respondents reported their purchases of twenty-two brands in eleven household product categories during the preceding four weeks. The dependent variable, then, was the percentage who purchased the brands during the past four weeks. At the second interview, the respondents were divided ex post facto into two groups: those who had been exposed to magazine and television advertising for the relevant products and those who had not been exposed. The results were:

[18]Donald T. Campbell and Julian C. Stanley, *Experimental and Quasi-Experimental Designs For Research* (Chicago: Rand McNally and Company, 1963).

[19]Thomas E. Coffin, "A Pioneering Experiment in Assessing Advertising Effectiveness," *Journal of Marketing,* Vol. 27 (July 1963), pp. 1-10.

	Experimental Group (Percent)	Control Group (Percent)
Before measurement	19.4	19.4
Experimental variable	Advertising	No advertising
After measurement	20.5	16.9
Change	+1.1	−2.5
Effect of experimental variable	+3.6	

Securing Information Through Surveys

Surveys obtain information by means of questionnaires. These questionnaires are administered by one of the major survey methods: mail surveys, telephone interviews, and personal interviews. Surveys are usually conducted on a sample. No matter what sampling plan is chosen, there will be sampling error. Moreover, nonsampling errors will also be present. Careful questionnaire construction is a key step in reducing measurement bias.

Survey Methods. The three most prevalent methods of directly questioning a respondent are the mail questionnaire, the telephone interview, and the personal interview. Each method has its own strengths and weakenesses.

A mail survey requires mailing questionnaires to respondents. These questionnaires are then self-administered by the respondents. No personal interviewer is involved. The advantage of mail surveys include wider geographic coverage; less distribution bias by type of neighborhood, family, or individual; no interviewer bias; better chance of thoughtful answers; time saving (over personal interview); centralized control; and cost saving. Mail surveys are inappropriate when no mailing list is available or is acceptable because of incompleteness or bias, when the subject matter requires a trained interviewer, when the questionnaire is too long or too difficult, when the respondent is not the addressee, and when the available time is insufficient.[20]

Information on changes in the attitudes and purchase behavior of an individual is available only if the same questions are repeated on the same respondents. In longitudinal analysis, this is called a panel design. The Market Research Corporation of America (MRCA) collects data on the purchases of nondurable consumer products. In this context, the mail survey instrument is called a diary. A sample page from a diary is shown in Figure 2-3.

Personal interviews are characterized by face-to-face interaction between the interviewer and the respondent. The physical presence of the interviewer permits flexibility in asking questions, creates motivation for cooperation that leads to high response rates, and allows for longer interviews. On the other hand, the same physical presence limits the geographic spread of the respondents, precludes respondent anonymity, induces response bias, and necessitates expensive interviewing costs, training costs, and control costs.[21]

Group interviewing occurs when respondents are interviewed in groups rather than individually. Respondents are interviewed at a central site rather than in the field. Thus,

[20]Paul Erdos, *Professional Mail Surveys* (New York: McGraw-Hill, 1970).

[21]Charles S. Mayer, "Data Collection Methods: Personal Interviews," in Robert Ferber, ed., *Handbook of Marketing Research* (New York: McGraw-Hill, 1974), pp. 2-82 to 2-89.

TOILET BOWL CLEANERS, BATHROOM CLEANERS   None ☒

Columns: (Brand) | Check FORM (Liquid or Foam / Dry / Pressurized Can Aerosol) | Check TYPE of CONTAINER (Other Can / Plastic Bottle with Spray Top / Other Plastic Bottle / Glass Bottle with Spray Top / Other Glass Bottle / Other—Describe) | QUANTITY (How many pkgs. or items of each kind) | WEIGHT (SIZE) (Of each pkg., item, lbs., ozs., etc.) | PRICE PAID (DON'T INCLUDE TAXES — For Each / Total if more than one) | Newspaper—Store's Ad / Newspaper—Manufacturer's Ad / Magazine / Direct Mail / From Prior Purchase Same Item / From Other Purchase / Off, Other Special Offer / Write in Value of Coupon, Off, etc. | WHERE BOUGHT (NAME OF STORE OR DELIVERY COMPANY / TYPE OF STORE Grocery, Drug Department, Home Delivery, Carry-Out, Other (Describe))

OTHER CLEANING and LAUNDRY PRODUCTS   For laundry, floors, walls, plumbing fixtures, furniture, pots and pans, appliances, hands, etc.   None ☐

BORAX (Like Borateem, Arm & Hammer, etc.) (Brand)
Check FORM (Powder, Granules, Flakes or Chips / Liquid / Paste / Cake / Other) | Check TYPE of CONTAINER (Box or Bag / Pressurized Can (Aerosol) / Bottle with Spray Top / Other Bottle / Other Type) | Does Label mention Special GIFT OFFER (YES—Describe / NO (✓))

HEAVY DUTY HAND CLEANERS (Brand)
3/1 BOOSTER ✓ (Liquid) ✓ (Pressurized Can) ✓ (NO) 1 9oz .43   RED DRUG

OTHER CLEANERS and SOFTENERS (Brand)

DISPOSABLE DIAPERS, LINERS   None ☐
Check as Many as Apply (✓) (Disposable Diaper / Liner / Pre-Folded / Pinless) | Intended User Write in: Age (Years / Months) / Weight | Number in each Package

3/1 TENDER ✓✓ 2   12 1 — .99   ✓ .13 RED DRUG

TOILET TISSUES   None ☐
Check ONE (Solid Color / Print or Pattern) | Write in Color(s) (Solid or Pattern) | Does Package Give Ply of Tissues? (✓) Yes/No | If "Yes" Write in Ply. (For example: 2-Ply, 3-Ply, etc.) | How Many Single Sheets in Each Roll? | How Many Rolls in Each Package? | Write in Total Square Feet if shown on label

3/8 PRIM ✓ YEL. ✓ 2 Ply 1000 2 — 1 2 Rolls .33   PETE'S MKT.

Figure 2-3 Sample Diary Page.

group interviewing can be conducted quickly and inexpensively. Group interviewing generates qualitative rather than quantitative results. It is best used when research is at an exploratory stage and idea generation is desired. The group interviews are often used in new product studies.

Telephone interviews represent a compromise between mail surveys and personal interviews. The primary advantages of a telephone interview are speed and efficiency. Telephone interviews are also more economical than personal interviews. The main drawbacks of telephone interviews center around having incomplete frames because everyone does not have a telephone, because some subscribers have unlisted telephone numbers, and because telephone directories become obsolete over time. Telephone interviews are also limited because the interview length must be kept brief and only short comments can be elicited.[22]

Questionnaire Construction. Having decided on what information should be sought and which survey method should be used, the next step is the development of the data collection form. The process of questionnaire construction consists of (1) deciding on the content of the individual questions, (2) determining their form, (3) deciding on

[22]Stanley L. Payne, "Data Collection Methods: Telephone Surveys," in Robert Ferber, ed., *Handbook of Marketing Research* (New York: McGraw-Hill, 1974), pp. 2-105 to 2-123.

their wording, (4) placing these questions in sequence, (5) specifying the layout of the questionnaire, (6) pretesting the questionnaire and (7) preparing the final version of it.[23]

The form of the question can be either check or open-end. The Newsweek Survey, shown in Figure, 2-4, contains check questions. These check questions can be either dichotomous (Question 1) or multiple-choice (Question 5). Check questions provide fixed alternative answers among which the respondent must choose. In contrast, the open-end question permits the respondent to give any answer. Open-end questions are often used when the alternative answers to a question are not known to the researcher. Otherwise, check questions are usually used because they can be answered more quickly and they are easier to tabulate and analyze. Most questionnaires contain both forms of questions.

The wording of the question must be chosen with care.[24] Questions should contain words that are familiar to the respondent. Furthermore, each word should hold the same meaning among all respondents. Questions should not be too complex or too long. In particular, each question should make only one query. On the other hand, questions should be specific enough that the respondent knows what is being asked.

Questions should be placed in the sequence that will promote respondent cooperation while avoiding order bias. The first question should create respondent interest in the questionnaire. This is very important for mail surveys. In general, the questions should appear in logical sequence. This aids the respondent's train of thought. Difficult or confidential questions should be asked only after the respondent has become involved in the questionnaire. Caution must be exercised to make sure that a question does not bias the answers to questions that follow it.

The questionnaire should appear short and easy to complete in order to encourage its acceptance by the respondents.[25] The layout should make clear where the answer is to be checked or where an answer is to be written. The space for answering should be to the right of the question since the question must be read before it can be answered. This was not done in the Newsweek survey. When the answer involves frequency intervals as with classification questions such as age and income, these intervals must be exhaustive and mutually exclusive as shown in Question 5 of the Newsweek Survey. If a portion of the questions need not be answered by a respondent, then instruction should indicate what to skip.

Have you heard of Cantrece Nylons?   Card #04 (cols. 5-6)

Yes _____-1   No _____-2   (col. 7)

IF NO, GO TO THE NEXT SECTION

Note that this personal interview questionnaire was also precoded to simplify data processing.

The questionnaires should be pretested under field conditions to insure that the respondents hold the same understanding as the researcher concerning what is being asked and what the answers mean. The pretest is a check against taking something important for granted. Any deficiencies found in the pretest should be corrected before distributing the final questionnaire.

Sampling Plan. Information may be obtained from the whole population by means of a census or from only a portion of the population by sampling. Temporal and monetary

---

[23]Harper Boyd and Ralph Westfall, *Marketing Research* (Homewood, Ill.: Richard D. Irwin, 1972), pp. 284-316.

[24]Stanley L. Payne, *The Art of Asking Questions* (Princeton, N.J.: Princeton University Press, 1951).

[25]Paul L. Erdos, *Professional Mail Surveys* (New York: McGraw-Hill, 1970), pp. 37-74.

NEWSWEEK SUBSCRIBER SURVEY

The following questions can be answered quickly and easily,
with a check or a word or two.

Please use the postage-paid envelope provided for your
convenience in returning the questionnaire to us

Your answers will, of course, be confidential.

1. In reporting matters of controversy, do you believe that NEWSWEEK is generally
even-handed and fair or that it takes sides?

A☐ Even-handed, fair   B☐ Takes sides

2. Which one category below best indicates how you would describe NEWSWEEK in terms of
being politically conservative or liberal?

A☐ Very conservative   C☐ Middle-of-the-road   E☐ Very liberal

B☐ Somewhat conservative   D☐ Somewhat liberal

3. What is your business, industry
or profession?

A☐ Agriculture/Forestry

B☐ Communications/Publishing/Advertising

C☐ Construction/Mining

D☐ Education

E☐ Finance or Banking

F☐ Government

G☐ Insurance or Real Estate

H☐ Manufacturing

I☐ Professional (MD, Lawyer, etc.)

J☐ Services to Business

K☐ Transportation or Public Utilities

L☐ Travel/Entertainment

M☐ Wholesale or Retail Trade

N☐ Other (please specify)

_____

4. What is your title or position? Please
check the most appropriate box.

A☐ Owner, Partner, Director

B☐ Company President

C☐ Other Company Officer
(Vice-Pres., Treasurer, etc.)

D☐ Department Head

E☐ Manager

F☐ Supervisor

G☐ Other administrative position
not mentioned above

H☐ Scientist or Engineer

I☐ Sales-Equipment

J☐ Technical Specialist

K☐ Sales-Merchandise

L☐ Clerical   M☐ Teacher

N☐ Foreman, Skilled Craftsman, Laborer

O☐ Housewife   P☐ Student   Q☐ Retired

R☐ Military (Rank: _____)

S☐ Other (please specify)_____

5. Which one of the following categories most closely approximates your total annual income,
from all sources, including salaries, dividends and so on?

B☐ Under $5,000   G☐ $15,000—$17,499   L☐ $40,000—$49,999

C☐ $ 5,000—$ 7,999   H☐ $17,500—$19,999   M☐ $50,000—$74,999

D☐ $ 8,000—$ 9,999   I☐ $20,000—$24,999   N☐ $75,000 or more

E☐ $10,000—$12,499   J☐ $25,000—$29,999

F☐ $12,500—$14,999   K☐ $30,000—$39,999

6. Please indicate the charity of your choice:

A☐ UNICEF   C☐ Red Cross

B☐ American Cancer Society   D☐ American Heart Society

(For every ten thousand mentions, we'll contribute $750.00 to the designated charity.
This could well mean a substantial donation to each charity, depending of course,
upon the number of subscribers responding. Thank you!)

Figure 2-4 One-Page Mail Survey.

costs usually preclude conducting a census. Thus, surveys are used to provide sample information from which inferences about the population can be made. The design of the sample survey and the determination of the sample size is beyond the scope of our coverage.[26] However, some of the basic concepts of sampling will be introduced.

The design of a sample survey begins with the definitions of the population or universe the researcher wishes to study. For example, the universe may be all car owners in the United States. An element of the population is the subject on which a measurement is taken. Sampling units are collections of elements. If each sampling unit contains one and only one element, then a sampling unit and an element are synonymous. However, quite frequently they are not identical. For example, it might be more efficient to sample households rather than individual car owners. The sampling units would be households and the number of elements would vary among households. The list of sampling units is called a frame. For households, the frame might be a telephone directory or a list of registered voters.

Each sample observation contains some information about the population. The amount of information contained in a sample depends on the size of the sample. It also depends on the extent of variability in the data. Note that the size of the universe is irrelevant.[27] Each sample observation also costs money. Thus, there is a trade-off between precision and cost.

A sample cannot provide perfect information about the population because of variability in the sampling process itself. Consequently, it is desirable to know at least approximately the magnitude of this sampling error. This is possible only when probability sampling is used. Probability sampling procedures are those in which every element has a known probability of being selected. The opposite is a convenience sample where elements are selected haphazardly, the probability of inclusion is unknown, and statements cannot be made about the statistical significance of the results.

The basic preferred design is simple random sampling. Simple random sampling draws a sample in such a manner that every sampling unit has an equal probability of being chosen. As long as the population is relatively homogeneous, a simple random sample contains as much information as any other survey design. When the population can be segmented into distinct groups that are more homogeneous than the population as a whole, then stratified random sampling is better because it yields greater precision for the same sample size. When an acceptable frame is unavailable or when the cost of obtaining observations is a function of the distance between sampling units, then cluster sampling is better because it yields a given amount of information at the minimum cost. Cluster sampling is simple random sampling in which each sampling unit is a cluster of city blocks or census tracts.

Nonsampling Errors. The accuracy of marketing research is not affected by sampling error alone. Total survey error also includes nonsampling errors. There are many types of nonsampling errors. Some of these are measurement error, frame error, noncontact error, and refusal error. Since these errors may be as large or larger in magnitude as sampling error, they should be evaluated if only subjectively.[28]

---

[26]A good introduction is provided in William Mendenhall, Lyman Ott, and Richard L. Scheaffer, *Elementary Survey Sampling* (Belmont, Cal.: Wadsworth Publishing Company, 1971).

[27]If the size of the sample is large relative to the universe, this must be taken into account by a finite population correction factor.

[28]The technical procedure for making such an assessment is given in two articles by Rex V. Brown: "Evaluation of Total Survey Error," *Journal of Marketing Research,* Vol. 4 (May 1967), pp. 117-127 and "Just How Credible Are Your Market Estimates?," *Journal of Marketing,* Vol. 33 (July 1969), pp. 46-50.

Measurement errrors can arise from defective questionnaire construction. They also can occur when the way the interviewer asks a question influences the respondent's answer. Many respondents wish to give the interviewer the answer they think the interviewer wants. Thus, interviewers must be carefully trained not to give cues to the respondent. Respondents might give incorrect answers in other situations as well. Under time pressure, the respondent might give less thoughtful replies in order to complete the interview as quickly as possible. Respondents tend to give a more favorable picture of themselves than is true when questions concerning their prestige are asked.

Frame error is usually present to some degree since a perfect listing is rarely available. For example, in a telephone survey a directory is likely to be used. One study found that about 12 percent of the households did not have a telephone, about 6 percent had unlisted numbers, and about 12 percent of the households had a telephone installed after the beginning of the directory year.[29]

Nonresponse error exists when some respondents cannot be reached. Noncontact occurs because the respondent is not at home, is away on business or a vacation, or has moved. Refusal occurs when the respondents are busy at some other activity, are ill, or consider the information sought as an invasion of their privacy.

These nonsampling biases arise in panel designs as well.[30] Panels inevitably experience mortality bias. Of those initially contacted, about 40 percent refuse to participate, and additional 15 percent drop out during the first few weeks, and thereafter 1 percent per month stop participating. Conditioning bias may occur if repeated questioning causes changes in the respondent. Inaccuracies by respondents in recalling and recording their purchase behavior is the origin of more bias.

Securing Information Through Observation   — A.C. Nielsen Co.

More accurate information on the behavior of respondents can be achieved by observing the behavior than by relying on reports by the respondents. Sometimes respondents will not remember their own behavior. Other times they will claim behavior that will give themselves a better image. For example, people were observed buying cut-rate gasoline during the day. Their telephone numbers were obtained using their license plate numbers. That same night in response to a telephone survey, many of these people stated that they bought a name-brand gasoline that day.

Pantry audits can be used to confirm reported consumer purchase behavior. Field-workers enter the home and conduct an inventory of the brands on hand, their quantities, and their prices.[31] The Johnson Wax Company has discovered that reported brand purchases of floor wax vary greatly from the actual brand in inventory.[32]

Audits can also be performed on retail stores. The A. C. Nielsen Company conducts an audit on a representative cross-section of retail outlets every sixty days. The type of data obtained for a brand is shown in Figure 2-5. These data are available not only for our own brand but for competitive brands as well.

[29]Sanford L. Cooper, "Random Sampling by Telephone—An Improved Method," *Journal of Marketing Research,* Vol. 1 (November 1964), pp. 45-48.

[30]Louis P. Bucklin and James M. Carman, *Research Program in Marketing* (Berkeley, Cal.: Institute of Business and Economic Research, 1967).

[31]For instance, Haug Associates, a commercial marketing research firm, conducts a home audit bimonthly for the Los Angeles Times.

[32]Paul Green and Donald S. Tull, *Research for Marketing Decisions* (Englewood Cliffs, N.J.: Prentice-Hall, 1975), p. 154.

"Alpha" Brand of Cake Mix (39¢ Size) in Super X Market

		FOR JUNE-JULY
	PKGS.	VALUE
INVENTORY:		
July 9	114 Pkgs.	
Sept. 10	93 Pkgs.	
Change	21	
PURCHASES		
From manufacturer (1 order)	12	$ 3.72
From wholesalers (4 orders)	48	15.00
Total	60	$18.72
CONSUMER SALES		
Packages	81	
Price, per pkg.		$ .39
Dollars, total		$31.59
STORE PROMOTION		YES NO
Goods display		☒ ☐
Local advertising		☒ ☐
Inad coupons		☒ ☐
Feature pricing		$ .33

Figure 2-5 A Store Audit.
Source. Nielsen Retail Index Service (Chicago: A. C. Nielsen Company, 1965), p. 6. Courtesy of the A. C. Nielsen Company, Retail Index. Division, Nielsen Plaza, Northbrook, IL 60026.

Securing Information From Existing Sources

Often data is already available in records kept within the firm or held by external organizations. Sales and marketing cost information are generated regularly as a by-product of the firm's usual course of business. This internal information might have to be restructured into a more useful form.

The primary sources of external information are the government and commercial services. The government publishes statistics and special reports on many topics. Commercial services such as Nielsen and MRCA provide information through panels and store audits. Trade associations are also important sources of secondary information.

ANALYTICAL TOOLS

Managerial decisions are based on data gathered by the firm's marketing information system. Frequently the raw data have to be processed to convert them to a more useful form. Two of the more common techniques used for this purpose in marketing are cross classification analysis and regression analysis. Regression analysis will be discussed in Chapter Three.

Cross Classification

The simplest way to examine data for relationships among variables is by means of cross-classification analysis. Each variable is divided into a number of categories or attributes. Each observation simultaneously falls into one category on each of the variables. In a table, the intersection of categories across variables is called a cell. Cross tabulation involves counting the number of observations that occur in each cell.

Bucklin, for example, studied the relationship between product price levels and the degree that consumers checked advertising.[33] The first variable had four categories while the second variable had two. Thus the cross tabulation shown in Table 2-3 has eight cells. An unequal number of observations in each price category made visual interpretation of the raw data difficult and so the data were transformed into percentages. The results indicate that advertising is used much more frequently in the search for higher-priced products.

Table 2-3
The Checking of Advertisements by Product Price Level

Product Cost (Dollars)	Checked (Percent)	Not Checked (Percent)	Total (Percent)	Base
5-9	14	86	100	(370)
10-19	22	78	100	(198)
20-49	31	69	100	(176)
50 or more	46	54	100	(123)
Total	24	76	100	(867)

SOURCE. Louis P. Bucklin, "The Informative Role of Advertising," *Journal of Advertising Research,* Vol. 5 (September 1965), pp. 11-15.

When the values of two or more variables tend to vary together, there is said to be association among these variables. On rare occasions variables will exhibit concurrent movement even though no real association exists. Consequently, a significance test is necessary to provide reassurance that any observed covariation is greater than could reasonably be attributed to chance.[34]

A chi square test can be used to examine the reality of any association. This test assumes that the variables are statistically independent. The actual cell frequencies (O_{ij}) are compared with those frequencies (E_{ij}) that would be expected if the variables were independent. The expected cell frequencies are calculated according to the rules of probability. Under the null hypothesis of independence, the joint probability of the variables is the product of the marginal probabilities. The formula for the two variable case is

$$E_{ij} = \left(\frac{R_i}{n}\right)\left(\frac{C_j}{n}\right)n = \frac{R_i\,C_j}{n} \qquad (7)$$

[33]Louis P. Bucklin, "The Informative Role of Advertising," *Journal of Advertising Research,* Vol. 5 (September 1965), pp. 11-15.

[34]M. J. Moroney, *Facts From Figures* (Baltimore, Md., Penguin Books, 1965), pp. 246-270.

where R represent the ith row total, C_j represents the jth column total, and n represents the grand total, that is, the sample size.

Observed and expected cell frequencies can be compared using the formula

$$\chi^2 = \sum_{i=1}^{r} \sum_{j=1}^{c} \frac{(O_{ij} - E_{ij})^2}{E_{ij}} \tag{8}$$

where r = number of rows and c = number of columns in the table. The formula requires that raw data, not percentages, be used. The expected value for χ^2 is zero. The question is whether the calculated value of χ^2 is sufficiently great to refute the null hypothesis that the observed discrepancy could have arisen by chance.

The distribution of the statistic is approximately chi square.[35] The significance level of the test is usually chosen to be .05. This is the probability of rejecting the null hypothesis by mistake when it is true. If the value of calculated χ^2 is greater than the value of the tabulated $\chi^2_{.05}$, then the null hypothesis of statistical independence is rejected. If the calculated value is less than the tabulated value, the null hypothesis cannot be rejected.

Suppose that a product manager is interested in whether customer's sex affects product usage rates. A survey is conducted and the results are shown in the top half of Table 2-4. The expected frequencies are calculated and are shown in the bottom half. For instance, the expected number of customers out of a sample size of 200 who are both light users and male is (80) (100)/200 or 40. The value of chi square for data in Table 2-4 is thus

Table 2-4
Cross Tabulation of Sex Versus Product Usage Rate

Observed Frequencies

| | Sex | | |
Usage Rate	Male	Female	Total
Light	32	48	80
Medium	42	38	80
Heavy	26	14	40
Total	100	100	200

Expected Frequencies

| | Sex | | |
Usage Rate	Male	Female	Total
Light	40	40	80
Medium	40	40	80
Heavy	20	20	40
Total	100	100	200

[35]The chi square distribution has been extensively tabulated. Tables can be found in the appendices of almost any statistics book. The degrees of freedom equals $(r-1)(c-1)$ for two-way classification. The χ^2 test is only an approximation. This approximation is satisfactory only if each *expected* cell size is five or more.

$$\chi^2 = \frac{(32\text{-}40)^2}{40} + \frac{(48\text{-}40)^2}{40} + \frac{(42\text{-}40)^2}{40} +$$
$$\frac{(38\text{-}40)^2}{40} + \frac{(26\text{-}20)^2}{20} + \frac{(14\text{-}20)^2}{20}$$

$$\chi^2 = 7.0$$

Since the observed value of chi square (7.0) is greater than a critical value (5.99) obtained from a chi square table, we can say that a relationship exists between sex and product usage.

When a number of complex relationships are being evaluated, computer programs such as Contingency Table Analysis (BMD02S) are often used.[36] Additional variables can be included in cross-classification analysis. However, as more variables are added, the analysis becomes unwieldly and better results may be obtained by least squares regression.

Summary

This chapter focused on the method of decision theory in marketing problem solving. The emphasis was on consistent choice among courses of action. The decision process was shown to involve (1) recognition and definition of the central problem, (2) formulation of the alternatives, (3) analysis of the alternatives, (4) specification of a solution, and (5) implementation of a plan of action. Personal decision analysis permits the manager to include subjective probabilities about the occurrence of various events in the environment.

Decision making generates information needs. This chapter discussed how information can be elicited from experts, through experimentation, through surveys, or from existing sources. The manager must assess whether reducing the uncertainty inherent in a decision by some amount is worth spending money to obtain additional information and is also worth delaying the decision in the meantime.

Appendix

Elicitation of Personal Probabilities. Different techniques are available for assessing probabilities.[37] The manager can assess either the probability density distribution or the cumulative distribution function for the quantity about which there is uncertainty. The manager can start with certain values of this uncertain quantity and then assign corresponding probabilities or start with fixed values of the probabilities and specify corresponding values of the uncertain quantities. We will consider the technique that involves both second options.

[36]W. J. Dixon, ed., *BMD Biomedical Computer Programs* (Los Angeles: University of California Press, 1970).

[37]This section is based on Robert Schlaifer, *Analysis of Decisions Under Uncertainty* (New York: McGraw-Hill, 1969). See Robert L. Winkler, "The Assessment of Prior Distributions in Bayesian Analysis," *Journal of the American Statistical Association,* Vol. 62 (September 1971), pp. 776-800 for some evidence on the viability of the various techniques.

This technique assesses the cumulative distribution function by means of fractiles. The cumulative distribution function gives the probability that the uncertain quantity will take on a value less than or equal to some specified value. The value of the uncertain quantity that partions the distribution, so that the probability of obtaining a value less than k, is called the kth fractile.

Consider how a brand manager might assess the cumulative distribution for first year sales of a new product. First, the manager can determine the median, or the .50 fractile, level of sales. Suppose the manager believes this value to be four million units. This means that the manager has the opinion that chances for actual sales above or below four million units are equally likely. Next, the manager can divide the halves above and below the median themselves into equally likely halves. This gives the upper quartile, the .75 fractile, and the lower quartile, the .25 fractile. The manager judges five million units to be the upper quartile and three and one half million to be the lower quartile. As a check, the manager should believe that the actual value of sales is just as likely to fall within this interval as that it will fall outside this interval. Finally, the manager expresses beliefs about upper and lower limits between which sales almost certainly will fall. These are usually the .99 and .01 fractiles. The manager assesses that there is one chance in a hundred that sales will exceed eight million units. A similiar assessment indicates sales are unlikely to fall below two million.

A graph of the cumulative distribution of sales fitted from the manager's assessments is shown in Figure 2-6. The manager could make assessments on other fractiles as well.

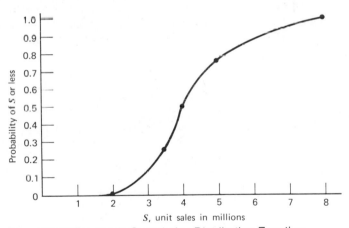

Figure 2-6 Manager's Cumulative Distribution Function.

QUESTIONS

1. Suppose a manager wants to choose between three different campaigns. The first campaign is a modest one involving limited use of national media. The second campaign follows a segmentation strategy in which heavy local media advertising is directed toward concentrated areas where high response is anticipated. The third campaign seeks saturation by means of extensive national media advertising.

   Buyer reponse to a campaign is uncertain because response is also a function of many other factors. Therefore, the manager has converted his personal judgment into probability statements about the likelihood of three different response rates. These probabilities, along with the discounted profits for each campaign in each possible environment, are given in Table 2-5.

What are the expected monetary values of each campaign? Which campaign should the manager choose? What is the most the manager would pay for market research?

Table 2-5
Payoff Matrix and Expected Monetary Values for Campaign Selection Problem

Potential Response (States of Nature)	Probabilties	Campaign Alternatives (Courses of Action)		
		Modest	Segmented	Saturated
Low: less than 15 percent	.3	$2000	-1000	-5,000
Moderate: 15 to 25 percent	.5	3000	4000	3,000
High: more than 25 percent	.2	4000	9000	11,000

2. The 1963, conventional-ply tires and belted tires were being reinforced with rayon and nylon. However, research was being conducted on four other materials: steel wire, Fiberglas, modified nylon, and polyester. A man-made fibers company wants to know what material to choose as a primary target. Internal and external experts identifed key factors about which there was uncertainty and estimated the 1978 market share of each material given assumptions about these key factors. Their results are shown in Figure 2-7. What material would you recommend?

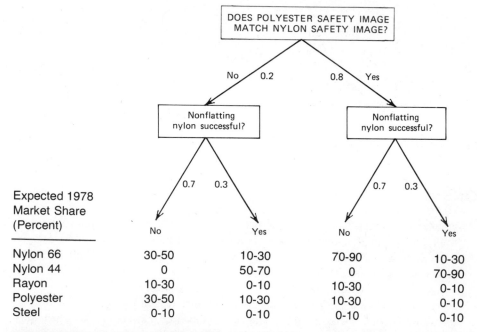

Figure 2-7 Decision Tree for 1978 Automobile Tire Replacement Market.

3. Show how well you can assess the probability function of an uncertain quantity or event. First, answer the following three questions: Did you vote for the Democratic party candidate in the last presidential election? Should it be possible to advertise on behalf of some ends and not others? Will consumerism be enduring? Then, provide the information sought in Table 2-6 without consulting any source material.

   The true values of the uncertain quantities are known. For the first three questions, the responses of the class will determine the true values.

4. Often when making decisions under uncertainty, a manager must make personal probability assessments. What determines whether a manager is a "good" or "bad" assessor?

5. A probability is negligible on the human scale if reasonable men and women act as if this probability can be disregarded. What value would you assign to this probability? Why? If an action has as a posssible outcome the bankruptcy of the firm, what value of the ruin probability would lead you to reject the act out of hand? Why?

Table 2-6

Fractile Uncertain Quantity	.01 One chance in 100 actual below this value	.25 Lower quartile: actual 3 times as likely above as below this value	.50 Median: actual equally likely above or below this value	.75 Upper quartile actual 3 times as likely below as above this value	.99 One chance in 100 actual above this value
1. The percentage of the class who voted for the Democratic party candidate in the last presidential election	——	——	——	——	——
2. The percentage of the class who felt that it should be possible to advertise on behalf of some ends and not others	——	——	——	——	——
3. The percentage of the class who consider that consumerism will be enduring	——	——	——	——	——
4. Total 197__ toy and game sales (in billion dollars)	——	——	——	——	——
5. Coca Cola's 197__ sales (in billion dollars)	——	——	——	——	——
6. Coca Cola's 197__ advertising expenditures (in million dollars)	——	——	——	——	——
7. Coca Cola's 197__ advertising/sales ratio (percentage)	——	——	——	——	——
8. Pepsi's 197__ advertising/sales ratio (percentage)	——	——	——	——	——
9. General Motor's 197__ advertising/sales ratio (percentage)	——	——	——	——	——
10. Listerine's 197__ share of the mouthwash market (percentage)	——	——	——	——	——

6. The manufacturer of a nationally advertised and distributed toilet bowl cleaner wants to obtain information on consumer attitudes about dry versus liquid versus automatic toilet bowl cleaners. The manufacturer is also interested in if the users of those different product types have different characteristics. Design a short mail questionaire to obtain this information. Redesign the questionnaire so that it can be used in a telephone survey.

7. The Chef Boy-Ar-Dee Pizza Company wants to conduct a mail survey on in-home preparation and consumption of pizza. The questionnaire shown in Figure 2-8 has been proposed by an outside market research firm. Comment on any errors that you find in this questionnaire. Construct a revised questionnaire.

Chef Boy-Ar-Dee Market Survey

1. Do you or any of your family eat pizza prepared in the home?
   □ Yes   □ No
2. Do you prefer pizza made from frozen pizza or from pizza mix?
   Frozen pizza □   Pizza mix □
3. What brand of pizza mix did your household last buy?
   Appian Way □   Chef Boy-Ar Dee □
4. Below is a list of frozen pizza. Tell me which is your family's first, second, and third choice.
   Celeste _____
   Gino's _____
   Jeno's _____
   John's _____
   Oh-Boy _____
5. Information on the following questions would be helpful to us in classifying the results of the questionnaire. Please check one answer in each group that best applies to you.

Age		Income Per Year	
Less than 20	□	500-7500	□
20-30	□	7500-10,000	□
30-50	□	10,000-20,000	□
50-65	□	20,000 or over	□
Over 65	□		

Figure 2-8 Mail Survey.

8. A large consumer goods firm wants to know whether customers in the deal prone segment of a market differ significantly on demographic characteristics from customers in the market taken as a whole. The firm conducted a survey. One demographic characteristic, age, is cross tabulated against deal proneness in Table 2-7. Is the relationship between age and deal proneness significant at the .05 level?

Table 2-7
Age and Deal Proneness

	Sample Groups		
Age	Deal Prone	Random	Total
35 and younger	44	13	57
36-50	64	32	96
51 and older	40	36	76
Total	148	81	229

Case 2-1
Lectromatic Corporation[1]

The Lectromatic Corporation, a large manufacturer of electrical appliances, was organized on July 15, 1925, as the result of the merger of two companies with complementary technological expertise. The Thomas W. Wilson Company had been founded in 1884 for the purpose of developing an electrical light. The Charles B. Bronson Company was organized in 1915 in order to adapt refrigeration processes to household use.

The company's growth has been steadily upward with the exception of the depression years. By 1929, it had attained a sales volume of $150 million. By 1933, however, sales had dropped to $43 million, and the company, like many others in the industry, did not recover until the end of the decade. By 1968, the company's sales volume had grown to $4.3 billion.

The company produced all its appliances for the United States market from its manufacturing complex in Georgia. Major subsidiaries include Lectromatic-Canada and Lectromatic Europe. United States facilities for many consumer goods are currently being expanded in anticipation of long-term growth. The company also planned to intensify distribution in Asia and South America by 1970.

The company's financial condition compares favorably with its major competitors. Like many other companies in the industry, Lectromatic's profit margin has declined in recent years. Net profit as a percent of sales was 4.8 percent in 1967 compared with 5.9 percent in 1965.

MARKETING STRATEGY AND ORGANIZATION

Product Line

Lectromatic enjoys a reputation for high-quality appliances. The company has pioneered improvements in its existing product line, and, particularly since the 1950's has developed many new small electrical appliances.

The company produces approximately thirty different types of appliances. Major appliances produced include refrigerators, freezers, washers, dryers, ranges, dishwashers, waste disposals, room air conditioners, and other commercial appliances. The company manufactures both black-and-white and color television sets as well as electric radios, phonographs, tape recorders, mixers, blenders, knives, irons, hair dryers, blankets, toasters, coffee makers, skillets, waffle irons, toothbrushes, and clothes and shoe brushes.

Each appliance comes in a variety of models, price ranges, and colors. For example, the company manufactures twenty-seven models of refrigerators, thirty-two ranges, thirty-one washer and dryer models, twelve different dishwashers, and thirty-two different types of air conditioners. The total product line, excluding color availabilities, consist of slightly over seven hundred models.

Pricing Strategy

Lectromatic follows a regionally oriented, rather than a standardized, pricing policy. Prices to retailers vary from region to region, according to the costs involved in servicing the region and according to other considerations.

Retail prices also vary by region and type of retail outlet. Each individual retailer sets his own prices based on what he pays for the product and on the markup that he needs to implement his particular retailing strategy. The company has not actively pursued a retail price maintenance policy because of the problems and costs involved in enforcement. Generally, retail prices of Lectromatic appliances are either competitive or slightly higher (5 percent) than those of competing brands.

Promotional Strategy

In the past, the company's advertising expenditures have varied between 0.5 percent and 1.5 percent of sales. In 1968, the advertising budget totaled $29,875,000. In 1966, when the company's sales were $3.9 billion, it spent $27,300,000 on advertising. By contrast, the 1966 advertising expenditures of major competitors were (1) General Electric, $22,901,166; (2) Radio Corporation of America, $14,540,513; (3) Zenith, $5,140,644; and (4) Motorola, $5,989,277.[2]

[1]From *Cases in Consumer Behavior,* by Roger D. Blackwell, James F. Engel, and David T. Kollat. Copyright © 1969 by Holt, Rinehart and Winston, Inc. Reprinted by permission of Holt, Rinehart and Winston, Inc.

[2]*National Advertising Investment* (January-December 1966).

The company advertises in a variety of media. In 1968, 28.2 percent of the budget was invested in newspapers, 32.3 percent in magazines, 24 percent in network television, 7.5 percent in spot television, 2 percent in network radio, and 6 percent in spot radio. Major competitors typically spend a smaller percentage in newspapers and spot television and a larger percentage in business publications. This is primarily because of the fact that many competitors produce products for the industrial market.

The company also has a cooperative advertising program with its dealers. The terms are fifty-fifty—the dealer and the company split the cost of the dealers advertising— provided that the dealer meets certain standards established by the company and that the dealer submits acceptable proof of the advertising. Most competitors have a comparable cooperative arrangement with their dealers.

Channels of Distribution

Appliances are shipped from the company's manufacturing facilities in Georgia to five regional, company-owned, distribution centers located throughout the United States. Domestic, nonprivate-brand appliances are sold through twenty-five zone sales offices. The products are distributed through department stores, furniture stores, appliance stores, discount department stores, television and radio shops, and television repair shops. The company also produces private-brand merchandise for several chain organizations. This merchandise is shipped directly from the firm's plant or a regional distribution center to the chain's warehouse.

Marketing Organization

The marketing department is organized on a functional-product basis (Figure 1). The directors of advertising and sales promotion, product planning, field sales, private brands, marketing intelligence, and two product group directors report to the marketing vice president, Jack A. Wilson. The regular force is organized on a regional basis except for quantity sales to business and institutional customers, and national accounts that handle sales of regular merchandise (nonprivate brands) to retailers operating in several geographic areas. Ten product mangers are responsible for making certain that their products receive the proper amount of research, advertising, and sales effort. All research activities are coordinated by the director of marketing intelligence, Harold Wilcox. Bruce Hansen is responsible for the consumer behavior research program.

Harold Wilcox = mkt Resh (Intell)
Bru Hansen Consumer Behavior

CONSUMER RESEARCH PROGRAM

Background and Problems

In the fall of 1965, Wilcox asked Hansen to critically evaluate the company's consumer research program and submit recommendations outlining the ways that it could be improved. In a meeting that lasted nearly three hours, Wilcox outlined some of the problems to Hansen.

"Last week Jack Wilson asked me to review my operation and reevaluate the role that marketing intelligence should play. Jack is under a lot of pressure, you know. Since our profit margin has declined, top management is looking for ways to tighten up expenses. That huge advertising budget of ours is a prime candidate. Wilson's ability to sell the budget in the future is going to require more hard facts than we've had before.

Probs

There are other problems too. The product managers say they aren't getting the kind of information they want in time to make decisions. The advertising and sales promotion manager says he needs more information. And, of course, in our own shop, we either don't have the right kind of information or don't know how to use what we have, or both, because our sales forecasts get worse each year. At any rate I want you to really look into this thing. You've got six months."

Hansen, a young Ph.D from a large midwestern university, took the request seriously. He and his assistants interviewed every member of the marketing department in order to determine the amount and type of information needed and when it was needed. They reviewed journal articles, attended professional meetings, conferred with advertising and marketing research agency executives, and contacted research departments of noncompeting firms that Hansen thought might face similar types of problems.

Six months later Hansen submitted his report. It concluded that the current consumer research program was not meeting the needs of the organization. By depending almost entirely on outside data collection and research groups, operating managers were not getting the kind of information that they needed. Even the useful information commonly reached managers too late.

The report continued by stating that an information system that meets the collective needs of the company has to have several characteristics. First, it ① must be efficient, that is, capable of providing answers to questions in time for managers to use the information before it becomes obsolete. Second, it ② must be flexible enough to answer the variety of

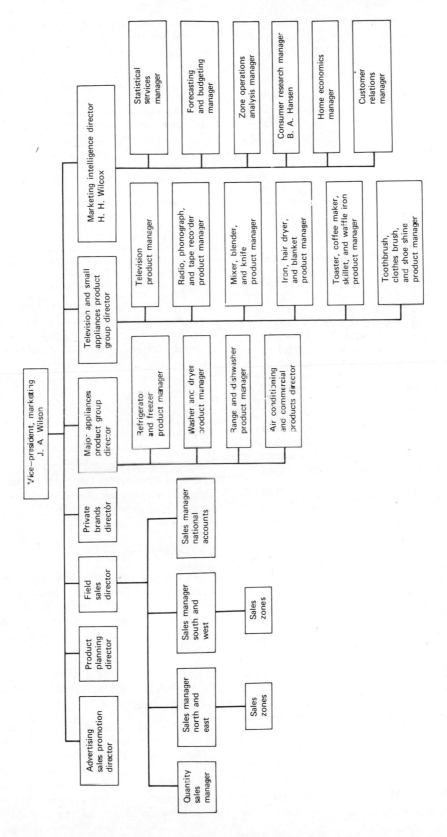

Figure 1 Lectromatic Corporation—Marketing Department.

questions that the organization asks. Finally, it must produce relevant and valid results. With respect to the latter requirement, the report stated:

"Our entire research program utilizes what many psychologists, sociologists, and marketing-behaviorists refer to as a distributive strategy of inquiry. In plain English, this means that we are analyzing only the purchase itself— trying to find out how Lectromatic buyers differ from consumers buying other brands.

While this is a legitimate concern, it has certain limitations. First, we must infer why consumers buy or do not buy our products. If they don't buy we don't know why and if they do buy we still don't know why. This suggests the second limitation: namely that our approach generates limited insights about how our operating managers can go about convincing more consumers to buy our product. It seems to me that a far more useful approach would be to determine, or simply describe if you will, the steps that consumers go through in purchasing appliances. In other words, instead of focusing only on the purchase itself, we should find out what happens *before* that time. For example, what activities and events result in consumers recognizing that they need an appliance? What sources of information are used to learn about different brands? What is the relative importance of these sources? What features are they looking for? Which features are most important? Answers to these questions will provide relevant data for management decisions. This is called a decision process approach and I recommend that we initiate a research program based on this point of view."

The final conclusions of the report were

"If we are to effectively service the consumer behavior information requirements of the organization, and if we are to initiate a Decision Process Research Program (DPRP), and the other programs that will overcome our current deficiencies, our internal organization must be expanded. Outside organizations simply do not presently do the kind of research that we need."

Excerpts of Hansen's report were included in Wilcox's report to Wilson. In May of 1966 Hansen was directed to initiate a DPRP and was authorized 90 percent of the additional personnel, facilities, and financial resources that he had requested.

LECTROMATIC'S DECISION PROCESS RESEARCH PROGRAM[3]

Research Design

The research needs of the company as well as the logic of decision-making itself led Hansen to the

[3]Only selected parts of this program are reported in this case.

choice of a longitudinal design rather than a cross-sectional survey. Hansen justified his selection of longitudinal design as follows:

"Longitudinal analysis of reinterview data is the best available method for understanding changes that occur over time. The span of time that we are concerned with is the time that it requires an average buyer to reach a decision regarding the purchase of one of our products. This time span begins with the emergence of an intention to purchase a product and ends with a decision to purchase or not to purchase.

A national probability sample of 7500 households was designed. Personal interviews were conducted by a New York based interview firm with an established reputation for quality research. Precautions were taken to minimize the possibility that respondents would know that Lectromatic was sponsoring the study.

Each respondent was interviewed once each three months over a two-year period. During each interview, respondents were shown a list of household appliances (those produced by Lectromatic) and asked whether or not they planned to buy any of them some time during the next year. Respondents planning to buy were asked when they anticipated acquiring the item and the brand that they thought they would purchase. During each reinterview, each respondent was asked whether the appliances that he had previously stated he intended to purchase had actually been purchased. Respondents purchasing appliances without previously stated purchase intentions were asked to describe the circumstances and events that led them to buy. Selected findings from the study are discussed below.

Length of Planning Period

The time span between purchase intentions and a decision to purchase varied considerably across products (see Table 1). Clothes dryers have the longest planning period (seventeen weeks) while many appliances have average planning periods of one week or less.

Relationships between Market Share and Purchase Intentions

The respondents intending to purchase an appliance during the next three months were asked to indicate which brand they thought they would purchase. The percentage of respondents intending to purchase Lectromactic appliances was computed and compared with the firm's current market share in each product category. This type of comparison is made available to product managers, advertising

Table 1

Average Length of Planning Period of Selected Appliances

Appliance	Average Length of Planning Period (Weeks) [a]
Clothes dryer	17
Electric range	14
Tape recorder	12
Refrigerator	11
Room air conditioner	5
Electric iron	3
Electric skillet	2
Radio	1

[a] *Planning period* is defined as "the period of time between a stated purchase intention and a purchase."

personnel, and other interested managers every three months.

Table 2 shows the relationship between market share and share-of-purchase intentions from the latest survey. Wide variations exist across products; in some instances purchase intentions exceed market

Table 2

Relationships between Lectromatic's Market Share and Share of Intentions

Appliance	Market Share	Share of Purchase Intentions
Refrigerators	12	21
Freezers	14	19
Washers	10	14
Dryers	8	12
Ranges	14	17
Dishwashers	13	16
Room air conditioners	18	19
Television: black-and-white	21	18
Television: color	17	23
Radios	22	14
Tape recorders	23	31
Mixers	19	20
Blenders	22	14
Knives	21	27
Irons	20	21
Hair dryers	23	28
Blankets	21	6
Toasters	17	12
Coffee makers	18	24
Skillets	17	18
Waffle irons	26	10
Toothbrushes	24	34
Clothes brushes	27	12

share, although for other product categories the opposite relationship exists.

Relationships between Buying Intentions and Purchasing Behavior

Overall, 46 percent of the respondents fulfilled their purchase intentions by buying a brand in the product category for which they had purchase plans. However, as Table 3 indicates, wide variations in fulfillment rates were found. Of those respondents intending to purchase a Lectromatic appliance, only 40 percent actually purchased any brand. Fulfillment rates for respondents originally preferring other brands was much higher—48 percent. Lectromatic also had a lower brand-preferred/brand-purchased rate. Of the respondents originally preferring Lectromatic, only 37 percent eventually purchased the brand. In contrast, on the average, 45 percent of the respondents originally intending to purchase other brands actually purchased them.

Net Gain and Loss Analysis

Although the percentage of respondents who switched away from a particular brand is important, it reveals only part of the behavior that is relevant for management decisions. A more comprehensive, and hence more germane, measure is *net change for a brand*. For example, of those who originally intend to purchase Lectromatic, some will fulfill their intentions, some will purchase another brand, and some will not purchase at all. Similarly, of those originally intending to purchase other brands, some will purchase the brand that they originally preferred, some will purchase another brand (perhaps Lectromatic), and some will not purchase at all. The statistic—net gain or loss—includes the intenders who originally planned to purchase Lectromatic but who actually purchased another brand, as well as the respondents who originally preferred another brand but actually purchased Lectromatic.

Table 4 itemizes net gains and losses from stated brand intentions for each of the products produced by Lectromatic. It is again clear that Lectromatic products differ widely in the net percentage that they gain or lose from original brand intentions.

Unplanned Purchase Analysis

Before reinterviewing respondents, interviewers reviewed the purchase intentions obtained during the previous interview(s). During each reinterview, respondents were shown a card itemizing the products produced by Lectromatic and were asked whether or not they had purchased any of these products since

Table 3

Relationship between Buying Intentions and Purchasing Behavior

Purchase Intention	Purchasing Behavior	
Lectromatic	40 percent purchased the appliance	37 percent purchased the brand intended
	60 percent did not purchase the appliance	63 percent changed brands
Average for all other brands	48 percent purchased the appliance	45 percent purchased the brand intended
	52 percent did not purchase the appliance	55 percent changed brands

the last time they were interviewed. If the respondent purchased one or more of the products but had not previously expressed a purchase intention, he or she was asked, "During our previous conversations you expressed no intention of buying (*insert product*). Would you please tell me the conditions or circumstances that led you to purchase (*insert product*)?"

Purchases without previously stated purchase intentions were classified as *unplanned*. Table 5 summarizes the reasons for these unplanned purchases cross-classified by whether the appliance is a necessity or a luxury.

QUESTIONS

1. What are the advantages of the longitudinal method of consumer research?
2. Under what conditions should this approach be used?
3. What marketing problems are suggested by the data in Tables 1 through 5?
4. What changes in Lectromatic's marketing program would you recommend on the basis of your analysis of the data in Tables 1 through 5?

Table 4

Net Gains and Losses Resulting from Switching from Stated Brand Intentions[a]

	Number of Respondents Switching to Lectromatic and Other Brands for Each 100 Respondents Switching[a] from the Brand	Net Percentage Gain or Loss
Refrigerators		
Lectromatic	60	−40
Average for other brands	95	−5
Freezers		
Lectromatic	90	−10
Average for other brands	99	−1
Washers		
Lectromatic	86	−14
Average for other brands	103	+3
Dryers		
Lectromatic	87	−13
Average for other brands	106	+6
Ranges		
Lectromatic	95	−5
Average for other brands	103	+3
Dishwashers		
Lectromatic	97	−3
Average for other brands	101	+1

Table 4 (continued)

Product and Brand	Number of Respondents Switching to Lectromatic and Other Brands for Each 100 Respondents Switching[a] from the Brand	Net Percentage Gain or Loss
Air Conditioners		
Lectromatic	99	−1
Average for other brands	99	−1
Television: Black-and-White		
Lectromatic	110	+10
Average for other brands	106	+6
Television: Color		
Lectromatic	94	−6
Average for other brands	101	+1
Radios		
Lectromatic	113	+13
Average for other brands	104	+4
Tape recorders		
Lectromatic	92	−8
Average for other brands	97	−3
Mixers		
Lectromatic	101	+1
Average for other brands	104	+4
Blenders		
Lectromatic	107	+7
Average for other brands	102	+2
Knives		
Lectromatic	90	−10
Average for other brands	104	+4
Irons		
Lectromatic	98	−2
Average for other brands	104	+4
Hair dryers		
Lectromatic	92	−8
Average for other brands	98	−2
Blankets		
Lectromatic	112	+12
Average for other brands	102	+2
Toasters		
Lectromatic	107	+7
Average for other brands	103	+3
Coffee makers		
Lectromatic	91	−9
Average for other brands	102	+2
Skillets		
Lectromatic	101	+1
Average for other brands	101	+1
Waffle irons		
Lectromatic	114	+14
Average for other brands	97	−3
Toothbrushes		
Lectromatic	85	−15
Average for other brands	102	+2
Clothes brushes		
Lectromatic	113	+13
Average for other brands	98	−2
Average for all products		
Lectromatic	92	−8
Average for other brands	102	+2

[a]Purchasers only.

Table 5
Reasons for Unplanned Purchases (Percent)

Product and Brand	Type of Appliance[b]		
Reason(s) Given[a]	Necessity	Luxury	All Purchases
Old appliance not available	47	13	35
Dissatisfied with old appliance	10	3	8
Wanted or needed it	21	57	36
Special opportunity to buy	10	18	14
All other reasons	25	28	26

[a]Responses total more than 100 percent because many respondents gave more than one reason.
[b]Appliances classified as necessities include (1) refrigerators, (2) washers, (3) ranges, (4) black-and-white televisions, (5) radios (regular, not FM or transistor), (6) irons, (7) toasters, and (8) coffee makers. The luxury classification includes (1) freezers, (2) dryers, (3) dishwashers, (4) air conditioners, (5) color television, (6) FM and transistor radios, (7) tape recorders, (8) mixers, (9) blenders, (10) knives, (11) hair dryers, (12) blankets, (13) skillets, (14) waffle irons, (15) toothbrushes, and (16) clothes brushes.

Case 2-2
Armengee Clothing, Inc.[1]

Early in 1972 Alchian Armengee, President of Armengee Clothing, Inc., attended a conference at Miami Beach, Florida. One of the sessions he attended was a preview of a Department of Commerce Report on "Demand Equations and Projections for Detailed Items of Expenditure" written by H.S. Houthakker and Lester D. Taylor.[2] One of the demand equations for women's clothing had a positive price coefficient, and it seemed to Mr. Armengee that the equation said that the more you raised price, the greater the revenue.[3] "Suppose you doubled your price every year," he wondered, "wouldn't you be better off?"

The Armengee Clothing Company produced women's clothing with two principle operating divisions, one of which manufactured outerwear, such

[1]This case was prepared by Professor George H. Haines, Jr., of the University of Toronto. All characters and incidents described in the case are fictional. However, the data are real and were collected as part of a research project on clothing purchasing conducted by Leonard S. Simon and Marcus Alexis and supported by a grant from the Chemstrand Foundation. Reproduced by permission.

[2]Later published in *Consumer Demand in the United States, 1929-1970: Analyses and Projections,* Harvard University Press, pp. 68-69.

[3]The equation took the form:
Sales of Women's Clothing $= -7.97 +$
$.567q_{t-1} + .039\Delta X_t + .012X_{t-1} +$
$(.250)\quad (.005)\quad (.007)$
$.034\Delta P_t + .144P_{t-1} -6.21d_t$
$(.086)\quad (.106)\quad (3.84)$
$R^2 = .96$

where q_t was per capita expenditures for clothing, X_t was total per capita consumption expenditures, P_t was relative price, d_t was a dummy variable for prewar and postwar periods, and the numbers in brackets were the standard errors of the regression coefficients, and R^2 is the proportion of the variation in clothing sales explained by the independent variables.

as ladies' sweaters, man-tailored blouses, skirts, slacks, and raincoats. The other division manufactured underwear for the specialty trade. Mr. J. C. Kroll headed the first; Mr. F. Q. Wrigley, affectionately known as "F. Q." about the shop, the second.

Upon his return Mr. Armengee set up a conference with Mr. Kroll and Mr. Wrigley where he showed them the demand equation for women's clothing and asked for their opinion on his plan of doubling the price of all their items every year. After he had said this there was a distinct moment of silence. "But, Alchian," said Mr. Kroll, "these prices are all relative. You could get the same result if prices of other things were all going up faster than clothing prices, but that wouldn't mean we should double our prices every year."

"Let's do a survey," said F. Q. "We can put some questions in about that line of rubber underwear, too, to see if we should produce it." F. Q. had been an enthusiastic believer in market research ever since he had flown out to Los Angeles to interview shoppers in one of the lingerie stores that bought from the Armengee Clothing Company. In fact, it has become a bit of a joke around the company. After some more discussion, it was decided F. Q. could do his own survey, and that a commercial firm would be hired to do a survey for Mr. Kroll. It was decided that a typical American city should be chosen, rather than attempt a national sample, and after some discussion they settled on Rochester, New York.

The Babbitt Barnett Company was engaged to perform the survey. Mr. Armengee stipulated that the raw data were to come to the Armengee Clothing Company for analysis. After several conferences and a pretest of a preliminary version of the questionnaire, Mr. Barnett proposed an area sampling plan designed to ensure adequate coverage of all races and social classes. As a first step Mr. Barnett selected eighteen census tracts within the city limits and twelve tracts from the surrounding suburbs. Next he picked sample blocks from each tract and assigned a quota of interviews to be completed in each area. Instructions given to the interviewers on the selection of individual respondents are shown in Exhibit 1 and the revised questionnaire is given in Exhibit 2.

Exhibit 1

Sampling Instructions for Clothing Study

Go to the designated corner of the assigned block in your area. Be sure of your boundaries and that you are in the right block. Start at the corner marked with the asterisk and go clockwise around the block. Ring every doorbell until you complete an interview. Skip three dwellings and start ringing doorbells until another completed interview is obtained. Continue around the block, interviewing in houses on your right until quota is filled. Be careful that every doorbell is rung. Look for basement apartments, rear entrance apartments, apartments over stores, garages, or any other multiple dwelling. Be sure to skip three dwellings after completing an interview. *Do not* interview occupants of sorority or fraternity houses, dormitories, hotels, motels, hospitals, boarding houses, or rooming houses. If a trailer park falls in your area, conduct only one interview in that park and continue on to next populated area. Record all information on your *Area Sheet.* Print addresses on Area Sheet of each doorbell rung. Interview only female heads of household or single women over 20 years of age who have their own residences.

Explanation of terms follows:

Interviewer Record initials *ONLY.*

Quota Five interviews from each census tract.

N.H. When no one answers the doorbell.

Fold When part way through interview, respondent refuses to continue, record question, number at which she folds. *DO NOT COUNT IN QUOTA.*

Refusal When respondent refuses to be interviewed.

N.E. No eligible respondent available. Respondent must be female head of household or a single woman over 20 years of age with her own residence.

C.I. For each completed interview insert check mark on Area Sheet.

Total of columns across must total number of contacts. Continue around block until quota is filled. If quota is not filled, so note on the Area Sheet and move to the next adjacent block in any direction and proceed around that block in the previous manner. Record on the back of the Area Sheet the block to which you have moved by drawing a diagram of the block that shows its boundaries and that indicates your starting point and direction of movement away from it. If you are still unable to fulfill your quota in this second block, repeat the above process for moving to another block. If area is commercial or razed, contact office. If streets do not exist, contact office. If area is commercial, look for dwellings over stores before leaving area.

Exhibit 2

Clothing Study Questionnaire

Hello. My name is _____ . I am representing the Babbitt Barnett Marketing Research Company. May I speak to the lady of the house? We are doing a study to find out how people shop for clothing and what they buy. Would you help us by answering a few questions? Thank you.

If no, terminate: Thank you.
If yes, obtain:
Name: _____

Address _____
           Number and Street

           _____
           City or Town

Phone Number (if any) _____
Thank you for your cooperation. Let's begin with the questions now.

KEYPUNCHER: START CARD 1 HERE

Questionnaire code _____ (Cols. 1-3)
Card number   (4-1)
I.   PROPENSITY TO SHOP
     1. Approximately what percentage of *your own* clothing do you make yourself?
     Variable Number 1-1.

		$\overline{X}$	σ
0-20% __(5-1)	21-40% __(5-3)	1.71	1.93
41-60% __(5-5)	61-80% __(5-7)		
81-100% __(5-9)			

     2. How frequently do you shop for clothing for yourself?
     (HAND CARD A)
     Variable Number 1-2.

	Cols. 6-7		$\overline{X}$	σ
Less than once a year	_____	(0)	14.64	15.56
One to five times per year	_____	(3)		
Once every two months	_____	(9)		
Once a month	_____	(18)		
Two to four times a month	_____	(38)		
Once a week or more	_____	(52)		

     3. Does your husband usually accompany you when you shop for clothing?

     Variable Number 1-3.
     Yes____(8-1)   No____(8-2)   Not married____(8-3)

	$\overline{X}$	σ
	1.85	.47

     4. Approximately what percentage of the time do you shop for *your own* clothing with friends?
     Variable Number 1-4.

		$\overline{X}$	σ
1-20%_____(9-1)	21-40%_____ (9-3)		
41-60%_____(9-5)	61-80%_____ (9-7)	1.88	2.45
81-100%_____(9-9)	Never_____ (9-0)		

5. Several things are probably important to you in deciding whether or not you will shop for clothing articles for yourself at a particular store. Would you please indicate which number on this card best describes the importance of each of the following things to you when you decide whether or not you will shop for clothing for yourself at a particular store. For example, if you considered it very important to shop at a store that offered baby-sitting service, you would indicate a "1"; if baby-sitting were very unimportant to you, you would indicate a "5", etc. (HAND CARD B).

Variable Number 1-5.

Item	Rating	Col.	$\overline{X}$	σ
Alterations	____	(10)	3.77	1.42
Variable Number 1-6.				
Latest styles or fashions in women's wear	____	(11)	2.39	1.38
Variable Number 1-7.				
Variety or depth in type of merchandise	___	(12)	2.09	1.19
Variable Number 1-8.				
Quality of merchandise	____	(13)	1.64	1.02
Variable Number 1-9.				
Value of merchandise for prices paid (obtaining your money's worth)	____	(14)	1.48	.95
Variable Number 1-10.				
Charge accounts	____	(15)	2.81	1.58
Variable Number 1-11.				
Budget accounts	____	(16)	3.73	1.57
Variable Number 1-12.				
Delivery	___	(17)	3.26	1.56
Variable Number 1-13.				
Accepting returned goods	____	(18)	1.88	1.32
Variable Number 1-14.				
Phone orders	____	(19)	3.58	1.57
Variable Number 1-15.				
Mail orders	____	(20)	4.28	1.26
Variable Number 1-16.				
Evening hours	____	(21)	2.91	1.58
Variable Number 1-17.				
Self-service	____	(22)	3.50	1.41
Variable Number 1-18.				
Helpfulness of salesclerks	____	(23)	2.09	1.23
Variable Number 1-19.				
Convenient location—easy to get to	____	(24)	2.02	1.16
Variable Number 1-20.				
Parking available	____	(25)	2.32	1.50

6. How would you rate your feelings about shopping for:
(HAND CARD C)
Variable Number 1-21.

Own clothes		Col.	Others' clothes	Col.
Really enjoy	____	(26-1)	_____	(27-1)
Don't mind	____	(26-2)	_____	(27-2)
Dislike	____	(26-3)	_____	(27-3)
Don't know	____	(26-4)	_____	(27-4)
No answer	____	(26-5)	_____	(27-5)
		$\overline{X}$ 1.43		1.67
		σ .66		.77

II. EXPENDITURES FOR CLOTHING

1. Approximately how many dollars did the following members of the family spend for clothes last month, either for themselves or other members of the family?

		$\overline{X}$	σ
Variable Number 1-23.			
Your husband	$_____(cols. 28-30)	36.93	51.09
Variable Number 1-24.			
Yourself	$_____(cols. 31-33)	47.20	57.92
Variable Number 1-25.			
Children	$_____(cols. 34-36)	39.40	69.79
Variable Number 1-26.			
Other (specify)	$_____(cols. 37-39)	19.89	22.19

2. Approximately how many of these dollars were spent in the following types of stores? (HAND CARD D)

Variable Number 1-27.

Stores	Amount	$\overline{X}$	σ
Discount stores (such as Arlan's, Gem. Field)	$_____(cols. 40-42)	28.79	25.02
Variable Number 1-28.			
Department stores (such as Sibley's, McCurdy's, Edwards, Sears, Penney's)	$_____(cols. 43-45)	55.72	56.88
Variable Number 1-29.			
Specialty stores (such as Forman's, Flah's, Kroll's, National)	$_____(cols. 46-48)	47.10	61.91
Variable Number 1-30.			
Chain stores (such as Lerner Shops, Lane-Bryant, Robert Hall, Bond's, Three Sisters)	$_____(cols. 49-51)	23.38	19.78

3. Approximately how many of these dollars were spent last month on the following items?

Item	Amount	$\overline{X}$	σ
Variable Number 1-31.			
Ladies' sweaters	$_____(cols. 52-54)	8.80	8.91
Variable Number 1-32.			
Ladies' man-tailored blouses	$_____(cols. 55-57)	7.64	5.99
Variable Number 1-33.			
Ladies' skirts	$_____(cols. 58-60)	10.25	7.18
Variable Number 1-34.			
Ladies' slacks	$_____(cols. 61-63)	10.16	6.77

KEYPUNCHER: START CARD 2 HERE
Questionnaire Code_____(cols. 1-3)
Card Number   (4-2)

IV. CLOTHING ATTRIBUTES
   I am now going to ask you some questions about your shopping for your own sportswear. First, I have some questions about ladies' sweaters.
   A. Sweaters
   1. When you buy a sweater *for yourself,* what is the price that you usually pay?
Variable Number 2-1.

	$\overline{X}$	σ
$_____(cols. 5-7)	7.95	3.38

2. What is the *most* you would normally pay for a sweater?
Variable Number 2-2.

$_____(cols. 8-10)	12.41	6.26

3. What is the *least* you would normally pay for a sweater?
Variable Number 2-3.

$_____(cols. 11-13)	5.02	2.55

4. Would you please indicate which of these fall *colors* you prefer most, second most, etc. when shopping for seaters? (HAND CARD E)

Color	Col.	$\overline{X}$	σ
Variable Number 2-4.			
Brown _____	(14)	3.28	1.40
Variable Number 2-5.			
Navy _____	(15)	2.64	1.31
Variable Number 2-6.			
White _____	(16)	2.57	1.36
Variable Number 2-7.			
Grape _____	(17)	3.84	1.39
Variable Number 2-8.			
Green _____	(18)	2.71	1.23

5. Would you please indicate which of these *styles* you prefer most and least when shopping for sweaters? (HAND CARD F)

Style	Col.	$\overline{X}$	σ
Variable Number 2-9.			
Cardigan (buttons down the front, long sleeves) _____	(19)	1.27	.54
Variable Number 2-10.			
Poor Boy (short sleeves, ribbed, pullover) _____	(20)	2.62	.62
Variable Number 2-11.			
Pullover (long sleeves) _____	(21)	2.07	.68

6. Would you please indicate which of these *fabrics* you prefer most, second most, etc. when shopping for sweaters? (HAND CARD G)

Fabric	Col.	$\overline{X}$	σ
Variable Number 2-12.			
100% wool _____	(22)	2.37	.89
Variable Number 2-13.			
Acrilan (Orlon/nylon blend) _____	(23)	1.70	.68
Variable Number 2-14.			
Orlon _____	(24)	1.93	.74

7. When you buy a sweater you are probably interested in its fabric, style, color, and price. Would you please look at this card (HAND CARD H) and tell me which number on it best describes how important these things are to you? First, how important is *color* in selecting a sweater?

Respondent's Rating	Col.		
Variable Number 2-15.			
	(25)	1.56	.90

8. Would you please indicate which number on this card best describes your feelings on how important *fabric* is in selecting a sweater?

Variable Number 2-16.			
	(26)	1.91	.95

9. Would you please indicate which number on this card best describes your feelings on how important *price* is in selecting a sweater? (REFER TO CARD H)

Variable Number 2-17.			
	(27)	2.11	1.04

10. Would you please indicate which number on this card best describes your feelings on how important *style* is in selecting a sweater? (REFER TO CARD H)

Variable Number 2-18.			
	(28)	1.69	.98

B. Ladies' Man-tailored Blouses

Now, may I ask you some some questions about ladies' man-tailored blouses?

1. When you buy a man-tailored blouse for *yourself*, what is the price that you usually pay?

	Amount	Col.	X̄	σ
Variable Number 2-19.	_____	(29-31)	4.65	1.76

2. What is the *most* you would normally pay for a man-tailored blouse:

		Col.	X̄	σ
Variable Number 2-20.	_____	(32-34)	6.65	2.71

3. What is the *least* you would normally pay for a man-tailored blouse?

		Col.	X̄	σ
Variable Number 2-21.	_____	(35-37)	3.01	1.40

4. Would you please indicate which of these *colors* you prefer most, second most, etc. when shopping for ladies' man-tailored blouses? (HAND CARD I.)

	Color		Col.	X̄	σ
Variable Number 2-22.	Yellow-gold	_____	(38)	2.82	1.14
Variable Number 2-23.	Beige	_____	(39)	2.89	.96
Variable Number 2-24.	White	_____	(40)	2.06	1.07
Variable Number 2-25.	Light blue	_____	(41)	2.20	1.09

5. Would you please indicate which of these *styles* you prefer most, second most, etc. when shopping for ladies' man-tailored blouses?
(HAND CARD J)

	Style		Col.	X̄	σ
Variable Number 2-26.	Roll-sleeve, V-neck with collar	_____	(42)	2.37	1.05
Variable Number 2-27.	Roll-sleeve, button front, bermuda collar	_____	(43)	1.83	.99
Variable Number 2-28.	Roll-sleeve, pointed convertible collar	_____	(44)	2.71	.88
Variable Number 2-29.	Long-sleeve, French cuff, convertible collar	_____	(45)	3.09	1.15

6. As you did with sweaters, would you please indicate which number on this card (HAND CARD K) best describes how important style, color, fabric, and price are to you in selecting a ladies' man-tailored blouse. First, how important is *price*?

Respondent's Rating	Col.	X̄	σ
Variable Number 2-30.			
	(46)	2.20	1.08

7. Would you please indicate which number on this card best describes your feelings on how important *color* is in selecting a ladies' man-tailored blouse? (REFER TO CARD K)
Variable Number 2-31.

(47)	1.66	.92

8. Would you please indicate which number on this card best describes your feelings on how important *fabric* is in selecting a ladies' man-tailored blouse? (REFER TO CARD K)
Variable Number 2-32.

(48)	2.11	1.06

9. Would you please indicate which number on this card best describes your feelings on how important *style* is in selecting a ladies' man-tailored blouse? (REFER TO CARD K)
Variable Number 2-33.

(49)	1.80	1.07

C. Skirts
Now, I have some questions for you about skirts.
1. When you buy a skirt for yourself, what is the price that you usually pay?

	Amount	X̄	σ
Variable Number 2-34.	$_____(cols. 50-52)	8.72	3.49

2. What is the *most* you would normally pay for a skirt? $\overline{X}$ σ
Variable Number 2-35. $_____(cols. 53-55)   12.06   5.04

3. What is the *least* you would normally pay for a skirt?
Variable Number 2-36. $_____(cols. 56-58)   5.56   2.39

4. Would you please indicate which of these fall *colors* you prefer most, second most, etc. when shopping for skirts? (HAND CARD L)

Variable Number 2-37.	Green	_____(col. 59)	2.44	.89
Variable Number 2-38.	Brown	_____(col. 60)	2.40	1.15
Variable Number 2-39.	Navy	_____(col. 61)	1.95	.98
Variable Number 2-40.	Grape	_____(col. 62)	3.20	1.08

5. Would you please indicate which of these *styles* you prefer most, second most, etc. when shopping for skirts? (HAND CARD M)

Variable Number 2-41.	Pleated	_____ (63)	2.83	1.25
Variable Number 2-42.	Slim, waistband, side-zip	_____ (64)	1.82	.96
Variable Number 2-43.	Slim, no waistband, side-zip	_____ (65)	2.78	.87
Variable Number 2-44.	A-line, no waistband	_____ (66)	2.53	1.09

6. Would you please indicate which of these *fabrics* you prefer most, second most, etc. when shopping for skirts? (HAND CARD M)

| Variable Number 2-45. | 100% wool flannel | _____(67) | 1.38 | .56 |
| Variable Number 2 46. | Wool basketweave | _____(68) | 1.66 | .48 |

7. As before, would you please indicate which number on this card (HAND CARD O) best describes how important style, color, price and fabric are to you in selecting a skirt? First, how important is *fabric*?

Respondent's Rating   Col. $\overline{X}$ σ
Variable Number 2-47.
                          (69)   1.93   1.13

8. Would you please indicate which number of this card best describes your feeling on how important *price* is in selecting a skirt? (REFER TO CARD O).
Variable Number 2-48.
                          (70)   2.07   1.09

9. Would you please indicate which number on this card best describes your feelings on how important *color* is in selecting a skirt?
Variable Number 2-49.
                          (71)   1.77   1.05

10. Would you please indicate which number on this card best describes your feelings on how important *style* is in selecting a skirt? (REFER TO CARD O).
Variable Number 2-50.
                          (72)   1.74   1.01

KEYPUNCHER: START CARD 3 HERE

Questionnaire Code_____(cols. 1-3)
Card Number   (4-3)

D. Slacks
Now, may I ask you some questions about slacks?
1. When you buy slacks *for yourself,* what is the price that you usually pay?
                          Amount   X σ
Variable Number 3-1. $_____(cols. 5-7)   8.61   4.05

2. What is the *most* you would normally pay for slacks?

			$\overline{X}$	σ
Variable Number 3-2.	$_____(cols. 8-10)		11.72	4.41

3. What is the *least* you would normally pay for slacks?

Variable Number 3-3.	$_____(cols. 11-13)		5.55	2.99

4. Would you please indicate which of these fall *colors* you prefer most, second most, etc. when shopping for slacks? (HAND CARD P).

Variable Number 3-4.	Green	_____	(14)	2.54	.92
Variable Number 3-5.	Navy	_____	(15)	1.87	1.06
Variable Number 3-6.	Brown	_____	(16)	2.34	1.11
Variable Number 3-7.	Grape	_____	(17)	3.12	1.12

5. Would you please indicate which of these *styles* you prefer most, second most, etc. when shopping for slacks? (HAND CARD Q)

	Style		Col.	$\overline{X}$	σ
Variable Number 3-8.	Vertical stretch pant, detachable stirrup	_____	(18)	2.20	1.15
Variable Number 3-9.	Western-Levi look	_____	(19)	3.25	.97
Variable Number 3-10.	Straight leg, front zip, beltless	_____	(20)	2.46	1.01
Variable Number 3-11.	Tapered leg, side zip, beltless	_____	(21)	1.99	1.02

6. Would you please indicate which of these *fabrics* you prefer most, second most, etc. when shopping for slacks? (HAND CARD R).

	Fabrics		Col.	$\overline{X}$	σ
Variable Number 3-12.	Corduroy	_____	(22)	2.74	1.02
Variable Number 3-13.	Cotton demin	_____	(23)	2.51	1.12
Variable Number 3-14.	Rayon/Acetate blend	_____	(24)	2.26	1.15
Variable Number 3-15.	100% wool flannel	_____	(25)	2.34	1.24

7. Again, as before, would you please indicate which number on this card (HAND CARD S) best describes how important color, price, fabric, and style are to you in selecting slacks? First, how important is *color*?

Respondent's Rating	Col.	$\overline{X}$	σ
Variable Number 3-16.			
	(26)	1.81	1.08

8. Would you please indicate which number on this card best describes your feelings on how important *fabric* is in selecting slacks? (REFER TO CARD S).

Variable Number 3-17.			
	(27)	2.08	1.09

9. Would you please indicate which number on this card best describes your feelings on how important *style* is in selecting slacks? (REFER TO CARD S).

Variable Number 3-18.			
	(28)	1.81	1.09

10. Would you please indicate which number on this card best describes your feelings on how important *price* is in selecting slacks?

Variable Number 3-19.			
	(29)	2.06	1.07

E. Raincoats
Finally, may I ask you some questions about ladies' raincoats?

1. When you buy a raincoat *for yourself,* what is the price that you usually pay?

	Amount	Col.		
Variable Number 3-20.	$ _____	(30-32)	19.58	10.80

2. What is the *most* you would normally pay for a raincoat?
Variable Number 3-21. $ _____   (33-35)   25.97   15.17

3. What is the *least* you would normally pay for a raincoat?
Variable Number 3-22. $ _____   (36-38)   12.42   7.08

4. Would you please indicate which of these colors you prefer most, second most, etc. when shopping for a raincoat? (HAND CARD T)

	Color		Col.	$\bar{X}$	σ
Variable Number 3-23.	Light blue	_____	(39)	2.80	1.22
Variable Number 3-24.	Navy	_____	(40)	2.72	1.14
Variable Number 3-25.	Beige	_____	(41)	2.43	1.32
Variable Number 3-26.	Yellow	_____	(42)	4.10	1.24
Variable Number 3-27.	Black	_____	(43)	2.88	1.54

5. Would you please indicate which of these *styles* you prefer most, second most, etc. when shopping for a raincoat? (HAND CARD U).

	Style	Col.	$\bar{X}$	σ
Variable Number 3-28.	London Fog *style* with raglan sleeve and button-fly front	_____(44)	1.63	.82
Variable Number 3-29.	Shirtwaist (set-in sleeve, nine buttons exposed down front, pointed collar)	_____(45)	2.13	.75
Variable Number 3-30.	Trench coat (epaulets, belted, double-breasted, leather buttons)	_____(46)	2.26	.76

6. Would you please indicate which of these *fabrics* you prefer most, and which you prefer least when shopping for raincoats? (HAND CARD V).

	Fabric			
Variable Number 3-31.	65% Dacron, 35% cotton in poplin weave	_____(47)	1.24	.43
Variable Number 3-32.	Raylon blend (poplin-like)	_____(48)	1.75	.43

7. As you have done previously, would you please indicate which number on this card (HAND CARD W) best describes your feelings on how important style, fabric, color, and price are in selecting a raincoat? First, how important is *style*?

Respondent's Rating	Col.	$\bar{X}$	σ
Variable Number 3-33.	(49)	1.69	.95

8. Would you please indicate which number on this card best describes your feelings on how important *price* is in selecting a raincoat? (REFER TO CARD W).

Variable Number 3-34.
(50)   2.13   1.07

9. Would you please indicate which number on this card best describes your feelings on how important *color* is in selecting a raincoat? (REFER TO CARD W).

Variable Number 3-35.
(51)   2.04   1.16

10. Would you please indicate which number on this card best describes your feelings on how important *fabric is* in selecting a raincoat? (REFER TO CARD W).

Variable Number 3-36.
(52)   2.13   1.15

III. CONSUMER CHARACTERISTICS
1. How long have you lived at this address?

			$\bar{X}$	σ
Variable Number 3-37.	_____Years	(cols. 57-58)	7.31	7.33

If less than three years, what was your previous place of residence? (Check)

<u>Variable Number 3-38.</u>

In the city of Rochester	_____	(59-1)	1.73	1.20
In the country of Monroe, but not in the city of Rochester	_____	(59-2)		
Other areas in New York State	_____	(59-3)		
Outside New York State	_____	(59-4)		

2. What is your marital status?

$\overline{X}$ σ

<u>Variable Number 3-39.</u>   Married _____(60-1)   Single _____(60-2)   1.31   .99
                                       Divorced_____(60-3)   Separated _____(60-4)
                                         Widowed _____(60-5)

3. (a) How many children are there in your family?
<u>Variable Number 3-40.</u>   _____   (col. 61)   2.64   1.56

    (b) What are the ages of your oldest and youngest children?

<u>Variable Number 3-41.</u>	Oldest_____	(cols. 62-63)	14.38	10.30
<u>Variable Number 3-42.</u>	Youngest____	(cols. 64-65)	8.19	10.65

4. a. How many automobiles are owned by the immediate members of this family?
<u>Variable Number 3-43.</u>   0____(66-0) 2____(66-2)   1.23   .70
                                   1____(66-1) more than 2____(66-3)
                                   NOTE: Skip 4b if 4a answered "0."

4. b. What percentage of the time do you use your automobile for clothing shopping?
<u>Variable Number 3-44.</u>   1-20%____ (67-1)   21-40%____ (67-3)   6.74   4   3.27
                                   41-60%____ (67-5)   61-80%____ (67.7)
                                   81-100%____ (67-9)   Never____ (67-0)

5. Do you have a telephone in your home?
<u>Variable Number 3-45.</u>   Yes____(68-1)   No____(67-2)   1.13   .34

6. Which member of the family earns the major part of the total family income?
<u>Variable Number 3-46.</u>   Husband_____(69-1)   1.12   .35
                                     Wife or self____(69-2)
                      Child or children____(69-3)

7. (a) What is the occupation of the principal wage earner as above?

$\overline{X}$ σ

<u>Variable Number 3-47.</u>   _____   (cols. 70-71)   4.20   3.27

    (b) Is the other spouse employed?
<u>Variable Number 3-48.</u> Yes____(72-1)   No____(72-2)   Not married____(72-3) 1.89 .50

8. What is the last year of school completed by the principal wage earner (as above)? (HAND CARD X)

<u>Variable Number 3-49.</u>   (cols. 73-74)

0-8 (grammar school)	_____	(8)	13.47	6.65
9-10	_____	(10)		
11-12 (12-completion of high school)	_____	(12)		
13-14	_____	(14)		
15-16 (16-completion of college)	_____	(16)		
17 or more years (graduate school)	_____	(18)		

9. Into what age group does the principal wage earner (as above) fall? (HAND CARD Y). Variable Number 3-50.

		(Col. 75-76)	$\overline{X}$	σ
A. 20-29 years	_____	(25)	40.22	12.38
B. 60 years or over	_____	(67)		
C. 40-49 years	_____	(45)		
D. 30-39 years	_____	(35)		
E. 50-59 years	_____	(55)		

10. In which of these groups does your total family income before taxes fall? (HAND CARD Z). Variable Number 3-51.

Per Week	Per Year		(Cols. 77-78)	$\overline{X}$	σ
A. $78 to $115	$4000 to $5999	_____	(5)		
B. $0 to $77	$0 to $3999	_____	(2)		
C. $270 and over	$14,000 and over	_____	(18)	9.64	4.70
D. $155 to $192	$8000 to $9999	_____	(9)		
E. $193 to $269	$10,000 to $13,999	_____	(12)		
F. $116 to $154	$6000 to $7999	_____	(7)		

—END OF INTERVIEW—

Check from observation:
Race of respondent
Variable Number 3-52.

			$\overline{X}$	σ
White _____(79-1) Negro _____(79-2) Other _____(79-3)			1.13	.36

Date of interview: _____ _____ _____
                      Month   Day   Year

Time of interview: _____ A.M.
                            P.M.

Interviewer's initials: _____

The interviewers (all women) were trained by Mr. Barnett. One hundred and twenty-nine interviews were completed and shortly thereafter the results came in for tabulation. The data processing department keypunched the interview forms, calculated means and standard deviations of the responses, and turned the results over to Mr. Armengee (the raw data are given in Exhibit 3).

Mr. Armengee had recently hired his daughter's husband after he graduated from business school. Armengee decided to give him the results of the study for analysis after making the following points:

1. The material in Part I, Propensity to Shop, was designed to help retailers as well as to help Armengee understand their customers.
2. The attributes in Part IV were chosen because of current sales popularity (the most popular attributes being included).
3. All man-tailored blouses were made from one material, so no questions about fabric were asked.

4. An unanswered question was whether they should double the price of all their items every year.

"But, really, " Mr. Armengee said, "what I want, now that we have all these data, is to know what it tells me about what we should do in the future."

QUESTIONS

1. What information did Armengee need to make their marketing plans?
2. Did the questionnaire collect the data needed and was the sample of consumers obtained in the survey representative of shoppers in the Rochester area?
3. What did Armengee learn from the results of the survey?
4. What changes should be made in Armengee's marketing programs?

Exhibit 3

Data Listing and Technical Notes on Data

1. Occupation is coded 1 to 14, on the basis of judged socioeconomic status of the occupation. One is high; fourteen is low.
2. Any questions where the respondent did not respond are left blank; if the respondent's response was 0, a zero is punched. However, on a number of questions, such as Question No. 2 (Cols. 40-51, at Card 1), a blank means the respondent did not shop at these stores; a zero here would mean the respondent did shop, but did not spend any money for clothing in the store type last month. Such a distinction, where appropriate, is followed throughout the results.
3. In cases where data were grouped within a range, the number punched refers to the midrange value. Examples would be Income (Col. 77-78, Card 3), Age (Col. 75-76, Card 3), and Education (Col. 73-74, Card 3).
4. The mean and standard deviation of respondents' responses are recorded on the questionnaire.

```
                          CLOTHING STUDY DATA LISTING

0021118305131113533253521512      105          105               008
0022008012004234151323121231003005003341241233141008010008423112431222312
0023008012009421314233412122230350350104215313212132   04 5233300 1 1231667071
003110321+3344151111141112300411203S   012135   004   010
0032008010007421351322312212002005002341213242240100120054213412312222224
0033005010004412334122431233102003002032541123122124   05 10170729110121845181
004130329425311531151513122C50007         057
0042              004010001342131243113012015008321421341212\?
0043008012005312414324312124303503502012543123121213   08 1101  19110221435121
005111831522112521454422122   050        025025
0052010015007451631321232142004005003231413241233010015006213442132122\?1
0053012015008132424341234132120250350155412313212?222   09 5111  19120831635021
006111811222312332221112112030032      062        010   015
0062010025003514321323121234008015003243131422123012022200321342431122415
0063014020003312 1324321422510120200043245123112?412   16 1201011911042142505\?
0091109213242222543223551103603000\?   030036
0092006012006412531233122211005006004413221343220100150072314413212322\?
0093              01901901524153132122222   07 1316071111081123509\?
0101103214232255435552222211   020008035014   032015
0102008008000042453113 3121122005007004412321342112013015008231 13212?111
0103              01702001532451132121122   05 1318151011082085502\?
0111152292232341535553253110501S0   03005002002S   015010
0112006018003521432133121231003006003243132413121006010006321441232134\?
0113006015300641321234321421230200200?032451231122322   0111  19210721225091
0121118155221555545522212\?   097   060   037   006   010
0122003007003241532313121252003004003412331242111005006004213441232114\?\?
0123010010000423141342321422\?4          031140905192107210350S1
0131303255111155516555514512030050   010070          015
01320100150062345123123123112110040080034312124331?100900900621344231122\?\?
0133012013009231543214231211203503502023154123122222   03 12131113110311235091
01515032042122445144241242101035   005040     003
0152008012006124531323122221002004002342131241221007010005312421341212\?1
015300701200531241432143213211\?   02001054231321212212   06 15120115110321245091
0161103203422222542555522223
0162006007005       1 3 1111
0163              020020007   1231 1112   25 1236332911052146712\?
0171118 5112221111141222211   030       020010      010005
01720120150104315213213231131008008005234114323121015016008243143212113\?\?
0173015015010234124314321211130350350152531413212131\?   12 15301729110221467121
0181109215122235515535522242   100      015075010
018?              00500800432141234313\?
01830100150083412134242131314045030010452313122114\?\?   11 1213072911022124505\?
01911032132211355135551321\?   020       015
0192010015003431521233121321003005002432132142311010015010234412312222\?\?
0193              05007002023154213   1222 .   03 12272429110121655091
02011092031112355155551332206502\?   255085 . 006020020
02020120150101543213212312310110110073214342131210130150112143412312231?
0203020020015241334214231122?   0250204325121312?2312   10 1317102911012165518\?
0211109215541111445521122310060064   004   014         004
02120040050035324123112314210030070014321423111420050080024131342214112
0213005007002213442314231121100901500612352431212122   0121404011911062122507\?
02219182153111221122452422201001502000\?   051   006   006
0222010012004243511323211131003005001312421433221007010003321441231243\?1
0223              01502001031452213211323   22 1218131911032124509\?
0231103213111113441445321112204004001\?   090
02320100100006321451322311231004006003432112343111008010000542134132213332
0233              01501501012435123121332   21 1321115191101212451\?1
```

```
0241138214121133112325321111          005010    005010
024201001800532451123123222100400400224314231111100701200512342143211321
024301001200623143421342121230120160083215423112132         20 12030119110321225   1
0261118211331112211522111230050300200200200200030025          010
0262010010005325141322131231005008003214221342121
0263008010005243114322134121202502501534251132121212         07 14221119110321245071
0271103214331122117234334511
0272008011005423511323211221005012002142342312132008015008132441322112011
0273                     011011008145232131212221         07 13388213110321255051
0281103154511111111115353111101501203020         107
028200701000331524123321212220050070034231213342122008012005431242311212222
0283008012005413224313124122202002001523451132121221         08 14090229110821225071
0291118213511131315513121210200200010         050
02512007011000452412331213121300500807033412124323440090130052431312421244
02930090130062341431234124324015020015342511231212243         02212 30219110811235091
0311118201111135555555511523    022015      015022
0312007008006421531323211122004004003234121342112010012008321423412122211
031300600600343124123212312201201501013425132124252     15 1115  11110411245091
032110321211111223223132212305002003           020050    030
0322004018008123541323121231005005000440123124312101601600831244231211312
032301601600632144132312421213020025015343125132121312         10 12070619110321235091
0301118015021111131331311112020050030001004005002001        014010
033200601600483615223112311141006008003431221343111008080050512342143121311
0333005016005123413424321111301602001613452321121311         3 13140619110821235071
0341109216441144515544111220007         007
0342005010003124531321231111005005002134221431111005010004312431241211111
0343010012004312114323412111101901901535142132121111       0111       19110321225071
0351103213111111151115332332  019   008010
035201101100621534132312112100701000513421234211101101100632144132215111
0353                  025025011  1  21321213111     35 13110329110821235091
0361103253221133515555315115025060050012090090        006012
03620060150043125412332121343008010004324141323224010010004312441232122225
0363010010015321414324213225303904001334215132123222     0211409030 110810825052
03711522121411222254232321  020015    025      010010005  003
0372005006005431521323121422004005003243142314211005009004321412       1122
03730090120083124243132141211060080050123452131212220      0111304011321041122505
03811092955333555155511115511028015015   058
0382003003001412532132211133002002002432121344433003004002231441231245420
0383                          05 1406010 21070825021
03911032131111111145552115120150250100   035010    005     011
0392006006004215431323215131005005002413241332210100120083124412321231
039301501500932141423432122210100150082315431212322220      0214520110 120831255052
04211092153333555325515133220120050100  010017    003
0422004006002142533213212220030040011243312422220060080022134413221222
042300601000213243421123422201002000543152132122222     05 120604151101210163507
04311032053341112111552113202502  020   035
0432007010005341522313211221005006004123431242121008013005231412541222110
0433007014005213424312143121202003001243251231122112      0121111  11110311235091
0441503295 2145552552555521101  020   005010    015    006
04420080150084125312233122151005007003341213425121010010015008321431241215120
0443010010005312442312341115502002001523154123125111     36 12040119110421235051
0451138295111115511533111211010010035    055      004005
0452008010007432511321231221005010002241213421310100200061234413212311110
0453                 0200350203412513212111111     11 1119   2911012144509
0461138112111115555555111111   060   030030    005005
0462005010004143522313122251002005002243124132222100600700441231234212411
0463               0140200144315231221242220      0211329221111103108450720
```

```
04711182155255555553251451102502504500610                                     006
0472005005002453121323121323004004002142332142133004005003231421433112
047300406003312412433142232101201500835142132212123        05 13100319110711035091
04811032152211335111111141!    013010005023        050    004    005
048200500300341253123321122200300400113423142222200600800431241243121222
04830060070043124124341231212005006003412351321212t2        01112010111210821225052
0491103214111122214433133110200150250200060020             008
049200600600421354231321222200400500243212134321200700900623144312211211
04930080100063124123432141113                              09111  0109110321225051
051113820511111532253332211    060        030030    004008
05120100150065412313212311320040060024213241331110100130062431412321121t
05130150130081342143223411113030060030341251231211511        08 13140329110121635121
0521103113211135511111411122075025        050050
052201001000351423231312222200600800334121234322101101500534122 13421
052300701000531421432142332210200200101243512317333        07 14120419110121635121
054110921231112322353522212025050̇        050025    010010
05420100150053245112312111100600800314322134111101001500513244231211111
0543010015005123434214321111102003002032154123121111        02411  0129110121825121
0551103205331125211223121111    075        075
0552008010005523141323211121005008003132123142111010020̇0053421423112221t
05530080150053241432113421212        07 16140329110121845181
05611182124221225255542221̇2    030050    030015    040005    015010
05620050100035124312332122220050060034321423122220050070033412412321222Z
05630060070043142142313242220300400203245132121222    0213316021912043123509̇2
05711381122222222225522221302503̄5        015040        010005
0572005010002231451232312222003004002432121432220050060022134123412222Z
05730070100033214124314322220150200101325423112222        03 1305011911032142505Z
0581103254222222255222222̇3    056020    065        001    004
05820030070013415213231222220010020004132213422222C03004001312421342122̇2̄
0583006010002123414323214222200701000342153132122222    0115628060 121221045092
0591103155322151235222222t1    030        030    001    010
0592005005002513241323122222005005003423143212222006010002341221̇34    2̇222
05930050100023142314231242220010010005124533121222̇2    01113220519110321235071
06011032022222222355522222t105002o    030    100    030    005006
0602006008002142531233212222005008003132141243222200801000431241324122222
06030060100063124431241322222018030010523411321222̇2    04 10    15110721055051
06211032511111551255123152̇105̇8        058
06220090090053245112332131310040040043421123413210080100052314142312415t
0623                015020015432512312121̇32        031161302101107t0845092
06411032511111111111313115t1    080    005060 · 012
06420120120055142313231222311003005003243112431322006010004341241322211133̇
06430060100054123123441231311010010005423513212112̇3    08 440905̇0 22112102505Z
06511032041111111111111111t    075026    013026008022    004005
06520060150032415313212324110030050013412312413450030080033412123412121t
06530030060013421412351510080100051354231212112Z    0141316011111081123505Z
0661703105331135513311121110100t5        01001000̄5    003
06620120120063451221313222110020020021342213431210080080052431342121222̇2
06630120150102431234124312222018022015512433212t1222        03 120201191101216250gt
0671109201111153115523111t1    125    080        020
06720150250102435132131212120050070034132124322220050070032314314221122̇2
06730100110052134243131241222020030015314521321212z2    0111304012011032142501
06811132144222542245244221205017500̄6    006    006
06820060100045341212331211110030060024312314221210090120032431214321211Z
068300501200323412341213412120200250152315421312222Z    10 12080429110421445071
069110321511111254545533444404004ô        020075008    003        012
06920090303044532123131221220040040021342132422220070090051342213421222Z
069300700700621432431321422220150150071423523121222Z    10 12080729110221245121
```

```
070115211221115531511511111    185060   010060175
070200601500115432123312113100600600024132342111110100100042143213421111
070300900900241231243341211110350350203425112312111     07 14100529110111635121
071113821522215554554333311020030040    050040          014016
071200801000554231123312122100400500343212314212100801500514323421122211
071300601000513421234421312120150250151534221312121     014120701291103212235181
072110311533415543555452110100100100    005020005
072200301000224153213312231400300500242133124324100701500521341342123124
0723               0100150081423512321321    03 1101  29110821235071
073110320555412215425235521    102    022080       012
073200500500542153132512421.4               00800800832144231124241
0733               010010010312543211245.1.1  14  141408111101311245121
074111821232211142145133111203007501.2    020067030       006015
074201501504103124513233121211100600600034312432122210080100053214413212.3112
074300601200431243421243122120120200071315223121.1222   37 171.70123110221435121
075110329552211142222511111010025       015020
075200801000413452123231211110060060022314213411120C09009005231412341211.22
075301201200531243421243111210120480112314513212.2121   04 1407011111022.1425091
0761100215542145516552223513
076200500800552143132312232300500700543121234.1244
0763               07 1136  0 221221067051
077115220555544422222233413    150    150    008010
077200501200352143132312111100701000223142341111110080100052413123.412.1111
0773               01502501032145123121111  04 50  15121231655051
078110021552315552553333522    040    040       009
078200600800343152132321423400400500243212134333300500600223141342123333
078100800000000311241243284412..501001501500813453132123333  03 4224220 220421245051
079111831325115552555341512    001    001
079200400500042513.41  142222200200300232144123222200500500421342341122222
079300400500043314312441322222201001000554123231121222   05 20  0 221231055021
080170310554315554553214533045045    045045
080200900100042435113231213350050050022341214321350100100053124413221325
0803               012015007431253321124345  0141132 15110321255051
081190320554511245155451212.2    008    008
081200400700315432123123131100300400011234123422330080120053241134212.1122
081300501200032431143232125311101501500553142231122223   07 150902111102.21235051
082133310512223355552323513
082200500800443152132    2231
082300300700033214    4213.2142               0111101 19110320825071
083113821522115531552523211    500    350150    035040030
083201102501045312123123124200700800724312413422100801100713424213212311
083301101100714323421432111140200200154235112312142.2  03 131002191102210.25121
084110320222112242452332322    030    030       009
084200701000512453312321111100300700312343214112200701000631244123212211
084300501000541231324321422220100120074325131212122222   0211205041911  21235091
085110311332212233243332212    036    036       006
085200802000735241132312122200501200324132314211100801300531244231122111
085300701200431244312321412220320320201543152123121111  14 131005191104.21245051
087110311533123252552313521
087200801500445312123213232110050050022134132432120080100042341124312.1222
087301001500523141324321422130100100104315212312321.2  014122018111103821245051
088110910543323344231325122
088200600900035234113232132140030050022143413212130060110031423213412312.3
088300400600231422431124313310110180084235132123132  04 131404151101214352121
089110920222211514455331513    030    030       012010
089200600800642135132312111100600700523142134121100801000634124123121121
089300600800521436213134212110070070051243532122111112  16 1    10110321245  1
```

```
09019032154421555154234111111    090        090              003
090200600800432154132312111100400500334213241222
0903005005003312434212143211101101501012354312121111    03 13050211110111425121
09111032113211152112551112301010    910
0912010012008321451323211131008010008431231243111012015010421341231213111
0913        035035006341521231223211    10 14211139110121645  1
09211091132223344135541231102005005010    003017100    008008    012
0922015030008135421321231222200801100413242143123201301600821342134122132
09230110150082413241334212221015040011451231232121221    12 1216141110221645  1
09411182042111132245351212201006003510    095010    004
0942010010007413521321322121004006003321431241212007012004123441321221211
0943        020020015321541231221211    07 1416091711012164518181
095110330121111551155522213
0952010020000742135132132133100801200442133124511101201500832142431121512
0953        250153125421312151101    06 5139 1912123125507101
0961103305221115213525121111    060050040    10005010
0962012012000351234132321112200701000643123214121101201500634124312121111
0963        020025012314523122111111    21 5136 29121231267181
0971118102211124112554222221
0972010015005542312311321222005005003341224314132012015010134212432112121
097301001500087134431242311123005015005312452132111121    16 1136 19111221267091
0981309203111135514415122111162030520    005212
0982009012006243511323211222100400800314324132212201201500713244231121212
09830070120052314431212431212035040025314251231213111    05 12030239110121635121
09911092053211253155532521202506015010    235        004005    004
0992005010004241531322314420006008004431212345143012015008312423411255121
09930150220083214142343215414012015004214531321215421    22 12262229110121455121
1001509215211155513323312210051000501    005150    020
1002007015005213541323211231005010005432142311212007025005412321431212321
1003010015004312414234324312122020035010324511321222221    05 15150339110121845181
10111382023111153155551113303101    015015    007009
101201501801252314123123113100700800442133124113101502001434214231121111
1013.        035099006132542131211131    10 1 29110121655181
10211182151111155125453121101010    010
1022        0080100064213342111111
10230100150054123341223412122025040015413522131212211    08 1121 39110121855181
1031103212222252235552232200501510    010010
1032012020000521453132312213210050100033241312431310150220053214413212341313
1033        0350400103412512312132101    13 12161319110121855181
104113820213111511223511111110010020001    005035C    040
104201804001514253132123122100701400532143242121110180180132134312412121101
10430200200152314243124311212030300204513212312121201    12 14180829110121645181
1051138213121125313535231110100100301    010040    008
10520180250102145323112321320070070004312231442110200350103214134212142101
1053020030010312432142343211403003500443152132122421    014120604191101218351818181
10711032141111252145441222201501801501    030018
10720150400104253112313222221008014006321441233131018025012142324311222221
1073018020015321443212341221203504507543251132123322    03 1101 29110121825181
108110921542114551253311211050050090    140050    008
10820180200104315213212321420100150005421312434121018025008312434211214211
10830150150102314341224312123025040002043152132123421    07 14120729110121845181
1091103204322235415555222210100100501    035035    010010010
1092012015008514231321232232005008003243113243231010015008341214321222321
10930120160103142342124313335030035020213451231223231    03 12232039110121655181
11011093041111152115542211201    050100    150
11020050170034135212331212220050050054321243122210100180053214312412321101
11030100140006313413422134221201    10 231107171211313435121
```

```
11111092533111115111155312112080035055025015100    080    005005010
11120080120055412312332111210040050033412123411110120150084123124312121 1
11130120150034123342123411311037040015143251231212 11    06 12151215110121655181
11215032953211253355355311 C10020010    002026    014005    009
11220090160055143212321 31231005012004432121433122014020005 24134321212311
11230000000000000000000000000000032050007312451231213 31    09 12161219110211645121
11317092151312554123351222 1 C12002015005    030004    002
11320099120024532123211234321004007002241332411242008010006 2341413221 3212
11330080120062431431204212122032032020351241231 2232 1    06 121108231102212450 91
11411032151111111113515111 22    001    001
114201501500552314 31323211 111100400500324131324 11110080120052413123432111 11
11430080100052143341243211111025025015312451231211 11    09 13050111110221845091
11515382141211253135451321 2    032012    024020
1152010012005132541323321122100500600432142134212100800800631242341122211
1153008015005321424312431222 10200350153214512312112 2    12 141709191101114450 181
1161103211111111511115551112102502 5    015    065
11620060100055314212321221 21005007002432121430 11110100100082413421312111 11
1163                 01202001232451123121111    34 15442529110320867091
117110382351111153115531 1112    025025100    075075
1172    143252311231113005007004312442131111015018008413241231210 11
117301301500343123412243113111    12 13181229110121645121
11811382321221352115151 11112    020015    010015010
1182001001500543215137132331 20040060024213213411420120180063421432 11212 41
11830150150084231342143211 42203503501013452123121255    06 1309051711 0321435121
1191318245151231655353551232213080010    005    025060
119200500700353121321321131 20030040021432213413330060090043412415 2125133 2
1193007010005310234211347141101001500523415173211155    16 1519101711 0321245181
12011092151311115431511112015006    006    015    003
1202009001000341352321213112320050050003341222134312100700800043214 41321233 12
12030040100043214341223144311015030015235412312131 1    0121103 19110121625121
1211152115113555555551151111110010005 0    100100    050    024    020
1212011013009421352311321 11100600900643122134111009001100631324123412111 1
12130060080062143143231425 11011011901113154331 2121113    02113080219210421025052
1221152115555151515515511 11020010025    055    004002005
12220050110052154310032113510050050005431212345535500500700532144123125151
1223    016025006324512312150 155    011131712 0 210820867071
12311321755555554515555555111053031    069    006    003010
12320060100045124332132115130030050003243112345555006010003431231241251 55
1233003010003216343123214555500300800033254131221515 5    0111505010 210421025021
1241118215551155515555515110140 10    005    024    005
1242004006003412531321321515001 00300134122134155400300300033214213412512 51
1243003003000231241423241355510150150102134531221115 5    01110    0121071082502 1
12511381153331553155113111 11010010005    010005    010
12520050080025324113232115130030050022431213411430050070032413324121311 3
12530040060033142243132142431018020010134253212111 25    03 1107 19110420845051
12611181321111111155131111112040040    010    040020    015010005
12620050200054215313232111220050050034321243131320080150063214324112221 1
12630080150053124342134121222020002501532451132211212    0111    15110421225071
12711092551111551555315151 1    025030020075    009    030
12720040080025123513232124 4 13003004002142321341331002006000234211324122121
1273    31474312341232 11005007005342152131211 45    01149401601130421025091
128115225311111555155511 11111010    025    035    010
1282004006003421531323211 11100200400243212134131400400600033214123412113 5
1283004006002312424313214554100400500032341523121234 2    014141304192103214350 51
12911381151115515155115111 1035030030    060    005008004
12920060080041425312331251110030040022431213411510040080082134132412513 1
1293003006003132423413214351101202001024351312215 155    08 13050119210411025073
```

```
13015182155143515155115151     020008          020008                                              .
13020030050034215313231211130020040014321341211320050080023214231412l253
13030040060022134123431241111005008004143523212l 355        0541101  0 110821025051
131110321153224342352423412   040040   026   054
1312
1313                           012013008432511231223221    11 15170629110321445121
13211032114112455111551112403515O         110075
1322009012005243511321231141
1323                           01502001042153123211141    10 1134  23110121467091
13311382152111151155552251240005004O        014035         011
133201001000652341132312221.2               0100100061423412312l.222
13330100150073124243134l221220250350254315212321222 4  0111218092311082123518l
13411032554522255555554221.2   025          020005
1342
1343                           035035035423511231211312   09 14210529110221245091
13519002054411154145254221l030075         105
13520150300154315213231223420050080043142412323 32
13530150150102314143224312311042050020123451232l3452    0211205022911012163512l
1361103115241325134324221111010     100           004005
1362006007004452311231235435004006003042312341534005005003023143124211534
1363004006003142312434231453200300500315324312124524    0111203011711042102509 2
142110921552222222255242221l070         035035
142200600800623541123321214200300300313421423421401001300512344123122412
14230070100051234243131422124               01110   13210111225181
14311032122224222242222212   050009   024035     .   014
14320080120055312412321322320060060042413124322220140140083412432112222l
14330100100053142421332142l2201201200823541231122212   08 1112  19110711245091
14411032511111133155141331l045040       030045010
144201002000542531213123321100501200313244132312100601000413244312121111
14430080080051243241324131223015020015421531221222l33    0211202011911041123509l
14511522351111555155414151l007040020   030037   006
145200400400321543231321111100400600242314231411006009004123441322lllll
14530050120021324142343121414007071005143521321211 44   03 1110  13210720825071
146l900205222255355515111330500 40      015012063   005008   007
14620050150054315212331222320060090053412413232 23
14630100150091243342141322222037037025423511231223 22    08 1239361112032105507l
14811032952111535155212112 2  006          006        006
14820080130061235423112311210040060033214412321110060080043124413221121l
14830130150083124134242131211015020013513421231212ll    0121101  29110421225051
14911032551111!111111155111l2   025015   025   015
1492005009003!43521323211l11100500600042314432111110100150083124413212111l
14930090110053124243132142l110140150104315212312111l    07 1218122911072104509l
15011182533111111133153213203001.0       034   006   006
1502006015005215341323121212003006002324112343121007012005412341232l2311
15030090100074213243142131222302003501842153,123121322    05 120502151102218251 21
```

Three

Demand Analysis and Forecasting

No one regards what is before his feet; we all gaze at the stars.
Quintus Ennius

Demand analysis is the assessment of the amount prospects are ready and able to buy under specified market conditions. Changes in market conditions cause changes in demand. The level of demand is affected by the marketing activities of the firm and its competitors and by environmental factors such as economic conditions. Moreover, the needs of customers alter over time.

Detection of market changes permits the identification of new product opportunities. Discovery of relationships between demand and marketing instruments such as price and promotion allows the determination of the optimal marketing mix. Learning about the location of demand in time and space permits the establishment of sales goals and standards.

Demand analysis involves economic studies, market potential studies, consumer surveys, industrial surveys, and sales studies. Economic studies deal with business conditions and forecasts, industry product forecasts, special market studies, and capital budget coordination. Market potential studies are done by products, by territory, and by channel of distribution and involve consideration of profit potentials and potential competition. Consumer surveys research buying habits, motivation, and attitudes. Similarly, industrial surveys investigate buying requirements, buying influences, and attitudes. Sales studies involve determination of potential, territory boundaries, quotas, forecasts, product mix, and market share.[1]

Thus, demand analysis engages in the estimation of the size and location of markets. The analysis can take place at different levels of aggregation from the national economy down to the sales of individual models as shown in Figure 3-1. Influences vary in importance according to the level in the hierarchy being studied. Moreover, demand analysis attempts to identify trends in the market. In order to take the correct marketing actions, the manager must know not only what is occurring in the marketplace, but why it is happening. The quality of decision making is a function of the quality of the demand analysis.

Demand analysis provides a key input to the marketing plan. It is logically done prior to the identification of problems and opportunities and to the determination of strategy and tactics. In subsequent chapters, demand analysis will be shown to play an

---

[1]Extracted from Table 1-2 in G. David Hughes, *Demand Analysis for Marketing Decisions* (Homewood, Ill.: Richard D. Irwin, 1973), p. 13.

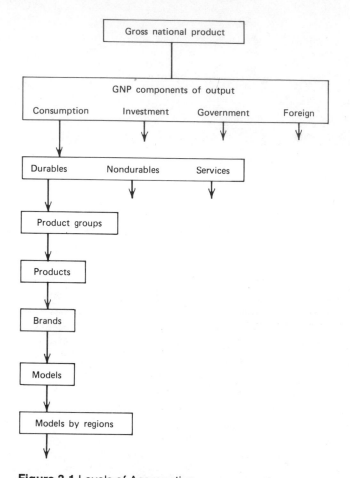

Figure 3-1 Levels of Aggregation.
Source. M. F. Elliott-Jones, *Economic Forecasting and Corporate Planning* (New York: The Conference Board, 1973), p. 26.

important role in the allocation of resources among the various elements of the marketing mix and in market segmentation. This chapter focuses on the sales potential and forecast aspects of demand analysis.

Effective planning and control of marketing activities often requires that managers collect data on sales potentials and make predictions on the actual volume of business they expect to achieve in the future. Where sales potentials represent the maximum volume an industry or firm can sell under the best of conditions, sales forecasts are realistic estimates of the goods businessmen expect to sell in the next quarter or the next year. We will explain both of these concepts and describe a variety of methods that can be used to obtain numerical values for potentials and sales forecasts. But first, we will discuss briefly the determinants of demand.

THE DETERMINANTS OF MARKET DEMAND

According to economists, the primary determinants of demand are the price of the product, the prices of other products, the incomes of the buyers, and the tastes of these buyers.[2] To these, one must add nonprice determinants such as advertising and sales force effort.

The conventional demand curve shows the relationship between the quantity demanded and the price of the product. This price is the actual market price, not the list or posted price. The demand curve for a supermarket's private label bread is shown in Figure 3-2. The price of the competing manufacturer's brand is held constant at 32¢ per loaf. All promotional factors remain constant. The demand curve is for average weekly sales. Demand curves always are for a given time period. One role of promotion is to make the buyer less sensitive to price changes. This implies that the demand curve changes with changes in promotion. This notion will be pursued in ''Advertising'' (Chapter 10).

The demand for a particular product is affected by prices of any related products that a buyer might purchase. With a fixed budget, the purchase of one product changes the availability of funds for the purchase of another item. When an increase in the price of one product produces an increase in demand for another, or has the opposite outcome for a price decrease, then the two products are said to be substitutes. Increases in beef prices usually cause homemakers to buy more chicken. On the other hand, when an increase in the price of the product results in a reduction of demand for the other, or has the opposite outcome for a price decrease, then the products are complements. If the demand for a product is derived from the demand of another, then the two are complements. For

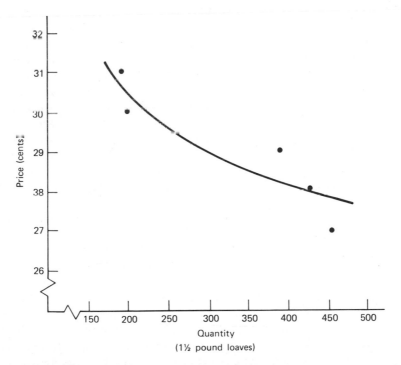

Figure 3-2 Demand Curve for Private Label Bread.
Source. Keith Cox, "The Role of Experimentation in the Information System of a Retailer" in L. George Smith, ed., *Proceedings* (Chicago: American Marketing Association, December 1964), p. 386.

[2]Kristian S. Palda, *Economic Analysis for Marketing Decisions* (Englewood Cliffs, N.J.: Prentice-Hall, 1969).

instance, lower prices for pets lead not only to higher sales of pets, but also to expanded sales of pet food and pet accessories.

The demand for a product may be influenced by consumers' disposable personal income. The demand for most products does rise along with increases in income. For industrial products, profits or cash flow is used instead of income. Products that are little influenced by these variables are called necessities.

Buyer's tastes and preferences underlie demand relationships. Taste is an all-encompassing concept for such determinants of demand as socioeconomic factors, nondemographic factors, financial factors, expectations, and other determinants. Many of these factors will be expanded on in Chapters Four and Five, "Segmentation" and "Buyer Behavior." Preferences, not only of consumers, but also of "rational" indusrial buyers, are very important. For instance, one steel industry observer believes that American steel users are, on average, willing to pay 25 percent more for domestic steel than for the identical steel from foreign producers.[3] Tastes and preferences tend to be stable in the short run, but change slowly over time.

ESTIMATING POTENTIALS

Potentials can be expressed on an industry basis as the maximum possible sales for all sellers of goods or services or more narrowly as the maximum sales opportunities for an individual firm. The relationship between industry and company potentials is described in Figure 3-3. We have shown the larger industry potential growing slowly in response to increased per capita consumption of the product. Company A's potential, on the other hand, is expanding rapidly because of growth in their manufacturing, sales, and distribution facilities. The actual sales levels achieved in any period are determined by the intensity of the marketing programs employed by individual firms (e.g., price, promotion, and advertising), actions of competitors, and general economic conditions. Realized sales are normally less than potential figures, but sales may approach potential as promotional efforts convert more and more prospects into users of the good or service (Figure 3-3).

Although potentials represent the maximum sales levels that can be achieved under ideal conditions, forecasts are predictions of the actual volume that is expected in a future time period. Thus despite a company potential of $38 million in period 12, a consideration of past sales levels, planned marketing efforts, and general business conditions has led to a sales forecast of only $34 million for company A during period 12 (Figure 3-3).

Potentials derived for an individual firm are usually broken down into subcategories for planning purposes. Estimates of *product* potentials are also expressed in terms of *geographic* areas such as states, counties, and sales territories. Geographic potentials can be quite helpful in making decisions on the allocation of salesmen and advertising efforts. Managers who know where potential customers are located can do a better job of designing sales territories and scheduling advertising to hit target markets. Geographic potentials are particularly useful in decisions on whether to expand into new foreign or domestic markets. A knowledge of geographic potentials can also be helpful in setting quotas for salesmen. Quotas are short-run sales goals for particular areas and they should reflect potentials if they are used to reward performance. It is often useful to look at geographic sales potentials when a company is setting up or reorganizing their distribu-

[3]John P. Davine, "Pricing Strategy for the Steel Industry in Meeting Foreign Competition," in Charles H. Hindersman, ed., *Proceedings* (Chicago: American Marketing Association, June 1962), pp. 340-365.

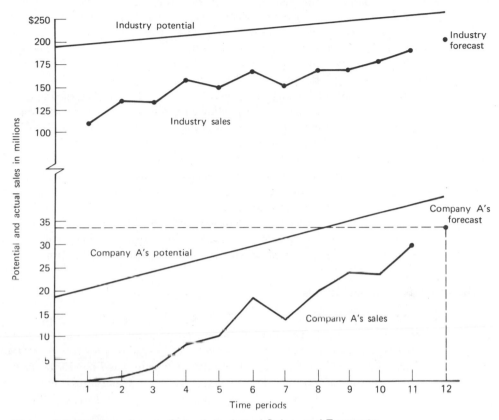

Figure 3-3 Relations Among Potentials, Actual Sales, and Forecasts.

tion system. Concentrations of potential demand may be best served by direct distribution channels whereas a more dispersed market potential would call for wholesalers or other agent middlemen.

A third way to break out sales potentials is by individual *customers*. This can be difficult because it is hard to identify all potential users and get them to accurately estimate their needs. When reliable customer potentials can be obtained, they are valuable in scheduling the frequency of sales calls and direct mail promotions.

Chain Ratio Method

Sales potentials for individual products can be determined by applying a series of ratios or usage rates to an aggregate measure of demand. A firm might start with a total population figure for an area and then multiply by average annual per capita expenditures to give an estimate of maximum possible sales for a general product class (i.e., boats). This number could then be reduced by multiplying by a percentage that reflected sales of a particular type of boat (sailboats) and still further by a percentage of customers that bought a particular size (12 to 15 feet). The resulting estimate of total potential sales for small sailboats could then be divided among the firms in the industry.

When companies operate in relatively mature markets, it may be possible to derive potential figures for new items from current industry sales. For example, in 1964 General

Foods was considering adding a freeze-dried instant coffee (Maxim) to its product line. Potential sales for the new item were derived by multiplying annual total coffee sales of 174.5 million units by a series of percentages.[4] The first step involved multiplying total sales by 83.5 percent to remove out-of-home coffee consumption. The remaining 145.7 million units were then multiplied by 93.7 percent to eliminate purchases of decaffeinated coffee. This left a total demand for soluble and regular coffee of 136.5 million units. Since instant brands already had 30 percent of the coffee market, the improved flavor of the freeze-dried Maxim should have allowed a soluble-market share of about 40 percent. When the 40 percent market share was multiplied times the 136.5 million units, an industry soluble-market potential of 54.6 million units was obtained. An estimate of the potential first year sales of General Food's new freeze-dried instant could then be made by predicting the proportions of consumers that would try the product and repurchase it over the long run.[5] If 40 percent of the instant coffee drinkers tried the new brand and 20 percent of these became regular purchasers, then the market potential for Maxim would be 40 percent × 20 percent × 54.6 or 4.37 million units. General Foods was now in the position to determine whether the revenues and costs associated with producing and selling 4.37 million units of Maxim would yield a profit for the firm.

Buying Power Index Method

Market potentials for consumer goods are usually estimated by constructing indexes from basic economic data. Perhaps the most popular multifactor index of area demand is the Buying Power Index published in June of each year by *Sales Management* magazine. This index combines estimates of population, income, and retail sales to give a composite indicator of consumer demand in specific counties and cities in the United States.

The Buying Power Index for a particular area (i) can be calculated using the formula:

$$BPI_i = \frac{5\,I_i + 3\,R_i + 2\,P_i}{10} \tag{1}$$

where I_i is the percentage of U.S. disposable personal income in area i, R_i is the percentage of U.S. retail sales, P_i is the percentage of U.S. population and the values 5, 3, and 2 are weights to reflect the relative importance of the three factors. For example, Table 3-1 shows some figures indicating that Indianapolis has 0.410 percent of U.S. income[6], 0.466 percent of retail sales, and 0.363 percent of the population. The Buying Power Index for this area would then be [5(0.410) + 3(0.466) + 2(0.363)]/10 or about 0.417 percent. Thus a city with only 0.365 percent of the U.S. population has 0.417 percent of the national sales potential due to higher than average income and retail sales.

Note that the Buying Power Index expresses sales potentials in *relative* rather than absolute terms. Although the index does not tell a firm how many units it can sell in an area, it does help managers allocate advertising and selling efforts across geographic regions. Thus, the BPI suggests that Indianapolis with 0.417 percent of the U.S. sales potential should receive about 0.417 percent of the total advertising and selling budget

[4]The situation is described in the "General Foods-Maxim" case that appears in Harper W. Boyd, Jr., and Robert T. Davis, *Marketing Management Casebook* (Homewood, Ill.: Richard D. Irwin, 1971), pp. 267-306 and the derivation of market potential is discussed in the teachers manual on page 40. A unit of coffee is either 48 ounces of soluble or 12 pounds of ground.

[5]Specific methods of estimating penetration and repeat purchase ratios will be described in Chapter 7, "Product Policy."

[6]Not shown for this particular year. It can be found by dividing Indianapolis figure (3,242,679) by the total U.S. figure (791,506,134) and multiplying by 100 percent.

Table 3-1
Population, Income, and Sales Data Used to Calculate the Buying Power Index

Indiana ESTIMATES Counties Cities	Met. Area Code	Population 12/31/72			EBI 1972		Percent Hslds. By Cash Income Groups: (A) $0-2,999; (B) $3,000-4,999; (C) $5,000-7,399; (D) $8,000-9,999; (E) $10,000-14,999; (F) $15,000 and Over						Retail Sales—1972							
		Total (Thousands)	Percent of U.S.A.	Households (Thousands)	Net Dollars (000)	Median Hsld. Cash Income	A	B	C	D	E	F	Total Retail Sales ($000)	Percent of U.S.A.	Food ($000)	General Mdse. ($000)	Furn.-House.-Appl. ($000)	Automotive ($000)	Drug ($000)	Buying Power Index
Marion 113		809.4	0.3864	268.2	3,465,423	9662	10.7	8.1	18.5	15.2	26.1	21.4	2,186,316	0.4928	413,224	531,772	97,001	432,038	97,709	0.4440
▲Indianapolis		760.4	0.3630	251.4	3,242,679	9548	11.2	8.5	8.8	15.0	25.1	21.4	2,069,471	0.4664	384,735	498,123	93,954	415,100	92,501	0.4174
State Totals		5314.3	2.5372	1716.8	19,587,623	8,702	14.1	9.7	20.8	15.7	23.1	16.3	11,504,622	2.5927	2314,113	205,914	482,447	2,219,368	427,366	2.5235

Source. Copyright © 1973. *Sales Management Survey of Buying Power;* further reproduction forbidden.

for products in national distribution. When items are only available in certain regions, the BPI for each area would be converted to a percentage of the total BPI for all areas covered.

The most critical steps in the construction of an index of sales potential are the selection of the variables to be included and the determination of the weights used to adjust the impact of the factors. The trick is to find variables that are related to the sales of your product or service and have published figures available for different geographic regions. If factors other than population, income, and retail sales are important for a particular product, it is easy to make substitutions and calculate new BPI values. The weights used in the Buying Power Index were originally based on a multiple regression formulation[7], but they are sure to vary for different products and services. The creators of the BPI suggest that the variables and the weights used in the index reflect the potential for mass products sold at popular prices. If a firm discovers that the BPI weights are inappropriate, it can determine its own weights and calculate new values using data from the Survey of Buying Power or other sources. The Buying Power Index is not a sophisticated device, but it does combine several important variables into a convenient form for estimating potentials for local demand.

SIC Method

Industrial market potentials can be built up from data made available through the U.S. Census of Manufacturers. The census combines businesses into *S*tandard *I*ndustrial *C*lassifications (SIC) according to products produced or operations performed. The 1967 Census of Manufacturers classified firms into twenty-one major industry groups using two-digit codes. These major groups were broken down into 147 subclassifications using three-digit codes and 420 product categories carrying four-digit code numbers. For example, SIC #20 stands for all manufacturers of food and kindred products, #202 represents the subclass of companies that produce dairy products, and #2026 includes the firms that produce fluid milk.

One advantage of estimating sales potentials from the Census of Manufactures is that it allows figures to be developed for geographic areas such as states, counties, standard metropolitan statistical areas, and cities. Geographic potentials are quite valuable in making allocations of advertising and personal selling activities to reach target market segments. For example, Table 3-2 shows the types of data that are available for selected SIC codes in the Indianapolis metropolitan area. Potentials can be estimated on the basis of number of companies or employees, production man hours, wages, value added, cost of materials, value of shipments, or new capital expenditures.

The first step in estimating potentials from census data is to identify all the SIC codes that make use of the product or service. This is usually accomplished by looking at the types of firms sold in the past, asking salesmen to identify other industries that are likely customers, using judgement to pick likely codes from the SIC manual, and running surveys of different types of firms to see where products are employed. Next the firm must select an appropriate data base for estimating the amount for the product that will be used by each SIC code. A food machinery manufacturer, for example, could review past sales data to find out the relationship between the number of its machines in use and the number of production workers in a particular industry. If the manufacturer found that 7 machines were used for every 1000 grain milling employees, 10 for every 1000 bakery workers, and 2 for every 1000 beverage workers, then the market potential for the

[7]Harry D. Wolfe, *Business Forecasting Methods* (New York: Holt, Rinehart and Winston, 1966), p. 195.

Table 3-2

Selected Industry Statistics for the Indianapolis Standard Metropolitan Area, 1967

SIC Index Code	Industry	Establishments		All Employees		Production Workers			Value Added by Manufacture (Million Dollars)	Cost of Materials (Million Dollars)	Value of Shipments (Million Dollars)	Capital Expenditures, New (Million Dollars)
		Total (Number)	With Twenty Employees or More (Number)	Number (1,000)	Payroll (Million Dollars)	Number (1000)	Man-Hours (Millions)	Wages (Million Dollars)				
20	Food and kindred products	99	58	8.5	56.4	5.4	11.4	31.9	148.2	311.7	460.3	9.7
202	Dairy products	16	12	1.3	9.3	0.5	1.2	3.1	22.3	47.9	70.1	0.5
2026	Fluid milk	10	8	1.2	8.1	0.4	1.0	2.5	18.1	36.2	54.1	0.5
203	Canned, cured, and frozen foods	10	5	1.1	4.8	1.0	1.9	3.7	13.9	32.2	46.1	0.4
204	Grain mill products	8	6	1.0	7.2	0.7	1.7	5.4	31.3	52.3	83.3	5.3
205	Bakery products	13	11	1.9	12.8	1.1	2.4	7.3	26.4	23.0	49.4	0.9
208	Beverages	11	7	1.0	6.4	0.5	0.9	2.2	12.7	11.7	24.4	1.6
209	Misc. foods and kindred products	21	9	0.8	4.9	0.6	1.2	3.2	23.5	59.0	82.9	0.6
23	Apparel, other textile products	23	8	0.9	3.6	0.8	1.4	2.2	6.0	9.8	15.8	0.3
239	Misc. fabricated textile products	18	4	0.4	2.1	0.3	0.7	1.2	3.4	6.4	9.7	0.3
24	Lumber and wood products	58	18	1.4	7.8	1.1	2.6	5.4	15.0	15.9	50.8	0.6
243	Millwork, plywood, related products	24	12	0.9	5.7	0.7	1.7	3.7	10.9	11.4	22.3	0.5
2432	Veneer and plywood	9	9	0.7	4.5	0.6	1.3	3.0	8.9	9.0	18.0	0.4
249	Miscellaneous wood products	12	3	0.3	1.1	0.2	0.5	1.0	2.6	2.7	5.2	0.1
3441	Fabricated structural steel	11	6	0.6	4.6	0.4	0.8	2.3	7.7	8.4	16.7	0.4
3443	Fabricated platework	8	5	0.3	2.3	0.3	0.5	1.7	2.7	3.9	7.4	0.1
3444	Sheet metal work	19	5	0.3	2.8	0.3	0.5	2.2	5.2	3.7	8.4	0.1

Source. Census of Manufactures, Area Statistics (1967).

Indianapolis area could be determined as shown in Table 3-3. Since grain milling (SIC #204) has 700 workers and 7 machines are used per 1000 workers, the market potential would be 0.7 × 7 or 4.9 machines. Similar calculations for other codes yields a total market potential of about 17 machines for the Indianapolis area. The potential built up for Indianapolis would then be added to estimates derived for other areas to give state and national figures.

Another way to build potentials using census data is by conducting surveys of purchase intentions among firms in selected SIC codes. Bursk and Greyser describe a company that sent questionnaires to 14,000 prospects in 100 SIC codes.[8] The mailing list was specially prepared by *Iron Age* magazine to cover the intended market and 65 percent of the questionnaires were returned. The survey made it possible to calculate the percentage of firms in each SIC code that were interested in the product. These percentages could then be used to estimate the market potential for the product in a given area. For example, Table 3-2 shows there were nineteen sheet metal plants (SIC #3444) in the Indianapolis metropolitan area in 1967. If the survey revealed that 31 percent of the firms in SIC 3444 planned to buy the product, then the Indianapolis potential would be 19 × 0.31 or 6 plants. The actual number of machines that could be sold to these six prospects could be estimated by looking at the relationship between size of firm and past purchasing behavior. If the average order from sheet metal plants with sales of less than $500,000 is 1.4 machines, then the Indianapolis potential is SIC 3444 would be 6 × 1.4 or about 8 machines. The same procedure would be employed with other SIC codes and the results totaled to give regional and national potential figures.

Table 3-3

Estimating the Market Potential for Food Machinery in Indianapolis

SIC Code	Industry	1 Production Employees[a] (1000)	2 Number of Machines Used per 1000 Workers[b]	Market Potential (1 × 2)
204	Grain milling	0.7	7	4.9
205	Bakery products	1.1	10	11.0
208	Beverages	0.5	2	1.0
				16.9

[a] From Table 3-2.
[b] Estimated by manufacturer from past sales data.

Input-Output Method

Industry sales potentials can also be derived from input-output tables for states and nations that show how businesses buy and sell goods from one another. A portion of a U.S. input-output table[9] indicating how the production of twelve industries is distributed among fifteen economic categories is shown in Table 3-4. The table reveals that in 1963

[8] See the "Seaborg Machine Tool Company" case that appears in Edward C. Bursk and Stephen A. Greyser, *Advanced Cases in Marketing Management* (Englewood Cliffs, N.J., Prentice-Hall, 1968), pp. 18-21.
[9] A complete set of tables for 370 industries in the United States is available in *Input-Output Structure of the U.S. Economy: 1963*. (Washington: Office of Business Economics, U.S. Department of Commerce, 1969), three volumes.

Table 3-4
Abbreviated United States Input-Output Matrix[a] (Millions of Dollars)

For the distribution of output of an industry, read the row for that industry.

For the composition of inputs to an industry, read the column for that industry.

Column industries (Industry No.):
1. Livestock and livestock products
2. Other agricultural products
3. Forestry and fishery products
4. Agricultural, forestry and fishery services
5. Iron and ferroalloy ores mining
6. Nonferrous metal ores mining
7. Coal mining
8. Crude petroleum and natural gas
9. Stone and clay mining and quarrying
10. Chemical and fertilizer mineral mining
11. New construction

Industry No. / Industry	1	2	3	4	5	6	7	8	9	10	11	Personal consumption expenditures	Net exports	Federal government purchases	State and local government purchases	Total
1 Livestock and livestock products	4,750	1,819	117	192	—	—	—	—	—	—	—	1,762	38	5	12	26,684
2 Other agricultural products	7,897	769	117	550	—	—	—	—	—	—	323	2,868	2,917	92	88	27,266
3 Forestry and fishery products	—	—	35	—	—	—	—	—	—	—	3	420	46	172	2	1,751
4 Agricultural services	445	1,053	74	—	—	—	—	—	—	—	—	15	11	17	33	1,772
5 Iron and Ferroalloy ores mining	—	—	—	—	55	25	5	—	—	—	1	—	118	9	—	1,429
6 Nonferrous metal ores mining	—	—	—	—	1	263	1	(b)	5	5	—	—	1	242	—	1,519
7 Coal mining	6	1	—	—	5	1	410	(b)	5	5	165	1	305	35	2,637
8 Crude petroleum and natural gas	—	—	—	—	—	—	1	297	—	1	—	—	12	(b)	—	12,265
9 Stone and clay mining	1	85	—	(b)	(b)	(b)	1	—	1	17	478	15	38	3	14	2,024
10 Chemical and fertilizer mining	—	35	—	—	—	5	(b)	—	5	31	5	—	62	(b)	—	696
11 New construction	—	—	—	—	—	—	—	—	—	—	—	—	2	4,010	15,356	65,519
31 Petroleum refining	170	954	34	3	11	7	23	64	52	6	1,119	8,232	678	711	301	21,837
Petroleum transactions percent total	0.779	4.368	0.002	—	—	—	0.001	0.003	0.002	—	5.125	37.70	3.105	3.256	1.378	—

[a] Some industries have been eliminated so the table could be shown on a single page and the rows do not sum to the totals shown.
[b] Less than $500,000.

Source: *Survey of Current Business* (November 1969), pp. 30 and 35.

petroleum refining (industry 31) sold $170 million of its production to the livestock industry (column 1), $954 million to other agricultural industries (column 2), and $34 million to the forestry industry (column 3). In addition, a large portion of the petroleum output was sold in the final demand sector with consumers taking $8232 million, export $678 million, and governmental agencies $1012 million.

Potentials can be extracted from input-output data by dividing sales to particular industries by the total sales made to all sectors of the economy. For example, the $170 million of petroleum products purchased by the livestock industry represents 0.779 percent of total petroleum demand of $21,837 million. Thus by converting the dollar figures shown in an input-output table to percentages, a firm can obtain estimates of the relative potential of different market segments (bottom line Table 3-4). In the case of petroleum, the two agricultural markets represent 5.1 percent of current sales and should therefore, receive 5.1 percent of the advertising and personal selling expenditures of the firm. The petroleum figures also suggest that although the consumer market is large (37.7 percent), the industrial sector has more than half of all sales (53 percent). Furthermore the current overseas market for petroleum products is small (3.1 percent), indicating that export does not offer much potential.

The derivation of relative market potentials from input-output tables allows a firm to compare its own sales to particular market segments with the levels achieved by all firms in the industry. Although these comparisons look backward in time, they can reveal important market sectors that have been ignored by current marketing programs. Input-output tables thus provide a useful way to construct relative sales potentials for areas based on current levels of sales achieved by different industries.

Input-output tables can also help in estimating the impact of some change within the market. The process of manufacturing gasoline once required tetraethyl lead. The manufacture of tetraethyl lead consumed lead. Then legislation required automobiles to have catalytic exhaust systems as a means of reducing pollution. Since lead reduced the effectiveness of these catalytic systems, legislation required nonleaded gasoline. The consequences of the legislation on lead markets can be evaluated by means of the input-output tables. Similarly, the market for platinum, the most common catalyst, can be assessed.

SALES FORECASTING

Accurate forecasts of the goods and services firms expect to sell in the future are vital to almost all phases of business planning. Marketing executives must have sales forecasts to set quotas, guide product development, plan promotions, and allocate personnel. Sales forecasts are employed by many areas within the firm and it is common to find several departments contributing to their preparation.

Sales forecasting activities are normally controlled by company policies with regard to timing, coverage and detail. The time dimension refers both to the frequency with which forecasts are prepared and the length of the period covered by the projections. A Conference Board survey revealed that most manufacturers and service companies[10] prepare sales forecasts on an annual basis. The actual time periods covered by these forecasts varies from as little as one month to five years or more. Although a one-year

---

[10]Service companies include insurance, banking, transportation, and utility firms. From Stanley J. PoKempner and Earl L. Bailey, *Sales Forecasting Practices* (New York: The Conference Board, Experiences in Marketing Management, No. 25, 1970), p. 21.

forecast period was typical, most firms break the annual forecast down into monthly or quarterly estimates. Sales forecasts are reported for products, product lines, and total company sales as forecasts are often built up from estimates for individual items.

The accuracy of the forecast usually declines as the time period forecast becomes more distant from the present. The forecast is often expressed as a range of possible values around an expected value. Thus, this range becomes larger as the length of the forecast increases. This phenomenon is shown in Figure 3-4 for an n-period forecast. For simplicity of exposition, we will focus on different methods for forecasting the "expected value" and delete consideration of the range. However, the existence of the range is implicit.

Sales Forecasting Methods

Despite considerable talk about sophisticated techniques, sales forecasting is more of an art than a science in most firms. A Conference Board survey, for example, has shown that *Executive Opinion* was the most frequently used sales forecasting technique among consumer products manufacturers and service companies (Table 3-5). This technique involves soliciting the judgement of a group of experienced managers. This seems to indicate that many businessmen rely on the art of the educated guess rather than on statistical analysis of data. However, executives and salesmen use implicit models in making their "subjective" judgements, so the distinction between them and a "mathematical" model may be less than one might assume.[11] The evaluation of the quality of the manager's judgmental information was discussed in the last chapter, "Decision Making."

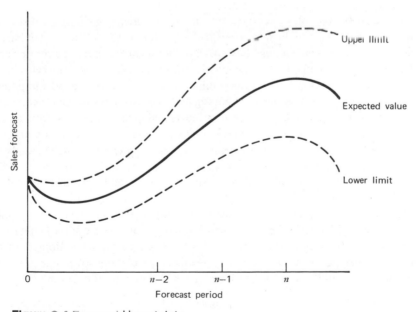

Figure 3-4 Forecast Uncertainty.

[11]For example, see George Schussel, "Sales Forecasting With the Aid of a Human Behavior Simulator," *Management Science,* Vol. 13 (June 1967), pp. B-593-B-611.

Table 3-5

Utilization of Alternative Sales Forecasting Methods by 161 Companies

	Percentage of Firms Reporting Heavy or Moderate Usage		
Method	Industrial Manufacturers	Consumer Manufacturers	Service Companies
Executive opinion	81	77	80
Sales force composite	86	51	70
Survey of Users	59	37	25
Time series projection	52	57	71
Mathematical models	32	35	44
Methods used per company	3.1	2.5	2.9

Source: Adapted from Table 1 in *Sales Forecasting Practices* (New York: The Conference Board Experience In Marketing Management, No. 25, 1970), p. 10.

The favorite forecasting technique employed by industrial manufacturers appears to be the *sales force composite* method. With this procedure, salesmen project volume for customers in their own territory and the estimates are aggregated and reviewed at higher management levels.[12] Some sales force systems use subjective probabilities and expected values. The sales force composite method is popular with industrial concerns because they have a limited number of customers and salesmen are in a good position to assess customer needs. Forecasts prepared by salesmen may be biased, however, since the projections are often used to set quotas and salesmen hesitate to predict more volume than they can deliver. One benefit of the sales force composite method is that participation in the forecasting process may increase the salesman's confidence in his sales quota and may give him a greater incentive to achieve it.

The derivation of sales forecasts from *Surveys of Buying Intentions* was stressed by 59 percent of the industrial manufacturers in the Conference Board study, but the technique had only limited usage among consumer product manufacturers and service companies (Table 3-5). This method asks a sample of customers (via personal interviews, phone, or mail questionnaires) to indicate the products and amounts they expect to purchase in a future period. Responses are then aggregated and estimates of total demand for each product are prepared. Sales forecasts for individual firms are derived from total demand using market share estimates. Buyer surveys are often time consuming and expensive and there is always a question of whether the persons interviewed will actually buy what they intended to purchase. User surveys have been most successful in industrial markets where limited numbers of firms have specific needs and tend to follow through on purchase intentions.

The U.S. Department of Commerce has conducted annual surveys of the capital equipment buying plans of businessmen for many years. These surveys have been quite accurate and are widely used to build sales forecasts for capital equipment manufacturers. The average error in business investment predictions over one seventeen-year period, for example, was less than 5 percent.[13] Although the Commerce Department

[12]Selection of the best level of aggregation in light of total forecast error is discussed in Richard Staelin and Ronald E. Turner, "Error in Judgmental Sales Forecasts: Theory and Results," *Journal of Marketing Research,* Vol. 10 (February 10, 1973), pp. 10-16. They point out that the salesmen's forecasts are seldom independent. The salesmen may use some of the same inputs, for instance, GNP, in making their forecasts.

[13]Morris Cohen, "Surveys and Forecasting," *How Business Economists Forecast,* William F. Butler and Robert A. Kavesh, eds., (Englewood Cliffs, N.J.: Prentice-Hall, 1966), pp. 60-62.

investment survey has been a good predictor, it is not available until March and many firms use the earlier McGraw-Hill survey, which is published in November for the following calendar year. This survey has somewhat larger errors (about 6 percent) but the loss of precision may not be serious.

Consumer surveys of buying intentions have been most often used to forecast sales of durable goods. Maynes, for example, has shown that the Quarterly Survey of Buying Intentions published by the Census Bureau is closely related to consumer expenditures on new cars.[14] These results suggest that intentions data can be used to make accurate forecasts of aggregate sales of consumer durables. Another set of data that is available to forecast the sales of consumer goods is the Index of Consumer Attitudes published by the Survey Research Center at the University of Michigan. This index is derived from consumer surveys that probe consumer attitudes towards personal finances, business conditions, buying opportunities, but does not ask about buying plans for specific products. For example, in the fourth quarter of 1970 the Survey Research Center reported that the Index of Consumer Attitudes reached a low of 72.4[15] for the year. This value was down considerably from the base of 100 recorded in February 1966 and reflected a loss of consumer confidence caused by depressed business conditions. Typically, surveys of buying intentions are used along with other information to prepare sales forecasts for industrial goods and consumer durables.

The use of *mathematical models* to predict sales was emphasized by only 32 to 44 percent of the companies in the Conference Board survey. Forecasting models usually combine several explanatory variables in the form of one or more equations. Once an acceptable model has been created, parameters and variables are estimated and inserted in the model to crank out the sales forecasts. Mathematical forecasting models are normally tailor-made to meet the needs of individual firms and tend to be costly and complex. In addition, they require highly trained personnel and computers to develop the models and prepare the forecasts. An example of a sales forecasting model designed for new products will be discussed in the "Product Policy" chapter.[16] Although businessmen have been slow to adopt mathematical models for sales forecasting, this method has become more popular as computer software has become more widely available and the models have proven they are fast, cheap, and accurate.

One universal trait of business forecasting revealed by the Conference Board survey is that firms employ several methods to make a given sales prediction. This allows managers to check the estimates provided by alternative techniques and hopefully improves the reliability of the final sales projection. The average company in the Conference Board survey, for example, utilized two or three different approaches to predict sales. The most popular numerical approach to forecasting mentioned in the Conference Board survey, *time series projection*, will be discussed in the next section.

Time Series Forecasting

Time series forecasts rely on past data to provide a base for making projections about the future. This method assumes that significant relationships exist between time and other variables and these can be used to make accurate predictions about coming events.

[14]E. Scott Maynes, "An Appraisal of Consumer Anticipations Approaches to Forecasting," *American Statistical Association Business and Economic Statistics Section–Proceedings*, 1967, pp. 114-123.
[15]"Study Finds Buyers' Confidence at '70 Low in the Fourth Quarter," *The Wall Street Journal* (December 17, 1970), p. 8.
[16]See Chapter Seven, page 310.

Perhaps the most popular series used in business forecasting is the record of past sales achieved by the firm. Time series forecasting is widely accepted by businessmen and over half of the manufacturers and service companies in the Conference Board survey placed heavy or moderate reliance on this method.

Leading Indicators. There are many time series that have forecasting value for businessmen. The best series are those that are closely related to company sales and are available several months in advance. Changes in the series can then be used to predict sales directly or the series can be combined with other variables in a forecasting model. For example, if sales of the firm were found to be correlated with orders for durable goods, then a 5 percent gain in durable orders could indicate a 5 percent increase in company sales. Obviously the key issue is finding indicators that have forecasting value for particular products. Fortunately the National Bureau of Economic Research (NBER) has analyzed business cycles for more than thirty years and has done a good job of identifying series with forecasting merit.[17] Twelve of the best leading indicators reported by NBER are:

1. Prices of 500 common stocks.
2. New orders, durable goods.
3. Ratio price/unit labor cost, manufacturing.
4. Nonagricultural placements.
5. Index of net business formation.
6. Corporate profits after taxes.
7. New building permits, private housing units.
8. Industrial materials prices.
9. Average work week, manufacturing.
10. Change in manufacturing and trade inventories.
11. Contracts and orders, plant and equipment.
12. Change in consumer installment debt.

Time Series Components. The usual approach with time series forecasting is to break a series down into seasonal *(S)*, trend *(T)*, cyclical *(C)*, and irregular *(I)* components. Seasonal variation represents fluctuations that repeat themselves over a fairly short period such as a week or several months. Trend, on the other hand, is a structural change in a series that persists over a long period of time. Cyclical components resemble seasonal variation, but are indeterminate in length and are usually spread over several years. The chance or irregular variation in a series is caused by unpredictable factors such as war, weather, strikes, and fashion.

The trick is to separate the variation caused by seasonal, trend, and cyclical components from a chance variation so a series can be used for forecasting purposes. To accomplish this task, a model is needed to show how the factors are related. One approach assumes the components are independent and equal to the sum of the four elements or $Y = S + T + C + I$. If there is reason to believe that the components are interrelated, a multiplicative model of the form $Y = S \times T \times C \times I$ can be used. Most

[17]Geoffrey H. Moore and Julius Shiskin, *Indicators of Business Expansions and Contractions* (New York: Columbia University Press for the National Bureau of Economic Research, Occasional Paper 103, 1967). Also see Robert S. Sobek, "A Manager's Primer on Forecasting," *Harvard Business Review,* Vol. 51 (May-June 1973), p. 6.

Current values for leading indicators can be obtained from U.S. Department of Commerce publications such as *Survey of Current Business, Manufacturer's Shipments, Inventories, and Orders,* or *Business Cycle Developments.* Other sources include the Federal Reserve Bulletin put out by the Board of Governors of the Federal Reserve System and the numerous reports of the Bureau of Labor Statistics in the U.S. Department of Labor.

sales forecasting is concerned with short-run projections and cyclical factors normally do not have much impact on these predictions. Thus cyclical components are often combined with irregular variation and the analyst focuses his attention on the seasonal and trend factors.

Adjusting Time Series Data. Sometimes time series data are not expressed in a form that is appropriate for forecasting purposes. Often the necessary adjustments are simple, such as converting from sales in dollars to sales expressed in tons or units. On other occasions it may be necessary to perform a series of changes such as combining two or more series to create a forecasting index. Frequently it is desirable to modify time series data to correct for price changes. Price inflation is a perennial problem and is normally controlled by expressing dollars in terms of values established in a base year. Population growth is another factor that can cause serious distortion of time series data. Disturbances caused by population changes can be minimized by dividing by appropriate population figures and placing the series on a per capita basis.

Perhaps the most common data adjustment in sales forecasting is eliminating seasonal effects. Since business forecasts are often prepared monthly or quarterly, seasonal factors are frequently responsible for many of the short run changes in volume.

Consumer Durables Forecast. Consumer durables include such products as automobiles, appliances, and furniture. They are distinguished from nondurables by the fact that they are not consumed in a single instance and by the fact that they have special use requirements. Television has a useful life of at least several years and requires a wired home and leisure time on the part of the user. The market for durables is made up of three submarkets: the initial purchase market, the replacement market, and the multiple-ownership market as illustrated in Table 3-6. Since substantially different trends could be operating in each submarket, each submarket should be forecast separately.

New-owner durable sales can be forecast by one of the methods to be presented in subsequent sections. The most prevalent technique is regression analysis. For instance, refrigerator demand might be determined by the number of wired dwelling units, the level of income, the net extension of installment credit, and the price index of household furnishings. Replacement durable sales can be found by relating the life expectancy of the durable to the number of new sales in each prior year. A survival or life table is shown in Table 3-7. This table shows, for various maximum estimated lives, the fraction of products still surviving at different ages. The maximum estimated life is about twice the average estimated life. One minus the survival rate is the death rate. Those products that die and are scrapped may be replaced.

Table 3-6
AGB Research Survey of Recent Acquisitions (Percent)

		Acquisitions			
	Penetration	Initial	Replacement	Additional	Total
Cookers	96	28	70	2	100
Vacuum cleaners	76	42	53	5	100
Washing machines	49	61	37	2	100
Refrigerators	35	89	10	1	100

Source. D. A. Brown, S. F. Buck, and F. G. Pyatt, "Improving the Sales Forecast for Consumer Durables," *Journal of Marketing Research,* Vol. 2 (August 1965), p. 230. Published by the American Marketing Association.

Table 3-7
Durable Goods Survival Coefficients

Age in Years	6-Year Life	11-Year Life	14-Year Life	20-Year Life	25-Year Life
1	1.000	1.000	1.000	1.0000	1.0000
2	.996	.9995	1.000	.9998	1.0000
3	.908	.9946	.998	.9992	.9999
4	.500	.9656	.989	.9965	.9997
5	.092	.8621	.957	.9878	.9989
6	.000	.6406	.874	.9641	.9965
7	—	.3594	.716	.9115	.9904
8	—	.1379	.500	.8159	.9762
9	—	.0344	.284	.6736	.9474
10	—	.0054	.126	.5000	.8962
11	—	.0000	.043	.3264	.8159
12	—	—	.011	.1841	.7054
13	—	—	.002	.0885	.5714
14	—	—	.000	.0359	.4286
15	—	—	—	.0122	.2946
16	—	—	—	.0035	.1841
17	—	—	—	.0008	.1038
18	—	—	—	.0002	.0526
19	—	—	—	.0000	.0238
20	—	—	—	.0000	.0096
21	—	—	—	—	.0035
22	—	—	—	—	.0011
23	—	—	—	—	.0003
24	—	—	—	—	.0001
25	—	—	—	—	.0000

Source. Milton H. Spencer, Colin G. Clark, and Peter W. Hoguet, *Business and Economic Forecasting* (Homewood, Ill.: Richard D. Irwin, 1961), p. 256.

Suppose we have a small appliance with an estimated average life of three years. New sales are forecast to increase by one million units each year. If every customer is satisfied and will repurchase the product when it wears out, then we can derive the replacement demand using the six-year life coefficients given in Table 3-7. The results are shown in Table 3-8. Replacement sales in 1985 are forecast to be:

$$(.092-.000)(2000) + (.500-.092)(3004) + (.908-.500)(4096) + (.996-.908)(5596) + (1.000-.996)(7504) + (1.000-1.000)(9517) = 3604$$

Note that after awhile replacement units themselves have to be replaced. Thus, replacement demand is determined by the total numbers of units of the product functioning and their life expectancy. In this example, replacement sales will eventually be greater than initial sales.

Moving Averages. One of the simplest methods used to follow trends in sales data is the moving average. The analyst merely computes the average volume achieved in several recent periods and uses it as a prediction of sales in the next period. This approach assumes that the future will be an average of past achievements. Although moving averages can provide good forecasts when sales are stable, they are apt to lag behind when there is a strong trend in the data. A crucial issue in using moving averages is determining the ideal number of periods (N) to include in the average. With a large

Table 3-8
A Small Appliance's Eight-Year Forecast (Thousands)

Year	New Sales	Replacement Sales By Product Age in Years					Sub total	Total Sales
		2	3	4	5	6		
1978	1000	—	—	—	—	—	—	1000
1979	2000	—	—	—	—	—	—	2000
1980	3000	4	—	—	—	—	4	3004
1981	4000	8	88	—	—	—	96	4096
1982	5000	12	176	408	—	—	596	5596
1983	6000	16	264	816	408	—	1504	7504
1984	7000	22	361	1226	816	92	2517	9517
1985	8000	30	493	1671	1226	184	3604	11604

number of periods, forecasts tend to react slowly whereas low values lead to predictions that respond more quickly to changes in a series.

   Exponential Smoothing. A characteristic of moving averages that distracts from their ability to follow trends is that all time periods are weighted equally. This means that information from the oldest and newest periods is treated the same in making up the forecast. A popular forecasting method that emphasizes recent data and discounts old information is known as exponential smoothing. An exponentially smoothed forecast can be derived using the formula:

$$\overline{S}_t = \alpha S_t + (1-\alpha)\,\overline{S}_{t-1} \tag{1}$$

where $\overline{S}_t$ is the sales forecast for period $t + 1$, α is the smoothing constant, S_t is actual sales in period t, and $\overline{S}_{t-1}$ is the smoothed forecast obtained for period t-1. The formula combines a portion (α) of the sales achieved in the current period with a discounted value of the smoothed average calculated for the previous period to give a forecast for the next period ($t+1$).

   The main decision with exponential forecasting is selecting an appropriate value for the smoothing constant (α). Smoothing factors can range in value from zero to one with low values providing stability and high values allowing a more rapid response to sales changes. Forecasts based on smoothing factors of .2 and .8 have been plotted against a set of sales data in Figure 3-5. The forecasts for period 2, for example, were derived by plugging the smoothing constants, the demand observed in period 1 ($S_t=80$), and the smoothed sales computed for the previous period ($\overline{S}_{t-1} = 70$) into equation 1, [. 2 $\times$ 80 + $(1-.2)$ 70 = 72, .8 $\times$ 80 + $(1 - .8)$ 70 = 78]. Note that the forecasts lagged behind actual sales due to the strong trend in the data. The .8 smoothing constant produced the most accurate forecasts and the .2 factor gave the most stable projections. This suggests that large smoothing factors are needed when a series is changing and low values when sales are more stable. Perhaps the best way to select a smoothing constant is to take some representative sales data and measure the forecasting errors produced by smoothing constants of different sizes. The optimum smoothing factor would be the one that gave the smallest forecasting error.

   The weights assigned to past sales data by exponential forecasting methods vary with the size of the smoothing constant (α). Sales in the most recent period (S_t) are multiplied directly by the smoothing constant and sales in previous periods, (S_{t-1}, S_{t-2}, $\ldots S_{t-n}$) are assigned weights that decline geometrically with age. Since each exponentially smoothed sales forecast is based on a smoothed average from a previous period, it is

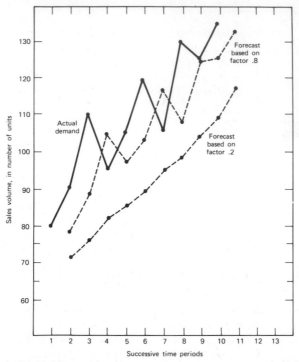

Figure 3-5 Forecasting Sales Using Exponential Smoothing Factors of .2 and .8. *Source.* Norbert L. Enrick, *Market and Sales Forecasting* (San Francisco: Chandler Publishing Co., 1969), p. 10.

not immediately clear how the process gets started. One possibility is to simply take the average of sales observed in the first few periods and use this as an estimate of the initial smoothed sales.

A disadvantage of exponential sales forecasts is they tend to lag behind when there is a trend in the data. This is shown clearly by the forecast calculated with a smoothing factor of .2 in Figure 3-5. One remedy is to simply use a higher value of the smoothing constant. This approach gives more accurate tracking of the data, but the forecast loses much of its stability. Forecasts that jump around in response to random elements are a nuisance as the firm must continually expand and contract production activities. A better remedy for lags in the smoothed forecast is to adjust the exponential average to account for the trend in the data.[18] In the case of the data in Figure 3-5 a trend-corrected smoothed forecast was more accurate than a simple smoothed forecast. Also both of the smoothed forecasts were considerably better than a sales forecast based on a two-month moving average.

Thus we may conclude that exponential smoothing provides a forecasting procedure that is simple, adaptable, and one that gives good tracking of historical data. Despite these benefits, marketing managers sometimes use several independent variables to project sales and regression techniques have advantages for this type of forecasting.

Forecasting with Regression Methods

Sales forecasts are often prepared using equations that show how demand is related to its determinants. These relationships are found by statistical analysis using a technique

[18]First calculate the changes between successive values of smoothed sales. Then smooth the changes using equation 1 to give an estimate of the trend. Since the lag in smoothed sales varies inversely with the size of the smoothing constant (α), multiply the smoothed trend by $(1-\alpha)/\alpha$. Next add the lag-adjusted trend to smoothed sales and include an estimate of trend for the succeeding period.

called regression analysis. The analyst first selects those factors that might explain sales of the product. Then, regression methods are employed to explore the covariations among these variables in data. Thus, regression analysis shows the impact of the determinant variables on demand. Forecasts are obtained by evaluating the regression equation using estimates of future values of the explanatory variables.

Many companies use the regression technique to predict sales.[19] American Can has found that beer can demand is related to income levels, the number of drinking establishments per thousand persons, and the age distribution of the population. Eli Lilly has discovered a relationship between pharmaceutical sales and disposable income. Armour forecasts the number of cattle to be slaughtered in future months. RCA forecasts the sales of television sets, radio sets, and phonographs. One of the strengths of regression analysis is its ability to assimilate large quantities of data.

Linear Regression. In simple linear regression, the relationship between the dependent varible (Y) and some independent varible (X) can be represented by a straight line. The equation of this line is $Y = a + bX$ where a is the intercept and b shows the impact of the independent varible. The key step in deriving linear regression equations is finding values for the coefficients (a, b) that give the best fit to the data. One way to determine these coefficients is to plot the data on a graph and make a freehand estimate of the line that represents the relationship between the two variables.

Although this approach may give satisfactory results, the best fit can be obtained by employing *least squares* procedures. "Least squares" estimates of the coefficients are values that minimize the squared differences between the actual sales observations and the values predicted by the equation. This can be explained by referring to Figure 3-6 where the prices (Y) paid for a new winter coat have been plotted against the consumers' income (X). Note that for the individual who had an income of $3000, the error between the actual and predicted price was $14. The least squares procedure minimized the sum of the squares of all the errors to calculate the coefficients of the regression line. The computer output for the regression equation is shown in Figure 3-7.[20] The equation ($Y = 40 + 6X$) says that the price for a coat is $40 plus $6 for every thousand dollars of income. Thus, if a consumer's income was $7500, then our estimate of the price that this consumer would pay is $85.

Regression analysis assumes that the dependent and independent variables are interval scaled. However, many marketing variables are qualitative (race, sex, occupation) and are represented by dummy variables. When a particular characteristic is present, the value of the dummy variable is given a value of one and when it is absent the value is zero.[21] In the coat example, the price paid can be made a function of the respondent's income and sex. Let the value of the dummy variable (Z) take on a value of one if the respondent is male, and be zero if the respondent is female. The coefficient obtained for the dummy sex variable will indicate the *difference* in the price paid between a man and a woman. The equation showing the impact of sex and income on coat purchases is approximately:

---

[19]George G. C. Parker and Edilberto L. Segura, "How to Get a Better Forecast," *Harvard Business Review,* Vol. 49 (March-April 1971), pp. 99-109.

[20]W. J. Dixon, ed., *BMD Biomedical Computer Programs,* (Los Angeles: University of California Press, 1973), 773 pages. The printout shown in Figure 3-7 has been edited slightly so it would fit on a single page. Figures for sums, sum of squares, cross-product sums, cross products of deviations, and the inverse of the correlation matrix have been deleted. Also the variables have been labeled where they are shown by number in the actual printout.

[21]When the dependent variable is qualitative, regression analysis is not appropriate and either discriminant or canonical analysis must be used. For a discussion of these techniques, see Donald F. Morrison, *Multivariate Statistical Methods* (New York: McGraw Hill Book Company, 1967).

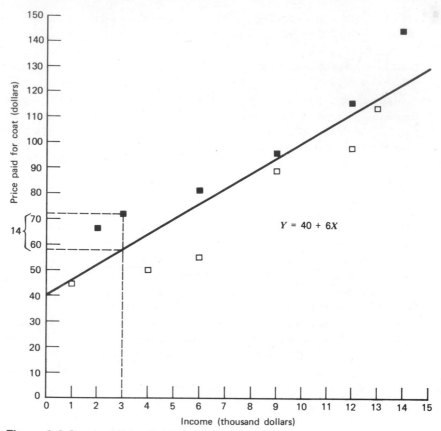

Figure 3-6 Graph of Price Paid Versus Income.

$$Y = 30 + 6X + 20Z \tag{2}$$

This suggests, in this hypothetical example, that men pay $20 more than women for top coats.

Aluminum Siding Forecasts. Assume a manufacturer of aluminum siding needs a method to predict sales in prospective territories. Reliable sales forecasts would allow the firm to make better decisions on expansion in new areas and help determine the number of salemen to assign to territories. Suppose that a search of company records revealed first-year sales figures for twenty new territories as shown in Table 3-9. In addition, a review of census and business publications provided comparable figures for interest rates on home mortgages, family income, and the number of marriages in each territory. The firm can now develop an equation to predict siding sales on the basis of the variation observed in income, interest rates, and marriages across twenty territories.

Before building an equation, it may be useful to plot the relationships between sales and the independent variables to see if they are linear. Scatter diagrams suggest that the linear assumption holds for the income and marriage variables, but the relationsip between sales and the interest rate appears to follow a curvilinear model (Figure 3-8). If changes in sales are associated with relative rather than absolute changes in the interest rate, then a better forecasting equation will be obtained if the logarithms of the interest rates are used instead of the actual values shown in Table 3-9.[22]

[22]Ronald E. Frank, "The Use of Transformations," *Journal of Marketing Research,* Vol. 3 (August 1966), pp. 247-253.

```
BMD03R - MULTIPLE REGRESSION WITH CASE COMBINATIONS
HEALTH SCIENCES COMPUTING FACILITY, UCLA

SAMPLE SIZE      12
NO. OF VARIABLES 2
DEPENDENT VARIABLE IS NOW PRICE

COEFFICIENT OF DETERMINATION  0.825
MULTIPLE CORR. COEFFICIENT    0.908

SUM OF SQUARES ATTRIBUTABLE TO REGRESSION      8301.519
SUM OF SQUARES OF DEVIATION FROM REGRESSION    1755.480

VARIANCE OF ESTIMATE    175.548
STD. ERROR OF ESTIMATE   13.249

INTERCEPT (A VALUE)      39.632
```

ANALYSIS OF VARIANCE FOR THE MULTIPLE
LINEAR REGRESSION

SOURCE OF VARIATION	D.F.	SUM OF SQUARES	MEAN SQUARES	F VALUE
DUE TO REGRESSION.........	1	8301.519	8301.519	47.289
DEVIATION ABOUT REGRESSION.	10	1755.480	175.548	
TOTAL..	11	10057.000		

VARIABLE	MEAN	STD. DEVIATION	REG. COEFF.	STD. ERROR OF REG. COE.	COMPUTED T VALUE
INCOME	7.583	4.541	6.048	0.879	6.876
PRICE	85.500	30.236			

Figure 3-7 Computer Printout for Coat Example.

A multiple regression equation created to forecast sales of aluminum siding from the logarithm of the interest rate, income, and marriage variables is shown in the printout in Figure 3-9. In the middle of the figure, the constant for the regression equation (204.757) is listed alongside the heading INTERCEPT (A VALUE). This represents the theoretical value of sales when the other variables are zero. The regression coefficients are shown under the heading REG. COEFF. When these coefficients are placed in equation form we have:

$$Y = 204.8 - 87.12 \log_{10} X_1 + 1.930 X_2 - .018 X_3 \qquad (3)$$

where Y is sales of aluminum siding, X_1 is the interest rate, X_2 is family income, and X_3 is the number of marriages. This equation suggests that siding sales increase with income and decline with growth in the interest rate and the number of marriages. Thus if the firm was considering entering a new territory where the interest rate on home mortgages was 10 percent, average family income was $15,000 and 100,000 marriages were performed annually, a sales forecast for the territory could be prepared by inserting these values in equation 3. Since the logarithm of the interest rate is 1, we have $\{204.8 - 87.12(1) + 1.930(15) - .018(100)\}$ or a sales estimate of 1,448,000 square feet of siding for the new territory. Before our analyst shows this equation to his boss, he should check to see how good a forecasting device he has created.

Table 3-9

Economic Indicators and Sales of Aluminum Siding in Twenty Territories[a]

Average Interest Rate on Home Mortgages[a]	Average Family Income[a] (1,000)	Marriages per year[a] (1,000)	Sales of Aluminum[b] (10,000 ft²)
8.50%	$14.3	62.0	142
9.40	9.5	55.5	138
6.43	17.8	76.5	177
7.40	11.5	45.8	156
6.50	13.0	90.3	158
10.40	11.6	35.0	144
7.41	14.7	93.1	150
10.60	11.1	33.5	136
8.00	13.1	90.0	140
7.05	16.9	75.2	157
7.80	11.2	97.0	153
7.95	12.7	75.6	147
6.75	16.5	99.5	170
6.30	18.4	89.5	165
6.75	16.0	110.9	160
6.56	13.3	30.6	153
7.25	13.8	21.2	146
9.85	9.6	25.1	140
6.85	18.2	52.7	173
6.50	14.8	50.0	167

[a] Data derived from business and census publications.
[b] Company sales records.

Measuring Efficiency. Perhaps the most important measure of the forecasting ability of regression equations is the standard error of the estimate. This statistic tells the analyst the range of error he can expect around his sales forecasts and is calculated by taking the standard deviation of the variation about the regression line. The usual assumption is that deviations from the regression are normally distributed. Then the standard error reported in Figure 3-9 (6.732) means there is a 68 percent chance that the true value of sales will be within ±67,320 of any forecast made with equation 3. Another way to evaluate a forecasting equation is with the cofficient of determination (R^2). This statistic shows the proportion of the variance in sales that is explained by the independent variables in the equation. The value of R^2 will always lie between 0 and 1. The R^2 obtained suggests that the equation was able to explain 74.5 percent of the total variation in the sales of aluminum siding.

The forecasting ability of our equation can also be judged by looking at the errors in the coefficients derived for interest rate, income and marriages. These errors indicate the expected dispersion around the coefficients and are shown under the heading STD. ERROR OF REG. COE. Usually regression coefficients are evaluated by dividing by their errors to give a T value. This T ratio provides a standardized measure of the precision with which the coefficient has been estimated. A good rule of thumb is that the value of the T ratio for each variable in the equation should be greater than 2.00 in absolute value.

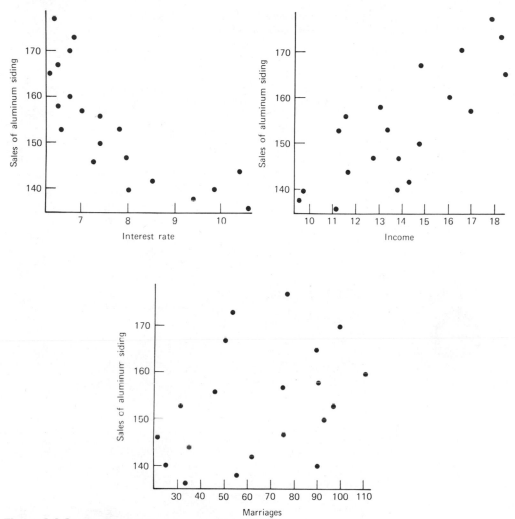

Figure 3-8 Scatter Diagrams.

When the assumption that the deviations from the regression line are normally distributed is made, the quantity T follows the t distribution. This permits us to construct significance tests for individual regression coefficients. Each coefficient measures the contribution of its associated independent variable to the analysis. The hypothesis to be tested is that the independent variable has no linear influence on the dependent variable, that is, that the coefficient is really zero. If the computed T statistic is greater than the tabulated t at the chosen level of significance, then the null hypothesis of no contribution can be rejected.[23]

For example, the computed T value for the interest variable in equation 3 was -2.64. Since this exceeds the critical value of 2.58 associated with a 1 percent chance of error, we can say that the regression coefficient for the interest variable was significant. The T value for the income variable (2.27) was not significant at the 1 percent level, but it did

---

[23]The degrees of freedom are $n - k$ where n = number of observations and k = number of coefficients estimated.

BMDO 3R— MULTIPLE REGRESSION WITH CASE COMBINATIONS
HEALTH SCIENCES COMPUTING FACILITY, UCLA

TRANS CARD NO.	GENERATOR NEW VARIABLE	CARD(S) TRANS CODE	ORIG. VAR(A)	ORIG. VAR(B) OR CONSTANT
1	1	3	1	0.0000

CORRELATION COEFFICIENTS

	LOG_{10}INTEREST	INCOME	MARRIAGES	SIDING SALES
LOG_{10} INTEREST	1.000	−.743	−.459	−.814
INCOME		1.000	.431	.795
MARRIAGES			1.000	.380
SIDING SALES				1.000

SAMPLE SIZE   20
NO. OF VARIABLES   4
DEPENDENT VARIABLE IS NOW SIDING SALES

COEFFICIENT OF DETERMINATION   .745
MULTIPLE CORR. COEFFICIENT   .863

SUM OF SQUARES ATTRIBUTABLE TO REGRESSION   2119.579
SUM OF SQUARES OF DEVIATION FROM REGRESSION   725.221

VARIANCE OF ESTIMATE   45.326
STD. ERROR OF ESTIMATE   6.732

INTERCEPT (A VALUE)   204.757

ANALYSIS OF VARIANCE FOR THE MULTIPLE LINEAR REGRESSION

SOURCE OF VARIATION	D.F.	SUM OF SQUARES	MEAN SQUARES	F VALUE
DUE TO REGRESSION	3	2119.579	706.526	15.588
DEVIATION ABOUT REGRESSION	16	725.221	45.326	
TOTAL	19	2844.800		

VARIABLE	MEAN	STD. DEV.	REG. COEFF.	STD. ERROR OF REG. COE	COMPUTED T VALUE
LOG_{10} INTEREST	.881	.072	−87.118	32.950	−2.644
INCOME	13.900	2.744	1.930	.851	2.269
MARRIAGES	65.450	27.863	−.018	.063	−.292
SIDING SALES	153.600	12.236			

Figure 3-9 Sample Printout From Multiple Regression Program.

exceed the critical T value at the 5 percent level of significance ($T=1.746$, $P=.05$, 16df). The weakest regression coefficient in the equation showed the impact of marriages and it had an error that was three times the coefficient. This suggests the marriage variable was irrelevant and could be dropped from the forecasting equation. If this is done, the equation reduces to:

$$Y = 202.1 − 84.91 \log_{10} X_1 + 1.892 X_2 \tag{4}$$

where X_1 and X_2 are the same as before.

The most interesting feature of the new equation is that it has a lower standard error of the estimate than equation 3. With the new equation, there is a 68 percent chance that the true value of sales will be within ±65,000 of any forecast. Thus the marriage variable not only failed to increase the proportion of sales explained, but it actually reduced the ability of the equation to predict sales of aluminum siding. These results suggest that analysts should look carefully at the contribution of each variable in explaining sales, the errors in the coefficients, and the standard error of the estimate before they use equations to predict sales.

Traps to Avoid. The ease with which a relationship between sales and other variables can be found with regression masks potential problem areas.[24] The inclusion of variables spuriously related to sales and the omission of variables causally related to sales may lead to serious forecast errors. Futhermore, the system may change over time, which may mean that the assumptions underlying the forecast no longer hold.[25]

Regression results apply only to the range of data upon which they were constructed. Caution must be exercised in forecasting outside of this observed range. The actual demand function could be highly nonlinear while the segment of it that was examined could be approximately linear. Experimentation is one way to extend the range of the observations. Overall, there should be at least five times as many observations as there are independent variables in the regression equation.

Another problem can occur with uncertainty over the direction of causation. The usual assumption is that sales are influenced by the independent variables, such as income, that appear on the right side of the equation. However, sales are often used to set advertising and price levels and these factors in turn affect sales. When variables like these appear in a forecasting equation, influence flows in both directions and a single equation model is inadequate. An example, showing how a system of equations can be used to trace the relationship between sales and advertising is explained in "Advertising" (Chapter Ten).

COMPUTER-ASSISTED FORECASTING

Computers are frequently used in sales forecasting because they are fast and they can make predictions from masses of figures using complex procedures. This allows the firm to make more frequent forecasts for a much wider range of products. The computer can

[24]A subtle problem with time series regression, called autocorrelation, occurs when the differences between sales predicted by an equation and actual sales are correlated over time. This tends to overstate the explanatory power of the regression and can lead to errors in predictions for future periods. The presence of autocorrelation may suggest that important variables have been left out or that the equation was constructed improperly. Sometimes an autocorrelation problem can be solved by using the differences between successive data points rather than the actual values themselves to build a forecasting equation.

Another problem, called multicollinearity, occurs when variables used to explain sales are strongly related to each other. In which case, the influence of one can not be separated from another. Consequently, the explanatory power of the regression is unaffected, but the estimates of the coefficients are not precise. The usual solution for this problem is to drop one or more of the offending variables from the equation. There is no impact on forecasting ability unless the relationship between included and excluded variables change over time.

Detailed discussions of autocorrelation and multicollinearity can be found in texts such as J. Johnston, *Econometric Methods* (New York: McGraw-Hill, 1972). These concepts have been introduced only as warning to the user of their existence.

[25]A procedure for adjusting forecasts to take into account unusual happenings has been proposed by James E. Reinmuth and Michael D. Geurts, "A Bayesian Approach to Forecasting the Effects of Atypical Situations," *Journal of Marketing Research,* Vol. 9 (August 1972), pp. 292-297.

also be programmed to make adjustments in raw data, compare predictions generated by alternative techniques, and keep track of forecasting errors. A computer program that accomplishes all these tasks has been developed by Robert McLaughlin and James Boyle for the Scovill Manufacturing Company.[26]

A sample printout from the Scovill computer forecasting program is shown in Figure 3-10. The simplest forecasts prepared by the Scovill program are shown under the heading HORIZONTAL CONTINUATION. This approach assumes that the future sales will remain at current levels. Thus, the forecasts for one, two, and three months into the future are identical. The first set of forecasts (7549) is merely the most recent sales figure. The second set (7772) is an average of sales in the most recent two periods and the third set (7966) is an average of the most recent three periods. A similar procedure was used to derive forecasts for orders and these are shown in the next three columns.

Sales forecasts prepared using time series models are grouped under the TREND PROJECTION heading of the Scovill printout. The first set of forecasts was based on an exponentially smoothed average adjusted for trend. The next set of forecasts was based on an exponential model that used separate parameters for smoothing sales and tracking the trend.[27] A naive rate of change model was used to develop the third set of forecasts. The initial prediction was obtained by subtracting average sales over the past three months from sales in the last month and adding 70 percent of this difference to sales achieved in the last month. Forecasts for the second and third months in the future were obtained by adding 70 percent of the projected change to the previous forecast. The last forecasting model included under the TREND PROJECTION heading was based on regression analysis. Sales forecasts were prepared using an equation that related sales to orders received in past months. The Scovill program used a simple two variable equation, but the program can be modified to include other variables and equations.

Final sales forecasts are not produced automatically by the Scovill computer program. Normally the analyst reviews the graphs showing past sales and orders, the rate of change, and the sales and order projections shown in the printout before making his own forecast. A record of the actual sales forecasts made by the analyst over the last twelve months is maintained by the Scovill program under the heading FINAL FORECASTS.

Percentage errors in the analyst's final sales forecasts are shown under the heading FORECAST ACCURACY in the Scovill printout. Note that the average error in the two-month forecast was less than 2 percent, suggesting that Scovill's analysts were able to make accurate sales predictions. The precision of the forecasts prepared by the computer are shown under the headings ACCURACY LAST 12 MONTHS. Forecasts based on moving averages of recent sales figures produced errors ranging from 3 to 6 percent and were clearly inferior to the forecasts derived from the TREND PROJEC-TION methods. Suprisingly the naive rate of change model had smaller average errors (2.2 percent) than either of the exponential smoothing models (averaging errors of 2.7 percent and 2.3 percent). The mistakes produced by the regression model were even larger (3.0 percent), suggesting that additional variables were needed in the forecasting equation.

Perhaps the greatest advantage of the Scovill forecasting model is that it routinely

---

[26]Robert L. McLaughlin and James J. Boyle, *Short-Term Forecasting* (Chicago: American Marketing Association, Marketing Research Technique Series No. 13, 1968). The Fortran listing of the program is described in Appendixes A, B, C, D, and E, on pp. 85-107 of the report.

[27]The model used here was derived from an article by Peter R. Winter, "Forecasting Sales by Exponentially Weighted Moving Averages," *Management Science,* Vol. 6, No. 3 (April 1960), pp. 324-342. Winter's model actually had a third parameter for seasonality, but this was ignored in the Scovill program.

A — ORDERS RECEIVED / FORECASTS OF CYCLE / PRESSURES

A	-0-	S-TD	-CI-	-TC-	%CHG	3MMT	Cycle 1ST	Cycle 2ND	Cycle 3RD	Cycle TOTAL	D-CHG	Cycle %	CHG	3 MO	BACK LOG
APR	7978	100.1	7970	8012	3.84	24313	7899	7900	7899	23698	34	99.7	101.9	98.5	27497
MAY	7343	89.0	8250	8330	3.97	23303	8000	8130	8200	24300	234	101.2	101.5	94.2	28198
JUN	9477	107.0	8857	8616	3.43	24798	8400	8500	8600	25500	1234	102.7	101.5	98.9	27853
JUL	8303	94.3	8804	8726	1.28	25123	8400	8500	8600	25500	1234	102.4	99.7	103.2	28586
AUG	8511	95.7	8893	8718	-0.09	26291	8600	8600	8599	25799	1234	101.3	98.9	106.2	26626
SEP	8733	104.3	8372	8529	-2.18	25547	8600	8700	8800	26100	34	98.6	97.4	101.8	28247
OCT	8585	100.1	8576	8314	-2.52	25829	8600	8600	8600	25800	123	96.4	97.7	97.3	28513
NOV	7938	100.5	7898	7968	-4.16	25256	8600	8600	8600	25800	1234	93.3	96.8	94.9	25708
DEC	7175	93.6	7665	7638	-4.14	23698	8200	8100	8000	24300	1234	90.7	97.2	91.3	26601
JAN	7045	98.3	7166	7269	-4.83	22158	8000	7900	7800	23700	1234	88.4	97.5	90.0	26172
FEB	8051	114.3	7043	6940	-4.53	22271	7800	7700	7600	23100	12	87.1	98.5	91.9	24911
MAR	6803	102.9	6611	6775	-4.75	21899	7700	7600	7500	22800	1	87.6	100.5	91.9	23501

B — MANUFACTURERS SHIPMENTS / FINAL FORECASTS / FORECAST ACCURACY

B	-0-	S-TD	-CI-	-TC-	%CHG	3MMT	Final 1ST	Final 2ND	Final 3RD	Final TOTAL	Acc 1ST	Acc 2ND	Acc 3RD	-I- TOTAL	3 MO SR%
APR	8303	104.7	7930	8040	1.92	24684	8271	7624	8208	24103	0.4	5.5	6.3	4.0	0
MAY	8045	96.5	8336	8235	2.43	24726	7720	8416	7249	23385	4.2	3.7	4.4	4.1	0
JUN	8725	103.9	8397	8389	1.87	25073	8624	7426	8373	24423	1.2	1.9	1.1	1.3	0
JUL	7566	88.4	8558	8522	1.58	24336	7426	8373	8944	24743	1.9	1.1	1.3	1.4	
AUG	8461	98.5	8589	8606	0.99	24752	8471	8944	8875	26290	-0.1	1.3	1.7	1.0	337
SEP	9060	104.0	8711	8647	0.48	25087	8944	8978	8862	26784	1.3	0.6	-3.9	-0.7	348
OCT	9029	103.2	8749	8627	-0.23	26550	8875	8660	8548	26083	1.7	-1.6	-1.5	-0.4	359
NOV	8519	100.7	8459	8542	-0.99	26608	8660	8548	7903	25111	-1.6	-1.5	-2.9	-2.0	368
DEC	8420	99.4	8470	8420	-1.43	25968	8151	7444	8144	23739	3.3	3.1	0.0	2.1	378
JAN	7677	91.9	8353	8222	-2.35	24616	7352	8042	8276	23670	4.4	1.2	-3.2	0.7	369
FEB	8140	101.8	7996	7966	-3.12	24237	7940	8170	7957	24067	2.5	-2.0	0.0	0.0	363
MAR	8010	106.1	7549	7838	-5.23	23827	8170	7957	7238	23365	-2.0	0.0	0.0	0.0	375

C — HORIZONTAL CONTINUATION / TFEND PROJECTION / SUR / CONTRIBUTIONS

C	BC1	BC2	BC3	AC1	AC2	AC3	EX1	EX2	NF2	EP1	SUR D-CHG	Contrib S-TD	Contrib -TC-	Contrib -I-	5 MO BIAS
1ST	7549	7772	7966	6611	6827	6940	7169	7562	7257	7459	90%	89	52	48	-1.2
2ND	7549	7772	7966	6611	6827	6940	6782	7241	7053	7408	100%	79	83	17	0.2
3RD	7549	7772	7966	6611	6827	6940	6394	6920	6910	7398	90%	68	92	8	2.4
TOTAL	22647	23316	23898	19833	20481	20820	20345	21723	21220	22265	90%	58	98	2	0.1

D — ACCURACY LAST 12 MONTHS / REALIZATION PENTAD

D (NEXT)	S-TD	BC2	BC3	AC1	AC2	AC3	EX1	EX2	NF2	EP1	-C-	Pentad -CI-	Pentad FINAL	Pentad OPT	SR%
1ST	100.0	2.9	3.6	4.8	3.7	3.5	1.9	2.1	1.8	1.7	5.7	2.1	2.1	1.1	303
2ND	100.0	4.4	4.9	4.0	3.5	3.8	3.1	2.8	2.5	3.1	6.5	3.8	2.2	1.1	358
3RD	100.0	5.5	6.0	4.6	5.2	6.2	4.2	4.0	3.8	4.6	7.5	5.0	3.2	1.1	344
TOTAL	100.0	3.7	4.2	4.2	3.7	4.2	2.7	2.3	2.2	3.0	6.1	4.2	2.1	0.4	355

Figure 3-10 Sample Printout from the Scovill Sales Forecasting Program.
Source. Robert L. McLaughlin and James J. Boyle, *Short-term Forecasting* (Chicago: American Marketing Association, Marketing Research Technique Series No. 13, 1968), p. 19.

predicts sales using seven different methods and keeps track of their accuracy. This allows the analyst to compare alternative approaches and provides support for final sales predictions. Although most businesses use more than one method to forecast sales, the Scovill program provides an unusual variety of supporting figures to help speed the forecasting task.

Summary

Demand analysis forms the foundation for understanding potentials and forecasts. The determinants of demand include the elements in the marketing mix of the firm and of its competitors, the characteristics of the buyers, and environmental factors. The primary methods for estimating potentials include the chain ratio, the Buying Power Index, the SIC, and input-output. For forecasting, many business executives take pride in their intuitive ability to foresee the future. Others rely on procedures that systematically collect and process data on sales and other variables. The most widely used time series methods include moving averages, exponential smoothing, and regression. Many of these techniques can be employed in both potential and sales forecasting.

Some evidence suggests that regression models provide more accurate forecasts than subjective models based on expert judgement.[28] The expansion of marketing information systems that provide more and better data for forecasting purposes has led to the growth of computer-assisted forecasting. Despite some advantages, computer models are not a panacea and the forecaster still has to select the "right" variables and combine them in appropriate form. This requires imagination, a background in statistics, and a willingness to experiment. Also, the forecaster must know how to measure accuracy and the cost of errors so that alternative models can be compared in terms of predictive efficiency. Perhaps the ideal forecasting procedure combines a computer model based on past data with a manager's interpretation of current developments.

The only thing certain about the future is the inevitability of change. The enterprise must constantly exert an effort to know its customers and their needs and to provide them with the right product at the right time. Thus, ensuring flexibility in marketing is a major management task.

Questions

1. What are the limitations of the SIC method in estimating industrial sales potential? The input-output method?
2. Why might a forecast not be accurate?
3. What is meant by a short-term forecast? A long-term forecast? For which marketing activities is each used?
4. The input-output matrix for a simplified economy is given in Table 3-10. Assume that consumer expenditures for manufactured products increases by $100 million.

What would be the direct and indirect effects on sales of services?
5. Hovercraft provides a new capability for travel over water at speeds up to 70 knots without the drag associated with displacement vessels. Thus, one possible use for hovercraft is as high-speed passenger and car ferries. The demand for high speed services is shown in Figure 3-11. Assess the prospects for a hovercraft that, utilized for 2000 hours p.a., can carry 500,000

[28]J. Scott Armstrong and Michael C. Grohman, "A Comparative Study of Methods for Long-range Market Forecasting," *Management Science,* Vol. 19 (October 1972), pp. 211-221.

passengers in one year over a route of 20 miles, at a 50 percent load factor.

6. Pacific Gas and Electric Company serves central and northern California. This region had a population of 9,171,600 in 1969. The Company estimated the demand for household durables. The regression equation for washing machines is

$$Q = 210,739 - 702.59P + 69H + 20Y$$
$$(t - \text{statistic}) \quad (-6.34) \quad (4.61) \quad (5.39)$$

where Q = annual retail sales of washing machines

       P = average installed price

       H = new single-family housing units connected to utilities

       Y = California per capita income

The R^2 was .95 and the standard error was 5773. The regression was based on annual data for the period 1948-1969.

What is your interpretation of the regression results?
How could Pacific Gas and Electric make use of these results?

7. In 1963, Sperry and Hutchinson Company (S&H Green Stamps) conducted a survey of households concerning weekly expenditures on food for home consumption. Data was collected on family size, presence of children under 6 (Yes=1, No=0), presence of children between 6 and 18 (Yes=1, No=0), schooling of household head (None=1, Some but not more than 8 years=2, 9-11 years=3, High school graduate, but no college=4, Some college=5, College graduate=6,) income, and price consciousness (Yes=1, No=0).

The regression model of food expenditures was run on 312 families. The results are shown in Figure 3-12. Does the model explain food expenditures? What are the important factors in explaining food expenditures?

8. A supplier of components for factory installed air conditioners for passenger cars wants a forecast of installations in 1966. Fit the information in Table 3-11 with a regression equation. Given 1966 factory sales of passenger cars of 8,598,000 and 1965 disposable personal income of $431

Table 3-10
An Input/Output Table For A Simplified Economy
(Million Dollars)

Purchases By / Sales By	Primary Industry	Manufacturing Industry	Service Industry	Final Buyers			Total Output
				Consumer	Investment	Government	
Primary Industry	50 (.125)	250 (.167)	10 (.020)	60	0	30	400
Manufacturing Industry	100 (.250)[a]	500 (.333)	40 (.080)	500	200	160	1500
Service Industry	70 (.175)	200 (.133)	100 (.200)	100	0	30	500
Primary Inputs	180	550	350	Gross domestic product = 1080			
Total Inputs	400	1500	500				2400

[a] Figures in parentheses are the derived input/output coefficients.

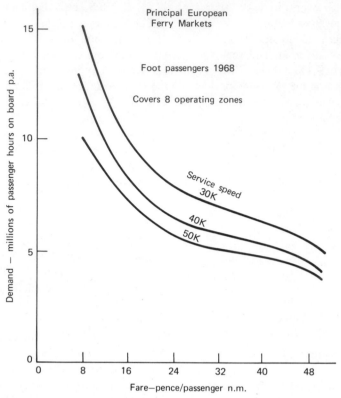

Figure 3-11 Demand for High-Speed Services.

billion, how many air conditioning units do you expect to be installed? The range?

9. Information on variables that might influence the demand for dishwashers is given in Table 3-12. First, find the relationship between sales and price. Then, estimate the demand equation with all of the potential explanatory variables included. Forecast 1971 dishwasher sales.

Table 3-11
Passenger Car Air Conditioning Units

Year	Factory Installations of Air Conditioning Units in Passenger Cars, in Thousands	Factory Sales of Passenger Cars, in Thousands	Disposable Personal Income (in 1958 Dollars) for Previous Year, in Billions
1965	2061	9306	407
1964	1412	7752	381
1963	1032	7638	367
1962	757	6933	351
1961	438	5543	340
1960	414	6675	333
1959	345	5591	319
1958	195	4258	316

BMDO3R — MULTIPLE REGRESSION WITH CASE COMBINATIONS
HEALTH SCIENCES COMPUTING FACILITY, UCLA

SAMPLE SIZE   312
NO. OF VARIABLES   7
DEPENDENT VARIABLE IS NOW WEEKLY FOOD EXPENDITURES

COEFFICIENT OF DETERMINATION   0.4199
MULTIPLE CORR. COEFFICIENT   0.6480

SUM OF SQUARES ATTRIBUTABLE TO REGRESSION   22303.69531
SUM OF SQUARES OF DEVIATION FROM REGRESSION   30808.11719

VARIANCE OF ESTIMATE   101.01021
STD. ERROR OF ESTIMATE   10.05038

INTERCEPT (A VALUE)   7.56862

ANALYSIS OF VARIANCE FOR THE MULTIPLE
LINEAR REGRESSION

SOURCE OF VARIATION	D.F.	SUM OF SQUARES	MEAN SQUARES	F VALUE
DUE TO REGRESSION	6	22303.695	3717.282	36.801
DEVIATION ABOUT REGRESSION	305	30808.117	101.010	
TOTAL	311	53111.812		

VARIABLE	MEAN	STD. DEVIATION	REG. COEFF.	STD.ERROR OF REG. COE.	COMPUTED T VALUE	PARTIAL CORR. COE.
FAMILY SIZE	3.842	1.947	2.700	0.483	5.586	0.304
TODDLERS	0.378	0.485	-1.247	1.470	-0.848	-0.048
YOUNGSTERS	0.461	0.499	4.474	1.609	2.780	0.157
SCHOOLING	3.689	1.209	0.728	0.551	1.320	0.075
INCOME (OOO)	7.091	4.597	0.752	0.147	5.086	0.279
PRICE CONSCIOUS	0.448	0.498	-0.436	1.156	-0.377	-0.021
FOOD EXPENDITURES	27.366	13.068				

Figure 3-12 Sperry and Hutchinson Computer Print-Out.

10. Sales for the Chester Furniture Company
for the past fifteen time periods have been
(with sales in dollars):

Period	Sales	Period	Sales	Period	Sales
1	227,500	6	236,000	11	344,200
2	235,000	7	235,400	12	294,800
3	164,000	8	268,200	13	312,000
4	187,000	9	250,400	14	309,900
5	228,500	10	232,900	15	327,500

Prepare sales forecasts for period 16 using the
moving average, weighted moving average,
naive rate of change, exponential smoothing,
and regression techniques.
Which method does the best job of tracking
the data over the fifteen time periods?

Table 3-12
Dishwasher Sales

Year	Dishwasher Sales, Millions of Units	Average Dishwasher Price, Dollars	U.S. Personal Disposable Income, Billions of Dollars	Stock of Dishwashers, Millions of Units	Households U.S., Millions	Nonfarm Housing Starts, Millions
1970	2.116	220.	687.8	14.90	62.875	1.434
1969	2.118	224.	634.2	12.70	61.805	1.482
1968	1.961	220.	591.2	10.90	60.44	1.524
1967	1.585	213.	546.3	9.20	58.84	1.299
1966	1.511	216.	505.3	7.80	58.09	1.173
1965	1.260	219.	469.1	6.70	57.25	1.488
1964	1.050	221.	435.8	N.A.	55.99	1.535
1963	0.880	240.	403.8	3.92	55.18	1.615
1962	0.720	242.	385.3	N.A.	54.65	1.469
1961	0.620	250.	364.4	3.66	53.46	1.337
1960	0.555	256.	350.0	3.20	52.79	1.274
1959	0.547	256.	337.1	2.88	51.30	1.531
1958	0.400	275.	317.9	2.52	50.40	1.209
1957	0.390	267.	308.7	2.20	49.54	1.042
1956	0.400	290.	287.2	1.83	48.78	1.118
1955	0.295	306.	275.3	1.57	47.87	1.329
1954	0.215	300.	254.8	1.38	46.89	1.220
1953	0.180	300.	250.3	1.25	46.33	1.104
1952	0.210	300.	236.7	1.05	45.50	1.127
1951	0.260	300.	226.0	N.A.	44.65	1.091
1950	0.230	291.	206.9	N.A.	43.55	1.396
1949	0.160	N.A.	187.4	N.A.	42.18	1.025
1948	0.225	N.A.	188.4	N.A.	40.53	0.932
1947	0.120	N.A.	169.5	N.A.	39.10	0.849

N.A.—not available.

Case 3-1
The Duport Company[1]

The Duport Company manufactured the concentrate for Genii, a bottled carbonated grapefruit drink. The company had franchised bottlers in forty-four states but had varying coverage of the population of these states. In planning future expansion and franchising of new bottlers, Mr. Herbert Walker, president of Duport, thought that the company should have some idea of the potential of each state. By concentrating on those areas where the potential was the greatest, Mr. Walker believed that Duport could make the greatest gains at the least cost.

The Duport Company was not a bottling company. It manufactured concentrated flavors that were used in making carbonated soft drinks. Bottlers purchased the concentrate and mixed it with carbonated water to produce a soft drink. This was then bottled for distribution. Besides the Genii concentrate, Duport also sold assorted flavors (e.g., ginger ale, root beer, and orange) for bottling in 24-ounce bottles under the Walker label. The Walker brand was not nationally advertised but had a strong following in several of the major metropolitan markets.

Duport had 150 bottlers franchised to bottle Genii in the United States. The company also had bottlers in South America, Canada, and Western Europe. Duport had established a distinctive bottle design and labels, which all bottlers used. An 8-ounce bottle was used for Genii. The terms of the franchise required bottlers to use only concentrate purchased from Duport for bottling Genii,[2] to use the bottle and label specified for Genii by Duport, and to maintain certain standards of quality. The bottlers were required to send periodic samples of bottled Genii to Duport for quality checks. The franchise granted the bottlers an exclusive territory.

The bottlers were also expected to promote Genii in their area through sales effort and advertising. Duport participated in cooperative advertising with the bottlers. Most of the franchised bottlers had an advertising account with Duport. The bottler paid an extra charge of one dollar for each gallon of concentrate. This was matched by Duport and set aside in the advertising account. The bottler would then forward any bills for advertising Genii to Duport for payment out of his advertising account. Also the cost of displays and other promotional materials provided the bottler by Duport were deducted from this account. Duport allowed the bottlers, particularly newly franchised bottlers, some latitude in drawing against future accruals in their advertising accounts.

Duport conducted a national advertising campaign for Genii. It advertised regularly in the *Saturday Evening Post* and had occasional television spots. Also, regional campaigns were conducted from time to time primarily through newspapers. Duport provided bottlers with mats and ideas for local advertising.

The first step in determining potentials was to attempt to isolate those factors that affected soft drink sales. Mr. Walker had learned of studies by other soft drink companies that had found that temperature and income were factors that affected soft

[2]Imitations were available from competitive companies.

drink sales. He asked his statistical department to do a correlation analysis involving per capita consumption in bottles of all soft drinks, mean annual temperature, and per capita income, by states (Table 1). They found that there was a significant correlation among these factors but that temperature was by far the most important factor. Appendix A is a summary of their results.

From the estimating equation developed in the calculations, the statistical department calculated the expected demand, by states, based on the mean annual temperature and per capita income. This was then compared with sales to determine what states were above or below the expected demand (Table 1).

Having these data, Mr. Walker asked that Genii sales in bottles per capita be analyzed with temperature and income to see what correlation existed. Since Duport in no case had 100 percent coverage of a state, per capita consumption in bottles was estimated for that portion of the population that was reached by franchised bottlers. A summary of the results is shown in Appendix B.

QUESTIONS

1. What do the coefficients in the equations shown in Appendix A and B suggest about the relationship between consumption of Genii and other soft drinks and the independent variables temperature and per capita income?
2. How much confidence should Duport place on the results of the analysis?
3. Where should Duport located new franchises?

Table 1

Correlation of Per Capita Soft Drink Consumption and Selected Factors

State	Bottles of All Soft Drinks Consumed Annually per Capita[a] X_1	Mean Annual Temperatures[b] X_2	Annual Income per Capita[c] X_3 (Hundreds)	"Expected" Sales Y_{123}	Actual Sales Less Expected Sales $X_1 - Y_{123}$	Bottles of Genii Consumed Annually Per Capita[d] X_4	Expected Sales Y_{423}	Percent of State Population under Franchise by Duport
Alabama	200	66°	$13	253	−53	1.8	4.1	63.9
Arizona	150	62	17	216	−66	9.4	3.9	18.8
Arkansas	237	63	11	236	+1	3.3	4.2	55.9
California	135	56	25	158	−23	8.2	3.5	8.4
Colorado	121	52	19	146	−25	3.3	3.7	83.4
Connecticut	118	50	27	114	+4	2.1	3.3	4.9

State	Bottles of All Soft Drinks Consumed Annually per Capita[a] X_1	Mean Annual Temperatures[b] X_2	Annual Income per Capita[c] X_3 (Hundreds)	"Expected" Sales Y_{123}	Actual Sales Less Expected Sales $X_1 - Y_{123}$	Bottles of Genii Consumed Annually Per Capita[d] X_4	Expected Sales Y_{423}	Percent of State Population under Franchise by Duport
Delaware	217	54	28	138	+79	—	—	—
Florida	242	72	18	277	−35	3.7	4.0	23.4
Georgia	295	64	14	277	+18	1.3	4.1	18.0
Idaho	85	46	16	114	−29	5.5	3.7	70.8
Illinois	141	52	24	134	+7	3.0	3.5	75.8
Indiana	184	52	20	144	+42	2.2	3.6	28.9
Iowa	104	50	16	140	−36	3.0	3.8	30.3
Kansas	143	56	17	177	−34	3.7	3.8	18.6
Kentucky	230	56	13	186	+44	5.1	4.0	66.4
Louisiana	269	69	15	265	+4	3.1	4.1	33.9
Maine	111	41	16	82	+29	2.4	3.7	88.3
Maryland	217	54	21	154	+63	14.4	3.6	5.4
Massachusetts	114	47	22	107	+7	2.8	3.5	38.6
Michigan	108	47	21	109	−1	1.0	3.5	75.6
Minnesota	108	41	18	77	+31	4.2	3.6	85.6
Mississippi	248	65	10	251	−3	4.8	4.2	57.2
Missouri	203	57	19	178	+25	3.6	3.7	35.2
Montana	77	44	19	94	−17	4.0	3.6	89.0
Nebraska	97	49	16	133	−36	2.7	3.8	39.0
Nevada	166	48	24	108	+58	2.8	3.4	16.3
New Hampshire	177	35	18	38	+139	3.7	3.5	67.9
New Jersey	143	54	24	147	−4	0.9	3.5	66.2
New Mexico	157	56	15	181	−24	—	—	—
New York	111	48	25	106	+5	4.0	3.4	30.2
North Carolina	330	59	13	205	+125	6.4	4.0	42.3
North Dakota	63	39	14	74	−11	2.5	3.7	68.7
Ohio	165	51	22	133	+32	1.9	3.6	24.3
Oklahoma	184	62	16	218	−34	1.0	4.0	66.1
Oregon	68	51	19	140	−72	2.4	3.7	74.3
Pennsylvania	121	50	20	131	−10	1.8	3.6	28.1
Rhode Island	138	50	20	131	+7	—	—	—
South Carolina	237	65	12	247	−10	3.3	4.2	73.0
South Dakota	95	45	13	115	−20	7.8	3.8	44.5
Tennessee	236	60	13	212	+24	4.0	4.0	96.6
Texas	222	69	17	261	−39	3.7	4.0	36.6
Utah	100	50	16	140	−40	5.7	3.8	81.3
Vermont	64	44	16	101	−37	—	—	—
Virginia	270	58	16	191	+79	5.8	3.9	26.7
Washington	77	49	20	124	−47	3.4	3.6	38.6
West Virginia	144	55	15	174	−30	1.2	3.9	65.2
Wisconsin	97	46	19	107	−10	2.2	3.6	55.2
Wyoming	102	46	19	107	−5	2.5	3.6	18.6

[a]*Source. National Bottler's Gazette,* "The Soft Drink Industry—A Market Study."
[b]*Source.* U.S. Weather Bureau, *Climatological Data–National Summary,* Vol. 7, No. 13, (1956).
[c]*Source.* U.S. Department of Commerce, *Office of Business Economics, U.S. Income and Output,* a supplement to the *Survey of Current Business* (November 1958).
[d]Based on percentage of population under franchise in each state.

Appendix A

Correlation Analysis of Bottles of All Soft Drinks Consumed Annually Per Capita (X_1), Mean Annual Temperature (X_2), and Annual Per Capita Income (X_3), By States [a]

Simple Correlation. Bottles of all soft drinks consumed per capita (X_1) and mean annual temperature (X_2) by states:

Estimating equation: $Y_{12} = 6.81X_2 - 206.7$

Standard error of estimate: $S_{12} = 40.5$

Coefficient of correlation: $r_{12} = .804.$

Simple Correlation. Bottles of all soft drinks consumed per capita (X_1) and per capita income (X_3) by states:

Estimating equation: $Y_{13} = 257 - 5.51X_3$

Standard error of estimate: $S_{13} = 78.4$

Coefficient of correlation: $r_{13} = -.29$

Multiple Correlation. Bottles of all soft drinks consumed per capita (X_1), mean annual temperature (X_2), and per capita income (X_3) by states:

Estimating equation: $Y_{123} = 6.46X_2 - 2.37X_3 - 145.5$

Standard error of estimate: $S_{123} = 39$

Cocfficient of correlation: $r_{123} = .814$

Coefficients of partial corrclation: $r_{12.3} = .784, r_{13.2} = -.258$

[a]Forty-seven states only. New Hampshire was eliminated from calculation because of extreme variation.

Appendix B

Correlation Analysis of Bottles of Genii Consumed Annually Per Capita (X_4), Mean Annual Temperature (X_2) and Annual Per Capita Income (X_3) by States.

Simple Correlation. Bottles of Genii consumed per capita (X_4) and mean annual temperature (X_2) by states:

Estimating equation: $Y_{42} = .019X_2 + 2.74$

Standard error of estimate: $S_{42} = 2.48$

Coefficient of correlation: $r_{42} = .065$

Simple Correlation. Bottles of Genii consumed per capita (X_4) and per capita income (X_3) by states:

Estimating equation: $Y_{43} = 4.33 - .032X_3$

Standard error of estimate: $S_{43} = 2.48$

Coefficient of correlation: $r_{43} = -.053$

Multiple Correlation. Bottles of Genii consumed per capita (X_4), mean annual temperature (X_2), and per capita income (X_3) by states:

Estimating equation: $Y_{423} = 3.764 + .0136X_2 - .0409X_3$

Standard error of estimate: $S_{423} = 2.46$

Cocfficient of correlation: $r_{423} = .081$

Case 3-2
Mustang Aviation Corporation II[1]

A long-range planning meeting has been called by the Board of Directors of the Mustang Aviation Corporation. The purpose of the meeting is to discuss the future of the utility aircraft business and to outline the various plans and objectives that the Mustang Corporation should implement in order to ensure itself a strong position in the industry's future.

As marketing information director for the Mustang Corporation, Mr. Richard T. Lange has been asked to accumulate as many data as possible and from these data to make sales forecasts both for Mustang Aircraft and for the civil aircraft industry as a whole. Mustang's president has asked the marketing information director to prepare three-year, five-year and ten-year forecasts for single-engine aircraft of the type produced by the Mustang Corporation.

Mustang Aviation was originally founded on the West Coast in early 1946 by two World War II veterans—James Haste and Paul Early. Both Mr. Haste and Mr. Early had been air force pilots during the war and prior to the war had received degrees in aeronautical engineering. Although the company was originally set up as a partnership, the capital requirements of meeting postwar demand for single-engine aircraft had forced the partners to incorporate their business in 1947. The new corporation was called The Mustang Aviation Corporation.

Immediately after the war there was a fantastic boom in civil aircraft demand. Not only was there general economic prosperity, but substantial amounts of money were available to war veterans who wished to continue their flying careers outside the military. Unfortunately, Mustang Aviation, like most light-aircraft manufacturers, had neither the production facilities nor the financial resources to meet the great demand for private and business aircraft. As a result of this shortage, the greater part of the postwar aircraft demand was filled by military surplus craft. In 1946 and 1947 alone nearly 50,000 aircraft were sold from military surplus stockpiles.

In the few years following the fantastic postwar demand for light aircraft there was a serious recession in the demand for these airplanes. This recession left the Mustang Corporation in a particularly difficult situation. The company had made major capital investments in order to "beef up" their production facilities, which had consistently operated at capacity during 1946 and 1947. During 1948, 1949, and 1950 the Mustang Aviation Corporation was able to avoid financial disaster only by laying off the bulk of their employees and by accepting whatever contract work they could muster from larger aircraft manufacturers. This contract work for the most part consisted of precision machining and assembly of parts for commercial and military aircraft.

The major stockholders had blamed the losses incurred in these three years on poor management planning. As a result of this, there had been some drastic changes in management personnel in the early fifties. Mr. Lange had come to Mustang in 1953 and since that time had found the corporate owners very unreceptive to proposed changes. This conservatism, he felt, was a direct result of the company's financial crisis in the late forties.

From 1951 to 1969 there had been a relatively slow but consistent increase in the dollar volume of new aircraft sales. At the same time, there had also been a slower, but general, increase in the total number of new aircraft sold. In 1969 and 1970 the aircraft industry was severely affected by a general economic and business recession. Tight money, rising unemployment, and the repeal of the investment tax credit that had stimulated business purchases caused a steep decline in sales and profits. The number of new aircraft units sold declined from a high of 15,768 in 1966 to 13,000 in 1969 and 7292 in 1970 (Exhibit 13). The industry made a rapid recovery and expected to sell 14,000 units in 1973. An FAA study indicated that there would be an upward trend in deliveries to a record 16,600 aircraft in 1974 and further steady rise to 20,500 units by 1977.[2] It is significant to note a trend in the average cost of new aircraft. In 1954 the average price of the 3089 new units sold in the general aviation class was $13,000. The average price of the 9459 units sold in 1964 was in excess of $28,000 and current prices are shown in Exhibit 5. In addition, the total number of active civil aircraft had increased from 60,921 in 1950 to 134,500 in 1970.

The Mustang Aviation Corporation manufactured only single-engine aircraft for either private or busi-

[1]Bertram Schoner and Kenneth P. Uhl, *Marketing Research: Information Systems and Decision Making,* 2nd ed., John Wiley and Sons, 1975, pp. 516-526. Reproduced by permission. The name of the company and some of the figures are disguised.

[2]*Barron's,* April 10, 1972, p. 11.

Exhibit 1
Summary of Civil Flying

Item	1940	1950	1960	1962	1963	1964	1965	1967	1968	1969	1970	1971
Airports in operation	2,331	6,403	6,881	8,084	8,814	9,490	9,566	10,126	10,470	11,050	11,261	12,070
Public	1,031	2,272	2,780	3,178	3,451	3,644	3,570	3,830	3,986	4,155	4,260	4,418
Private	1,300	4,131	4,101	4,906	5,363	5,346	5,996	6,296	6,484	6,895	7,001	7,652
Total civil aircraft	17,928	92,809	111,580	124,273	129,975	137,189	142,083	166,600	179,300	190,700	154,500	N.A.
Eligible aircraft	N.A.ᵃ	60,921	78,760	86,287	87,267	90,935	97,743	116,800	127,200	133,800	134,500	N.A.
Total pilots	N.A.	N.A.	348,062	365,971	378,700	431,041	479,770	618,000	692,000	720,000	733,000	741,000
Airline transport	1,431	N.A.	18,279	20,032	20,269	21,572	22,440	26,000	29,000	31,000	34,000	36,000
Commercial	18,791	N.A.	89,904	96,047	96,341	108,428	116,665	150,000	164,000	177,000	187,000	192,000
Private	49,607	N.A.	138,869	149,405	152,209	175,574	196,393	253,000	282,000	299,000	304,000	313,000
Student	110,938	44,591	99,182	95,870	105,298	120,743	139,172	181,000	209,000	204,000	196,000	186,000
Other	N.A.	N.A.	1,828	4,617	4,583	4,724	5,100	—	—	—	—	—
Hours flown (1000's)												
General aviation	3,200	9,650	13,121	14,500	15,106	15,738	16,733	22,153	24,053	25,351	26,031	N.A.
Business	314	2,750	5,699	5,431	5,740	5,823	5,857	6,578	6,976	7,064	7,204	N.A.
Commercial	387	1,500	2,365	3,051	3,172	3,305	3,348	3,918	4,810	4,928	6,849	N.A.
Instructional	1,529	3,000	1,828	2,385	2,417	2,675	3,346	6,262	6,494	7,023	4,524	N.A.
Personal	970	2,300	3,172	3,489	3,626	3,777	4,016	5,173	5,532	5,999	6,896	N.A.
Other	—	100	57	144	151	158	166	222	241	337	557	N.A.

ᵃN.A.: information not available.

Source. U.S. Department of Commerce, Bureau of the Census, *Statistical Abstract of the United States—1972*, Washington, D.C.

Exhibit 2
Civil Aircraft Shipments,[a] 1950 to 1971

Type	1950	1955	1959	1960	1962	1963	1964	1965	1966	1967	1968	1969	1970	1971
General aviation	3391	4563	7802	7726	6797	7629	9459	12,053	15,723	13,536	13,749	12,581	7,381	7,450
Single-engine	N.A.[b]	3755	6785	6438	5765	6317	7812	10,023	13,226	11,530	11,479	10,193	6,029	6,277
1-3 pass.	N.A.	786	1649	1366	1247	1404	2187	3,545	5,744	4,873	4,507	4,447	1,981	1,948
4 pass. +	N.A.	2969	5136	5072	4518	4913	5625	6,478	7,482	6,657	6,972	5,746	4,048	4,329
Multiple-engine	N.A.	808	1017	1288	1036	1311	1647	2,030	2,497	2,006	2,270	2,388	1,352	1,173
Commercial transports	129	113	262	238	146	80	158	221	322	500	702	509	313	230
Rotorcraft	N.A.	144	178	217	306	413	450	372	352	518	518	510	496	463

Source. U.S. Department of Commerce, Bureau of the Census, *Statistical Abstract of the United States—1972,* Washington, D.C.
[a]Shipments of complete aircraft.
[b]N.A.: information not available.

ness use. The company manufactured six basic models: the Mustang 10, 15, 20, 25, 30, and the Mustang 40. The Mustang 10 was a small, economical two-passenger plane, which was used principally as a training aircraft. In contrast, the Mustang 40 was a powerful single-engine plane, which was sold either for business use or as a luxury private plane. Additional data on the various Mustang models are shown in Exhibit 5.

Mr. Lange has been able to accumulate the data displayed in Exhibits 1 to 12 in order to assist him in his analysis and forecasts.

Questions

1. Estimate the demand for all single-engine civil aircraft for 1975, 1977, and 1982.
2. Estimate the sales volume for the Mustang Aviation Corporation for 1975, 1977, and 1982.
3. What qualifications would you make concerning your forecasts?
4. What other data do you think would be helpful?

Exhibit 3

Value of Civilian Aircraft Shipments—1969-1972

Year	Number	Value of Shipments (Civilian)
1969	13,197	3,593,393
1970	7,858	3,605,035
1971	7,634	2,972,913
1972	9,375	3,273,900

Source. U.S. Department of Commerce, Census of Industry, 1972, Washington, D.C.

Exhibit 4

Selected Financial Items for the Aircraft Industry, 1964 and 1971 (Includes Aircraft Parts)

Year	Assets Per Employee	Sales Per Employee	Sales Per $ Investment	Return on Capital Investment	Return on Sales
1964	$9,430	$19,465	3.29	11.0%	3.7%
1971	19,600	31,073	3.10	0.5	2.3

Source. U.S. Department of Commerce, Bureau of the Census, *Statistical Abstract of the United States 1966 and 1972,* Washington, D.C.

Exhibit 5

General Aviation Classes

Class	Some Representatives	Characteristics	Price Range
I	Cessna 150 Piper Commanche 140 Champion Mustang 10 Mustang 15	2-passenger, light, economical, good training craft, good for private owners	$13,000—$15,000
II	Beechcraft Musketeer Piper Cherokee 180 Mustang 20 Mustang 25	1 to 4-passenger, greater speed than class I, only light baggage capacity	$19,000—$22,000
III	Cessna 180 Piper Cherokee 235 Mustang 30	4-passenger, increased speed and load capacity, used for personal transportation and limited freight hauling	$28,000—$31,000
IV	Beechcraft Bonanza Cessna 210 Piper Commanche 260 Mustang 40	4-passenger, largest single-engine craft, used as a small business craft or as luxury transportation for private owners	$42,000—$47,000

Exhibit 6

All Aircraft—Value of Backlog Orders, Net New Orders, and Sales, (Value in Millions of Dollars)

Year	Net New Orders	Net Sales	Backlog December 1
1951	11,100	3,473	12,666
1955	9,323	8,470	15,705
1960	11,373	10,999	15,452
1961	13,418	14,948	14,147
1962	14,963	15,972	13,137
1963	17,637	16,407	13,904
1964	17,970	16,686	15,188
1965	22,183	17,016	20,385
1968	27,168	25,592	30,749
1969	22,005	24,648	28,297
1970	21,161	24,752	24,705

Source. U.S. Department of Commerce, Bureau of the Census, *Statistical Abstract of the United States—1972,* Washington, D.C.

Exhibit 7

United States Registered Civil Aircraft by Engine Power and Number of Seats—1968 and 1969

Type of Aircraft Total	Total	1969 Eligible	Total	1968 Eligible
	179,063	125,041	169,207	119,320
By total rated takeoff engine power				
1 engine	157,318	108,633	149,005	103,761
Up to 100 hp	49,301	28,262	47,059	27,229
101-200 hp	63,258	47,018	59,282	44,408
201-350 hp	39,694	31,231	37,703	29,950
351-500 hp	3,363	1,328	3,326	1,393
501-700 hp	1,070	559	1,002	548
Over 700 hp	632	235	633	233
By number of seats				
1 engine	157,318	108,633	140,005	103,761
1-3 seats	77,312	44,965	72,620	42,806
4 and 5 seats	73,811	58,194	65,190	51,429
6-20 seats	6,195	5,474	11,195	9,526

Source. FAA—Office of Management Services, *Census of U.S. Civil Aircraft,* December 31, 1969.

Exhibit 8

Eligible U.S. Civil Aircraft in Relation to Population and Area by FAA Region—1969

FAA Region	Per 1,000 Sq. Miles	Per 10,000 Popula- tion	Total Eligible Aircraft	State Area Sq. Miles	Estimated 1969 Population (000)
Eastern	90.0	4.0	29,576	328,669	74,347
Southern[a]	51.3	5.6	17,760	346,214	31,558
Central	39.5	7.5	34,408	871,446	46,034
Southwest	31.9	8.7	17,878	560,551	20,489
Western	34.3	10.1	31,529	918,949	31,210
Alaskan	3.9	80.6	2,272	586,412	282
Pacific	35.0	2.8	226	6,450	794
U.S. Total[a]	37.0	6.6	133,649	3,618,691	201,924

Source. FAA—Office of Management Services, *Census of U.S. Civil Aircraft,* December 31, 1969.
[a]Includes Puerto Rico and the Virgin Islands.

Exhibit 9

General Aviation Aircraft by Type of Flying—1965 and 1969

Type	Number of Aircraft 1965	1969	Per Cent of Total 1965	1969
Executive	—	2,320	—	2
Personal	46,721	70,500	53	55
Business	21,127	22,068	24	17
Instructional	6,855	15,655	8	12
Air taxi	5,267	5,642	6	4
Aerial application	4,901	5,788	5	4
Industrial special	1,811	409	2	0.5
Use not reported	—	632	—	5
Other	2,060	6,365	2	0.5
Total	88,742	129,372	100	100

Source. FAA–*Statistical Handbook of Aviation,* September 1965 and 1970. Washington, D.C.

Exhibit 10

Population (in Millions), Income, and Savings (Current Prices, Billions)—1945-1972

Year	Population	National Income	Personal Income	Disposable Personal Income	Personal Savings
1945	139,928	181.5	171.1	150.9	29.6
1950	152,271	241.1	227.6	206.9	13.1
1955	165,931	331.0	310.9	275.3	15.8
1956	168,903	350.8	333.0	293.2	20.6
1957	171,984	336.1	351.1	308.5	20.7
1958	174,882	367.8	361.2	318.8	22.3
1959	177,830	400.0	383.5	337.3	19.1
1960	180,671	414.5	401.0	350.0	17.0
1961	183,691	427.3	416.8	364.4	21.2
1962	186,538	457.7	442.6	385.3	21.6
1963	189,242	481.9	465.5	404.6	19.9
1964	191,889	518.1	497.5	438.1	26.2
1965	194,303	564.3	583.9	473.2	28.4
1966	196,560	620.6	587.2	511.9	32.5
1967	198,712	653.6	629.3	546.3	40.4
1968	200,706	711.1	688.9	591.0	39.8
1969	202,677	766.0	750.9	634.4	38.2
1970	204,879	798.6	806.3	689.5	54.9
1971	207,049	855.7	861.4	744.4	60.9
1972	208,837	934.9	935.8	795.1	54.8

Source. Economic Report of the President, U.S. Government Printing Office, Washington, D.C., January 1973.

Exhibit 11

Annual Sales of Mustang Aircraft Units

Class	Model	1947	1950	1955	1960	1962	1964	1966	1968	1970	1971	1972	1973
I	10	48	11	51	137	193	287	318	296	164	182	204	326
	15	36	3	62	152	192	278	292	259	136	152	176	272
II	20	15	5	23	98	157	362	471	446	235	261	292	467
	25	13	6	31	84	140	218	318	261	148	169	183	293
III	30	7	2	34	127	227	323	403	388	208	231	303	413
IV	40	0	0	5	138	251	306	459	383	203	225	268	421
Total		119	27	203	736	1160	1774	2261	2033	1094	1220	1426	2192

Source. Mustang Aircraft Corporation records.

Exhibit 12

A Comparison of Total U.S. Eligible Civil Aircraft and General Aviation
Aircraft by Type of Aircraft; December 31, 1959-1969 (1959 = 100)

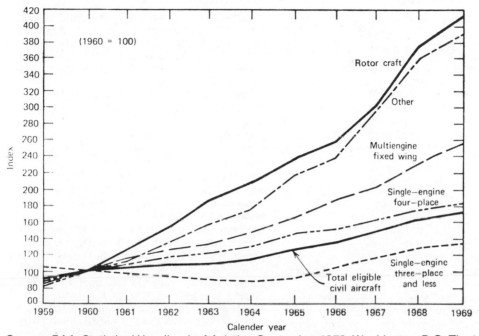

Source. FAA–Statistical Handbook of Aviation, September 1970, Washington, D.C. The term "rotor
craft" includes gliders, dirigibles, and balloons. The term "other" includes autogiros, excludes
air-carrier helicopters.

Exhibit 13
General Aircraft Sales.

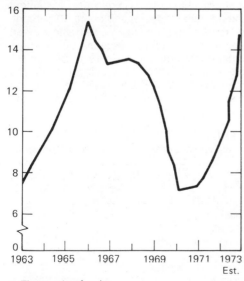

△ Thousands of units

Source. "Sales Zoom for the Light-Plane Makers," Business Week. (March 10, 1973), pp. 154-160.

Case 3-3
Ajax Cement, Inc.[1]

Memorandum

To: Peter Donald
From: Marvin Sklar
Subject: Portland Cement Forecast

Jim Avery, in our last planning session, wanted a breakdown of cement consumption by major markets, and a forecast of cement demand for our area. Please get to work on this problem immediately, and report your progress to me before the next planning session, which is two weeks from today.

Memorandum

To: Marvin Sklar
From: Peter Donald
Subject: Portland Cement Forecast: Preliminary Investigation

Shipments of Portland Cement averaging over 5 million tons have been valued at about $84 million for each of the past five years. Thirty-five percent of shipments from the Lehigh Valley are consumed in Pennsylvania. Sixty-five percent goes out of the state to New York, New Jersey, and several other northeastern states. The Valley accounts, in total, for about 71 to 73 percent of the State's production.

About 50 percent of cement production is directed to concrete ready-mix plants whose activities are closely linked to the level of building and highway construction. Large amounts are also purchased by concrete products manufacturers. In normal years, about one-quarter of sales goes to residential construction. However, in the past year in Pennsylvania this has decreased 18 percent as a result of tight money conditions.

Market Background

It is estimated that about 5.25 barrels of cement are used for each $1000 spent on new construction. Although residential construction has been the largest dollar expenditure, it by no means accounts for the largest consumption of cement and cement products. State or federal

[1]H. Lee Mathews, Ira J. Dolich, and David T. Wilson, *Analysis and Decision Making: Cases for Marketing Management,* Copyright © 1971, pp. 73-79. Reprinted by permission of Prentice-Hall, Inc., Englewood Cliffs, N.J.

projects such as dams, highways, and airports have a proportionately higher level of cement consumption per dollar of construction value.

The market for new construction in Pennsylvania can be divided into the general-use sectors shown in Table 1.

The market for construction materials in Pennsylvania has been extremely sensitive to small changes in the economy. Between 1946 and 1952, the level of construction, measured in constant dollars, rose at an average year-to-year rate of about 10 to 15 percent. During this same period cement consumption increased at 5 to 7 percent. As shown in Table 3 both construction expenditure and cement consumption declined between 1950 and 1954, and again between 1955 and 1958, during slack periods in the economy. Since 1958, construction has shown a somewhat irregular but persistent increase paralleling personal income. In contrast, cement continued its decline until 1961. This decline is considered to be the result of increased use of substitute products. Both series again turned down in 1967 under tighter credit conditions.

Reductions in construction expenditure are often characterized by periods of anti-inflationary policies and a general tightness in money supply. Currently this effect appears to have resulted in the diminishing supply of personal credit. In 1966, residential construction, which in recent years has normally been 30 to 40 percent of the aggregate, decreased about 10 percent. The recent decline in housing has been triggered by a sharp increase in average mortgage rates (as shown in Table 3) from 5.8 percent in late 1965, to a high of about 6.8 percent in late 1966. By mid-1967, this rate had decreased to 6.7 percent with some moderate

Table 1
Pennsylvania Cement Use Sectors (Percent)

Market	Construction Expenditure	Consumption Of Cement
Residential	43	25
Nonresidential	40	42
Business structural		
Farm		
Nonprofit (schools, etc.)		
Highways	11	22
Water resources (dams)	6	11

Table 2
Statistical Series Completed, 1946-1966

Population
Family formations
Personal income
Construction contracts
Total construction (highway and building)
  Highway construction
  Building construction
    Residential
      One-family homes
      Apartments
    Nonresidential
      Schools
    Improvements
Employment manufacturing
Weekly earnings manufacturing
Unemployment
Bond issue municipal governments
Freight-car loadings
Interest rate short-term bank loans
Home mortgages
Production of cement
Consumption of cement

increase in housing starts over the early part of the year.

Despite the current slack in the construction markets in Pennsylvania, the long-term trend in construction and cement demand can be expected to increase markedly over the next period. This is suggested by continued increase in personal income, a general decrease in residential vacancy rate, and projection of federal aid schemes.

In Table 2, construction activity has been broken down into its component markets. Personal income, population, employment, and the cost of money (interest and mortgage rates) appear to be strong determinants of construction activity in the State during the period analyzed. Table 3 shows the state's basic market patterns for different construction groupings and their overall relation to other factors.

Changes in the share of market held by cement, vis-à-vis substitution, is suggested by the trend line of demand for cement per $1000 of construction expenditure. As illustrated in Table 3, this series shows a persistent decrease since 1952, and can probably be used with confidence in weighing a forecasting index.

Table 3
Statistical Series for Pennsylvania, 1950-1967

Time	Cement Consumption[a]	Cement Consump. Per $1000 Construction Expenditure	Personal Income[b]	Total Construction[c]	Resident	Nonresident	Highway	Improvement
1950	0	15,093	17.20	$19,528	878,127	433,223	250,727	102,900	91,277
1951	1	16,133	24.80	19,401	649,386	313,872	142,304	106,800	86,410
1952	2	15,133	23.50	20,824	645,245	328,038	139,424	94,000	83,783
1953	3	15,229	21.40	22,129	710,648	310,598	195,764	105,400	98,857
1954	4	15,160	20.40	21,587	849,469	370,909	260,806	107,200	110,753
1955	5	16,083	17.90	22,369	1,011,854	490,117	290,895	114,500	116,342
1956	6	15,540	19.10	23,104	903,195	391,010	304,366	90,800	117,019
1957	7	14,354	18.40	23,603	878,608	374,205	285,789	96,800	121,815
1958	8	15,276	20.80	23,673	879,478	343,652	266,674	145,800	123,352
1959	9	15,844	19.10	24,355	1,047,384	409,724	290,556	219,900	127,204
1960	10	13,721	15.70	25,069	1,051,173	405,697	329,745	176,300	139,430
1961	11	13,238	15.30	25,492	1,010,536	410,616	303,299	144,700	151,922
1962	12	14,766	15.70	26,666	1,133,424	413,691	393,351	190,500	135,881
1963	13	15,316	15.40	27,653	1,224,887	408,287	436,731	228,200	151,669
1964	14	15,848	14.90	29,542	1,275,748	469,636	469,636	212,500	153,957
1965	15	16,826	14.00	31,078	1,439,988	498,158	564,633	239,700	137,497
1966	16	16,780	13.00	32,888	1,568,749	449,783	718,217	274,100	126,649
Estimated									
1967	17		13.50	34,336	1,532,832	400,949	698,183	303,900	129,800

[a]Cement in 376 lb barrels.
[b]Personal income in millions; all other values in thousands.
[c]Includes highway and building construction.
Constant dollars: 1957-1959 = 100.

Table 3 (Continued)

	Population	Marriages	Av. Weekly Employment Manufacture	Earnings Manufacture	Unemployment	Municipal Bond Issue	Freight Carload	Short-Term Interest Rate	Home Mortgage Rate
1950	10,520	89.23	1,481	68.48	32.0	74.45	38.90	2.70	4.95
1951	10,404	83.86	1,588	69.63	213.7	43.93	40.50	3.10	4.93
1952	10,542	79.00	1,558	74.01	236.5	67.55	37.99	3.50	5.03
1953	10,592	80.32	1,648	78.57	223.8	143.01	38.22	3.70	5.09
1954	10,798	72.93	1,489	76.85	410.4	192.56	33.92	3.60	5.15
1955	10,814	77.54	1,510	81.38	345.8	119.47	37.64	3.70	5.18
1956	10,854	77.68	1,535	83.10	276.5	185.65	37.85	4.20	5.19
1957	10,946	75.21	1,536	83.83	301.0	227.25	35.50	4.60	5.42
1958	11,058	67.20	1,397	82.97	498.2	193.37	30.22	4.30	5.58
1959	11,235	71.72	1,408	87.56	423.8	181.81	31.02	5.00	5.71
1960	11,333	71.84	1,440	88.70	375.4	159.34	30.44	5.20	5.85
1961	11,410	69.62	1,378	90.92	427.1	209.61	28.59	5.00	5.87
1962	11,363	68.92	1,399	94.19	363.7	313.06	28.72	5.00	5.87
1963	11,425	72.02	1,397	97.52	322.9	659.85	28.87	5.00	5.84
1964	11,491	76.66	1,429	100.79	275.7	253.35	29.03	5.00	5.78
1965	11,520	80.19	1,490	105.10	205.9	271.03	29.25	5.09	5.76
1966	11,601	82.00	1,556	105.99	163.3	248.33	29.62	6.60	6.70
est.									
1967	11,626	84.00	1,542	105.47	165.2	252.00	27.84	5.80	6.60

Sources. Business Survey and Survey of Current Business, Center for Research College of Business Administration, The Pennsylvania State University, *Statistical Abstracts of the United States; Statistical Biennial Reports,* Pennsylvania State Highway Department; *Mineral Industry Surveys and Mineral Yearbook,* United States Bureau of Mines.

Statistical Information

The statistical period has been taken back only to 1950 as a result of discontinuous elements in many of the lesser series. Most series also show an abnormally high rate of increase in the early postwar years.

Table 3 summarizes the 20 statistical series that were collected for the period 1946 to 1966. (I have made the estimates for 1967.) A number of other series including population by age groupings and the industrial index were not documented for the complete period, and as a result had to be dropped.

With the exception of population, no projections are available for these series. Total population and division by age groupings have been estimated by the Commerce Department and Temple University in separate studies through 1985. These can be useful for long-term forecasting of economic activity. Personal income commonly shows a close correlation with population and may be safely projected for five to ten years in determining general levels of construction.

Method of Analysis

The basic approach used for developing forecasting models will be to equate the demand for cement with economic factors such as population, income, employment, wages, availability of credit and so on. This leads to forecasting equations that take the form:

$$Dc = f(CI, I, P, E, M, HV, R, T, \underline{\hspace{1cm}})$$

where:

Dc = total demand for cement
CI = total construction (nonresidential, residential, improvements, and highways)
I = personal income
P = population
E = employment
M = family formations
HV = housing vacancy rate
R = cost of money
T = time

Demand at the firm or regional level might be expressed as a percent market share: as:

$$LV = Dc \times \%M$$

where:

LV = cement provided by the Lehigh Valley
D_c = total demand for cement in the state
$\%M$= percent market share

Several series that are desirable, such as housing vacancy rate and the business index, are not available in statistical form and could be substituted by proxy measurements. These include employment manufacturing, average weekly earnings in manufacturing, freight-car loadings, and others. Marriage was used as an indication of family formations, and indirectly as a demand factor for new housing. Cost of money can be implied by figures on short-term rates, on bank loans, and new home mortgage rates. From trends developed, it appears that share of market can be closely predicted by time series projection. This would be modified, of course, by capital changes in producing areas such as new plant or equipment, but will not be considered for this problem.

If this approach seems reasonable, I will proceed to develop several models.

Memorandum

To: Peter Donald
From: Marvin Sklar
Subject: Portland Cement Forecast

I reported your findings to Jim Avery, and he wants your forecast by the next session in two weeks.

Questions

1. Calculate a weighted moving average of cement consumption in Pennsylvania and use it to predict cement usage in 1967.
2. Estimate 1967 cement consumption using exponential smoothing.
3. What independent variables in Table 3 are most closely related to cement consumption?
4. Select what you feel are the most useful variables for 1950-1966 and construct several multiple regression equations to predict cement consumption in Pennsylvania. Then use the estimated values of the independent variables to prepare cement forecasts for 1967.
5. Are your forecasting equations improved by lagging variables or using the logarithms of the factors?
6. Construct confidence intervals around your regression forecasts for 1967.

Four
Segmentation

Small opportunities are often the beginning of great
enterprises.
Demosthenes

The central focus of a marketing organization must be on identifying and exploiting transitory opportunities. However, this mission is often pushed into the background by the press of day to day problem solving. Managers become occupied with manipulating elements of the marketing mix to achieve short-run tactical advantages over the competition. Therefore, a conscious effort must be made to take a broader-strategic viewpoint.

This chapter focuses on the opportunities originating from the fact that most markets are heterogeneous. Segmentation is the strategy of allocating the marketing resources of the firm on the basis of variations in the level of demand associated with this heterogeneity.

A market can be described in terms of the array of products available to a buyer or in terms of the group of prospects looking for a product. One definition of a market is "the interrelated class of brands or products whose relations of substitution and competition are powerful enough so that the sales of each are strongly influenced by the sales of other."[1] Another definition is "a market is a group of potential purchasers of a given product and brand."[2] However, identification of these prospects does not, in itself, constitute a strategy. Thus, segmentation needs to take into account diversity among product offerings and among prospects. In the extreme, segmentation involves designing a unique product and marketing program for each buyer.

The characteristics of the product that are salient to buyers provide a way to describe the structure of a market. These characteristics relate directly to the benefits sought by the buyers. Consequently, the dimensions can be either real or imaginary. Products or brands have positions within the market structure on the basis of the amount of each salient characteristic that buyers perceive them to possess. Each buyer has a location in the market structure which corresponds to the characteristics of that buyer's ideal product.

There are two complementary segmentation strategies: market segmentation and product positioning. The distinction is that in market segmentation the product's position

[1] Volney Stefflre, "Market Structure Studies: New Products for Old Markets and New Markets (Foreign) for Old Products" in Frank M. Bass, Charles W. King, and Edgar A. Pessemier, eds., *Application of the Sciences in Marketing Management* (New York: Wiley, 1968), pp. 251-268.
[2] Jack Z. Scissor, "What is a Market," *Journal of Marketing,* Vol. 30, (July 1966), pp. 17-21.

is assumed to be fixed while in product positioning it is assumed to be a variable. A product's position is variable when it is new or when it is being repositioned through product modification or change in promotional policy.[3] These strategies build upon the concept of a differentiated product versus an undifferentiated product or commodity.

PRODUCT DIFFERENTIATION

Product differentiation provides one basis upon which a supplier can appeal to selective buying motives. Chamberlin has defined this concept by saying that:

"A general class of product is differentiated if any significant basis exists for distinguishing the goods (or services) of one seller from those of another. Such a basis may be real or fancied, so long as it is of any importance whatever to buyers, and leads to a preference for one variety of a product over another."[4]

Thus products are different if the consumer believes that they are different.

Undifferentiated products (i.e., salt and cement) are called commodities. They usually earn a satisfactory profit only if demand exceeds supply. Thus, the appropriate marketing strategy is to stimulate demand while limiting supply. For example, DeBeers Consolidated Mines buys most of the diamonds produced in the world and sells them along with its own. When supply exceeds demand, DeBeers holds the excess off the market to keep prices high. They also attempt to stimulate demand through advertising centered around the theme, "Diamonds are Forever."

Profits from commodities are often cyclical. When demand exceeds supply, profits are very high. This encourages firms to expand capacity resulting in excess supply. When many firms sell the same product, price cutting occurs as each firm tries to obtain enough orders to efficiently utilize production facilities. The resulting narrow profit margins rarely permit significant promotional expenditures and each firm must make a strategic decision on whether to remain in the marketplace. Withdrawal allows assets to be redeployed immediately. Firms that continue believe they will survive the price competition and will resume more profitable operations at a latter date. In the short run, those who stay attempt to maintain price stability and stress customer service.[5]

Where possible, a better strategy would be to turn the commodity into a differentiated product. One way to do this is to broaden the concept of the product in the eyes of the buyer. For example, the Signode Corporation sells steel strapping for packing goods for shipment that is similar to that offered by other manufacturers. To help differentiate their product, Signode began selling strapping systems rather than just strapping materials. Signode offered to design and build special equipment to solve the material handling problems of each of their customers. These unique machines automatically package the product by attaching the appropriate number of straps in the correct position. The customer could either buy or lease the machines and although customers were free to buy strapping from competitors, Signode stressed its product's suitability for *its* machines. This approach resulted in Signode securing about half of the strapping market in the United States.

[3]Henry Assael, "Segmenting Market Segmentation: Strategies and Techniques," *European Research,* Vol. 1 (September 1973), pp. 190-194.

[4]Edward H. Chamberlin, *The Theory of Monopolistic Competition,* (Cambridge: Harvard University Press, 1956), p. 56.

[5]See the Dow Chemical Company (A) case in E. R. Corey, *Industrial Marketing: Cases and Concepts* (Englewood Cliffs, N.J.: Prentice-Hall, 1962), pp. 8-12. Also see Theodore D. Frey, "Forecasting Prices for Industrial Commodity Markets," *Journal of Marketing,* Vol. 34 (April 1970), pp. 28-32.

Signode's strategy is a variation of Gillette's traditional practice of stimulating demand for razor blades by giving away razors.[6] Earnings are derived from selling high-margin consumable supplies rather than from sales of machines that use the supplies.

MARKET SEGMENTATION

Where product differentiation is based on distinctions among products, market segmentation is based on distinctions among prospects who constitute the market.[7] Recognition of the heterogeneity of customers has led firms to appeal to segments of what once might have been considered a homogeneous market. Market segmentation requires that the firm first specify operational market segments and then allocate resources to these segments.

Segmentation involves a process of aggregation. The firm could consider each buying unit a segment. However, at least some economies of scale should be possible if these buying units are clustered into fewer groups. Buying units are aggregated in segments in such a way that there is maximum homogeneity of demand within segments and maximum heterogeneity of demand between segments. Continuation of the aggregation process eventually leads to the formation of a single segment: the market as a whole. The firm must determine the level of aggregation which will generate the optimal profits.

From a different perspective, segmentation has a somewhat negative connotation in that it implies the firm is deliberately abandoning part of the market to the competition. Mass market opportunities need not be ignored. Perhaps the timing of a brand's entry into the product class prescribes whether a firm should segment a market or treat it as a whole. The original entrants probably should seek to dominate the entire market, while latecomers might do better to attempt to dominate an identifiable submarket.

For example, in the ready-to-eat cereal market, segments can be defined on the basis of the age of the consumer as shown in Table 4-1. Kellogg's Corn Flakes, a pioneer brand, is highly ranked in all age categories. Captain Crunch is sold to children under twelve while Special K and Grapenuts are sold to adults. These late entrants have successfully concentrated in particular market segments. To determine whether segmentation makes sense for a particular brand, a firm needs a set of evaluation criteria.

Segmentation Criteria

A number of criteria have been suggested to determine if segmenting a market would place management in a better position than treating the market as a homogeneous entity. The members of each segment must be identifiable in terms of measurable characteristics. The average level of customer demand for the brand must vary from one segment to another. Customer sensitivity to changes in the firm's promotional and marketing policies as well as those of competitor's must vary from one segment to another.[8] In

---

[6]Although Gillette has 60 percent of the razor blade market and sells more double-edge stainless-steel blades than all its competitors, Schick dominates the $50 million injector blade segment of the market. Until recently Gillette did not have an injector blade with a *demonstrable difference* and its market share was less than 20 percent compared to Schick's 70 percent.

[7]Wendell R. Smith, "Product Differentiation and Market Segmentation as Alternative Marketing Strategies," *Journal of Marketing,* Vol. 21 (July 1956), pp. 3-8.

[8]Ronald E. Frank, "Market Segmentation Research: Findings and Implications" in Frank M. Bass, Charles W. King, and Edgar A. Pessemier, eds, *Applications of the Sciences in Marketing Management* (New York: Wiley, 1968), pp. 39-68. Also see Henry J. Claycamp and William F. Massy, "A Theory of Market Segmentation," *Journal of Marketing Research,* Vol. 5 (November 1968), pp. 388-394.

Table 4-1

Rankings of Top Ten Cereal Brands by Age Groups[a]

Brand	Age				
	<6	6-12	13-20	21-44	>44
Corn Flakes	4	2	1	1	1
Cheerios	1	1	2	4	13
Rice Krispies	2	3	4	6	9
Frosted Flakes	3	4	5	5	10
Wheaties	8	6	3	2	6
Nabisco Shredded Wheat	21	8	6	3	3
Special K	25	21	8	10	2
Toasties	16	10	7	7	4
Captain Crunch	5	5	9	21	36
Grapenuts	42	27	10	11	7

[a]Sixty-seven brands were ranked.

addition, specialized advertising and promotional media (such as regional editions of magazines) should be available so the segments can be reached efficiently. Finally, the segments must be large enough so that a segmentation strategy will lead to increased profits.[9]

Measurable Characteristics

The major alternative bases for segmentation are geographic, demographic, psychographic, and behavioralistic. These bases along with their typical breakdowns are shown in Table 4-2.[10] Many of these characteristics of the buyer will be discussed in detail in the next chapter.

Geographic Basis. Markets can often be segmented on the basis of geography and population density. There exists product usage variations among homemakers on these dimensions. For instance, usage rates of eye makeup are higher in metropolitan areas and in the West than other areas while the usage rates of shortening are higher in areas outside of metropolitan areas and in the Southeast.[11] Geographical segmentation permits some efficiencies in media selection. Spot TV, spot radio, local newspapers, and regional editions of magazines can be used differentially across geographic segments.

Multinational firms may be interested in segmenting markets on the basis of national boundaries. The attractiveness of an overseas country market environment is a function of political stability, market opportunity, economic development and performance, cultural unity, legal barriers, physiographic barriers, and geocultural distance.[12] In

[9]Leland L. Beik and Stephen L. Buzby, "Profitability Analysis by Market Segments," *Journal of Marketing*, Vol. 37 (July 1973), pp. 48-53.

[10]Many of these breakdowns are from William M. Weilbacher, "Standard Classification of Consumer Characteristics," *Journal of Marketing*, Vol. 31 (January 1967), pp. 27-31.

[11]This example, which will be carried throughout this section, is from William D. Wells, "Segmentation by Attitude Types" in Robert L. King, *Proceedings* (Chicago: American Marketing Association, 1968), pp. 124-126.

[12]James E. Hansz and James D. Goodnow, "A Multivariate Classification of Overseas Country Market Environments" in Boris W. Becker and Helmut Becker, eds., *Proceedings* (Chicago: American Marketing Association, 1972), pp. 191-198.

Table 4-2
Alternative Bases For Segmentation

Basis	Typical Breakdown
1) Geographic	
Region	New England, Metro New York, Mid-Atlantic, East Central, Metro Chicago, West Central, Southeast, Southwest, Pacific
County size	A, B, C, D
S.M.S.A. population	Under 50,000; 50,000-99,999; 100,000-249,999; 250,000-499,999; 500,000-999,999; 1,000,000-3,999,999; 4,000,000 or over
2) Demographic	
Age	Under 6; 6-11; 12-17; 18-34; 35-49; 50-64; 65 and over
Sex	Male; female
Family life cycle	Young, single; young, married, no children; young, married, children; older, married, children; older, married, no children; older, single; other
Family income	Under $5000; $5000-$7999; $8000-$9999; over $10,000.
Education	Grade school or less; some high school; graduated high school; some college; graduated college
Occupation	Professional and technical; managers, officials, and proprietors; clerical; sales; craftsmen, foremen; operative; farmers; armed services; retired; students; homemakers; unemployed
Social class	Lower; working; lower-middle; upper-middle; upper
Manufacturer's total assets	Under $5000; $5000-$9999; $10,000-$24,999; $25,000-$49,999; $50,000-$99,999; $100,000-$299,000; $300,000-$499,999; $500,000-$999,999; $1,000,000 and over
Manufacturer's industry	Standard Industrial Classification (SIC) code
3) Psychographic	
Personality	(Each of the psychographic categories is multidimensional. Results for each dimension are broken down into thirds)
Life-style	
Needs/values	
4) Behavioralistic	
Decision-making unit	(Product specific)
Usage rate	Nonuser; light; medium; heavy
Readiness stage	Unaware; aware; interested; intending to try; trier; repeat purchaser
Benefits sought	(Product specific)
End use	(Product specific)
Brand loyalty	Nonloyal; loyal
Response function	(Sensitivity to changes in marketing mix)

addition, the multinational firm must take into account factors specific to the firm and its industry.

Demographic Basis. Consumer markets can be segmented according to the age, sex, stage in the family life cycle, family income, education, occupation, and social class of the consumers. For instance, eye makeup usage rates tend to be higher for the young, the well-educated, and the working wife. The shortening usage rates tend to be higher for those who are older and have larger families. Industrial markets can be segmented according to the total sales, total assets[13], or total number of employees of the manufacturer.

Psychographic Basis. Psychographics provide a useful supplement to demographics. Psychographics focus on general buyer habits, life styles, and attitudes as they might relate to a specific product class. Life-style is concerned with the activities, interests, and opinions toward leisure time, work, and consumption of the buyer alone or with others with respect to both general behavior and the specific product class.[14]

Returning to our homemakers once again, we find that the heavy eye makeup user is fashion conscious, considers appearance important, is cosmopolitan, is active socially, and is not an enthusiastic housekeeper. On the other hand, the heavy shortening user likes housekeeping, sewing, and taking care of children. This user is also health conscious.

Behavioralistic Basis. Markets can be segmented by the decision-making unit, the usage rate, the end use, the degree of brand loyalty, the response to changes in our and our competitors' marketing mix, and the readiness stage.

A common way to segment a market is by volume. Marketing managers obviously distinguish between users and nonusers of their product or service. However, users consume different amounts. A small proportion of users might account for a large share of our sales. Thus, the importance of a buyer is represented by the associated purchase volume. The importance of the heavy users is indicated in Figure 4-1. Note that for colas one heavy-half household is equivalent in purchase volume to nine light-half households. Strategies based on the heavy half are easier to implement if these users have clearly defined demographic profiles.[15]

Rather than segmenting a market on the basis of descriptive factors such as geographic, demographic, or volume, causal factors related to the reasons for purchase might be more appropriate. These causal factors are the benefits sought by the buyer. Once the benefit segments have been constructed, they can be characterized further using conventional descriptive factors. As an example, consider the toothpaste market. Four benefit segments can be identified: (1) flavor, product appearance; (2) brightness of teeth; (3) decay prevention; (4) price. These segments have different demographic strengths, special behavioral characteristics, brands disproportionately favored, and personality and life-style characteristics as shown in Table 4-3. This information is suggestive about how copy directions and media choices might be tailored to reach different target segments.[16]

[13]Data on total assets are given in the *Thomas Register* (New York: Thomas Publishing Company, current year).

[14]Jerry Wind, "Life Style Analysis: A New Approach" in Fred C. Allvine, ed., *Proceedings* (Chicago: American Marketing Association, 1971), pp. 302-305. This idea is developed further in Joseph T. Plummer, "The Concept and Application of Life Style Segmentation," *Journal of Marketing,* Vol. 38 (January 1974), pp. 33-37.

[15]Ronald E. Frank, "But the Heavy Half is *Already* the Heavy Half" in Keith Cox and Ben M. Enis, eds., *Proceedings* (Chicago: American Marketing Association, 1968), pp. 172-176.

[16]Russell I. Haley, "Benefit Segmentation: A Decision-Oriented Research Tool," *Journal of Marketing,* Vol. 32 (July 1968), pp. 30-35.

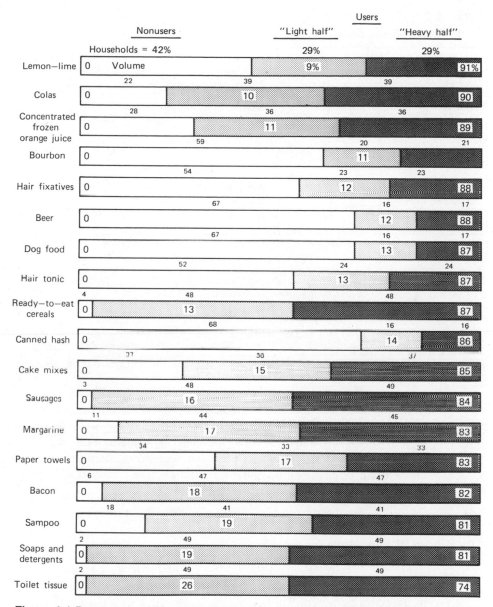

Figure 4-1 Percentage of Purchase Volume Accounted for by Different Usage Groups. *Source.* Dik Warren Twedt, "How Important to Marketing Strategy Is the 'Heavy User'?," *Journal of Marketing,* Vol. 28 (January 1964), pp. 72. Published by the American Marketing Association.

The most common way of segmenting an industrial market is by end use. An industrial marketer might want to segment the pollution-control market. Some of the ways this market could be segmented are by the type of pollutant (e.g., odors), by the medium being polluted (e.g., water), by the source of the pollution (e.g., municipality), by the entity requiring the control products (e.g., federal), and by the type of control product (e.g., biological organisms).[17] With more generality, an industrial market can be

[17]Thomas S. Bry, "Pollution Control Market Definitions, Subsegments, Opportunities" in Boris W. Becker and Helmun Becker, eds., *Proceedings* (Chicago: American Marketing Association, 1972), pp. 201-207.

Table 4-3
Toothpaste Market Segment Example

Segment Name	The Sensory Segment	The Sociables	The Worriers	The Independent Segment
Principal Benefit Sought	Flavor, product appearance	Brightness of teeth	Decay prevention	Price
Demographic Strengths	Children	Teens, young people	Large families	Men
Special Behavior Characteristics	Users of spearmint flavored tooth-paste	Smokers	Heavy users	Heavy users
Brands Dispropor-tionately Favored	Colgate, Stripe	Macleans, Plus White, Ultra Brite	Crest	Brands on sale
Personality Characteristics	High self-involvement	High sociability	High hypochon-driasis	High autonomy
Life-Style Characteristics	Hedonistic	Active	Conservative	Value oriented

Source. Russell I. Haley, "Benefit Segmentation: A Decision-oriented Research Tool," *Journal of Marketing,* Vol. 32 (July 1968), p. 33. Published by the American Marketing Association.

segmented by (1) the buyers' purchasing strategies, (2) the buyers' risk preferences, role types, and cognitive styles, (3) the problems and risks perceived by different buyers, (4) differences among purchase requisitions, and (5) differences in the environmental forces affecting different buyers.[18]

In summary, the bases for segmentation may be objective and general such as demographic factors (age, income, education), objective and situation specific such as consumption patterns (usage rate, brand loyalty, benefits sought), inferred and general such as personality traits (interests, self-concept, venturesomeness), or inferred and situation specific such as attitudes (intentions, perceptions, preferences).[19] Properties of the buyer will be discussed in detail in Chapter Five. The cost of obtaining information on these characteristics is an important element in calculating the potential profitablity of segmentation.

Traditional Stratification

Marketing segmentation has traditionally focused on forming groups and *then* determining the purchase of each group. Furthermore, these groups are defined *a priori* using management judgement. The choice of the appropriate bases is somewhat conditioned by the manager's prior beliefs about the product class. Recently, analytical techniques have been developed that search for natural groupings in large quantities of data.[20] Sometimes, these analytic approaches will provide better definitions of segments than will judgemental approaches.

[18]Richard N. Cardozo, "Segmenting the Industrial Market" in Robert L. King, ed., *Proceeding* (Chicago: American Marketing Association, 1968), pp. 433-440.

[19]Ronald E. Frank, William F. Massey, and Yoram Wind, *Market Segmentation,* (Englewood Cliffs, N.J.: Prentice-Hall, 1973), p. 27.

[20]Cluster analysis is a generic expression for a set of procedures for grouping things together on the basis of their similarities and differences. One special case of cluster analysis is called factor analysis. Factor analysis is a data reduction technique in which a set of variables is resolved into a small number of "factors." For more detailed information refer to Robert C. Tryon and Daniel E. Bailey, *Cluster Analysis* (New York: McGraw-Hill, 1970).

The judgemental approach has been used in a study of a frequently purchased food item sold primarily through grocery outlets.[21] Three different bases were chosen *a priori* to build market segments. One basis was the loyalty of a family toward a particular brand. Nonloyal families were found to be more responsive to changes in price than loyal families. A second basis was the size of the package that the family bought. No useful results were found because of frequent substitution among container sizes. The third basis was the type of retail store where the family made the purchase. Dealing activity[22] was found to be more effective in chain stores than in independents. Overall, the research suggested that effects of price and dealing activity vary across market segments.

The formation of meaningful market segments by traditional methods must be considered fortuitous. There is little evidence to support the basic assumption that individuals possessing the same characteristics will actually be similar in purchase behavior. A better course of action is to group customers on the basis of their similarity of their purchase behavior and then to determine the characteristics of each group.

Response Functions

The difficulty with using even this better approach for segmentation is that two households may exhibit the same purchase behavior for a given marketing mix, yet they may respond differently to changes in the mix. This is illustrated in Figure 4-2. The Smith and Jones households both purchase the same amount at the price level P_0, but the Smith family is more sensitive to changes in price. Thus, customers should be aggregated

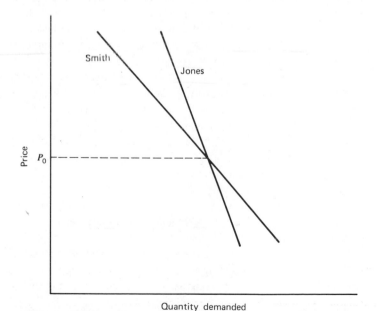

Figure 4-2 Two Response Functions.

Source. Parker Lessig and John Tollefson, "Market Segmentation Through Numerical Taxonomy," *Journal of Marketing Research,* Vol. 8 (November 1971), p. 481. Published by the American Marketing Association.

[21]William F. Massy and Ronald E. Frank, "Short-Term Price and Dealing Effects in Selected Market Segments," *Journal of Marketing Research,* Vol. 2 (May 1965), pp. 171-185.

[22]Deals are special promotions and include such things as cents-off packages, 1¢ sales, and special coupons.

on the basis of response functions instead of a single purchase variable. A response function can be defined as an expression relating a consumer's buying behavior to levels of all marketing stimuli such as price, advertising, and product alternatives.[23]

Response funtions are most easily calculated for consumer packaged goods. For less frequently purchased products, the appropriate data are often not available or are available only at a high cost (through experimentation). Thus, the remaining sections on market segmentation focus on consumer packaged goods.

Patterns of Purchase Behavior

The relationship between market segments and brand choice needs clarification. Only rarely does a market segment buy one brand and rarely is a brand bought by only one segment. Occasionally a segment may confine its purchases to one brand of a new product or a consumer durable. However, for established convenience goods, consumers are likely to purchase many brands. Typically the percentage of buyers who are loyal to one brand of convenience items drops as the time horizon is lengthened. One survey found that brand loyalty was 46 percent over four weeks, 25 percent over twelve weeks, 15 percent over twenty-four weeks, and 8 percent over forty-eight weeks.[24] This suggests that individual *patterns* of purchase behavior must be identified.

Patterns of repeat purchasing and brand switching can be found by studying sequences of purchases using panel data. Suppose a consumer has to choose between three available brands A, B, and C. The individual happens to belong to a consumer purchase panel.[25] The consumer records purchases for the product class in a "diary" and submits them periodically. Thus, the following ten week purchase sequence is known: AAABAACAAA. This individual tends to make repeat purchases on A.

There are several alternative explanations of this repeat purchase behavior; brand loyalty, habit persistence, maximization of value to price, shifts in brand availability. Brand loyalty indicates a repeat purchase on the basis of preference rather than habit. Maximization of value to price indicates a repeat purchase on the basis that the brand gives the consumer the most for the money. Brand availability indicates a repeat purchase on the basis that the brand is the only one stocked by the store regularly patronized. The manager needs to be concerned with not only the number of repeat purchasers but also with the underlying reasons for such behavior.[26]

Patterns of purchase behavior do vary in response to changes in marketing policies. The probability of switching from the brand last purchased to another brand is a function of the current values for each of the market variables for the brand last bought relative to the current average values of these variables for all brands in the evoked set and the response coefficients for these market variables. The relationship is thought to be approximately linear. Thus, if the price of Brand A is high in relation to the price of Brand B, a high probability of switching from Brand A to Brand B might be expected. Response coefficients show the purchase response of a consumer to a unit change in a market variable of the brand last bought and can be calcualted from panel data. Consumers are then classified into homogenous groups on the basis of these coefficients.

[23]Parker Lessig and John Tollefson, "Market Segmentation Through Numerical Taxonomy," *Journal of Marketing Research,* Vol. 8 (November 1971), pp. 480-487.

[24]Martin Collins, "Market Segmentation: The Realties of Buyer Behavior", *Market Research Society Journal,* Vol. 13 (July, 1971), pp. 146-157.

[25]The best-known panel is maintained by the Market Research Corporation of America (MRCA).

[26]Philip Kotler, *Marketing Decision Making: A Model Building Approach* (New York: Holt, Rinehart and Winston, 1971), p. 498. Also see Jacob Jacoby and David B. Dyner, "Brand Loyalty Vs. Repeat Purchasing Behavior," *Journal of Marketing Research,* Vol. 10 (February 1973), pp. 1-9.

Response Coefficients in The Chicago Coffee Market

A study of the coffee market in Chicago shows how response elasticities can be used to segment a market.[27] In this study response coefficients for price and deal market variables for Hills Brothers, Folgers, Maxwell House, private brands (such as A & P's Eight O'Clock), and other brands (such as Manor House) were calculated for each consumer. The price response coefficients show the impact of regular shelf prices. Deal coefficients show the impact of cents-off packages, 1¢ sales, and special coupons.

The purchase behavior of one family, the Browns, is diagrammed in Figure 4-3. There is a high probability that the Browns will purchase A & P's Eight O'Clock whether or not Eight O'Clock was the last brand bought. Eight O'Clock is a low-priced brand. On the other hand, Eight O'Clock appears vulnerable to dealing activity by Hills Brothers and Folgers. Both Manor House and Maxwell House are frequently repurchased by the Browns on deals. However, an initial purchase of either brand is unlikely. Sample families like the Browns can be grouped with other families with similar response coefficients to form a segment.

The Chicago coffee market produced five major segments. The segments were characterized as (1) oriented toward other brands, (2) sensitive to Hills Brothers market-

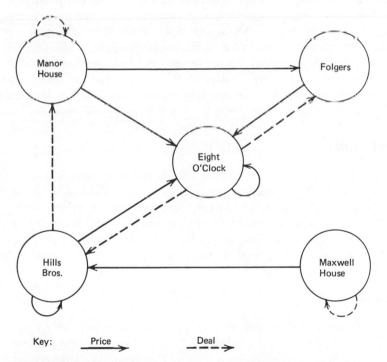

Figure 4-3 Diagram of the Brown Family's Purchase Behavior.
Source. Adapted from W. F. Duhamel, "The Use of the Variable Markov Processes as a Partial Basis for the Determination and Analysis of Market Segments," unpublished doctoral dissertation, Stanford University, 1966, p. 92.

[27]This section is drawn from W. F. Duhamel, "The Use of Variable Markov Processes as a Partial Basis for the Determination and Analysis of Market Segments," unpublished doctural dissertation, Stanford University, 1966. He studied the regular coffee market in Chicago using 100 families from the *Chicago Tribune's* consumer panel.

ing activity and Maxwell House deals, (3) susceptive to Hills Brothers prices and other-brand deals, (4) strong loyalty to Folgers on deals, and (5) responsive to private prices and Hills Brothers deals. This suggests that Folgers should avoid deals because they encourage existing customers to repurchase rather than attracting buyers from other brands. The analysis thus far provides group membership for the 100 consumers in the sample. Clearly, the process is too costly and complex to allow its use for all coffee drinkers. Thus, implementation depends on finding some demographic traits which easily identify the market segments.

One way to classify consumers into segments on the basis of demographic attributes utilizes linear discriminant analysis.[28] Discriminant functions are developed with weights for the demographic factors so that the probability of misclassifying any family is minimized. The relation between response profiles and socioeconomic factors is shown in Table 4-4. These results suggest that Folgers should direct their deals toward suburban families with more teenagers and lower-status occupations.

In this particular case, discriminant analysis using the demographic information was not completely effective in classifying prospects into the five purchase-behavior groups. The failure of consumer characteristics to provide a basis for identifying segments, with similar purchase behavior, has been an obstacle to implementing market segmentation strategies.

Moreover, in the long run, individuals may well move from one segment to another and the boundaries among segments may change. Thus, market segmentation is dynamic. Management must be careful so as not to orient their strategy to their past or present accomplishments instead of their future opportunities.

Market segmentation assumes that the product is fixed. Now consideration will be given to the situation where the product itself can vary. Products can be new or an existing product which is to be repositioned by means of changes in design or promotion policy.

PRODUCT POSITIONING

The merging of product differentiation with market segmentation is called product positioning. Instead of just measuring preference in terms of consumer characteristics, product characteristics are allowed to vary. Product positioning focuses on buyers' perceptions and preferences about the place a product (or brand) occupies in a specified market. Product segmentation couples product positioning with market segmentation. There is a change in marketing emphasis from ''whom you reach'' to ''what characteristics you build into the product.''[29]

Perceptual Mapping

Although a given product will possess many characteristics, only a few will be important in the consumer's decision-making process.[30] These critical attributes are used to differentiate among the competitive offerings. The remaining characteristics are often

---

[28]A discussion of linear discriminant analysis can be found in Paul Green and Donald Tull, *Research for Marketing Decisions,* (Englewood Cliffs, N.J.: Prentice-Hall, 1975), pp. 441-465.

[29]Norman L. Barnett, ''Beyond Market Segmentation,'' *Harvard Business Review,* Vol. 47 (January-February 1969), pp. 171-185.

[30]James H. Myers and Mark I. Alpert, ''Determinant Buying Attitudes: Meaning and Measurement,'' *Journal of Marketing,* Vol. 32 (October 1968), pp. 13-20 and David Klahr, ''A Study of Consumers' Cognitive Structure for Cigarette Brands,'' *Journal of Business,* Vol. 43 (April 1970), pp. 190-204.

Table 4-4

Correspondence Between Behavioral and Socioeconomic Profiles
By Market Segment

Segment Number	Response Characteristics	Socioeconomic Profiles
I	Extremely sensitive to the marketing activity (price and deal) of the other brands	Older families with grown children at home
II	Very responsive to Hills Brothers and Maxwell House dealing activity but oriented toward Hills Brothers on price alone	Older, educated, high income Protestants with smaller families
	Strongest attraction toward Stewarts	
	Not oriented toward toward private brands	
III	Loyal to Hills Brothers but can be switched to other brands with deals	South Side apartment-dwellers
	Only slightly influenced by private brands	Diverse occupational classes
IV	Very conscious of Folgers and extremely loyal to Folgers on deals	Suburban families with more teenagers and lower-status occupations
	Nondeal emphasis on private and other brands	
V	Oriented toward private brands but susceptible to Hills Brothers dealing activity	Suburban homeowners with young children

Source. W. F. Duhamel, "The Use of Variable Markov Processes as a Partial Basis for the Determination and Analysis of Market Segments," unpublished doctoral dissertation, Stanford University, (1966), p. 179.

related to basic performance and are presumed to be equal among all brands. For example, the basic function of a refrigerator is to preserve food, but this attribute is unimportant in brand choice. Meanwhile, features such as an automatic icemaker and decorator color panels might be very important.

Every market has a structure that can be expressed in terms of these crucial characteristics. Within this structure, the locations of brands are determined by the strength of the attributes they are perceived to possess. The closer brands are in this space, the greater the likelihood that consumers will perceive them as similar. These multidimensional configurations are called perceptual maps.

Multidimensional scaling techniques[31] can be used to build perceptual maps. The procedures involve algorithms that start with some measure of similarity between pairs of products and work backward to find a geometric representation of the product category. These techniques position products that are perceived as similar near one another and locate dissimilar products far apart.

[31]Roger N. Shepard, A. Kimball Romney, and Sara Beth Nerlove, eds., *Multidimensional Scaling: Theory* (New York: Seminar Press, 1972); Paul E. Green and Frank J. Carmone, *Multidimensional Scaling and Related Techniques in Marketing Analysis* (Boston, Allyn and Bacon, 1970); Paul E. Green and Vithala R. Rao, *Applied Multidimentional Scaling* (New York: Holt, Rinehart and Winston, 1972).

The relationship among seven Southern California tourist attractions was investigated in a recent pilot study.[32] Respondents were presented with series of triads. For each triad (e.g., Disneyland, Marineland of the Pacific, and Knott's Berry Farm), the respondent had to choose the two attractions that were most similar and then to choose the two that were least similar. The perceptual map constructed from these data is shown in Figure 4-4. The map helps explain why Magic Mountain, the newest attraction, has been experiencing lower-than-expected attendance. Consumers view Magic Mountain simply as an imitation of the long-established and successful Disneyland attraction.

Dimensions of perceptual maps are not named by the multidimensional scaling programs. Additional information must be gathered from consumers to find the critical dimensions and locate them on the maps. For example, respondents in the tourist attraction study were asked to indicate as many or as few benefits (e.g., fun rides, economical, plenty of animals) as they associated with each attraction. These ratings were then fitted to the perceptual space as shown by the arrows in Figure 4-4. Thus, the attributes that are most important in consumers' perceptions of a product category can be determined from field research.

Perceptual maps can also be used to identify new product opportunities.[33] New

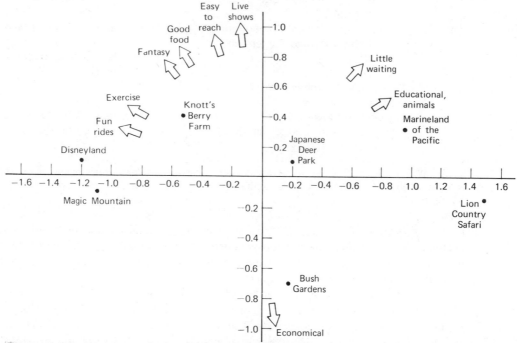

Figure 4-4 Perceptual Space for Major Tourist Attractions.

[32]Conducted by Professor Robert V. Stumpf, California State Polytechnic University—Pomona, and one of the authors. Alternative data collection procedures and preprocessing steps are discussed in Green and Rao, pp. 22-26. Green and Rao also discuss the computer programs used in this research: INDSCAL, PROFIT, PREFMAP, HOWARD-HARRIS CLUSTER.

[33]Volney Stefflre, "Market Structure Studies: New Products for Old Markets and New Markets (Foreign) for Old Products" in Frank M. Bass, Charles W. King, and Edgar A. Pessemier, eds., *Applications of the Sciences in Marketing Management* (New York: Wiley, 1968), pp. 251-268 and Alvin J. Silk, "Preference and Perception Measure in New Product Development: An Exposition and Review," *Industrial Management Review,* Vol. 11 (Fall 1969), pp. 21-37.

products can be positioned in gaps that appear in the market. However, a product will not succeed just because it is unique. For example, American drinkers have been moving away from bourbon and U.S. blends and toward Scotch, vodka, and Canadian blends. In response the industry has introduced light whiskies, such as Four Roses Premium, that are pale brown in color and bland in taste. To capitalize on this trend, Brown-Forman Distillers brought out a dry, white whiskey, called Frost 8/80. Although consumers rated Frost 8/80 high on uniqueness, they did not know what to make of a product that looked like vodka, but tasted like whiskey. Consequently, sales over the first two years were less than one third of the company's forecast and the product was withdrawn. This suggests that gaps in perceptual space are meaningless unless potential consumers are to be found in them.

Joint Space

While consumers tend to agree about what brands are similar, they often disagree about their own personal preferences. Thus consumers' evaluative space needs to be superimposed upon their similarities space to get a joint space. Each consumer is represented in this space by a point representing that individual's ideal product. Ideal points are person points. Variation in the location of person points over this joint space indicates where there are sufficient prospects to justify current and new products.

When consumers are asked directly they usually have difficulty describing the ideal product.[34] This occurs because the ideal product is something that is likely not to have been previously considered. Fortunately, the ideal product can be derived using preference data. Suppose, for a four-brand category, perceptual mapping using similarities data gives a one-dimensional map:

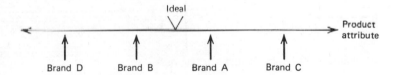

In addition, consumers are asked for their rank-order preferences of the four brands. Suppose a consumer prefers Brand A to Brand B, which is preferred more than Brand C, which is preferred more than Brand D. This means the consumer's ideal brand must be located between Brand A and a point midway between Brand A and Brand B. The approach can be generalized to more than one dimension.

Product segments can be interpreted in two ways. When consumers do not have the same perceptual map, a market segment can be defined as a group of consumers who use the same perceptual map. However, when consumers possess the same map they can be formed into homogeneous preference groups. This is done by cluster analysis using information on the distances between brands and individual ideal points.

The cluster procedure was followed in the tourist attraction study to form the segments shown in Figure 4-5. For Segment I preferences decrease as the distance from the ideal point increases. The converse is true for Segments II and III and they are said to be negative ideal points. The share of the potential market available for each segment is 29, 37, and 34 percent, respectively. The most preferred attraction for each segment is correspondingly Knott's Berry Farm, Lion Country Safari, and Disneyland.

[34]Martin Christopher, "Nonmetric Scaling: The Principles and Marketing Possibilities," *European Research*, Vol. 1 (May 1973), pp. 108-144.

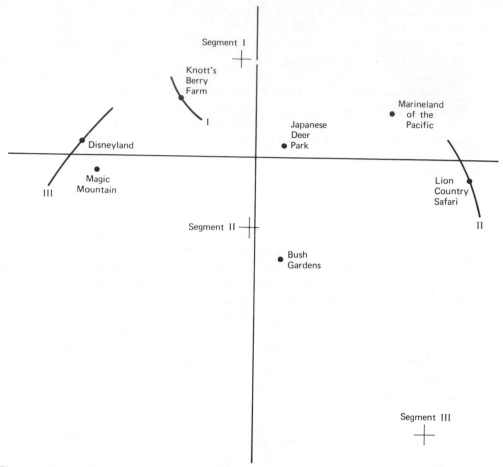

Figure 4-5 Joint Space for Major Tourist Attractions.

Knowledge of buyer perceptions and preferences allow firms to identify new product opportunities. Note that knowledge not conjecture, is required. Consider the following example.[35] One firm sought to create the "better brownie." It believed strongly that sweetness, chocolateyness, and moistness were the factors determining consumers' preference for brownies. Consumers were asked to taste various existing brands of brownies and rate them on each of these three dimensions as well as on an overall preference scale. The data were plotted in three dimensional space and each brand was numbered according to its overall preference. The results indicated that consumers' preference for a brownie were positively related to how sweet and how moist they perceived it and not related to how chocolatey they perceived it. Thus, the firm concluded that the "better brownie" was sweeter and moister and instructed its kitchen to make such a brownie. A memo came back from the kitchen saying "Congratulations, you have just reinvented chocolate milk!"

The firm assumed that it knew the most important dimensions of preference. These dimensions may or may not be relevant to the consumer. Furthermore, the firm assumed that these dimensions were independent. In fact, chocolateyness is highly correlated with

[35]Charles Ramond, "Some Do's and Don't's of New Product Research," in Russell I. Haley, ed., *Attitude Research in Transition* (Chicago: American Marketing Association, 1972), pp. 186-206.

sweetness. After a certain point in order to make a brownie more chocolately, ingredient formulation requires that more sugar, not more chocolate, be added. Finally, the firm failed to take into account the boundaries imposed by the actual physical ingredients. The moistest brownie evaluated may well be as moist as one can make a brownie.

In addition, information on perceptions and preferences shows when existing brands need repositioning. Sometimes one brand in a company's product line may be perceived as close to another causing an unacceptable level of cannabalism. For example, Proctor and Gamble found that consumers perceived two of its detergents as being identical. In this particular case, Proctor and Gamble dropped one brand rather than attempt repositioning. In another case Nestle's exploited regional differences in perceptual maps for a beverage to reposition brands through selective advertising changes.[36]

The Majority Fallacy

Marketing executives must determine the characteristics of a product to be introduced in an established field. Companies that are first in a market can set characteristics that appeal to the majority of the customers, but this has less attraction for firms who enter late. Some of the factors influencing this decision can be shown using the preference distribution described in Figure 4-6. The distribution shows the proportion of consumers that prefer each of three different grades of brown sugar. Consumer preferences are displayed both as a histogram and as the smooth distribution that would result if a great many grades of sugar had been evaluated by consumers. The diagram suggests that if three grades of brown sugar were available, 60 percent of the consumers would choose medium, 20 percent would select light, and 20 percent would pick the dark grade. With these preferences known, the first company to enter the market would maximize revenue by selling a medium grade of brown sugar. However, if four companies divide the medium-brown sugar market equally, then the optimum characteristics for succeeding entries is not immediately clear. If a new firm compared consumer preferences for a

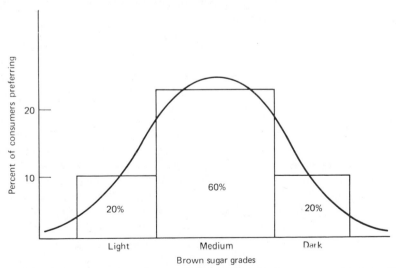

Figure 4-6 Consumer Preferences for Light, Medium, and Dark Grades of Brown Sugar.

[36]Henry Assael, "Perceptual Mapping to Reposition Brands," *Journal of Advertising Research,* Vol. II (February 1971), pp. 39-42.

light brand of brown sugar with the medium grades already on the market, the medium grade would be preferred by most consumers. Unfortunately the firm might interpret these results to mean that the best way to enter the market would be with a medium grade. A new medium brand might be expected to capture one fifth of the 60 percent in the middle or only about 12 percent of the total market. The potential for a new light grade, by comparison, is a full 20 percent of the consumers. This example shows how the "majority fallacy" can trap an unwary firm into merely duplicating existing characteristics. The "fallacy" is that competition is ignored. Obviously the "majority" of consumers do not have to prefer a particular product for it to be a successful.[37]

One product category that clearly illustrates the majority fallacy is spaghetti sauce.[38] Consumers prefer sauce with different degrees of thickness, redness, sweetness, richness, spiciness, or cheesiness. Although some variation in characteristics is present among existing brands, most sauces imitate the dominant brand, Ragu. Ragu occupies a position near the center of a continuum from heavy, rich, spicy, sauces to light thin, and sweet sauces. Heinz, Hunt, Chef-Boy-Ar-Dee, and others similar to Ragu have consistently failed when they have attempted to compete with Ragu in the New York market. Meanwhile a local firm, Ronzoni, has gained a significant market share by selling a product that contains twice as much meat as Ragu and is spicier and thicker. Ronzoni wisely chose a flavor area sufficiently distant from Ragu so that a sizable potential market existed for its own distinctive taste.

Summary

Marketing managers must continually assess which product-market growth strategy is appropriate for their product. An undifferentiated product or commodity permits little marketing initiative. With these items the goal is usually just to maintain the status quo. In contrast, the complete gamut of the marketing mix can be used for a differentiated product. Given this differentiated product, the firm must decide whether it should seek to dominate the whole market or only a distinct market segment. A product that has been positioned with knowledge of the market structure has tremendous initial advantage.

Questions

1. Compare and contrast advertising strategy and tactics for undifferentiated brands and differentiated brands. For which is advertising content important? Frequency of exposure? Recentness of exposure?

2. How might the markets for the following products be segmented: clothes dryer, watches, frozen vegetables, cat food, airline travel?

3. A salad dressing manufacturer wants to assess trends in container sizes in its market. The manufacturer found government reports on shipments of mayonnaise, salad dressing, and related products by size of container. This information is shown in Table 4-5. Recommend which container sizes should be sold and in what proportions.

4. A textile company is in the process of evaluating the market for terry woven to-

[37]This discussion of the "majority fallacy" is adapted from an article by Alfred A. Kuehn and Ralph L. Day, "Strategy of Product Quality," *Harvard Business Review,* Vol. 40, (November-December 1962), pp. 100-110.

[38]David A. Schwartz, "Sometimes It Doesn't Pay to Follow the Leader," *Sales Management,* Vol. 109 (October 16, 1972), pp. 42-44.

Table 4-5
Shipments of Mayonnaise, Salad Dressing, and Related Products
by Size of Container
(Percent of Shipments)

Container Size	1971	1970	1969	1968	1967	1966	1965	1964	1963	1962
6 ounces or less	0.3	0.3	0.4	0.3	0.4	0.5	0.5	0.6	0.4	0.4
8 ounces (half pint)	12.0	12.4	12.8	13.0	13.2	12.8	12.8	13.3	13.3	14.0
12 ounces	0.2	0.7	0.7	0.8	0.2	0.4	1.0	0.3	0.3	0.2
16 ounces (pint)	13.7	14.0	13.6	14.0	15.3	15.9	16.9	17.5	18.6	20.9
24 ounces	0.7	0.7	0.7	0.9	1.2	1.0	1.5	1.9	2.6	2.9
32 ounces (quart)	37.3	37.7	38.7	39.4	38.8	39.0	38.3	39.8	40.3	39.1
64 ounces (half gallon)	0.5	0.5	0.5	0.5	0.5	0.4	0.5	0.4	0.8	0.4
128 ounces	22.7	22.5	21.8	21.6	21.0	29.6	19.8	19.3	18.3	17.5
Other sizes:										
Less than one gallon, n.s.k.	3.9	3.7	3.6	2.9	2.4	—	—	—	—	—
More than one gallon	8.7	7.5	7.2	6.6	5.8	—	—	—	—	—
N.s.k. [a]	—	—	—	—	1.2	9.4	8.7	6.9	5.4	4.6

[a] N.s.k. Not specified by kind.

wels. Historical data are given in Table 4-6. Are the concepts of product differentiation and market segmentation being applied? What channel mix and finish mix should the company have?

5. Market segments can be constructed by cross-classifying various variables considered important. What problems might arise in attempting to cross-classify more than a few variables?

6. How might packaging be used to position a product?

7. A survey was conducted to determine how people perceive soft-drink brands in relation to each other. Subsequently, the perceptual map shown in Figure 4-7 was developed. Label each dimension. Name the brands to which a Pepsi drinker might switch. Discuss how diet drinks are perceived. Identify new product opportunities.

8. Bird's Eye Foods, Ltd. mapped the fish product market (illustrated in Figure 4-8). A technological breakthrough enabled the

Table 4-6
Value of Shipments of Terry Woven Towels
(Millions of Dollars)

Year	Total Value of Shipments	Distribution Channel			Type of finish		
		Branded Retail	Private Ticket Retail	Institutional and Other	In White	In Solid Colors	In Fancies
1972	302.3	165.3	65.8	71.2	64.6	130.5	107.2
1971	274.3	149.9	60.1	64.2	63.8	118.9	91.6
1970	259.6	142.3	47.0	70.2	54.4	119.1	86.1
1969	248.3	135.7	43.4	69.1	61.7	106.6	80.0
1968	244.2	131.4	46.0	66.1	79.7	91.4	73.2
1967	226.7	124.7	41.7	60.4	78.7	81.4	66.6
1966	221.8	103.1	46.6	72.1	78.9	76.3	66.5
1965	203.4	95.6	38.6	69.2	77.3	71.2	54.9
1964	178.4	83.9	35.7	58.9	64.2	60.7	53.5

company to quick freeze fish in batter. Should the company introduce Cod in Batter? Should the company withdraw any of its current quick frozen fish products?

9. Should product differentiation be restricted? In particular, analyze whether there should be a moratorium on style changes in the automobile industry.

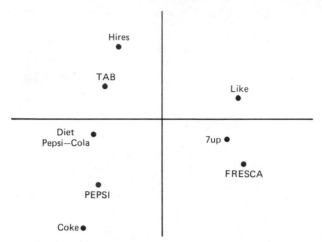

Figure 4-7 Mapping of Soft Drinks.

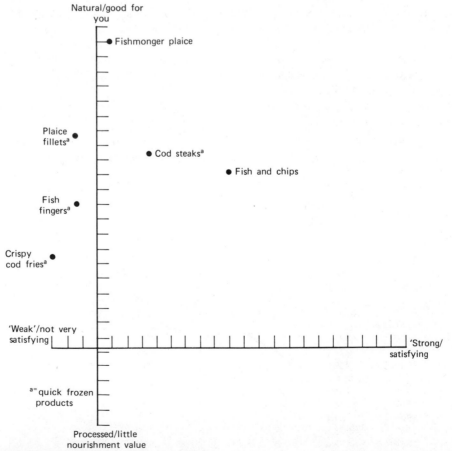

Figure 4-8 Mapping of Fish Products.

Case 4-1
Atlas Steels, Ltd.[1]

Early in 1969, Atlas Steels was approached by a medium-sized trailer van manufacturer who had been producing limited quantities of stainless-steel trailer vans and wanted the support of Atlas Steels for further market development. Consequently, the marketing manager asked Mr. Harris, Product Manager of Stainless Steels, for a brief report stating his feelings regarding the potential of the trailer van industry.

The issue was how, if at all, Atlas Steels should attempt to increase its sales of stainless-steel sheet and strip to the transportation industry, and to the trailer van industry specifically. If the decision was to attempt to gain a substantial portion of these markets, it would be necessary to determine at whom promotion should be aimed and what approach should be used.

THE COMPANY AND PRODUCT LINES

Atlas Steels was firmly established among world industry as a leading producer and supplier of stainless, tool, and alloy specialty steels. The company was a division of Rio Algom Mines, Ltd., a major Canadian natural resource development company. Close to 3600 employees made up the Atlas organization, which maintained marketing facilities or was represented throughout the world. The company's main production facilities were located at Welland, Ontario, and more recently at Tracy, Quebec. Both were fully integrated plants, incorporating all phases of production from melting to finished product. A wide range of specialty steel product, including stainless-steel strip up to 18 inches wide, was manufactured at the Welland plant where the company had its beginning. Production at the Tracy Plant was entirely devoted to the manufacture of stainless-steel continuous sheet, in width up to 48 inches. Auxiliary production, such as the cold drawing of wire, was also conducted by Atlas Steels in Melbourne, Australia.

The major producing competitors of Atlas Steels in the Canadian stainless-steel market were com-

panies located in the United States, Europe, and Japan. Although Atlas did, in some cases, price its product somewhat higher than the competition, management felt that the company's proximity to the market and thus the availability of the desired service more than compensated for any price differential.

DISTRIBUTION

Atlas Steels' stainless-steel products were distributed in Canada by Atlas Alloys, a subsidiary of Atlas Steels; Firth Brown Steels; Drummond McCall; and Wilkinson Company (Exhibit 1). These distributors serviced the smaller volume customers on a day-to-day basis from their inventories. Their services included sawing, flame cutting, shearing, and grinding. In addition to these distributors, Atlas maintained a mill sales force that serviced large-volume customers directly and sold products that required special mill processing.

ADVERTISING POLICY

Prior to 1965, Atlas Steels had employed an advertising strategy designed to promote the widespread recognition of the properties of their stainless-steel lines. Advertisements in this period illustrated applications of stainless in an attempt to demonstrate the metal's properties and to suggest further applications. Appeals were general and not directed at any specific market segments.

In addition to various trade journals, magazines such as *Time, Canadian Business,* and the *Financial Post* had been used for these types of advertisements. In the words of Mr. J. G. Brammall, Manager of Sales Promotion, "we wanted to tell everybody that stainless was great."

However beginning in 1965, the company's philosophy was changed to one of using market research to identify promising market segments and then "hitting those segments with all available resources."

An example of this philosophy in action was the company's approach to the architectural field. Atlas management, recognizing the potential market for stainless steel in the construction of high-rise buildings, established an Architectural Development Department that worked closely with architects and architectural component manufacturers to promote

Exhibit 1
Distribution Chart—Stainless Steel

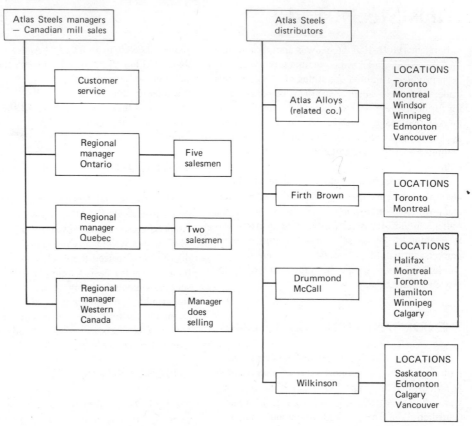

the specification of stainless-steel for construction. Prior to this time, other materials such as aluminum and concrete had been more commonly used by the construction industry. The new department was supported by advertising in the appropriate trade media including trade journals, direct mail, trade shows, and architecturally oriented technical literature. The efforts of the Architectural Development Department led to a number of very large orders for stainless-steel. One such order was for the exterior walls of the new Canadian Imperial Bank of Commerce head office building in Toronto. This order represented over two million pounds of Atlas stainless-steel.

THE TRANSPORTATION INDUSTRY

Mr. Ohlson, the Marketing Manager, felt that the trends to urbanization and rapid transit systems, plus the need to distribute products to the people living in the fringe areas, supported the growth of the trans-

portation industry. Consequently, there appeared to be a significant amount of potential for the company's stainless-steel sheet and strip.

Prior to the completion of the new Tracy Plant in 1967, Atlas Steels had not been able to produce stainless-steel sheet with the required strength qualities or in the necessary width required by the trailer van, truck body, and container markets. The new plant had given the company this capability.

Stainless steel had been used with much success in the transportation industry in a number of markets inluding Europe and Australia. It had also been used in Canada and the United States for some segments of the transportation industry. For example, stainless steel was used in the production of the Canadian Pacific Railway's luxury cross-Canada train, the Canadian. It was specified by the Department of Health and Public Welfare for vehicles used for the bulk transportation of milk on the highways. In addition, the CPR had ordered double-decker suburban coaches in stainless steel for the Montreal suburban transit system and it had been used in growing proportions in the manufacture of buses.

Mr. Harris said that there were ten major manufacturers of transportation equipment in Canada. Among the difficulties he saw in persuading some of these manufacturers to switch to stainless steel were the tooling up expenses the manufacturer would have to incur and the lack of a developed market for stainless-steel equipment. In 1967, Metropolitan Toronto purchased aluminum coaches for its subway and Mr. Brammall said that this resulted in Atlas management developing a "let's get our case before more people" attitude.

About this time, Atlas Steels was approached by a medium-sized trailer van manufacturer who wanted to offer a superior product to the trade as a means of increasing his market penetration. For this reason, he chose stainless steel, but required a stainless-steel sheet with special strength characteristics and requested Atlas Steels to develop it in their new plant. Atlas agreed and the product was made. The manufacturer produced a few stainless-steel trailer vans and sold them, but market penetration was minimal.

In view of his initial success, he again approached Atlas Steels, this time requesting Atlas's help in developing a market for the product. "I'm running into opposition because people just don't know enough about stainless steel," he pointed out.

More specifically he asked Atlas Steels to help him make a call on a major buyer. The company consented and the mill account manager, Inco's[2] market development manager, and the president of the van manufacturing company met with the vice-president of the company interested in purchasing trailer vans to explain the advantages of stainless steel. The call was a success and an order was subsequently placed with the manufacturer for 63 trailers.

THE TRAILER VAN INDUSTRY

Trailer vans represented a major potential market for stainless steel in the transportation field. In the trucking business, the profitability of an operation hinged on the operator's ability to keep equipment on the highway with as little downtime for maintenance as possible. Fleet operators in increasing numbers were looking for strength and durability, light weight, low maintenance, attractive appearance, and ease of repair when they purchased trailer vans. Approximately 7 percent of all van trailers in

[2]Inco—The International Nickel Company of Canada, which was Atlas' supplier of nickel used to make stainless steel.

North America were being fabricated from stainless steel. From 1964 to 1968, its use had increased by more than 1000 percent. Many owners considered their trailers as mobile billboards that created an image of efficient, dependable service. In 1968 the majority of trailer vans in Canada were being manufactured from aluminum with a small portion in painted mild steel.

TRAILER VAN MANUFACTURERS

There were seven manufacturers in the Canadian trailer van industry (Exhibit 2). These manufacturers were believed to be interested primarily in the price of materials and the technical assistance and service they would receive from the supplier. Typical questions raised by the manufacturers included: "What type of tooling should I use to corrugate the panels?" "How does a manufacturer overcome springback when corrugating stainless?" "Can stainless steel be successfully painted?" Atlas had worked with the one manufacturer they had sold in developing the required answers.

The mill salesforce called on trailer van manufacturers intermittently to stress the following special advantages offered by stainless steel:

1. Stainless was corrosion resistant. It never demanded special treatment, and resisted grime, soot, and corrosive urban atmospheres.
2. Stainless was durable and permanent—it outlasted the anticipated life of all rolling stock. Many installations twenty to thirty years old were as good as new.
3. Stainless was extra strong, was ideal for applications where high strength and light weight had to be combined for efficient operation. Its high strength-to-weight ratio, as illustrated by its resistance to puncturing and tearing, permitted the use of thinner gauges for strength characteristics equal to or better than competitive materials.
4. Stainless was readily fabricated by conventional means.
5. Stainless was easy to weld and required no costly, special techniques. Weld joints were compatible with other steels.
6. Stainless was attractive. Its soft, lustrous quality reflected beauty and richness.
7. Stainless blended in with other materials. Its natural, soft-neutral, silvery color blended in beautifully with other materials such as wood, glass, and plastics.

Exhibit 2

Companies Manufacturing Trailer Vans in Canada

Company	Location	Number of Employees	Description
Abbot Truck	Winnipeg, Manitoba	75	Canadian owned— production primarily trailer vans
Brantford Trailer and Body	Brantford, Ontario	355[a]	Subsidiary of Canadian Trailmobiles—recently converted to dump-truck production
Can-Car	Thunder Bay, Ontario	1275[a]	Division of Hawker Siddley —production was primarily subway and railway cars— using aluminum and painted steel
Canadian Trailmobiles	Scarborough, Ontario	315[a]	Subsidiary of Pullman in the United States
Fruehauf	Cooksville, Ontario	358	Subsidiary of Fruehauf in the United States
Highway Trailer	Cooksville, Ontario	106[a]	Canadian-owned manufacturer of trailer vans
Zeigler Trailer	Sault Ste. Marie, Ontario	150	Canadian-owned manufacturer of trailer vans and mobile homes

[a]*Source.* Scott's *Ontario Industrial Directory,* 1966-1967 edition.

8. Stainless' smooth surface was easy to clean. Its tough, hard, glasslike surface resisted grime and dirt. A fast wash or wipedown restored its like-new appearance.

9. Stainless was economical. Its low maintenance cost, plus no need for painting, made stainless the most economical metal to use over the long haul.

10. Trade-in value was higher for stainless vans.

The Atlas salesmen, for the most part, called on purchasing agents who were responsible for buying the materials the engineering department specified at the best price. To date, the manufacturers had shown little interest in stainless steel because, as they put it, "we are doing well enough in aluminum so why should we cannibalize our own market."

In addition, salesmen enountered the problem of tooling-up costs. Mr. Harris estimated that it would cost a manufacturer about $100,000 in new tooling to switch production from aluminum to stainless steel. This expense included the purchase of corrugating equipment, new dies, and the rearranging of all the equipment and fixtures. Mr. Harris thought that perhaps 75% of the $100,000 figure was related to the use of stainless-steel skin. He said that

stainless-steel skin could be used with extruded aluminum structural members but cautioned that "aluminum when joined to stainless steel could result in galvanic corrosion of the aluminum if the joining area were not properly shielded in its design."

Stainless-steel trailer vans were being sold for a $500 premium. Roughly $200 of this premium would be used to cover the extra skin material cost and about $150, exclusive of depreciation, would be required for the additional manufacturing expenses involved with the use of stainless steel.

Two of the largest manufacturers were subsidiaries of United States corporations. Their parent companies had tooled for stainless steel fabrication in the United States but, to date, had limited their sales to the U.S. market. Because these companies were located in the United States they purchased their stainless steel from U.S. producers. Finished vans were not included in the Canada-United States Agreement on Automotive Products[3]; in fact, they

[3]An agreement between Canadian and U.S.A. governments by which various automotive parts and completed units may be transported between the two countries, duty free.

were specifically excluded from the duty-free arrangement.

Truckers, Atlas executives believed, were not buying stainless-steel vans for two reasons:

1. The purchase price of aluminum vans was approximately $500 lower per unit.
2. Stainless-steel vans were not readily available in Canada. Only one company manufactured stainless-steel vans in Canada, and this company was one of the smaller trailer van manufacturers. The duty of 20.5 percent[4] on U.S. manufactured trailer vans further increased the price differential.

ALTERNATIVES

Mr. Ohlson felt that there were two broad courses of action open to the company. The first was to wait for more information in order to define the market more accurately, and the second was to take immediate action to gain a portion of the market. He recognized that if he chose to wait for additional information the company "would not spend a lot of money attempting to develop a market that wasn't really there." On the other hand, he believed failure to move immediately would result in lost sales. Aluminum and other metals were being used to produce transportation equipment and the longer Atlas waited, the stronger these forms of competition would become. In addition, the trailer van manufacturer mentioned earlier had "his foot in the door," but without the assistance of Atlas Steels "he would fail to make major in-roads into this market and would lose interest."

Without further study, Mr. Harris estimated that a minimum of two month's time would be required to gain "adequate" information on the trailer van industry and that such information would cost at least $7000. The estimates for obtaining similar information for the entire transportation industry were at least six months and $50,000.

Although Atlas Steels was currently operating at near capacity, the sale of stainless steel to the transportation industry would enable the company to replace lower margin products with a specialty product that commanded a higher margin. In the case of stainless steel, the margin was 30 percent or $360 per ton; that is, the direct manufacturing costs

amounted to 70 percent of the $1,200 per ton average selling price.[5]

Mr. Ohlson felt that the alternative of taking immediate action could be broken down into the following considerations:

1. Price.
2. Product.
3. Distribution.
4. Promotion.
   (a) Target audience.
   (b) Media.
   (c) Message.

Atlas could cut the price of its stainless steel in order to gain acceptance for the product with the idea of raising it later when the market developed.

Changes in the product, such as making it thinner in order to reduce the price, would be impossible with the existing state of technology if the quality demanded was to be maintained. Mr. Harris explained that flatness could not be currently ensured for a thickness of less than 0.023 inches.

Mr. Ohlson considered the present distribution system to be fixed since the company's mill sales force would handle the sales of stainless-steel sheet to the transportation industry. There would not be any advantages to selling large orders through distributors and Atlas wanted to maintain its existing close direct association with the transportation industry.

Atlas could attempt to reach the manufacturers and their customers by advertising in trade journals. Mr. Brammall felt that for "minimum to good coverage" this would require the use of six publications with six advertisements in each. These advertisements would cost about $500 each for space and production.[6]

A directmail campaign would cost about $20,000 if an "adequate" job were to be done. This cost included the development of a mailing list of all personnel in the transportation industry who might influence the purchase of vans or other similar equipment. Mr. Brammall believed that if this was to be an effective approach, it would be necessary to use an "attention getter" for added impact. This might take the form of a stainless-steel trailer-van model that would cost between $20 and $50 each.

Another possibility was to attempt to influence the major trend setters in the industry by using seminar programs in which a film on stainless steel and its

---

[4]*Source.* McGoldrick's *Canadian Customs and Excise Tariffs,* 1969-1970 edition.

[5]Typical industry figures—not specifically Atlas.
[6]Production costs were those incurred in the preparation of the advertisement.

advantages would be shown. Such a film would cost about $15,000 to produce. The seminar approach could be supplemented by holding a convention for the manufacturers, end users, and government and municipal purchasers. To be effective, Mr. Brammall felt that a minimum of 200 senior management people and purchasing agents should be invited. He anticipated a cost of $10,000 plus the cost of a follow-up campaign of small group seminars for interested companies or agencies.

Before making a decision, Mr. Ohlson, reviewed, once again, Mr. Harris's report on trailer vans (Exhibit 3).

QUESTIONS

1. What is the market potential for stainless-steel sheet in the trailer van industry?
2. Does the truck operator or the trailer manufacturer make the final decisions on whether stainless-steel sheet is used in trailer vans? Why should Atlas be concerned with this issue?
3. What are the key arguments for and against the use of stainless-steel in truck trailers?.
4. How can these arguments be presented most effectively to fleet owners and trailer manufacturers?
5. Should Atlas go after the trailer van market? If so, what price should they charge for stainless-steel sold to this market?

Exhibit 3

Interoffice Correspondence
To: C. E. Ohlson
From: W. D. Harris
September 11, 1969

Subject: Report on Trailers and Trailer Van Sheet
A. U.S. Market

1. Trailer van production—United States—all materials.

   1963 43,000 units 1966 71,000 units
   1964 48,000 units 1967 56,000 units
   1965 61,000 units 1968 Not available
   U.S. market growth—7.1 percent per annum

2. In 1968, stainless penetration of total U.S. market of trailer van construction was approximately 7%. (*Source.* Inco.)
3. The U.S. stainless-steel van market was "Ohio" and "Michigan" oriented in market penetration due to the location of trailer van manufacturers using stainless (i.e., Fruehauf and Ohio Body). (*Source.* Trade journal.)
4. In 1968, stainless van production capacity was 400 units/month. There were four manufacturers: Fruehauf, Ohio Body, Trailmobile, and Great Dane. (*Source.* Trade journal.)
5. In the United States there was a price premium of up to 20 percent for stainless versus aluminum trailer vans. (*Source.* Trade journal.)
6. Fifteen to twenty-year economic life in stainless versus five to ten years of aluminum. (*Source.* Trade journal.)
7. Stainless benefits: durability, low maintenance, ease of cleaning, high resale value.
8. Reported strong market division between

consumer preference on low initial cost versus low total cost. (*Source.* Trade journal.)
B. Canadian Market
1. Trailer Van Production—Canada—all materials.

   1963 1645 units 1966 2624 units
   1964 2096 units 1967 2606 units
   1965 2193 units 1968 2800 units
   at estimated 7 percent U.S. growth

   Canadian market growth 1963-1967—16.1 percent per annum.
2. Only one manufacturer in stainless.
   Other manufacturers reportedly resist entry due to tooling costs. The one manufacturer's capacity is currently limited to 240 vans per year (less than 10 percent of the total market).
3. For each trailer van unit approximately 850 pounds of stainless sheet is used for the "skin" panels. For structural sections, such as corner posts and vertical members, a minimum of the same weight per unit is required. Most roof sheet for aluminum trailers is 0.032 inch, imported in 100-inch-wide coils to provide a one-piece roof. There is no comparable offering in this width in stainless.
   Most panel sheet for aluminum trailers is 0.050 inch thick. Assuming equal covering areas of aluminum and stainless, and comparing 0.050 inch aluminum with 0.023 inch stainless, there is a 32.4 percent weight advantage to aluminum skin. At this time no assessment of the relative weight advantages of the structural members is available.
4. Aluminum has an advantage over stainless in rub rails, posts, and so on, as many sections can be extruded, reducing fabrication expense to the manufacturer. At the present time, stainless strip has to be custom fabri-

cated but, if extrusion technology focuses on stainless, extrusions may become available. In most cases, dies for the extruded aluminum sections are the trailer van manufacturers' property and cost in the neighborhood of $300 to $500.

5. In Canada, the premium for a stainless van is $500 per unit over aluminum. A typical aluminum van sells for about $9000. On the basis of an 850-pound stainless trailer there are about 900 square feet per van. Again assuming equal covering areas, comparative costs for skin are:

Stainless 900 square feet
  @52.3¢ $470.70
Aluminum 900 square feet
  @30.80¢   277.20
                    $193.50

Therefore, the $500 stainless premium would result as follows: roughly $200 extra skin material cost, $300 extra fabrication or structural member cost and/or profit. The extra profit on a stainless van would probably be no more than $50 and may be nil.

6. Contingent potential for stainless sheet for skin panels in the Canadian markets.

	Stainless Van Potential at Assumed 50 Percent	Stainless Sheet Potential at 850
Van Production (Units)	Share of Market (Units)	Pounds/ Unit (Tons)
1968 2600	1400	595
1978[a] 5500	2750	1165

[a] Assumes 7 percent annum growth (U.S. growth).

7. Major promotion objective: to influence more trailer van manufacturers to offer a stainless van alternative, produced in Canda.

C. Additional Points Requiring Clarification

1. Confirmation of U.S. trailer van market data and specific penetration in stainless.

2. Duty drawback and duty-free entry on parts fabricated in the United States for Canadian assembly, and vice versa.

3. Is long economic van life versus low initial cost desirable from a Canadian operator's point of view?

4. What is the user's definition of low maintenance costs? Frequency of repairs, cost of repairs, or downtime due to the inactivity of a trailer that is being repaired?

5. A figure on the amount of aluminum extrusion tooling owned by the van manufacturers in Canada and the cost of replacing this tooling. Also required is a fix on what percentage of present tooling would be made idle by a switch to stainless steel.

6. Broader analysis of the van consumer (large versus small) as to the benefits of stainless steel, so as to enable more accurate judgment of ultimate sales potential.

Case 4-2
North Branch Paper[1]

In 1970 a small regional producer of industrial and consumer paper products, North Branch Paper Mills, Inc., was purchased by American Food Products Corporation (AFP). AFP produced and marketed several nationally known brands of canned fruits and vegetables, prepared frozen foods, and snack items. Sales in 1969 were over $275 million, and the net profit margin was 3.5 percent. Industry observers considered this profit margin adequate, but it certainly was not outstanding. In order to improve profits, the firm decided to seek acquisi-

[1]Case prepared by Frederic B. Kraft of Wichita State University. Demographic data were collected by John A. Miller of Indiana University. Copyright © 1974 Frederic B. Kraft. Reproduced by permission.

tions that would allow it to sell high margin, nonfood items through established marketing channels. It was this strategy that led to the acquisition of North Branch Paper Mills, Inc. in 1970.

North Branch Paper Mills, Inc. had grown from a small producer of newsprint, groundwood paper, and unbleached kraft paper to a middle-sized, but relatively unknown, company. Major products included a wide range of industrial paper products and a somewhat smaller number of consumer items, including bathroom and facial tissues, paper napkins, and paper towels. Consumer products either carried distributor's labels or were sold under the company's Countess label. Sales of North Branch consumer products were well over $1 million in

1969, through very little effort had been made by the company to promote the Countess label.

The North Branch Paper Mills was operated as a separated division by AFP. AFP grouped related products in separate divisions and brand managers were made responsible for individual brands. Staff functions, such as marketing research and advertising, were centralized at the AFP corporate level.

The North Branch Paper Division had four brand groups and the responsibility for the Countess brand of paper towels was given to Dan Orr. Orr had been an assistant brand manager for a major consumer products company, and AFP hired him to develop and test a marketing program for the Countess brand. Orr was asked to build sales of Countess in the Midwest as a prelude to a large-scale national marketing effort. When he began this task in early 1971, Orr was aware that brand managers at AFP were usually given no more than eighteen to twenty-four months to develop a profitable product. The AFP president had made it clear that he did not intend to "waste dollars propping up dead products."

PAPER TOWEL INDUSTRY

Rapid increases in sales, and intense competition marked the paper towel industry in the 1960's. In 1963, two major competitors (Laddy and Vera) accounted for over 76 percent of total market sales of $144 million. By 1970 the paper towel market was shared by eight major competitors, with the largest market share 22 percent. The sales volume for the eight producers totaled $418 million, a sizable increase over the 1960 figure. Although industry analysts projected annual increases in paper towel consumption of 10 percent, some paper towel producers were having difficulty maintaining their market share. Laddy, for example failed to meet the growing competitive emphasis on coupons, price deals, and increased advertising and suffered serious erosion of its market position.

The entry of new competitors in the national market was prompted by the traditional high profits of paper products. The newcomers included small regional firms, such as the maker of Conserve, who first established its product in one region and then began to enter other regional markets. A second type of competitor was the large established consumer products company, such as the maker of Bouquet. These companies purchased regional paper producers to acquire trade names and production capacity and then rapidly introduced their brands nationally through established marketing channels.

Product and promotional appeals also changed during the 1960s. In the early 1960s advertising stressed absorbency, with conflicting claims made by each of the two larger competitors. In order to increase the absorbency of its product, Vera introduced the first two-ply towel nationally during 1963 and 1964 using a vigorous mail coupon campaign. An East Coast regional brand (Swan) followed with a regional introduction of a three-ply towel it claimed was more absorbent than the two ply.

Later in the 1960s towel strength became an important advertising theme. The maker of Tuffi introduced the ultimate in durability with a nylon reinforced four-ply towel. When Tuffi's initial sales were somewhat lower than expected, its maker considered stressing the reusability of the product. By late 1971, it was rumored that the makers of Laddy were about to test a four-ply product.

Another trend in the paper towel market was the introduction of colors and patterns. Originally a white commodity, the paper towel became available in "decorator," colors, bright patterns, and border stripes. The makers of Laddy successfully tested a four pattern, four-color towel in the western states, while the makers of Regal introduced a "color-on-color" towel with daisies imprinted on a colored background.

CURRENT SITUATION

In January, 1972, Dan Orr asked his assistant, Fred Ballinger, to help him review the progress made by Countess paper towels. "I'm afraid we're going to have to improve these reports if headquarters is going to let us go national," Orr said, as he handed Ballinger the report on market shares for the last three months of 1971 (Exhibit 1). Ballinger was aware that Countess paper towels had not made much progress despite fairly extensive promotional efforts aimed at establishing Countess as a colorful new towel. He suggested that an indepth study of their product and of the paper towel market was in order.

Orr agreed, stating, "We've got to come up with some more facts. For one thing, Nielson data are expensive and usually consistent, but here's a report from Compusamp showing that Vera is outselling Bouquet by 10 percent, the direct opposite of the Nielson figures. Besides, I'd like to have more detail so we can really analyze our customers! The Nielson figures show we're in sixth place in our region, with a 6 percent of the market. Unless we can get that up to at least 8 or 9 percent, I don't think we'll get the go-ahead. However, the market share figures don't tell us what the consumer is thinking. If we spend some money and find out what's going on out there, maybe we can make some adjustments and get things moving." Orr telephoned the marketing research manager to set up a meeting to discuss a research plan for Countess towels.

CONSUMER RESEARCH PLAN

When Orr met with the corporate research manager, O. C. Thomas, he outlined his needs for a thorough analysis of the paper towel consumer. He was concerned with the success of the recent couponing campaign which featured a 7¢ offer. Orr was also interested in determining the level of awareness of Countess and other brands, the relative brand preferences, the perceived importance of product features, and the ratings of available brands on these features. Thomas suggested that demographic data be collected to determine whether the competing brands appealed more to one group of consumers than another.

"Why not just ask the housewife what she usually buys, or maybe even see what brand she's got on hand?" asked Ballinger. Orr responded. "I want to know more than simply the housewife's most recent purchase because the purchase could be an exception to her usual buying pattern. I think the biggest differences among consumers are shown by their purchasers over a period of time. For example, we could determine which housewives were heavy users and which were light users and then compare their preferences to determine who responds best to our brand."

Thomas agreed, and he suggested that a fairly small panel study would be appropriate. "If we draw a sample from just one town, say Fort Wayne, Indiana, where we feel that buying habits are representative, we can get useful information and keep costs down." Although research funds for the study were limited, enough money was allocated to permit an eighteen week longitudinal panel study. Futhermore, the panel study of paper towel purchases was to be preceeded by interviews with housewives to determine their attitudes toward the available brands.

RESULTS OF THE STUDY

Professional interviewers were hired by AFP to collect the data and in February they interviewed 500 Fort Wayne housewives. Of these, 217 agreed to fill out the questionnaire, and to record their purchases for the duration of the eighteen-week study. At the end of the eighteen weeks, 132 of the participants had made one or more towel purchases. Women who claimed to be paper towel users but who did not purchase during this time were not retained for the final analysis.

The questionnaires completed at the beginning of the study were designed to collect six types of information:. (1) the first brand of paper towels the housewife could mention, (2) her statement of her favorite brand of paper towels, (3) her recall of the brand she had most recently purchased, (4) her perception of the importance of four paper-towel attributes (absorbency, strength, color, and economy) in her choice of brands, (5) her evaluation of each of the nine leading brands on these attributes, and (6) the categorization of her family on eleven demographic variables.

The average ratings of the importance of the four attributes in brand choice (Exhibit 2) and the average rating of each brand on these attributes (Exhibit 3) were combined to give a special "summated index" of the housewifes's evaluation of each brand. This index was calculated for each housewife by multiplying her satisfaction ratings of the four attributes of each brand times her perceived importance of each attribute, and then adding together the four scores. The summated scores were then converted into index form by dividing by the highest summated rating made by the housewife. Thus, the highest evaluation had an index value of 100, and lower rated brands were some fraction of 100. The summated indexes, first brand mentioned, stated favorite brand, and most recently purchased brand were keypunched along with the purchase information recorded by each housewife in the eighteen weeks following the completion of the questionnaire. Information was also collected at the time of the February interviews on the average selling prices in Fort Wayne grocery stores for the nine leading brands of towels. Thomas had suggested that these data might aid in interpreting consumers' brand evaluations.

DATA ANALYSIS

When the data collection was completed in May, Orr and Ballinger met with Thomas to discuss the analysis plan. Orr was anxious to analyze the data as soon as possible, since competitive brands were becoming more aggressive. He was particularly concerned with Laddy, who was beginning a new promotional program stressing economy. Furthermore, a new three-ply towel was being tested in several markets, including some in which Countess was sold. Also, it had recently been rumored that the price of Tuffi would be reduced in all markets to bring it in line with competitive brands. The need to develop a coherent marketing strategy was clear. Heavy competitive advertising, such as Bouquet with its liquid absorption test, had been very successful. Countess had developed no particular strategy other than using a promotional theme based on Countess's colorful new towel designs. Orr began his analysis by examining the prices and package sizes of his competitors (Exhibit 4).

QUESTIONS

1. Have the Countess marketing efforts been effective in establishing brand awareness?
2. What level of brand preference for Countess has been established?
3. Should Countess attempt to appeal to a particular market segment? (Perhaps segments might be defined by demographics or by extent of paper towel usage.)
4. Should attention be given to changing any specific product attributes of Countess?
5. Should the "cents-off" deal be offered again?
6. What attributes of Countess should receive particular emphasis in a new promotional campaign?
7. Is the Countess brand ready for national promotion?

Exhibit 1
Average Market Shares for Paper Towels in the Midwestern States (Fourth Quarter, 1971)

Brand	Percentage
Bouquet	25
Laddy	22
Vera	16
Regal	12
Softex	9
Countess	6
Old South	4
Tuffi	2
Conserve	2
Others	2
	100

Exhibit 2
Perceived Importance of Atributes Used in Selecting a Brand of Paper Towels

Attribute	Average Rating[a]	Standard Deviation
Absorbency	4.50	.75
Strength	4.20	.96
Color	2.41	1.34
Economy	4.07	1.03

[a]Each individual rated the perceived importance of each attribute on a five-point scale on which 1 signified "not at all important," and 5 signified "very important."

Exhibit 3
Average Ratings of Towel Attributes by Brand

Brand[a]	Absorbancy		Strength		Color		Economy	
	Rating[b]	Rank	Rating	Rank	Rating	Rank	Rating	Rank
Bouquet	4.01	(2)	3.84	(3)	4.07	(1)	3.39	(3)
Laddy	3.92	(4)	3.86	(2)	3.91	(5)	3.46	(2)
Regal	3.78	(6)	3.67	(5)	3.97	(3)	3.31	(5)
Vera	3.66	(7)	3.70	(4)	3.73	(6)	3.14	(8)
Softex	3.00	(9)	2.82	(9)	3.46	(9)	3.57	(1)
Countess	3.80	(5)	3.66	(6)	3.94	(4)	3.23	(7)
Old South	3.53	(8)	3.35	(7)	3.64	(7)	3.30	(6)
Tuffi	4.24	(1)	4.17	(1)	3.97	(2)	2.93	(9)
Conserve	3.99	(3)	3.13	(8)	3.62	(8)	3.34	(4)

[a] Brands are presented in order of the number of purchases during the study.
[b] Each individual rated her satisfaction on a five-point scale on which 1 signfied "very unsatisfactory," and 5 signified "very satisfactory."

Exhibit 4
Prices of Paper Towels in Fort Wayne
Stores, February 1972

Brand Number	Brand Name	Average Price Per Roll (Cents)	Roll Length (Feet)
1	Bouquet	37.5	100
7	Laddy	37.6	120
10	Vera	37.4	100
3	Regal	36.0	100
11	Softex	31.2	100
5	Countess	37.3	110
6	Old South	32.5	100
8	Tuffi	45.5	50
4	Conserve	34.4	100

Appendix A

Format for Data Analysis—Countess Paper Towel Study[1]

Card 1		*Variable*	*Variable Number*
Col.	1- 4	Questionnaire identification number	
		(Number of purchases in first month—cols. 5-22)	
Col.	5- 6	Number of purchases of brand 1 in first month	1
	7- 8	Number of purchases of brand 3 in first month	2
	9-10	Number of purchases of brand 4 in first month	3
	11-12	Number of purchases of brand 5 in first month	4
	13-14	Number of purchases of brand 6 in first month	5
	15-16	Number of purchases of brand 7 in first month	6
	17-18	Number of purchases of brand 8 in first month	7
	19-20	Number of purchases of brand 10 in first month	8
	21-22	Number of purchases of brand 11 in first month	9
		(Number of purchases in second month—cols. 23-40)	
Col.	23-24	Number of purchases of brand 1 in second month	10
	25-26	Number of purchases of brand 3 in second month	11
	27-28	Number of purchases of brand 4 in second month	12
	29-30	Number of purchases of brand 5 in second month	13
	31-32	Number of purchases of brand 6 in second month	14
	33-34	Number of purchases of brand 7 in second month	15
	35-36	Number of purchases of brand 8 in second month	16
	37-38	Number of purchases of brand 10 in second month	17
	39-40	Number of purchases of brand 11 in second month	18
		(Number of purchases in third month—cols. 41-58)	
Col.	41-42	Number of purchases of brand 1 in third month	19
	43-44	Number of purchases of brand 3 in third month	20

[1]Brands 2 and 9 are not included in the study as no purchases were made of these brands.

Card 1		*Variable*	*Variable Number*
	45-46	Number of purchases of brand 4 in third month	21
	47-48	Number of purchases of brand 5 in third month	22
	49-50	Number of purchases of brand 6 in third month	23
	51-52	Number of purchases of brand 7 in third month	24
	53-54	Number of purchases of brand 8 in third month	25
	55-56	Number of purchases of brand 10 in third month	26
	57-58	Number of purchases of brand 11 in third month	27
		(Number of purchases in fourth month—col. 59-76)	
Col.	59-60	Number of purchases of brand 1 in fourth month	28
	61-62	Number of purchases of brand 3 in fourth month	29
	63-64	Number of purchases of brand 4 in fourth month	30
	65-66	Number of purchases of brand 5 in fourth month	31
	67-68	Number of purchases of brand 6 in fourth month	32
	69-70	Number of purchases of brand 7 in fourth month	33
	71-72	Number of purchases of brand 8 in fourth month	34
	73-74	Number of purchases of brand 10 in fourth month	35
	75-76	Number of purchases of brand 11 in fourth month	36

Card 2

Col.	1- 4	Questionnaire identification number	
Col.	19-20	First brand mentioned	37
		Code	
		0 Respondent couldn't answer	
		12 Brand number 12 (IGA) named	
	21-22	State favorite brand	38
		Code	
		0 Respondent couldn't answer	
		98 Don't know (although claimed to have favorite brand)	
		99 Don't care, or no preference	
	23-24	Most recent brand purchased (prior to start of study)	39
		Code	
		0 Respondent couldn't or wouldn't answer	
		15 Brand number 15 (Scot Lad)	
		98 Don't know (although claimed to have made a recent purchase)	
		Summated attitude index of 9 brands. 100 represents highest score given by subject. Lower numbers represent a proportion of 100. Cols. 25-51.	
Col.	25-27	Attitude rating on brand 1	40
	28-30	Attitude rating on brand 3	41
	31-33	Attitude rating on brand 4	42
	34-36	Attitude rating on brand 5	43
	37-39	Attitude rating on brand 6	44
	40-42	Attitude rating on brand 7	45
	43-45	Attitude rating on brand 8	46
	46-48	Attitude rating on brand 10	47
	49-51	Attitude rating on brand 11	48

Card 2   *Variable*   *Variable*
                                                                                          Number

52	Marital status	49
53-54	Wife's age	50
55-56	Husband's age	51
57	Number of children	52
58-59	Age of youngest child	53
60-61	Total number of persons in household	54
62-63	Total years of schooling—wife	55
64-65	Total years of schooling—husband	56
66	Wife work?	57
67	Husband's occupation	58
68	Income	59

Appendix B
Codes for Demographic Data

Variable
Number

49   Marital status: 1 = married   3 = widow
                       2 = single   4 = divorced

50   Wife's age: 01 = <20   05 = 35-39   09 — 55-59
                   02 = 20-24 06 = 40-44   10 = 60-64
                   03 = 25-29 07 = 45-49   11 = >64
                   04 = 30-34 08 = 50-54

51   Husband's age: 01 = <20   05 = 35-39   09 = 55-59
                      02 = 20-24 06 = 40-44   10 = 60-64
                      03 = 25-29 07 = 45-49   11 = 164
                      04 = 30-34 08 = 50-54

52   Number of children: 1 = 1, 2 = 2 . . . 9 = 9 or more

53   Age of youngest child: 01 = 1, 02 = 2 . . . to 99 years

54   Total number of persons in household: 01 to 99 persons

55   Total years of schooling, wife: 01 to 20 is same as the number of years
                        21 = 21 or more years

56   Total years of schooling, husband: 01 to 20 is same as the number of years
                        21 = 21 or more years

57   Does the wife work? 1 = yes 2 = no

58   Husband's occupation:
     1 = Professional, technical   6 = Unskilled worker
     2 = Proprietor, manager, official, wholesale/retail   7 = Student, military
         dealer   8 = Retired, disabled
     3 = Clerical or sales   9 = Unemployed
     4 = Craftsman, skilled worker, foreman   Blank = not reported
     5 = Semiskilled worker, operatives

59   Total family income
     1 = $ 0-2,999   4 = $ 7,500-9,999   7 = $15,000-19,999
     2 =   3,000-4,999   5 =   10,000-12,499   8 =   20,000-24,999
     3 =   5,000-7,499   6 =   12,500-14,999   9 =   25,000 and over

Appendix C
Data Listing—Countess Paper Towel Study

```
Column  6   10   14   18   22   26   30   34   38   42   46   50   54   58   62   66   70   74   78
  1   0 0 0 0 0 0 0 1 0 0 0 0 0 0 0 1 0 0 0 0 0 0 0 1 0 0 0 0 0 0 0 0 0 0 0 0 0
  1   0 0 0 0 0 0 0101010 60 60 71100 80 69 65100 69110110  021608283
  2   1 0 0 0 0 0 0 0 0 1 0 0 0 0 0 0 0 0 2 2 0 0 0 0 0 0 0 1 0 0 0 0 0 0 0 0 0
  2   0 0 0 0 0 0 0039998 64 64 76 86 86100  0  0 010607306041719117
  3   2 0 0 0 0 0 0 0 0 0 0 0 0 0 0 0 0 1 0 0 0 0 0 0 0 0 0 1 0 0 0 0 0 0 0 0 0
  3   0 0 0 1 0 0 0010101100  0 0100 0100  0  0 010607210041419219
  4   0 0 0 0 0 2 0 0 0 0 0 0 0 4 0 0 0 0 0 0 0 3 0 0 0 0 0 0 0 2 0 0 0 0 0
  4   0 0 0 0 0 0 0070707 60  0  0 80 0100  0 80 010606304051721219
  5   3 0 0 0 0 0 0 0 0 1 0 0 0 0 0 0 0 0 4 0 0 0 0 0 0 0 3 0 0 0 0 0 0 0 0 1 0
  5   0 0 0 0 0 0 0010101100  0 0 38 0 38  0  0 010607509071820217
  6   2 0 0 0 0 0 0 0 0 1 0 0 0 0 0 0 0 1 0 0 0 0 0 0 0 0 0 1 0 0 0 0 0 0 0 0 0
  6   0 0 0 0 0 0 0010101100 88  0 73 64 64 97 80 010504102031720218
  7   0 0 0 0 0 0 0 0 1 0 0 0 0 0 0 0 0 1 0 0 0 0 0 0 0 1 0 0 0 0 0 0 0 1 0 0 0
  7   0 0 0 0 0 0 0079907  0 87 84  0 0100  0 87 84104040 · 021821118
  8   0 0 0 0 0 0 0 0 0 0 0 0 0 0 0 0 0 0 0 0 0 0 0 0 0 0 0 0 0 0 0 0 0 0 0 0 0
  8   0 0 0 0 0 0 0100710100 98100 93100 93  0100  0110100 031610286
  9   0 0 0 0 0 0 1 0 0 0 0 0 0 0 0 1 0 0 0 0 0 0 0 1 0 0 0 0 0 0 0 0 0 0 0 0
  9   0 0 0 0 0 0 0100810  0 91  0  0  0 91100 91 010404602081216214
 10   0 0 0 0 0 0 0 0 0 1 0 0 0 0 0 0 0 1 0 0 0 0 0 0 0 0 1 0 0 0 1 0 0 0 0 0
 10   0 0 0 0 0 0 0080808100  0  0  0  0 0100  0 010909616041312145
 11   0 0 0 0 0 0 1 0 0 0 0 0 0 0 0 0 0 0 0 0 0 0 0 0 0 1 0 0 0 0 0 0 0 0 0 0 0
 11   0 0 0 0 0 0 0079998  0  0  0 0 87100  0  0 0103030  022121172
 12   0 0 0 0 0 0 0 0 0 0 0 0 0 1 0 0 0 0 0 0 0 0 0 0 0 0 0 0 0 0 0 0 0 0 0 0 0
 12   0 0 0 0 0 0 0079907100100100100100100  0100  0104062090021821119
 13   0 0 0 0 0 0 1 0 0 0 0 0 0 0 0 0 0 0 0 0 0 0 0 0 0 0 0 0 0 0 0 0 0 0 0 0 0
 13   0 0 0 0 0 0 0010808100  0 0100 0100100  0 0109080  02 12156
 14   0 0 0 0 0 0 0 0 0 0 0 0 0 0 0 0 0 1 0 0 0 0 0 0 0 0 0 0 0 0 0 0 0 0 0 0 0
 14   0 0 0 0 0 0 0079806100  0  0 89 75 63  0  0 0102020 021618173
 15   0 0 0 0 0 0 0 0 1 0 0 0 0 0 0 0 0 0 0 0 0 0 0 0 0 0 0 0 0 0 0 0 0 1 0 0 0
 15   0 0 0 0 0 0 0070715 89 85 89 96  0 89  0 85 0103030  022021113
 16   0 0 0 0 0 0 0 1 0 0 0 0 0 0 0 0 0 0 0 0 0 0 0 0 0 0 0 0 0 0 0 0 0 0 0 0 0
 16   0 0 0 0 0 0 0070707  0 77  0 87 87 90100  0 010909132022112135
 17   0 0 0 0 0 0 0 0 0 1 0 0 0 0 0 0 0 0 0 0 0 0 0 0 0 0 0 0 0 0 0 0 2 0 0 0
 17   0 0 0 0 0 0 0070707 82 32  0 82 82100 99100 010303203041212244
 18   2 0 0 0 0 0 0 0 0 4 0 0 0 0 0 0 0 0 0 0 0 0 0 0 0 3 0 0 0 0 0 0 0 0 0 0 0
 18   0 0 0 0 0 0 0010107100 57 75 55 86 77 57 77 6310911427041208164
 19   1 0 0 0 0 0 0 0 1 0 0 0 0 0 0 0 0 2 0 0 0 0 0 0 0 2 1 0 0 0 0 0 0 0 0 0 0
 19   0 0 0 0 0 0 0079907100100100100100100  0 010506506071009155
 20   2 0 1 1 0 0 0 0 0 1 0 0 0 2 0 0 0 1 0 0 1 0 1 0 0 0 0 1 0 0 3 0 0 0 0 0
 20   0 0 0 0 0 0 0050105100 87 91 87 97 99 80 74 010406310051112155
 21   0 0 0 0 0 0 0 0 0 2 0 1 0 0 0 0 0 0 2 0 0 0 0 1 0 1 0 0 0 0 0 1 0 0 1 0 0
 21   0 0 0 0 0 0 0079907 68 61  0 45  0 84 35 0100105063050512  244
 22   0 0 0 0 0 0 0 1 0 0 0 0 0 0 0 0 0 1 0 0 0 0 0 0 0 1 0 0 0 0 0 0 0 1 0 0 0
 22   0 0 0 0 0 0 0101010 68 63 60 60 60 68 69100 010809315041010281 .
 23   0 0 0 0 0 1 0 0 0 0 0 0 0 0 0 0 0 0 0 0 0 0 0 0 0 0 0 0 0 0 0 0 0 0 0 0 0
 23   0 0 0 0 0 0 0079907100  0 58 0100100 90  0 010505306041712126
 24   1 1 0 0 0 0 0 0 0 0 0 0 0 0 1 0 0 0 0 0 0 0 0 0 0 0 0 0 0 0 0 0 0 0 1 0 0
 24   0 0 0 0 0 0 0070101100 64  0  0  0  0 0100 010202101031519171
 25   0 0 0 0 0 0 0 0 0 0 1 0 0 0 0 0 0 0 0 0 0 0 0 0 0 0 0 0 0 0 0 0 0 0 0 0 0
 25   0 0 0 0 0 0 0129912 91 98 0100 76 98 98 98 0102030  021417272
 26   0 0 0 1 0 2 0 0 0 0 1 0 0 1 0 0 0 0 0 0 0 0 0 1 0 0 3 0 0 0 0 0 0 0 0
 26   0 0 0 0 0 0 0070808  0  0 0100 0100100 0 010807203041313135
 27   0 0 0 0 0 4 0 0 0 0 0 0 0 0 4 0 0 0 0 0 0 2 0 0 0 0 0 0 0 2 0 0 0 0 0
 27   0 0 0 0 0 0 0070707  0  0  0  0 0100  0 50 010303207041212146
```

```
28   2 0 0 0 0 0 0 0 0 1 0 0 0 0 0 0 0 0 1 0 0 0 0 1 0 0 0 1 0 0 0 0 0 0 0 0 0 0 0
28   0 0 0 0 0 0 0 0030303100100 63 58 63100 46  0 010707217031214115
29   0 0 0 0 0 0 0 0 0 0 0 0 0 0 0 0 0 0 0 0 0 0 0 0 0 0 1 0 0 0 0 0 0 0 0 0
29   0 0 0 0 0 0 0 0010101 67  0 33100  0100  0  0 01111124003080828
30   1 0 0 0 0 0 0 0 0 0 0 1 0 0 0 0 0 0 0 0 0 0 0 0 0 0 1 0 0 0 0 0 0 0 0 0
30   0 0 0 0 0 0 0 0079901100  0  0 91  0 91  0100  0102030  021721215
31   0 0 0 0 0 0 0 0 1 0 0 0 0 0 0 0 0 0 0 0 0 0 0 0 0 0 0 0 0 0 0 0 0 0 0 0
31   0 0 0 0 0 0 0 0071010  0 85  0 87 77100  0100  0105060  021821117
32   0 1 0 0 0 0 1 0 0 0 0 0 0 0 0 0 0 1 0 0 0 0 0 0 0 0 0 1 0 0 0 0 0 0 1 0 0 0
32   0 0 0 0 0 0 0 0070708 69 67  0 88  0 91100 64 010404407061212155
33   2 0 0 0 0 0 0 0 0 2 0 0 0 0 0 0 0 0 2 0 0 0 0 0 0 0 0 2 0 0 0 0 0 0 0 0 0
33   0 0 0 0 0 0 0 0010101100 78  0  0  0 77  0  0 0104040  021716225
34   0 0 0 0 0 0 0 0 0 0 0 0 1 0 0 0 0 0 0 0 0 0 0 0 0 0 0 0 0 0 0 0 0 0 1 0 0
34   0 0 0 0 0 0 0 0070810 95 95  0 95 95 95100 95 010405307051216226
35   0 0 0 1 0 0 0 0 0 0 0 0 0 0 0 0 0 0 0 0 3 0 0 0 0 0 0 0 3 0 0 0 0 0 1 0
35   0 0 0 0 0 0 0 0050501100 92  0100  0  0  0  0 010909231021213145
36   0 0 0 0 0 0 0 0 0 0 0 0 1 0 0 0 0 0 1 0 0 0 0 0 0 0 0 0 0 0 0 0 0 0 0 0
36   0 0 0 0 0 0 0 0019901 97 84 89100 85 79 77 32  0309 4200215  1 3
37   0 0 0 0 0 0 0 0 0 0 0 0 0 0 0 0 0 0 0 0 0 0 0 0 0 0 0 1 0 0 0 0 0 0 0 0
37   0 0 0 0 0 0 0 0100505  0  0  0100  0  0 96 81 010404201041714217
38   0 0 0 0 0 0 0 0 0 0 0 0 0 0 0 0 0 0 0 0 0 0 0 0 1 0 0 0 0 0 0 0 3 0 0
38   0 0 0 0 0 0 0 0 2039903 67100  0  0 67100  0 85 010405405061416214
39   0 0 0 0 0 0 0 0 1 0 1 0 0 0 0 0 1 1 0 0 0 0 0 1 0 0 0 0 0 0 0 0 0 0 0
39   0 0 0 0 0 0 0 0050303 60100 54 81  0 76  0 66 010202102031516253
40   0 2 0 0 0 0 0 0 0 0 0 0 0 0 0 0 0 0 0 0 0 0 0 1 0 0 0 0 0 0 0 0 0 0 0 0
40   0 0 0 0 0 0 0 0039901 83100  0 92  0  0 0100 01110913202161522
41   0 0 0 1 0 0 0 0 0 0 0 0 0 0 0 0 0 0 0 0 0 0 1 0 0 0 0 0 0 0 0 0 0 0 0
41   0 0 0 0 0 0 0 0070505 94 73 67100 94100  0 69 010908227021021217
42   0 0 0 0 0 0 0 0 0 0 0 0 0 1 0 0 0 0 0 0 0 0 0 0 0 0 0 0 1 0 0 0 0 0 0
42   0 0 0 0 0 0 0 0070707  0  0  0 75 75100  0  0 010909320021620217
43   0 0 0 0 0 0 0 0 0 0 0 0 0 0 0 0 0 0 0 0 0 0 0 0 0 0 0 0 0 0 1 0 0 0
43   0 0 0 0 0 0 0 0  0 89  0  0  0 79 79100 010404405061619117
44   0 0 0 0 0 0 1 0 0 0 0 0 0 0 0 0 0 1 0 0 0 0 0 0 0 0 0 1 0 0 0 0 0 0 0 0
44   0 0 0 0 0 0 0 0101008 89100  0 89 89 97 97100 010505205041221216
45   0 0 0 0 0 0 0 0 0 0 0 0 0 1 0 0 0 0 0 0 0 0 0 0 0 0 0 0 0 0 0 0 0 0 0 0
45   0 0 0 0 0 0 0 0070707 93 82 75100 82 91  0  0 010808318041518217
46   0 0 0 0 0 0 0 0 0 0 0 0 0 0 0 0 0 0 0 0 0 0 0 0 0 0 0 0 0 0 1 0 0 0
46   0 0 0 0 0 0 0 0070707 78 82 78 85 78100  0100  0102030  021616153
47   0 0 0 0 0 0 0 0 0 0 0 0 0 0 0 2 0 0 0 0 0 0 0 0 0 0 0 0 0 0 0 0 0 0 0 0
47   0 0 0 0 0 0 0 0010101100 75 58 48 69 85 82 79 011111443020808283
48   0 0 0 0 0 0 0 0 0 0 0 1 0 0 0 0 0 0 0 0 0 0 0 0 0 0 0 0 0 0 1 0 0 0
48   0 0 0 0 0 0 0 0030803 67 92  0 66  0 0100 66 010505111031212144
49   4 0 0 0 0 0 0 0 0 0 0 5 0 0 0 0 0 0 3 0 0 0 0 0 0 0 4 0 0 0 0 0 0 0 1 0
49   0 0 0 0 0 0 0 0010101100  0 74 74 74 67 84  0 010505305051212244
50   0 0 0 0 0 0 0 0 0 0 3 0 0 0 0 0 0 0 0 0 0 0 0 0 0 0 1 0 0 0 0 0 0 0 0
50   0 0 0 0 0 0 0 0050101 98 98 80 94 82  0 0100 8210708316031008156
51   0 1 0 0 1 0 0 0 0 0 0 0 0 0 0 0 0 0 0 0 0 0 0 0 0 0 0 0 0 0 0 0 0 0 0 0
51   0 0 0 0 0 0 0 0069906100  0 0100100 86 88  0 010811317041314145
52   0 0 0 0 0 1 0 0 0 0 0 0 0 0 2 0 0 0 0 0 0 0 1 0 0 0 0 0 0 0 2 0 0 0
52   0 0 0 0 0 0 0 0101010 85 95 85100 85 92 51 92 010506511061618118
53   0 0 0 2 0 0 0 0 0 0 1 0 0 0 0 0 1 0 0 1 0 0 0 1 0 0 0 0 0 0 0 0 0 0 0
53   0 0 0 0 0 0 0 0080103 97  0 0100 69 74100  0 01091023102121214
54   0 0 0 0 0 0 0 0 1 0 0 0 0 0 0 0 0 0 0 1 0 0 0 0 0 0 0 0 0 0 0 0 0 0 0 0
54   0 0 0 0 0 0 0 0070593100 85 85100 89 89 94  0 010404203041921217
```

```
55  1 0 0 0 0 0 0 0 0 0 0 0 1 0 0 0 0 0 0 0 0 0 0 0 0 0 0 0 1 0 0 0 0 0 0 0 0 0
55  0 0 0 0 0 0 0 0070707 87  0  0 87 87 87100  0  010909128021620217
56  0 0 0 1 0 0 0 0 0 0 0 0 0 0 0 2 0 0 0 0 0 0 0 2 0 0 0 0 0 0 0 0 1 0 0 0 0
56  0 0 0 0 0 0 0080808 74 74 74 64 74 64100 74 7410404301051620126
57  0 0 0 0 0 0 0 0 0 0 0 0 0 0 0 0 0 0 0 0 0 0 0 0 0 0 0 0 0 1 0 0 0 0 0
57  0 0 0 0 0 0 0     100  0100100100100  0  0  010606312051720117
58  0 0 0 0 1 0 0 0 0 0 0 0 0 0 0 0 0 0 0 0 0 0 0 0 0 0 0 0 0 0 0 1 0 0 0
58  0 0 0 0 0 0 0100707100100 88 60100100  0 86  010404304051414245
59  0 0 0 0 0 0 0 1 1 0 0 0 0 0 0 0 0 0 0 0 0 0 0 0 0 1 1 0 0 0 0 0 0 0 0 0
59  0 0 0 0 0 0 0010111100 76  0 83 59 80  0 56  011011233021516136
60  0 0 0 0 0 0 0 0 0 0 0 0 0 0 0 1 0 0 0 0 0 0 0 0 0 0 0 0 0 0 0 0 0 0 0
60  0 0 0 0 0 0 0079910  0 89  0100 89 89  0 91  010607516071214228
61  0 0 0 0 0 2 0 0 0 0 0 0 0 0 0 0 0 0 1 0 0 0 0 0 0 0 0 0 0 0 0 0 0 0 0
61  0 0 0 0 0 0 0050598 74100 86 79 74 89 33  0  010809210041316137
62  0 0 0 0 1 1 0 0 0 0 0 0 1 0 0 1 0 0 0 0 0 0 1 0 0 0 0 0 0 0 0 1 0 0 0 0
62  0 0 0 0 0 0 0070507  0  0  0 89100100  0 91  010404205042020219
63  0 0 0 0 0 0 0 0 0 0 0 0 0 0 0 0 0 0 0 0 0 0 0 1 0 0 0 0 0 0 0 0 1 0 0 0
63  0 0 0 0 0 0 0101010 94 94 94 88 88100  0100  010609413061820119
64  0 0 0 0 0 0 0 1 0 0 0 0 0 0 0 0 0 0 0 0 0 0 0 0 0 0 0 0 0 0 0 0 0 0 0 0
64  0 0 0 0 0 0 0050505 71 7110010010010010010094 9410808510051420219
65  0 0 0 0 0 0 0 0 0 0 0 0 0 1 0 0 0 1 0 0 0 0 0 0 0 0 0 0 0 0 0 0 0 0 0
65  0 0 0 0 0 0 0010101100  0  0 48  0 69  0  0  010304203041516117
66  0 0 0 0 0 0 0 2 0 0 0 0 0 0 0 0 1 0 0 0 0 0 0 0 0 0 0 0 0 0 1 0 0 0 0
66  0 0 0 0 0 0 0070798100 93  0 71 64100  0100 83103020  021518115
67  2 0 0 0 0 0 0 0 0 1 0 0 0 0 0 0 2 0 0 0 0 0 0 2 0 0 0 0 0 0 0 0 0 0 0
67  0 0 0 0 0 0 0010101100 31 41 66 60 69 69 26 2611010325021210115
68  0 1 0 0 0 0 0 0 0 0 0 0 0 0 0 1 0 0 0 0 0 0 0 0 0 0 0 0·1 0 0 0 0 0 0
68  0 0 0 0 0 0 0030303  0100  0 84  0 84  0  0  0110100  021011216
69  0 0 0 0 0 2 0 0 0 0 0 0 0 0 0 0 1 0 0 0 0 0 0 0 0 0 0 0 0 1 0 0 0 0 0
69  0 0 0 0 0 0 0079907 94 94 89 89 89100 89 89  010403101031417272
70  0 4 0 0 0 0 0 0 0 3 0 0 0 0 0 0 0 3 0 0 0 0 0 0 0 3 0 0 0 0 0 0 0 0 1
70  0 0 0 0 0 0 0030303 77100  0 83 60 60  0 60  010202102031212132
71  0 0 0 0 0 0 0 0 1 0 0 0 0 0 0 0 0 0 0 0 0 0 0 0 0 0 0 0 0 0 0 0 0 0 0
71  0 0 0 0 0 0 0010101100  0  0  0  0  0  0  0  0102030  0213181 2
72  0 1 0 0 0 0 0 0 0 4 0 0 0 0 0 0 0 2 0 0 0 0 0 0 2 0 0 0 0 0 0 0 0 0 0
72  0 0 0 0 0 0 0030303100 92  0 75  0  0  0 63  040303102031415242
73  1 0 0 0 0 0 0 0 1 0 0 0 0 0 0 0 0 0 0 0 0 0 0 0 0 0 0 0 0 0 0 0 0 0 0
73  0 0 0 0 0 0 0010101100 91  0  0  0  0  0  0  0103030  021620174
74  0 0 0 0 1 1 0 0 0 0 0 0 0 2 0 0 0 0 0 0 0 0 2 0 0 0 0 0 0 0 0 0 0 0 0
74  0 0 0 0 0 0 0070707 73 73  0  0  0100  0  0  011111227031919219
75  0 0 0 0 0 0 0 1 0 1 0 0 0 0 0 0 0 0 0 0 0 0 0 0 1 0 0 0 0 0 0 0 0 0 0
75  0 0 0 0 0 0 0019901100  0  0  0  0 89  0  010304101031818215
76  0 0 0 1 0 0 0 1 0 0 0 0 0 0 0 0 0 0 0 0 2 0 0 0 0 0 0 0 1 0 0 0 0 0 0
76  0 0 0 0 0 0 0101010  0  0  0100 82 88  0100  0109090  022119219
77  0 1 0 0 0 0 0 0 0 0 0 0 0 0 0 0 0 0 0 0 0 0 0 0 0 0 0 0 0 0 0 0 0 0 0
77  0 0 0 0 0 0 0059898  0  0  0  0  0  0  0  0  010404207041720216
78  0 0 0 0 1 0 1 0 0 0 0 0 0 0 0 0 0 0 0 0 0 0 0 0 0 0 0 0 0 0 0 0 0 0 0
78  0 0 0 0 0 0 0070798  0  0  0 91 91100 91 85  010405201061716216
79  0 0 0 0 0 1 0 0 0 0 0 0 0 1 0 0 0 0 0 0 0 0 0 0 0 0 0 0 0 0 0 0 0 0 0
79  0 0 0 0 0 0 0070701 47  0  0  0  0100 92  0  010304201041717227
80  0 0 0 1 0 0 0 0 0 0 0 1 0 0 0 0 0 0 0 1 0 0 0 0 0 0 0 0 0 0 0 0 0 0 0
80  0 0 0 0 0 0 0050505  0  0  0100  0 93 95  0  010505303051619218
81  1 0 0 0 0 0 0 0 0 0 0 0 0 0 0 0 0 0 0 0 0 0 0 0 0 0 1 0 0 0 0 0 0 0 0
81  0 0 0 0 0 0 0070707100 82 82 82 88100  0  0  01070721604314227
```

```
 82   0 1 0 0 0 0 0 0 0 0 1 0 0 0 0 0 0 0 0 0 0 0 0 0 0 0 0 0 0 2 0 0 0 0 0 0 0 0 0
 82   0 0 0 0 0 0 0100707 88 96  0 96 88 96100 88  010202102031413233
 83   1 0 0 0 0 0 0 0 1 2 0 0 0 0 1 0 0 0 2 0 0 0 0 0 0 0 4 0 0 0 0 0 0 0 0 0 0
 83   0 0 0 0 0 0 0 0070707100 76 58 67 94100 69 60  0109100  021313244
 84   0 0 0 0 0 0 0 0 0 0 0 0 1 0 0 0 0 0 0 0 0 0 0 0 0 0 0 0 0 0 0 0 0 0 0 0
 84   0 0 0 0 0 0 0070606  0  0100 93100 93  0  0  010707706061616225
 85   0 0 0 0 0 0 0 0 0 0 0 0 0 2 0 0 0 0 0 0 0 0 0 0 0 0 0 0 0 0 0 1 0 1 0 0 0 0
 85   0 0 0 0 0 0 0079907  0  0  0  0100100  0 80  010606118032021118
 86   1 0 0 0 0 0 0 0 0 2 0 0 0 0 0 0 0 0 1 0 0 0 0 0 0 0 1 0 0 0 0 1 0 0 0 0 0
 86   0 0 0 0 0 0 0010101100  0  0100  0100  0  0  010607318031212243
 87   1 0 0 0 0 0 0 0 1 3 0 0 0 0 0 0 0 0 0 1 0 0 0 0 0 0 0 0 0 0 0 1 0 1 0 0 0
 87   0 0 0 0 0 0 0010101100 60  0 60 60 66  0  0  010303203041212246
 88   0 0 0 0 0 0 0 0 0 0 0 0 0 0 0 0 0 0 0 0 0 0 0 0 1 0 0 0 0 0 0 0 0 1 0 0 0 0 0
 88   0 0 0 0 0 0 0010101100 95 29 79 79 90 98 55  010404407061212145
 89   1 0 0 0 0 0 0 0 0 0 1 0 0 0 0 0 0 0 0 0 0 0 0 0 0 0 0 1 0 0 0 0 0 0 0 0 0
 89   0 0 0 0 0 0 0059905 79100 63 93 63 63 86 79  010405402061321217
 90   0 0 0 0 0 1 0 0 1 0 2 0 0 0 0 0 0 0 0 0 0 0 0 0 1 0 0 0 0 0 0 0 0 0 0 0
 90   0 0 0 0 0 0 0010303 94100 81 60 81 81 81 92  010606313051216127
 91   0 0 0 0 0 0 0 0 0 0 0 0 1 0 0 0 0 0 0 0 0 0 0 0 0 0 0 0 0 0 0 0 0 0 0 0 0
 91   0 0 0 0 0 0 0050505 82 84 71100  0 82 73 93 44  011011335021411281
 92   0 0 0 0 2 0 0 0 0 1 0 0 0 0 0 0 0 0 0 1 0 0 1 0 0 0 0 0 0 0 0 0 0 0 0 0
 92   0 0 0 0 0 0 0070101100100  0100100100100  0  010708314031112146
 93   0 0 0 0 0 0 0 0 1 0 0 0 0 0 0 0 0 0 1 0 0 0 0 0 0 2 0 0 0 0 0 0 0 0 0
 93   0 0 0 0 0 0 0010101100 84  0 81  0 73 84 31  010911231021208182
 94   0 0 0 1 0 0 0 0 1 0 0 0 0 0 0 0 2 0 0 0 0 0 0 0 8 0 1 0 0 0 0 0 0 0 0 0
 94   0 0 0 0 0 0 0109998  0  0  0100  0  0  0  0  011111243020812253
 95   3 0 0 0 0 0 0 0 0 3 0 0 0 0 0 1 0 0 4 0 0 0 0 0 0 0 2 0 0 1 0 0 0 0 0 0
 95   0 0 0 0 0 0 0030303100100  65100100  55100100  821060651205121622
 96   1 0 0 0 0 0 0 0 0 0 0 0 1 0 0 0 0 0 0 0 0 0 0 0 1 0 0 0 0 0 0 0 0 0 0 0
 96   0 0 0 0 0 0 0010101100  0  0  0  0  0 86 86  0110090  021408253
 97   0 0 0 0 0 0 0 0 0 0 0 0 0 0 0 0 0 0 0 1 0 0 0 0 0 0 0 2 0 0 0 0 0 0 0 0 0
 97   0 0 0 0 0 0 0060806 73 73 73 77 84 67100 67  010807321041210146
 98   3 0 0 0 0 0 0 0 0 1 0 0 0 0 0 0 1 1 0 0 0 0 0 0 0 1 0 1 0 0 0 0 0 0 0
 98   0 0 0 0 0 0 0010801 79 77  0  0  0 77100 84  010607501061012224
 99   0 0 0 0 0 0 0 0 0 0 0 0 0 0 0 0 0 0 0 0 0 0 0 0 0 0 0 0 0 0 0 0 0 0 0
 99   0 0 0 0 0 0 0100110100100  0 82 52 74 77 35  010303206041213205
100   0 0 0 0 0 0 0 0 0 1 0 0 0 0 0 0 0 0 0 0 0 0 0 0 0 0 0 0 0 0 0 0 0 0 0
100   0 0 0 0 0 0 0101010 96 94 86 86 86100 89 86  8010506601081314245
101   0 0 0 0 0 0 0 0 0 0 1 0 0 0 0 0 0 0 0 0 0 0 0 0 0 0 0 0 0 0 0 0 0 0 0
101   0 0 0 0 0 0 0010103100 80 55 60 60 55 83 55  010808222031312247
102   1 0 0 0 0 0 0 0 1 1 0 0 0 0 0 0 0 0 0 0 0 0 0 0 0 0 1 0 0 1 0 0 0 0 0
102   0 0 0 0 0 0 0010101 99100 83 88 88 94 83  0  010708222041212129
103   1 0 0 1 0 0 0 0 1 0 0 1 0 0 0 0 1 1 0 0 0 0 0 0 0 2 0 0 0 0 0 0 0 0
103   0 0 0 0 0 0 0013501 88 88 76100 88 88100 76  6410607216031212244
104   0 0 0 1 0 0 0 0 0 0 1 0 0 0 0 0 0 0 0 0 0 0 0 0 1 0 0 0 0 0 0 0 0 0 0
104   0 0 0 0 0 0 0059998  0 93  0100 21100100  0  011111335021408253
105   0 0 0 0 0 0 0 0 1 0 0 1 0 0 0 0 0 0 0 0 0 0 0 0 0 0 0 0 0 0 0 0 0 0 0
105   0 0 0 0 0 0 0070711 81100 76 87 88 87 87 39  6510809329021214215
106   0 0 0 0 0 3 0 0 0 0 0 0 0 0 2 0 0 0 0 0 0 0 4 0 0 0 0 0 0 0 0 2 0 0 0
106   0 0 0 0 0 0 0070707  0  0  0  0100  0  0  010404103031920215
107   0 1 0 0 0 0 0 0 0 0 0 0 0 0 0 0 0 0 0 0 0 0 0 0 0 0 0 0 0 0 0 0 0 0 0
107   0 0 0 0 0 0 0070808 65 75 65 65 65 72100 65  6510304302051212117
108   1 0 0 0 0 0 0 0 0 1 0 0 0 0 0 0 0 1 0 0 0 0 0 0 1 0 0 0 0 0 0 0 0 0
108   0 0 0 0 0 0 0050505  0  0  0100  0  0  0  0  011111241021713224
```

```
109  0 0 0 0 0 0 0 0 1 0 0 0 0 0 0 0 1 0 0 0 0 0 0 0 1 0 0 0 0 0 0 1 0 0 0
109  0 0 0 0 0 0 0079915  0 86  0 86 86 86 93  0  010606308051819116
110  0 1 0 0 0 0 0 1 0 0 1 0 0 0 0 0 0 0 0 0 0 0 0 0 0 0 0 0 0 0 0 0 0 0 0
110  0 0 0 0 0 0 0039903  0100 80 80 80 80  0  0  010709108031921218
111  0 0 0 0 0 3 0 0 0 0 1 1 0 0 0 0 0 0 0 0 0 2 0 0 0 0 0 0 0 0 2 0 0 0 0
111  0 0 0 0 0 0 0079910 85 95100 85 85 90  0100  01080911803121223
112  0 0 0 0 0 0 0 0 0 0 0 0 0 1 0 0 0 0 0 0 0 0 0 0 0 0 0 0 0 0 0 0 0 0 0
112  0 0 0 0 0 0 0079907  0  0  0  0 0100  0100  010404201041621218
113  0 0 0 0 0 0 0 0 0 0 0 0 0 0 0 0 0 0 0 0 0 1 0 0 0 0 0 0 0 0 0 0 0 0 0
113  0 0 0 0 0 0 0050505 75 75 75100 75 75  0  0  010505208041621116
114  0 0 0 0 0 2 0 1 0 0 0 0 0 1 0 2 0 0 0 0 0 3 0 0 0 0 0 0 1 0 0 0 0 0
114  0 0 0 0 0 0 0070707 42  0 42 46 40100 40 75  010605304051921118
115  0 0 0 0 0 0 0 0 0 0 0 0 0 0 0 0 1 0 0 0 0 0 0 0 0 0 0 0 0 0 0 1 0 0
115  0 0 0 0 0 0 0100111100100 75 75 75 75 75 83 83110100  021721219
116  0 0 0 0 0 0 0 0 0 0 0 0 0 0 0 0 0 1 0 0 0 0 0 0 0 0 0 0 0 0 0 0 0 0
116  0 0 0 0 0 0 0019901100  0 0100  0100  0  0  010711209041821218
117  0 0 0 0 0 2 0 0 0 0 1 0 0 0 0 0 0 0 0 0 0 1 0 0 0 0 0 0 0 1 0 0 0 0
117  0 0 0 0 0 0 0070707  0 87  0  0 60100  0  0  010809315031612227
118  0 0 0 0 0 0 0 0 0 0 0 0 0 0 0 0 0 0 0 0 0 0 0 0 0 0 0 0 0 0 1 0 0 0
118  0 0 0 0 0 0 0081010 87 95  0 95  0  0 91100  010505312041518229
119  0 0 0 0 0 0 0 0 0 0 0 0 0 0 0 0 0 0 0 1 0 0 0 0 1 0 0 0 0 0 0 0
119  0 0 0 0 0 0 0079905  0  0 0100  0100  0 96  0102030  021621218
120  0 0 0 0 0 0 0 0 0 0 0 0 2 1 0 0 0 0 0 0 0 0 0 0 0 0 0 1 0 0 0
120  0 0 0 0 0 0 0059998  0  0  0  0  0100 91 911040821304  19117
121  0 0 0 0 0 0 0 0 0 0 0 0 0 0 0 0 0 1 0 1 0 0 0 0 0 0 0 0 0 0 1 0 0
121  0 0 0 0 0 0 0070707 73  0 68 62  0100 95 89 63308  2150318  1 6
122  0 0 0 0 0 0 0 0 0 0 1 0 0 0 0 0 0 1 0 0 0 0 0 0 0 0 0 0 0 0 0 0
122  0 0 0 0 0 0 0050707 80  0 80 80 73100 87  0 010707410061616217
123  0 0 0 1 0 0 0 0 0 2 0 0 0 0 0 0 0 0 0 0 0 0 0 0 0 1 1 0 0 0 0 0
123  0 0 0 0 0 0 0050505 75 88 91100 91 97 84  0  0106070  021214115
124  0 0 0 0 1 0 0 0 0 0 0 0 0 0 0 0 0 0 1 0 0 0 0 0 0 0 0 0 0 0 0
124  0 0 0 0 0 0 0070707  0  0 85 85  0100  0  0  0308  1170213  1 8
125  0 0 0 0 0 0 0 1 0 0 0 0 0 0 0 0 1 0 0 0 0 0 0 0 0 0 0 1 0 0 1 0 0
125  0 0 0 0 0 0 0  0  0  0  0  0  0  0  010707311041719217
126  0 0 0 0 0 0 0 0 0 0 0 0 0 0 0 0 0 0 0 0 0 0 0 1 0 0 0 0 0
126  0 0 0 0 0 0 0060707 67 67  0  0 83100  0  0  01050730505121621
127  1 0 0 0 0 0 0 0 0 0 0 0 0 0 0 0 0 0 0 0 0 0 0 0 0 0 0 0 0 0
127  0 0 0 0 0 0 0010801100 92  0  0 76  0100  0 010607605081212245
128  0 0 0 0 0 0 2 0 0 0 0 0 0 1 0 0 0 0 0 0 0 2 1 0 0 0 0 0 0 0 0
128  0 0 0 0 0 0 0019905100 94 59 83 76 65 94 94  010304202041612244
129  1 1 0 0 0 0 1 0 1 0 0 0 0 1 0 1 0 0 0 0 0 0 0 0 0 0 0 0 0 0 0
129  0 0 0 0 0 0 0010101100100  0 88  0 88  0 94  01080815061314117
130  0 0 0 0 0 1 0 0 0 0 0 0 1 0 0 0 1 0 0 0 0 0 0 0 0 0 0 0 0 0 0
130  0 0 0 0 0 0 0069906 91 91  0 0100 94  0  0 010405307051318216
131  0 0 0 0 0 1 0 0 0 0 0 0 0 0 0 0 0 0 0 0 0 0 0 0 0 0 0 0 0 0 0
131  0 0 0 0 0 0 0030808 79 84 79 79 79 79100 84 79102033040509091 4
132  0 0 0 0 0 0 0 0 0 0 0 0 0 0 0 0 0 0 0 0 0 0 0 0 0 0 0 0 0 1 0 0 0
132  0 0 0 0 0 0 0070501 87 82 82 97 89 82 85100  0109090  031712129
```

Five

Buyer Behavior

The consumer is not a moron. She is your wife.
David Ogilvy

The objective of marketing activity is to influence customers to pick your product or service instead of other merchandise when they enter the marketplace. This means it is important for marketing managers to understand the "whys" and "hows" of buyer behavior so they can do a better job of developing, pricing, promoting, and distributing products to groups of consumers. By carefully studying buyer behavior, managers can better recognize new product opportunities associated with unfulfilled needs, and identify meaningful bases for market segmentation.

The many books and articles written on buyer behavior have resulted in a large number of rather specific and limited conclusions, but few generalizations. Buyer behavior is affected by many factors that are specific to the particular product and situation, so that broad conclusions and predictions will probably never be possible. Yet, researchers have developed many conceptual models and research techniques that are useful for studying specific aspects of buyer behavior, and many relevant variables have been explored.

The goal of this chapter is to develop an understanding of these variables and models. We begin by looking at a simple flow diagram that describes the purchase of a new car, move on to a discussion of factors influencing buying decisions, and conclude with a review of several comprehensive models of buyer behavior.

BUYING A NEW CAR

Some of the basic dimensions of buyer behavior can be explained by referring to a flow diagram that shows how one of the authors purchased a new car (Figure 5-1). The process began in this case with a suggestion by the wife that in view of the impending gasoline shortage it might be wise to consider replacing the old car with something more economical. Obviously pleased with the call to action, the husband rushed off to see what he could find. Less than twenty-four hours later he drove home with a new Datsun that he found at the first dealer visited.

This example suggests that buying often can be usefully studied as a *sequential* process that operates over a limited *time* span. It also appears that large buying decisions ($2500) are sometimes made on the basis of *limited* or even incorrect *information* (Figure 5-1). Thus, in the present case the buyer thought the Toyota was high priced when in fact both

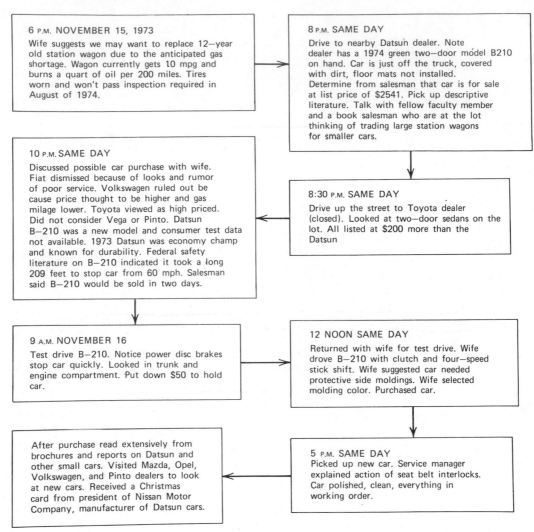

Figure 5-1 New Car Purchase by Author.

Toyota and Fiat had models priced lower than the Datsun. Another factor influencing this purchase was the *fear* (encouraged by salesman) that the car under consideration would be sold to someone else if the decision was delayed. The buyer knew that the B-210 was the most economical Datsun and he would probably have to wait several months for another car if he passed up this opportunity. The decision was also affected by the *availability* of the product and the *location* of the dealers. If the buyer had gone to the Toyota dealer first and they had been open for business, he might have purchased a Toyota instead of the Datsun.

Another subtle motivating factor was that two of the buyer's friends were also looking for new small cars. The accidental meeting of these people at the Datsun lot provided the buyer with *social approval* for the purchase decision. Interestingly, both friends subsequently bought other brands of small cars. The book salesman bought a Fiat because he wanted maximum gas mileage and the dealer gave him a good price for his trade-in. The other friend already owned one Opel and he bought a second because he liked the brand and the dealer gave him a good deal. Note that the size of the trade-in, maximum gas mileage, and previous ownership were not key factors in the sale of the Datsun. (Figure 5-1).

The buying process described in Figure 5-1 is summarized in Figure 5-2. Recognition of a problem or need leads to a search for alternatives. This is followed by a mental evaluation of the alternatives, purchase, and post purchase behavior. The buying process takes place over time and is influenced by a variety of interacting factors shown in the middle of Figure 5-2. In the next section we will review some of these modifying forces.

FACTORS INFLUENCING BUYING DECISIONS

The factors that influence buyers vary from person to person and there is no typical set of forces that affects all decisions. This is partially due to differences that exist among buyers, products, and time periods and is also related to the multidimensional character of the factors. Examination of the decision process suggests that some influencing forces are objective and others are more subjective. Some operate occasionally and some work all the time. Where one factor may work by itself, others interact with several variables. Sometimes influencing forces work slowly and at other times they work quickly to produce an impulse sale. On another level, some factors can be viewed as personal and internal while others operate outside the individual. Whatever the character of the

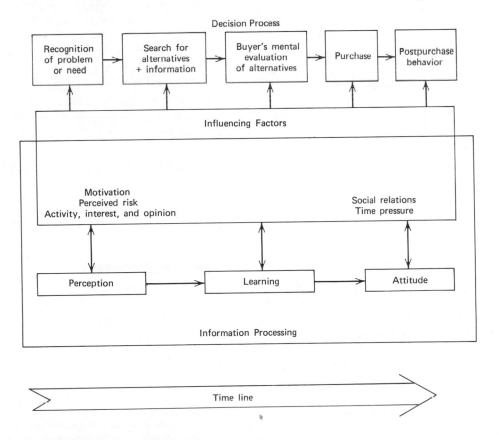

Figure 5-2 Simplified Buyer Behavior Model.

factors, we will try to explain these forces and show how they operate to modify the actions of buyers. Although influencing forces often operate in concert, we will treat them individually for purposes of discussion.

Motivation

Motives are forces that activate goal directed behavior on the part of customers. Needs are aroused either internally or by outside stimuli (such as advertising) and the individual seeks to satisfy them by purchasing goods or services. Thus when a person becomes thirsty he buys a drink and if he is lonely he joins a club.

A useful classification of motives has been developed by Maslow (Figure 5-3). This theory suggests that needs are arranged in a hierarchy and consumers satisfy needs on one level before moving on to higher levels. Once a comsumer has filled his requirements for food and shelter he becomes more concerned with safety and products such as fire extinguishers and radial tires. At the next level a need for belongingness is filled by churches, clubs, and family associations. The fourth level in the hierarchy is concerned with status and some people satisfy this need by buying paintings or boats. The highest need level is for self-actualization and this implies doing something to use the talents of the individual such as taking art lessons or working towards a new occupation. The top levels of the hierarchy are most likely to be attained in developed economies that have discretionary income. Maslow's hierarchy of needs is not a rigid system and individuals may operate on several levels and products can be sold to fill a variety of needs.[1]

Although basic needs explain a lot of buying, we all purchase many things for other reasons. For example, some people have an unusually strong concern for their *health* and buy a lot of vitamins and books on nutrition. Others are *anxious* in small groups and purchase quantities of deodorants and mouthwash. Still others are interested in *excitment* and take up sky diving and travel to exotic locales. Marketing managers can also appeal to *pride* in personal appearance or possessions to sell soap, cosmetics, and house paint. Another powerful motivating factor in buying situations is *economy*. When gasoline was

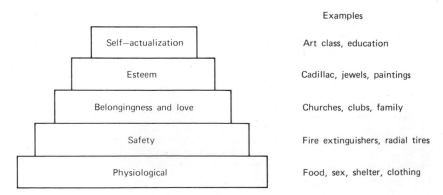

Figure 5-3 Maslow's Hierarchy of Needs.

[1] An excellent summary of theories of motivation and their influence on early research on consumer behavior can be found in William W. Wells and Arthur D. Beard, "Personality and Consumer Behavior" in Scott Ward and Thomas Robertson, eds., *Consumer Behavior: Theoretical Sources* (Englewood Cliffs, N.J.: Prentice-Hall, 1973), pp. 141-199.

cheap, Detroit sold cars on the basis of horsepower and comfort. As gasoline became less abundant and higher priced, auto advertising emphasized miles per gallon and the size of the gas tank. This quest for economy was shown to be a motivating factor in the purchase of the Datsun B-210 described in Figure 5-1.

One motivating force that has not been widely used in marketing communications is *fear*. The problem is that high levels of fear may cause consumers to distort advertising messages and actually reduce the sales of the product. For example, auto manufacturers could use films of cars being smashed and burned in wrecks to sell safety features. However, consumers might be so horrified by the pictures that they would refuse to buy a car at all and instead do their traveling by train or airplane. Lower levels of fear, on the other hand, can help sales by creating interest in the product message. The inhibiting and facilitating effects of fear appeals may balance each other out as shown in Figure 5-4. In this case a moderate level of fear is optimal as demonstrated by the peak in the *Total Effect* curve. Research on response to fear appeals suggests that the optimal level varies with the salience or relevance of the topic for the audience member and with personality.

Once a person is motivated by needs or other factors, his search for alternatives and their evaluation is influenced by his perceptions of the world around him.

Perception

Perception is the process by which the buyer becomes aware of and interprets some aspect of his environment. In a marketing setting this means attaching values to communications about products received from salesmen, friends, advertisements and independent test reports. Variations in the behavior of buyers in the marketplace can be

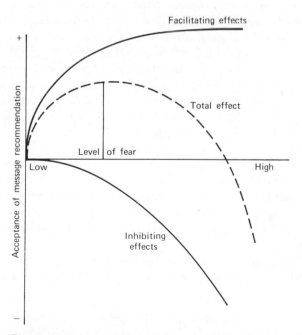

Figure 5-4 Message Acceptance as a Function of the Level of Fear.
Source. Reprinted from Michael Ray and William Wilkie, "Fear: The Potential of an Appeal Neglected by Marketing," *Journal of Marketing,* Vol. 34 (January 1970), p. 56. Published by the American Marketing Association.

partially explained by individual differences in the ways products and services are perceived. In the previous chapter, differences among the perceptual maps of buyers were found to be one basis for segmenting a market.

For example, the Datsun buyer perceived that the Toyota, Fiat and Volkswagon cars were all higher priced than the B-210 (Figure 5-1). The buyer obtained his information on the Volkswagon from newspaper reports, the price of the Fiat was mentioned by a friend, and the Toyota prices were observed on cars at the Toyota lot. As it turned out, these perceptions of price were not correct. Although the Vokswagen was higher, both Fiat and Toyota had models that were priced higher and *lower* than the Datsun. In this case the buyer's perceptions of price levels were based on incomplete information due to his rush to make a decision.

The perceptual process controls both the quantity of information received through attention and the quality or meaning of information as it is affected by bias. Attention is the mechanism governing the receptivity of the buyer to ads and other stimuli to which the buyer is exposed. Bias, on the other hand, is distortion of incoming data caused by previous exposure to the product or other promotional material. Three aspects of the perceptual process that have important marketing implications are selective attention, perceptual bias, and attitude change.

Selective Attention. In the case of selective attention, the consumer has frames of reference that he uses to simplify the information that he is continually receiving from his friends and marketing communications. Although the sorting out process prevents the consumer from being overwhelmed by his experiences, it does mean that he is sensing only part of his environment. For example, a person can sit in front of a television set and read a newspaper in a room full of children. When the person is called to dinner, he often doesn't hear the summons because he has effectively "tuned out" all sound messages and is only receptive to what he sees in the paper. In addition, he is likely to notice only some of the ads in the paper depending on his preferences for sports or news coverage.

Since marketers cannot afford unlimited advertising exposure, they try to design ads that stand out and will not be ignored by consumers. This approach is supported by McGuire's theory of selective attention that states that an individual tends to see in any complex stimulus those features that are the most unusual.[2] In a marketing context this could mean creating ads that employ distinctive colors instead of the usual black and white found in newspaper ads. Other approaches to break through the consumer's perceptual screen would be to use ads that are larger than your competitors or use more white space or print with white type on a black background.

Research on value-related words has shown that the buyer will perceive words that are important to himself, such as preferred brand names (Buick), more rapidly than words of lesser importance. This selective attention has obvious advertising implications and it has been suggested that ads should emphasize brand names only when reinforcing favorable preference.[3] When the goal of the ad is to change preference, some other form of attention attraction is necessary.

Perceptual Bias. An example of perceptual bias can be described by referring to some research conducted by the Carling Brewing Co. showing that brand names

---

[2]William J. McGuire, "The Guiding Theories Behind Attitude Change Research" in Charles W. King and Douglas J. Tigert, eds., *Attitude Research Reaches New Heights* (Chicago: American Marketing Association, 1970), pp. 26-48.

[3]Homer Spence and James Engel, "The Impact of Brand Preference on the Perception of Brand Names: A Laboratory Analysis" in David Kollat, Roger Blackwell, and James Engel, *Research in Consumer Behavior* (New York: Holt, Rinehart and Winston, 1970), pp. 61-70.

influence taste perception.[4] Carling first asked consumers to explain their preferences for beer and found the answers centered on the physical attributes of the product such as flavor. Then an experiment was conducted to determine if the beer drinkers could distinguish among major brands when they were not labeled. The consumers failed this test and when these same drinkers were subsequently asked to rate labeled beers, their ratings differed from those in the unlabeled experiment. These results suggest that brand names influence preference and the success of the brand of beer may be highly dependent on the effectiveness of its marketing effort. The sense of taste is especially subject to perceptual bias and distortion and product development for products for which flavor is an important attribute must be designed to accomodate this phenomenon.

Attitude Change. Theories of attitude change assume that a person's favorable or unfavorable feelings exert a direct influence on the purchase behavior by determining the perception of various alternatives. This information processing approach suggests that it is easier to change the category that the consumer perceives as appropriate for a stimulus than it is to change the evaluation of categories. Thus, one author notes that dietetic fruits and vegetables sell better in the fruit and vegetable aisle of supermarkets than in a special dietetic section.[5] Occasionally, broader reorganizations of categories occur such as the expansion of tire and auto accessory sales by department store chains and the loss of this business by the traditional service stations. Sometimes prexisting cateogries can be split or relationships between categories can be altered.[6] For example, many successful fast food outlets were built around the sale of a single food item (soft ice cream, pizza, roast beef sandwich), but their survival in the long run depended on their ability to broaden their menus.

Perceived Risk

The amount of risk a buyer believes is associated with a purchase decision also affects his behavior. The degree of risk varies with the costs at stake in a decision and the degree of certainty the buyer places on his belief that the outcome of the decison will be satisfactory.[7] The costs of a bad decison include monetary loss, time loss, ego loss, and losses related to the failure to satisfy the aroused need.[8]

For example, perceived risk was quite high during the Datsun purchase described in Figure 5-1. Not only was a substantial amount of money involved ($2500), but all of the cars being considered were manufactured overseas. This raised doubts about parts availability, commitment of the manufacturer to the U.S. market, training of mechanics, and accessibility of repair service in other communities. Most of these fears about service could have been reduced if the buyer had purchased a Volkswagen, which has a large and reputable service organization. Since the Volkswagen price was considered too high, the buyer could have reduced his perceived risk by purchasing a Toyota, which was the second-largest-selling imported car and had a fairly large dealer network. Unfortunately, the local Toyota dealer had just opened for business and did not have an established

---

[4]Ralph Allison and Kenneth Uhl, "Influence of Beer Brand Identification on Taste Perception," *Journal of Marketing Research,* (August 1964), pp. 36-39.

[5]Thomas S. Robertson, *Consumer Behavior* (Glenview, Ill.: Scott, Foresman, 1970), p. 59.

[6]Edgar Crane, *Marketing Communications* (New York: Wiley, 1965), p. 55.

[7]Raymond A. Bauer, "Consumer Behavior as Risk Taking" in Robert S. Hancock, ed., *Proceedings* (Chicago: American Marketing Association, 1960), pp. 389-398.

[8]Donald F. Cox and Stuart V. Rich, "Perceived Risk and Consumer Decision-Making—The Case of Telephone Shopping," *Journal of Marketing Research,* Vol. 1 (November 1964), pp. 32-39.

reputation for service. Datsun, on the other hand, was number 3 in sales, had 1000 U.S. dealers, a computerized parts distribution network (according to ads), and a well-established local dealer. In this case the buyer attempted to minimize his perceived service risk by purchasing a popular brand (Datsun) that *Consumer Reports* magazine said required few repairs.

Two levels of risk can be distinquished in purchase situations.[9] First, inherent risk expresses the basic risk existing in a product class. Second, handled risk expresses the risk remaining after information processing and risk reduction by the buyer. For example, a consumer could associate a great amount of risk with the product razor blades. On the other hand, a consumer might purchase a favorite brand with confidence. For this individual, inherent risk is high, but handled risk is low.

Individuals often pursue different risk reduction strategies. Some buy only for cash, others buy the most expensive item as an assurance of quality, still others buy the least expensive to minimize dollar investment, or frequent stores carrying advertised brands, and so on. Some risk reduction actions by consumers are perverse. Frequently, the amount of deliberation for an expensive product is less than for an inexpensive one. Some buyers seem to be unable to live with an upcoming decision involving high perceived risk and act hurriedly.[10]

Personality

Personality has to do with those enduring qualities of the individual that underlie consistent responses to the environment such as achievement, dominance, exhibition, and so on. However, attempts to relate measures of personality with various buying actions of consumers have generally been unsuccessful. The reason for this apparent inconsistency may lie with measures of personality that have been tried.

Personality scales have usually been developed from empirical studies where a large number of variables have been measured quantitatively. Statistical techniques are used to select those variables that best discriminate among individuals for some specified characteristic such as dominance. After checking the validity and reliability of the measures, a standard questionnaire is developed.

The inability of these personality measures to explain consumer buying behavior can often be traced to their misuse. Frequently, little thought is given as to why personality factors should be related to a particular purchase phenomenon. An instrument designed to measure some gross psychological trait perhaps should not be expected to predict market behavior.

One well-known study compared owners of Chevrolets and owners of Fords in terms of personality traits as measured by the Edwards Personality Preference Schedule.[11] Another study, using the same measures of personality, attempted to explain variations in brand loyalty and quantities purchased for bathroom tissue in terms of personality.[12] Neither study found personality significantly related to the phenomena investigated. It has been argued that marketing people must learn to develop their own instruments.

---

[9]James R. Bettman, "Perceived Risk and Its Components: A Model and Empirical Test," *Journal of Marketing Research,* Vol. 10 (May 1973), pp. 184-190.

[10]Ted Roselius, "Consumer Rankings of Risk Reduction Methods," *Journal of Marketing,* Vol. 35 (January 1971), pp. 56-61.

[11]Franklin B. Evans, "Psychological and Objective Factors in the Prediction of Brand Choice," *Journal of Business* (October 1959), 340-369.

[12]Advertising Research Foundation, *Are There Consumer Types?* (New York: Advertising Research Foundation, 1964).

Those who only modify some known instrument without regard to the implications for its validity and reliability may be in error. Thus, careful development of market-oriented instruments is needed.[13] One example of such specialized instruments is the activity, interest, and opinion scale.

Activity, Interest, and Opinion. Activity, interest, and opinion (AIO) measures are at an early stage of development, but they hold promise for helping managers analyze market behavior. Individuals can be described in terms of their activities or how they spend their time, their interests or what is important to them in their immediate environment, and their opinions.[14] Statements used in AIO instructions vary according to the characteristics of the product and its prospects. Some representative statements which a housewife would be asked on a six-point agreement scale are given in Table 5-1.

The AIO approach has been employed successfully to describe heavy users of Kentucky Fried Chicken.[15] Based on a sample of 1000 female homemakers, relative to

Table 5-1
Activity, Interest, and Opinion Statements

Dislikes Housekeeping	Community Minded	Information Seeker
I must admit I really don't like house chores.	I am an active member of more than one service organization.	I often seek out the advice of my friends regarding which brand to buy.
I find cleaning my house an unpleasant task.	I do volunteer work for a hospital or service organization on a fairly regular basis.	I spend a lot of time talking with my friends about products and brands.
I enjoy most forms of housework. (Reverse scored)	I like to work on community projects.	My neighbors or friends usually give me good advice on what brands to buy in the grocery store.
My idea of housekeeping is "once over lightly."	I have personally worked in a political campaign or for a candidate or an issue.	
Sewer	**Self-Confident**	**Self-Designated Opinion Leader**
I like to sew and frequently do.	I think I have more self-confidence than most people.	My friends or neighbors often come to me for advice.
I often make by own or my children's clothes.	I am more independent than most people.	I sometimes influence what my friends buy.
You can save a lot of money by making your own clothes.	I think I have a lot of personal ability.	People come to me more often than I go to them for information about brands.
I would like to know how to sew like an expert.	I like to be considered a leader.	

Source. William D. Wells and Douglas J. Tigert, "Activities, Interests, and Opinions," *Journal of Advertising Research,* Vol. 11 (August 1971), p. 35.

[13]Harold H. Kassarjian, "Personality and Consumer Behavior: A Review," *Journal of Marketing Research,* Vol. 8 (November 1971), pp. 409-418.

[14]Joseph T. Plummer, "Life Style Patterns and Commercial Bank Credit Card Usage," *Journal of Marketing,* Vol. 35 (April 1971), pp. 35-41.

[15]Douglas J. Tigert, Richard Lathrope, and Michael J. Bleeg, "The Fast Food Franchise: Psychographic and Demographic Segmentation Analysis," *Journal of Retailing* (Spring 1971), pp. 81-90. Customers buying the product at least once a month were considered heavy users.

light users, heavy users were found to be comparatively:

"Demographic Profile. More likely to be working full time; young; in a family with slightly more children than the sample average; in a family with total family income significantly higher than the sample average. In spite of the large income, undoubtedly due in part to the working status of some heavy users, this family is not upscale in terms of either educational or occupational status of the husband or wife . . . . Not only are the heavy users about twice as likely (compared to nonusers) to be working wives, but they are also more likely to live in large cities or their suburbs and to have their own car. In addition, per capita consumption appears to be higher in the South and Pacific regions of the United States and lower in the Northeast and Middle Atlantic regions.

"Other Products Consumed. Heavy users of fried chicken are also heavy users of eye make-up, nail polish, perfume, cologne, toilet water, regular soft drinks, chewing gum, and candy. They are above average in town driving, frequent buyers of gasoline and shoes—a young homemaker fits this description.

"They also buy other convenience food items: frozen cakes, frozen fruit, TV dinners, frozen side dishes, frozen maincourse dinners, refrigerated biscuits and rolls, canned spaghetti, toaster pastries, layer-cake mix, and frosting.

"For the carry-out chicken purchaser, both the means and the need have determined their purchasing behavior. In other words, their working status has both eliminated time available for preparing meals and provided the income necessary for purchase of a wide variety of convenience food.

"AIO Profile. Heavy users exhibit a zest for life. They are optimistic about their personal and financial futures, fashion and appearance conscious, pro credit, active, influential and risk takers. They are not afraid to borrow or invest and they like to go to exciting parties. Although they are above average income, they are not on top of the social ladder."

A list of a strategic marketing implications suggested by the results of the AIO study includes:

1. Accept charge cards in chicken outlets.
2. Maintain an informal atmosphere. Patrons like to dress and shop in casual and comfortable clothes.
3. Tie in promotional activities with bowling alleys, beauty parlors, dress shops, etc.
4. Don't stress cents-off promotion. Heavy users do not seem to be price conscious.
5. Consider home delivery as an added time saver.

Self-Concept. Finally, buyer behavior may be more closely related to self-concept, or perceived self, than it is to personality.[16] Consumers may prefer products whose brand images are most similar to their own self-concept. The problem is whether to use the self that the individual wants to be or the self that the individual is. This discrepancy between ideal and actual self could provide an opportunity for making product appeals. Some empirical evidence suggests that consumers are basically satisfied with themselves. Even for conspicous products, actual self-concept is more similar to brand preference than is ideal self-concept.

Attitude Formation and Change

Since attitudes often affect buyers' decisions (Figure 5-2), managers must understand attitude formation and attitude change if they expect to direct marketing activities to

[16]Ivan Ross, "Self-Concept and Brand Preference," *Journal of Business,* Vol. 44 (January 1971), pp. 38-50.

influence sales. One definition of attitude suggests it is a mental state of readiness, organized through experience, exerting a directive and/or dynamic influence upon the individual's response to all objects and situations with which it is related.[17] This implies that attitude is a hypothetical construct that intervenes between marketing communication inputs and an observable output such as product purchase. Most discussions of attitude recognize three components: *cognitive* (perceptual), *affective* (like-dislike), and *conative* (intentions). Attitude research in buyer behavior has sometimes focused on measures of a single component of attitude; other research applications have been concerned with the structural relationships among two or even all three of these components. Several examples of these applications follow.[18]

Single-Component Measures

Measures of individual attitude components have been sought as response measures to marketing stimuli, such as advertising themes and package designs, since measures of sales effectiveness in the market are sometimes too difficult and time-consuming to be practical. Axelrod has argued the need for such response measures, which he labels Intermediate Criteria, and has published results of a study sponsored by Lever Brothers in which the alternative Intermediate Criteria were field tested in terms of several criteria.[19] Descriptions of these ten measures appear in Figure 5-5. It may be noted that advertising recall and awareness are measures of *cognition* (perception or awareness of brands); Predisposition-to-Buy Scale, Constant Sum Scale, First and Second Choices, and Buying Game are alternative measures of *intentions;* and the +5 to −5 rating scale is a measure of *affect.*

Axelrod's study provided means for judging these measures in terms of sensitivity (ability to discriminate between stimuli such as commercials), stability (ability to provide the same answers on repeated testing), and power to predict ultimate brands purchased. Although the study was limited to a small number of product categories, it is interesting to note that first-brand awareness (first brand named on the awareness measure) was the best measure for the prediction of short-term trends, particularly for brand switching, and the constant sum scale was judged better for diagnostic purposes, since it spread responses along a continuous scale.[20] Thus, these two scales could well be used in combination.

Assael and Day tested the predictive power of unaided brand awareness and brand attitude (defined as degree of agreement with statements favorable toward the brands studied) for deodorants, analgesics, and instant coffee in a unique study utilizing measures taken repeatedly from periodic national surveys.[21] In terms of predicting market share, brand attitude was important for analgesics and instant coffee, but was not very predictive for deodorants.[22]

[17]George W. Allport, "Attitudes," in C. Murchison, ed., *Handbook of Social Psychology* (Worcester, Mass.: Clark University Press, 1935), pp. 798-884. This definition seems to be related to the learned behavior paradigm of attitude change.

[18]One of the best reviews of the application of attitude research in consumer behavior is George S. Day, "Theories of Attitude Structure and Change" in Scott Ward and Thomas S. Robertson, eds., *Consumer Behavior: Theoretical Sources* (Englewood Cliffs, N.J.: Prentice-Hall, 1973), pp. 303-353.

[20]*Ibid.,* p. 17.

[19]Joel Axelrod "Attitude Measures that Predict Purchase," *Journal of Advertising Research,* Vol. 8 (March 1968), pp. 3-18.

[21]Henry Assael and George S. Day, "Attributes and Awareness as Predictors of Market Share," *Journal of Advertising Research,* Vol. 8 (December 1968), pp. 3-10.

[22] *Ibid.,* p. 10.

1. The Lottery Measure

For your cooperation, we would like to give you a chance to win a drawing of $5.00 worth of [product class]. If you are a winner, we will send you the brand you choose. If you are the winner of $5.00 worth of [product class], what brand do you want?

2. The +5 to −5 Rating Scale

I would like you to rate some brands of [product class] from +5 to −5. The more you think a brand is above the average for all [product class] brands, the higher the plus number you should give it, up to +5. The more you think a brand is below average the bigger the minus number you should give it, all the way down to −5. Remember, you can use *every* number between +5 and −5.

3. The Predisposition-to-Buy Scale

Now I would like you to tell me about your interest in purchasing various brands of [product class] by using this card. Tell me which statement describes your feelings about each brand as I name them.

I will definitely buy the brand next time.

I will probably buy the brand in the near future.

I might buy the brand in the future.

I don't know whether or not I will buy the brand.

I will probably not buy the brand.

I will certainly not buy the brand.

I would not use this brand under any circumstance.

4. The Constant Sum Scale

Here's a sheet on which I have listed several brands of [product class]. Next to each brand is a pocket. Here are eleven cards. I would like you to put these cards in the pockets next to the brands to indicate how likely it is that you would buy each brand. You can put as many cards as you want in front of any brand, or you can put no cards in front of a brand.

5. Paired Comparisons

I'm going to name some pairs of brands of [product class]. I'd like you to tell me which of each pair you would be more likely to purchase.

6. Forced Switching

Please tell me what your regular brand of [product class] is. Now, for your cooperation, we would like to give you a chance to win a drawing for $5.00 worth of [product class]. If you're the winner we'll send you the brands you choose. You can select any brand except (REGULAR BRAND). What brand do you want?

7. Advertising Recall

What brands have you seen or heard advertised for [product class] in the past three months? Are there any others?

8. First and Second Choices

If you were to go out shopping right now for [product class], what brand do you think you would buy? If that were not available, what brand would you be most likely to consider as a substitute for the one you wanted?

9. Awareness

Considering [product class], please tell me all the brands you can think of.

10. Buying Game

I am going to give you some cards showing different situations you might run into if you were shopping for [product class]. The prices and brands available will vary from card to card. In each case I would like you to tell me which brand you would be most likely to purchase. Here is the first card. What brand would you buy? Here is the second. . . .

Figure 5-5 The Ten Intermediate Criterion Measures Tested.
Source. Joel Axelrod, "Attitude Measures that Predict Purchase," *Journal of Advertising Research,* Vol. 8 (March 1968), pp. 3-18.

This finding suggests that single-component attitude measures, though easily administered and interpreted, may not have equal predictive power for all product categories. Furthermore, the predictive ability of attitude measures is limited by situational factors that occasionally intervene and prevent consumers from purchasing the most preferred brand. Stores may be out of stock or special incentives for brand switching may be present. Also, choice behavior may be dependent upon specific use situations.[23] For instance, a family might buy one brand of beer for everyday consumption and another for parties.

Finally, using simple attitude measures for judging response to marketing stimuli seems to assume that attitude change is always a worthwhile goal for marketing activity and that favorable attitude change toward a brand necessarily precedes purchase of that brand. There is some evidence that attitude change may *follow* a change in behavior, at least under certain circumstances, implying that the proper goal for marketing sometimes may be to induce trial purchase of the brand rather than to improve attitudes toward the brand.

Benjamin Lipstein has suggested that both the degree of economic risk and the anxiety level associated with the product determine the likelihood of attitude change prior to purchase.[24] In general, the greater the economic risk and the higher the anxiety level, the greater will be the importance of attitude. Anxiety is related to consumers' ability to quickly perceive results of using the product and the perceived variability in performance among brands. Where product performance is variable and/or difficult to judge, anxiety associated with the product is high.[25]

Another advertising agency researcher, Kenneth Longman, suggests that attitude change as a goal for promotion is most appropriate for products with relatively long purchase cycles (the time elapsing between purchases), where many sources of information are sought out by buyers, and where the purchase occasion is dependent upon some other event (such as purchases of proprietary drugs and replacement purchases of appliances and autos).[26]

Attitude Structure. Attitude research in consumer behavior has recently focused heavily on the *components* of attitude, especially the cognitive component. One approach views the consumers' process of judging brands as based on the characteristics or attributes relevant for the product category and perceptions or evaluative beliefs about each known brand in terms of these attributes.[27] Affect or liking is commonly assumed to be a function of these evaluative beliefs.

The crucial attributes are often determined by depth interviews with small numbers of consumers or by group depth interviews.[28] The number of significant characteristics tends to vary by product class, and often may be surprisingly small—perhaps three to seven. Product attributes and brands used in one of the earliest consumer research applications of this approach appear in Figure 5-6.

For diagnostic purposes, understanding of all the product attributes considered salient by consumers is essential, and research at this stage should explore the possibility that the

---

[23]Rolf Gunnar Sandell, "Effects of Attitudinal and Situational Factors on Reported Choice Behavior," *Journal of Marketing Research,* Vol. 5 (November 1968), pp. 405-408.

[24]Benjamin Lipstein, "Anxiety, Risk and Uncertainty in Advertising Effectiveness Measurements" in Lee Adler and Irving Crespi, eds., *Attitude Research on the Rocks* (Chicago: American Marketing Association, 1968), pp. 11-27.

[25]*Ibid.,* p. 18.

[26]Kenneth Longman, *Advertising* (New York: Harcourt Brace Jovanovich, Inc., 1971), p. 146.

[27]A number of issues in this conceptualization of attitude structure and in methodology have been extensively explored. An excellent review is provided in William L. Wilkie and Edgar A. Pessemier, "Issues in Marketing's Use of Multi-Attribute Attitude Models," *Journal of Marketing Research,* (November 1973), pp. 428-441.

[28]Additional methods, together with many examples of actual consumer attitude research instruments, can be found in G. David Hughes, *Attitude Measurement for Marketing Strategies* (Glenview, Ill.: Scott, Foresman and Company, 1971).

market may consist of subgroups or segments differing in the clusters of attributes of importance.[29] For example, Table 4-3 illustrates possible segmentation of the toothpaste market by clusters of attributes or benefits.

If the purpose of the research is to find evaluative beliefs that predict brand choice, product attributes viewed by consumers as not varying over brands may be dropped from the analysis. Such attributes are not *determinant* of consumer brand choice, and so are not useful either for predicting choice or as the basis for promotional themes.[30] The attribute set may also be reduced by dropping attributes perceived by consumers as being highly intercorrelated with other attributes.

Product characteristics can be described in terms of the importance *weight* (value) assigned to each attribute of a product by an individual (i.e., his choice criteria), and *amount* of each attribute a brand is perceived to have; and the *uncertainty* an individual has about his perception of the amount of an attribute.[31] The weight assigned to each

Frozen Orange Juice	Mouthwash	Toothpaste
Taste/flavor	Kills germs	Decay prevention
Price	Taste/flavor	Taste/flavor
Texture	Price	Freshens mouth
Nutritonal value	Color	Whitens teeth
Packaging	Effectiveness	Price
Minute Maid	Micrin	Pepsodent
Snow Crop	Cepacol	Crest
Birds Eye	Listerine	Gleem
A & P	Lavoris	Colgate
Sunkist	Colgate 100	Macleans

Toilet Tissue	Lipstick	Brassieres
Texture	Color	Style
Color	Taste/flavor	Price
Price	Prestige factor	Comfort
Package size	Container	Fit
Strength	Creaminess	Life
Aurora	Hazel Bishop	Penneys
Delsey	Max Factor	Playtex
Northern	Avon	Lovable
Scot Tissue	Coty	Maidenform
Charmin	Revlon	Sears

Figure 5-6 Product Attributes and Brands.
Source. Frank M. Bass and W. Wayne Talarzyk, "Using Attitude to Predict Individual Brand Preference," *Occasional Papers in Advertising,* No. 4 (May 1971), p. 67.

[29]Russell Haley, "Benefit Segmentation: A Decision-Oriented Research Tool," *Journal of Marketing* (July 1968), pp. 30-35.

[30]James H. Myers and Mark I. Alpert, "Determinant Buying Attitudes: Measuring and Measurement," *Journal of Marketing* (October 1968), pp. 13-20.

[31]For a discussion of the relationship of these components to the concepts found in social psychology see Joel B. Cohen, Martin Fishbein, and Oeli T. Ahtola, "The Nature and Uses of Expectancy-Value Models in Consumer Attitude Research," *Journal of Marketing Research,* Vol. 9 (November 1972), pp. 456-460.

attribute has often been measured with bipolar or rank order scales. For example, a bipolar scale used to assign attribute weights to two brands of beer and a hypothetical "ideal beer" took the following form:

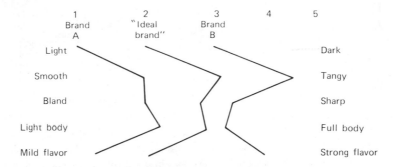

The amount of each attribute can be found by asking consumers to look at the set of characteristics for each brand and decide how well the characteristic describes the brand:

For BOLD Laundry Detergent

		Does Not Describe Brand		Describes Brand Well	
Cuts grease	1	2	3	4	5
Works in cold water	1	2	3	4	5
Whitens clothes	1	2	3	4	5

Several measurement problems with this procedure shall be mentioned. Some authorities urge the use of constant-sum scales, rather than bipolar scales, because the latter tends to lead to badly skewed distributions and a lack of variance.[32] When respondents currently use one of the brands being evaluated, there is a strong tendency for them to overrate the currently used brand, reflecting a sort of "halo effect."[33] It is sometimes difficult to state attributes verbally in such a way that all respondents interpret them in a similar way. Finally, respondents may tend "to give socially acceptable or function-oriented responses in an attempt to appear highly rational."[34]

Uncertainty about amounts of attributes can be found by using a constant-sum probability scale in conjunction with the attribute amount scale. When uncertainty is taken into account, the perceived amount of each attribute is an expected value.

Building an Attitude Index. The weight and amount components can be combined to produce an aggregate attitude index to predict individual attitudes and preference toward a brand. For example, Table 5-2 gives the basic component scores for three attributes that were important in the car purchase described in Figure 5-1. The *weights* shown were determined by asking the buyer to allocate the constant sum of 1.00 across

[32]George S. Day, op. cit., p. 312. David S. Hughes, op. cit, provides an excellent summary of attitude scaling methods.

[33]Frank M. Bass and W. Wayne Talarzyk, "Using Attitude to Predict Individual Brand Preference," *Occasional Papers in Advertising,* No. 4 (May 1971), pp. 69-71.

[34]Marshall Greenberg and Paul E. Green, "Multidimensional Scaling" in Robert Ferber ed., *Handbook of Marketing Research* (New York: McGraw-Hill, 1974), pp. 3-52.

Table 5-2
Attribute Scores for Automobile Customer

Weight	Atribute	Amount		
		Fiat	Datsun	Toyota
.45	Good service	1	4	2
.35	Low price	2	5	3
.20	Miles per gallon	5	4	3

the three attributes to indicate their relative worth. In this case, the buyer attached the highest weight (.45) to Good Service and Parts, the second highest weight (.35) to Low Price, and the smallest weight (.20) to Miles Per Gallon. Next the *amount* of each attribute displayed by each brand was obtained by asking the buyer to assign numbers from 1 (does not describe brand) to 5 (describes brand well) to the different products.

An adequacy-importance attitude index can be constructed for the car buyer by combining the data in Table 5-2 using the formula:

$$A_j = \sum_{k=1}^{n} a_k x_{kj} \tag{1}$$

where:

A_j = Attitude index for brand j
a_k = Weight assigned to attribute k
x_{kj} = Amount of attribute k assigned to brand j
n = Number of attributes

Thus, attitude index values can be obtained for the three brands of cars being considered by the customer as follows:

Fiat = $(.45)(1) + (.35)(2) + (.20)(5) = 2.15$
Datsun = $(.45)(4) + (.35)(5) + (.20)(4) = 4.35$
Toyota = $(.45)(2) + (.35)(3) + (.20)(3) = 2.55$

In this case brands with an attitude index of 5.0 would possess ideal quantities of the attributes desired by the customer and brands with an index of 1.0 would have none of the attributes desired by the customer. The index values obtained suggest that the buyer had the most positive attitude toward the Datsun (4.35) with lower scores for Fiat and Toyota. The analyst is now in a position to ask the customer for his rankings of the brands to see if they agree with predictions based on the attitude index. The final step is to establish the relative importance that market segments attach to different attributes, build some of these characteristics into the brand, and then advertise to show customers that the product has these attributes.

An alternative to the adequacy-importance model would be an expectancy-value model:

$$A_j = \sum_{k=1}^{n} b_{jk} e_k \tag{2}$$

where:

A_j = Attitude index for brand j
b_{jk} = Belief that brand j possesses attribute k
e_k = Evaluation of the desirability of attribute k
n = Number of attributes

Information on beliefs and evaluations are usually measured using bipolar scales (-2, $-1,0,1,2$) rather than nonnegative scales (1 to 5). Buyers are asked whether they believe that a brand is very likely ($+2$) to very unlikely (-2) to possess a particular attribute that they evaluate as very good ($+2$) to very bad (-2). This formulation means that if a brand is believed unlikely to possess an attribute that is very bad, then the contribution to the attitude index is positive.[35]

Managers take the practical view that attitude is a measurable construct that can be used to evaluate the effects of persuasive communications. However, these managers might improve their decision making if they would take into account explicit theories of attitude change. The most important are learned behavior, consistency, and social judgement.

Learned Behavior

Learning occurs when customers respond to a stimulus and are rewarded with need satisfaction or are penalized by product failure. For example, a consumer may be stimulated by a need for a cool drink on a hot day. The consumer's response may be to try different brands of soft drinks until he finds a product that fills his need. After this, he will tend to make a similar response on future occasions. The consumer has learned. Theories that explain this adaptive behavior include problem solving, stimulus response, and reinforcement. Examples of the use of learning theory in marketing programs include techniques such as giving out free samples of new products, 30¢-off coupons, and refund offers that are designed to get product trial.

A learning view of attitudes would claim that an attitude is an intervening variable between an objective stimulus, and an overt response. In this chain reaction, attitude is not only an implicit response to the objective stimulus, but is itself a stimulus to the observable response.[36] Because of delays in the mechanism, the magnitude of attitude change is an effect of a stimulus on a buyer that, if known, could be used to predict subsequent behavior. This approach emphasizes the stimulus characteristics of the communication situation: the order and arrangement of persuasive communications, the credibility of the communicator, and the characteristics of the audience.

The Consistency Paradigm

The consumer attempts to maintain consistency among attitudes, among behaviors, and among attitudes and behaviors. Exposure to conflicting information produces internal strain. The consumer seeks to find a solution that minimizes this tension. Conflict reduction alternatives available to the consumer include (1) changing his behavior to conform to new information, (2) changing his attitudes, (3) discrediting the source of the conflict-causing new information, (4) acquiring additional information to reinforce his original position, (5) avoiding the information sources that contribute to the dissonance (selective exposure), (6) distorting the new information, and (7) forgetting the content of the new information (selective recall).

Cognitive Dissonance. The best known consistency theory in marketing is cognitive dissonance.[37] Cognitive dissonance is concerned with postdecision doubt. Making a

---

[35]James R. Bettman, Noel Capon, and Richard J. Lutz, "Cognitive Algebra in Multi-Attribute Attitude Models," *Journal of Marketing Research,* Vol. 12 (May 1975), pp. 151-164.

[36]L. W. Doob, "The Behavior of Attitudes," *Psychological Review,* Vol. 54 (May 1947), pp. 135-156.

[37]Leon Festinger, *A Theory of Cognitive Dissonance* (Evanston, Ill.: Row, Peterson, 1957) and *Conflict, Decision, and Dissonance* (Stanford: Stanford University Press, 1964).

purchase decision usually does not eliminate dissonance as the consumer remains aware of the favorable features of the unchosen brands and must reconcile this knowledge with his own decision. The process of reconciliation often involves a search for new information.

The likelihood that a consumer will search for information after purchase increases with the importance of the decision, with the number of negative attributes of the chosen alternative, with the number of positive attributes of the unchosen alternatives, and with the dissimilarity of the alternatives. The kind of information sought depends on the confidence the consumer has in his initial decision. The more certain the consumer is that he has made the correct decision, the more likely he will try to find differing information and refute it. On the other hand, the less confident the consumer is, the more likely that he will only look for information that supports his decision.

The car purchase described in Figure 5-1 produced a great deal of dissonance because the buyer quickly spent $2500 on the basis of only limited information on alternative brands or models. After the purchase, the buyer attempted to reduce his dissonance by reading performance literature on different cars and by visiting dealers to gather data on prices. The manufacturer (Datsun in this case) recognized that dissonance could occur and made several attempts to reassure the buyer that he had made the right choice. First, the warranty card was not given to the buyer at the time of purchase (this seemed odd at the time), but was sent to his home several weeks later. Included with the card was a questionnaire that asked the buyer to evaluate the way the dealer prepared the car for delivery. This allowed the buyer to express any frustrations he had encountered during the purchase or with subsequent service. The manufacturer also took the trouble to send the buyer a Christmas card from the president of the company and have the dealer invite the buyer to have recommended service work done at periodic intervals.

Advertising sometimes produces dissatisfied customers by creating expectancies that are not fulfilled by product performance. The resulting dissonance can be reduced by returning the product or by brand switching. Engel and Light relate an anecdote in which a new, sporty make of automobile was rejected during trial when its performance did not live up to its advertising claims. Advertising must create realistic expectancies in order to achieve product repurchase and use.[38]

Consistency and Product Introduction. Dissonance theory also provides insight for planning new product introductions. Often a new product is temporarily offered at a low introductory price. The reason is to encourage trial of the product. While many marginal users will be lost when the price is raised, some of these consumers, who would not have tried the product at the regular price, hopefully will be retained. Although this reasoning seems quite plausible, dissonance theory suggests that the effort may be counterproductive and lead to lower rather than higher eventual sales.

Some researchers[39] suggest that the higher the price a consumer pays for a new product, the greater will be the pressure on him to justify the purchase by liking the product. This greater liking will in turn produce greater repeat purchases. On the other hand, a consumer who buys the product on a cents-off promotion can justify his purchase as a bargain and does not need to alter his attitude toward the product. An experiment was conducted to test this hypothesis. Higher sales in the long run were indeed achieved by

[38]James F. Engel and M. Lawrence Light, "The Role of Psychological Commitment in Consumer Behavior" in Frank M. Bass et. al. eds., *Applications of the Sciences in Marketing Management* (New York: Wiley, 1968), pp. 193-194.

[39]Anthony N. Doob, J. Merrill Carlsmith, Johnathan L. Freedman, Thomas K. Landauer, and Soleng Tom, "Effect of Initial Selling Price on Subsequent Sales," *Journal of Personality and Social Psychology,* Vol. 11 (April 1969), pp. 345-350.

introducing the product at its normal selling price rather than by introducing it at a low price for a short time and then raising the price to its regular level. This is shown for aluminum foil sales in Figure 5-7.

Thus, attempts to change attitudes by first changing behavior must involve commitment to product trial. This suggests that sampling a new product would be ineffectual where consumers have established preferences. In one case housewives resisted cold water detergents and stated they would not use a free sample. Some commitment was achieved by using cents-off coupons in the initial advertising and forcing the consumer to pay most of the purchase price.[40]

Social Judgement

The attitude structure of the consumer usually contains a range of acceptable positions, not just a single position. Attitudes toward brands in a product class can be divided into the latitude of acceptance, the latitude of rejection, and the latitude of noncommitment. The latitude of acceptance is the range of acceptable positions (including the most acceptable) on an attitude toward a product. The latitude of rejection is the range of

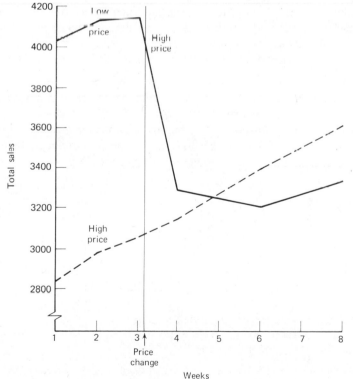

Figure 5-7 Aluminum Foil Sales.
Source. Doob et al., "Effect of Initial Selling Price on Subsequent Sales," *Journal of Personality and Social Psychology,* Vol. 11 (April 1969), pp. 345-350. Copyright © 1969 by the American Psychological Association. Reproduced by permission.

[40]James F. Engel and M. Lawrence Light, "The Role of Psychological Commitment in Consumer Behavior" in Frank M. Bass et. al., eds., *Applications of the Sciences in Marketing Management* (New York: Wiley, 1968), pp. 194-195.

objectionable positions (including the most objectionable) on an attitude toward a product. Any remaining positions fall within the attitude of noncommitment.[41] The attitude structure for a hypothetical toothpaste buyer is shown in Figure 5-8.

The boundaries between the categories are determined by the degree of involvement of the consumer in the product class. The more involved a consumer is in his own position, the broader will be his latitude of rejection. This provides a definition of commitment which can be used in the consistency paradigm.

Latitudes of acceptance have been used to measure price thresholds.[42] Consumers have been found to have ranges of acceptable prices for given products. A buyer will often reject purchase of a product if its price is below his low price threshold and above his high price threshold. This price-limit concept implies a backward bending demand curve.

The theory also has applications in persuasive communications. When a consumer receives a persuasive communication, he makes a judgement about the position of the message relative to his own position. Predictions about the nature of his attitude change can be derived from social judgement theory:

1. When persuasive attempts fall within his latitude of acceptance, an individual's attitude changes.
2. When they fall within his latitude of rejection, he does not change his attitude.
3. As discrepancy between the consumer's own stand and the position advocated by the communication increases, the greater will be the attitude change provided that the advocated stand does not fall within the latitude of rejection.
4. For communications that advocate positions within the latitude of rejection increased discrepancy produces less attitude change.[43]

Thus, attitude change can be induced under conditions of commitment by accurate placement of appeals relative to commitment.[44]

Suppose that the attitude structure for the toothpaste buyer represented in Figure 5-8 holds for the market segment where decay prevention is the most important brand choice attribute.[45] What promotional tactics should each firm adopt? Crest, as the most prefer-

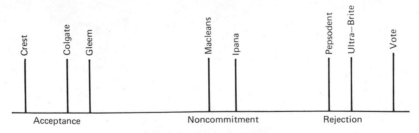

Figure 5-8 One Toothpaste Buyer's Attitude Structure.
Source. Adapted from Jacob Jacoby, "A Model of Multi-Brand Loyalty," *Journal of Advertising Research,* Vol. 11 (June 1971), pp. 25-31.

[41]C. W. Sherif, M. Sherif, and R. E. Nebergall, *Attitude and Attitude Change* (Philadelphia: W. B. Saunders, 1965).

[42]Kent B. Monroe, "Measuring Price Thresholds by Psychophysics and Latitudes of Acceptance," *Journal of Marketing Research,* Vol. 8 (November 1971), pp. 460-464.

[43]Charles Kiesler, Barry Collins, and Norman Miller, *Attitude Change* (New York: Wiley, 1969), p. 248.

[44]James F. Engel and M. Lawrence Light, "Role of Psychological Commitment in Consumer Behavior" in Frank M. Bass et al., eds., *Applications of the Sciences in Marketing Management* (New York: Wiley, 1968), pp. 199-202.

[45]The example is taken from Jacob Jacoby, "A Model of Multi-Brand Loyalty," *Journal of Advertising Research,* Vol. 11 (June 1971), pp. 25-31.

red brand, should emphasize the dominant attribute. Where possible, Crest should indicate how it differs from competing brands on this dimension (i.e., contains decay-preventive Fluoristan). Colgate and Gleem, the other acceptable brands, should attempt to minimize the perceived differences between their brands and the most preferred brands on this same dimension. Comparability should be stressed. Macleans and Ipana, neutral brands, could adopt similar tactics. However, their best approach would be to attempt to make some other attribute dominant, such as breath freshener or tooth whitener. This would be the only hope for the rejected brands: Pepsodent, Ultra Brite, and Vote.

Social Relations

In addition to the individual personal variables we have discussed, variables measuring consumers' interpersonal relationships have been found relevant in a wide variety of purchase decisions. Three of the more important variables are social stratification, family relationships, and opinion leadership.

Social Stratification. The primary theory of social class stratification states that members of society must be distributed in a manner that results in all the positions within society being filled and the corresponding duties being performed. The mechanism for accomplishing this is economic advantage and prestige. Differences in the demands of these various positions lead to stratification within society.

The first research in this area was done by Warner[46] and his colleagues who derived the relative social positions of members of small towns using intensive interviews. These individuals were grouped into five social classes. Four objective measures—occupation, source of income, type of housing, and location of residence—were used to determine class membership. Similar work by Hollingshead resulted in an Index of Social Position based on occupation and education.[47] The population distribution for his classes is presented in Table 5-3. Recently, more sophisticated techniques (including factor analysis) have been applied to census data to determine social class membership.[48]

Table 5-3
Hollingshead's Socioeconomic Class Structure

Class Ranking	Percentage of Population
I (Upper)	2.7
II	9.8
III	18.9
IV	48.4
V (Lower)	20.2

Source. August B. Hollingshead and Fredrick C. Redlich, *A Community Study* (New York: Wiley, 1958), p. 395.

[46]W. Lloyd Warner, *Social Class in America* (New York: Harper & Row, 1949).

[47]Jerome K. Myers and Lee L. Bean, *A Decade Later: A Follow-up of Social Class and Mental Illness* (New York: Wiley, 1968), pp. 235-237.

[48]James M. Carman, *The Application of Social Class in Market Segmentation* (Berkeley: University of California, The Institute of Business and Economic Research, Research Program in Marketing, 1965).

Within each social class some families are overprivileged relative to others in their class. That is, their incomes are above the group median.[49] Thus, they can meet the basic norms of their group and still have discretionary income. The overprivileged segment may be the largest market for quality products and brands. A study of the automobile market found that, for each social class, the overprivileged segment bought more medium-sized and large cars and fewer foreign economy cars. Futhermore, the purchase behavior of relatively prosperous, blue-collar workers was found to be more like the behavior of affluent, white-collar and professional workers than that of less propserous, blue-collar workers.[50]

Social class concepts have also been applied to understanding commercial bank credit card usage. Members of lower classes tend to use their credit cards for installment financing and less for convenience than do those in upper classes. Futhermore, differences in opinion about what is acceptable to charge exist between groups. Those in the upper classes are more likely to charge items such as gasoline, restaurant expenses, and entertainment while those in lower classes are more likely to purchase consumer durables such as furniture and appliances on credit.[51]

Family Influence. The role and influence of family members in consumption decision making will vary depending on the product and family characteristics. The purchasing behavior of a family also changes as it progresses through its life cycle. Six major stages of life cycle are (1) young single people, (2) young married couples with no children, (3) young married couples with dependent children, (4) older married couples with dependent children, (5) older married couples with no dependent children, and (6) older single people.[52] The distinctive characteristics of the family at each stage are given in Table 5-4.

Joint decision making by the husband and wife tends to decline over the family life cycle as each of the partners becomes more aware of what the other considers acceptable. Usually, one partner will be responsible for decisions concerning a given product class. For example, the husband may make decisions on what brand of car to purchase while the wife may select the wallpaper patterns. This division of responsibility is based on relative expertise. Joint decision making is more important where large expenditures are involved.[53]

Influence of Opinion Leaders and Innovators

Personal influence can be defined as a change in an individual's attitude or behavior as a result of interpersonal communication.[55] The buyer can receive a communication about a product either gratuitously or as a result of information seeking. Furthermore, the buyer can influence others while being influenced himself.

Buyers who exert the most influence are called opinion leaders or influentials. The

[49]Richard P. Coleman, "The Significance of Social Stratification in Selling" in Martin L. Bell, eds., *Proceedings* (Chicago: American Marketing Association, December 1960), pp. 171-184.

[50]William H. Peters, "Relative Occupation Class Income: A Significant Variable in the Marketing of Automobiles," *Journal of Marketing,* Vol. 74 (April 1970), pp. 74-77.

[51]H. Lee Mathews and John W. Slocum, "Social Class and Commercial Bank Credit Card Usage," *Journal of Marketing,* Vol. 33 (January 1969), pp. 71-79.

[52]William Wells and George Gubar, "Life Cycle Concept in Marketing Research," *Journal of Marketing Research,* Vol. 3 (November 1966), pp. 355-363.

[53]Donald Granbois, "The Role of Communication in the Family Decision-Making Process" in Stephen A. Greyser eds., *Proceedings* (Chicago: American Marketing Association, December 1963), pp. 44-57.

[54]Harry L. Davis, "Dimensions of Marital Roles in Consumer Decision Making," *Journal of Marketing Research,* Vol. 7 (May 1970), pp. 168-177.

[55]This section is based on Thomas S. Robertson, *Innovative Behavior and Communication* (New York: Holt, Rinehart, and Winston, 1971) and Everett M. Rogers, *Diffusion of Innovations* (New York: The Free Press, 1962).

Table 5-4
An Overview of the Life Cycle

Bachelor Stage; Young Single People Not Living at Home	Newly Married Couples; Young; No Children	Full Nest I; Youngest Child Under Six	Full Nest II; Youngest Child Six or Over	Full Nest III; Older Married Couples with Dependent Children	Empty Nest I; Older Married Couples; No Children Living with Them; Head in Labor Force	Empty Nest II; Older Married Couples; No children at Home; Head Retired	Solitary Survivor; in Labor Force	Solitary Survivor; Retired
Few financial burdens Fashion opinion leaders Recreation oriented Buy: basic kitchen equipment basic furniture, cars, equipment for the mating game, vacations	Better off financially than they will be in near future Highest purchase rate and highest average purchase of durables Buy: cars, refrigerators, stoves, sensible furniture, vacations	Home purchasing peak Liquid assets low Dissatisfied with financial position and amount of money saved Interested in new products Like advertised products Buy: washers, dryers, TV, baby food, chest rubs and cough medicine vitamins, dolls, wagons, sleds, skates	Financial position better Some wives work Less influenced by advertising Buy larger-sized packages, multiple-unit deals Buy: many foods, cleaning materials, music lessons, pianos	Financial position still better More wives work Some children get jobs Hard to influence with advertising High average purchase of durables Buy: new, more tasteful furniture, auto travel, non-necessary appliances, boats, dental services, magazines	Home ownership at peak Most satisfied with financial position and money saved Interested in travel, recreation, self-education Make gifts and contributions Not interested in new products Buy: vacations luxuries, home improvements	Drastic cut in income Keep home Buy: Medical appliances, medical care, products that aid health, sleep, and digestion	Income still good but likely to sell home	Some medical and product needs as other retired group; drastic cut in income Special need for attention, affection, and security

Source. William Wells and George Gubar, "Life Cycle Concept in Marketing Research," *Journal of Marketing Research*, Vol. 3 (November 1966), p. 362.

term opinion leader should be used carefully since it is often interpreted as meaning that influence trickles down from members of upper social classes to members of lower social classes. Empirical evidence, however, suggests that influence more often occurs horizontally within strata.[56] Influentials tend to be more gregarious than their peers. They possess more knowledge in their area of influence. Often this knowledge has been obtained through greater exposure to relevant mass media.

According to the two-step flow of communication, the firm directs its advertising to the influentials in its product category and these people influence their followers by means of word-of-mouth communication. These influentials do not simply transmit the advertising message, but add their own evaluation of it. The influentials also tend to receive more word-of-mouth communications; perhaps implying a multistep flow. Marketing managers must identify influentials and determine how to encourage them to transmit a favorable evaluation of their product.[57]

Rather than trying to identify influentials, the manager might attempt to create them.[58] The manager could select individuals who possess a high degree of mobility, status, and confidence and then employ tactics that reinforce these attributes. For example, a record company was able to place some of its rock-and-roll songs on the top-ten charts without any promotion using this approach. The company recruited social leaders from high schools in different areas. These leaders were identified by school administrators. These students participated in a panel that evaluated records. The introductory letter stressed that they as leaders should be better able to recognize potential rock-and-roll hits. Participants were given supplementary information about each song and singer. They were told that the average level of expertise for this product class was low, thus suggesting that their own expertise was relatively high. The firm sought individuals who met basic prerequisites for being influentials in the product class. Then, it endeavored to enhance the appropriate characteristics of these individuals.

The amount of word-of-mouth communication varies according to adopter categories. The purchaser of a product can be classified into one of five groups on the basis of the time of his adoption relative to that other buyers, as shown in Figure 5-9.[59] The five categories are: innovators, early adopters, early majority, late majority, and laggards. A summary of some representative features of the membership of each group is given in Table 5-5. Individuals who buy later are more likely than earlier buyers to receive word-of-mouth communications.

The innovators are important in new product introductions because they affect later adopters and retail availability. However, innovators are usually not influentials. They are too innovative, or different, to be credible. They do help create awareness of a new product and perform a product testing function which is observed by the influentials.

[56]Charles W. King, "Fashion Adoption: A Rebuttal to the 'Trickle Down' Theory" in Stephen A. Greyser, eds., *Proceedings* (Chicago: American Marketing Association, 1963), pp. 108-125.

[57]Elihu Katz, "The Two-Step Flow of Communication," *Public Opinion Quarterly,* Vol. 21 (Spring 1957), pp. 61-78 and Johan Arndt, "Testing the 'Two Step Flow of Communication' Hypothesis" in Johan Arndt, eds., *Insights in Consumer Behavior* (Boston: Allyn and Bacon, 1968), pp. 189-202. For a summary of the evidence supporting a more complex "multistep" model, see James F. Engel, David T. Kollat, and Roger D. Blackwell *Consumer Behavior,* 2nd ed. (New York: Holt, Rinehart and Winston, 1973), pp. 403-408.

[58]Joseph R. Mancuso, "Why Not Create Opinion Leaders for New Product Introductions?" *Journal of Marketing,* Vol. 33 (July 1969), pp. 20-25.

[59]The traditional bell-shaped curve does not always hold for marketing-related innovations. See Robert A. Peterson, "A Note on Optimal Adopter Category Determination," *Journal of Marketing Research,* Vol. 10 (August 1973), pp. 325-329.

Figure 5-9 Adopter Category as a Function of the Relative Time of Adoption.
Source. Everett M. Rogers, *Diffusion of Innovations* (New York: The Free Press, 1962), p. 162.

Time Pressure

The time available to a buyer to conduct a search for information on a product or service is not unlimited, as shown by the car purchase described in Figure 5-1. Incomplete information introduces uncertainty into the decision making process. Instore bargaining influences the outcome of the process as well.

The way individuals allocate their time affects purchase behavior because product usage involves an expenditure of time. The buyer's perception of the magnitude of this time often influences his choice behavior. The buyer trades money expenditures off against time expenditures. For example, the consumer pays a higher price for a convenience product than he would for its ingredients, but receives a compensating reduction in his outlay of time. Gathering information about a product, however, also requires an expenditure of time.[60]

While home appliances, prepared foods, no-iron fabrics, and other labor-saving technology have saved the homemaker both time and drudgery, these time savings have not been translated into leisure time. In part, the reason seems to be that expectations about the level of household care have risen and that the average size of the home and the number and complexity of its contents have risen. However, the most important factor is the increase in time spent shopping.[61]

The real price that a buyer pays for a product is equal to its market price plus the opportunity cost of time. Thus, the manager needs to be aware of the implications of the theory of the economics of information. Farley provides this summary:

1. The larger the quantity purchased, the more searching is expected since the total

[60]Philip B. Schary, "Consumption and the Problem of Time," *Journal of Marketing,* Vol. 35 (April 1971), pp. 50-55.

[61]John P. Robinson and Philip E. Converse, "Social Change Reflected in the Use of Time" in Angus Campbell and Philip E. Converse, eds., *The Human Meaning of Social Change* (New York: Russell Sage Foundation, 1972), pp. 74-75.

Table 5-5
Summary of Selected Characteristics of Adopter Categories

Adopter Category	Salient Values	Personal Characteristics	Communication Behavior	Social Relationships
Innovators	"Venturesome"; willing to accept risks	High education; highest social status; high upward mobility; high empathy; low dogmatism; high rationality; high achievement aspirations	Closest contact with scientific information sources; interaction with other innovators; relatively greatest use of impersonal sources	Some opinion leadership; very cosmopolite
Early adopters	"Respect"; regarded by many others in the social system as a role model	High social status; large and specialized operations	Greatest contact with local change agents	Greatest opinion leadership of any category in most social systems; very localite
Early majority	"Deliberate"; willing to consider innovations only after peers have adopted	Above average social status; average-sized operation	Considerable contact with change agents and early adopters	Some opinion leadership
Late majority	"Skeptical"; overwhelming pressure from peers needed before adoption occurs	Below average social status; small operation; little specialization; small income	Secure ideas from peers who are mainly late majority or early majority; less use of mass media	Little opinion leadership
Laggards	"Tradition"; oriented to the past	Little specialization; lowest social status; smallest operation; lowest income; oldest	Neighbors, friends, and relatives with similar values are main information source	Very little opinion leadership; semi-isolates

Source. Everett M. Rogers and F. Floyd Shoemaker, *Communication of Innovations* (New York: The Free Press, 1971), pp. 195-196 and Everett M. Rogers, *Diffusion of Innovations* (New York: The Free Press, 1962), p. 185.

expected gain is higher. Heavy buyers should tend to pay less than light buyers for a given item.

2. The higher the household's income, the more a family member values his time. Higher-income families search less and appear more brand loyal.

3. The larger the family, the greater the necessity of efficiently using a given dollar of income. Larger families search more and appear less brand loyal.[62]

Empirical evidence suggests that the theory is reasonable. One oddity was that high-income families tended to be brand *dis*loyal. Apparently the superior information processing skills of these families had not been taken into account.[63]

The outcome of any shopping trip is also affected by the store environment. Management seeks to control this environment to its own advantage. In full-service stores, salesmen must know the importance to consumers of selected product attributes and of their images of various brands. For many consumer durables, the salesmen must also understand the bargaining process. While display and layout factors are important in these stores, they become crucial in self service stores.

Retailers' and consumers' perceptions often differ. One study revealed that appliance retailers tend to understate the importance to the consumer of service, warranty, and ease of use, and to overstate the importance of extra gadgets.[64] Underestimation of these attribute strengths may result in a less effective promotional mix. Furthermore, many retailers possess misconceptions about brands carried by competitive stores. As an example, retailers felt that Sear's appliances were less trouble free than did the consumers. Retailers seem to lag consumers in updating images of particular brands.

Models of Buyer Behavior

Models can provide a broad overview of the mutal relationships among the factors influencing buyer behavior. In the piecemeal study of individual components of buyer behavior, the subtleties of complex interactions and feedbacks among variables may be missed. Unfortunately, attempts to represent buyer behavior by mathematical methods have run into measurement and estimation difficulties. Although these models are presently unable to accurately predict buyer behavior, they can be used to help explain and understand behavior.[65]

A number of large-system models of consumer buying behavior have been developed.[66] We have selected the Howard-Sheth model for discussion because it is com-

[62]John U. Farley, " 'Brand Loyalty' and the Economics of Information," *Journal of Business,* Vol. 37 (October 1964), pp. 370-381.

[63]The theory has been broadened to take into account other factors. See Louis P. Bucklin, "Consumer Search, Role Enactment, and Market Efficiency," *Journal of Busineess,* Vol. 42 (October 1969), pp. 416-438.

[64]Peter J. McClure and John K. Ryans, "Differences between Retailers' and Consumers' Perceptions," *Journal of Marketing Research,* Vol. 5 (February 1968), pp. 35-40.

[65]James R. Bettman and J. Morgan Jones, "Formal Models of Consumer Behavior: A Conceptual Overview," *Journal of Business,* Vol. 45, (October 1972), pp. 544-562.

[66]Alan Andreasen, "Attitudes and Customer Behavior: A Decision Model" in Harold H. Kassarjian and Thomas S. Robertson, eds., *Perspectives in Consumer Behavior* (Glenview, Ill.: Scott, Foresman, 1968), pp. 498-510; James Engel and Lawrence Light, "The Role of Psychological Commitment in Consumer Behavior: An Evaluation of the Theory of Cognitive Dissonance" in Frank M. Bass, Charles W. King, and Edgar Pessemier, eds., *Applications of the Sciences in Marketing Management* (New York: Wiley, 1968), pp. 179-206; Flemming Hanson, *Consumer Choice Behavior* (New York: The Free Press, 1972); John A. Howard and Jagdish N. Sheth, *The Theory of Buyer Behavior* (New York: Wiley, 1969); Francesco Nicosia, *Consumer Decision Processes* (Englewood Cliffs, Prentice-Hall, 1966).

prehensive and well known. Some models that have been specifically developed to represent industrial buying behavior will be reviewed later in the chapter.[67]

Howard-Sheth Consumer Model. The Howard-Sheth theory of buyer behavior (Figure 5-10) contains four basic elements: (1) inputs, (2) internal processes, (3) outputs, and (4) exogenous influences. Inputs to the model include both stimulation from marketing sources (i.e., advertising) and the social environment (i.e., reference groups). Much of the input information is concerned with the price, quality, availability, and service offered by various brands. The primary output of the model is the purchase decision. Note that a dotted line goes back into the central box from purchase (Figure 5-10) to provide feedback on performance for subsequent decisions.

The internal processes of the buyer are classified in the Howard-Sheth model as either perceptual or learning. The perceptual process deals with information processing and learning deals with concept formation. Perceptual factors include overt search, stimulus ambiguity, attention, and perceptual bias. *Overt search* refers to the intensity of the buyer's quest for information when he is uncertain about alternative brands. *Stimulus amibiguity* means that known information is ignored and new relevant data are passed along to other stages of the model. *Attention* is concerned with the consumer's intake of information and serves as a gate keeper on the amount of data absorbed. *Perceptual bias* deals with the buyer's selective attention to data and his distortion of information to make it fit his own frame of reference.

The learning constructs of the model include motives, brand comprehension, choice criteria, attitude, confidence, intention to buy, and satisfaction with the product. *Motives* are forces that activate goal directed behavior on the part of customers. A useful classification of physiological and other motives was described earlier in Figure 5-3. *Brand comprehension* is concerned with the buyer's knowledge about brands and their characteristics. *Choice criteria* are the factors used by consumers to select brands for purchase. These tend to change with experience and the acquisition of data. The *attitude* variable refers to the brand preferences of the buyer. *Intention to buy* is simply an estimate of the time and place of purchase. *Confidence* is a summary factor that describes the buyer's conviction about brands. *Satisfaction* combines the buyer's expectations with product experience obtained after purchase.

The consumer decision process in the Howard-Sheth model starts with inputs of information that are filtered by the attention and perceptual bias factors. The remaining data then move on to influence motives, choice criteria, and brand comprehension. Attitudes toward brands are modified by several variables and this affects intentions to buy. Confidence supports the intentions factor and helps influence information gathering for subsequent purchases. The most important output is the purchase decision and its subsequent effect on satisfactions.

Exogenous influences (shown at bottom of Figures 5-10) are not part of the decision-making process, but are taken into account in the decision. These external influences include the importance of the purchase, culture, social class, personality traits, social and organizational setting, time pressure, and financial status. They often provide bases for market segmentation.

An important part of the Howard-Sheth model is the concept that the buyer strives to simplify his buying environment. The model suggests that decision making for a product class evolves from *extensive problem solving* to *limited problem solving* to *routinized*

---

[67]Frederick E. Webster and Yoram Wind, "A General Model for Understanding Organizational Buying Behavior," *Journal of Marketing,* Vol. 36 (April 1972), pp. 12-19; Jagdish N. Sheth, "A Model of Industrial Buyer Behavior," *Journal of Marketing,* Vol. 37 (October 1973), pp. 50-56.

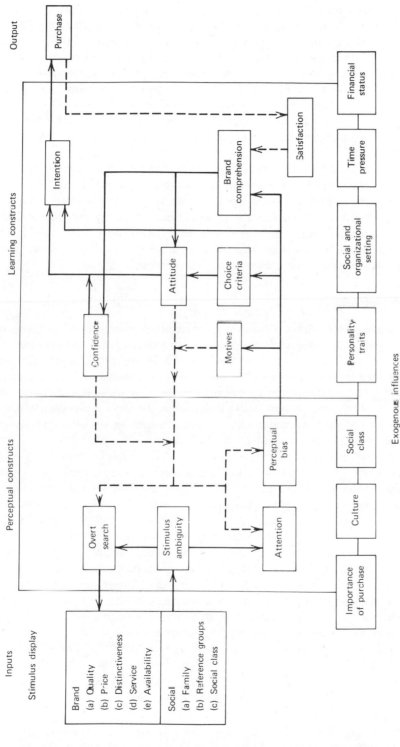

Figure 5-10 Howard-Sheth Model of Consumer Buyer.
Source. Adapted from John A. Howard and Jagdish N. Sheth, *The Theory of Buyer Behavior* (New York: Wiley, 1969), p. 30.

response behavior. In extensive problem solving, the choice criteria are not well developed and the buyer has no strong feelings toward any brands. This means the buyer has to gather a great deal of data before a decision can be made. Although the choice criteria are structured in limited problem solving, no one brand emerges predominant. Finally, with routine response behavior the buyer has a strong predisposition toward one brand. In this case, the consumer buys the same brand again and again without gathering additional data. The farther along that the buyer is in this simplification process, the less receptive he will be to environmental stimuli such as advertising. New products will not be successful when the buyer uses routinized response behavior unless they possess significant new attributes. These new attributes cause the choice criteria to be reconsidered.

A version of the Howard-Sheth model has been formulated as a system of equations using test market data for a new branded product sold in supermarkets.[68] When the test started, only one other brand was in the same product class. Unfortunately, the fit of the Howard-Sheth model to the test data was poor. These results may have occurred because the linkages among the variables in the model were not precisely defined and there is no way to select stimuli to produce desired results. Despite these limitations, the model is a useful guide to help explain consumer buying decisions.

Industrial Buying Models

Industrial marketers (firms whose customers are other business firms or organizations) attempt to sell goods and services by developing awareness of their product offerings and building favorable attitudes at key points in the buying organization. Competitive advantages are gained by offering a combination of quality, service, and price that provides the best solution to the customer's problems. Success in industrial marketing often depends on how well the seller understands the buying process including the indentification of the buying authority, the establishment of decision criteria, and the procedures for evaluation and selection of suppliers.

The industrial buying process tends to be much more complex than purchase decisions made by individual consumers. With industrial products there are usually a number of persons within the firm that participate in the buying decision. Often the buyer is not the user of the product and final buying authority frequently rests with another executive who relies on the advice of engineers and other experts. The technical nature of most industrial products also adds to the complexity because a great deal of factual information must be reviewed within the firm and agreements reached on precise product specifications. Normally this technical evaluation and coordination of interested parties requires considerable time and as a result industrial buying takes longer than consumer purchase decisions. A more serious problem is that industrial buying procedures vary widely across firms and even within companies so industrial suppliers must tailor their sales presentations to the needs of particular buying situations.

A flow diagram showing how one firm purchased a test stand for automobile engines is shown in Figure 5-11. In this case the need for the product came from a request from an affiliated company. The next step in the process was the assignment of buying responsibility to the group head of the mechanical division and his technical buyer. Once the

[68]John U. Farley and L. Winston Ring, "An Empirical Test of the Howard-Sheth Model of Buyer Behavior," *Journal of Marketing Research,* Vol. 7 (November 1970), pp. 427-438. Additional tests of the model appear in John U. Farley, John A. Howard and L. Winston Ring, *Consumer Behavior: Theory and Application* (Boston: Allyn and Bacon, 1974).

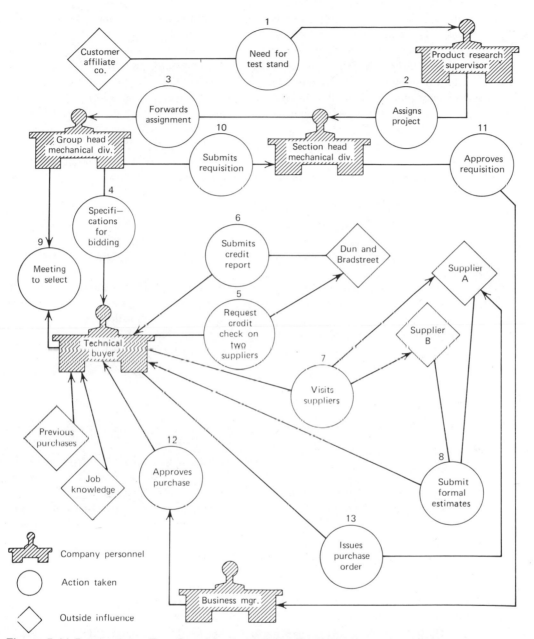

Figure 5-11 Purchasing a Test Stand for Automotive Engines.
Source. Murray Harding, "Who Really Makes the Purchasing Decision?" *Industrial Marketing,* Vol. 51 (September 1966), p. 77. Copyright © 1966 by Advertising Publications Inc., Chicago, Ill.

buyer received the specifications for the test stand, he began to gather data on possible suppliers. The buyer was very thorough and actually visited two potential suppliers and obtained credit checks on them. A more typical sequence would have the supplier salesmen visit the buyer. After bids had been received from two potential suppliers, the buyer met with the group head of the mechanical division to decide on awarding the contract. The process did not end here and three more approvals were needed before the purchase could be completed. Altogether five executives of the company were involved in buying the test stand and the buying process went through a total of twelve steps.

A generalized model of the industrial buying process developed by Sheth is described in Figure 5-12. The Sheth theory begins by representing participants (i.e., buyers, engineers, users) by a model of individual behavior similar to the original Howard-Sheth consumer model (Figure 5-10). The actions of the buyers are thus influenced by their education, life-style, role orientation, and satisfaction with previous purchases. In the industrial model information sources tend to be more specific and include salesmen, catalogues, trade shows, journal advertising, and direct mail. The next stage in the model involves the identification of the conditions that cause joint decisions among the participants. These include product related factors such as delivery requirements and company variables such as organization size and degree of centralization. The focus of the model is on the process of joint decision making: assimilation of information, deliberation, and conflict resolution. Up to this point, the model assumes that the choice of a supplier is the result of a rational and systematic decision making process. Sometimes, however, industrial purchase decisions are determined by external situational factors such as strikes, price controls, recession, mergers, or foreign trade.

The primary motive for building models of consumer and industrial buying behavior is to gain a better understanding of the decision process. Managers who know what is going on are in a better position to supply the right kind of information to the right persons at the appropriate time. Models are not a "cure all," but they can help direct marketing activities to better serve consumer and industrial buyers.

Summary

The marketing manager must understand buyer behavior in order to recognize new product opportunities, to identify meaningful bases for market segmentation, and to improve existing marketing activities. Two internal processes of the buyer are important. The perceptual process deals with information processing and the learning process with concept formation. Attitude formation and change is part of the latter process. External influences such as the organizational and social setting are also important. The manager needs to know how the firm's marketing stimuli, in the presence of other external influences, interact with the internal processes. This knowledge permits the manager to assess the probability that the buyer will purchase the firm's product.

Questions

1. Under what circumstances can fear appeals be used? Is it ethical to use such appeals?
2. Compare and contrast the major theories of attitude change. What factors govern the marketer's choice of an appropriate attitude change theory?
3. Extend the adequacy-importance model given in equation (1) to include uncertainty. Show how you would collect the necessary data.
4. Describe the family life-cycle and its influence on consumption patterns and consumer decision processes.
5. When should a firm introducing a new product attempt to identify innovators and influentials for the product category? How can the firm use this knowledge about their identities?

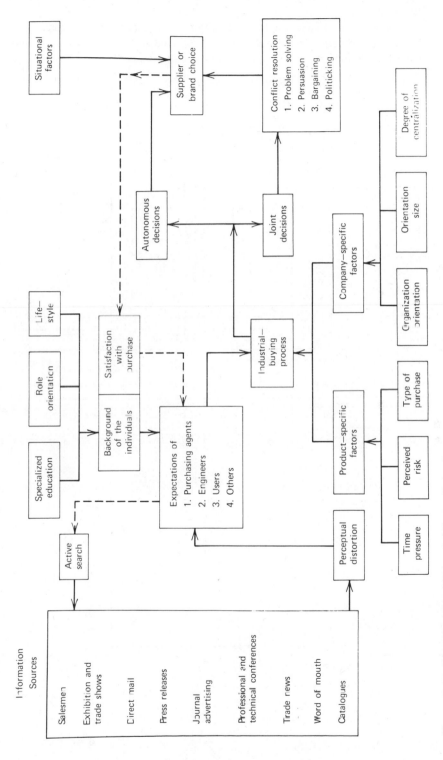

Figure 5-12 Sheth Model of Industrial Buyer Behavior.
Source. Reprinted from Jagdish N. Sheth, "A Model of Industrial Buyer Behavior," *Journal of Marketing,* Vol. 37 (October 1973), pp. 50-56. Published by the American Marketing Association.

6. Recall the most recent purchase that you have made. Construct a flow chart of your decision process.

7. Perkins Engine's analysis of the diesel-engine market is diagrammed in Figure 5-13. Is this representation of the market sensible? What additional information would be useful in developing a marketing communications plan?

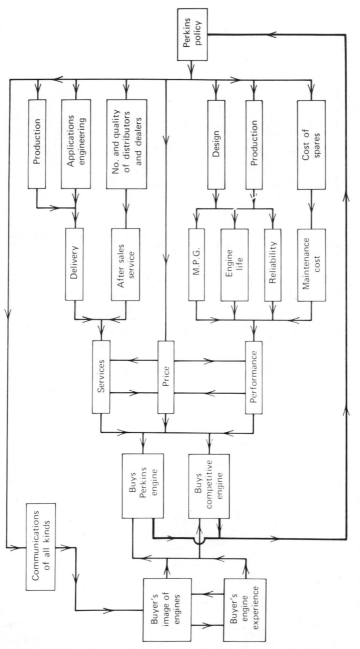

Figure 5-13 The Diesel Engine Market.

Case 5-1
Bank of Minneapolis and Trust Company[1]

A group of business and professional men were gathering some information to support a proposal to start a new bank in downtown Minneapolis. Most existing banks in the general area were large national banks and were well established. The proposed operation was to be an independent state bank located at 922 Nicollet Avenue.

The statute governing the conditions for the issuance of bank charters in Minnesota provides five criteria that, if satisfied, require the state to grant a charter. These are as follows:

"If the applicants are of good moral character and financial integrity,

"If there is a reasonable public demand for this bank in this location,

"If the organization expenses being paid by the subscribing shareholders do not exceed the neces sary legal expenses incurred in drawing incorporation papers and the publication and the recording thereof, as required by law,

"If the probable volume of business in this location is sufficient to insure and maintain the solvency of the new bank and the solvency of the then existing bank or banks in the locality without endangering the safety of any bank in the locality as a place of deposit of public and private money, and

"If the Department of Commerce is satisfied that the proposed bank will be properly and safely managed."

PROPOSED MANAGEMENT

The primary ingredient of a successful bank is sound business judgment on the part of the board of directors and the operating officers. The group that combined to form the staff and board of directors of the proposed bank represented a cross section of business and professional men. In addition, the personal financial statements filed by these men disclosed individual net worths that indicated financial integrity. Thomas Scallen, the proposed president of the bank, has had formal banking education and experience in the management and operation of two independent banks. He suggested that the new

[1]This case was prepared by Charles C. Nicholson for Professor Robert L. Johnson of the University of South Dakota School of Business. Reproduced by permission.

bank's stock be shared with the public so that a broad ownership among the people in the area be obtained.

PROPOSED LOCATION

The group that wanted to start the new bank at 922 Nicollet Avenue believed the area in downtown Minneapolis was presently without a convenient, pleasant, readily available all-service bank. The area to be served had an estimated population of 50,000 spread over forty square blocks. It was thought to be the fashion center of the upper midwest retail clothing trade. The specific location of the proposed bank was in the Nicollet Arcade Building facing Nicollet Avenue at the southern end of the 900 block. The rear of the facility opened into a parking lot that offered ample parking at least for the near future. The center of Minneapolis is the Nicollet Avenue shopping area, running from 4th to 12th Street, and bounded at the north end by the Gateway redevelopment and at the south end by the convention hotel complex and parking centers around the interstate freeway's major downtown outlet. It was in the center of this southern end that the proposed bank was to be located, the only bank on Nicollet Avenue. There were seven banks in the general area and two were located approximately four blocks from the proposed location on Nicollet Avenue.

POPULATION AND ECONOMIC FACTORS

The metropolitan area of Minneapolis-St. Paul ranked third in growth among large cities in America. On the other hand, the population of the City of Minneapolis had decreased and it was thought that the greatest decreases had been in the residential areas near the so-called "core area" or that area to be served by the proposed bank. The population of the City of Minneapolis had decreased from 482,872 in 1960 to 434,000 in 1970.

In addition to the decrease of the residential population in the area to be served by the bank there was disagreement as to the economic condition of the neighborhood. Some people that were questioned had stated that the southern Nicollet area where the proposed bank was to be located had deteriorated in recent years. The retail sales in the City of Minneapolis had also declined and this was attributed to the growth of the suburban areas. Approximately forty industrial concerns had moved out of the heart of the city and had relocated in the suburbs since 1947.

The men organizing the proposed bank felt that these factors were somewhat irrelevant and misleading. They thought that the area held a great potential for a new bank. There were a multitude of privately owned independent businesses that flourished in the area. The area, even though well established, had recently undergone an expansion with the introduction of new businesses and the remodeling and expansion of old businesses. In particular, the Mar-Ten Parking Ramp at 10th and Marquette handled approximately 1500 vehicles a day and had ten new businesses on its main floor. The Eberhardt Company had recently built a new building between 10th and 11th on Marquette. There were also three buildings primarily devoted to medical and dental services near the location of the proposed bank. There were over 450 doctors and dentists located in the buildings. These professional people were independent businessmen, each having their own separate business and private banking needs.

The potential for the new bank would be enhanced by numerous projects which were contemplated or near reality. The highlight of the proposed projects in the area was the pedestrian mall that was to be built on Nicollet Avenue and would be directly in front of the proposed bank location. The group of men starting the proposed bank had to constantly remind themselves that the Minnesota statutes do not speak in the future tense. There must be a present public demand and a present probable volume of business sufficient to insure and maintain the solvency of the new bank.

DEMAND

In an attempt to measure the probable demand for a bank at the proposed location, an independent research firm was retained to conduct a survey on attitudes toward banking on south Nicollet Avenue. The results of the survey are shown in Exhibit 1. In addition to the survey, a pedestrian traffic count was made of traffic flowing by the front entrance of the proposed bank. This traffic came from existing auditorium facilities, the hotels and motels in the area and the surrounding parking facilities. The count showed that approximately 9000 people per day pass the front door of the proposed bank.

An inquiry was made also on certain trends with other banks in the downtown Minneapolis area. It was found that the total deposits of downtown banks had increased substantially over the past ten years but that the number of demand deposit accounts and the demand deposit balances had decreased. Most of the increase in total deposits was accounted for by the increase in corporate time money from large national corporations.

FINANCIAL CONSIDERATIONS

The group of men that were proposing the new bank on Nicollet Avenue had over 200 separate inquiries concerning the purchase of stock in the proposed bank. This amount of interest seemed ample proof that the public and businessmen in the area were convinced of the bank's prospects of success.

The estimated expenses for the first two years of operation were determined to be:

	First Year	Second Year
Interest on time and savings deposits	$ 9,000	$ 20,000
Salaries, wages and fees	45,000	60,000
All other expenses	53,000	60,000
	$107,000	$140,000

The estimated deposits for the first three years of operation were as follows: (assuming F.D.I.C. deposit insurance)

After six months of operation	$ 700,000
After one year of operation	1,530,000
After two years of operation	3,495,000
After three years of operation	5,425,000

The organization expenses could be paid by the subscribing shareholders and would not exceed the necessary legal expenses incurred in drawing corporation papers and the publication of recording thereof as required by law.

The terms of the lease agreement for the property to be occupied by the bank required the occupants to make all leasehold improvements. Moreover, a lease could not be arranged for any longer than seven years and no renewal option could be obtained. The proposed lease required rent of $1500 per month and the estimated cost of necessary furniture and equipment was $30,000.

QUESTIONS

1. What do you think of the sampling procedures

and questionnaires used to gather data for the proposed bank?

2. Do the data collected indicate a bank is needed on Nicollet Avenue?

3. Should the board of directors proceed with their plan to establish a new bank? If so, how should they market their services to potential customers?

Exhibit 1
Attitudes Toward Banking on Southern Nicollet Avenue

Part I. The first part of the survey consists of "street corner" interviews with 600 women who were shopping on south Nicollet Avenue. The interviews were conducted at the eight corner locations at 9th and 10th streets and Nicollet Avenue.

A. For what purpose do you usually come to downtown Minneapolis?

Purpose	Percentage Distribution
Shopping	55.9
Work	29.0
Doctor	12.5
Meals	33.4
School	3.2
Beauty shop	2.9
Banking	2.3
Pay bills	2.3
Movies	1.9
Library	1.1
All others	4.6
	119.1%[a]

Base for percentages—(617)

B. Which of these do you conduct with financial institutions in downtown Minneapolis?

Service	Percentage Distribution
Savings account	57.2
Checking account	41.2
Safety deposit box	13.1
Home loan or mortgage	11.2
Personal loan	5.0
None conducted downtown	26.5
	154.2%[a]

C. Which of these do you conduct at financial institutions *not* in downtown Minneapolis (elsewhere)?

Service	Percentage Distribution
Savings account	23.3
Checking account	34.9
Safety deposit box	9.6
Home loan or mortgage	6.6
Personal loan	3.0
None conducted elsewhere	59.2
Base for percentage—(502)	136.6%[a]

[a]Multiple response

D. Would you say that the place where you now conduct your banking business is _____ to the other activities you usually include in your trip downtown?

Very convenient	63.1
Somewhat convenient	10.1
Neither convenient nor inconvenient	2.0
Somewhat inconvenient	2.7
Very inconveneint	0.8
None—banking only	17.1
Banking done by mail	3.5
No answer	0.7
	100.0%

Base for percentage—369 respondents who indicated they do some banking at a downtown financial institution.

E. If a new bank were to be located on Nicollet Avenue between 9th and 10th streets, would it be _____ ?

	Total	Downtown Only	Elsewhere Only	Downtown and Elsewhere	Does no Banking
Very convenient	24.6	29.0	16.6	33.3	17.4
Somewhat convenient	17.4	18.9	12.8	16.7	19.1
Neither conv. nor inconv.	31.9	32.0	27.8	29.2	38.3
Somewhat inconvenient	11.4	12.1	15.0	8.3	7.0
Very inconvenient	14.4	8.0	27.8	12.5	16.5
Don't know	0.3	—	—	—	1.7
	100.0%	100.0%	100.0%	100.0%	100.0%
Base for percentage	(617)	(297)	(133)	(72)	(115)

F. If this new bank were open in this area, how likely is it that you would open an account or do business there?

Definitely would	6.8
Probably would	21.6
May or may not	19.0
Probably would not	28.8
Definitely would not	23.3
Don't Know	0.2
No Answer	0.3
	100.0%

Base for Percentage—(617)

Part II. The second part of the survey consisted of 200 "street corner" interviews with women shoppers at the same eight corners that were used for the first part of the survey. The object was to determine the attitudes toward two proposed names for the bank.

Here are two names that have been proposed for a new bank, which one do you prefer?

	Number	Percent
Bank of Minneapolis and Trust Co.	101	50.5
Bank of Nicollet Ave. and Trust Co.	61	30.5
No Opinion	38	19.0
	200	100.0

Part III. The third section of the survey consisted of a personal interview survey with 50 doctors and dentists plus 50 businessmen.

A. In your opinion, are the banking survices in this area _____ ?

	Doctors and Dentists	Businessmen	Total
Very Good	62	50	56
Good	36	42	39
Fair	—	4	2
Poor	—	2	1
Very Poor	—	2	1
Don't Know	2	—	1
	100%	100%	100%

B. Are there any banking or financial services that your business uses that you feel are *not adequately* handled now?

	Doctors and Dentists	Businessmen	Total
No	94	90	92
Yes	6	10	8
	100%	100%	100%

C. What are they?

	Doctors and Dentists	Businessmen	Total
Loans, too small, too much security	2	2	2
Charge exchange on out-of-town checks	2	—	1
Trust department	2	—	1
Make greater effort to collect	—	2	1
Exhorbitant charges	—	2	1
Foreign exchange charges too high	—	2	1
Prefer not to specify	—	2	1
	6%	10%	8%

D. Some businesses conduct all of their banking at one financial institution while others use several financial institutions. How many do you use in your business?

	Doctors and Dentists	Businessmen	Total
1	70	72	71
2	16	18	17
3	10	4	7
4	—	4	2
5	2	2	4
Not answered	2	—	1
	100%	100%	100%

E. Thinking back to the time your business banking was first conducted at _____, how was it that it was started there rather than at some other bank?

	Doctors and Dentists	Businessmen	Total
Convenience of location	28	38	33
Personal contact	24	10	17
Family/relatives	12	4	8
Favorable loan experience	2	8	5
Reputation of bank	6	2	4
Bank used by business before	4	4	4
To keep business and personal accounts at different banks	6	2	4
Interest rates good	4	2	3
Convenience of branch	2	4	3
Had other account there	2	4	3
All others (2% or less each)	12	16	14
Don't know, no answer	26	26	26
	128%[a]	120%[a]	124%[a]

[a]Some named more than one reason, or had more than one account.

F. Which category best describes the convenience of _____ for your present business banking?[a]

	Doctors and Dentists	Businessmen	Total
Very convenient	76.4	57.5	66.9
Somewhat convenient	11.2	21.9	16.6
Neither conv. nor inconv.	5.5	8.2	6.9
Somewhat inconvenient	5.5	8.2	6.9
Very inconvenient	—	4.2	2.0
Not answered	1.4	—	0.7
	100.0%[a]	100.0%[a]	100.0%[a]

[a] Combined ratings of convenience for all banks used.

G. If a new bank were to be located on Nicollet Avenue between 9th and 10th Streets, which category describes the convenience of that location for your business banking?

	Doctors and Dentists	Businessmen	Total
Very convenient	88	48	68
Somewhat convenient	6	26	16
Neither conv. nor inconv.	6	16	11
Somewhat inconvenient	—	6	3
Very inconvenient	—	4	2
	100%	100%	100%

H. Would you consider doing business banking at a bank on Nicollet Avenue between 9th and 10th Streets?

	Doctors and Dentists	Businessmen	Total
No	60	58	59
Yes	34	30	32
Yes, if branch of present bank	—	4	2
Yes, if company decided	—	2	1
Don't know	6	6	6
	100%	100%	100%

I. Would the business banking you would consider doing at this new bank be transferred from a bank you are using, or would this be an additional account?

	Doctors and Dentists	Businessmen	Total
Transferred account	20	26	23
Additional account	14	6	10
Don't know	—	4	2
	34%	36%	35%

J. Would you consider doing personal banking at a bank on Nicollet Avenue between 9th and 10th Streets?

	Doctors and Dentists	Businessmen	Total
No	70	52	61
Yes	28	46	37
Don't know	2	2	2
	100%	100%	100%

K. What type of business should I classify this as?

	Doctors and Dentists	Businessmen	Total
Retail	—	34	17
Wholesale	—	18	9
Manufacturer	—	6	3
Services	—	34	17
Insurance	—	8	4
Physician	70	—	35
Dentist	30	—	15
	100%	100%	100%

Case 5-2
Blitz-Weinhard[1]

In the middle of 1964, Mr. William Floyd, who had been appointed Director of Market Planning for Blitz-Weinhard in March, was concerned about the future of Blitz Beer in the Chico-Redding area of Northern California. The company had begun marketing operations in the Chico-Redding-Mt. Shasta market late in 1960, using a marketing mix almost identical to the one that was proving so successful in Oregon.[2]

In reviewing the decision to enter this market, it appeared to Mr. Floyd that the company had done little market research before entry into the five-county area in Northern California. Within a month of the decision to market Blitz Beer in that area, distributors had been appointed in Chico, Redding, and Mt. Shasta, and the Southern Oregon sales ter-

[1]Reprinted from *Stanford Business Cases 1967,* Volume II, with the permission of the publishers, Stanford University Graduate School of Business © 1967 by the Board of Trustees of the Leland Stanford Junior University.

[2]See map of Northern California market in Exhibit 1 and selected area statistics in Exhibit 2.

Exhibit 1
Blitz Northern California Market

ritories had been revised so that the company could appoint a full-time saleman to cover the new market.

In the last three months of 1960, the company spent $17,000 in the new market on advertising and promotion in support of the newly introduced Blitz Beer. No new advertising copy was designed, however, and essentially the same commercials and point-of-purchase displays were used as those being used in Oregon.

Mr. Floyd understood that the primary factors that in 1960 led the company to "import" its Oregon marketing strategy into California were first, the proximity of the proposed market to Oregon and second, the proven success of the "mix" in Oregon. The first point was significant because the company had been advertising on television and radio stations in Klamath Falls, Medford, and Grants Pass in Oregon for several years. The major stations in all three cities could be received in parts of Northern California, and the company had felt that it would be inappropriate to use two sets of copy in overlapping markets.

It seemed to Mr. Floyd that one of the mistakes the company had made was to equate geographic boundaries with marketing boundaries. He commented, "If they (the company) were advertising over the border and creating demand in California, why weren't they selling there too?" He believed that, in fact, the company might easily have created some adverse feeling in the fringe markets (where Blitz beer was advertised but not available), which would be difficult to overcome.

In the first week of April, 1964, some three weeks after his appointment ot the position of Director of Marketing Planning, Mr. Floyd sent the following information in a memorandum to Mr. Wessinger, President of Blitz-Weinhard:

Chico-Redding (California)—New Market

"Market Size: The Chico-Redding market encompasses Shasta, Tehama, Glenn, Butte, and half of Trinity counties. There are approximately 700 licensed beer accounts in this area; the 215,000 people residing here provide an annual beer potential of 108,000 barrels.

"History: During the past four years, our brewery has attempted to establish Blitz-Weinhard Beer in this market. Approximately $148,000 of advertising and sales support have been spent; our current market share is 0.7 percent. At present, we hold 95 percent off-premise distribution and 20 percent on-premise distribution.

"No real concentrated marketing effort was made to expand sales until April 1962; results were favorable through June. Then sales slipped, and have never reached their 1962 level. There seems to be a direct relationship between per

capita advertising expenditures and sales. (See Exhibit 3.)

"Objective: The purpose of entering the Chico-Redding market was threefold:

1. To achieve additional sales volume and provide a stepping stone into the entire Northern California market.
2. To strengthen Blitz-Weinhard's market position in Southern Oregon.
3. To gain new market experience from which a sound marketing program could be developed for expansion into key Northwest markets.

"Selling Support: The full-time salesman working the area has performed well above average. Considerable time and effort has been spent in consumer sampling, display work, and gaining additional cooler facings. Periodically, brewery crews have been sent to augment the resident salesman's work. A brewery-subsidized driver-salesman in Redding has greatly improved service—however, his consumer/sales effectiveness is marginal.

"Advertising Support: Initially, our entrance into the market was haphazard. No unique introductory advertising was used. In April, 1960, our campaign was initiated with a high per capita expenditure. This showed good promise at first but appeared to irritate consumers within three months. The campaign used for the past nineteen months has not created high consumer demand.

"Difficulties Encountered:

1. Until January, 1963, our service to accounts was poor. We experienced frequent out-of-stocks.
2. Although no complaints have been noted, it is highly probable that old beer reached consumers. Old beer was due to inadequate service during our early stages and to absence of code dates.
3. Prior to mid-1963, we enjoyed 50 percent on-premise distribution with packaged beer and had created some on-premise demand. However, several breweries moved into the Chico-Redding area with draft beer which eliminated the majority of our on-premise business. Obviously, introducing draft beer initially would have helped establish ourselves.
4. We were the last brewery, by several months, with flip-top cans.
5. There seemed to be consumer antagonism toward our initial advertising campaign; also, there has been mild adverse reaction toward our present announcer and our lack of variety.
6. Due to slow sales, we have experienced some difficulty maintaining our present cooler space, are prevented from gaining additional cooler space, and have encountered resis-

Exhibit 2

Blitz Northern California Market

Information distributed by Mr. Floyd at the meeting that produced the second 1966 plan for the Northern California market.

I. Countries	1965 Population (Estimate)	Potential (Barrels)
Siskiyou	34,200	16,650
Trinity	9,700	4,720
Shasta (Redding)	70,000	34,100
Tehama	28,100	13,700
Glenn	18,800	9,160
Butte (Chico)	93,500	45,530
	254,300	123,860

II. Economic outlook: good—20 percent increase by 1970 (an additional 311,500 people, 148,630 barrels). Area ties in with Southern Oregon—high Oregon tourist.

III. Marginal income per barrel: assume $8.00 through 1970.

Note: The meeting had access to additional information that is given in Exhibit 4 (market shares of selected brands in the Northern California market), on page 223 of this case (the extent of Blitz distribution in Northern California).

Exhibit 3

Blitz Northern California Sales (Cases)

	Redding[a]			Chico		
Distributor	1961	1962	1963	1961	1962	1963
January	107	160	285	94	271	270
February	186	179	347	47	268	333
March	236	227	368	76	427	349
April	308	810	490	80	484	377
May	394	979	833	88	1211	681
June	695	945	879	349	1051	573
July	569	813	875	129	957	850
August	680	810	897	155	877	620
September	524	467	511	137	622	392
October	393	539	381	85	340	332
November	198	363	199	388	455	258
December	189	307	292	264	289	187
	4479	6599	6357	1892	7242	5222

	Per Capita Expenditures (Cents)					
	Redding			Chico		
	1961	1962	1963	1961	1962	1963
Advertising	9.1	21.6	10.2	8.9	20.3	9.8
Sales	5.8	6.8	19.1	5.3	5.3	5.6

[a]Tehama County switched to Chico in latter part of 1962.

tance in expanding on premise distribution.

"Favorable Factors: Presently, Blitz-Weinhard Beer has much more cooler space than sales warrant. In Redding, our cooler position and facings are exceeded by only three or four other brands. We have continually upgraded our distributors and offer excellent service.

"Our product name is known throughout the market. We have excellent trade relations, and in some cases, retailers volunteer display and POS space. We offer the consumer a twelve-ounce can at competitive prices.

"Observation:

1. Blitz-Weinhard Beer has become a factor in the Chico-Redding market: with correct pressure, our sales will increase. However, the present sales volume and growth rate precludes expansion into adjacent areas for some time to come.
2. After two years of time and effort, our service and direct sales support are efficient and exceed most brands outselling us. Our advertising, however, does not seem to create sufficient consumer demand. We have made little attempt to alter our advertising message and experiment with various media combinations.
3. We have not developed an effective marketing program in Northern California; we have little favorable experience from which a marketing program can be developed for expansion into Northwest markets.

"Recommendations:

1. Review our brand image projection. If possible, research our advertising effectiveness and devote time to developing an effective program for use here and in other new markets.
2. Direct sales effort should be directed towards specific groups—college groups, bowling teams, etc.
3. Consider taking some emphasis away from Glenn and Butte counties and directing more towards Shasta, Tahama, and Siskiyou. (See map, Exhibit 1).
4. Without revisions in our present program, initial expansion effort into new markets should be directed away from the off-premise accounts. Direct sales and personal relationships are more productive with the on-premise consumer. However, by-passing the grocery trade eliminates well over half of the potential in any new market selected.

REVISION OF THE INITIAL PROGRAM FOR THE CHICO-REDDING MARKET

After further research into the condition of Blitz beer in each of the "fringe markets," Mr. Floyd presented a series of proposals dealing with the fringe markets to the other marketing department personnel.[3] His presentation included the outline of the position of Blitz-Weinhard in the Chico-Redding market. With regard to this market, Mr. Floyd commented as follows:

"The most important immediate steps are to determine, first, the prices we should charge for our price beer, and, second, what our volume will be at these prices. This information, coupled with our Blitz-Weinhard sales trend, should allow us to establish a break-even budget for at least the remainder of 1964. I propose that our basic objectives in the Chico-Redding market should be:

1. To introduce price beer and malt liquor into Northern California in an effort to break-even.
2. To hold Chico-Redding as a test market at the least possible cost.

"To hold accomplish our objectives, we should take the following steps:

1. Determine the price beer and malt liquor potential in this market.
2. Accurately estimate our anticipated price beer and malt liquor sales volume.
3. Adjust our prices to remain competitive.
4. Prepare a minimum Blitz-Weinhard advertising holding program which would include outdoor and radio (for example, a whisper commercial). The budget for this holding program will be approximately $8500 from June 1 to December 31, 1963.[4]

"The whole emphasis, " Mr. Floyd went on, "is on holding the Chico-Redding market for the next six months, maybe longer, until we reach our break-even point on a total beer basis. At this time (June, 1964), although operations in Northern California are definitely unprofitable, we do not have either the understanding of the market or the means by which we could make it into a profitable operation in less than six months. Since we are unwilling to withdraw completely, I believe that this program represents the only reasonable course of action."

The program was accepted by Mr. Wessinger, and the advertising budget was approved. The company succeeded in persuading its distributors in Redding and Mt. Shasta to carry both Cascade and Olde English malt liquor; the Chico distributor, whose total beer sales as well as his Blitz volume had been deteriorating since June, 1963, relinquished

---

[3]Besides Northern California, the company was interested in expanding Blitz sales in Boise (Idaho); Yakima, Walla Walla, and Puget Sound (Washington).

[4]Nearly $15,000 had been spent on all forms of advertising and promotion in the first six months of 1964.

the account, and the company transferred to a second distributor in Chico who was willing to carry all three brands of the company's beer.

During this period, the company's salesman wanted to hold as many retail accounts as possible, in spite of much-reduced advertising and sales promotion allowance. The company was especially anxious to retain representation in the on-premise accounts, partly because of the small proportion of such accounts in which Blitz was represented (20-25 percent of those available) and partly because Mr. Floyd believed that the initial expansion effort should be directed towards channels in which direct sales and personal relationships were more productive.

CHANGES IN THE COMPANY, 1964-1965

It was not until May, 1965, that Mr. Floyd was able to report to Mr. Wessinger that both the market situation in Chico-Redding and the over-all ability of the company to better exploit this market had improved.

During the year that had elapsed since the inception of the "holding" operation in the Northern California market, the company had undergone several important changes in both the organization of its marketing department and in its marketing strategies. The sales manager, who now had a staff rather than a line assistant, was directly responsible for five sales area supervisors, each of whom had control over three or more field salesmen. Direction and control of the salesforce had correspondingly improved during the year: three new salesmen had been hired; an improved bonus system had been devised; and a series of sales training programs had been initiated in late 1964.

An important development during the year had been the hiring of a new advertising agency; one that, Mr. Wessinger felt, "offered more experienced account personnel and greater skills in the production of commercials at a time when we most needed a fresh approach to advertising our products." He went on: "The salesmen began selling the price beers themselves, instead of letting the distributor do the job. At the same time the distributor's task was more clearly determined, and he had more specific targets to aim for and bonuses to earn. We increased our point of sale allocation from 30¢ to 45¢ a barrel and the agency developed some bright new displays that proved very effective. Total sales were currently (June, 1965) running 12 percent higher than this time last year."

DEVELOPMENTS IN THE NORTHERN CALIFORNIA MARKET

During the year ending June, 1965, the company increased its on-premise distribution in the Chico-Redding market, but lost representation in off-premise accounts. In June, 1965, the company beers were represented in 502 off-premise outlets in Northern California (87 percent of the total available, versus 95 percent a year earlier), and 208 on-premise outlets[5] (32 percent versus 25 percent in June, 1964). The company sold Blitz draft in only 4 out of the estimated 160 draft accounts in the area in June, 1965.

Competitive positions in the market had changed during the year. Mr. Floyd believed that of the five leading brands, only Olympia had gained significantly in the market share; Coor's and Hamm's were both in approximately the same position as a year earlier, while Lucky Lager, Burgermeister, and Falstaff had declined. The brand shares of the leading beers in the Chico-Redding-Mt. Shasta market in June, 1965, were estimated as shown in Exhibit 4.

PROPOSED DEVELOPMENT OF THE CALIFORNIA MARKET

A meeting was held in July, 1965, between the marketing department personnel and agency executives at which the future development not only of the California market, but also of markets in Boise, Yakima, Walla Walla, and Spokane was discussed. Mr. Floyd prefaced the discussion in this way:

"In the event that we select a market or markets and commit a full scale marketing program including high advertising intensity and sales help, we should expect and 8-10 percent market share within three years to consider this program a success.

"Many subjective judgements must be made including distribution strength, service, additional expansion, effect in Oregon, etc. I hope you will use this information (Exhibit 2) plus your experience to aid in the formation of reasonable objectives for attainment during 1966."

It was eventually decided at the meeting that, with regard to the California market, the following objectives would be set up:

"First, to use the Northern California area (specifically, Shasta County) as a market in which to test new market expansion advertising.

[5]On-premise outlets sold packaged Blitz Beer.

Exhibit 4

Brand	Market Share Percent Packaged (est.)	Market Share Percent Draft (est.)
Olympia	23	16
Coor's	19	22
Hamm's	16	15
Lucky Lager	14	13
Burgermeister-Schlitz	11	15
Falstaff	8	5
Pabst	2	10
Price Beers	5	2
Others[a]	2	2
	100	100

[a]Blitz beer was estimated to hold less than 0.6 percent of the total market in June, 1965.

"Second, to take maximum advantage of all sales opportunities and to gain 4,000 barrels during 1966 (a 3.2 percent market share)."

The meeting defined Blitz-Weinhard's strategy, designed to accomplish these objectives, as follows:

"A full-scale advertising campaign specifically for market expansion will be directed primarily to the Redding market.

"Constant strong sales and point-of-purchase pressure will be maintained on the Redding market during the test period; at the same time, sufficient sales pressure will be maintained on adjacent California markets to ensure that all sales opportunities are exploited.

"A preliminary market plan will follow."

THE DEVELOPMENT OF A MARKET PLAN FOR 1966

It was not until late September that Mr. Floyd received word that the advertising agency had been doing some "preliminary work" on the proposed Northern California market.

In his letter to Mr. Floyd, the account executive pointed out that the two objectives of the 1966 Market Plan were incompatible. "The 4000 barrel goal," he remarked, "apparently refers to the whole of the six counties—Siskiyou, Trinity, Shasta, Tehama, Glenn, and Butte-and not just to Shasta County (Redding). I am assuming that we are talking in terms of the *six*-county area, since TV was the chosen media and this area is *one* TV market. In fact, the market should include not only the six counties above, but also Colusa, Modoc, Sutter, and

Larsen counties.'' The executive went on: ''These last four counties don't add much population, but do get TV coverage and should be counted in the test area. In other words, TV coverage is the basic contour of our market. We can't confine our advertising expenditures to Redding (Shasta County).'' The account executive further asked Mr. Floyd to consider the development of a three-year plan, over which period the company's market share would, he proposed, rise from 3.2 percent in 1966 to 5 percent in 1967, and to 8 percent in 1968. Mr. Floyd agreed with the market share projections and proposed that the agency should undertake a survey of 200 beer drinkers in the Redding area in order to determine the true position of Blitz Beer in the market. Mr. Floyd proposed that the results of this survey would depend on the extent and depth of the 1966 campaign and, hence, on the amount of money that would need to be spent over the next three years in order to achieved the proposed market share.

A CHANGE IN STRATEGY

In mid-December, Mr. Floyd received both the results of the survey[6] and, based on these findings, details of the proposed budget for the three years 1966-1968 (Exhibit 5).

It came as something of a shock to Mr. Floyd to learn that the agency estimated that more than $200,000 would need to be spent in the next three years in order to establish an 8 percent share for Blitz Beer by the end of 1968. He and Mr. Wessinger came quickly to the conclusion that in view of the additional cost of salesmen, and the budgeted revenue of $170,400 expected over the three years, the agency's proposals were not economically feasible.[7]

With the rejection of the agency's proposals, and the firm refusal of the company to spend anything like the large sums of money over the next three years that a conventional advertising effort would require, Mr. Floyd turned to alternative strategies that could lead to success in the Redding market.

He was interested in the possibility of using word-of-mouth communication to promote Blitz' sales in Redding. During the course of a conversation with the executives of the advertising agency, a

[6]See Appendix A.

[7]The company had used the original market share data supplied by the agency (1960, 3.2 percent; 1967, 5.0 percent; 1968, 8.0 percent) together with a 20 percent increase in population by 1970, to arrive at a total revenue figure for the three-year period 1966-1968 of $170,400. (1966, $32,000; 1967, $52,000; 1968, $86,400).

number of points were made in favor of using the technique.

First, the word-of-mouth method was relatively inexpensive; second, it seemed reasonably well suited to promoting acceptance of a new product or changing the image of an existing product whose market share was relatively small; third, if the technique were used, Blitz-Weinhard would be the only company using it in the Northern California area.

The agency executive explained that the effectiveness of word-of-mouth communication depended primarily on the existence in the market place of horizontal social networks. The members of each network tended to have a common social status; networks were, he said, generally fragmented on a neighborhood basis—especially for low-middle and upper-lower class families.

It had been found that if a ''compelling'' message was initiated by key members of a network (individuals who were perceived as having better-than-average-knowledge of the product and its usage) then over a period of time a ''multiplier'' concept operated to produce changes in the behavior of a large proportion of the network in the direction advocated by the ''source.''

The agency executive suggested that the task of delivering the initial message could be performed either by a number of Blitz-Weinhard executives or could be delegated to influential local personnel (e.g., bartenders or retail store personnel).

He also suggested that the effectiveness of the word-of-mouth campaign would be increased if, at the end of the introductory period, selective media advertising was used to reinforce it. He pointed out that since beer drinking was, for many people, a fairly frequent event, the very act of consumption should provide operative conditioning. That is, the reward (drinking beer) should reinforce the stimulus (the message and source), as well as providing the occasion for influencing others.

The most important criteria for success were the message content, the availability and credibility of the source, the sample of people contacted, the experience of tasting the product, and other agents who validated the message (e.g., bartenders). It was vital, the executive concluded, to develop a unique message that would lose little in its transmission from one person to another.

Mr. Floyd was convinced that a word-of-mouth campaign had a sufficient chance of suceeding in the Redding market to warrant trying it. He believed, however, that to be successful, the company should use messages that not only were related to the proven attributes of Blitz-beer, but also took into account the attitudes of the Redding consumer towards Blitz (Appendix A).

"The results of the December survey," Mr. Floyd remarked: "indicated that Blitz-Weinhard Beer does not enjoy a favorable brand image in the Redding market. Whether this is due to previous brewery mistakes or is a result of low market share is debatable. Nevertheless, a brand image change is needed before a satisfactory upward sales trend can be expected, no matter what promotional techniques we use.

Exhibit 5
Proposed Northern California Budget

Expenditures	March-August 1966	Sept.-Feb. 1966-1967	1966 Total
Media			
TV	11,440	5,720	15,260
Radio	9,672	4,836	12,896
Outdoor	7,512	7,512	12,520
Newspaper	1,920	1,920	3,200
Point-of-purchase			10,000
Public relations			5,000
Total			58,876
Market research			8,000
Production costs[a]			
TV			20,000
Radio			3,000
Outdoor			5,000
Newspaper			5,000
Total			33,000
Fee			13,000
Total, 1966			112,876

[a]The agency anticipated that the production costs of $33,000 would be incurred only once in the period 1966-1968. However, media costs (not including point-of-purchase and public relations expenditures) in 1967 and 1968 should be $40,000 per year.

The agency proposed that at least $10,000 and $5000 should be budgeted in 1967 for point-of-purchase and public relations expenditures. The grand total of expenditure for the three year period then proposed was $207,876.

"It seems prudent to 'chip away' at the present image rather than attempt to change the consumer's attitude 'overnight' using a heavy advertising schedule.

"I propose that we should begin at once seeking a number of special representatives to act as message-carriers in the Redding market for the next six months. Our 1966 plan for the Redding market will be as follows:

1966 Redding Market Plan

I. Objective: During 1966, the objectives of this program are:
   A. To sell 1300 barrels of Blitz-Weinhard Beer in the two-county Redding market.
   B. To use the Redding area as a "word-of-mouth" test market—experience gained here could facilitate efficient expansion elsewhere.

II. Market size: The Redding market consists of Shasta and Tehama Counties. 82,400 people reside here; they consume 41,463 barrels of beer annually. The 1966 goal of 1300 barrels represents a 3.1 percent market share.

III. Basic Strategy: A comparatively small expenditure will be made to start a "word-of mouth" campaign in the Redding market. Once the campaign has been in practice three to six months, special messages on selective advertising media will be used to reinforce the word-of-mouth effort. Sales and POS support will be kept at the 1965 level.

IV. Market Plan: Approximately one-half of resident sales supervisor's time will be spent in the two-county Redding market. POS coverage will be roughly 50 percent of that targeted for established Oregon markets.

Ten to fifteen influential beer drinkers will be appointed as special representatives to start the word-of-mouth campaign. Each representative will spend a weekend in Portland touring the brewery and familiarizing

Proposed Revenues	1965	1966	1967	1968	1969	1970
Population[a]	124,000	129,000	134,000	139,000	144,000	148,000
Market share:	3%	4%	7%	10%	12%	14%
Market share: barrels	3,720	5,160	10,380	13,900	17,280	20,720
Contribution per barrel	$8.00	$8.00	$8.00	$8.00	$8.00	$8.00
Revenue before sales expenses and tax	29,760	41,280	83,040	111,200	138,240	165,760

[a]A 20 percent increase in population was expected by 1970.

himself with our product, our sales objectives, and our personnel. After their return to Redding, the representatives will receive $10.00 per week as allowance for six months. This allowance will be used for his personal consumption and to influence other typical consumers to switch to Blitz-Weinhard Beer.

V. Word-of-Mouth Campaign: The key to the success of the word-of-mouth campaign is largely dependent on the individuals selected and the effectiveness of their communication. Among the many points to be considered in effectively executing this program are:

A. Type. The representative selected must be very similar to the consumers with whom he associates insofar as income, education level, type of employment, etc. are concerned.

B. Influential. Every effort must be made to select those individuals that are well liked and have some "stature" among their circle of friends. This does not mean that a person with a supervisory position is required—it does mean a person whose opinions are respected by his peers.

C. Acquainted. Preferably, each representative should not be personally acquainted with any of the other representatives thus increasing the chance that their sphere of friends will not cross.

D. Employment. During the initial interviewing stage, it would be advisable to give the prospective representative the idea that he is "applying" for the job rather than being "sought out" and appointed. Thus, he "discovered" the Blitz-Weinhard "word-of-mouth" experiment and was fortunate enough to volunteer and be selected.

E. Not Salesmen. The special representative under no circumstances should consider himself a Blitz-Weinhard salesman. Instead, he should be *sold* on the merits of our product. He must convey his message to his friends and acquaintances in a sincere manner rather than in an artificial sales presentation.

F. Brewery Tour. During the brewery tour, it is essential that four or five definite easy-to-understand *product attributes* be presented that are *unique* to Blitz-Weinhard Beer and the Blitz-Weinhard Brewery. When the tour is completed, an attempt should be made to get a "read back" from the representatives to insure effective communication (high alcoholic content, superior quality control, etc.).

G. Participation. Each representative should be encouraged to participate in the formulation of the program and volunteer suggestions to more effectively market our beer in the Redding area.

H. Incentive. At the onset, the representatives should be clearly instructed that this is a three-month program depending on their *effectiveness*, it may be extended through the summer months. This should provide a subtle incentive to do a good job.

I. Long-Term Inducement. Upon completion of the program (approximately six months), a special award or long-term relationship with the brewery must be developed to insure continued support of our product (brewmaster wall plaque, free six-pack per month, Bandwagon subscription, etc.).

VI. Budget: The following budget reflects minimum sales and maximum expenditures involved with the Redding proposal:
1300 Barrels at $7 barrel marginal
income. . . .$9,100

Manpower (one/two		
sales supervisors)	$7,500	
Point of sale		
(approximate)	3,750	
12 special		
representatives	5,920	
Advertising	4,800	21,970
		($12,870)

Special Representatives		
12 people at $10/		
week for 26 weeks	$3,120	
18 people to Portland		
(air, room, etc.)	1,800	
Miscellaneous	1,000	
	$5,920	

Advertising		
Outdoor (50 percent—		
12 months)	$1,800	
Radio (special—13 weeks)	3,000	
	$4,800	

QUESTIONS

1. What useful ideas for selling Blitz Beer can be gleaned from the consumer survey and the other exhibits in the case?
2. Evaluate the word-of-mouth promotional campaign suggested for the Redding market.
3. Design your own marketing program to increase the market share and profits for Blitz-Weinhard Beer in Northern California.

Appendix A

Survey of the Redding Beer Market

Background. Historically Blitz-Weinhard Beer has had distribution with limited sales in the Redding, California, market. Recently the management of Blitz initiated a marketing plan that will establish Blitz as a major brand in this market.

To assist both the client and the agency in developing their related responsibilities for the success of this plan, the following survey has been commissioned.

Purpose. The purpose of this study is to measure the beer drinkers' current imagery evaluation of Blitz-Weinhard and the other competitive beers found in the Redding market.

The specific objectives are to ascertain:

1. Brand preference and awareness of all major beers currently sold in the market.
2. The beer drinker's attitude toward and image of these beers.
3. The extent that Blitz has established its image in the market (whether positive or negative).

Summary of Findings

Olympia Beer is the major selling beer in the market. It is recognized as the leading brand and consumers associate it with all types of beer drinkers. It is rated the closest of any beer to an "ideal" beer. Because of its dominance in the market, it is most vulnerable when out-of-stock brand switching occurs. However, it is drunk by more as the second beer.

Coor's and Hamm's follow respectively as leading brands. These three beers enjoy approximately two-thirds of the market's sales. All three beers emphasize one common feature: water.

Advertising recall was highest for Hamm's Beer followed by Olympia, Falstaff, Lucky and Blitz.

The most important features determining brand image are:

Quality of the beer.
Degree of harshness/smoothness.
Consistency of taste.
Aging.

In all instances Olympia, Coor's and Hamm's were rated similar to the "ideal" beer. Blitz was least like an ideal beer with reference to quality, aging, and consistency of taste.

What is Blitz-Weinhard's Position?

At the present, Blitz holds a minor position in the Redding Market—4 percent of the respondents have drunk it in the last four weeks. Three percent usually drink Blitz.

The level of advertising recall for a product with this share is considerable. Approximately half of the respondents claim to recall Blitz's advertising in the last four weeks.

A summary of facts on Blitz are:

89 percent are aware that Blitz is sold in the markets.[1]
47 percent of all respondents recall Blitz advertising

---

[1]Forty-six percent claimed awareness when provided with ended recall.

31 percent of all respondents have tried Blitz at sometime in the past

12 percent have tried Blitz in the past and recall some advertising

4 percent have drunk Blitz in the past four weeks

3 percent usually drink it

5 percent would not recommend Blitz because they dislike the flavor, saying it was bitter and/or green. Half of these comments came from beer drinkers under 29 years of age.

2 percent stated they would buy Blitz if their own favorite brand was not available.

A. *The Market*

The leaders. The Redding market is dominated by beers that emphasize the importance of water.

Olympia: "It's the Water."
Coor's: "Rocky Mountain Spring Water."
Hamm's: "From the Land of Sky Blue Water."

These brands emjoy over two-thirds of the market's "usually drunk" beer volume.

Table 1 is a breakout of each brand in the market, rating each by the percentage of respondents that (1) have ever tried, (2) tried in the past four weeks, and (3) usually drink or favorite brand.

Table 1

Brand	Percent Ever Tried Brand	Percent Tried in Past Month	Percent Usually Drink Brand
Olympia	89	43	31
Lucky Lager	79	15	10
Hamm's	78	22	16
Coor's	72	23	19
Burgermeister	59	9	6
Falstaff	43	3	2
Budweiser	39	6	6
Schlitz	35	3	2
Blitz-Weinhard	31	4	3
Pabst	28	9	8
Miller	26	9	7

Segregation of the participants in the survey on a demographic basis indicated the *Olympia's* overall strength or appeal appears to be universal. It is attracting above-average support from the white-collar and skilled craftsman while *Coor's* appears to be attracting above average support from the skilled and semiskilled. In effect, Olympia and Coors, the leading two beers in the market, are effectively, by accident or design, reaching and attracting a major portion of the occupational scale of drinkers.

Hamm's has above average appeal from the professional men. By age group, Coor's and Lucky's strength increases among the younger consumers while Hamm's declines. Olympia is equally preferred by all age groups.

B. *Brand Switching*

If their favorite brand is not available, 79 percent of the beer drinkers will buy another brand at the store they are in, while 21 percent would attempt to locate their favorite brand in another store. The ultimate in brand loyalty is exemplified by those who will go to another store. Among the leading four brands, this claim of loyalty is:

	Usually Drink Brand (Percent)	Percentage Who Would Go to Another Store
Coor's	19	21
Lucky	10	21
Olympia	31	19
Hamm's	16	16

One out of the five Blitz drinkers claimed he would go to another store.

As expected, a large portion, 79%, will select another brand.

The regular *Olympia* drinker tends more towards Hamm's, Coor's and Lucky in that order.

The regular *Coor's* drinker tends toward Lucky, Olympia and Hamm's.

The regular *Hamm's* drinker will select Olympia, then Burgermeister.

The regular *Lucky* drinker will seek Olympia or Hamm's.

C. *Ad Recall*

Recall through any media was claimed by a large portion of the respondents for only two brands: Hamm's and Olympia. Total awareness recall (both aided and unaided combined) indicates that 90 percent of the respondents recall having seen and/or heard Hamm's beer advertising in the last four weeks, 84 percent recall Olympia.

(Moderate beer drinkers tended to recall more ads regarding Lucky, Blitz, Burgermeister, and Budweiser while the heavier drinkers tended toward Olympia. See Table 2.)

Table 2

What Beer Advertising (any media) Have Your Seen in Last Four Weeks? (Percent) [a]

Brand	Unaided	Aided	Total Awareness-Recall
Hamm's	79	11	90
Olympia	64	20	84
Lucky Lager	45	14	59
Falstaff	39	26	65
Blitz-Weinhard	36	11	47
Budweiser	20	11	31
Coor's	18	11	29
Burgermeister	17	20	37
Schlitz	17	13	30

[a] Sample size 198

D. *Beer Disliked*

Lucky Lager and Burgermeister are the two beers that received the most negative comments. The third beer was Blitz-Weinhard. Table 3 shows the percentage of respondents that made adverse remarks about a beer; their primary reasoning is shown in the right column.

Table 3

Brand	Percent	Reasoning
Lucky Lager	11	It's bitter, too strong, makes one sick
Burgermeister	9	It's bitter, it's green
Blitz-Weinhard	5	It's bitter, it's green
Falstaff	4	It's bitter
Coor's	3	It's green
Schlitz	3	Too strong
Budweiser	2	It's bitter
Hamm's	2	Too strong
Olympia	2	It's flat

It was found that of the sixty-two drinkers who had *ever tried* Blitz (Table 1), ten would not drink it again (or would not recommend the beer). Blitz was in the least favorable position followed closely by Lucky Lager and Burgermeister. Olympia, Coor's and Hamm's held the most favorable positions (Table 4).

Table 4

	Percent of Total Consumers That Have Ever Drunk the Brand	Percent Who Would Not Recommend the Beer	Approximate Ratio
Blitz-Weinhard	31	5	6:1
Lucky Lager	79	11	7:1
Burgermeister	59	9	7:1
Falstaff	43	4	11:1
Schlitz	35	3	12:1
Budweiser	39	2	20:1
Coor's	72	3	24:1
Hamm's	78	2	39:1
Olympia	89	2	45:1

E. *Stereotype of Beer Drinkers*

The respondents were asked what type of people they thought would drink a particular brand of beer.

Among all beer drinkers, *Olympia* is considered a favorable beer for the young as well as the retired, men as well as women, as well as being drunk by hunters, fishermen, loggers and truck drivers. In summary, the image of Olympia is all encompassing—a beer acceptable to a majority of the Redding community.

Lucky Lager is creating an association with the ruggedness of the outdoors with fishermen, hunters, loggers and truck drivers being the nucleus of the image for Lucky Lager.

Coor's has women in general and the professional man, while *Hamm's* has attracted the men and truck drivers.

The young beer drinkers see young people and students drinking Olympia. He, himself, has a strong association with Olympia, a feeling he does not hold toward any other brand of beer.

Similarly, the beer drinker over 39 years associates the retired person with Olympia as well as the young of either sex and all outdoor individuals.

F. *Brand Image*

The results showed that respondents discern degrees of difference in four areas:

A. Quality of beer.
B. Degree of harshness/smoothness.
C. Consistency of taste.
D. Aging.

The brand's relative differences from the ''ideal'' for these features are shown below. The brand on the left is most like the ideal beer.

Quality:	Olympia	Coor's	Hamm's	Lucky	Blitz
Harshness/smoothness:	Olympia	Coor's	Hamm's	Blitz	Lucky
Consistency:	Olympia	Coor's	Hamm's	Lucky	Blitz
Aging:	Olympia	Coor's	Hamm's	Lucky	Blitz

Among all beer drinkers Olympia is considered the closest to the ideal on these features. The rest fall into the same descending pattern as is found for brands usually drunk. An exception is Harshness/Smoothness where Blitz outperforms Lucky Lager. (Similar results were found for both heavy and moderate drinkers.)

Six
Product Development

No war, no panic, no bank failure, no strike or fire can so completely and irrevocably destroy a business as a new and better product in the hands of a competitor.

F. Russell Bichowsky

Product development is the process of finding ideas for new goods and services and converting them into commercially successful product line additions. Managers of the process attempt to maximize returns on funds invested in new merchandise, minimize the risk of loss, and efficiently use the human and physical resources of the firm. The quest for new products is based on the assumption that customers want new items and that the introduction of new products will lead to greater total sales and profits for the firm. The history of American business is littered with the skeletons of companies who mistakenly believed that their products or services were immune from the ravages of time and competition.[1] The destruction of old economic structures and their replacement is a driving force in a capitalistic society and businesses are constantly being reshaped by new products, new methods, new markets, and new forms of organization.[2] The objective of this chapter is to show how business firms can react to these changes with well-managed product development programs.

WHY DEVELOP NEW PRODUCTS?

"New" products can be defined as goods and services that are basically different from those already marketed by a firm. This means "new" products include the truly innovative items like the Polaroid camera as well as items that are new to a company but not new to the marketplace. On the other hand, a redesign of an existing item introduced at an annual model changeover would not be considered a "new" product.

Many businessmen believe that in the long run there is a positive correlation between the introduction of new products and increases in total sales and profits for the firm. One study of fifty-seven companies has shown that high research and development expenditures are positively related to profitability when market position is strong.[3] General

[1]See Theodore Levitt, "Marketing Myopia," *Harvard Business Review* (July-August 1960), pp. 45-56.
[2]Joseph A. Schumpeter, *Capitalism, Socialism, and Democracy* (New York: Harper and Brothers Co., 3rd ed., 1950), p. 83.
[3]"PIMS: A Breakthrough in Strategic Planning," *Marketing Science Institute Research Briefs* (July 1974), p.1.

Mills, for example, achieved a 17 percent sales increase in 1971 and attributed most of the gain to the introduction of four new breakfast foods.[4] Kodak is so committed to product development that they introduce a new or improved product once every three days. The tie between product development and profitability is often difficult to establish because of the years that usually elapse between expenditures and their return. However, a second study has shown a simple correlation of +.65 between returns on invested capital and research spending as a percent of sales for fifteen manufacturing industries.[5] These results suggest that product development can lead to improved sales and profits for business firms.

The Product Life Cycle

Perhaps the most important concept supporting product development activities is the life-cycle hypothesis. This proposition suggests that products follow patterns of birth, growth, and decline much like those observed for plants and animals.[6] A hypothetical

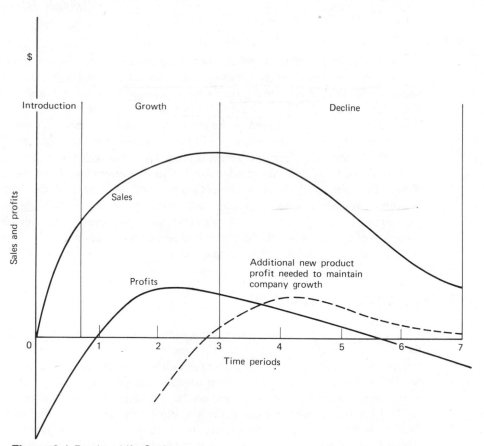

Figure 6-1 Product Life Cycle.

[4]"Business Bulletin," *Wall Street Journal* (April 13, 1974), p.1.

[5]Data shown in *Journal of Business,* Vol. 33 (July 1960), p. 205. Correlation calculated by the authors.

[6]A check on the validity of the product life cycle has been made by Polli and Cook and they concluded that the concept is valid in many market situations. See Roland Polli and Victor Cook, "Validity of the Product Life Cycle," *Journal of Business,* Vol. 42, No. 4 (October 1969) pp. 385-400.

product life cycle is shown in Figure 6-1. Note that sales grow rapidly during the introductory period and eventually decline due to the appearance of competitive products and price cutting.[7] Profits are negative at the start of the cycle due to introductory expenses and they also come under pressure later because of price reductions and advertising designed to maintain market shares. This diagram suggests that companies must continually introduce new items if they expect the growth of sales and profits of the firm.

There is some evidence that product life cycles are becoming shorter in some lines of trade.[8] Competitors have been increasingly quick to copy new items and introduce their own brands at low prices. This can lead to rapid declines in profit margins and market shares for innovators. If the life expectancy of new products continues to decline, firms will need to develop even greater numbers of new items to maintain their market positions.

What Price Success?

The creation and marketing of new products is an expensive and risky task. One study of 111 new food items revealed that preintroduction research and development expenses averaged $94,000.[9] Many of these items were also placed in test markets at an additional expense of $248,000 each and the products actually placed on the market incurred first-year promotional expenditures of $1.4 million. Given the magnitude of these costs, the prudent businessman will want to know the proportion of new products that can be expected to succeed. In the case of the food products, 79 percent were kept on the market after being placed in regular distribution.[10] In another study reported by Booz, Allen & Hamilton, 67 percent of 366 recently marketed products were classified as successful.[11]

New product failure rates tend to vary widely among individual firms, but there is relatively little variation among industries (Table 6-1). These data also indicate that a large number of new products are lost in the idea and development stages. This means that a great deal of money is spent developing products that never reach the marketplace. One estimate is that 70 percent of development expenditures are made for products that are unsuccessful.[12] Because of the high risks associated with product development, businessmen must understand the different strategies that can be employed to bringing out new items.

NEW PRODUCT STRATEGIES

The most popular new-product growth strategies were described briefly in Chapter 1 (Figure 1-1). Perhaps the simplest approach is a policy of improving present products.

[7]The shape of the product life cycle in Figure 6-1 is typical of those for new food items and consumer expendibles. The sales of durables grow more slowly and the life cycle is apt to be "S" shaped as shown in Figure 7-1 in the next chapter.

[8]Joseph C. Seibert, *Concepts of Marketing Management* (New York: Harper & Row, Publishers, 1973), p. 166.

[9]This includes $26,000 for market research, Robert D. Buzzell and Robert E. M. Nourse, *Product Innovation in Food Processing* 1954-1964 (Boston: Harvard University, Graduate School of Business Administration, Division of Research, 1967), p. 113.

[10]Robert D. Buzzell and Robert E. M. Nourse, *Product Innovation in Food Processing 1954-1964* (Boston: Harvard University, Graduate School of Business Administration, Division of Research, 1967), p. 123.

[11]*Management of New Products* (Chicago: Booz, Allen & Hamilton, Management Consultants, 1968), p. 11.

[12]*Ibid.*, p. 11.

Table 6-1

New Product Success Rates as a Percentage of Product Ideas, Development Projects, and Products Introduced

Industry	New Product Ideas, Commercially Successful	Product Development Projects, Commercially Successful	New Products Introduced, Commercially Successful
Chemical	2	18	59
Consumer packaged goods	2	11	63
Electrical machinery	1	13	63
Metal fabricators	3	11	71
Nonelectrical machinery	2	21	59
Raw material processors	5	14	59

Source. Management of New Products (Chicago: Booz, Allen & Hamilton, Management Consultants, 1968), p.12.

This strategy relies on existing facilities and technology to bring out product variations and is a fairly low-risk procedure. The approach is defensive, however, and is unlikely to lead to the dramatic growth sometimes associated with totally new products.

A second possibility is to pursue a strategy of expanding product or service assortments. The idea is to take a basic product (a refrigerator or insurance policy) and offer the customer several new and different variations. A refrigerator manufacturer, for example, could remove some features and offer a stripped-down economy model, or bring out a two-door model for those interested in a separate freezer, or add an ice maker and cold-water dispenser for more affluent customers. The objective of these changes is to bring out models that will attract previously untapped segments of the market.

Another approach is to follow a strategy of product line extension. This technique utilizes existing salesmen, promotional methods, and distribution channels to offer customers a broader choice of services or merchandise. Thus, a refrigerator manufacturer could build sales by expanding his line to include freezers, dishwashers, and room air conditioners. In the case of services, a life insurance company could expand its line by offering fire insurance and mutual funds in addition to its regular policies. Frequently, items used to extend product lines are purchased from other companies.

Some companies believe that the relationship between product development expenditures and future profits is so uncertain that a policy of *copying* your competitors is a more profitable strategy in the short run. Levitt suggests that no single firm can be first in everything and a policy of imitation can be lucrative if the firm moves in quickly on developing markets before profit margins deteriorate.[13] Thus although Schick was the first to introduce the electric razor, Norelco was able to come in later and dominate this market.

Perhaps the most risky new product strategy is to introduce items or services that are completely different from present lines of business. This is an expensive process because these items often require entirely new production, promotion, and distribution facilities. Thus to be successful, a diversification new product strategy must generate additional revenue to pay the extra costs of product development. Although diversification

[13]Theodore Levitt, *The Marketing Mode* (New York: McGraw-Hill, 1969), p. 59.

strategies are risky, they sometimes open the door to fantastic growth opportunities. Remember it was two small firms that gambled on new products for instant photography and electrostatic copying that became the giant Polaroid and Xerox corporations of today.

We have discussed five separate new product strategies, but it is obvious that a firm with ample resources could pursue several different strategies at the same time. Frequently the successful implementation of a new product strategy depends on the organizational arrangements that are used to control this activity.

CONTROLLING PRODUCT DEVELOPMENT

Product development can be described as a sequential decision process based on limited information. It resembles a high-stakes poker game where the player makes bets (investments) that his cards (products) will be more successful than those of his competitors. Success at poker and product development both depend on luck and on the skill of the player in organizing and interpreting the information that is available.

The basic steps of product development are shown in Figure 6-2. The procedure begins with the *screening* of a relatively large number of product ideas gleaned from a variety of sources. The example in the chart suggests that out of every fifty-eight ideas, about twelve ideas were subjected to an intensive profitability evaluation during the *business analysis* phase. The six ideas that survived were then sent on to the *development* stage. The laboratory design and testing phase eliminated three more ideas leaving only three products for *testing.* The final step in the chain, *commercialization* involved taking the two products that succeeded in the test markets and launching the two through the regular distribution network. The end result of all these activities was the conversion of fifty-eight new product ideas into one commercially successful product.

The management of product development activities is not an easy task even for firms who have been successful with new products. Most of the problems have to do with assigning responsibilities, communications, and the coordination of working relationships among the various departments of the firm. For product development to be

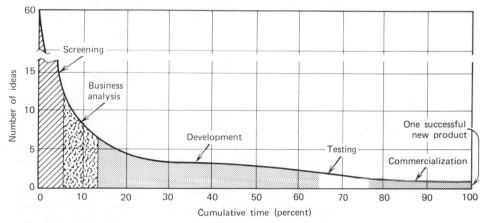

Figure 6-2 Stages in the Product Development Cycle.
Source. Average experience of fifty-one companies as reported in *Management of New Products* (Chicago: Booz, Allen & Hamilton, Management Consultants, 1968), p. 9.
© Booz, Allen & Hamilton.

effective, production, marketing, and research must work together despite conflicting objectives.

New Products Departments

The most popular method used to manage product development is the new products department. A 1968 survey reported that 86 percent of the firms studied had small new products departments reporting directly to the chief executive.[14] Typical activites per formed by new products departments include:

Recommend new product objective.
Plan exploration activities.
Make screening decisions.
Develop specifications.
Coordinate testing and precommercialization.
Direct interdepartmental teams.

The relatively small size of product development departments means their primary responsibility is to provide continuity of supervision and to coordinate the new product activities performed by other departments. While the product development departments may do some screening and product evaluation, they normally rely on sponsor groups and other areas of the firm for the bulk of the new product work. The introduction of a centralized new product department can simplify communications by reducing the number of interactions needed to send and receive messages on development projects. Another advantage of new products departments is that they tend to produce more new products than more informal methods. Grayson studied 125 packaged-goods manufacturers and found that firms organized with full-time new products executives produced 60 percent more new items than firms without any new products executives.[15]

Sponsor Groups

Sponsor groups represent a second type of organizational arrangement that has proved to be effective in the management of product development activities. The idea is to assemble a small team at the business analysis stage and give it the responsiblity for promoting and controlling the development of a single product. The project team usually includes one to five people from the major functional areas of the company and they stay with the product through its commercialization phase. The product teams normally report to the director of the new products department.

The use of separate teams for each product provides continuity and the extra push needed to gain acceptance for projects. It is a sad commentary, but most business firms and government agencies resist new ideas because of the changes required in existing methods and procedures. To overcome this resistance, a product champion is needed to help sell top management on the virtues of the new enterprise. Despite claims made by business firms that new ideas are welcome, many good ideas are lost because there is no one available to sponsor a particular innovation. Product teams help overcome this problem by specifically assigning each project to an individual or group.

Perhaps the most crucial problem with sponsor groups is where to get the people to

[14]*Management of New Products,* op. cit., p. 20.
[15]Robert A. Grayson, "If You Want New Products You Better Organize to Get Them," D. Maynard Phelps, ed., *Product Management: Select Readings 1960-1969,* (Homewood, Ill.: Richard D. Irwin, 1970, p. 47.

staff the new product teams. If these groups function as proposed, many of the individuals will stay with the projects permanently. This constant transfer of product development people into the operating divisions is apt to lead to serious staffing problems. The issue is compounded by a frequent shortage of individuals with the breadth of experience needed to work effectively in product development. Staffing problems have been serious enough in some firms to force them to abandon product teams in favor of other systems.

Budgets and Schedules

The product development process can be made more efficient by giving one individual overall responsibility and utilizing appropriate budgets and schedules. New products have a way of costing more and taking longer than anticipated and someone must keep track of these events if control is to be effective. Flow charts are one device that executives can use to manage the development process (Figure 6-3). These diagrams help provide sequencing for activities and an enumeration of all events that must be accomplished before a product can be placed on the market. Figure 6-3, for example, lists sixty-one events or factors that must be considered to move from selecting new product strategies to a reevaluation of the product after it has been introduced. A new product flow chart can be used as a sort of master checklist to make sure that all necessary work is completed in the proper sequence. Although flow charts provide a good description of the work to be done, they do not give exact sequencing of all events or provide estimates of times to complete each activity. These refinements are available with network analysis that will be discussed later in the chapter.

SEARCH AND SCREENING OF PRODUCT IDEAS

The management of product development has been described as a sequential process that converts ideas into commercially successful product line additions. The procedure is essentially a series of go, no-go decisions where the best ideas emerge as finished products. Ideas that fail to meet development criteria are either dropped or sent back for more testing. The developmental process demands a steady stream of new ideas from which a few choice projects can be selected for more intensive development.

Sources of Product Ideas

The most important source of ideas for new products lies within the individual company itself. A survey revealed that 88 percent of new product ideas came from the research staff, engineers, customers, salesmen, dealers, marketing research personnel, and other employees and executives of the firm.[16] The trick is to find a way of motivating people to suggest ideas and then organizing a systematic procedure for channeling the ideas to the product development department. Some firms show their appreciation by offering cash prizes, royalties, or promotions to employees who volunteer new concepts.

There are an almost endless number of external sources of new product ideas, some of which are in Figure 6-3. One of the most attractive ways to acquire new products is to simply buy up other companies that have developed new items. This procedure has the advantages of eliminating all of the costs of search, screening, testing and commerciali-

---

[16]John T. Gerlach and Charles A. Wainwright, *Successful Management of New Products* (New York: Hastings House, 1968), p. 61

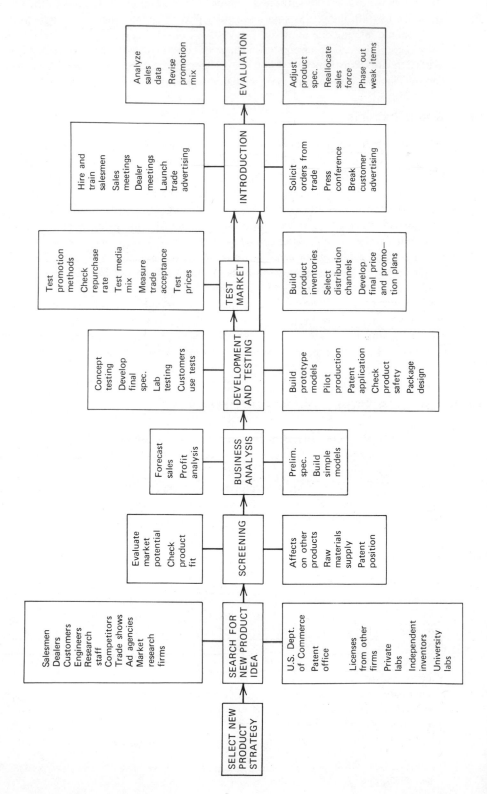

Figure 6-3 Flow Chart of the Product Development Process.

zation and involves fewer risks because someone else has already built up a satisfied group of customers and dealers. For example, the Rival Manufacturing Company bought Naxon Utilities Corporation in 1970 primarily as an entry into the sunlamp field and for a line of portable laundry equipment.[17] Neither of these products were particularly successful, but Rival also picked up a stoneware-lined electric slow cooker at the same time. This item turned out to provide an exceptionally fine way of cooking, so Rival redesigned the cooker and called it the Crock-Pot. The new item was well received by the trade and in the first year $10.5 million of the cookers were sold accounting for 40 percent of the total sales of the company. The main problems with this approach to product development are finding firms with innovations that are willing to be bought up and avoiding antitrust action if the purchase threatens to monopolize trade in individual markets.

Licensing of New Products

Obtaining new product ideas through licensing offers several advantages for firms that wish to avoid the high cost of product development yet lack enthusiasm for acquiring going conerns. Probably the most important attraction is that there are more firms willing to license their ideas than there are firms willing to sell successful new products. Also most license agreements involve the payment of royalties on a unit or percentage of sales basis so that initial costs are low and subsequent payments are due only when the product is actually sold. Futhermore, it is unusual for royalties paid on products obtained by licenses to exceed the saving achieved in research and development expenses. Licensing can also reduce lead time compared to the months or years that may be required to develop similiar products in the company's own laboratories. However, products obtained through licensing normally require a considerable investment of money before they become successful product line additions. Although basic research has been completed, the firm must still decide on what package, price, promotional campaign, and channel of distribution to use for the product.

New Product Scouts

Product scouts are employees or consultants whose primary job is to find ideas that offer commercial potential for their sponsoring companies. The primary advantage of scouts is that the cost of locating an externally developed product by systematic investigation is usually less than 2 percent of the cost of internal development.[18] Product scouts search through a wide variety of leads for new product ideas ranging from such obvious sources as trade publications to more obscure personal contacts with inventors and patent attorneys. The astute product scout also maintains close contact with the major university and independent research laboratories as well as other manufacturers who may have unusual products for sale or lease. Some new product scouts publish newsletters describing recent innovations. For example, Patents International Affiliates offers a monthly printout of new product information (PATINDEX) from a world wide computerized data bank.

One other area where product scouts can be used to advantage is searching through the maze of governmental agencies and publications for spin-offs from federal research

---

[17]*Wall Street Journal* (August 17, 1973) p. 9.

[18]Ralph G. Miller, "Domestic Product Scouting," *Utilizing R +D By-Products,* Jerome W. Blood, ed., (New York: American Management Association, 1967), p. 113.

projects. Product scouts can be used to help monitor the activities of the U.S. Patent Office. Occasionally good ideas can be obtained from the *Register* of patents available for licensing or sale and the listing of government owned or dedicated patents. Another good source is the *Official Gazette,* a weekly publication of the patent office that lists patents added to the *Register* plus new patents granted. Once the flow of new product ideas has been started, procedures must be established to select the most promising projects for more intensive analysis and development.

Screening Procedures

The objective of the screening process is to eliminate those new product ideas that are inconsistent with the goals or resources of the firm. Screening can be viewed as a two-stage filtering procedure. In the first phase, a fairly quick judgment is made to see whether the idea is compatible with the company's plans, technical skills, and financial capabilities. This evaluation is made by knowledgeable managers and staff specialists who weed out the obviously unsuitable ideas so that valuable resources will not be wasted reviewing impractical proposals. The second phase of the new product screening process is more detailed and is designed to establish a ranking for the remaining ideas. This ranking is based on an evaluation of the factors that are considered relevant for product development in the particular firm. One check list of seventeen factors that can be used to help assess the suitability of new product ideas is given in Table 6-2. The descriptions under the column headings show how individual products would be scored from very good to very poor on each of the seventeen factors. Obviously, the idea is to separate the new product proposals with high ratings from those with average or poor ratings. This can be accomplished by using a form with the seventeen factors listed on one side and a five-point scale across the top that could be checked to indicate relative positions. The problem with this approach is that it becomes extremely difficult to compare patterns of check marks and the method assumes all factors are equally important. Obviously, this is not the usual situation and additional refinements must be made in the screening process.

What is needed is a system that considers the relative importance of the evaluation criteria and converts all factor evaluations into a single index number for each product. The relative importance of development criteria can be resolved by introducing a system of weights for the seventeen factors. In Table 6-3 weights varying from .02 to .15 have been assigned to the factors indicating that management believes breadth of market, exclusiveness of design, and value added are more important to product success than raw material availability and number of sizes and grades. Then the five rating classifications (very good to very poor) could be assigned numbers and an overall profile obtained by multiplying the compatibility scores by their weights and summing (Table 6-3). Index numbers obtained in this manner would range in size from 1.0 for the weakest projects to 5.0 for the most attractive. The main value of a new product index is to quickly separate the best proposals so that priorities can be established for succeeding stages of development.

BUSINESS ANALYSIS

The business analysis stage of product development involves a detailed study of the potential *profitability* of new product ideas. The objective of business analysis is to eliminate unprofitable ventures before extensive development and market testing expenses are incurred. Presumably the screening phase has already rejected the most

Table 6-2

Factor Ratings for New Products

	Very Good	Good	Average	Poor	Very Poor
I. Marketability					
A. Relation to present distribution channels	Can reach major markets by distributing through present channels	Can reach major markets by distributing mostly through present channels, partly through new channels	Will have to distribute equally between new and present channels, in order to reach major markets	Will have to distribute mostly through new channels in order to reach major markets	Will have to distribute entirely through new channels in order to reach major markets
B. Relation to present product lines	Complements a present line that needs more products to fill it	Complements a present line that does not need, but can handle, another product	Can be fitted into a present line	Can be fitted in a present line but does not fit entirely	Does not fit in with any present product line
C. Quality/price relationship	Priced below all competing products of similar quality	Priced below most competing products of similar quality	Approximately the same price as competing products of similar quality	Priced above many competing products of similar quality	Priced above all competing products of similar quality
D. Number of sizes and grades	Few staple sizes and grades	Several sizes and grades, but customers will be satisfied with few staples	Several sizes and grades, but can satisfy customer wants with small inventory of nonstaples	Several sizes and grades, each of which will have to be stocked in equal amounts	Many sizes and grades that will necessitate heavy inventories

	Very Good	Good	Average	Poor	Very Poor
E. Merchandisability	Has product characteristics over and above those of competing products that lend themselves to the kind of promotion, advertising, and display that the given company does best	Has promotable characteristics that will compare favorably with the characteristics of competing products	Has promotable characteristics that are equal to those of other products	Has a few characteristics that are promotable, but generally does not measure up to characteristics of competing products	Has no characteristics at all that are equal to competitors' or that lend themselves to imaginative promotion
F. Effects on sales of present products	Should aid in sales of present products	May help sales of present products; definitely will not be harmful to present sales	Should have no effect on present sales	May hinder present sales some; definitely will not aid present sales	Will reduce sales of presently profitable products
II. Durability A. Stability	Basic product that can always expect to have uses	Product that will have uses long enough to earn back initial investment, plus at least 10 years of additional profits	Product that will have uses long enough to earn back initial investment, plus several (from 5 to 10) years of additional profits	Product that will have uses long enough to earn back initial investment, plus 1 to 5 years of additional profits	Product that will probably be obsolete in near future
B. Breadth of market	A national market, a wide variety of consumers, and a potential foreign market	A national market and a wide variety of consumers	Either a national market or a wide variety of consumers	A regional market and a restricted variety of consumers	A specialized market in a small marketing area
C. Resistance to cyclical fluctuations	Will sell readily in inflation or depression	Effects of cyclical changes will be moderate, and will be felt after changes in economic outlook	Sales will rise and fall with the economy	Effects of cyclical changes will be heavy, and will be felt before changes in economic outlook	Cyclical changes will cause extreme fluctuations in demand

D. Resistance to seasonal fluctuations	Steady sales throughout the year	Steady sales—except under unusual circumstances	Seasonal fluctuations, but inventory and personnel problems can be absorbed	Heavy seasonal fluctuations that will cause considerable inventory and personnel problems	Severe seasonal fluctuations that will necessitate layoffs and heavy inventories
E. Exclusiveness of design	Can be protected by a patent with no loopholes	Can be patented, but the patent might be circumvented	Cannot be patented, but has certain salient characteristics that cannot be copied very well	Cannot be patented, and can be copies by larger, more knowledge-companies	Cannot be patented, and can be copies by anyone
III. Productive Ability A. Equipment necessary	Can be produced with equipment that is presently idle	Can be produced with present equipment, but production will have to be scheduled with other products	Can be produced largely with present equipment, but the company will have to purchase some additional equipment	Company will have to buy a good deal of new equipment, but some present equipment can be used	Company will have to buy all new equipment
B. Production knowledge and personnel necessary	Present knowledge and personnel will be able to produce new product	With very few minor exceptions, present knowledge and personnel will be able to produce new product	With some exceptions, present knowledge and personnel will be able to produce new product	A ratio of approximately 50-50 will prevail between the needs for new knowledge and personnel and for present knowledge and personnel	Mostly new knowledge and personnel are needed to produce the new product

	Very Good	Good	Average	Poor	Very Poor
C. Raw materials' availability	Company can purchase raw materials from its best supplier(s) exclusively	Company can purchase major portion of raw materials from its best supplier(s), and remainder from any one of a number of companies	Company can purchase approximately half of raw materials from its best supplier(s), and other half from any one of a number of companies	Company must purchase most of raw materials from any one of a number of companies other than its best supplier(s)	Company must purchase most or all of raw materials from a certain few companies other than its best supplier(s)
IV. Growth Potential A. Place in market	New type of product that will fill a need presently not being filled	Products that will substantially improve on products presently on the market	Product that will have certain new characteristics that will appeal to a substantial segment of the market	Product that will have minor improvements over products presently on the market	Product similar to those presently on the market and that adds nothing new
B. Expected competitive situation-value added	Very high value added so as to substantially restrict number of competitors	High enough value added so that, unless product is extremely well suited to other firms, they will not want to invest in additional facilities	High enough value added so that, unless other companies are as strong in market as this firm, it will not be profitable for them to compete	Lower value added so as to allow large, medium, and some smaller companies to compete	Very low value added so that all companies can profitably enter market
C. Expected availability of end users	Number of end users will increase substantially	Number of end users will increase moderately	Number of end users will increase slightly, if at all	Number of end users will decrease moderately	Number of end users will decrease substantially

Source. John T. O'Meara, "Selecting Profitable Products," *Harvard Business Review*, (January-February, 1961), pp. 84, 85.

Table 6-3

New Product Evaluation Form Showing the Calculation of a Rating for Product X

Factors	1 Weight	2 Compatibility Rating Very Good (5)	Good (4)	Aver- age (3)	Poor (2)	Very Poor (1)	Factor Score 1 × 2
Relation to present channels	.05		√				.20
Relation to present products	.05			√			.15
Quality/price relationship	.05		√				.20
Number of sizes and grades	.02				√		.04
Merchandisability	.05	√					.25
Effects on the sales of present products	.05			√			.15
Stability	.05				√		.10
Breadth of market	.15		√				.60
Resistance to cyclical fluctations	.02				√		.04
Resistance to seasonal fluctations	.05			√			.15
Exclusiveness of design	.10	√					.50
Equipment necessary	.02					√	.02
Production knowledge and personnel	.02			√			.06
Raw material availability	.02				√		.04
Place in the market	.15	√					.75
Value added	.10			√			.30
Growth in users	.05		√				.20
Total	1.00			Product Rating Index			3.75

unsuitable projects so that the product development staff is in a position to focus its attention on the practical ideas that remain. A wide variety of techniques have been created to measure the profitability of product development projects and a number of these measures will be reviewed.

Break-Even and Payback

One of the simplest approaches to the evaluation of new product proposals is break-even analysis. Break-even volume (Q) is the number of units that must be sold to cover the fixed and variable costs involved in developing and producing new products. It can be calculated with the formula:

$$BE = Q = \frac{F}{P - V} \tag{1}$$

where Q is the break-even volume, F represents the average annual fixed costs associated with each product, P is the selling price, and V is the variable cost per unit. The break-even volume (Q) is obtained by simply dividing the annual fixed costs by the margin $(P-V)$ generated by the sale of each unit. For example, suppose fixed costs for research and development, production equipment, and nonrecurring introductory adver-tising and distribution expenses for a new cake mix are estimated to be $75,000 per year. If the item sells for $6 per case and variable costs of labor and materials are $3.50 per case, then the break-even volume Q would be $75,000/($6 - $3.50) or 30,000 cases. Thus the firm would have to sell 30,000 cases just to cover its fixed costs and the margin on any additional volume would be available for profits.

Once break-even volumes have been calculated for each new product, they can be compared against projected sales. The most desirable projects would be those that had the greatest excess of expected sales over the break-even volume. Break-even analysis assumes fixed values for price and unit variable costs although experience suggests that both of these factors have a tendency to vary over the life of the product. These deficiencies can be overcome by employing a variant of break-even analysis known as payback.

Payback is simply the number of years the company expects it will take for a new product to pay back the original investment. In making new product evaluations with this technique, management ranks projects on the basis of the length of the payback period. The shorter the payback period the sooner the product will enhance the profits of the firm. Payback is usually calculated by dividing total fixed costs of the project (F_t) by the estimated annual increase in cash flow generated by the product. This implies an averaging of sales, costs, and prices over the life of the project. A better approach is to find the payback period (N) that satisfies the following set of conditions where P_i is

$$\frac{F_t}{\sum\limits_{i=1}^{N} (P_i - V_i)\, Q_i} = 1 \tag{2}$$

the expected price in the year i, V_i is the expected unit-variable cost and Q_i is the anticipated sales as i goes from year 1 to the payback year N.

The objective of this formula is to find the payback period (N) where the accumulated margin is just equal to the total fixed costs of the project (F_t). The expected margin is calculated separately for each year and added up until it is equal to total fixed costs. The advantage of this method over traditional payback formulas is that price (P_i), unit variable costs (V_i), and unit sales (Q_i) can all change from year to year. For example, suppose total fixed costs for the new cake mix amounted to $250,000 and the price, variable costs, and expected sales were estimated as shown in Table 6-4. Under these conditions, the cumulative margin exceeds total fixed costs by the end of the third year. The three-year payback period derived for the cake mix could then be compared with figures estimated for other projects and the historical standards set by the firm.

One problem with payback is that it does not discriminate among projects according to their absolute size. Two new products could have the same payback period, but differ greatly in the size of the investment and potential dollar profits generated for the firm. Even more serious is the observation that payback does not adequately handle the opportunity cost of capital,[19] the time value of money, and risk.

Return on Investment

Return on investment (ROI) is frequently used in new product evaluations because it simplifies comparisons among projects and allows products to be checked against the opportunity cost of capital for the firm. This approach can be implemented by estimating the return on investment for each new product and comparing the results with other projects and the cost of capital. Those projects with the *highest* rates of return would move immediately to the development and testing phases of the program.

Return on investment can be calculated in a variety of ways depending on the treatment

[19]The rate of return the company foregoes when it invests in new projects. It represents the basic investment alternative to product development.

Table 6-4

Calculating the Payback Period for a New Cake Mix

Year	Price Per Case P	Variable Costs Per Case V	Quantity Sold in Cases Q	Margin Per Year (P-V)Q	Cumulative Margin	
1	$6.00	$3.50	20,000	$50,000	$50,000	
2	5.90	3.45	40,000	98,000	148,000	Total fixed
3	5.75	3.40	44,000	103,400	251,400	costs of
4	5.50	3.42	41,000	85,280	336,680	$250,000
5	4.69	3.55	25,000	28,500	365,180	
6	4.00	3.65	10,000	3,500	368,680	

of depreciation, taxes, and investment. The most popular method is the ratio of average annual earnings after taxes and depreciation to average investment. In symbols this would be:

$$\text{ROI} = \frac{E}{I} \tag{3}$$

where E is average annual earnings and I is the average investment required for the project. This approach requires an estimate of the expected life of the product and judgements on the probable sales and costs associated with the product each year. If average earnings after taxes for the cake mix were estimated at $10,000 per year and the average investment was $75,000, then the projected return on investment (ROI) would be $10,000/$75,000 or 13.3 percent.

The ROI model that has been described is widely used in the evaluation of new product proposals. Knopa found that twelve of seventy-one firms surveyed relied on simple return on investment calculations to discriminate among new ventures.[20] Although simple return on investment calculations are easy to understand and popular among businessmen, they do not adequately treat the problem of the time value of money. Two projects could have the same average rates of return, but have remarkable different patterns for the timing of investments and the return of earnings. Some projects may require a high initial investment and become profitable at the end of their life cycle whereas others may require a series of smaller investments and produce most of their profits soon after they are introduced. Common sense suggests that most businessmen would choose the second type of proposal regardless of similarities in the average rate of return. An objective way to consider the time value of money in new product evaluations is to employ a model that includes a discounted rate of return.

Discounted Rate of Return

The problem of comparing new products with different patterns of investment and revenues can be handled by adding a discount factor to the return on investment calculations. This allows future investment and income streams to be converted back to present-value terms so that alternative projects can be evaluated more objectively. The

[20]Leonard J. Konopa, *New Products: Assessing Commercial Potential* (New York: American Management Association, 1966), p. 15.

discounted rate of return (r) is obtained by plugging estimates of revenues and costs into the formula:

$$I = \frac{R_1 - C_1}{(1 + r)^1} + \frac{R_2 - C_2}{(1 + r)^2} + \cdots \frac{R_n - C_n}{(1 + r)^n} \qquad (4)$$

where I is the initial investment required for the product, R_1 is the total revenue in year 1, and C_1 is the total cost of the product for the first year. The idea is to find a discounted rate of return (r), such that the present value of the income stream (right side of the equation) is just equal to the initial investment (I). The usual solution for this problem is to substitute values of r into the formula until the present value of the earnings approximates the initial investment.

For example, suppose the intial investment for the new cake mix was $250,000 and the estimated income over the life of the project followed the pattern shown in Table 6-4 (column 5). The discounted rate of return (r) could then be calculated by substituting the income and investment figures into equation 4 to give:

$$\$250,000 = \frac{\$50,000}{(1 + r)^1} + \frac{\$98,000}{(1 + r)^2} + \frac{\$103,400}{(1 + r)^3} + \frac{\$85,280}{(1 + r)^4} + \frac{\$28,500}{(1 + r)^5} + \frac{\$3,500}{(1 + r)^6}$$

This expression can be solved by substituting in different discount values (r) until the present value of the income stream (right side of the equation) just equals the initial investment of $250,000. After three trials, the authors found that a discount rate of 15 percent was appropriate for the cake-mix problem. Thus the return generated by spending $250,000 on a new cake mix would be the same as making 15 percent per year on an investment of $250,000.

Konopa found that the discounted rate of return was the most popular single procedure used to evaluate new products. A total of twenty-one out of seventy-one firms used this approach to select projects for further development. In making "go" and "no go" decisions, some firms simply picked the products with the highest estimated returns. Others used cut off points and only accepted projects that exceeded a 15 or 20 percent discounted rate of return. Still other firms used a more general decision rule where new projects had to have a discounted rate of return that exceeded the current average for the company.

Project Numbers

While the discounted rate of return considers the opportunity cost of capital and the time value of earnings and investments, it does not deal directly with the problem of risk. Risk represents the chance that a new product will fail and it has been built into several return on investment models. For example, the American Alcolac Corporation model uses two probabilities in the calculation of project rating numbers.[21] The formula is set up in the following form:

$$\frac{\begin{matrix} \text{Chance of} \\ \text{technical} \\ \text{success} \end{matrix} \times \begin{matrix} \text{Chances of} \\ \text{commercial} \\ \text{success} \end{matrix} \times \begin{matrix} \text{Projected} \\ \text{annual} \\ \text{volume} \end{matrix} \times \text{(Price-variable)} \times \text{Life} }{\text{Total fixed costs}} = \begin{matrix} \text{Project} \\ \text{number} \end{matrix}$$

[21]Theodore T. Miller, "Projecting the Profitability of New Products," *The Commercialization of Research Results* (New York: American Management Association, Special Report No. 20, 1957, p. 31.

The basic structure of the model involves the multiplication of annual volume times the unit margin times the expected life to give a figure for the total earnings generated during the life of the project. Total earnings are then divided by total fixed costs to give the number of times the original investment is repaid over the life of the product. The chances of technical and commercial success included in the formula are subjective probabilities ranging from zero to one and are estimated by executives of the firm. The inclusion of the two probabilities is an attempt to handle risk by deflating the size of the project rating numbers. For example, if technical success is estimated at .9 and commercial success at .7 the calculation of a project number might go as follows:

$$\frac{.9 \times .7 \times 100,000 \times \$2.50 \times 7}{275,625} = 4$$

In this particular example, the influence of the two probabilities reduces the project number from a value of 6.3 to 4.0.

Project numbers are used in much the same manner as other evaluation criteria and products with the highest ratings tend to be preferred over those with low scores. However, the absolute size of project numbers carries less meaning than other return on investment ratios. A project number of 1, for example, represents a minimum level because these products just break-even at the end of their life cycle. Project numbers that exceed 1 suggest that profits are earned, but the rate is not specified. Perhaps the greatest value of these calculations is in making quick and easy comparisons among a large group of products. Although project numbers specifically include risk, they do not allow for variations in sales, costs, and prices over the life of projects and they do not consider the time value of money. These limitations have restricted the use of this model and Konopa found only four out of seventy-one firms using project numbers to evaluate new product ideas.

The procedures we have discussed for analyzing the profitability of new products are fairly simple and enjoy widespread acceptance by the business community. Because of the different types of information provided by each method, some firms calculate break-even, payback, and ROI rates for each new product being evaluated. The main limitations of these methods are that they do not allow for interactions among marketing variables and they do not adequately handle risk.

DEMON and SPRINTER

Two of the more sophisticated models available to help evaluate the potential of new products are DEMON and SPRINTER.[22] DEMON stands for *DE*cision *M*apping via *O*ptimum GO-NO *N*etworks and its basic dimensions can be shown by referring to Figure 6-4. This approach suggests that new product decisions are made in an information network where the choices are either GO (full-scale development), ON (investigate further), or NO (reject the product). A GO decision means the firm is committed to the project and can move to product or market testing before full commercialization is begun. With the ON decision, more data is gathered and the analysis is repeated until a GO or a NO decision is reached. The choice among the GO, ON, and NO decision is made on the basis of new product profitability and the degree of uncertainty associated

[22] A. Charnes, W. W. Cooper, J. K. DeVoe, and D. B. Learner, "DEMON: Decision Mapping via Optimal Go-No Networks—A Model for Marketing New Products," *Management Science,* Vol. 12 (July 1966), pp. B-865-B-888; Glen L. Urban, "A New Product Analysis and Decision Model," *Management Science,* Vol. 12 (April 1968), pp. B-490-B-527.

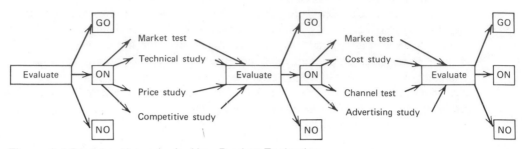

Figure 6-4 Decision Networks for New Product Evaluation.
Source. David B. Montgomery and Glen L. Urban, *Management Science in Marketing* (Englewood Cliffs, N.J., Prentice-Hall, 1969), p. 312. © 1969. Reprinted by permission of Prentice-Hall, Inc.

with these profits. Product profits are obtained by estimating the relations between sales and the marketing mix variables (advertising, price, selling and distribution) over the life of the product and subtracting costs. The uncertainties of the profits can be specified by establishing confidence limits around the best sales estimates for each year.

An example of a new product decision plot is shown in Figure 6-5. In this diagram, discounted differential profits are measured along the vertical axis. Since new products often hurt the profitability of older lines, they should be judged on the basis of the net increase (or differential) in the total profits of the firm. Also new product profits are received over a period of years and they should be discounted to reflect the time value of money. In this case differential profits are discounted at the corporate target rate of return to obtain a present value in dollars for the new product profit stream. In the example shown in Figure 6-5, the required new product investment was $5 million and this represents the dividing line between GO and NO decisions under conditions of certainty. Thus, if the discounted differential profit for a new item was less than $5 million, the rate of return would be less than the target return and a NO decision would drop the item from further consideration. If the differential profit exceeded the $5 million invested in the new product, then a GO decision would be indicated.

Most new products are introduced under conditions of uncertainty and this is measured in Figure 6-5 along the horizontal axis. Uncertainty can be described as the expected standard deviation in profits and is shown in dollars. The diagram is divided into three regions representing GO, ON, and NO decisions on the basis of the amount of risk the firm is willing to tolerate. The line dividing the GO and ON decision areas (Z_1) indicates the firm wants a 90 percent chance that differential profit will exceed the new product investment before a GO decision can be made. Thus at point *Y,* with an expected differential profit of $10 million and a standard deviation of $2 million, the decision would be GO as the probability exceeds the 90 percent cut off. However, if the differential profit dropped to only $7 million, then the point would fall into the ON decision area and more data would have to be gathered and the analysis repeated. Note that the greater the expected uncertainty, the higher the level of profit needed to give a GO decision. The lower boundary between the ON and NO areas (Z_2) suggests the firm expects a 40 percent chance of reaching the target rate of return before an ON decision is made. The calculations required to maximize the expected value of discounted differential profit as modified by risk, investment, and other constraints are extremely complex. One way to simplify this problem is to use a trial-and-error search routine called

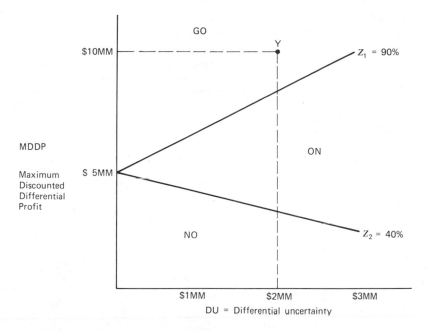

GO

$10MM

Y

$Z_1 = 90\%$

MDDP

ON

Maximum
Discounted
Differential
Profit

$ 5MM

$Z_2 = 40\%$

NO

$1MM $2MM $3MM

DU = Differential uncertainty

Figuro 6 5 An Examplc of a New Product Decisiun Plot.
Source. Glen L. Urban, "SPRINTER: A Tool for New Product Decision Makers," *Industrial Management Review,* Vol. 8 (Spring 1967), p. 48. Reprinted with permission form *Sloan Management Review.*

SPRINTER.[23] SPRINTER stands for *S*pecification of *PR*ofits with *I*nteraction under *T*rial and *E*rror *R*esponse. This routine evaluates a wide range of marketing programs and identifies the best price, advertising, and distribution levels for the new product in each planning period. The output of the model includes a GO, ON, or NO decision and the maximum level of the differential profit generated by the item.

SPRINTER has been successfully employed to help evaluate a new nylon compound for a chemical company. The company had tentatively decided to GO with the product even though it would compete directly with two other plastics marketed by the firm for use in small gears and bearing linings. Data for the SPRINTER program were provided by marketing executives and included estimates for the effects of price, advertising, and salesmen on new and existing products over a ten-year planning period. The company had planned to price the product at $350 a carton for three years and then drop to $250 for the next seven years. In addition, 1 percent of the sales force was delegated to push the new probuct and $10,000 per year allocated for advertising.

When the figures supplied by the executives were fed to the SPRINTER program[24] the results shown in Table 6-5 were obtained. The first column of output shows the effects of implementing the company planned marketing program for the new nylon compound. The discounted differential profit ($6 million) was less than the planned investment ($8 million) resulting in a NO decision for the product. SPRINTER searched for a better solution and was able to raise expected profits to $10.8 million by making substantial

Table 6-5

SPRINTER Output for Proposed Nylon Compound

	Reference Program	Search Program	Larger Plant	Larger Sales Force
Discounted differential profit	6,000,000	10,833,000	11,561,000	12,219,000
Investment	8 mm	8 mm	8.3mm	8.4mm
Probability of achieving target rate of return	Less than 50%	86%	88%	91%
Advertising level per year	10,000	10,000	10,000	10,000
Percent of sales effort per year	1.0	1.0	1.0	1.3
Price in year				
1	350	250	250	250
2	350	250	250	250
3	350	250	250	250
4	250	180	170	190
5	250	200	160	200
6	250	210	170	210
7	250	170	170	180
8	250	180	180	180
9	250	180	180	190
10	250	190	190	200
Recommended decision	No	On	On	Go

Source. Glen L. Urban, "A New Product Analysis and Decision Model," *Management Science,* Vol. 14 (April 1968), p. B-514.

cuts in the price of the new item. Even more money was generated by relaxing the constraint on plant capacity. The highest expected profit ($12 million) was produced by cutting price, enlarging the plant, and adding one more salesman to sell the product. The probability of achieving the target return exceeded 90 percent in this case and SPRINTER recommended GO.

Although SPRINTER helped improve the quality of the new product decision for the nylon compound, the results were only as good as the input data. Since the chemical company had introduced similar items, they were in a good position to describe accurately the impact of marketing variables and effects on other lines. If executives do not have a good understanding of the impact of price, advertising, and distribution factors on new products, then other simpler evaluation methods should be used.

DEVELOPMENT AND TESTING

Development and testing are concerned with establishing physical characteristics for new goods and services that are acceptable to consumers. The objective is to convert ideas into actual products that are safe, provide customer benefits, and can be manufactured economically by the firm. Usually development includes concept testing, consumer preference tests, laboratory evaluations, use tests, and pilot plant operations (Figure 6-3).

Concept Testing

The first step in the development process often includes measuring customer reactions to descriptions of new products. Promising ideas are converted into concept statements that are printed on cards and shown to small groups of customers. Sometimes pictures or preliminary models of the product are included along with the written descriptions. Participants are asked if they would buy the item and are requested to give reasons for their decisions. Modifications are then made in the product concept and the revised statement is tested with another group of customers. When a product concept appears well defined in terms of customer acceptance, a real product is developed to go along with the concept.

For example, concept testing has been used by the Post Division of General Foods in the development of a new type of dog food.[25] General Foods needed something different to compete with canned dog food and a new process suggested that a meat product with 25 percent moisture could be developed that would not require refrigeration. Concept statements describing the new product in the form of sausages and dried beef were tested on groups of consumers. This led to a revised concept with the product formulated as a hamburg patty. The laboratory then made up some sample patties and the concept and the new product were tested with sixty dog owners. Forty of the respondents were first shown the following concept statement:

DOG PATTIES
"Here is a new natural way to feed your dog all his nutritional requirements—all the proteins a dog likes and needs. These new patties are deliciously attractive and for the same amount of food value as a can of the best dog food, they have only one-third the weight and bulk.[26]

and then were questioned concerning their perception of the product. Next the dog owners were shown the actual product and requestioned. The remaining twenty owners were shown the product first and then asked to give their attitudes towards the dog patties. As a result of these tests, General Foods learned that the dog-patty concept was acceptable to most dog owners and they also gathered some useful information on packaging, pricing, and promotion.

Preference Tests and Product Quality

Preference tests are employed to compare consumer reactions to different product attributes or quality levels. Consumers are usually given two samples of the product with different characteristics to taste or use and are then asked which they prefer and why? The idea is to isolate the most desirable characteristics and quality levels so they can be built into the new product.

Consumer preference tests are often helpful in determining specifications for new items because product standards developed by laboratory technicians can be different from the more general standards used by consumers. An example of conflicting quality standards was shown by an applesauce preference test conducted by one of the authors.[27]

[25]See the *General Foods–Post Division (A)* case developed by the Harvard Graduate School of Business Administration and distributed by the Intercollegiate Case Clearing House of Boston, ICH 10M8, copyright © 1964 by the President and Fellows of Harvard College, p. 7.

[26]See the *General Foods–Post Division (A)*, Appendix A, p. 17.

[27]Douglas J. Dalrymple, "A Study of Consumer Preference for Applesauce Using the Two-Visit Interview Technique," *Journal of Farm Economics*, Vol. 43, No. 3 (August 1961) pp. 690-697.

A blind taste test that exposed 652 consumers to pairs of applesauce brands revealed that 3 of the preferred brands had been graded C or Substandard according to the U.S. Grades. This implied that the federal standards for applesauce emphasized product characteristics that were not important to consumers. Subsequent research revealed that the preferred brands of applesauce were thinner and had more defects than the federal standards allowed for Grade A applesauce. Thus, a situation developed where products that failed to pass the standards set up by the industry, were actually the brands most preferred by consumers. The irony of this particular case was that only one manufacturer appeared to know enough about consumer tastes to produce a product tailored to the *real* consumer preferences. This manufacturer was shrewd enough to market the product under his own label so that federal grades were not needed to sell the product to retailers. The moral of this story is that manufacturers cannot ignore the quality standards held by final consumers if they expect to take maximum advantage of market opportunities.

A variety of methods have been developed to identify product features that are important to consumers and to estimate the numbers of persons who prefer different variations or quality levels. Perhaps the simplest approach is to interview potential customers and ask them to rate product features on a scale 1 (unimportant) to 5 (very important). This makes it possible to compare the relative value of product attributes and to construct distribution of customer preferences. Another approach suggested by Benson builds preference distributions for product attributes from consumer's comparisons of a few existing or sample products.[28] Individual product attribute scores can then be grouped into clusters to identify market segments based on benefits or other factors.[29]

A third method recommended by Day submits a full range of sample products to groups of consumers using a forced choice paired comparison technique.[30] For example, Figure 6-6 shows the preference expressed by 928 consumers for five levels of chocolate flavoring for ice cream. Note that the largest group of consumers preferred ice cream with less than the normal amount of chocolate, but 15 percent preferred 40 percent more chocolate flavoring. Thus an ice cream manufacturer could avoid the "majority fallacy" by introducing an extra-rich chocolate ice cream to appeal to the top segments of the market.[31]

Consumer preferences for product attributes can also be obtained be ranking procedures and the multiple dimensional scaling techniques described in Chapter 4 (pp. 152-157). Whatever the method employed, marketing managers need accurate preference data so they can set product specifications to achieve the best possible market positions.

Use Tests

Once a firm has established a viable product concept and a set of specifications, the next step in the developmental process is to test samples of the product to see if they meet the needs of the customer. Usually this is done through a combination of laboratory and field testing. Lab tests offer the advantage of controlled conditions and they can often simulate usage of the product and obtain results quicker than field trials. Car doors, for example, can be slammed thousands of times in the lab to see if they are designed to last

---

[28]Purnell H. Benson, "Fitting and Analyzing Distribution Curves of Consumer Choices," *Journal of Advertising Research,* Vol. 5, No. 1 (March 1965), pp. 28-34.

[29]Benefit segmentation is discussed in Chapter 4, p. 16.

[30]Ralph L. Day, "Systematic Paired Comparisons in Preference Analysis," *Journal of Marketing Research,* Vol. 2 (November 1965), pp. 406-412.

[31]The "majority fallacy" is discussed in more detail in Chapter 4.

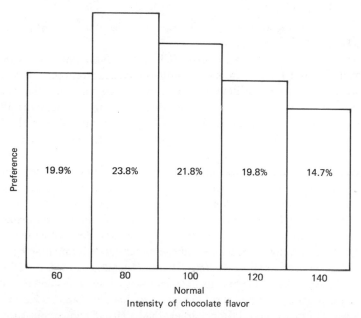

Figure 6-6 Consumer Preferences for Five Levels of Chocolate Flavoring for Ice Cream. *Source.* Reprinted from Ralph L. Day, "Systematic Paired Comparisons in Preference Analysis," *Journal of Marketing Research,* Vol. 2 (November 1965), p. 411, published by the American Marketing Association.

the life of the automobile. Despite these advantages, laboratory tests are artificial and most new products are also subjected to testing by potential customers.

Customer use tests are designed to find out how a product performs under the realistic conditions encountered in the home or factory. General Electric, for example, tested its electric slicing knife among 800 persons in twenty-six different cities before introducing it to the marketplace.[32] In another case, a food manufacturer offered 738 women from four cities sample bottles of a new pourable mayonnaise.[33] After ten days, personal interviews were conducted to gauge customer reactions and give the women a chance to purchase some of the product at the regular price. Women who bought samples of the new pourable mayonnaise were contacted three additional times to see if they wanted more of the item. In addition, the respondents were asked to keep a diary to show how they used the product. This research indicated that although consumers liked the pourable mayonnaise, they tended to use it like a liquid salad dressing rather than a mayonnaise replacement. Thus the use test suggested some changes were needed in packaging and promotional appeals if the firm expected the item to complete with the more traditional mayonnaise products.

Selecting a Name

New products and services are given names so they can be more easily identified and promoted to consumer and industrial buyers. The best names tend to be short, distinctive, and easy to pronounce and remember. Also, desirable names often suggest action (i.e.,

---

[32]*Advertising Age* (May 11, 1964), p. 74.

[33]See the *Hamilton Division* case prepared by Neil H. Borden, Jr. of the University of Virginia and distributed by the Intercollegiate Case Clearing House of Boston, no. 9-571-705, pp. 18-20.

Whirlpool, Cougar, Roto Rooter) as well as show the intended usage of the product or service (i.e., Drano, Sinex, U-Haul).

Suggestions for names are frequently provided by the advertising agency that writes the promotional material for the product and by computers programmed to make up nonsense words. Sometimes consumers are interviewed to find out what images are associated with prospective brand names and to measure preferences for alternative names. Words that are made up, such as the Exxon name recently adopted by Standard Oil of New Jersey, are likely to have fewer negative connotations than words that are already in use.

A good description of the procedures used to select a name for a new product is provided by the dog food example mentioned earlier.[34] Concept tests had suggested that a concentrated dog food could be marketed in a form of hamburger patties. Four potential names for the new item (Dog burgers, Dog patties, Prime burgers, and Prime patties) were picked from lists prepared by an advertising agency and Post Division executives. Next the names were tested with consumers and General Foods found that the "burger" suffex had a "hearty" connotation whereas "patties" tended to have a "diminutive" image. The most popular name in the consumer tests was Dog burgers and Prime burgers was second. Unfortunately, further checking revealed that Dog burgers had been registered by another company and Prime burgers had caused some confusion among potential buyers. At this point the name Gaines burgers was suggested to tie the hamburg concept to an established dog food already marketed by the firm. Thus the name finally adopted for the new product combined a descriptive term (burger) with an existing company brand name (Gaines).

Companies must be careful to avoid selecting names that are similar to those used by other firms. Several years ago Colgate introduced a liquid cleaner called Gene and was surprised to find another company was already selling a cleaner under the registered name Jenie. Although the names were not spelled the same, Colgate was forced to withdraw its product from the market at a substantial financial loss. Sometimes brand names become so popular they are used by the public to describe a whole class of products (i.e., Scotch Tape). When this occurs the manufacturer can lose his rights to the name as happened in the case of aspirin and escalator. One way to avoid the problem is to insert the word "brand" after the name as in Scotch Brand Cellophane Tape to show that the word Scotch is not a generic term.

Packaging

The main concern in designing packages for new products is to protect the merchandise on its journey from the factory to the customer. This is particularly true for industrial goods and for items such as appliances where sales are made from display models. However, when consumers select products off store shelves, packaging becomes an important promotional tool. Dik Twedt suggests that sales are enhanced by packages that are visible, informative, emotionally appealing, and workable.[35]

Packages with high visibility tend to be easy to find when they are displayed on store shelves. Some of the laboratory instruments that can be used to test packages for visibility include the *tachistoscope* (how many seconds to identify the elements),

---

[34]See page 255. Name selection described in *General Foods–Post Division* (B), case no. 10M9, prepared by the Harvard Graduate School of Business Administration, 1964.

[35]Dik Warren Twedt, "How Much Value can be Added Through Packaging?" *Journal of Marketing,* Vol. 32 (January 1968), pp. 58-61.

distance meter (how far away can the design be identified), and the *apparent size meter* (which package appears larger at equal distance. The idea is to expose alternative package designs to small groups of consumers and select the design with the best scores. If these instruments are not available, the measurements can be simulated by more informal means.

Package designs with good informational value tell the consumer at a glance what the package contains. In addition, packages are required by federal laws to provide information on food additives, flammable materials, net weight, name of manufacturer or distributor and other factors. The Fair Packaging and Labeling Act (1967) also has provisions designed to help standardize package sizes and make comparative shopping easier for the consumer.

The emotional factor in packaging refers to the image that consumers form after viewing a product. Emotional appeals can be measured by asking respondents to rate packages using simple scaling techniques. Thus consumers could be asked to indicate whether a package was ''very modern'' on one extreme or ''old-fashioned'' at the other. Emotional reactions to packages can be critical in the sale of certain prestige products. For example, the bottles used to hold Avon cosmetics are so pleasing to the eye that many of them became collectors items.

Workability in packaging means that containers not only protect the product, but are easy to open and reclose, are readily stored, and have utility for secondary uses once the product is used up. Examples of package designs that have these characteristics includes tear-top pudding cups, reclosable pop bottles, and the drinking mugs used to hold margarine.

TEST MARKETING

Test marketing is an optional phase of the product development cycle that is designed to measure customer reactions to new products and their supporting marketing programs in selected market areas. It is conducted under realistic sales conditions with consumers making purchases from retail stores in response to regular advertising and promotional activities. A decision to enter test markets implies a basic uncertainty about how well a new item will be received by consumers.

Test markets are most often used when new products are radically different and companies do not know how to promote them or whether customers will buy the product. Low cost consumer items are the most common products placed in test markets. High tooling costs make it impractical to test market appliances or automobiles. Industrial goods manufacturers work closely with their customers and rely on feedback from use tests to determine when a new product is ready for national distribution.

A good example of the need for test marketing occurred a few years ago when Brown-Foreman Distillers developed a mild, light-colored whisky to compete with the rapidly expanding vodka segment of the market.[36] They spent lavishly on concept tests and taste tests to derive the ideal specifications for the new product. The name for the new whisky (Frost 8/80) was picked by experts and the package was designed to give the brand a quality image. Brown-Foreman was eager to beat their competitors to the market and Frost 8/80 was quickly placed in national distribution. However, after two years the product had achieved only one-third of its anticipated volume and the company dropped

[36]*Wall Street Journal* (January 5, 1973), p. 1. This example was described earlier in another context in Chapter 4, Segmentation (p. 155).

Frost 8/80 after losing over $2 million. This loss could have been partially or completely avoided if the product had been placed in test market. Consumers were confused about Frost 8/80 because it looked like vodka, but it tasted like whisky. A test market would have picked this up in time for the company to have changed the product or modified the advertising program before funds were committed for national distribution. On the other hand, when new products are not radically different from existing items (i.e., new flavor of a cake mix) test markets can be a waste of time and money. Polaroid, for example, is so confident that the latest versions of its cameras for instant photography will succeed that they do not bother with test markets.

Test Procedures

One of the first steps in designing a test market is selecting a representative group of test cities. The objective is to find stable communities where age and income statistics are typical of the anticipated buyers of the product. Several years ago, for example, the American Dairy Association selected a city to test market butter where most of the workers were employed by one firm. Right in the middle of the test the company went on strike, butter sales plummeted, and the market test was ruined. Test cities must also have cooperative merchants and good media coverage to facilitate promotional activities. In addition, test cities should be isolated from each other so that promotional campaigns run in one city do not influence sales in other test areas.

A related issue is deciding the optimum number of test communities. Although large samples increase the *reliability* of test results and raise the number of merchandising variations that can be evaluated, they also increase *costs*. Test marketing is so expensive that most firms utilize only a limited number of cities. One study of 102 firms revealed that about half of the companies used less than four test cities.[37]

Test markets typically vary in length from a few months to one or two years. A key factor in determining the length of a particular study is the repurchase cycle of the product. Some items, for example, are used infrequently and may be repurchased only every three or four months. A test market must be long enough so that it measures repeat buying as well as trial purchases. Other factors influencing the length of a study are the availability of research funds and the threat of retaliation by competitors.

One of the most crucial elements in test marketing is obtaining accurate data on product acceptance. While figures on factory shipments are easy to collect, they are a poor measure of consumer purchase rates because of initial stocking by stores and delays in reorders from retailers. The usual procedure is to conduct special store audits that show sales at the retail level. Additional information on customer characteristics and the number of repeat buyers can be obtained by having groups of consumers record their purchases over a period of time. Consumer panel data can also provide information on the number of customers that stay with their old brands and show how buyers switch from brand to brand when a new product is introduced to the market. If a firm needs data on customer attitudes, then actual buyers of the product can be interviewed to measure their reactions.

The concept of test marketing has great appeal among marketing executives because it reduces uncertainty and may improve chances for new product success. Not only does it allow the firm to measure customer acceptance under actual sales conditions, but it makes it easy to evaluate alternative promotional programs. The firm can try different combinations of coupons, free samples, and advertising in the test cities and see what

---

[37]*Printers Ink* (April 13, 1962), p. 22.

generates the greatest sales. In addition, the use of controlled test markets encourages the employment of sophisticated experimental designs and rigorous statistical measures of significance.

Test Marketing the Princess Phone

The introduction of the Princess phone a few years ago by AT&T provides an example of a well-run test marketing program.[38] The compact Princess phone was designed to use in bedrooms and had a light to make it easier to use in the dark. The first stage of the market test involved selling the new phone on a door-to-door basis to customers in Norristown, Pennsylvania and Peoria, Illinois, at two different prices. In Norristown the phone carried an initial charge of $8.50 plus a $.30 per month charge and in Peoria they used a $29.50 initial charge and no recurring fee.[39] The high initial price encountered substantial sales resistance and considerably more phones were sold per sales call at the lower price. After the sales test, a sample of 164 Princess phone buyers was interviewed to obtain customer reactions and information on where the new set was installed. Most of the buyers were satisfied with their new phones, but a number indicated that the base was not steady and the tone ringer was too loud. The survey also revealed that 37 percent of the Princess phones were installed in other rooms than the bedroom. This result had a direct affect on the selection of a brand name for the new product and the advertising messages used to promote the phone to consumers.

The second phase of the Princess phone experiment included a four-month sales test designed to find the optimum level of advertising support and the best media mix for the new product. AT&T also hoped to determine the approximate size of the market for the phone so they could set production schedules at their Western Electric subsidiary. The sales test evaluated four combinations of television and newspaper advertising support using sixteen cities (Table 6-6). Advertising impact was measured both in terms of Princess phone sales and in terms of consumer recall of the ads. Data on recall were gathered using telephone interviews with 300 randomly selected customers in each test city. In addition, all persons who installed Princess phones during the test were asked to complete a questionnaire.

Table 6-6

Test Cities and Ad Combinations Selected for Princess Study

Treatment	Colorado	Georgia	Illinois	Pennsylvania
Low TV—low newspaper	Denver	Savannah	Danville	Altoona
Low TV—high newspaper	Greeley	Albany	Peoria	Scranton
High TV—low newspaper	Pueblo	Atlanta	Decatur	Harrisburg
High TV—high newspaper	Colorado Springs	Macon	Springfield	Lancaster

Source. "American Telephone & Telegraph Company-Princess Telephone (B)," *Advanced Cases in Marketing Management* Edwin C. Bursk and Stephen A. Greyser (Englewood Cliffs, N.J.: Prentice-Hall, 1968), p. 76.

[38] "American Telephone and Telegraph Company—Princess Telephone (A & B)," *Advanced Cases in Marketing Management* by Edwin C. Bursk and Stephen A. Greyser (Englewood Cliffs, N.J.: Prentice-Hall, 1968), pp. 21-27, 74-85.

[39] Both rate structures provided the same return on capital.

The results of the advertising market study suggested that high levels of ad support did not significantly raise Princess phone sales and a relatively low ad budget was probably best for the new product. Also the *high TV-low newspaper* treatment was slightly better than the others indicating that AT&T should put more emphasis on TV than newspapers. Overall, the market tests of the Princess phone provided a great deal of useful information on product improvements, pricing, advertising budgets, media allocations, and copy themes. Although the test markets were a success for the Princess phone, this technique has a number of limitations that are sometimes overlooked in the rush to gather additional data on new products.

Limitations

Perhaps the most serious drawbacks with test marketing are that it is expensive and potential sales are lost due to delays in getting the product to the marketplace. In addition, it is often difficult to interpret sales results produced by test markets. Since the products are new, there are no absolute standards of performance that can be used for comparison. Except for situations where sales are unusually high or low, test results may simply reflect the basic uncertainty that prevailed when the study was initiated. In addtion, the small number of test cities and the artificial nature of the testing process makes it hazardous to project results into national sales figures. A compounding factor is the realization that some products succeed in test markets and then fail when introduced nationally and vice versa.

An even more insidious problem is the response that competitors can take to test market activity. One possibility is a direct attempt to wreck the test by introducing price cuts or coupons that upset normal sales patterns. A more likely reaction is that competitors will audit your test markets and use the results to develop their own product. General Foods reportedly used this procedure to measure Lever Brothers' sales of a new pancake syrup and was able to introduce their own product to national distribution at about the same time.[40] The moral of the story is that firms that allow items that can be copied easily to languish in test markets for extended periods may find that competitors have stolen their ideas, their advertising copy, and their markets.

Test markets are also inappropriate for most industrial products and items that require extensive tooling and unique production equipment. It is simply too expensive to test market lift trucks, autmobiles, and large appliances and alternative measures of customer acceptance must be developed for these items.

Alternatives to Test Marketing

One alternative to test marketing involves the exposure of customers to product advertising and purchasing situations in a closed laboratory setting. This technique has the advantage that it can be done quickly, at relatively low cost, and without revealing the product or its performance to competitors. Walker Research, for example, offers a service called *Simulated Store Tests* that can be used to evaluate new items.[41]

Groups of consumers are recruited, prescreened to represent the target market, and invited to a central location. Next they complete a questionnaire detailing their experience with the product category and are shown a series of advertisements (print, radio,

[40]"Product Tryouts: Sales Tests in Selected Cities Help Trim Risks of National Marketings," *Wall Street Journal* (August 10, 1962), p. 1.

[41]Described in a brochure by Walker Research, of Indianapolis, Indiana.

televison) within the context of a program or publication. The consumers are then directed to a simulated grocery store where they are given the opportunity to purchase items on display. Next the consumers are asked to complete a postpurchase questionnaire and participate in focussed group interviews to probe in detail reasons for purchase and product attitudes. Finally buyers of the product are phoned two weeks later to ask about product satisfaction and repurchase intentions.

The Simulated Store Test does not predict ultimate sales levels for new products, but it does provide a useful way to compare alternative pricing, promotion, and packaging strategies in a closed environment. In addition, it can measure the effects of new items on the sales of existing products sold by the firm. Perhaps the most attractive feature of the laboratory studies is a firm can get reactions from 500 customers in six to eight weeks at a cost of only $10,000.

Another way to gather information on customer acceptance of new products and promotional programs is to go immediately to a regional market introduction. This involves promoting and selling the product in a two-or-three-state area rather than just a few test cities. Although regional introductions are more expensive than running a test market, it is cheaper than introducing a product nationally. Also, if successful items are moved quickly from regional to national distribution, competitive responses are likely to be weak and ineffectual.

Too often new products are routinely shipped off to test markets without a realistic analysis of the potential cost or benefits of such a procedure. Test marketing is not a "cure-all" for product development problems, but simply one of many ways to gather data on new items.

COMMERCIALIZATION

The next step in the product development process is the introduction of new items to the dealers and then to the ultimate buyers of the product. The objective of commercialization is to get the dealers to stock the item and persuade the ultimate consumer to purchase the item for the first time. Previous stages have eliminated undesirable projects and have established the specifications, prices, and promotional arrangements most suitable for the new venture. The remaining commercialization phase is concerned with implementing the plans that have been made.

The Importance of Timing

The success or failure of many products often depends on when the product is introduced. If it is too soon, customers may reject it because it is not fully developed or because it is too far ahead of its time. For example, several years ago Philco introduced an ultra modern line of television sets that appeared to be of good quality, reasonably priced, and supported by an adequate promotional budget. The new line failed, however, because customers felt the line was too extreme to fit in with existing furnishings.

A more frequent error is to introduce a product too late, after competitors have captured a dominant market position. An example of the problems of late entry occurred not long ago in the dry-soup market, an area long dominated by Lipton. Corn Products introduced its Knorr dry-soup mixes to the United States market and six months later Campbell brought out its Red Kettle line.[42] Lipton responded by increasing the number

---

[42]John T. Gerlach and Charles A. Wainwright, *Successful Management of New Products* (New York: Hastings House, 1968), p. 125.

of soups in its line and by raising its advertising budget by 50 percent. After three years of lavish advertising by Corn Products and Campbell, the Knorr soups had gained 12 percent of the market and Red Kettle only 6 percent. Corn Products stopped production of the soups in the United States and began importing them while Campbell dropped its dry-soup line entirely.

A graphic description of how timing can affect the profitability of new products is given in Figure 6-7. Company A's product began at time zero as a quarterly expenditures for research and development. The product started to contribute profits soon after it was introduced and the profit line moved into the positive quadrant. Company A's initial investment was recovered in a little over two years as shown by the vertical dotted line. The second product was introduced by Company B at year seven and required two and three-quarters years to break even. The last product entered the market during the eighth year and over three years were needed to recoup the initial investment. Since the area under the curves represents total profits, profitability in this case was a function of the time of introduction. If the superior new product, for example, had arrived earlier, then it is quite possible that Company C's product would have failed to reach its break-even point. This discussion suggests that products that reach the market first are apt to enjoy greater sales, profits, and have a longer life cycle than those that follow.

Another problem is timing new product introductions so they do not merely replace the sales of existing company products. Many firms develop a number of new product ideas and then keep them in "cold storage" until they are needed. This allows new items to be released as interest declines in current products or when competitors come out with an innovation. IBM's Office Products Division follows this strategy and it allows the

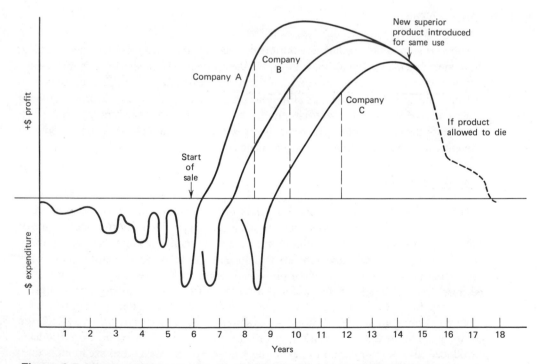

Figure 6-7 Affects of Timing on the Profitability of Three Competitive Products. *Source.* C. F. Rassweiler, "Product Strategy and Future Profits," *Research Review* (April 1961), p. 6. Reproduced with the permission of the John Manville Co.

company to squeeze maximum profit out of current machines before they are replaced by new models. Once the importance of timing is understood, the question is how to manage product development activities so that products arrive on the market at the "right" competitive moment.

Coordinating Product Introductions

Timing is crucial during commercialization because goodwill and sales can be lost if the product fails to reach the dealers on schedule. Optimum coordination of commercialization activities can be achieved by monitoring the introduction of new products using a PERT (Program Evaluation and Review Technique) type control procedure (Figure 6-8). This approach helps identify critical operations and the status reports produced by the system keep the project director informed of delays in completion times.[43]

Developing a Network. The first step in the application of PERT techniques is the development of a detailed activity network. This is based on a listing of all activities that must be performed and a careful analysis of the sequential and concurrent relationships that exist among the activities. For example, the flow diagram in Figure 6-3 gives many of the essential activities in product development and shows the general order in which they must be completed. This basic information can be combined with estimates of completion times to derive a new product development network as shown in Figure 6-8.

This diagram is made up of a series of arrows that represent activities or jobs to be completed. Each activity is labeled and begins and ends at points called events (circles with numbers in them). The relationship of the arrows to the events indicates the sequential and frequently parallel character of different product development activities. For example, the screening of product ideas, which occurs between events 1 and 2, must precede all of the other steps of the development process. The number 2 in brackets located below the first arrow indicates the time in weeks that the company expects will be needed to complete the first activity.[44]

The most important path through the product development network is known as the *critical path*. This represents the *longest* sequence of activities to be completed in the development cycle and it determines the earliest date that the project can be completed. The critical path is obtained by adding up and comparing activity completion times for all possible routes through the network. In the present example, the critical path is shown by the dark arrows and it is estimated to require a total of 134 weeks for all work to be finished. The critical path is important because delays in completing activities on this route will mean slippages in the schedule for the entire project. Also if competitive pressure makes it necessary to speed up the introduction of a new product, the critical path will show the activities that will have to be expedited or left out entirely.

Controlling the Network. The successful control of product development networks involves a delicate balancing of time, expense, and risk. The management of these factors can be made more efficient by utilizing the analytical ability of the computer. For

[43]*See An Introduction to PERT/Cost System for Integrated Project Management,* Special Project Office, U.S. Navy Department, Oct. 15, 1961. Also reproduced in Edgar A. Pessemier's *New Product Decisions: an Analytical Approach* (New York: McGraw-Hill Book Co., 1966), pp. 24-38.

[44]The times shown in the diagram are the most likely estimates prepared by individuals assigned to complete the work. PERT networks typically show three time estimates for the completion of each activity: Optimistic, Most Likely, and Pessimistic. An expected time (te) can then be calculated using the formula:

$$te = \frac{to + 4\,tm + tp}{6}$$

Initial screening and management approval (2)

Check patent position (3)

R+D technical evaluation (6)

Marketing suggestions (1)

Preliminary specification (2)

Build simple model (2)

Estimate competitive behavior (2)

Estimate market potential (2)

Estimate advertising and distribution costs (2)

Check manufacturing facilities (1)

Estimate manufacturing costs (2)

Set preliminary price (1)

Estimate demand (1)

Profit analysis (3)

Management evaluation (1)

Complete design and manufacture samples (18)

Sales plans (3)

Patent and copyright applications (3)

Preliminary package design (4)

Engineering tests (6)

Consumer panel evaluation (12)

Check product safety (2)

Revise product specifications (4)

Test package design (2)

Additional lab tests (5)

Preliminary advertising program (4)

Select brand name (2)

Critical Path Activity
Dummy Activity
Estimated Activity
Completion Times in Weeks
( )

Search and screening

Business analysis

Development

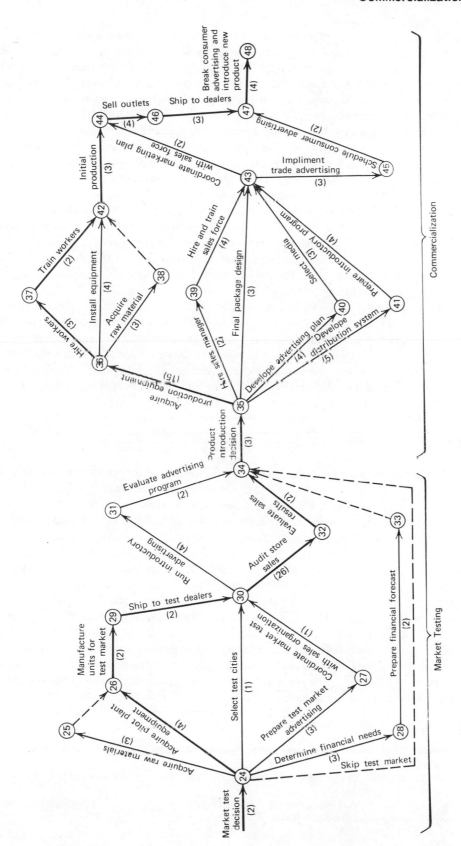

Figure 6-8 New Product Development Network.

example, once a new product network has been developed and estimates of completion times have been obtained, computer routines can be used to derive a critical path. The computer can also be used to keep track of the costs associated with each activity and to print out periodic status reports. Perhaps the most valuable contribution of the computer is that it can quickly simulate the cost and time implications of changes and revisions in new product networks.

Three approaches can be used when competitive pressure or slippages in critical path activities make it necessary to save time on a project. One is to convert sequential activities into projects that can be run in parallel. A second approach is to simply eliminate certain activities entirely. This method has the advantage that it saves both time and money. Uman gives an example where network analysis indicated that it would take two years for an improved product to reach national distribution.[45] A simulation was run with the test market removed and the length of the development schedule was reduced to nine months. In this case, management was willing to accept a greater risk of failure in order to get their product on the market quickly. A third way to speed the completion of activities in development networks is to simply apply additional resources such as money, manpower, materials, machines, or space.

Although network analysis has been used effectively in product development by Lever Brothers, Diamond Alkali, American Cyanamid, Sealtest, and other companies, there are limits to what this or any other control technique can accomplish.[46] Network analysis is a fairly expensive procedure and potential benefits must be significant if the technique is to pay its way. Because of the cost and problems of implementing network analysis, one author has suggested that unless a project involves the investment of $1 million, network analysis is probably not justified.[47]

Summary

Product development is an exciting, creative process that converts ideas into commercially viable goods and services. Product development is also expensive and the likelihood of increasing sales and profits from new items is enhanced by careful attention to the organization and control of this activity. A key ingredient is a full time director of product development to expedite and coordinate the many jobs and individuals needed to bring out new merchandise. Flow diagrams and PERT type control procedures are particularly useful in making sure projects reach the market on time and at an acceptable cost. In addition, the firm must foster a climate that is receptive to new ideas and develop screening criteria that are appropriate to its own objectives and resources. Also new products need to be carefully tested so that they reflect the attributes and quality levels actually desired by the ultimate consumer. This means concept tests to gauge customer reactions to product ideas, preference tests to select product attributes, and use tests to evaluate packaging and long run customer acceptance. Where new products are radically different, sales tests may be needed to measure repurchase rates and alternative promotional appeals. Finally, products must be introduced to the marketplace so that dealers and customers will become aware of the new items and begin to purchase them on a regular basis.

[45]David B. Uman, *New Product Programs: Their Planning and Control* (New York: American Management Association, 1969), p. 133.
[46]John T. Gerlach and Charles Anthony Wainwright, *Successful Management of New Products* (New York: Hastings House, 1968), p. 83.
[47]B. W. Badenoch, "Development Projects and Profit Objectives," *New Products–New Profits* (New York: American Management Association 1964), p. 49.

Questions

1. What are the different ways in which a company can find new products to develop? What are the risks involved?
2. A cynic, after analyzing the product life cycle concept stated: ''The only difference between a successful product and a failure is a couple of years.'' Comment on this statement. What implications does it have with regard to measurements of profitability?
3. Given the following activities what is the earliest time the product can be introduced? What is the critical path?

Activity	Must Follow	Weeks to Complete
A	—	5
B	A	2
C	B	3
D	B	8
E	C, D	4
F	E	3
G	F	2
H	F	3
I	H	2
J	G, I	4

   What is the latest week that activity C can start without delaying the total project?

4. Describe four products that, in your opinion, failed due to poor timing. What could have prevented these failures?
5. Rank the following products according to:
   (a) Payback period.
   (b) Average annual return.
   (c) Discounted rate of return.

Product	Initial Investment	Year 1	Returns in Year 2	Year 3
A	$100,000	$ 40,000	$50,000	$ 60,000
B	100,000	50,000	80,000	20,000
C	100,000	70,000	70,000	10,000
D	100,000	20,000	30,000	100,000
E	100,000	100,000	0	0

   Why are there differences in the rankings?
   As a marketing manager which method would you prefer to use?
6. What factors must be considered when the decision of whether or not to test market is being made?

7. Evaluate the procedures for analyzing the profitability of new products as to:
   (a) Time value of money.
   (b) Consideration of risk.
   (c) Contributions to other products.
   (d) Comparability of product ratings.
8. What impact does the shortage of raw materials and energy have on the product development process?
9. What are the objectives of the screening and business analysis phases of product development? Why do firms spend so much time and money on these activities?
10. Explain the differences among use tests, concept tests, preference tests, and market tests.
11. A competitor is running a sales-response test to pick the best of two advertising campaigns to use to introduce a new product. The company has spent $35,000 to date in three test markets and you know that some minor changes in your advertising in the test cities can ruin the test results. Those changes will cost about $1500. What should you do?

Case 6-1
M-Tron Industries[1]

In April 1971, the management of M-Tron Industries was evaluating a proposed marketing plan for their E-Z Breathe electronic air cleaner. Since late 1969 M-Tron management had made several attempts to market a portable electronic air cleaner for home use. Total factory sales since April 1970, were between 5000 and 6000 units. Mr. Kornelius Mooibroek, marketing manager of M-Tron, believed that 2500 to 3000 units were still in the inventories of distributors and dealers. The 5000 to 6000 total sales represented about three to four months' production capacity.

BACKGROUND

M-Tron Industries, Inc. was founded in 1965 by the efforts of a development company in Yankton, South Dakota. Manufacturing operations began in April 1965. The company began with approximately 30 employees, and grew to 190 employees in 1970. In July 1969, M-Ton acquired all of the outstanding stock of Min-Max of Kansas City, a company producing ultraprecision machined parts.

[1]This case was prepared by Professors James Taylor and Bertil C. Nyman with the assistance of Terry McClain, of the University of South Dakota. Reproduced by permission.

M-Tron's primary product is a piezoelectric quartz crystal component used for frequency control in all military and commerical communications equipment. In addition to piezo quartz products. M-Tron produced an electrostatic air purifier in a separate plant. With the exception of the production manager, no production facilities or personnel making quartz crystals are involved with E-Z Breathe. The size and financial position of the firm are described in Exhibits 1, 2, and 3.

M-Tron currently has three buildings in Yankton. Two buildings house the manufacturing and storage facilities for the quartz crystals and the third houses the offices and production facilities for E-Z Breathe. Sales of the crystals are through manufacturers' representatives and through the efforts of the sales manager.

DEVELOPMENT OF E-Z BREATHE

Mr. William Liggett, President of M-Tron in 1968, believed that M-Tron needed products to act as a hedge or balance against variations in demand for quartz crystals. He also wanted products that would allow M-Tron to grow. M-Tron was approached by a person with the idea of making electronic air cleaners for home and office use. This seemed to be the type of product that was now going to be in demand because of increased severity of air pollution. Hand-made models were demonstrated and reworked until, by October 1969, M-Tron had developed a model of the air cleaner that was ready for home-use testing. The trademark was applied for and hand-assembled units were placed in homes in the area at a nominal cost to the user.

COMPETITIVE SITUATION

At the time M-Tron was developing and initially selling E-Z Breathe, there were several competitive air cleaners on the market. Dome Laboratories had an air cleaner based on the same principle selling for $150 through medical marketing channels. S.C.S., a company in Minneapolis, had a portable model on the market. Minneapolis Honeywell has had a model on the market for several years. Emerson Electric and Sears, Roebuck market models, but have never put forth much effort to sell them. In 1970 Hoover began selling an air cleaner that also deodorizes for $119 retail. M-Tron management believes that the models currently on the market lack convenient portability, are too large, and are inconvenient in shape or unattractive in design. These models also lack convenience in maintenance.

PRODUCT DESCRIPTION

The E-Z Breathe electronic air cleaner measures $12'' \times 12'' \times 6''$ and weighs only 12 pounds. It is available in two finishes: walnut woodgrain in washable vinyl and stainless. The E-Z Breathe is intended to remove up to 99 percent of all airborne particles including pollens, lint, fog and mist, fly ash, dust, mold spores, bacteria, oil smoke, and tobacco smoke and can completely filter the air in a $15' \times 25'$ room three to five times per hour.

The E-Z Breathe removes air particles through a process known as "Electrostatic Precipitation." Air drawn into the filter cell passes through a series of ionizing wires. These wires impart a positive charge to particles suspended in the air. The air then passes between a series of parallel aluminum plates that are alternately charged positive and negative. The positively charged particles are repelled by the positively charged plates and attracted to the negatively charged plates in the same way iron is attracted to a magnet.

To keep the E-Z Breathe operating effectively, the electronic filter cell needs to be pulled out once or twice a month and soaked in a dishwasher detergent solution, or washed in an automatic dishwasher. After the filter cell has been thoroughly dried, it can easily be reinserted into the unit. Since each unit has only one moving part (the fan), the only additional maintenance required is to place a drop of oil on the fan once a year. M-Tron provides a one-year guarantee against defects in materials and workmanship, and the factory or authorized service station will repair the unit free of charge.

In reponse to some consumer complaints about difficulties in cleaning the filter cell and about the high noise level of the unit, M-Tron engaged in a series of product improvements designed to reduce these complaints. Most E-Z Breathe buyers were apparently well satisfied with their purchase.

MARKETING EXPERIENCE

Initial marketing efforts for E-Z Breathe began in late 1969. A few salesmen who were distributors of other products became convinced that E-Z Breathe had a good future and agreed to act as distributors. Attempts to market E-Z Breathe through heating and air conditioning dealers in South Dakota and Nebraska were not successful. One dealer's attempt at selling through direct mail failed. A Texas distributor attempted sales to doctors and consumers through Sunday Supplement advertising, but discontinued the effort. A Des Moines, Iowa, firm attempted to set up a house-to-house selling organization, but without success. M-Tron rented a booth at a home show in Sioux City, Iowa, and sold only three machines at $69.95. During this initial sales period, retail prices ranged from $69.96 to $99.95.

In February 1970, M-Tron contracted with an independent marketing research analyst to conduct a study to determine consumer reaction to E-Z Breathe and help M-Tron decide how to market the product.

In April 1970, before the results of the research were available, M-Tron decided to test market E-Z Breathe through a department store. Rike's Department Store in Dayton, Ohio, was selected to stock E-Z Breathe in their major appliances department. An advertising agency in Dayton was engaged to develop TV commercials and set up the TV schedule. The agency recommended a thirteen week program at $10,000 as the minimum necessary to gain adequate sales for E-Z Breathe in the Dayton area. Print ads were run in the *Dayton Daily News*.

A local distributor was sought and found to establish other dealers in the area, Rike's received their stock of E-Z Breathe cleaners, and the ads were run on schedule. In the first week Rike's reordered twice. The second week the ads were not run. The third week the ads were again run and Rike's reordered once. From that time on Rike's reordered once after a considerable length of time. The Rike's advertised price was $99.50. After eight weeks the advertising was pulled off the air since sales had fallen off. M-Tron figured the cost of selling the units (advertising to sales ratio) was $50 per unit.

Meanwhile, M-Tron decided to place an ad in *Salesman's Opportunity* magazine. The advertisement attracted several distributors, some of whom are still selling E-Z Breathe after nearly a year. The ad in *Salesman's Opportunity* ran in the April, May, and June 1970, editions. One east-coast distributor who was attracted by the ad is gaining some department store distribution. A dealer is using small ads in the *Denver Post* to get sales leads and follows them up with a direct sales demonstration in the home. She has been able to sell the product successfully and is still in business.

In July and August an Albuquerque distributor was established. He used local television advertising in two cities. Distributors were obtained in various cities thinly scattered throughout the nation. In Atlanta a medical personnel agency sold some to medical people. A distributor on the east coast used in-store demonstrations in several major department stores and in some cases was able to sell from twenty-five to forty per two-day demonstration period. These sales fell soon after demonstrations ceased.

Some housewares representatives (agents) were used to try to gain distribution through department stores. Beauty supply representatives were used to try to gain sales to beauty salons for the stainless model, which was priced to sell for $129. In December 1970, Brandeis Department Store in Omaha was sold directly by M-Tron. M-Tron advertised for Brandeis in newspapers and on TV. The price was set and advertised at $99.50. The results, just as the past experience, were good sales at first, then they tapered off. One medical supplier has ordered his fourth dozen E-Z Breathe cleaners for a rental-purchase plan he has been using. This medical supplier has good connections with doctors.

MARKET RESEARCH DATA

During the period of early May 1970, the market research results contracted for in February were received by M-Tron.

The research techniques involved interviews with groups of men and groups of women, as well as individual family interviews in homes and individual housewife interviews in a school cafeteria in Ohio during February and March 1970. In the interviews the plastic dome test was used. Findings are summarized as follows:

1. Women sinus sufferers are as conscious of air pollution in the home as they are of general air pollution problem outside the home.
2. Sleeping in clean air would be beneficial to health, especially for people with "breathing problems," such as asthma, sinus, hay fever, and "allergies."
3. E-Z Breathe would be used in the bedroom at night and in the kitchen and living room during the day.
4. (a). One-third of the interviewees would want an E-Z Breathe in their home. (Enthusiastically.)

   (b). One-third would want one in their home. (Not enthusiastically and with reservation.)

   (c). One-sixth would not want it in their home. The reasons were that there was no one in the family with a respiratory problem, they would rather have a central unit for the whole house, or they believe air conditioning filters the air sufficiently.

   (d). Those who are enthusiastic about wanting E-Z Breathe want it for relief of breathing problems: sinus, hay fever, bronchitis, and enphysema, in that order.
5. E-Z Breathe would be bought primarily for health reasons (respiratory problems). It would also be bought to help keep a clean house.
6. The women urged the importance of a home demonstration lasting several days to demonstrate its value.
7. E-Z Breathe would be bought primarily for the family. Protecting babies and small children from health hazards was frequently given as a reason for buying.
8. The wife would become interested in E-Z Breathe before the husband in two-thirds of the family interviews.
9. The buying decision would be a joint decision in two-thirds of the cases, and the wife's decision alone in about one-fourth of the cases.
10. "If I did not buy an E-Z Breathe it would probably be because the price is too high" was given as the reason for not buying by two-thirds of the families. Other reasons were lack of need, and the belief that furnace filters and air conditioning will do the job. (In the interviews

no price information was given and no sales promotion had been presented.) Some people were disappointed that it was not an odor remover also.

11. Most respondents indicated they would expect to buy E-Z Breathe in department stores. Some named appliance, hardware and discount stores.

12. The appearance and compactness are features that people liked about E-Z Breathe.

13. Consumers expect to pay from $60.00 to $75.00 for E-Z Breathe.

14. The E-Z Breathe has a very broad consumer market appeal. It is greatest in large urban areas, particularly in residential districts located near industrialized areas or areas of heavy traffic flow, and where household incomes are relatively high.

In the summer of 1970, M-Tron contracted for a marketing research study designed to measure attitudes and buying motivations of E-Z Breathe owners. The study involved sending questionnaires to E-Z Breathe owners who had previously returned their warranty cards to M-Tron. A total of thirty-four forms were returned and about two-thirds of the forms were from respondents living in Dayton or Kettering, Ohio.

This survey was followed by a warranty card survey by M-Tron using the same questionnaire. M-Tron's survey was nationwide and involved seventy-two returns. With few exceptions both survey results agree. A summary of the findings is given below:

1. The E-Z Breathe is bought for specific family members rather than for general family use.

2. The E-Z Breathe is bought to cope with health problems (of a respiratory nature) of specific members of the family.

3. Buyers of the E-Z Breathe are concerned about the health of specific family members; they are not worried about the dust, dirt, smoke in their homes; and they do not buy the E-Z Breathe for the well-being and comfort of their families in general.

4. Chronic diseases directly related to breathing problems—that is, sinus, asthma, and hay fever—induce people to buy the E-Z Breathe. To a lesser extent, heart disease, bronchitis, and emphysema also trigger purchases.

5. The E-Z Breathe is bought primarily for women.

6. The E-Z Breathe is bought for elderly people. Over three-fifths are bought for people in their fifties or older, and over four-fifths are bought for persons in their forties or older.

  (a) The median age of women for whom the E-Z Breathe is bought is 57—thus the product has appeal to elderly women.

  (b) Men for whom the E-Z Breathe was bought have a median age of 63.

7. The E-Z Breathe is very well liked by those who have bought it. Over nine-tenths of them either think it is "wonderful" or "like it very much."

8. Four features or characteristics of the E-Z Breathe are liked best by its owners in the following order: (a) it cleans the air, removes dust, and makes it easier to breathe; (b) it removes smoke from the air; (c) it operates quietly; and (d) it is portable and can be moved about easily.

9. Few product problems have been experienced by E-Z Breathe owners. Of the few mentioned the most common are problems involving cleaning the filter cell, and some instances of product defects when purchased.

10. Increase the capacity of the E-Z Breathe so it will handle more than one room and make it quieter—these were the most frequently suggested improvements for the E-Z Breathe. The general high level of satisfaction with the E-Z Breathe is brought out by the fact that two-thirds of the respondents could think of no improvements or did not answer the question.

11. In the Dayton area warranty card study the great majority of owners learned about the E-Z Breathe on TV, primarily on evening and to a lesser extent on afternoon TV. (In the nationwide survey, word of mouth from friends and relatives and newspaper advertising were checked as the main sources of product knowledge.) Relatively little TV advertising was done outside of Dayton. Local news shows and Rike's commercials were about the only specific shows respondents remembered as being the ones where they first learned about the E-Z Breathe.

12. A wide variety of occupations is represented among the E-Z Breathe owners. The older age characteristic is again indicated by the fact that about two-fifths of them are retired.

13. Modest income families are buying the E-Z Breathe. Over two-fifths of them are in the two-lowest income categories: under $5000, and $5000 to $7500. This again reflects the fact that many of the buyers are elderly people past their peak earning years or retired. In the nationwide survey, 29 percent were in the lower two income groups. Another 29 percent were in

the $15,000 and over group, whereas in the Dayton study 15 percent were in this group. The income groups involving families earning $7500 to $15,000 accounted for approximately 42 percent in both studies.

PROPOSED NAME CHANGE

On the basis of this experience with the electronic air cleaner, Kase Mooibroek felt that the E-Z Breathe name might restrict their market too narrowly to those customers who bought the product for health reasons. As a result of a brainstorming session with the firm's advertising agency, the following list of potential brand names for M-Tron's "new" product was developed.

Nature-Aire	Electro-Fresh	Vistatronic
Sani-Aire	Airtron	Ultraronic
Fresh-Aire	Airtronic	Electromatic
Cleer-Aire	Electro-Airtron	Air Guard
Crystal-Aire	Micro-Tronic	Air Stream
Tropic-Aire	Mini-Tronic	Spring Air
Islandaire	Electropure	Spring Time
Ecolo-Aire	Environmenta	Air Pac
Airalator	Refreshaire	Alpine
Aller-Out	Recycle-Aire	North Wood
Allergex	Futuraire	The Nordic
Electro-Breeze	Smog-Ex	The Viking
Electro-Kleen	M-Tronic-Aire	
Relieftronic	Vista-Aire	

1971 SALES PLAN

Sales of E-Z Breathe were disappointing to the management of M-Tron. Total factory sales from April 1, 1970 to March 31, 1971, were between 5000 and 6000 units, of which Mr. Mooibroek estimated about half were still in the inventory of the channel members. However, this was about 10 percent of the estimated total industry sales of air cleaners for that year. The 1970 sales of all air cleaners were about 50,000 units. *Chain Store Age* predicts sales of air cleaners will double in 1971 and may expand to 500,000 units by the middle 1970s. At least one major chain is considering setting up a separate "ecology appliance" section in its major appliance department.[2]

[2]*Retail Memo,* Bureau of Advertising, New York, July 16, 1971.

In planning for the future of E-Z Breathe the management of M-Tron was presented with a sales plan in March, 1971, by Mr. Mooibroek.

E-Z Breathe
Sales Plan
April 1971 - March 1972

This plan is based on what we have learned from the past experimentation with test markets, distribution, and advertising programs.

This plan calls for setting up national distribution on E-Z Breathe through (1) medical equipment dealers, (2) department and appliance stores, and (3) pharmacies and drug stores.

Advertising will be done by M-Tron on a national basis. Advertising dollars will be built into the price that distributors and dealers pay for the units.

1. Any money we get over and above our cost plus normal profit based on return on investment can be used for two advertising funds. One fund will be for the national advertising and one for local. The margins will be as follows:
   (a) Retailers' margin will be 30 percent of their selling price.
   (b) Distributors' margin will be 20 percent of their selling price.
   (c) M-Tron's margin *for advertising* will be 35 percent of their selling price.
2. The margin for advertising will be used in national advertising directed at:
   (a) Doctors, who often influence the purchase of an electronic air cleaner.
   (b) Medical equipment dealers, who will rent or sell E-Z Breathe to doctors' patients (about 6000 such dealers in the United States).
   (c) Consumers, primarily middle-aged and elderly people who we've found represent the majority of E-Z Breathe buyers. (Over 80 percent of E-Z Breathe buyers are people in these age groups, with modest incomes. They buy the E-Z Breathe for a specific health problem.)

M-Tron must take over complete control of E-Z Breathe advertising because local retail advertising that's been done so far in a number of cities around the country has not paid off. The main reason for this is that all of the local advertising has been directed at the general public whereas follow-up surveys have shown that most people who actually buy the unit are respiratory sufferers. Thus, much of the local advertising has been wasted on people who are not really good prospects. By concentrating our advertising on people who are known to be the

Sales Forecast
E-Z Breathe

	Expected Number of Units Sold	Dollar Sales	Proposed National Advertising Expenditure (Dollars)
April	550	31,955	6,700
May	775	45,027	3,700
June	925	53,742	23,200
July	1300	75,530	32,700
August	1150	66,815	31,800
September	900	52,290	21,800
October	700	40,670	900
November	600	24,860	—
December	500	29,050	1,000
January	600	34,860	500
February	625	36,312	900
March	725	42,122	1,400
	9,350	533,233	124,600

best prospects we feel the advertising program will pay for itself in terms of increased unit sales.

The attached sales forecast is a realistic estimate of what this plan will produce in terms of sales during the period April, 1971 to April, 1972.

Questions

1. What are the most important market segments for E-Z Breathe?
2. Should M-Tron change the name of the product?
3. What should M-Tron do to successfully market the air cleaner? If you reject the proposed sales plan, what would you offer as a substitute?

Exhibit 1
M-tron Industries, Inc.

Consolidated Balance Sheet March 31, 1971

ASSETS	1971	1970	1969
Current assets:			
Cash	$ 56,564	$ 15,704	$ 14,968
Receivables net of allowance for doubtful accounts $3,569 1971; $3,792 1970	271,509	490,653	243,466
Total inventories	477,126	619,928	388,627
Recoverable income taxes	91,826	—	—
Prepaid expenses	11,601	3,574	3,819
Total current assets	908,626	1,129,859	650,880
Rental property, at cost less accumulated depreciation	—	45,499	20,722
Property, plant and equipment, at cost			
Land and improvements	8,875	4,080	3,942
Leasehold improvements	35,909	32,735	2,887
Building and improvements	126,412	104,221	100,595
Machinery and equipment	1,116,347	1,040,194	261,917
Office furniture and equipment	36,148	35,092	16,402
Automobiles	5,791	5,791	—
	1,329,482	1,222,113	385,743
Less accumulated depreciation and amortization	396,596	238,288	117,185
Net property, plant and equipment	932,886	983,825	268,558
Cost on excess of net assets of acquired companies	338,287	399,781	20,132
Other assets, net of amortization	32,956	51,963	2,206
Total other assets	371,243	451,744	22,338
	$2,212,755	$2,610,877	$962,498

LIABILITIES AND STOCKHOLDERS'S EQUITY

	1971	1970	1969
Current liabilities			
Current installments of long-term debt	$ 150,372	$ 88,411	$ 53,715
Notes payable to bank, secured	14,990	128,647	13,000
Accounts payable—trade	143,631	253,734	127,768
Accrued expenses	89,472	61,084	29,735
Federal and state income taxes	—	94,253	—
Total current liabilities	398,465	626,129	224,218
Deferred income taxes	7,200	8,100	—
Long-term debt			
Notes payable less current portion above	425,179	306,899	351,362
Equipment contracts payable less current portion above	42,692	57,375	315
6 percent convertible subordinated debentures	450,000	450,000	—
Total long-term debt	917,871	814,274	351,677
Stockholders' equity			
Common nonvoting stock of $1.00 par value per share Authorized 500,000 shares; none issued	—	—	—
Common voting stock of $1.00 par value per share Authorized 2,000,000 shares; issued 613,465 (591,599 in 1970)	613,465	591,599	408,428
Additional paid-in capital	502,958	502,958	—
Retained earnings (deficit)	(227,204)	67,817	(21,825)
Total stockholders' equity	889,219	1,162,374	386,603
	$2,212,755	$2,610,877	$962,498

Exhibit 2

Statement of Consolidated Earnings year ended March 31,1971

	1971	1970	1969
Net sales	$2,329,420	$2,603,049	$1,541,734
Cost of sales	2,096,998	1,943,884	1,154,857
Gross profit	232,422	659,165	386,877
Selling, general, and administrative expenses	562,455	463,136	202,985
Operating income (loss)	(330,033)	196,029	183,892
Other income	8,655	8,998	4,556
	(321,378)	205,027	188,448
Other expenses.			
Interest	74,763	57,067	23,164
Loss on disposal of equipment	2,991	1,367	575
Other	6,155	—	—
	83,909	58,434	23,739
Earnings (loss) before Federal and state income taxes and extraordinary item	(405,287)	146,593	164,709
Federal and state income taxes			
Current	(107,766)	54,451	—
Deferred	(2,500)	2,500	—
Tax effects of operating losses	—	7,945	81,500
	(110,266)	64,896	81,500
Earnings (loss) before extraordinary item	(295,021)	81,697	83,209
Extraordinary item-income tax benefit from operating loss carry forward	—	7,945	81,500
Net earnings (loss)	$ (295,021)	$ 89,642	$ 164,709

Exhibit 3

Financial Highlights

	1971	1970	1969	1968	1967	1966
Net sales	$ 2,329,420	2,603,049	1,541,734	1,220,198	1,001,998	171,029
Percent increase (decrease)	(10)	69	26	22	486	—
Earnings (loss) before taxes	(405,287)	146,593	164,709	73,627	(135,634)	(127,945)
Federal and state income taxes	(110,266)	64,896	81,500	—	—	—
Net earnings (loss)	(295,021)	81,697	164,709	73,627	(135,645)	(127,945)
Depreciation	161,456	121,854	45,411	38,057	25,371	1,723
Property, plant and equipment at cost	1,329,482	1,222,113	385,743	314,017	295,797	206,686
Stockholders' equity	889,219	1,162,374	386,603	130,294	24,375	46,718

Case 6-2
Choufont-Salva, Inc.[1]

Choufont-Salva, the Philippine subsidiary of A. L. Choufont, decided to add an oral contraceptive developed by the parent company to their product line. Choufont-Salva's marketing division (see Exhibit 1) now was faced with the task of designing a marketing plan that would effectively sell this product.

THE COMPANY

Choufont-Salva, Inc. was founded by Mr. Lorenzo J. Salva and became a subsidiary of A. L. Choufont, of Belgium in 1959. Many of the subsidiaries of A. L. Choufont marketed both ethical[2] and proprietary[3] drugs. Choufont-Salva, however, had followed the policy established by Mr. Salva of dealing only in ethical drugs.

[1]This case was prepared by Edward L. Felton, Jr., under the direction of Ralph Z. Sorenson. Copyright © by the Inter-University Program for Graduate Business Education. Reproduced by permission.

[2]Ethical drugs were promoted directly to the medical profession whose members in turn recommended or prescribed the drugs to the ultimate consumers.

[3]Proprietary drugs were promoted directly to the consumers, and the manufacturers of proprietary products usually engaged in heavy consumer advertising and promotional activities.

Choufont-Salva marketed sixty-seven different drug products and had sales of approximately ₱6,900,000.[4] Penicillin accounted for 47 percent of sales; and streptomycin, 16 percent. Thirteen other products were responsible for an additional 21 percent of the company's income.

For all products, Choufont-Salva had three prices: the retail price,[5] the semi-wholesale price, which was 5 percent less than the retail price, and the wholesale price, which was 10 percent less than the retail price. Because of the difficulty in determining whether a purchaser was functioning primarily as a wholesaler or a retailer, Choufont-Salva used the volume of business done actually with the company as the basis for determinimg which of the price lists was applicable to a customer. Approximately 30 percent of the company's sales were retail; 10 percent, semi-wholesale; and 60 percent, wholesale.

Choufont-Salva realized an average contribution of 59 centavos on every peso of sales. Five centavos

[4]Philippine ₱1.00 = U.S. $0.256; U.S. $ = Philippine ₱3.90

[5]Retail price, as used by Choufont-Salva and other drug companies, referred to the price charged to retail drug outlets and similar purchasers—not to the price paid by the ultimate consumers. The price paid by the ultimate consumers generally was about 10 percent higher than this retail price.

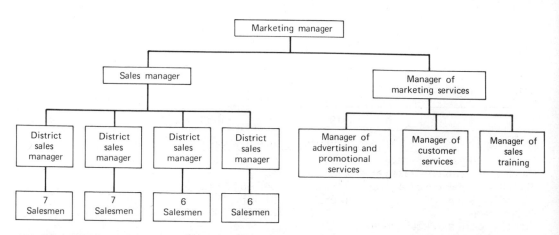

Exhibit 1.
Organizational Chart of the Marketing Division

of this contribution was paid out in commissions[6] 9½ centavos was spent on advertising and promotions; and 21½ centavos was expended on other marketing and administrative expenses. However, the contribution that the company received on sales of a particular product and the expenditures made in promoting the sale of a product frequently varied greatly from this average.

SALES ACTIVITIES

Choufont-Salva had divided the Phillippines into twenty-six territories. In each territory, there were between 150 and 300 doctors in private practice on whom the salesman called once per month. Since Choufont-Salva dealt only in ethical drugs, management believed that the doctor was the most important person to reach in the company's marketing activities. Salesmen in the provinces spent approximately 70 percent of their time calling on physicians. Salesmen in Manila and other large cities devoted an estimated 80 percent of their time to this activity.

Because of the busy schedules of the doctors, most visits with physicians lasted only fifteen minutes. During this time a saleman normally made two product presentations. During each presentation, the salesman described how the drug being discussed had been developed, noted the benefits of the product, pointed out how this drug differed from comparable products on the market, and presented clinical evidence attesting to the effectiveness of the drug. At the close of the visit, the salesman left samples of the two products he had discussed and also of two or three other drugs that the company marketed.

Approximately 40 percent of the doctors on whom Choufont-Salva salesmen called dispensed their own drugs. During visits to these doctors, the salesman also took orders and made collections for previous purchases.[7] Approximately 10 percent of Choufont-Salva's sales were made to this group of doctors, most of whom were located in the provinces. A salesman who had a territory in Manila or another large city and devoted his day exclusively to calling on doctors could make fifteen to eighteen calls if the doctors had their offices at a hospital and twelve to fifteen calls if the doctors had private offices away from a hospital. A provincial salesman calling only on doctors could average ten to twelve

[6]Salesmen received commissions of 4½ percent and district sales managers received commissions of ½ percent on all sales made in their respective territories.

[7]Commissions on a sale were not paid until the company had received payment.

calls per day. Choufont-Salva salesmen called on an estimated 25 percent of the doctors in the Philippines. Management believed, however, that these doctors were the ones with the highest professional standing and with the largest and most important practices.

In additon to the doctors, Choufont-Salva salesmen called monthly on 1500 of the estimated 5000 drug stores in the Philippines. Approximately 85 percent of the company's sales were made to these pharmaceutical outlets. When calling on drug stores, the salesmen answered any questions that the personnel had about different products, discussed new or improved products, took back old stocks of drugs, accepted orders, and made collections. The salesmen also called each month on approximately fifty clinics. Sales to these clinics, which were either government health centers or industrial clinics attached to large manufacturing facilities, were responsible for 5 percent of Choufont-Salva's sales.

Choufont-Salva supported the activities of its salesmen with advertising and promotional efforts. The company spent ₱8,000 on advertising in the last year. Since Choufont-Salva dealt only in ethical drugs, the entire advertising expenditure was for ads placed in the three leading professional medical journals—the *PMA*[8] *Journal, Family Physician, and The Philippine Journal of Surgeons* (See Exhibit 2 for circulation and rates).

Choufont-Salva also spent ₱650,000 on promotional activities. Of this amount ₱550,000 was invested in samples given to physicians. This reflected management's belief that samples were the most effective way of promoting the company's drugs. When samples of drugs were left with a doctor, it reminded him of the products and encouraged him to prescribe them to his patients. Also, the company believed that a doctor liked samples because samples enabled him occasionally to give away medicine free to patients, thus generating goodwill among the recipients. The remaining 100,000 spent on promotions was used to print cards, folders, and booklets about various drugs sold by Choufont-Salva. These printed materials were used by the salesmen in discussing the products with the doctors and were left with the doctor at the close of the call.

THE PHILIPPINE MARKET FOR CONTRACEPTIVES

When Choufont-Salva decided to enter the contraceptive market the population of the Philippines

[8]Philippine Medical Association.

was approximately 33 million. The country had an estimated 5 million households, 85 percent of which were located in rural areas. According to government statistics, the population was increasing at the rate of 3.2 percent per year, one of the highest population growth rates in the world. If this rate of population growth continued, the country would have 53 million inhabitants by 1980. Exhibit 3 provides some data on the female population of the Phillippines.

Recently the Family Planning Association of the Philippines, Inc. (FPAP) was organized by a group of Catholic laymen. Although three small Protestant family-planning groups were already in existence, the FPAP was the first nationwide family planning movement in the Philippines, a country in which 84 percent of the population was Catholic. By the time that Choufont-Salva decided to enter the market, the management of the company estimated that there were approximately 100 government or private clinics from which persons could receive information on family planning and, if they desired, birth control products. The majority of these centers were affiliated with either the FPAP or the Planned Parenthood Movement of the Philippines. Birth control products were also available at most drug outlets.

The management of Choufont-Salva estimated that in the past year Filipinos spent ₱5,000,000 on contraceptive products. Approximately 70 percent of these products were dispensed through drug stores; 25 percent, through clinics; and 5 percent, directly by doctors. Management predicted that in the current year the market for contraceptives would be ₱7,500,000 and that the market would continue to grow at least 50 percent per year for the next three years.

The company estimated ₱4,000,000 was spent on oral contraceptives in the Philippines in the past year. The popularity of this method of birth control was attributed to the fact that oral contraceptives were virtually 100 percent effective and extremely easy to use. Although there were fifteen brands of oral contraceptives on the Philippine market, five brands controlled 75 percent of the market (Exhibit 4).

The second most popular contraceptive product in the Philippines was the intrauterine device (IUD). Filipinos spent an estimated ₱750,000 per year on IUD's including fees paid to doctors for inserting the devices. The charges made by private doctors for this service ranged from a low of 5 pesos to a high of 100 pesos per patient. Planned parenthood clinics, on the other hand, had a policy of inserting IUD's completely free or at a charge of 5 pesos or less.

IUD's were in strong favor with governmental and private agencies in the Philippines who promoted planned parenthood to low-income groups. This method of birth control was inexpensive and did not require instructions that women had to remember. Yet, IUD's had a major draw-back. Approximately 20 percent of all women were unable to retain IUD's. This method of birth control, however, was 98 percent effective in preventing pregnancy among those able to use the device.

Condoms, diaphragms, and spermicidal jellies and creams were not very widely used in the Philippines. In the past year these products together accounted for only an estimated ₱250,000 of the total contraceptive market.

CHOUFONT-SALVA'S ORAL CONTRACEPTIVE

Choufont-Salva's oral contraceptive was developed in the A. L. Choufont laboratories in Belgium. The product was first introduced in Canada and was currently being marketed in fourteen countries. However, the parent company had not yet published any detailed information on the market performance of the contraceptive. The bits of data that had been received from the company's Brussels headquarters indicated that the acceptance of the new contraceptive had ranged from fair in Brazil to excellent in Mexico and Denmark.

Oral contraceptives were manufactured in the form of tablets that were taken by women for twenty to twenty-two days during each menstrual cycle. Most oral contraceptive tablets were a combination of a progestin and an estrogen, and tablets containing these two hormonal products were virtually 100 percent effective as contraceptives.

Oral contraceptives, however, produced undesirable side effects such as weight gain, nausea, and headaches in some women. In general the incidence of these side effects were related to the dose of the progestin in the oral contraceptive. As a result, pharmaceutical companies had been trying to develop new progestational agents that could be given in dosages of one milligram or less but still would be effective in controlling fertility.

A. L. Choufont was the first to achieve this breakthrough in steroid research. The company developed a new, totally synthesized and extremely potent progestational hormone. By using this new progestional agent, Choufont was able to produce a new oral contraceptive that combined in each daily dose only one milligram of progestin with one-tenth of a milligram of an estrogenic agent.

There was only one oral contraceptive compound available in the Philippines that contained as little as one and one-half milligrams of progestin per daily dose. This was a new contraceptive that had been on the market for less than three months. The strength of the progestin in the other compounds on the market varied from 2 to 10 milligrams per tablet.

The low dosage of progestin in the Choufont-Salva contraceptive lessened the chance that a patient would experience undesirable side effects from taking the medication. Clinical data compiled by A. L. Choufont indicated that only 4 percent of the patients taking the oral contraceptive developed by the company experience nausea, headaches, or similar unpleasantness. No other oral contraceptive had such a low incidence of side effects.

The Choufont-Salva oral contraceptive consisted of twenty-one tablets per course of medication. The woman was to take the first tablet on the fifth day of her menstrual cycle and take one tablet daily for twenty-one days. She was then to stop taking tablets for seven days. On the eighth day she was to start the next twenty-one-day series of tablets. This meant that each new course of medication started on exactly the same day of the week as the initial course. Always starting the medication on the same day of the week lessened the chance of a woman forgetting to begin the cycle anew. Choufont-Salva felt that this attribute would give the product a slight competitive advantage over the most of the other oral contraceptives on the market. Only two other contraceptives on the market had dosages of twenty-one tablets per twenty-eight-day period.

Because of the heavy financial investment in equipment required for producing oral contraceptives, Choufont-Salva had signed a contract with Companie Nationale de Pharmacie, S. A., the French subsidiary of A. L. Choufont. According to the contract, the French company would supply Choufont-Salva with the contraceptive tablets at a cost equivalent to ₱0.71 per course of medication. This price included shipping to Manila but did not include packaging.

DEVELOPING A MARKETING PLAN

Currently 63 percent of Choufont-Salva's revenue came from the sales of penicillin and streptomycin. Management wanted to lessen the company's dependence on these two products and felt that its new oral contraceptive had the potential of developing into a major drug in the company's product line. The marketing manager said that to help achieve this goal, the salesmen would devote at least 15 percent of their time to promoting the contraceptive during the first eighteen months that it was on the market.

The task of developing a marketing plan that would effectively promote Choufont-Salva's oral contraceptive was the responsibility of the company's marketing committee. Deciding on a name for the tablets, selecting the packaging that would be used, determining the price that would be charged, and deciding on what advertising and promotional activities to employ were among the decisions facing the committee.

Name

The oral contraceptive developed by A. L. Choufont et Fils, S. A. was marketed by the company's Canadian subsidiary under the brand name Controva. This name was formed by combining the prefix *contra,* which makes up the first half of the word *contraceptive* and means against, with *ova,* the plural of *ovum* which means egg. Since entering the market in Canada, the product had been introduced in three other English-speaking countries: Great Britain, the United States and Australia. In these three countries the product also was being sold under the name Controva.

Because *contraceptive* and *ovum* were not words commonly used by Filipinos some in the marketing organization at Choufont-Salva felt that the company should select another brand name for the product. These persons felt that the name should be easy to remember, be suggestive of a characteristic of the product, and sound western. Two names had been suggested: Combitabs, which was formed from the words *combination* and *tablets* and suggested that the tablets were a combination of progestin and estrogen, and Periodez, which suggested that the tablets were taken during a definite period in the menstrual cycle.

Packaging

Management was considering four packaging possibilities for the oral contraceptive: a glass bottle, a simple aluminum strip, a comb case, and a compact case (Exhibit 5). The company was also faced with the question of what color combinations to use on the package. Three combinations had been suggested: black and white, gold and white, and light pink and pale green. An advocate of the pastel colors claimed that they were "feminine and inviting to the woman."

Price

Primarily because of its lower progestin content, the progestin-estrogen compound developed by

Choufont cost less to manufacture than did other oral contraceptives. Since the tablets were costing Choufont-Salva only P.71 plus packaging for each dosage of twenty-one tablets, management was considering making the company's retail price.[9] for the medication P2.50 or P2.75 per bottle or package. This would give the company a competitive advantage in price since the retail price[10] of other oral contraceptives on the market ranged from P3.00 to P10.00 per course of medication.

Advertising and Promotional Activities

Choufont-Salva did not engage in consumer advertising. The company had the policy of advertising only in medical journals because management wanted Choufont-Salva to have the image of being a responsible pharmaceutical organization that worked closely with and through the medical profession. Some members of management, however, felt that the company should advertise its oral contraceptive directly to the general public. The decision made regarding this matter would influence the theme of the advertising campaign as well as the size of the advertising budget for the product.

Management also was undecided about how to promote Choufont-Salva's oral contraceptive. A memo from the company's advertising and promotional staff containing suggestions regarding promotional activities is reproduced in Exhibit 6. The cost of different consumer-oriented media are given in exhibit 7.

[9]Retail price referred to the price charged to retail drug outlets and similar purchasers—not to the price paid by the ultimate consumers.

[10]Price charged by the drug firms to retail drug outlets and similar purchasers.

NEW COMPETITION

A week after Choufont-Salva decided to enter the oral contraceptive market, the company learned that within a year T. T. Reyes, Inc., a competing Philippine drug company, probably would be marketing an oral contraceptive containing only one-half milligram of progestin. North American Drugs, Inc., the American parent company of T. T. Reyes, had just developed the new oral contraceptive in its laboratories. The American company planned to test market the product in the United States. If the test marketing was successful, North American Drugs would then release the product to is subsidiaries. Because of the test marketing, Choufont-Salva's management felt that it would be at least nine months and probably twelve months before T. T. Reyes could get the oral contraceptive on the Philippine market.

QUESTIONS

1. What cultural factors will be most important to Choufont-Salva in marketing birth control pills in the Philippines?
2. What are the prospects for first year sales of Choufont-Salva's oral contraceptive pills in the Philippine market?
3. Prepare a comprehensive marketing plan to sell Choufont's contraceptive pills in the Philippines including recommendations on packaging, pricing, advertising, sampling, and other promotional activity.
4. What changes would you make in Choufont-Salva's present marketing organization and compensation systems?

Exhibit 2

Journals in Which Choufont-Salva Advertised[a]

Journal	Frequency of Publication	Circulation	Cost per Page
Family Physician	Quarterly	3000	P225
The Philippine Journal of surgeons	Quarterly	3000	P225
The PMA Journal	Monthly	7000	P675

[a] The journals accepted only full-page advertisements.

Exhibit 3
Female Population of the Philippines (in Thousands)

| | Last Census | | Current |
Age	Total No. of Women	No. of Ever Married Women[a]	Estimated No. of Women
10-14 years	1705	2	2146
15-19	1401	174	1802
20-24	1158	689	1472
25-29	959	792	1208
30-34	796	691	996
35-39	675	664	822
40-44	580	497	689
45-49	489	464	585
50-54	384	312	493
55-59	288	218	389
60-64	214	180	284
65 years and over	409	334	462
Total	9058	5017	11348

[a] Women who currently were married or had been married at one time.
Source. Bureau of Census and Statistics.

Exhibit 4
Five Leading Brands of Oral Contraceptives

Brand	Usual Progestin Strengths	Estimated Market Share	Retail Price	Comments
Brand A	2.5 mg or 5.0 mg	35%	₱3.25 [a,b]	Company concentrated on drug outlets for promtion and distribution
Brand B	4.0 mg	17	3.00	Company concentrated on family planning centers for distribution
Brand C	2.0 mg or 10.0 mg	10	4.50	
Brand D	3.0mg	8	5.50	An improved version of brand B; made by same company
Brand E	10.0 mg	5	8.00	

[a] Price per course of medication.
[b] Retail price referred to the price charged by the drug firms to retail drug outlets and similar purchasers. The prices to the ultimate consumer generally were 10 percent higher than these prices.

Exhibit 5
Packages[a] Being Considered for Oral Contraceptive Pills

Glass Bottle. Label on the outside, cost [b]₱0.13, advantages: low cost, adequate protection, disadvantages: not attractive, little room on label for description or instructions on usage, no way to mark the package so the woman can easily ascertain the number of pills she has taken.

Aluminum Strip. 5 inches long and 1¾ inches wide to which the tablets would be affixed by thin plastic strip, strip packaged in aluminum foil, cost, ₱.22, advantages: low cost, permits instructions on a separate sheet to be enclosed with the strip, strip can be marked with the days of the week so the woman can easily ascertain the number of pills she has taken, disadvantages: inadequate protection to the tablets resulting in some breakage.

Comb Case. Tablets would be affixed to an aluminum strip and the strip would be placed in a comb-carrying case 5½ inches long and 2½ inches wide. The aluminum strip and carrying case would be packaged in a cardboard container 6 inches long × 2¾ × ½ inches cost, ₱0.29, advantages: excellent protection, attractive carrying case, permits ample room for instructions to be enclosed separately and/or printed on the package, aluminum strip can be marked so woman can easily ascertain the number of pills she has taken, disadvantage: high cost.

Compact Case. Tablets would be affixed (by being encased in plastic) to an aluminum disc 2¾ inches in diameter, disc would be placed in a compact 3¼ inches in diameter, perforated holes in the bottom of the compact would permit the woman to push the tablet through the bottom of the compact, separating the tablet from the aluminum disc, compact would be packaged in a cardboard container 3¾ inches × 3¾ inches × ¾ inches cost ₱0.76, advantages: very attractive carrying case, excellent protection, permits ample room for instructions to be enclosed separately and/or printed on the package, aluminum disc can be marked so woman can easily ascertain how many pills she has taken, disadvantage: very high cost.

[a]Each package would contain twenty-one tablets.
[b]This estimated cost included the price of the container and the cost of labor and other expenses involved in packaging the tablets.

Exhibit 6
Possible Promotional Activities

The sales promotional staff submits the following ideas for consideration in the formulation of the marketing plan for the new oral contraceptive product.

I. Sampling of all doctors on whom Choufont-Salva salesmen call. Almost every doctor in the Philippines has patients who are potential customers for our oral contraceptive. Extensive sampling will give broad coverage to our product.

To get desired support for our product and to develop brand loyalty among doctors, it might be desirable for the company to engage in heavy sampling for at least six months. This could be accomplished:

A. By giving to gynecologists, obstetricians, and general practitioners with clientele likely to use contraceptives from one to four dozen sample packets per month, depending on the doctor's location and practice. (We estimate that this group of doctors constitutes no more than one-fourth of the doctors on whom our salesmen call.)

B. By giving to all other doctors on whom our salesmen call four sample packets of our oral contraceptive during the product's introductory month and two packets per month for the next five months.

Heavy sampling of the approximately 100 government and private clinics disseminating birth control information and products. Most of these clinics recommend—and often insert either free or for a very nominal charge—IUD's. For example, at one Manila family-planning clinic last year, only 2 percent of the couples that came to the clinic decided to take oral contraceptives. The others are using IUD.'s To help alter this situation, the company might give one to four dozen samples monthly to each of the clinics, the number of samples depending on the size of the clinic.

II. The printing of both brochures and posters that will be used by the salesmen in describing to physicians our oral contraceptive and will be left with the physicians at the end of the visit. A five-color, eight-page brochure measuring 8 x 11 inches will cost approximately ₱590 per 1000 with a minimum order of 5000 required. A five-color 12 x 15 inch poster will cost approximately ₱500 per 1000 with a minimum order of 5000 required.

III. Mailing to all physicians on whom our salesmen do not call of the eight-page brochure mentioned above. The cost of printing a cover letter and mailing the brochure will be approximately ₱0.20 per physician, not counting the cost of the brochure.

IV. Outlet promotions. Because of the nature of the product and the large number of potential consumers, the company might consider altering its policy against outlet promotions and engaging in the following subtle promotional activities:

A. Encourage the salesgirls in drugstores to recommend our oral contraceptive to contraceptive customers. This could be accomplished (1) by the salesmen discussing with the girls both the characteristics of the product and its advantages over similar products on the market and (2) by giving the girls a sample packet of our contraceptive.

B. Print small booklets on family planning and have them displayed on the sales counter in an attractive heavy cardboard rack. The booklet would define family planning, discuss the various methods of birth control, give the answers to the questions people most frequently ask about family planning and contain humorous illustrations. Printing a three-color, thirty-page booklet that measures 5 x 3½ inches in size will cost approximately ₱250 per 1000 with a minimum order of 5000 required. Each display rack will cost approximately ₱5. Consideration might also be given to placing these racks in the offices of doctors. Both the booklets and the display racks would carry the name and trademark of Choufont-Salva.

Exhibit 7
Consumer-Oriented Media Costs

Print			
Publication	Circulation	Percent of Copies to Households Earning ₱15,000 & Above	Rate Per Column Inch
Newspapers			
Evening News	29,000	N. A.[a]	₱ 8.00
Manila Chronicle	72,000	22	11.00
Manila Daily Bulletin	59,000	71	9.50
Manila Times	120,000	31	19.00
Mirror	24,000	N. A.	6.00
Philippine Herald	47,000	18	8.50
The Sunday Times	155,000	48	21.00
Weekly Magazines			
Free Press	86,000	42	₱15.00
Graphic	88,000	55	12.00
Weekly Women's Magazine	93,000	65	14.00
Woman & the Home	81,000	22	13.00

[a] N. A. = not available.

Radio			
	Class A Time: 6:00 A.M.-9:00 A.M.		
Units	60 Sec.	30 Sec.	5-10 Sec.
1-12	₱12.50/spot	₱9.37/spot	₱3.12/spot
13-25	11.88	8.91	2.97
26-38	11.25	8.44	2.81
39-51	10.63	7.97	2.66
52-103	10.00	7.50	2.50
104-259	9.30	7.03	2.34
260-Up	8.75	6.56	2.19

Exhibit 7 (continued)

Class B. Time: 5:00 A.M.-6:00 A.M.
9:00 A.M.-2:00 P.M. & 5:00 P.M.-6:00 P.M.

Units	60 Sec.	30 Sec.	5-10 Sec.
1-12	₱7.50/spot	₱5.62/spot	₱2.28/spot
13-25	7.13	5.35	1.87
26-38	6.75	5.06	1.69
39-51	6.38	4.78	1.59
52-103	6.00	4.50	1.50
104-259	5.63	4.23	1.41
260 & Up	5.25	3.89	1.31

Class C Time: 2:00 P.M.-5:00 P.M.
6:00 P.M.-12:00 A.M. & 4:00 A.M.-5:00 A.M.

Units	60 Sec.	30 Sec	5-10 Sec.
1-12	₱4.50/spot	₱3.37/spot	₱1.12/spot
13-25	4.28	3.21	1.07
26-38	4.05	3.04	1.01
39-51	3.83	2.87	0.96
52-103	3.60	2.70	0.90
104-259	3.38	2.53	0.85
260-Up	3.15	2.36	0.79

Class D Time 12:00 A.M.-4:00 A.M.

Units	60 Sec.	30 Sec.	5-10 Sec.
1-12	₱3.00/spot	₱2.25/spot	₱0.75/spot
13-25	2.85	2.14	0.71
26-38	2.70	2.03	0.67
39-51	2.55	1.91	0.64
52-103	2.40	1.80	0.60
104-259	2.25	1.69	0.56
260 & Up	2.10	1.57	0.52

Production costs: the estimated costs[a] of producing a radio ad are as follows:

Length	Estimated Costs
60 seconds	₱500
30 seconds	500
10 seconds	400
5 seconds	400

[a]In estimating costs, it was assumed that (a) two announcers would be used in producing a 30- or 60-second ad and that only one announcer would be used in producing a 5-or 10-second ad and (b) a combo would furnish simple background music for the ads. The estimated costs also include the studio fees, the cost of tapes, and similar expenses.

Television

1. Rates
    (a) The rates for TV advertising spots are approximately the following:

Midprogram Breaks	Prime Time (6:30 P.M. till 10:00 P.M.)	Class B Time (All Other Hours)
60 seconds	₱500/spot	₱250/spot
30 seconds	250	125
10 seconds	125	65
5 seconds	65	35

Station Breaks (Between Programs)		
60 seconds	₱400/spot	₱200/spot
30 seconds	200	100
10 seconds	100	50
5 seconds	50	25

2. Production Costs
    (a) A 30-second film commercial would cost approximately ₱5000 to produce.
    (b) The estimated costs of producing a TV slide commercial are as follows:

Length	Estimated Costs
60 seconds	₱350
30 seconds	325
10 seonds	310
5 seconds	305

Case 6-3
Turtle Wax Limited[1]

In September 1961, Mr. Thomas Heywood joined N. Kilvert & Sons Ltd., of Manchester, as Marketing Director. Two months later he went to the United States to interview several U.S. companies who had shown some interest in licensing Kilvert as an import agent for the United Kingdom. Mr. Heywood became sufficiently interested to negotiate an exclusive licensing agreement with Turtle Wax, Inc. of Chicago, Illinois, a maker of a wide range of quality automobile waxes, cleaners, and other car-care products. On January 10, 1962, Mr. Heywood was reviewing his proposed program to test market Tur-

tle Wax Liquid Car Wax in Lancashire, as he was scheduled to present the program to the board of directors on the following day.

BACKGROUND[2]

N. Kilvert & Sons was a subsidiary company of Lloyd's Packing Warehouse (Holdings), Ltd. Originally Lloyd's had been involved in the packing, warehousing, and forwarding of the finished cotton products of the prosperous nineteenth century Lancashire cotton industry. The activities of the company grew to such an extent that almost every finished piece of cotton goods shipped overseas

[1]Case material of the Management Case Research Programme of the Dept. of Production and Industrial Administration, Cranfield, and prepared as a basis for class discussion. This case was made possible through the cooperation of Lloyd's Packing Warehouses. Cases are not designed to illustrate correct or incorrect handling of business situations. © The College of Aeronautics, Cranfield, January 1965. Reproduced by permission.

[2]Some of the figures and facts in this case have been disguised with the permission of Lloyd's Packing Warehouses. However, they are adjudged by the company to be useful for the purposes of class discussion.

from Lancashire was handled by Lloyd's. From this beginning the company diversified at first into transport services and subsequently into a wide range of activities. However, beginning about 1954 the Lancashire cotton industry fell into a protracted recession. Consequently the company found itself with empty warehouses and falling profits, while the market value of its outstanding shares fell to about £13 million. For a recent balance sheet statement, see Exhibit 1.

Beginning in the 1950's the Lloyd's management began an active diversification program. By 1960 the company had bought a number of companies whose activities fell into eight broad areas. These areas included packing, transportation, and travel, timber, paper, and packaging, consumer products, international operations, and engineering-industrial products and services. However, the rapid assimilation of these companies brought with it a series of new problems in respect to management and consolidation into the group. One purchase, a television manufacturing company proved to be unprofitable. As a result, by the early 1960's the group had lost money and management morale suffered.

In 1960, Lloyds purchased N. Kilvert & Sons, a manufacturer of lard, suet, and other products made from animal fats. By 1960, the Kilvert name had established, in the Midlands and the North, what executives believed to be a very good retail brand acceptance, especially in Lancashire and Yorkshire. In Lancashire the company had achieved distribution in about 79 percent of all food stores. Kilverts employed a sales force of ten men who sold directly to wholesalers and certain retail outlets. The salesmen would take customers' orders, which were then delivered primarily by wholesalers, although some retail business was done using the company-owned fleet of vehicles. Kilvert products were also marketed in other parts of the United Kingdom either under a private brand name or to institutional markets, which included restaurants, factories, and the armed forces.

However, in the few years prior to 1960, Kilvert sales had declined by 30 percent and profits had also fallen. In an attempt to improve Kilvert's position, Mr. William Kenyon, formerly production director for the Whiteside-Maconochie Company (manufacturers of pickles, sauces, cannet meats and vegetables, and soups) was brought in as managing director.

SEARCH FOR NEW PRODUCTS

Mr. Kenyon sought to stabilize Kilvert's sales by diversifying into products that were not affected by similar commodity-market fluctuations. Lard, which accounted for approximately 75 percent of all cooking fats sold in the United Kingdom, fluctuated considerably in price, reflecting the price of the raw materials. In his search for new products for Kilvert to market, Mr. Kenyon looked specifically for products that

1. Were not already well established or well known in England.
2. Were technically sound and firmly established in foreign markets,
3. Could use Kilvert's name and distribution network to the best advantage.

Because the United States appeared to be one of the most fertile sources of new products and ideas, Mr. Kenyon made a trip to the United States in 1961 to locate companies interested in marketing their products in the United Kingdom. During his trip, Mr. Kenyon initially selected two firms that seemed to have promising products. One was a frozen vegetables and desserts to the retail food trade, and the other was a Canadian firm that sold various specialty food items.

While visiting an advertising agency in Chicago, Illinois, Mr. Kenyon mentioned to the agency the purpose of his trip and asked if they might know of any companies interested in exporting. An account executive recommended that Mr. Kenyon visit a client of his, Turtle Wax, Inc., which manufactured and sold a variety of quality car-care products. Mr. Kenyon learned from the account executive that although automobile wax and similar car-care products in the United States were still sold through garages, that more recently they had also gained very heavy distribution through variety stores (e.g., Woolworth's), discount stores, and even in grocery supermarkets. When he subsequently visited Turtle Wax headquarters, Mr. Kenyon was told that five years ago an importer from Sweden had approached the company asking for exclusive distribution rights in Sweden. In three years this importer had achieved a 50 percent share of the auto wax market in Sweden, mainly at the expense of Johnson's auto wax.

On further discussion, Mr. Kenyon learned that Turtle Wax was a privately owned company that, while profitable, did not apparently seek outside sources of permanent financing and was therefore relatively restricted in its ability to expand. Turtle Wax had begun in the 1940's as a "backyard" operation, and although making a product which seemed to be widely regarded as being of very high quality, the company was never originally considered as a major threat to the larger auto wax producers in the United States. However, in 1961 Turtle

Wax claimed to be a leading company in sales of liquid car waxes with a 5 to 8 percent share of the total U.S. car-wax market. Besides liquid car wax, Turtle Wax also manufactured and sold a wide line of car-care products.

NEW MARKETING DIRECTOR

In September of 1961, Mr. Kenyon employed a new marketing director for Kilvert, Mr. Thomas Heywood. Mr. Heywood's primary responsibility was to improve sales of Kilvert lard products, but in November, Mr. Kenyon asked him to visit the United States to continue the investigations and negotiations with the three firms that Mr. Kenyon had contracted earlier in the year.

After demobilization from the Royal Navy soon after the end of World War II, Mr. Heywood attended the government-sponsored Business Training Scheme. This was a two-and-a-half year course initiated after the war for men demobilized from the Armed Forces and was designed to equip them for business. From 1949 to 1960, he worked for Proctor & Gamble, Ltd. In 1951, at the age of 25, he was appointed office manager of a new company sales office in Leeds, responsible for accounts, deliveries and sales administration for approximately 13,000 Proctor & Gamble customers. In 1952 he was assigned to the company's British head office in the public relations department. He remained in this department until 1958, when his final responsibilities as associate manager of the department included the designing and implementation of major public relations projects as well as answering the more complicated customer inquiries that were forwarded to his department. In this post he controlled a staff of some twenty people. Public relation projects were assigned to him by the various brand managers as part of their advertising expenditures.

Shortly afterwards, he transferred to the advertising department in the brand group responsible for a leading Proctor & Gamble toilet soap. In Proctor & Gamble the brand group had the ultimate responsibility for the marketing strategy of the brand. Mr. Heywood's initial training involved six months working as a salesman, selling soaps and detergents to grocery stores. On joining the brand group he assumed responsibilities over an eighteen-month period for advertising, research, budgeting control, packaging, display, sales promotion, product development and all other facets of brand management.

In 1960, Mr. Heywood left Proctor & Gamble to become marketing manager for a biscuit manufac-

turer in the northwest. Although this company was not profitable, Mr. Heywood had accepted the position as he believed it would round out his marketing experience and knowledge. It did in fact, enable him to control a sales force of over fifty men and forced him to operate with a negligible advertising appropriation. Eighteen months later, in the autumn of 1961, Mr. Heywood accepted Mr. Kenyon's offer of the post of marketing director for Kilvert & Sons.

MR. HEYWOOD'S TRIP TO AMERICA

Before Mr. Heywood went to the United States in November 1961, to follow up Mr. Kenyon's leads, he concluded, from the evidence available to him, that the frozen foods seemed the most attractive possibility, in contrast to Turtle Wax that seemed the least attractive. However, when he visited the frozen foods company, he discovered that the company was unwilling to risk any of its own funds abroad, nor make its terms particularly attractive to Kilvert. Moreover, Kilvert's anticipated profit margins on the frozen foods lines were not deemed sufficiently high, that is, it seemed improbable that the expenses that he foresaw he would incur in establishing distribution and sales for the new line would be paid back in less than five years. Mr. Heywood knew that this payback would not be satisfactory to the Lloyd's board of directors. The specialty foods company in Canada also proved unwilling to share any financial risks abroad, and again Mr. Heywood did not consider that the forecast margins for Kilvert justified the risk involved. Because his time in the United States was limited, Mr. Heywood concluded that it would be more expedient to follow up the Turtle Wax possibility than to search out other products.

Mr. Heywood was not very attracted to Turtle Wax since he believed that car-care products were not yet suitable for distribution through grocery stores. To initiate a change in the distribution pattern, he believed, would be expensive and time consuming, and neither Kilvert nor Lloyd's was currently in a position to initiate any major changes in this direction. He knew that car wax in England was sold exclusively through garages, service stations, and stores selling automobile parts and accessories. Within the latter, one large chain, Halford's, had 260 branches in England and accounted for approximately 15 percent total car wax sales. In addition, he appreciated that three large companies were already strongly entrenched in the English auto-wax market: E. R. Howard's "Auto-Brite," a liquid, with about 30 percent of the market; Johnson's "One-Step," a paste, with about 28 percent of the market; and Simoniz's ''Speedwax,'' a paste, also with about 28 percent of the market. All these companies had manufacturing facilities in England and all three were subsidiaries of very large and well-established American corporations. Mr. Heywood estimated that apart from these three manufacturers, the remaining 14 percent of sales were made by small manufacturers whose sales were based mainly on their local reputation or low prices. The three major manufacturers were together spending around £200,000 per year in advertising.

Mr. Heywood said that he was not able to discover the size of the English market for car waxes, although he did know that in 1962 there were about six million cars in England, and estimated that approximately 60 to 70 percent of the car owners bought car wax once a year. He also knew that the number of cars in England was increasing very rapidly, recalling that the increase was as large as 10 percent a year.

Kilvert's marketing director was told by the Turtle Wax executives that the company was willing to give Kilvert exclusive selling rights in the United Kingdom and would also agree to sell Kilvert at their standard export price. Even after making allowance for the 10 percent English import duty on car waxes, Mr. Heywood calculated that profit margins for Kilvert would be very attractive if Turtle Wax could be sold in England as a quality product with a price as high or even higher than the existing major car waxes. Confronted with the possibility of high gross margins in a potentially large and growing market for auto waxes, and recalling Turtle Wax's reputed success in Sweden, Mr. Heywood concluded that Turtle Wax warranted further investigation.

Soon after returning to England, Mr. Heywood went to Sweden to talk with the Swedish importer who was marketing Turtle Wax. He found that the importer was selling ''Turtle Wax at a price at least 50 percent higher than its major competitors, and along with this had supported his merchandising programme with what Mr. Heywood considered to be a ''fair-sized'' promotional campaign. There was real evidence that Turtle Wax in Sweden was making considerable inroads into a market that had once belonged exclusively to Johnson's.

After his visit Mr. Heywood was convinced that Kilvert should seriously consider test marketing the product in England, and he returned to England to discuss his findings with Mr. Kenyon. In their discussions, both admitted that to some extent common sense, and certainly the advice of many of their respected colleagues, told them to leave the Turtle Wax venture strictly alone. At this time, the parent company was losing money at the rate of £500

thousand a year and it would be very difficult to persuade the board to spend funds on a new product that might be better spent in improving the present lines. Moreover, the executives were reminded that such large and powerful companies as Du Pont of America and Rex of Germany had been unable to introduce successfully their own auto wax products into the U. K. market against the established positions of Simoniz, Johnson's and Howard's. Despite these warning signs, Mr. Kenyon and Mr. Heywood still believed that with proper promotion, and with correct pricing so as to produce a satisfactory margin, the product could be test marketed with only minor distraction from the executives' other responsibilities and with only temporary drain on the parent company's funds. Consequently, a decision to test market Turtle Wax on a limited basis was reached by mid-December of 1961.

At the end of 1961, Mr. Heywood engaged Mr. James Pert as his sales manager for the Turtle Wax venture. Mr. Pert has been an area sales manager for a company selling detergents for industrial use; outside of his sales management duties, however, Mr. Pert had only limited experience in other aspects of marketing. Mr. Heywood decided that he would have to rely for the time being on the appropriate departments in the Kilvert organization for the rest of the organization needed to manage the Turtle Wax test marketing (e.g., functions such as customer billing/shipping and general liaison activities with the American company). Mr. Heywood would continue to be marketing director for both the Kilvert Company and the Turtle Wax test-marketing program, but he hoped that with time he could delegate to his new sales manager, Mr. Pert, marketing responsibilities for Turtle Wax should the project prove to be successful.

DEVELOPING A MARKETING PROGRAM FOR TURTLE WAX

Mr. Heywood completed his negotiations with Turtle Wax Inc., of Chicago in late December. While Turtle Wax remained willing to franchise Kilvert as the sole distributor in England, the Turtle Wax executives did not feel that they were able to divert any of their resources from the much larger American market into speculative foreign ventures.

At the beginning of 1962, Messrs. Heywood and Pert were faced with several decision: How many of the various Turtle Wax car-care products should Kilvert offer, at what price, and with what promotional program? Mr. Heywood had already approached Lloyd's board of directors with his proposal for a test market, giving them preliminary costs and profit margin figures (see Appendix A). The response was that he could spend any reasonable sum provided he at least "broke-even" and sustained no loss by the end of Lloyd's next fiscal year, which ended September 10, 1962. Mr. Heywood believed that the major sales into the trade for the 1962 selling season would be in March, April, and May and he therefore realized that if he was to obtain the board's approval in time for his program to be given a fair chance to take effect before his "wholesale" selling season began, he must present his recommendations and full program to the board by the end of January. He also discussed with Mr. Kenyon how much money they would require from the parent company to conduct the market test. They agreed that they should not ask the board for a total of any more than £10,000 by September 30, the end of the first fiscal year.

On January 18, Mr. Heywood discussed possible strategies with Mr. Pert. After the discussion, Mr. Heywood asked Mr. Pert to incorporate their conclusion and to outline the details of the full marketing program in a report that Mr. Heywood would submit to Mr. Kenyon and the board. Some of the considerations that Mr. Heywood and Mr. Pert discussed are described below.

PRODUCT RANGE

Since it was not feasible for the Kilvert salesman to handle Turtle Wax Mr. Heywood planned to develop a separate Turtle Wax sales organization. It would be desirable, furthermore, for the new sales force to have a variety of products to sell. A full line of products would not only make more economical use of the salesman's time, thus giving the salesman more to talk about, but most importantly, he believed, it would establish the Turtle Wax Company as the supplier of a range of car-care products. Mr. Heywood reviewed the list of Turtle Wax products, but regarded this wide list of products: "As a real temptation in the wrong direction." He went on to say: "Obviously the product with the greatest appeal to the biggest market must spearhead the attack, as it would determine the success or otherwise of the venture. In his mind there was no doubt that he should concentrate his efforts on this one product during the initial sales drive. As regards the remaining Turtle Wax products, the question was rather how long he should wait before he introduced them."

It was decided, therefore, that at first only one product would be offered, Turtle Wax Liquid Car

Wax. It seemed clear that "certainly the most demonstrable product on the whole line" was the logical choice. It was further decided that after a few months, certain speciality items such as an upholstery cleaner would be added but that the car wax, including the ten-ounce size, should account for 85 percent of the test market's sales in the first full year. (See Appendix A, "Marketing Strategy".)

PRICING

Mr. Heywood concluded, on the evidence of his trip to Sweden, that the importer's higher price had not been a significant deterrent to sales. In fact, Mr. Heywood reasoned that a higher price reinforced the importer's advertising claim that Turtle Wax was a superior product. Looking at the British market, Mr. Heywood believed that a motor car had a strong emotional appeal in the lives of the people. This had been true especially since the war, for people who once thought they could never buy a car now found themselves owning one. He suspected that a man's approach and attitude toward car care products were not unlike those of woman toward beauty care products. Therefore, if someone waxed his car once or twice a year, 10/-d[3] to 12/-d was not too much to ask him to spend on the wax. Of the major competitors, Simoniz's Speedwax nine-ounce tin retailed for 10/-d and four-ounce tin for 5/-d. Johnson's One-Step eight-ounce tin retailed for 10/-d and four ounce tin for 5/-d. Auto-Brite Liquid (eight-ounce bottle) sold for 5/-d. Mr. Heywood and Mr. Pert decided that a ten-ounce bottle of Turtle Wax should sell for 12/6d (see Appendix A, "Price Structure").

DISTRIBUTION

One of the toughest hurdles Mr. Heywood expected to encounter in the initial stages was the problem of securing distribution outlets through the 35,000-odd garages in the United Kingdom. None of the major competitors sold direct to the garage or accessory outlets (except to some of the larger chain accessory stores such as Halford's) but instead preferred to use the services of about 250 wholesalers. About five of the larger wholesalers offered national

[3]£1(one pound sterling = 20s (shillings), 1s = 12d (pennies). In 1962, £1 = (£S.) $2.80, 1s = $.14, 7s = (approx) $1.00. The amount "10s/6d" should be read as "ten and six," that is, 10 shillings, 6 pence; and the amount "2/10s/6d" should be read as "2 pounds, ten and six."

coverage, and according to Mr. Heywood, together serviced about 60 percent of the retail outlets. Mr. Heywood expected that it would be very difficult to persuade wholesalers to take on his product no matter what margin of profit he offered them. In fact, exploratory interviews with two wholesalers confirmed this belief. Mr. Heywood commented: "We made the usual discovery; the wholesalers said that they already had too many brands to sell and continued: 'If we were to divert any of our time to your product, we wouldn't make a profit on any of our existing lines, furthermore, there is not room for another brand in this market.' "

At this time normal margins for the major brands of car wax were 20 percent for the wholesaler and 25 percent for the retailer, although less well-known brands usually gave the retailer a 33 percent suggested profit margin. Mr. Heywood decided that he would offer the wholesalers the traditional 20 percent discount but would offer retailers a 33 percent margin. (See Appendix A, "Price Structure"). This pricing structure was consistent with the decision not to try to "buy" the wholesalers through higher margins.

He estimated that a salesman of the requisite caliber would cost about £750 a year in salary plus £250 commission and about £1000 in expenses including a sales van. Furthermore, to gain maximum distribution coverage before the advertising and promotional campaigns were started would initially require more salesmen than later in the year. For the introductory campaign, lasting four weeks, he planned to use the services of Sales Force, Ltd; to augment his "pioneer sales force." This company charged a fee of £50 a week per man, or £250 a week for a five-man team, (including a supervisor for the five men). An important part of his strategy to secure distribution was the use of advertisements on regional television (see Appendix A, "Advertising and Sales Promotion Plan"). For the Manchester area, this meant using the services of the independent television network that covered the counties of Lancashire and Yorkshire (see Exhibit 2). During the weekdays the television service was supplied by the Granada network, and at weekends by the national ABC service.

Mr. Heywood's proposed strategy in direct selling was to combine an actual demonstration with a sample for the garage supervisor, and to emphasize the fact that "the product is advertised on television, therefore you've got to take it." Although other brands had used television advertising, Mr. Heywood thought that for the most part their brand images were lifeless and placed only minor emphasis on product quality. Therefore, he planned to

instruct his salesmen to obtain the largest advantages from the television campaign during the course of their presentations to the garage personnel. When making his presentation, a salesman would try to build up enthusiasm for Turtle Wax by waxing a section of a car standing in the garage, if possible the garage superintendent's own car. Mr. Heywood believed that his product was so demonstrably superior that the prospective customer could see the results for himself. Nevertheless, Mr. Heywood did not expect that demonstrations and sales presentations alone would necessarily result in an order. Throughout, the emphasis would be on quality: "An intelligent and distinctive sales presentation to be delivered on a superior product that is *new from America and is advertised on television.*"

Mr. Heywood remarked that it would have been simplest to test market the car wax in Manchester alone, but he thought it unwise to restrict the test market to an urban district, therefore, the whole of the county of Lancashire was chosen as the test-market area (see Appendix A, "Test Area", and "Market Details"). Since the counties of both Lancashire and Yorkshire came within the service area of the Granada Television Company, Mr. Heywood decided that television could be used as the major advertising weapon, even though the coverage afforded in Yorkshire would not be supported by a complementary sales effort. Furthermore, since the product (both for sale and stock) had to come from the United States, and this necessitated tying up capital, he reasoned that to extend the test base beyond Lancashire would spread the investment over too wide an area. There were about 2600 outlets in Lancashire that Mr. Heywood felt should all be covered by the end of February, or at least before the advertising began in March. However, he knew that his organization would not start selling in any significant quantity until the beginning of February. On a going basis, he calculated that about two company salesmen could cover this area, but that to gain sufficient distribution during the month of March in the test area would probably require an additional five salesmen from Sales Force Ltd. For each of the two company salesmen, he expected to buy an Austin Mini Van, on which he would receive about sixty-days credit before full payment was due.

ADVERTISING

Mr. Heywood felt that £10,000 was the maximum sum Kilvert could afford to spend on Turtle Wax promotion during the first year. He was able to convince a London advertising agency, with whom he had satisfactory dealings on previous occasions, that the Turtle Wax test-marketing program had considerable potential and would represent an excellent account for them as soon as Turtle Wax sales increased. "That afternoon" Mr. Heywood said, "about twelve people from the London agency sat around a table with representatives of Kilvert and discussed plans and strategy. As the discussion continued the agency suggested that there was a need for more research. The suggestion sounded reasonable enough to me, but I knew that we just couldn't afford to spend three months and £1000 of our promotional budget on research. This was the first time during my career in marketing that I had forsaken market research, but in this instance I felt we simply had to proceed without the use of this technique. I informed the agency, 'if we prove to be in business, we'll buy plenty of research later, but for the moment the test-market program and our own judgement will have to be our research'."

Mr. Heywood believed that the package used by the American Company could be a positive factor in his promotional campaign. He thought that the color of the bottle (green) was pleasing to the eye, while the written material was "fired on" (i.e., it comprised part of the bottle and was not just a paper sleeve placed over the bottle) The overall impression gave an appearance of high quality. Moreover, many features on the bottle emphasized the maker's claim that the wax was very durable. The printed material on the front stressed that the wax contained a special ingredient, "Sun-Stop," which the back of the bottle reinforced by a special "box" printed in yellow and red saying "Tested in Death Valley: Proven in Fiery Death Valley in 135°F Temperatures, Sun-Stop is a spectacular new *Turtle* Wax ingredient shielding your car finish from ultraviolet ray deterioration." Around the top edge of the bottle were the words "New 1 Year Car Wax, One Waxing Lasts up to One Year. Advertised in Sat. Eve. Post, Look, Life." The executives of Kilvert and the agency representatives decided to use these slogans, as well as emphasizing that Turtle Wax was a proven and successful American product, to create what they believed would be a very effective campaign.

The heart of the campaign would be to emphasize the "Once-A-Year Liquid Car Wax," a particular choice of words they believed to be stronger than the "Year Long Life" slogan found on the top of the bottle. The executives decided that a "Once-A Year Liquid Car Wax", conveyed through quality copy and colorful point-of-purchase display material, could be the foundation for a "dramatic and truly exciting advertising message." A carefully conceived strong claim, he thought, would stimulate the consumer's interest and also give him greater confidence in the product once he has actually used it. In the case of Turtle Wax, independent research in the United States of America confirmed the "Once-A-Year" statement.

Television, therefore, was the key to Mr. Heywood's stratey for obtaining distribution at the retail level. However, since television advertising was so expensive, the limited funds available for promotion made it impossible to employ any other advertising media if television were used. Moreover, the initial television commercial would have to be in a "magazine" program,[4] and would therefore require a studio announcer rather than a prefilmed presentation, since the latter would tie up too much capital in a fixed investment. The commercials would be presented on the Granada ABC networks six times during the months of March and April. In addition, for garage display small "crowners," that is, pieces of green printed cardboard that slipped over the necks of the bottle on display, would again emphasize the "Once-A-Year" theme.

PRESENTATION TO THE BOARD

On January 20, Mr. Heywood was due to present his plan to the board of directors. On January 19, Mr. Heywood received the report from Mr. Pert outlining a full test-marketing program. This report is reproduced in part as Appendix A. Mr. Heywood and Mr. Pert convened once more to reconsider their conclusions before making their recommendations to the board.

---

[4]There were two separate "magazine" programs taking place once every two weeks. The Turtle Wax advertising message would, therefore, be viewed weekly. These "magazine" programs lasted half an hour and took place at nonpeak viewing hours. Six different advertising messages, prepared by actors and lasting thirty seconds were shown during the program.

QUESTIONS

1. Evaluate Kilvert's program to test market Turtle Wax liquid car wax in the Manchester area.
2. How successful do you feel Kilvert's marketing program will be to import and sell Turtle Wax products in England?

Exhibit 1
Consolidated Balance Sheet, 30th September 1961

	1961			1960		
	£	£	£	£	£	£
Capital authorized						
5 percent cumulative preference	76,095			76,095		
6 percent cumulative preference	136,250			136,250		
Ordinary	2,287,655			2,287,655		
	2,500,000			2,500,000		
Capital issued and converted into stock						
5 percent cumulative preference	76,095			76,095		
6 percent cumulative preference	136,250			136,250		
Ordinary	1,700,000	1,912,345		1,700,000	1,912,345	
Share premium account		506,185			506,185	
Capital reserves						
Holding company	377,933			368,089		
Subsidiary companies	133,359	511,292		26,898	394,987	
Revenue reserves						
Holding company						
General reserve	500,000			550,000		
Stock and contingencies	—			100,000		
Profit-and-loss account	353,271			270,841		
Subsidiary companies						
General reserve	37,951			37,951		
Profit-and-loss account	(278,780)	612,442		181,936	1,140,728	
		3,542,264			3,954,245	
Reserve for staff benefit		17,881			23,695	
Taxation equalization reserve re initial allowances		43,389			57,579	
Reserve for future income tax		72,941			244,886	
Total capital and reserves		3,676,475			4,280,405	
Current assets						

Stock at or below cost	1,624,378		2,707,705	
Sundry debtors and payments in advance less provisions	2,979,081		3,075,688	
Bank balances	233,173		170,806	
Cash in hand	10,302		8,549	
		4,846,934		5,962,748
Deduct				
Current Liabilities				
Sundry creditors	1,594,922		1,894,026	
Bank overdraft and financial advances	1,283,383		1,314,992	
Bills payable	287,311		348,289	
Current taxation	76,864		271,577	
Recommended dividend (less tax)	26,031		93,713	
		3,268,511		3,922,597
		1,578,423		2,040,151
Fixed assets				
Freehold land and buildings leaseholds, plant, machinery, vehicles, etc.		1,691,566		1,940,987
Investments				
Associated company at par	400,000		300,000	
Quotec, at market price	30,726		55,712	
Trade, at or below cost	137		338	
		430,863		356,050
		3,700,852		4,337,188
Deduct				
Outside shareholders' interests in subsidiary companies share capital and proportion of capital and revenue reserves and undistributed profits attributable thereto		24,377		56,783
Total net assets		3,676,475		4,280,405

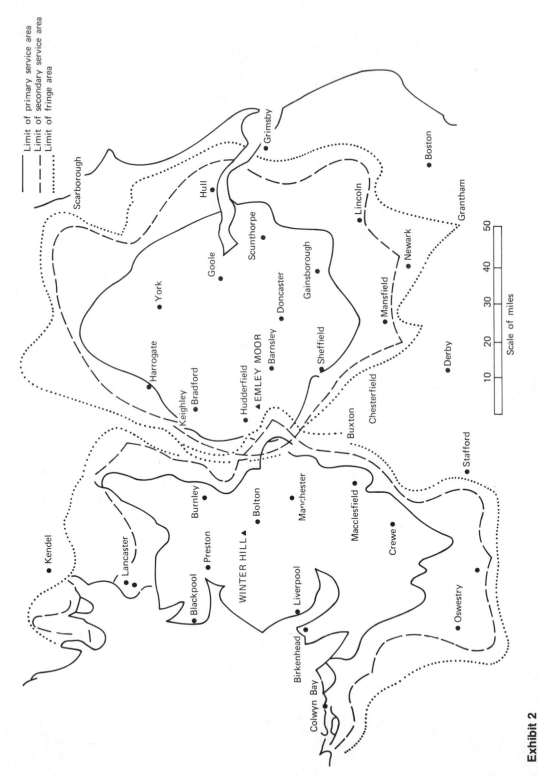

Exhibit 2

"Primary" and "Secondary" Service Areas Served by the Independent Television
Network for Lancashire and Yorkshire Counties.

Appendix A Mr. Pert's Turtle Wax Marketing Plan

RECOMMENDATION

It is proposed that we carry out a test-market campaign of Turtle Wax Liquid Car Wax and other Turtle Wax products in the Lancashire Television Area, commencing February 1962. This will require an appropriation of £10,000 (including all overheads) in fiscal 1962 and £17,000 in fiscal 1962/1963.

1.   MARKETING OBJECTIVE

To establish Turtle Wax products with the trade and the consuming public as the best automotive products available and to obtain the leading market share within a three-year period.

2.   MARKETING STRATEGY

We shall build our campaign on the Liquid Car Wax that will be the only product supported by advertising. It is anticipated that in the first year Car Wax will account for 85 percent of total sales.

Initially, we plan to sell our products direct to individual garages since we believe that this is the only satisfactory method of obtaining sufficient distribution and attracting the interest and support of the wholesaler. Assuming success in Year 1, we anticipate co-operation of wholesalers from Year 2 onward.

The range and introductory pattern will be as follows:

Month 1:	Liquid Car Wax	10 oz
	Liquid Car Wax	16 oz
	Liquid Car Wax	1 gal
Month 4:	Upholstery Cleaner	12 oz
	3 Minute Car Wash[a]	12 oz
	Zip Wax Car Wash[a]	20 oz
Month 7:	20/20 Windshield De-Icer	14 oz
	Bumper Wax	7½ oz

3.   TEST AREA
  Lancashire television area   Population: 7.5 million
4.   MARKET DETAILS
  (a)   Car ownership
        Estimated number of cars: 625,000
        (based on license figures 1960)
  (b)   Retail outlets
        (1)   Garages   Estimated 2400
        (2)   Accessory shops   Estimated   200
  (c)   Estimated market size
        Year 1   Assume 70 percent motorists purchase one item per year = 36,500 cases approximately.[b]
        Year 2   10 percent expansion of market = 40,000 cases
        Year 3   10 percent expansion of market = 44,000 cases.

[a]Case note: "Zip Wax Car Wash" was a car wash that also contained Turtle Wax Auto Wax; "3 Minute Car Wash" was a polisher that did not contain any wax.
[b]Each case contained 12 bottles.

5. PRICE STRUCTURE

	Product	Accessory Wholesaler	Retailer	Consumer
Turtle Wax	Liquid Car Wax 10 oz	6/8	8/4	12/6
	Liquid Car Wax 16 oz	9/4	11/8	17/6
	Liquid Car Wax 1 gal	52/0	65/0	87/6
	Upholstery Cleaner 12 oz	6/8	8/4	12/6
	3 Minute Car Wash 12 oz	5/0	6/4	9/6
	Zip Wax Car Wash 20 oz	5/10	7/4	11/0
	20/20 Windshield De-Icer 14 oz	6/8	8/4	12/6
	Bumper Wax 7½ oz	6/8	8/4	12/6

These prices show the following profit margins:

Retailers	33⅓%
Wholesalers	20%

6. HYPOTHETICAL PLAN

	Year 1		Year 2		Year 3	
	Turtle Wax	Other Products	Turtle Wax	Other Products	Turtle Wax	Other Products
Shipments	6,000	2,200	12,000	5,000	20,000	10,000
(cases)	£28,800 [a]	£9,240	£48,000	£18,500	£80,000	£37,000
Available average gross profit	40/-	45/-	36/-	35/-	36/-	35/-
Less 5/- per case admin.	5/-	5/-	5/-	5/-	5/-	5/-
	35/-	40/-	31/-	30/-	31/-	30/-
Total available	£10,500	£4,400	£18,600	£ 7,500	£31,000	£15,000
	£14,900		£26,100		£46,000	
Less salaries/ distribution	£ 6,000		7,000		7,000	
Available for profit and advt.	£ 8,900		19,000		39,000	
Promotional spending	£ 6,700		10,000		15,000	
Profit	£ 2,200		9,100		24,000	
Cumulative profit	£ 2,200		£11,300		£35,300	

Assumes   (a) Sales 4:1 garage: accessory in the first year.

(b)   Margin calculated on small size only.
         Large size brings in a slightly higher profit margin.

[a] £28,800 is based on an average price per case of £4. 16. 0.

Average Kilvert selling price per case:

Turtle Wax	Year 1	£4. 16. 0.
	2	£4. 0. 0.
Other products	Year 1	£4. 4. 0.
	2	£3. 14. 0.

The average gross profit calculation is reasonably conservative.

The drop in Year 2 is due to our change in selling pattern through the introduction of the wholesaler.

SALARY AND DELIVERY CHARGES

We have assumed the following organization requirements:

	Staff	Estimated Cost
Year 1	1 sales manager	£6,000
	2 sales/delivery men	
Year 2	½sales manager	£7,000
	3 merchandisers	
Year 3	½sales manager	£7,000
	3 merchandisers	

It is anticipated that further expansion areas will be charged with a proportion of sales manager's expenses from Year 2 onward.

7.   FISCAL PLAN

	Year 1961/2		Year 1962/3		Year 1963/4	
	Turtle Wax	Other Products	Turtle Wax	Other Products	Turtle Wax	Other Products
Shipments (cases)	5,000 £24,000	800 £3,360	12,000 £48,000	5,000 £18,000	20,000 £80,000	10,000 £37,000
Available average gross profit	40/-	45/-	36/-	35/-	36/-	35/-
Less admin.	5/-	5/-	5/-	5/-	5/-	5/
Total available	£ 8,750	£1,600	£18,600	£ 7,500	£31,000	£15,000
		£10,350		£26,100		£46,000
Less salaries		3,500		7,000		7,000
Available for profit & advt.		6,850		19,100		39,000
Promotional spending		6,700		10,000		15,000
Profit		250		9,100		24,000
Cumulative profit		£ 250		£ 9,350		£33,350

8.   ADVERTISING AND SALES PROMOTION PLAN

	Year 1 £	Year 2 £	Year 3 £
Television	2,300	5,000	8,000
Total advertising	2,300	5,000	8,000
Pioneer sales force	1,000		
Samples	500	500	500
Display	750	1,000	1,000
Garage promotion	150	2,000	3,000
September dealer offer	1,000		
Total sales promotion	3,400	3,500	4,500
Reserve	1,000	1,500	2,500
Total expenditure	6,700	10,000	15,000
Promotional spending per £ sales	3/6	3/1	2/7

8a.   ADVERTISING PLAN

The above schedule assumes television advertising over three years.
Year 1 plan makes provision for the following:

4 × 60 sec magazine program on Granada at £423		£1,692
2 × 60 sec magazine program on ABC at £274		548
		£2,240

Granada program in 1961 had a rating of 34 [a]
ABC program in 1961 had a rating of 27

8b.   SALES PROMOTION PLAN

One 10-oz bottle to every garage
              2,500 bottles at 4/8d .. .. £583. 6. 8.

9.   HYPOTHETICAL SHIPMENT

Period	Turtle Wax £	Remainder £	Total £	Turtle Wax Cases	Remainder Cases	Total Cases
February/March	7,200	—	7,200	1,500	—	1,500
April	4,800	—	4,800	1,000	—	1,000
May	2,400	420	2,820	500	100	600
June	2,400	420	2,820	500	100	600
July	2,880	420	2,820	600	100	600
August	2,400	420	2,340	500	100	500
September	1,920	1,680	3,120	400	400	700
October	1,920	2,100	4,020	400	500	900
November	960	2,100	3,540	200	500	800
December	960	840	2,280	200	200	500
January	960	840	2,280	200	200	500
	28,800	9,240	38,040	6,000	2,200	8,200

[a]Television "ratings" were a measure of a program audience size as measured by several commercial rating services, (such as Neilson's, Ltd.). For both networks ratings could range from 0 to 70.

10. ADVERTISING STRATEGY

Definition

Turtle Wax will be presented as a high-quality brand name. We aim to create the idea of Turtle Wax products being superior to any other on the market and worthy of commanding a premium price.

Execution

Initially, the liquid car wax will be the only product advertised.

Our copy strategy will stress:

    (a)   That Turtle Wax is a once-a-year wax,

    (b)   That Turtle Wax is already America's and Scandinavia's most popular wax.

11. PROMOTION STRATEGY

    1.   We shall obtain maximum distribution in months 1 and 2 by employing an outside pioneer sales force to supplement the Kilvert team.

    2.   By means of extensive sampling, we shall prove to all garage staff that Turtle Wax Liquid Car Wax is indeed the best and thereby ensure that it is enthusiastically offered to the customer.

    3.   We shall offer dealer loader incentives at the appropriate seasonal period of the year to obtain maximum loading of our products. We shall also make a special "offer" to dealers in the first month of sales. In this month dealers will be able to buy Turtle Wax at a much reduced price. The offer is expected to cost the company about £1000.

12. EXPENDITURE STRATEGY

We have chosen to test our plan in the Lancashire television area for the following reason: television advertising will influence the consumer, its main purpose is to influence the garage staff and also motivate them.

13. CHOICE OF TEST AREA

We have chosen to test our plan in the Lancashire television area for the following reason:

    (A)   By operating near Manchester we keep our distribution costs down and can test market on a small scale at the lowest possible cost.

    (B)   The name of Kilvert may help us to persuade garages to stock our products.

    (C)   Thirteen percent of the population of Great Britain reside within fifty miles of Manchester and 11 percent of the car population in that same area.

Seven
Product Policy

There is hardly anything in the world that some man cannot make a little worse and sell a little cheaper.

John Ruskin

Product policy is concerned with what products and services should be sold by the firm and how they should be marketed. Chapter Six discussed the development of new items, and this chapter emphasizes the management of products from the time they are introduced until they are removed from the marketplace. Our focus is on the specific plans and strategies needed during each phase of the product life cycle to improve the competitive position of the firm. The objective is to show how marketing executives work to control the destinies of products and services over their expected lifetimes.

EXPLOITING THE PRODUCT LIFE CYCLE

Most successful products follow a life cycle that includes introduction, growth, maturity, and decline stages (Figure 7-1). At the start products are unknown so the emphasis in the marketing mix is on promotion to acquaint customers with the product and gain product trial. As sales increase during the growth phase, emphasis shifts to opening new distribution channels and retail outlets. When a product reaches maturity,

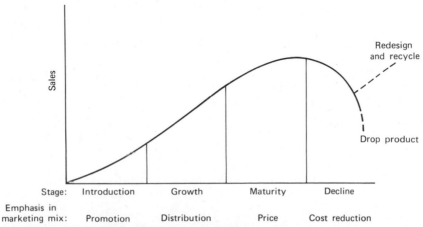

Figure 7-1 Product Life Cycle and the Marketing Mix.
Source. Reproduced with permission from G. David Hughes, *Demand Analysis for Marketing Decisions* (Homewood, Ill., Richard D. Irwin, © 1973), p. 138.

competition increases and marketing managers emphasize price, deals coupons, and special promotions to draw attention to their merchandise. Products in decline often need to be redesigned or cost reduced so they can continue to make a contribution to the company. When items become unprofitable, the company must decide whether the product should be carried at a loss or phased out to make room for more profitable lines.

Product life cycles vary in length from a few weeks for fashion merchandise up to fifty years or more for appliances and food items.[1] The amount of time a product stays in any one stage of the life cycle depends on customer adoption rates and the amount of new product competition. Since businessmen invest a great deal of money to gain consumer acceptance, it makes sense to try to extend the life of their products as long as possible.

Three strategies that can be employed to stretch product markets are promotion of more frequent and varied usage among current users, finding new uses for the basic material, and creating new users for the product by expanding the market. For example, nylon was first used in parachutes, rope, and women's stockings and demand for these purposes peaked in 1962 at about 50 million pounds per year (Figure 7-2). However,

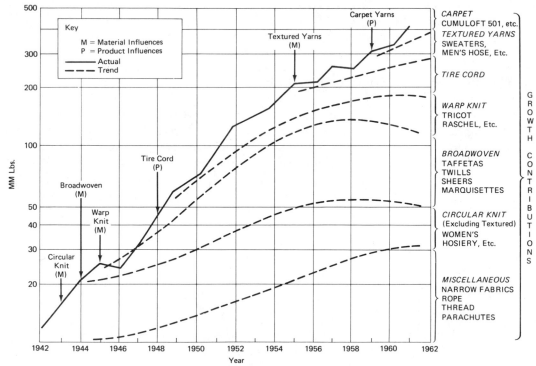

Figure 7-2 New Uses Extend Nylon Life Cycle.
Source. Jordan P. Yale, "The Strategy of Nylon's Growth: Create New Markets," *Modern Textiles Magazine* (February 1964), p. 33. Copyright © 1962 by Jordan P. Yale. Reproduced by permission.

[1]Products with short cycles include fad items like the hula hoop and eyeglass frames. Longer life cycles have been enjoyed by Coca Cola, corn flakes, the electric stove, and the zipper.

because of the development of new uses in tires, carpet, gears, sweaters, and other products, demand actually approached 500 million pounds per year. Some of the new uses resulted from changes in the product that allowed nylon to be molded and knit into new forms. Other applications resulted from demands by firms for high-strength fibers to help improve existing products (i.e., tires and carpet). Thus, instead of exhausting existing markets or giving way to competing products, nylon was able to achieve a spectacular increase in demand. In this case the search for new applications and new forms of the basic material greatly extended the life cycle of the product.

During the introductory phase of the product life cycle managers are often asked to estimate how well a new item will perform over the long run. A number of techniques that can be employed for this purpose will be reviewed in the next section.

PREDICTING SUCCESS FROM INTRODUCTORY SALES

Sales produced by newly introduced products are frequently used to estimate the shape of the revenue curve over the life of the product. Two critical factors in this analysis are the number of persons who make an initial purchase of the product and the number of persons who return to buy it again.

Penetration and Repurchase Ratios

Penetration and repeat purchase ratios provide a simple and practical way to predict the success of new products. Penetration refers to the proportion of buyers in a product class that try an item. Repeat purchase ratios show the percentage of these first time buyers that buy again within specified time periods. Both of these ratios can be estimated from sales figures from consumer panels and used to predict the long-run market shares of particular brands.

For example, a brand manager might have the responsibility for predicting the ultimate fate of the new brands shown in Figure 7-3. Both brands performed well in the first few months with sales rising quickly to a peak and then declining. The key factor explaining the difference in sales achieved by Brands A and B (Figure 7-3) was the repurchase rate. While the success of a product is partially determined by the number of persons who try the product, the key factor is the number who purchase it again.[2] In this case, Brand A was able to convert a much greater portion of those who tried the product into repeat customers (Figure 7-4). After five months, 50 percent of those who tried Brand A made a second purchase whereas less than 20 percent had repurchased Brand B. The failure of Brand B customers to repurchase suggests that there was something wrong with either the quality, price, or the usage concept of this product. If the brand manager had been able to predict the low volume of Brand B by the end of the fifth month, there might have been time to change the marketing program sufficiently to save the product.

Estimating Penetration and Repeat Ratios. Brand share forecasts for new products can be obtained by multiplying estimates of ultimate penetration ratios by the estimated long-run repeat purchase rates. The penetration ratio represents the maximum share of buyers that can be persuaded to try the product and the repeat rate shows the proportion of these customers that may be retained over time. Observation of empirical

---

[2]There are some cosmetic and appliance items that are designed for one-time purchase and repeat sales are not important. With these products success is a function of the firm's ability to continuously find new prospects and their skill at selling related items to previous customers.

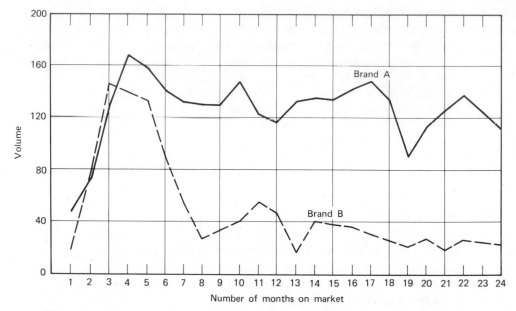

Figure 7-3 Monthly Sales Volumes Achieved by Two New Products.
Source. J. W. Woodlock, "A Model for New Product Decision," *New Product Development,* J. O. Eastlack, Jr., ed., (Chicago: American Marketing Assoc., Marketing for Executives Series, No. 13, 1968), p. 47.

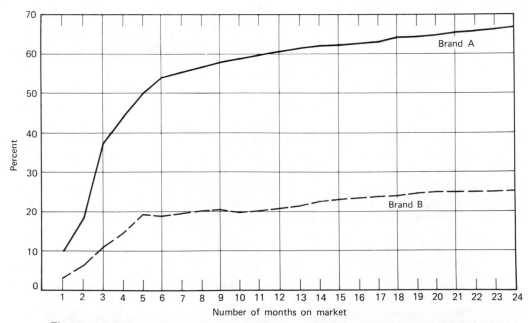

Figure 7-4 Percentage of Those Trying Brands A and B That Made a Second Purchase.
Source. Same as Figure 7-3, p. 51.

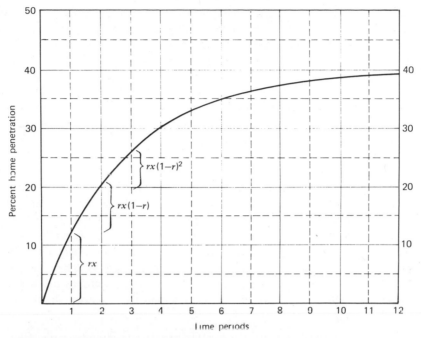

Figure 7-5 Hypothetical Cumulative New-buyer Penetration Curve.
Source. Reprinted from Louis A. Fourt and Joseph W. Woodlock, "Early Prediction of Market Success for New Grocery Products," *Journal of Marketing*, Vol. 25, No. 2 (October 1960), p. 33. Published by The American Marketing Association.

penetration curves suggests that successive increments to these curves decline and they approach a penetration limit that is less than 100 percent of the buyers in a product class. A representative curve is shown in Figure 7-5 with the penetration ratio nearing a limit of 40 percent. A simple growth model used to explain this behavior assumes that increments to penetration curves are proportional to the remaining distance to the upper boundary. In the example shown in Figure 7-5 a ceiling (x) of 40 percent was assumed and the constant fraction of the remaining distance (r) was set at 0.3. Thus, in the first period the number of new buyers was 0.3 (40 − 0) or 12 percent and in the second period it was 0.3 (40 − 12) or 8.4 percent. The formulas given in Figure 7-5 for the first three periods show that the increments to the penetration curve amount to $1 - r$ times the previous increment.[3]

The main problem with this model is obtaining accurate estimates of the penetration limit (x) and the constant incrementing fraction (r). Parfitt and Collins suggest that least squares procedures can be used to obtain relatively quick estimates of these parameters.[4] They used twelve weeks of new buyer data, for example, to estimate penetration levels at the end of the next sixteen weeks. When estimated levels were compared with the actual penetrations levels for five products, the errors were relatively small.

A more difficult problem is to derive values for repeat purchase rates. The first

---

[3]Since x is the limit and r is the constant fraction, the formula for the first period is rx. In the second period the remaining distance is $x - rx$ so the formula becomes $r(x-rx)$ or $rx(1-r)$.

[4]Their method discounts old data and gives additional weight to recent data in calculating least squares values for x and r, J. H. Parfitt and B. J. K. Collins, "Use of Consumer Panels for Brand-Share Prediction," *Journal of Marketing Research*, Vol. 5, No. 2 (May 1968), p. 144.

research in this area analyzed purchases according to depth of repeat class.[5] Buyers were grouped according to the number of repeat purchases they had made and predictions of future volume were made from these figures. However, depth of repeat classification depends on the shape of the penetration curves and the usage rate of the product, so forecasts made using this method may be subject to greater errors than with other procedures.

An alternative approach combines all repeat customers into one group and measures their purchasing patterns over time. The derivation of a repeat purchase rate using this method is shown in Figure 7-6. The diagram indicates that 40 ounces of Brand N were purchased for trial by five families during periods 1, 2, and 3. The first opportunities for repurchase thus occurred in periods 2, 3, and 4 as shown by the area set off by the staggered lines in the diagram. Note that in the first repeat period after trial, the five families bought 25 ounces of Brand N out of a total of 70 ounces purchased in the product class. This means that the repeat purchase rate was 36 percent of the total volume sold. In the second, third, and fourth repurchase periods after trial, the purchases of Brand N declined while the total sales of the product class remained about the same. The net result was a reduction in the repeat purchase rate as customers switched back to their old brands. The repeat rate shown in Figure 7-6 is not the same as the first repeat rate described in Figure 7-4. This earlier repeat rate was a cumulative ratio that increased as

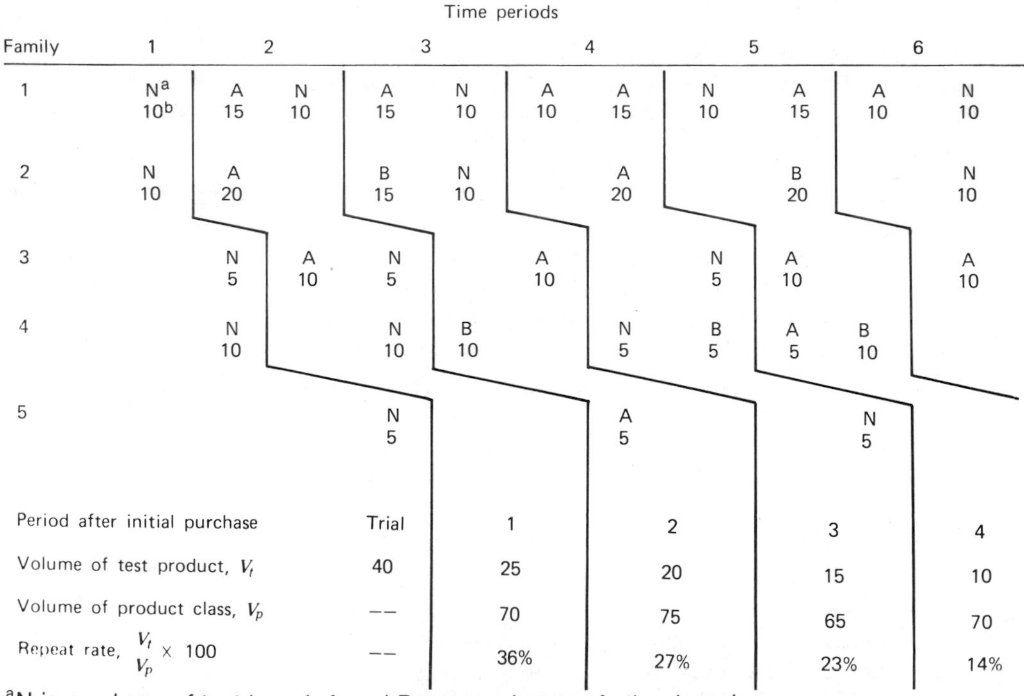

Time periods

Family	1	2		3		4		5		6	
1	N^a 10^b	A 15	N 10	A 15	N 10	A 10	A 15	N 10	A 15	A 10	N 10
2	N 10	A 20		B 15	N 10	A 20		B 20		N 10	
3		N 5	A 10	N 5		A 10		N 5	A 10	A 10	
4		N 10		N 10	B 10	N 5	B 5	A 5	B 10		
5				N 5		A 5		N 5			

	Trial	1	2	3	4
Period after initial purchase	Trial	1	2	3	4
Volume of test product, V_t	40	25	20	15	10
Volume of product class, V_p	--	70	75	65	70
Repeat rate, $\dfrac{V_t}{V_p} \times 100$	--	36%	27%	23%	14%

[a] N is purchase of test brand, A and B are purchases of other brands.
[b] Size of purchase in ounces is given below each transaction brand.

Figure 7-6 Deriving a Repeat Purchase Rate for Brand N From Panel Data.
Source. David H. Ahl, "New Product Forecasting Using Consumer Panels," *Journal of Marketing Research,* Vol. 7, No. 2 (May 1970), p. 162. Published by the American Marketing Association.

[5] Depth of repeat class or depth of trial (DOT) refers to the number of repeat purchases made. Described in Louis A. Fourt and Joseph W. Woodlock. "Early Prediction of Market Success for New Grocery Products," *Journal of Marketing,* Vol. 25, No. 2 (October 1960), pp. 31-38.

original buyers eventually came back to buy again. The repeat rate shown in Figure 7-6 included all depth of repeat buyers and it tends to decline as time from the trial purchase increases. The trick is to estimate the level at which aggregate repeat purchase rates stabilize so that a forecast can be made of the long run market share of the brand.

Forecasting with Penetration and Repeat Rates. Once estimates of ultimate penetration and repeat purchase rates have been obtained, they can be combined to yield a market share estimate. For example, the ultimate penetration ratio for Signal toothpaste was estimated by Parfitt and Collins to be 37 percent of the households buying in the product class[6] and the ultimate repurchase level was estimated to be 40 percent. Thus, the expected market share was 0.37 × 0.40 or 14.8 percent. The actual shares of the British dentifrice market obtained by Signal toothpaste are shown in Figure 7-7. Note that the Signal market share rose quickly to a peak of 24 percent and then declined much like the sales volumes shown by Brand A and B in Figure 7-3. If the brand manager had based his estimate of Signal's future performance on the market share obtained at the end of sixteen weeks, he would have overestimated the performance of the product. However, the estimate based on penetration and repeat rates (14.8) was very close to the actual long-run market share obtained by this product.

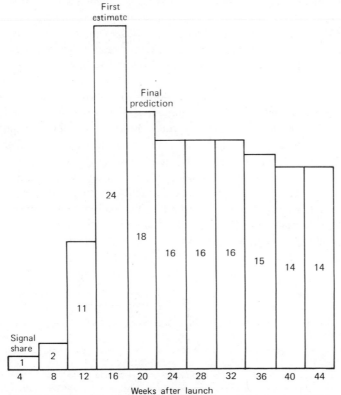

Figure 7-7 Signal's Share of the British Dentifrice Market for Eleven Periods After Launch. *Source.* J. H. Parfitt and B. J. Collins, "Use of Consumer Panels for Brand-Share Prediction," *Journal of Marketing Research*, Vol. 5, No. 2 (May 1968), p. 134. Published by the American Marketing Association.

[6]Signal toothpaste is a British brand and the data used to calculate the repeat purchase curve were taken from the Atwood Consumer Panel. The repeat purchase rate derived by Parfitt and Collins was based on the number of units purchased rather than ounces as used by Ahl in Figure 7-6. Ahl's method is better when the product is sold in more than one size and persons who try the product buy different quantities than regular buyers.

Although the penetration and repeat purchase models work fairly well, they are based on some tenuous assumptions about homogeneity of customer groups and stability of purchase probabilities. A detailed discussion of these problems is beyond the scope of this book and interested readers are referred to the work by Massy, Montgomery, and Morrison.[7] An alternative to the penetration and repurchase model utilizes a theory that new product acceptance spreads from person to person like an epidemic.

An Epidemic Growth Model

Bass has developed a new product-growth model that has proved to be useful in predicting the long-run sales of consumer durables.[8] The model is based on the assumption that the probability of an initial purchase is a linear function of the number of previous buyers. The relation takes the form:

$$S(T) = pm + (q-p)Y(T) - q/m[Y(T)]^2 \qquad (1)$$

where $S(T)$ is unit sales in period T. The beginning purchase probability (p) is a constant that represents the importance of innovators in the product category. The parameter m is the total number of initial purchases over the life of the product, and q is the coefficient of imitation. This equation says that sales in period T are equal to the innovative coefficient (p) times the expected total number of initial purchases (m) plus a percentage of all past sales. Since $Y(T)$ is a cumulative sum of past sales, the first two terms of equation 1 give a sales curve that grows at an increasing rate. The third term in the equation is negative and, when cumulative sales get large enough, this squared term will cause the sales curve to stop growing and eventually turn down.[9]

When Bass used the growth model on clothes-dryer sales data, he obtained the predictions shown in Figure 7-8. The simple correlation between predicted and actual sales was +.93 and the model seemed to track the clothes dryer data quite well. In addition, when the model was used to predict the time and magnitude of peak sales of eleven products,[10] the forecasts were only off by an average of 6 percent.

Although the growth model provided good forecasts when the three parameters were known, these would not be available before the product was placed on the market. Thus, marketing managers would be faced with guessing the sales curve for the new product or guessing the three parameters of the model. A more attractive alternative would be to wait until the product had been on the market for a short period and then use the sales data to predict long-run performance. For example, Bass used three years of color television sales[11] to generate values for p, q, and m and then inserted the numbers in the growth

[7]William F. Massy, David B. Montgomery, and Donald G. Morrison, *Stochastic Models of Buying Behavior* (Cambridge, Mass.: The M.I.T. Press, 1970).

[8]Frank M. Bass, "A New Product Growth Model for Consumer Durables," *Management Science*, Vol. 15, No. 5 (January 1969), pp. 215-227.

[9]This occurs when the square of cumulative sales exceeds m and the product of q times $[Y(T)]^2/m$ is greater than one.

[10]The products used were electric refrigerators, home freezers, black and white televisions, water softeners, room air conditioners, clothes dryers, power lawnmowers, electric blankets, automatic coffee makers, steam irons, and record players.

[11]Color TV sales were 0.7 million units in 1963, 1.35 million in 1964, and 2.5 million in 1965. Combining these values with a version of equation 1 we have:

$S_0 = 0.7 = a$

$S_1 = 1.35 = a + 0.7b + 0.49\,c$

$S_2 = 2.50 = a + 2.50b + 4.20\,c$

These three equations can be solved for the three unknowns, a, b, and c and then converted to the p, q, and m parameters.

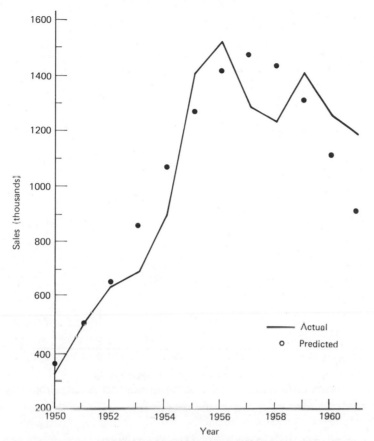

Figure 7-8 Actual and Predicted Sales of Clothes Dryers.
Source. Frank M. Bass, "A New Product Growth Model for Consumer Durables," *Management Science,* Vol. 15, No. 5 (January 1969), p. 224.

model to yield the sales forecasts shown in Figure 7-9. The model accurately predicted that color TV sales would peak in 1968 at less than seven million sets at a time when the industry was building plant capacity for fourteen million picture tubes.[12] The forecasts were reasonable except for 1971 when actual sales grew rapidly and predicted sales declined to less than four million sets.[13] This error shows that although the growth model can predict the time and magnitude of peak sales, it is inaccurate when it is used to forecast too far into the future. The reason is that the third term in the equation is negative and it eventually overpowers the rest of the factors and gives unrealistically low predictions. Thus, after the sales curve starts to decline and replacement sales become more important, the growth model must be replaced with other forecasting techniques.

Once a product has successfully made it through the introductory phase of the life cycle, managers begin to look for techniques that improve distribution and build repeat sales.

---

[12]Wellesley Dodds, "An Application of the Bass Model in Long-Term New Product Forecasting," *Journal of Marketing Research,* Vol. 10 (August 1973), p. 308.

[13]The 1971 forecast was made by the authors using data from the Bass article.

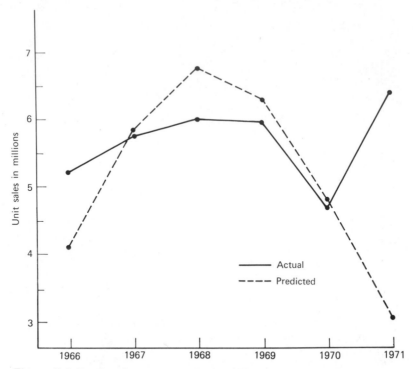

Figure 7-9 Predicted and Actual Sales of Color Television Sets.
Source. Prediction made by Bass, p. 225, and the authors; actual sales from *Merchandising Week,* February 22, 1971.

MANAGING PRODUCTS DURING GROWTH AND MATURITY

One way to increase customer interest during the growth and maturity phases of the product life cycle is to expand product lines and offer greater variety. Another possibility is to follow a strategy of market segmentation and sell the product under a variety of brands owned by distributors or other manufacturers. A third alternative is to engage in clever promotional campaigns devised to catch the eye of selected groups of customers. Managers can also manipulate the warranty and service dimensions of the product offer to build customer confidence and sales. We will discuss all of these strategies beginning with the issue of the size of the product line.

Product Line Strategy

Groups of products that are used together, sold to the same customer, or marketed through the same channels are known as *product lines*. One of the key jobs of the marketing manager is to select a mix of compatible products for the firm that promotes efficiency in selling, production, pricing, promotion, and distribution.

Product lines are usually described in terms of their width and depth. Width refers to the number of different product lines that are marketed by a single firm. For example, among other things General Motors sells cars, trucks, and buses and each of these could be thought of as a single line. Depth refers to the number of items sold by a company within each product line. Thus, depth in an automobile line could be represented by brands such as Cadillac, Buick, Oldsmobile, Pontiac, and Chevrolet (Figure 7-10). The third axis in Figure 7-10 has been labeled the model dimension. This suggests that each of the car, truck, and bus categories is available in several different shapes and model designations. The Chevrolet buyer for example, can purchase a large Caprice or a more modest Chevette. Similarly the light-truck buyer can select a panel, a camper, or a flat-bed design.

One of the major product policy decisions is whether to produce many lines of goods or to concentrate on a single product line. Gerber, for example, advertised for years that baby food and related products were their only business. The recent decline in the birth rate, however, suggests that a more diversified product line would offer Gerber a measure of protection against changes in life styles.[14]

A second question is how much variation to offer within each product line. The answer depends on the needs of the customer, the actions of competitors, and the goals and resources of the firm. One approach is to maximize customer satisfaction by carrying a full line of sizes, shapes, grades, and colors. For example, General Foods recently added a second brand of decaffeinated instant coffee (Brim). Decaffeinated coffee now accounts for over 10 percent of total coffee sales compared to only 5 percent a few years ago. General Foods wanted to strengthen its hold on this growing market segment, but its popular Sanka brand of decaffeinated coffee had a geriatic image and was bought primarily by older consumers. As a result, General Foods brought out Brim to expand its market coverage by appealing to the more youthful coffee drinker.

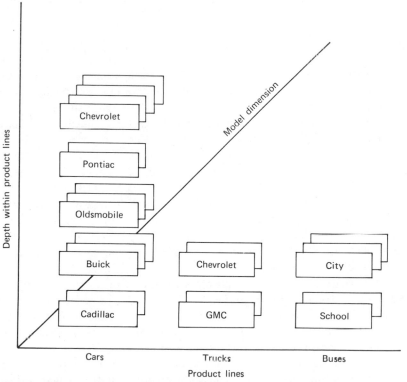

Figure 7-10 Hypothetical Product Line Strategy for General Motors.

[14]Gerber has, in fact, stopped the advertising theme and begun to diversify its product lines.

An alternative strategy would be to market only the most profitable items within each product line. In 1972, for example, a number of appliance manufacturers found that it was no longer profitable to market a full line of items. General Electric, Motorola, and Westinghouse dropped several small appliances so they could concentrate on products with higher returns.[15] An example showing how some grocery stores calculate product line profits is given in Table 7-1. The analysis begins with the gross margin produced by selling a case of each item and then subtracts warehouse, delivery, and store handling costs. Cash discounts are added back in to give estimates of profit per case. The store could then multiply the weekly sales of items times the profit per case to give dollar profit per item per week. This information could be used to decide which items in the product line should receive more display space and which items should be dropped. The figures in Table 7-1 suggest that the tuna fish and flavoring products had the most profit potential (DPP/Case $2.41, $1.84) and the flour and baby food items were losers (DDP/Case $[.06], $[.05]). Although a retailer would have to carry some flour and baby food items in his product line, the analysis indicates these items should be kept to a minimum.

Other product line strategies that could be followed would be to concentrate on the highest volume products or emphasize items that can be most easily manufactured with the skills and equipment of the firm. While a strategy of supplying a maximum of product variation seems desirable from a marketing standpoint, there is no assurance that this is the most profitable approach for all firms. Most firms must search for the degree of product line specialization that optimizes profits for their own particular manufacturing and marketing capabilities. The related issue of the total number of product lines is often resolved in favor of gradual expansion in an attempt to improve the long-run stability of the firm.

Brand Strategy

Brand strategy is concerned with deciding which products should be branded and whether they should be sold under your own label or labels controlled by other firms. Brands include all names, terms, signs, symbols, or designs that are used to identify and differentiate the goods of one seller from those of his competitors. Brands allow the consumer to recognize the product and increase the chances for repeat sales. Brands also encourage the use of preselling and reduce the need for personal contact at the retail level. In addition, brands facilitate the development of permanent price-quality images for products. Brands also simplify the introduction of new products and allow the manufacturer some control over the channel of distribution. Not all products can be branded and many raw materials are bought according to specifications and individual brands are meaningless. Branding is easiest where identifying tags or symbols can be attached directly to the product and where the consumer is willing to use brand designations to differentiate among products.

Family Brands. Brands are classified as family brands when a group of products is sold under one label by a single firm. Heinz and Del Monte are two companies that market a wide diversity of products under their own corporate name. Other firms, such as Proctor & Gamble prefer to use separate brand names for each product. Family brands have the advantage that advertising for one brand promotes the sale of all items that carry that particular label. Also family brands make it easier to introduce new products to distribution channels and the consumer. On the other hand, it is more difficult to create and maintain an identity for each item using a family brand strategy. One possible

[15]*Wall Street Journal* (March 9, 1972), p. 1.

Table 7-1

Calculating Product Line Profits for a Grocery Store

Product (Individual	Bulky Case Goods					Canned Goods[a]				Bottled Goods[b]			Small Case Goods			
	Paper	Cereal	Detergent	Flour	Coffee	Fruit	Soup	Tuna Fish	Ketchup	Baby Food	Flavoring	Vinegar	Bar Soap	Dry Soup	Dietary Specialty	Dessert
Brand Size	A	A	A	A	A	A	A	A	A	A	A	A	A	A	A	A
Gross profit per case	$2.39	$1.26	$.81	$.35	$1.79	1.36	$1.53	$3.13	$.86	$.22	$2.12	$.69	$2.46	$1.21	$1.72	$.88
Direct product costs per case																
Warehouse	.22	.16	.08	.10	.09	.12	.05	.09	.05	.04	.04	.07	.06	.06	.04	.04
Delivery	.24	.14	.08	.06	.06	.06	.05	.04	.05	.02	.01	.05	.03	.03	.02	.02
Store																
Unload, shelve	.29	.14	.12	.09	.11	.10	.14	.14	.10	.09	.07	.09[d]	.17	.10	.11	.13
Ring up and bag	.53	.24	.21	.10	.20	.14	.25	.24	.19	.08	.08	.11	.35	.18	.17	.18
Stamps	.30	.21	.18	.12	.38	.17	.20	.34	.10	.06	.14	.07	.32	.16	.16	.11
Space	.43	.28	.09	.05	.03	.20	.06	.11	.02	.02	.01	.17	.06	.09	.06	.02
Total	2.00[c]	1.17	.77	.51	.86	.79	.74	.96	.51	.32	.36	.57	.99	.61	.57	.49
Direct product profits per case (before cash discount)	.39	.09	.04	(.16)	.93	.57	.79	2.17	.35	(.10)	1.76	.12	1.47	.60	1.15	.39
Direct product profits per case (after cash discount)	$.61	$.25	$.18	$(.06)	$1.23	$.69	$.94	$2.41	$.42	$(.05)	$1.84	$.18	$1.70	$.71	$1.26	$.47

[a] Includes tins.
[b] Includes jars.
[c] Totals may not add precisely because of rounding.
[d] Baby food shelved by store personnel.

Source. McKinsey-General Foods Study (White Plains, N.Y.: General Foods Corporation, October 1963), p. 31. Reproduced with the consent of McKinsey & Company, Inc. and General Foods Corp.

compromise is to use separate brand names for each product and then tie them together with a unifying trade name. This is the strategy used by General Motors where cars are promoted under their own names and the GM symbol is used as a common point of reference.

Manufacturer Versus Distributor Brands.   Manufacturers have the choice of marketing products under their own labels or selling all or part of their output under brands controlled by distributors. Distributors' brands (A&P's Ann Page) have limited dissemination and are available only in stores that share a common wholesaler. Manufacturers' brands typically receive national advertising support, enjoy wide distribution, and are frequently stocked by competing retailers. The rivalry between manufacturers and distributors for retail shelf space has become so intense that it has become known as the "battle of the brands." Although manufacturers' brands have historically controlled sales in many product categories, distributors' brands are rapidly catching up. It has been shown that distributor brands have already captured the largest share of chain store sales of frozen juices and vegetables and are on their way towards complete domination in the sale of bakery and dairy products.[16]

A decision by a manufacturer to supply products for resale under his own and distributors' labels involves several complex issues including the question of whether the sale of the same product at different prices is legal. From a production standpoint, added sales from distributor brands can stabilize production schedules and help reduce unit costs as long as total volume increases. However, a strategy of selling some products under company labels and others under distributors' labels increases competition for your own brands and some manufacturer's labels will lose out in the battle for shelf space. One study concluded that despite the risks, many manufacturers have decided that a strategy or producing their own and distributor labels is the best approach.[17] This decision seems to be defensive and based on the assumption that if one firm refused to supply distributor brands, others would move quickly to fill the requirements of the market. Apparently, firms have been forced to produce private label merchandise by the realities of the marketplace although they might have preferred to maintain the historical dominance (and higher margins) of manufacturers' brands.

The growing use of private labels by retailers and other distributors is the result of a fight for control over the pricing and promotion of products at the retail level. With manufacturers' brands, prices are set by competitive forces and the same promotional materials are available to all dealers who handle the product. The situation is different with distributors' brands, because retailers set prices and promotional programs to maximize profits for the store as a whole rather than to stress the sales of individual items. Distributor brands also tend to be family brands that help build store loyalty and assist in the introduction of new items.

Another factor contributing to the growth of distributor labels is the attractive margin available on these products. Table 7-2 shows that eleven of thirteen private-label grocery items had higher margins than comparable manufacturers' brands. The lower margin on the manufacturers' brands is due to greater price competition on these items and the higher costs needed to cover national advertising programs. Although distributor labels usually carry higher retail margins, they tend to sell slower than manufacturers' brands so that gross margin dollars per shelf facing may be the same for both types of products (Table 7-2).

One important advantage of private labels is that they almost always carry lower retail

---

[16]*Organization and Competition in Food Retailing* (Washington, D.C.: National Commission of Food Marketing, Technical Study No. 7, June 1966), pp. 134-135.

[17]Victor J. Cook and Thomas F. Schutte, *Brand Policy Determination* (Boston: Allyn and Bacon, Inc., 1967), pp. 96-97.

Table 7-2

Comparison of the Performance of Distributor and Manufacturer Brands of Thirteen Grocery Products

	Frozen Orange Concentrate	Frozen Cut Green Beans	Cut Green Beans Canned	Canned Green Peas	Canned Sliced Cling Peaches	Canned Bartlett Pears	Canned Apple-Sauce	Catsup	Canned Tuna	Evaporated Milk	Frozen Sliced Strawberries	French Fried Potatoes	Spaghetti	Average
Margin, percent:														
Distributor brands	22.0	37.2	26.8	25.8	18.5	28.7	22.2	17.3	23.8	12.6	27.3	32.5	28.3	24.8
Manufacturer brands	23.0	30.5	23.7	21.2	18.1	24.0	23.3	16.5	19.2	11.2	26.4	29.1	25.6	22.4
Percent of total sales[a] of product														
Distributor brands	71	69	40	29	44	54	50	28	28	42	69	62	31	48
Manufacturer brands	29	31	60	71	55	46	50	72	72	58	31	38	69	52
Sales per facing (dollars):														
Distributor brands	1.94	.75	1.10	1.14	1.23	1.20	1.40	1.23	3.84	3.68	1.16	1.26	1.83	1.67
Manufacturer brands	.99	.91	1.30	1.44	2.07	1.22	1.20	1.28	3.30	2.03	.92	3.12	2.69	1.73
Cross margin dollars per facing:														
Distributor brands	.42	.29	.28	.29	.22	.34	.35	.20	.85	.44	.32	.40	.53	.38
Manufacturer brands	.23	.28	.31	.30	.36	.28	.28	.20	.61	.23	.24	.89	.70	.38
Percent of facings[a]														
Distributor brands	58	66	45	37	55	54	49	28	28	32	60	71	37	48
Manufacturer brands	42	34	55	63	45	46	51	72	72	68	40	29	63	52

[a] Simple averages were used. Totals may not add to 100 percent, because of rounding.

Source. Data summarized from a twelve-week analysis of operations of eleven retail chains in eleven cities. See *Organization and Competition in Food Retailing,* op. cit., p. 136.

prices. The National Commission on Food Marketing found that private label merchandise was about 20 percent lower in price than comparable manufacturer brands.[18] This means that retailers can broaden their market penetration by using private labels to appeal to price conscious customers. In addition, retailers can stock private label and manufacture brands and take advantage of the price umbrella established by the manufacturers' brand to push the sales of their own labels.

Promotional Strategy

The objectives of promotion during the growth and maturity phases of the product life cycle are to increase product trial and the number of stores handling an item by implementing a variety of merchandising activities. Promotional programs involving contests and coupons are usually undertaken in addition to expenditures for advertising and personal selling. In 1966, for example, an estimated $4 billion was spent on sales promotion or about one fourth as much as that spent for advertising.[19] However, because of the supplementary nature of promotional activities, it is often difficult to isolate the sales effects of individual promotional programs.

Dealer Promotions. These are designed to improve dealer cooperation and include such things as training sessions for sales personnel to make them more knowledgeable about the goods and services of a particular company. A related procedure is to give dealer salesmen special gifts or bonuses when they push the sale of certain products. Dealer interest can also be improved by providing them with attractive point-of-sale materials. As an added incentive, prizes are frequently offered to the merchants who construct the best displays utilizing the product and promotional materials. Perhaps the most popular promotional device directed at distributors is the "deal" or special reduced price offer. "Deals" are short-run discounts designed to build dealer stocks and to stimulate retail sales. They may be expressed in terms of lower prices or as "free" merchandise offered for minimum orders. Another effective promotional technique is a sales contest for distributors. Dealers who sell the most merchandise during a certain period are rewarded with vacation trips to Hawaii, mink coats, and cash bonuses. All promotional efforts are designed to raise sales, but most dealer programs have the goal of improving relations with those who sell the product to the final consumer. Better dealer relations can increase the number of distributors willing to carry the product, enlarge display areas, and gain acceptance of larger inventories and new items.

Consumer Promotions. Consumer-oriented promotional activities are designed to induce consumers to try products. Hopefully a proportion of those introduced to a product will become steady customers. The most effective way to get product trial is to mail or distribute free samples directly to customers' homes. Research has shown that 75 percent of the homes will try the free sample and 25 percent of these will go out and buy it. Up to 20 percent more users can be obtained by including a coupon with the free sample.[20] Sampling can be expensive, but it does assure that people will try the product and it has proved to be one of the most powerful promotional devices available to marketing managers.

Where promotional funds are limited, "cents-off" coupons can be an effective way to

---

[18]*Organization and Competition in Food Retailing,* op. cit., p. 137.

[19]John F. Luick and William L. Ziegler, *Sales Promotion and Modern Merchandising* (New York: McGraw-Hill Book Co., 1968), p. 7.

[20]Ogilvy & Mather ad, *Wall Street Journal* (April 16, 1973), p. 17.

get product trial. Over 21 billion of these coupons were distributed in 1972 and 58 percent of all households redeem them.[21] The coupons are typically sent by mail or attached to magazine and newspaper ads. This approach can be used regionally and the number of coupons returned is one measure of the effectiveness of the promotion. A slight variation is to offer the consumer a package with a special "cents-off" label. The "cents-off" designation indicates the amount the regular retail price is supposedly reduced during the special promotion. Although the manufacturer may lower the price to the dealer, there is no assurance that the retailer will pass the savings on to the consumer. The inability of the manufacturer to adequately control "cents-off" promotions makes this technique somewhat less desirable than couponing.[22]

In addition to promoting products with deals and coupons, manufacturers frequently try to build customer interest and sales volume with contests and games of chance. The idea is to attract consumer attention by offering substantial merchandise and cash prizes to a few lucky winners. Entry blanks and lottery tickets are dispensed at the retail level to tie the promotion to the sales of the product. The main objective of contests is to stimulate sales with in-store displays of the product rather than produce a large number of entries.

Since only a few people can win contests, a more positive approach is to give all persons making a purchase a free gift or novelty. For example, Frito corn chips has employed a promotion where they attach flower seeds to packages of the product. A classic novelty promotion was run a few years ago where gasoline customers were given a small plastic ball to mount on their radio antenna that resembled the "76" signs used to identify Union Oil stations.

A variation on the gift idea is the offer of merchandise at low prices to customers who send in labels from packages. Premiums are one of the least expensive of all promotional devices because the revenue derived from customers usually covers most of the costs of the promotion. This "self-liquidating" feature results from volume purchases and the elimination of the normally high retail margins on premium-type merchandise. The most desirable premiums are showy items that inspire retailers to build off-shelf displays and encourage usage of the product by the consumer.

Although premium promotions are inexpensive, there is some question whether a high response rate helps boost sales or merely represents bargain hunting by consumers. Several years ago one of the authors ran a study to measure the effects of premiums by inserting 37,000 coupons in bags of apples. One of the most interesting findings was that 25 percent of the returned coupons were from persons who had already acquired one premium. This obvious satisfaction with the premium merchandise made it difficult to explain why apple sales increased faster in control stores than it did in the stores where the premiums were used.

Defensive Promotions. There are a number of promotional tactics that can be used to protect the market positions of established brands from new product introductions. The idea is to attack new brands when they are vulnerable and forego short-run profits to retard or block the entry of competitive items. A classic approach is to introduce additional brands in the same product class to preempt shelf space and to deprive actual or potential competitors of profits or resources needed to compete in a market. Proctor & Gamble, for example, has successfully added other detergents to protect its leading brand, Tide.

[21]Ibid., p. 17.

[22]Because of abuses with "cents-off" promotions, both the Food and Drug Administration and the Federal Trade Commission have proposed regulations to control these promotions. The objective of the regulations is to make sure that the consumer receives a discount when one is promised. See the *Wall Street Journal* (May 22, 1970), p. 11.

Test markets also allow established firms to discourage new competitors with procedures that would be expensive if tried on a national scale. In one case, Vick Chemical ruined the test for a new Colgate cough preparation by dropping 25,000 Nyquil samples into Colgates' two test markets. In another test a coffee company put its premium grade in an elaborate cannister, raised the price, and began selling it in a large city. A competitor immediately copied the cannister design, added its cheapest coffee, cut its price, and placed it in the same market.[23]

Advertising can also be used to effectively blunt the introduction of new items. When Lever introduced Aim (a blue fluoride gel) with extensive sampling on a regional basis, Proctor & Gamble countered with heavy TV expenditures stressing the cavity-prevention properties of Crest. In one ad a postman was shown delivering an unnamed toothpaste sample to a housewife and in the ensuing conversation the importance of staying with Crest was stressed. As a result of these activities, much of Aim's 7 percent market share was cannibalized from Lever's other brand, Close-Up.

In another example, Sterling Drug Company utilized heavy television expenditures to protect Lysol's position in the spray disinfectant market. When Warner-Lambert tested Listerol in Dallas and Memphis, Sterling bought a lot of spot TV in these markets. In the first quarter of 1974, Warner-Lambert tried a heavier schedule spending $1.8 million on network TV. Sterling countered with an increase of $800,000 keeping Lysol's advertising expenditures twice those of Listerol. Sterling also accused Warner-Lambert of engaging in unfair competition and trademark infringement. As a consequence, Listerol's container was changed from dark to light blue. These efforts allowed Lysol to retain a market share of 75 percent compared to less than 10 percent for Listerol.

Hopefully these examples explain why some new products fail and also show how established products can protect themselves against the ravages of new competition by the effective use of promotion. The activities that have been discussed represent only a few of the many techniques that can be used to create a promotional strategy for the firm. The only real limit to the variety of promotions is the depth of the imagination of the managers in charge. The practical constraints on promotional efforts include the availability of funds and the need to find some reliable measure of sales effects.

Measuring Campaign Effectiveness.   A common criterion used to evaluate the success of promotional activity is plus sales per dollar of company expenditure. This ratio shows how sales respond to the prizes and trips used as incentives and allows comparisons to be made among different types of promotions. The Chevrolet Division of General Motors, for example, breaks historical sales data into trend, seasonal, and irregular components so that the plus sales produced by promotional efforts can be measured.[24] This method adjusts sales for seasonal factors and removes the trend so the remaining irregular component reflects the impact of the promotion.[25] Figure 7-11 shows the impact of Chevrolet's "Selling Showdown Campaign" on the sales of Chevelle cars in 1969. Note that the campaign produced losses in volume both before and after the effective dates of the promotion. The reduced volume before the promotion may have been due to the sales force holding back on deliveries to take advantage of campaign benefits. The drop after the promotion may indicate that the campaign had exhausted the available consumer demand. Total plus sales for the "Showdown Campaign" were

[23]Leonard J. Parsons, "Defensive Marketing." Paper presented at the Southwest Marketing Educators Annual Conference in Los Angeles, May 1974.

[24]James P. Wallace, letter to the marketing science editor, *Management Science,* Vol. 17, No. 4 (December 1970), pp. B-259-264.

[25]The method is based on a variant of the Census II Seasonal Adjustment Program and is similar to the Scovill computer forecasting model described in Chapter 3.

Figure 7-11 Irregular Changes in Chevelle Deliveries During "Showdown Campaign".
Source. James P. Wallace, Letter to the Marketing Science Editor, *Management Science,*
Vol. 17, No. 4 (December 1970), p. B-263.

obtained by adding in sales for the two ten-day periods before and after the promotion. If
the before and after losses were ignored, the estimate of plus sales in Figure 7-11 would
be inflated by 31 percent. Once a reliable figure for plus sales has been estimated, they
are divided by the costs of the promotion to get a ratio that can be used to evaluate the
results of current and past campaigns.

Aaker suggests that a promotion be evaluated on the value of new customers attracted
to it in addition to the immediate sales volume it generates.[26] New customers may like the
brand and buy it for years as a result. Thus immediate sales may not indicate the real
value of a promotion. Instead, it would be reflected by the number of new triers and their
acceptance of a brand. It is important to distinguish between gaining triers (the job of the
promotion) and gaining acceptance (the job of product development).

Multinational Product Strategies

Many firms attempt to expand sales during the growth and maturity phases of the life
cycle by looking for new markets in other countries. The trick is to find a product strategy
that meets the needs of foreign customers at a reasonable cost to the multinational firm.
Keegan, for example, suggests five policy alternatives that can be used to expand
international markets.[27]

The simplest (and often the most profitable) approach is to sell one product using one
message throughout the world. Pepsi Cola has been successful selling the same product
with standard promotional themes in a variety of markets. Pepsi has estimated that the
cost of preparing ads would be raised substantially by tailoring promotions to each
foreign market. Although this strategy has worked for soft drinks, other American firms
have run into problems trying to export prepared foods that do not fit local preferences.

A second strategy is to sell the same product in foreign markets, but adapt the
advertising message to local conditions. An American machinery manufacturer, for
example, has done quite well selling a line of suburban lawn and garden equipment as
basic agricultural tools in less well-developed countries. The company's products were

[26]David A. Aaker, "Toward a Normative Model of Promotional Decision Making," *Management Science,*
Vol. 19, No. 6 (February 1973), pp. 593-603.
[27]Warren J. Keegan, "Multinational Product Planning: Strategic Alternatives," *Journal of Marketing,* Vol.
33 (January 1969), pp. 58-62.

about one third cheaper than competing equipment and the only change required for this market expansion was a new advertising program designed to reach farmers. Also Lipton, which has had a great deal of success selling dehydrated soups in Europe, has expanded the sales of this product in the United States by emphasizing usage in sauces and dips.

Another approach is to modify the product to fit local conditions and leave the basic communications message the same. Esso, for example, adapted its gasoline to meet weather conditions in foreign markets, but used its famous "Put a Tiger in Your Tank" promotion in all areas. One of the more expensive multinational strategies is to change the product and the promotional program to meet the needs of local markets. American greeting card manufacturers found that Europeans expect cards to be wrapped in cellophane and have a space for the sender to write his own message. Thus, to enter this market, American manufacturers had to modify their cards and the advertising messages directed at customers.

Perhaps the most risky market expansion strategy is to try to invent something to meet the special needs of overseas customers. Colgate, for example, saw potential in the estimated 600 million people in the world who wash clothes by hand. To tap this market they developed an inexpensive (less than $10) plastic, hand-powered washer that has the tumbling action of a modern automatic machine. This product has sold well in Mexico and could help expand the demand for Colgate's laundry detergents. Obviously, no one multinational strategy can work for everyone and the astute manager must be able to select alternatives that are best for particular situations.

Warranty and Service Strategies

Warranty and service strategies represent commitments on the part of the seller to repair and adjust products that fail to perform after purchase. The main objectives of product warranties and service are to encourage sales by reducing consumer anxieties about postpurchase problems and to build repeat business from satisfied customers. The linkages between consumer attitudes about product performance and subsequent buying behavior were described earlier in the Howard-Sheth model (Chapter 5).

Historically warranties have been written statements that tell the buyer what steps the seller will take if the product fails within a specified time period. They were usually designed to limit the liability of the seller in case damage claims were filed by the buyer. In recent years, however, the courts have ruled that warranties do not have to be written and they do not limit the liability of the seller.[28] As a result, marketing managers have become more concerned with the promotional aspects of product warranties. For example, a warranty that offers "Double your money back" is clearly designed to boost sales by having the buyer try the product at little or no personal risk. Under these conditions, a warranty becomes a competitive tool designed to build customer confidence and steal buyers from firms with weaker warranty policies.

The automobile industry provides a good example of how warranties have been used to gain competitive advantages.[29] In 1961, Ford (the number 2 firm) was the first to adopt a twelve month-12,000 mile warranty for cars. This expanded warranty was copied by other firms and the industry went to a twenty-four month-24,000 mile warranty in 1963.

[28]State Farm Mutual Automobile Insurance Co. v. Anderson-Weber, Inc. and Ford Motor Co., 110 N. W. 2d 449, (Iowa, 1961).
[29]Described in Stewart H. Rewoldt, James D. Scott, and Martin R. Warshaw, *Introduction to Marketing Management: Text and Cases* (Homewood, Ill.: Richard D. Irwin, Inc., 1973), p. 276.

Chrysler (the number 3 firm) then introduced a five year-50,000 mile warranty on power train components. Chrysler had an exclusive on this warranty for several years and then in 1971 the power train warranty was dropped by all manufacturers. The high cost of this expanded coverage was apparently a factor in the return to a basic twelve month-12,000 mile warranty in 1969. In 1973, the warranty battle resurfaced when American Motors (the number 4 firm) began promoting an extended "Buyer Protection Plan." This program allowed buyers to extend their regular warranty to twenty-four months or 24,000 miles by paying an extra fee. In addition, the new plan provided parts and labor for all regular maintenance over the two-year period, free loan cars, trip interruption protection, and a toll-free hot line to AMC headquarters.

The introduction of expanded warranty coverage by the smaller auto companies suggests it was easier for these firms to compete with General Motors on the basis of a strong warranty than it was to play with the traditional marketing variables such as price, advertising, and dealer networks. Also the expansion and contraction of car warranties indicated that, like any promotional tool, warranty policies were constantly being evaluated on the basis of cost and their impact on sales. In addition to their immediate effects, strong product warranties build customer confidence over the long run and provide desirable social benefits in greater customer protection.

Service strategies are concerned with establishing procedures for repairing merchandise after the product has been sold to the consumer. Over the years, product complexity and high wages for repairmen created serious service problems for many manufacturers.[30] Consumers have found that it is difficult to get products repaired and the cost is often out of proportion to the value of the product.[31] As a result, consumers are now demanding and receiving better repair service from manufacturers. Many firms have expanded their regional repair centers and have installed "cool lines" so customers can call direct when they encounter repair problems (see Chapter One, p. 16).

In the past some manufacturers considered service a necessary evil and attempted to keep expenditures as low as possible. This raised profits in the short run, but eventually consumers began to rebel at the absence of local repairmen and parts. The failure of some foreign cars to successfully penetrate the U.S. market is a good example of how the lack of adequate *service facilities* can hurt sales.

An alternative service strategy is to consider repair work as a profit making opportunity. If most of the products owned by customers are out of warranty and require periodic repair, then the active solicitation of service work can be a lucrative business. Automobile manufacturers, for example make money on the sale of fenders and other parts to their dealers and independent service facilities. However, too great a reliance on service profits may stifle product improvements and allow competitors to grow by introducing new items.

A more desirable market-oriented strategy for service emphasizes fast, economical repairs with an objective of building long-run sales. Although a liberal factory service policy may cost more than other strategies, it can help protect the brand names owned by manufacturers and reduce problems caused by poor dealer service. Implementation of this strategy often requires extensive training of dealer repairmen and the establishment of regional service centers run by the company. In recent years the appliance industry has adopted a factory service policy of this type.

---

[30]E. B. Weiss, "Inconvenience and Expense of Home Appliance Servicing Grow," *Advertising Age,* Vol. 43 (March 13, 1972), p. 47.

[31]When a consumer finds that it costs $20 to clean and repair his watch he may be tempted to throw it away and buy a Timex for $12.

Manufacturers have used product service in a variety of ways to help promote the sale of merchandise. Sears, for example, emphasizes the nationwide availability of its service so that even if customers move to a new area repair service will be available. Maytag, on the other hand, takes a more whimsical approach and shows its repairmen sitting around with nothing to do, suggesting that Maytag appliances rarely break down. One of the most aggressive manufacturer service policies offers a lifetime of free repairs for all buyers of Zippo lighters. Gillette, on the other hand, minimizes its service costs by selling a disposable cigarette lighter that is simply thrown away when it breaks or runs out of fuel. These examples suggest that the choice of an optimum service strategy depends on the cost, complexity, and life expectancy of the product, the importance of repairs to the customer, and the concern of the manufacturer for building a satisfied group of repeat buyers. The last, and most neglected, phase of product management is the creation of strategies for products with falling sales.

PRODUCTS IN DECLINE

The theory of the product life cycle suggests that products are born, grow to maturity, and then enter a period of decline. The length of the decline phase is determined by changes in consumer preferences, activities of competitors, and the product elimination policies of the firm. While there is usually little that can be done about basic shifts in consumer preferences and the entry of competitive items, the firm has a wide range of alternatives that can be exercised for products with falling sales. Before discussing these alternatives, we need a system for identifying marginal products.

Identifying Weak Products

The problem of locating marginal products is most serious in multiproduct firms. In a small company declining products are known and there may be no need for a formal review procedure. With a broad product line, however, a committee may be needed to conduct a periodic check on product performance. The committee form of organization seems ideal for this task because it is temporary, provides anonymity, and allows representation from several departments within the firm. Product reviews should never be left entirely to the marketing department because of its known biases in favor of sales growth and maximum customer satisfaction. Also it is unlikely that a single individual would want to become known as the undertaker for declining brands. Indeed one reason weak products live so long is that no one wants to be associated with their funeral.

The composition of a product review committee varies among firms and one author recommends inclusion of executives from marketing, manufacturing, purchasing, control, personnel, and research and development.[32] The makeup of the group is not as important as the criteria and the procedures that are developed to evaluate product performance. Kotler suggests a two-stage review process where products are first screened on the basis of trends in sales, market share, gross margin, and overhead coverage.[33] Products that fail to pass minimum standards on these factors are subjected

---

[32]Philip Kotler, "Phasing Out Weak Products," *Harvard Business Review,* Vol. 43 (March-April 1965), p. 112.

[33]Kotler suggests that other factors could be included in the computer program designed to do the actual screening. The use of the computer in this instance seems warranted only where a large number of products are involved, *op. cit.,* p. 114.

to a more detailed analysis using seven additional criteria. Executives are asked to scale the products on the basis of market potential, utility of product or marketing program changes, release of executive time, alternatives, contribution, and relationship to the sales of other products. These scores are then weighted and summed to yield a product retention index that can be used to help eliminate marginal products.

An alternative approach suggested by Eckles[34] utilizes a four-level product-deletion system (Figure 7-12). The first stage is a monthly scan of the product line to find items that are performing poorly in terms of sales, profits, inventory, competitive activity, and total generic demand. In the second stage the weak products are matched against company objectives and those that pass are programmed for formula or package changes, extra promotion, cost reduction, or new market development. Unsuitable products move to stage III of the model where a detailed analysis is made using factors such as scope of the line, company new product research, customer satisfaction, utilization of facilities, and marketing problems. This step gives weak items another chance to redeem themselves and those that are salvaged are recycled through the corrective action phase of the program. The losers proceed to stage IV where the time of burial is determined from the stock on hand, holdover demand, effects on profits, and status of replacement parts. Eckles' system is comprehensive and offers businessmen a useful plan of action for product deletion decisions.

Strategies for Reviving Products

Perhaps the most important task of product review procedures is to separate the items that *can benefit* from a redesign of package or promotional plans from those that are on an irreversible slide towards extinction (Stage II, in Eckles' model). Too often vast sums of money are wasted trying to save products that have no future and should realistically be dropped from the product line. The job of identifying candidates for rescue operations is not easy and specific reasons behind sales declines must be identified. If quality is found to be inadequate and customers are shifting to improved versions, there may be little hope for the product. On the other hand, if the consumer is satisfied with the product but dislikes the package, price or distribution system then there may be a way to save the item so that is can continue to generate profits for the firm.

Perhaps the easiest solution to declining sales is to move the product into new foreign or domestic markets. This may require the addition of new distributors or the enlargement of the existing sales force. An alternative to greater breadth of market coverage is finding and promoting new uses for the product among existing customers. Manufacturers of packaged food products are particularly skilled at devising new recipes that help extend the life of old products. Also, minor adjustments in product specification (i.e., flavor or color) may lead to renewed interest among current users of the product.

A standard remedy used to revive aging products is to redesign the package to improve its appearance and increase the convenience for the consumer. For example, a declining market share prompted a manufacturer of fruit-flavored soft drinks to redesign the labels for the bottles using strong-deep colors.[35] The new labels were so attractive that sales increased 40 percent in two test markets while national sales advanced only 7 percent.

One of the most popular methods of rescuing declining products is to mount expensive promotional campaigns based on deals, displays, and coupons. However, most of these

---

[34]Robert W. Eckles, "Product Line Deletion and Simplification," *Business Horizons*, Vol. 14, No. 5 (October 1971), pp. 71-74.

[35]*Business Week* (April 21, 1973), p. 85.

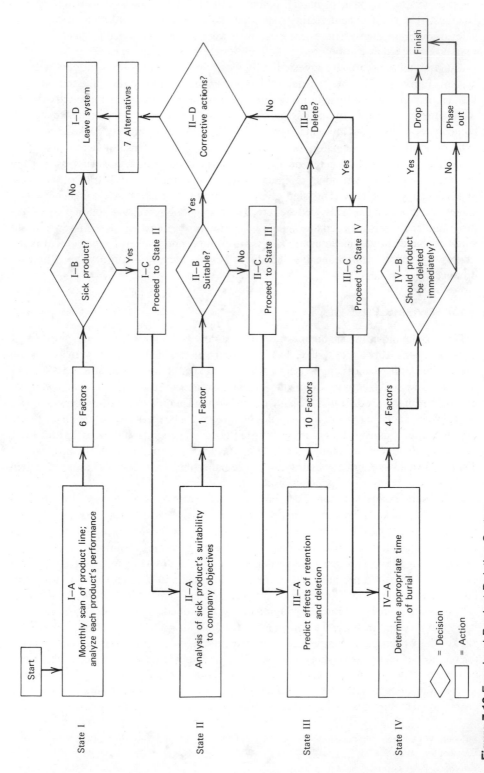

Figure 7-12 Four-level Product Deletion System.
Source. Robert W. Eckles, "Product Line Deletion and Simplification," *Business Horizons,* Vol. 14, No. 5 (October 1971), p. 73.

expenditures are wasted unless they emphasize something new in terms of market, package, or usage. Another standard remedy for declining products is switching advertising agencies in the hope that fresh ideas will lead to increased sales. The success of this approach, however, depends on the importance of advertising in the sale of the product and the ability of the new agency to come up with an original and effective advertising program. All marketing expenditures on declining products are risky and are justified only when there is reason to believe that the item can be saved.

Strategies for Dropping Products

A variety of strategies can be employed for those products that firms expect to drop from their product lines. Perhaps the simplest is to do nothing and wait until there are no longer any orders for the item. This approach cannot be recommended because it ties up capital, equipment, and manpower that might produce greater profits if utilized to promote other items. Experience has shown that company profits can often be increased despite substantial reductions in sales revenues resulting from discontinuing weak products. The business press periodically features stories of how individual firms have cut their product lines and raised profits.[36] The trick is to find a way to make money as the product is being phased out of production. One approach that has been successful is to drop all promotional activities and rely solely on repeat purchase from current customers. Where promotional expenditures have been substantial, sales are apt to decline slowly and the savings from discontinued advertising may make the item profitable in the short run. Talley describes an example where a match company had been unable to stop a sales decline despite a new package and a revitalized marketing program. However, when all promotional activities were stopped, the product became the most profitable (and most expendable) in the company's product line.[37]

Another useful strategy for declining products is to continue to sell the item, but to contract with another company for manufacturing. An alternative is to continue to make the product, but to license others to sell the item. A third possibility is to sell the product to another firm and let them worry about manufacturing and marketing the item. This procedure is attractive because it allows the seller to profit from the liquidation and may provide the buyer with a unique opportunity as well. For example, after Bristol-Myers dropped Ipana toothpaste from their product line they managed to sell the name to a nostalgic pharmacist and his partner. The new owners revised the formula to include the antidecay ingredient stannous flouride and packaged the product in the familiar blue-and-white tubes used by Bristol-Myers. Since they used no consumer advertising and subcontracted manufacturing to another firm, they were able to make a profit on a relatively small volume.[38]

In situations where nothing can save a declining product, the firm should dispose of the product with a minimum of inconvenience to the interested parties. This means notifying dealers in advance and helping them clear out old stock. Frequently special discounts are offered to dealers to stimulate the sale of discontinued items and it may even be necessary for the manufacturer to buy back the unsold merchandise. Dealers should also be informed about replacement items that are being promoted to take the place of the discontinued product. Finally the manufacturer should consider the negative effects that

[36]David C. Smith, ''Pruning Products: The Move Away from Full-Line Marketing,'' *Management Review,* Vol. 51 (October 1962), pp. 9-11.

[37]Walter J. Talley, Jr., *The Profitable Product* (Englewood Cliffs, N.J.: Prentice-Hall, 1965), p. 104.

[38]''Ipana Returns to Fray,'' *Advertising Age,* Vol. 40 (September 15, 1969), p. 2.

dropping items may have on customer good will and make arrangements to provide service and parts for recent buyers.

SUMMARY

In this chapter we have described some of the strategies used to manage products during the introductory, growth, maturity, and decline phases of the life cycle. New products are especially vulnerable to competitive pressures and a variety of repurchase and growth models have been discussed to make it easier for managers to predict long-run sales performance. Successful executives must also know how to manipulate product lines, brands, promotions, warranties, and repair services to optimize profits and social benefits. Finally, a variety of strategies for products with declining sales have been explained. We believe that the effective management of products in decline is an important activity for marketing managers and can increase sales and profits for the firm. Too often marketing executives become obsessed with the glamour of new products and fail to see the money that can be made in the declining portion of the product life cycle.

Questions

1. How can the concept of the product life cycle be used to manage items after they have been introduced to the marketplace?
2. Are warranties primarily designed to protect consumers and manufacturers against loss or to boost sales of goods and services?
3. Three months ago, your company introduced a revolutionary new cake mix. What methods can you use to estimate sales and market share for the remainder of the year?
4. What are the differences among deals, coupons, cents off, and premiums?
5. Should product lines be managed to maximize sales, profits per unit, or profit per unit of scarce resources?
6. Why are products that are still making a small profit sometimes removed from the product line?
7. Compare product strategies with market strategies.
8. Explain how penetration and repeat purchase rates can be used to project the sales of new items.
9. In what situations does a firm have a responsbility to keep selling a sick product?
10. During periods of shortages is it best to diversify product lines and enter new markets with better raw-materials availability or restrict product offerings to maximize short-run profits?

Case 7-1
Mured Valves, Inc.[1]

As the end of 1971 approached, Mr. Chester Johnson was considering what actions should be taken to improve the performance of Mured Valves, a small producer of component parts used by air conditioning and refrigeration manufacturers. In his 1970 report, Mr. Johnson had noted that the year had been difficult and sales had fallen $150,000 below his estimate. The performance of Mured during 1971 had been even more disturbing. While Mr. Johnson had submitted a sales estimate for 1971 of $2.2 million, he realized that actual volume would be in the neighborhood of $1.4 million despite a 9 percent increase in the total air-conditioning market. The dwindling sales volume had forced Mr. Johnson to reduce the firm's production and administrative staffs and Mured was currently operating at about 40 percent of capacity.

During 1969, Mured had been acquired by SRB, Inc., an international conglomerate with sales of more than $500 million. SRB placed Mured in its Howard Fluid Controls Division and appointed Mr. Johnson as general manager. In November 1971, Mr. J. W. Cain, Divisional Manager of Howard Fluid Controls, requested that Mr. Johnson arrange a meeting to present his plans and/or recommendations for "turning Mured around."

Mr. Johnson was convinced that product diversification was the answer to Mured's problems and was optimistic about the firm's future despite numerous unproductive attempts at product development. One of the major efforts in 1971 was to have been the development of a steel valve for automobile air conditioners. Unfortunately, the Ford Motor Company redesigned their unit and eliminated the valve and no other manufacturer used such a valve. Also, a considerable amount of time was spent developing an air-conditioning regulating valve at the request of a customer but the price was "out of line" and no bid was submitted. Such false starts caused some members of Mured's management to treat suggestions of product diversification with skepticism. Mr. Johnson felt, however, that a new idea for a pneumatic cylinder for a variety of equipment installed in aircraft offered great potential.

[1]This case was prepared by George Eddy and John Murphy under supervision of Professor Henry O. Pruden of The University of Texas at Austin. Copyright © 1972 by George Eddy and John Murphy. Reproduced by permission.

COMPANY ORGANIZATION

Mured was organized in Albuquerque, New Mexico, in 1956 by Mr. Albert Oakum and Mr. Phillip DeVan to manufacture a special reversal valve used by an original equipment manufacturer (OEM) of air conditioners. Since its first year of operation, the concern had developed a line of special valves and related equipment marketed to a number of U.S. OEMs of air conditioning and refrigeration products. In addition, through a licensing agreement, several of Mured's patented valves were manufactured and marketed by foreign producers.

Mured had developed a reputation as a quality producer, and Mr. DeVan's engineering expertise was widely recognized in the industry. Because of his special abilities, Mr. DeVan had been retained by SRB as vice-president of research and development of Mured after the SRB acquisition. Mured employed fifty-eight production workers and fourteen administrative personnel. A formal organization chart is shown in Figure 1. Mr. Johnson felt that since the firm was rather small, most communications and other management activity should be conducted on an informal basis.

PRODUCTS

Mured's basic approach was to custom engineer, produce, and sell high-quality valves to air conditioning producers. Considerable technical capability was necessary to design, test, and produce fluid control devices that met the demanding requirement of its customers. Mured concentrated its efforts on four primary valves: service valves, check valves, reversing valves, and compressor unloading valves.

The service valve was designed to allow factory sealing of the refrigerant in the condenser unit, and eliminated the need to charge the system at the point of installation. Check valves were installed to prevent the reversal of the refrigerant's flow within the system. Reversing valves have large bodies and numerous tubes; yet, they represent the most delicate and sophisticated of Mured's product line. Patented features permitted one unit to warm an office building in winter and keep it cool in summer, thus eliminating the need for separate heating and cooling units.

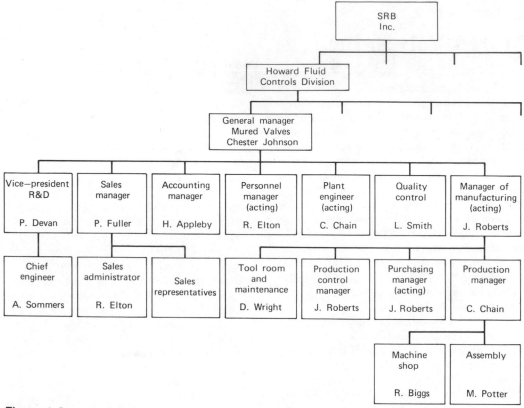

Figure 1 Organization Chart for Mured Valves.

COMPETITION

Mured was one of the smallest component producers for air conditioning equipment. Unlike most of its competitors, Mured dealt almost exclusively in valves for air conditioners. Competitors generally produced an extensive range of valve-type products for many market segments. The larger component producers made not only machined valves but also cast valves and a variety of related items.

All competitors offered about the same general services to the large air conditioning manufacturers. Each supplier tried to modify or design valves to suit detailed specifications determined by the larger OEMs. Suppliers tried to convince the large OEM's to "specify" their particular products whenever possible. Thus, information on new or changed OEM requirements was frequently critical in retaining market position. Mured did not publish standard catalog prices since they bid on specifications set by OEMs. Typically each customer had slightly different specs for each valve. Thus, each valve produced by Mured had as many as twenty-five varia-

tions and each was priced differently depending on the quantity requested. Once a supplier relationship had been established with an OEM, Mured's management considered it important to keep rival producers out even if it meant cutting price below costs on a particular order.

SALES

Approximately 80 percent of Mured's sales were made to OEMs and 20 percent to small dealers or replacement sales. A breakdown of the firm's sales by product line is shown in Table 1. The bulk of Mured's sales are made to the unitary air conditioning market.[2] During 1970, valves and related parts sold to the unitary market accounted for 69 percent of Mured sales and represented 14.5 percent of the total market (Table 2). Service valves and the fittings used in installing the valve were the only

[2] The unitary air conditioning market is primarily central air conditioning units for residences, apartment houses, and small commerical establishments.

Mured products sold to the unitary air conditioning market.

Mured experienced large fluctuations in sales to the unitary market, since demand in that industry is influenced by many factors including housing and building starts. In addition, demand was seasonal as major unitary customers cut production in the late summer and fall. These variations gave Mured serious inventory and production problems. A breakdown of Mured sales by customer accounts is given in Table 3 and Tables 4 and 5 present industry shipment data.

SALES MANAGEMENT

To handle sales efforts, Mured divided the United States into five sales districts. In each district, the firm's products were handled by one or more manufacturer's representatives who also sold other noncompetitive air conditioning components. These agents were compensated on a commission basis for sales made in their territories. The agents were located in California, Georgia, Illinois, New York, and Ohio to cover the primary areas where air conditioning OEMs were located. Mr. Johnson felt these agents should do more, and while he was generally satisfied with the efforts in the New York area, he was displeased with results in Georgia.

Most of Mured's contacts with sales agents occurred when the firm was contacted about filling a potential order, or when the agent placed an order for a manufacturer in his area. In addition, Mr. Johson and Mr. Fuller, the sales manager, attempted to make at least one visit per year to each principal sales office.

Mured's foreign sales were directed by three foreign firms who were licensed to manufacture Mured's patented valves. These firms were located in Formosa, Italy, and South Africa.

"We operate in a highly competitive industry," asserted Mr. Pete Fuller, "where we find ourselves the smallest producer in a field of forty firms. Of these forty, I would say that there are seven or eight who compete directly with us in service valves. Today, there is a lot of emphasis on price, as each OEM tries to reduce its costs. Our biggest customer, Airflow, continues to make valve analysis studies on component parts, and this keeps a lot of pressure on us to reduce our prices. This also means we are forced to redesign our valves more often and product life cycles are decreasing. For example, our valves now have a life cycle of about five years and not long ago, it was between five and ten years. I'd estimate

we make about seventy valves altogether." Mr. Fuller felt that the primary factors of concern to Mured customers were meeting specifications, price, and delivery.

Since demand for specific air conditioning units fluctuated widely, the OEMs frequently had to shift their own production schedules so suddenly that component suppliers like Mured were requested to meet very tight shipment requirements. Consistently meeting short deadlines was the basis for supplier "loyalty," as far as the air conditioning manufacturers were concerned. From time to time, the OEMs would alert a favored supplier that a competitor had offered to supply a similar valve at a significantly reduced price. This allowed the supplier time to make a counterproposal to try to preserve the "favored" position.

Mured recognized that its dependence on one customer for a large portion of its business could present problems in the future. Big OEMs preferred serveral sources of supply, and while Mured might be a primary source for a series of valves for a period of time, there was no long-term guarantee this would continue. Mured tried to be responsive to their largest account, but this made it very hard for Mured to become a primary supplier to another large OEM. Mr. Fuller believed that it would take years to become a principal supplier of another sizable OEM and that most potential customers considered a small component producer unable to satisfy more than one large OEM.

Mr. Fuller tried to concentrate on expanding Mured sales within the air conditioning industry, where the bulk of their products were utilized on residential units. Some of Mured's valves were utilized in commercial air conditioners, such as those installed in apartment and office buildings, but few were used in industrial applications. Mr. Fuller worked closely with OEM design and production engineers, from whom he tried to obtain potential future valve requirements and related, anticipated specifiations. He was able to establish and maintain these contracts as a result of years of reputable associations with the OEM's large industrial buyers. He also read numerous trade publications to see if he could detect trends, but he found it was very difficult to obtain projections of valve requirements from the big OEMs. Most seemed to forecast only three months ahead and these data fluctuated so much they were not very reliable for Mured's production planning.

Maintaining Mured's position with each of its principal customers, plus efforts to determine future requirements within the field, consumed practically all of Mr. Fuller's time. In addition, he was frequently called on to troubleshoot whenever a large OEM had a complaint about the performance of a Mured product. As a result, Mr. Fuller had little chance to develop new markets for Mured outside the air conditioning industry. He believed this should be done, but without extra assistance, he did not see what could be accomplished. He did not consider it worthwhile to hire anyone unless he had at least ten years' experience in an industry for which Mured had the capability to penetrate. For such expertise, he guessed Mured might have to pay as much as $15,000 a year. And before a likely prospect could be hired Mured had first to determine which new industry might offer the most advantages.

PRODUCTION

Mured's assets were valued at $1.5 million, of which plant and equipment accounted for nearly one half. Through experimentation Mured had developed a welding technique that allowed rapid, leakproof assembly of valves. Most competitors relied on casting procedures. Mured's special welding process enabled it to easily change final valve configurations to meet customer demands. For example, if an OEM wanted a vent moved slightly on a small valve, Mured could respond almost immediately (a rapid response is impossible with casting).

One of the problems Mr. Johnson, an industrial engineer, tackled on his arrival was slow delivery of finished products due to inefficient production operations. This was solved by realigning of assembly operations, replacing of some equipment, and increasing worker productivity. Production problems always intrigued Mr. Johnson and he devoted a considerable portion of his time to these issues. However, a continuing problem with sales forecasting made it difficult to schedule production efficiently. Table 6 shows the disparity between forecasted and actual sales of four products.

PRODUCT DEVELOPMENT

Mured's product development efforts centered around specifications and product requests sent to the firm by OEMs. These requests came from either the firm's sales agents or through management contacts. OEMs would forward specifications along with a set of drawings and an estimate of the number of units to be produced. Mr. DeVan and his assistant spent a great deal of time sifting through this information looking for opportunities to apply Mured's capabilities.

Requests for bids were reviewed by the sales manager and then turned over to Mr. DeVan for an evaluation of the technical feasibility of producing the item. Next the cost of materials and labor for manufacturing the item would be projected at the anticipated production levels. The final decision of whether to bid on an item or not rested with the General Manager. Mr. Johnson had two guidelines for making a decision on which products Mured should bid on. First, Mured's product must be better than any comparable product. Second, Mured must be able to recieve a normal profit.

Mured's search for diversification opportunities revealed that a Florida manufacturer of portable toilets for boats and motor homes was having trouble with a water valve. The brass valves were currently manufactured in Japan and 70 percent were being rejected because they failed to meet quality standards. Also boat manufacturers had been giving the Florida plant a hard time about excessive water leaks in their portable "johns." Mured acquired some of the water valves and found them similar to their current service valve. DeVan indicated the service valve could be redesigned to fit the Florida manufacturer's specifications and would offer greater reliability at a price 20 percent higher than the imported valve. The toilet manufacturer was actively looking for a new supplier and was soliciting bids on an initial order for 100,000 water valves. Mured estimated that the redesigned water valve could be manufactured for $.80 to $1.00 and would sell for about $1.20.

AN IMPROMPTU MEETING

"I have to satisfy Cain next week and I didn't think you'd mind if I whipped up a short preliminary session so we could 'synchronize' our watches," said Mr. Johnson to his assembled staff. "It's true I'm counting heavily on Phil's success in working out the bugs on the new hydraulic cylinder and the water valve. I believe we must diversify or perish, and I'm convinced these new products will be winners. . .But, I don't want to overly influence you and your ideas. I expect each of you to speak freely, and I know you will. Right, Bob?"

Mr. Robert Eton shifted in his chair slightly before responding. "I guess sometimes I'm too outspoken Chet, but I certainly agree that we've got to diversify, and I think your cylinder and the water valve have great prospects. I think Phil is a wizard engineer, so I'm optimistic about our chances for success. In fact, I—''

"Before you get carried away," interrupted Mr. Phil De Van, "you better realize there's a lot more to it than just working out some engineering bugs on the drawing board and in our model shop. It's got to be produced at the right cost, and then it's got to be sold. I think we may easily get out in deep water on this item, despite its potential. I've heard a lot of cries of alarm about our relationship with Airflow, but I'd like to remind you that if it hadn't been for our orders from Airflow we'd really have been in trouble. Pete, why don't you say something?"

"You've got a good point, Phil," responded Mr. Pete Fuller," and I think it's important to recognize that while our sales have been disappointing recently, the total economy has been slumping since the Administration started putting the brakes on defense expenditures and the supply of money. If you don't believe me, just look at the six percent unemployment figure. Frankly, I think we've done damn well to hold our own."

"But we haven't been holding our own, and *that's* the point," interjected Mr. James Roberts. "We've been losing orders and our production has dropped so much we may have to lay off more operators soon."

"Now, wait a minute, Jim," retorted Mr. Fuller, "I know as well as you that we've lost some orders when we couldn't reduce our costs, but at the same time I've worked out some new orders and I'm sure they'll be coming our way soon. These things take time, and—"

Mr. De Van hit the table hard with a clenched fist. "I don't see how I can be more specific for Chet than I already have been," he said loudly. "We've got the best valves on the market, and everybody knows it. And our welding techniques permit us to modify any valve we've got pronto, and none of our competitors can respond as fast as we to new OEM specs. So, I'll say it again: push the sales reps harder."

"You know damn well there's a limit to what we can do in that direction, Phil," Mr. Fuller reacted testily. "Some of these fellows in our regional sales offices can get pretty touchy, and if we antagonize them, we're worse off than before. They've got other suppliers to satisfy, too, you know. I've had Bob working on sales targets for each region, and he's been working up some data showing their performance" (Table 7).

"Have you got those target figures finished, Bob?" asked Mr. Johnson.

"Er, no, not quite, Chet," Mr. Elton seemed embarrassed.

"For your information, Chet," interposed Mr. Fuller, "I've seen estimates in reputable trade publications that project an average annual rate of increase of from 5 to 15 percent in total air conditioning shipments during 1971-1975. During the 1960s this market was growing at a 13 to 14 percent clip. Moreover, a recent industry survey I reviewed emphasized that only about 10 percent of all U.S. manufacturing plants are air conditioned. I'm convinced we can increase our sales with all this potential."

"That's all very interesting Pete, said Mr. Henry Appleby, "But I'm concerned the way our bar stock inventory has been building up in the face of declining production. Maybe we've got too much finished goods inventory."

"Are you saying we've overextended ourselves?" asked Mr. De Van.

"Well, no. I'm just not real sure," Mr. Appleby replied. "I'll have to run some more cost and profit-margin figures. With some seventy valves to monitor, this is a big job. Besides, I'm not convinced everyone really examines my reports that identify items that are losing us money, and—"

"I'm not worried about that," interrupted Mr. Johnson, "because I check our inventories, production, shipments and a lot of other things personally every day, so I'm satisfied our controls are okay."

"I know *you* do, Chet," said Mr. Appleby. "I know there's some skepticism about my reports because I've only just started working them up. I'm certainly not suggesting we make instant decisions on any item's future without further study. But I do think it would be worth our while to start testing some of our competitors' values on a regular basis. This would help us—"

"Have you got the money to finance the construction and equipping of the lab necessary to do all these wonderful things?" Mr. De Van spoke tartly. "And the money to hire another engineer?"

"No, Phil," Mr. Johnson addressed the questions. "We don't have such money, you know it, Henry know it, we all know it. But, let's sort of stop our discussion for a moment at this point. We don't seem to be getting very far. Now we've all pretty well agreed on these sales projections (Table 8), to which we've all made some input previously, based on our past sales performances and expectations of industry growth. You recall that these took account of our cost and selling price relationships on a valve-by-valve basis over the past year (Table 9). I think each of you agrees we need to break our dependence on Airflow, right? Then that means we've essentially got two main options: concentrate on diversification, or concentrate on developing more orders in the air conditioning industry other than Airflow. Agreed? So here's what I want you to do: prepare for another, and final, meeting, the end of this week by working up specific pros and cons on how each of these two main options might be accomplished.'' As they filed out of his office, Mr. Johnson looked at his calendar. He had eight days left to finalize his plan for Mr. Cain.

QUESTIONS

1. What are Mured's goals and marketing strategies?
2. How effective are Mured's procedures to develop new products and eliminate old items?
3. What can be done to improve Mured's sales forecasting procedures?
4. Will diversification solve Mured's problems?

Table 1
Product Line Sales Analysis
1969-1971

Product	1969 Actual	Percent of Total	1970 Actual	Percent of Total	1971 Pro Forma	Percent Total
Reversing valves	$ 185,000	12	$ 200,000	11	$ 225,000	10
Check valves	185,000	12	200,000	11	225,000	10
Unloader valves	55,000	3	15,000	1	110,000	5
Headers	90,000	5	80,000	4	90,000	4
Service valves (hand valves)	850,000	53	1,028,000	55	1,220,000	55
Fittings and nuts	165,000	10	250,000	13	250,000	11
Miscellaneous	74,000	5	80,000	4	80,000	4
Total	$1,604,000		$1,853,000		$2,200,000	

Source. Mured financial statements.

Table 2
Industry Sales Analysis
(Factory Shipments)

	1969 Actual	1970 Actual	1971 Pro Forma
Unitary air conditioning			
Installed sales (millions)			
Nonresidential	$1,028	$1,116	$1,183
Residential	824	890	943
Total	$1,852	$2,006	$2,126
Percent Change		8	6
Unitary valve sales (millions)	$8.175	$8.755	$9.280
Percent Change		7	6
Mured sales			
Unitary valve sales (millions)	$1.015	$1.278	$1.470
Percent change		26	15
Total sales (millions)	$1.604	$1.853	$2.300
Unitary sales as percent of total sales	63	69	67
Mured unitary market share (percent)	12.4	14.5	15.8

Source. Mured 1971 forward plan.

Table 3
Key Account Sales Analysis
1969-1970

Account Name	1969 Sales	Percent	1970 Sales	Percent
DOMESTIC				
AAA, Inc.	$ 16,600	1	$ 24,000	1
Airflow				
Syracuse	1,060,000	66	898,000	48
Tennessee	17,400	1	88,000	5
Tyler	83,000	5	88,000	5
Cox	58,700	4	27,500	1
Davis & Ragsdale				
California	88,700	6	92,500	5
Tennessee	63,000	4	150,500	8
Fedders	19,600	1	22,500	1
Holstead Mitchel	0	—	16,500	1
Hussmann	0	—	6,500	—
Holly Division Long Siegler	0	—	18,500	1
Transicold	66,000	4	15,500	1
Lennox	32,000	2	49,500	3
Goettl Brothers	0	—	12,000	1
Gaffers & Sattler	0	—	5,000	—
IBM	0	—	4,000	—
FOREIGN				
South Africa	1,000	—	5,000	—
Formosa	75,700	5	200,000	11
Italy	2,000	—	30,000	2
Airflow-Canada	0	—	6,000	—
Non Key Accounts	20,000	1	92,000	5
Total	$1,604,000		$1,853,000	

Source. Mured financial statements.

Table 4
Shipments Unitary Air-Conditioning Market 1953-1970

Year	Units	Percent[a]
1953	41,992	33.1
1954	80,001	49.7
1955	111,158	56.5
1956	147,224	57.9
1957	126,071	58.1
1958	140,988	61.2
1959	191,923	62.6
1960	217,148	63.7
1961	238,206	66.9
1962	305,190	67.0
1963	400,759	70.8
1964	483,593	70.7
1965	580,997	72.1
1966	652,736	69.6
1967	714,025	69.9
1968	847,387	70.4
1969	1,174,570	73.3
1970	1,172,223	74.6

[a] This represents the residential proportion of total shipments that also include commercial applications.

Table 5
Installed Value Of The Unitary Air-Conditioning Market (Factory Shipments Plus Extras)

Year	Residential	Commercial	Total
1956	$ 174,011,400	$290,796,100	$ 464,807,500
1957	176,230,800	226,582,300	402,813,100
1958	204,602,850	219,489,200	424,092,050
1959	266,675,850	283,136,700	549,812,550
1960	318,477,150	312,648,350	631,125,500
1961	338,139,000	280,286,300	618,425,300
1962	408,623,850	345,652,300	754,276,150
1963	451,360,800	390,610,800	841,971,600
1964	532,020,800	464,249,600	996,270,400
1965	632,567,600	543,029,600	1,175,597,200
1966	718,252,000	671,604,400	1,389,856,400
1967	783,604,000	749,020,000	1,532,624,000
1968	950,191,600	834,616,000	1,784,807,600
1969	1,295,766,400	981,417,200	2,277,183,600
1970	$1,287,433,600	$933,571,200	$2,221,004,800

Source. Mured sales analysis, 1971 forward plan.

Table 6
Forecasted And Actual Sales For Selected products

Month	#2523 Reversing Valve		#6344 Check Valve		#7004 Fitting		#6301 Check Valve	
	Fore.[a]	Act.	Fore.	Act.	Fore.	Act.	Fore.	Act.
Sept. '69	500	200	300	0	8,000	0	200	72
Oct. '69	400	0	500	0	15,000	8439	300	1,232
Nov. '69	400	0	500	0	15,000	32761	700	755
Dec. '69	0	0	100	0	23,000	8305	250	15
Jan. '70	400	0	200	0	35,000	11378	400	23
Feb. '70	0	0	300	0	20,000	18117	150	180
Mar. '70	b	0	b	0	b	4320	b	0
Apr. '70	200	0	100	0	15,000	0	100	85
May '70	200	0	200	90	16,000	0	125	168
June '70	b	0	b	0	b	0	b	0
July '70	200	0	0	35	5,000	0	1,080	1,790
Aug. '70	b	0	b	0	b	0	b	900

Source. Mured production control records.
[a]Forecasts selected were calculated two months in advance by the Sales Administrator, Mr. Elton.
[b]Indicates that no forecast was provided.

Table 7
Sales Performance By Regional
Representatives[a] (Dollars)

	North-east	South-east	Central/Southwest	West Coast
1969	1,100,000	12,000	18,000	248,000
1970	1,050,000	4,000	3,000	414,000
1971	900,000	1,000	19,000	280,000

Source. Mured sales manager records.
[a]Excludes sales by company headquarters direct and overseas sales. The newly formed "Fifth" territory is included in the figures for Central/Southeast. Sales made by the company directly reached $200,000 in 1971.

Table 8
Sales Objectives (Dollars)

1972	1,500,000
1973	1,800,000
1974	2,000,000
1975	2,300,000
1976	2,800,000

Table 9
Typical Cost Selling Price Relationships Representative Valves (Dollars)

	Manufacturing Cost[a] (Each)	Selling Price (Each)
Reversing Valves		
#2523	22.10	24.90
#2780	14.95	21.00
#2831	362.90	448.30
#2940	38.20	47.25
Check Valves		
#6301	2.30	2.85
#6344	4.60	3.65
#6347	1.30	1.85
#6422	2.50	2.75
#6510	1.62	2.08
#6602	1.18	1.82

[a]Excludes general and administrative costs.

Case 7-2
Armstrong Cork Canada, Ltd.[1]

"This Deltox rug problem is one of the toughest situations we have ever come up against," explained Mr. Donald H. Creech, manager of the Building and Floor Products Division, Armstrong Cork Canada, Ltd. "Our latest profit and loss statement shows that in the last four years we have lost a total of $221,000 on the product. We've made several changes in our marketing strategy for Deltox but we haven't discovered the right marketing mix to move the product in a really big way. Our production people have cut manufacturing costs to the bone.

"We've got to go over the Deltox marketing operation and try to work out a marketing plan that will get sales and profits up. If we can't come up with a good plan, I've got to recommend that we drop the product," concluded Mr. Creech.

[1]Case prepared by John Kennedy under the direction of Professor Donald H. Thain with the cooperation of Armstrong Cork Canada, Ltd. Copyright © by the University of Western Ontario. Reproduced by permission.

DELTOX RUGS

Deltox rugs were developed by a company in Oshkosh, Wisconsin, by treating sulphate kraft paper with chemicals to improve wearing properties, twisting it into strong cords, and weaving the cords into the finished product. At the time Deltox was acquired by the Armstrong Cork Company, the line had expanded to sixteen patterns, eight widths, and five price lines. Cut rugs were available in twelve sizes. According to company executives, a significant change in the use pattern of the product had taken place over the years. A transition from "summer only" to "year round" use had occurred and a survey indicated that 61 percent of all Deltox purchases were for all-year use. The survey also indicated that Deltox rugs were used in every room in the house (Exhibit 1). This versatility of use, together with the low price and attractive appearance of Deltox were the principal reasons for its success. In addition, the product was reversible, easy to clean, and extremely durable. There was no record of any customer complaint on a Deltox rug.

DELTOX IN CANADA

After Deltox was acquired by Armstrong, the rugs were distributed through the regular Armstrong wholesale organization, despite the practice of large retailers of buying direct from manufacturers. Armstrong Cork Canada, Ltd. imported rugs from the American plant for two years until the Deltox production facilities were completed in Canada. Financial data for the first five years of this operation are summarized in Exhibits 2 through 4.

Armstrong management knew that if the price was set above a certain level it would be more advantageous for both wholesalers and retailers to import Deltox rugs from the United States. Therefore, the product was priced slightly below U.S. landed prices. For example, the factory price to the wholesaler for a 9 x 12 foot Deltox rug was approximately $15.15. Rugs sold to retailers at $18.25, yielding the distributor a 17 percent margin on selling price. There was no suggested retail price. Wholesalers sometimes suggested that the dealer markup the rug 60 percent on his cost but the final selling price depended on the pricing policy of the individual retailer. A store selling a 9 x12 foot rug and taking a 50 percent markup on cost sold it for $27.50 while a store that wanted a 70 percent margin sold it for $31.50. Both wholesalers and retailers were offered volume discounts.

Initially Armstrong believed that the principal marketing problem was obtaining adequate distribution and the sales effort was directed towards achieving this objective. The company worked to build up wholesaler stocks because it was felt that such a move would encourage these firms to push Deltox. As an incentive to dealers, a Deltox retail display contest was run in year 3. This contest was backed up with a full-page advertisement in *Chatelaine*. All stores that entered the contest had to display the price and a number of selling points on the product. First prize was $500 cash. The wholesale salesman covering the winning account received $250 cash. This contest was believed to be well received and distribution was obtained in about 1,000 of Armstong's total of 6,000 dealers. Sales and profits for year 3, however, did not reach management expectations.

As a result, several changes in the Deltox operation were made during the next year. Cost reductions were effected through the consolidation of the line to thirteen patterns, four widths, and three price lines.

Product quality was improved with the use of a new latex adhesive binding process. In order to stimulate sales, the wholesale margin was increased to 18½ percent and extended credit was offered to wholesalers on orders of $2,000 or more. The wholesaler was supposed to pass on this special dating privilege to retailers by providing a billing date of April 1st on orders of $500 or more placed earlier in the year. Sales manuals and display units were made available to the retailers and a second retail window display contest was run.

In the fifth year of Deltox operations the line was further consolidated to ten patterns, four widths, and only one price. Extended terms were offered to wholesalers on all orders over $250. Later steps were taken to cut production costs by reducing to three the number of standard rug sizes available. Previously, the wholesaler could have odd-size rugs cut and bound at the factory on a special order basis. This service was discontinued. At the same time, wholesale margins were increased to 24 percent, the highest in the Armstrong line. This increased margin was effected through a 7 percent price increase to retailers.

Armstrong head office personnel asked each district manager to submit a memo that would outline his appraisal of Deltox and to comment on the ability of his office to sell rugs in the next period. Two replies are reproduced below.

Date: March 9
To: A. H. McNaughton Montreal Office
From: G. R. Winters Moncton Office
Subject: Deltox

The past performance of this product when Gulf Wholesale, Ltd. was handling it was only fair. However, the following yardage figures show that sales have increased each year since then:
Year 1—329 yards
    2—6,507 yards
    3—7,465 yards
    4—8,506 yards

As far as the three Maritime provinces are concerned, when Gulf Wholesale was handling Deltox, nearly all of the business obtained was sold by me personally as Gulf put very little effort on this product. With the complete coverage and proper sales effort that Ottawa Valley Lumber Co. can now give this product, its future prospects should be good.

Date: March 4
To: Alex McNaughton Montreal
From: R. Fletcher Montreal
Subject: Deltox

For the first month of this year, we sold over 22 percent of last year's total sales and with one exception, all four Montreal district wholesalers[1] are extremely confident of the future that exists for this product. The extremely small markup to be obtained by the wholesaler on all cut-orders supplied from his warehouse is the only disturbing feature of Deltox in this district at the present time, and this situation should and certainly can be remedied by increasing cut-order prices as soon as this can possibly be done.

At the present time, D.D.I. (Quebec wholesalers), who are new to the line, although they have handled fiber rugs in the past, feel that economically they can only justify the stocking and selling of rugs, although to keep up with the demand, they have been forced to stock and cut from full rolls during the past two months, due to our inability to supply cut-orders as quickly as we had first planned. They feel that if cut-orders were made as profitable for them as rugs, that the future of Deltox is unlimited.

Lino-Wood's position is similar to D.D.I., although they are still stocking and cutting rolls in the hope that this situation is only temporary. Lino-Wood are very pleased with the sales of Deltox to date, and they too feel that we have only begun to scratch the surface with this product.

Gauthier's purchases for the month of January were nearly half of last year's total purchases.

To summarize, we of the Montreal District would be extremely disappointed to see Deltox withdrawn from the Armstrong line of floor coverings. It is our opinion that this product will eventually become one of our top selling lines.

The ideas that the company might sell direct to selected retailers had been discussed with several wholesalers and all opposed the change. Mr. Creech believed that they were afraid that this might be "the thin edge of the wedge" in selling certain items direct to selected accounts. Some company officials were opposed to any course of action that might affect the company-wholesaler relationship. Nevertheless, Mr. Creech felt that a basic change in the distribution pattern might be the key to increasing Deltox sales and should be given serious consideration.

In reviewing the information available to him, Mr. Creech noted that the sales pattern, both by type of outlet and by volume, varied considerably across

[1]Two in Montreal, one in Quebec, one in Ottawa.

the country (Exhibits 5 and 6). The state of wholesaler and dealer enthusiasm for the product was reflected in the estimate that only 200 dealers now stocked and sold Deltox with another 300 selling the product but not stocking it. Mr. Creech knew that Deltox was competitive with natural-fiber floor coverings both in price and appearance. Retailers, however, were inclined to push these products in preference to Deltox because they were apparently easier to sell to the consumer. Many retailers had done exceedingly well with Deltox. Some stores inflated the "regular price" and promoted Deltox at a sales price that was represented as a savings of up to 50 percent of this "regular price." For example, one Montreal department store advertised 9 x 12 foot Deltox rugs for $26.25—one third off the regular price of $39.50—and sold 100 rugs in one hour. A large number of retailers had explained that there was sales resistance to Deltox because it was not well known to the consumer. Mr. Creech thought that a marketing program built around an extensive advertising program might be the solution to obtaining satisfactory long-run sales and profits for the Deltox operation.

On the other hand, the recent popularity of the somewhat higher-priced cotton and viscose-tufted floor coverings had begun to cut into the market formerly held by flat-weaved rugs. This posed a problem as to whether sales could ever be pushed up the point where the manufacturing operation was profitable. Armstrong Cork Canada, Ltd. could earn a 12 percent commission on sales of Deltox from the U.S. plant direct to Canadian wholesalers. The landed cost to the wholesaler on such purchases would be approximately 8 percent below the current Canadian factory price. Thus, one alternative open to Mr. Creech was to discontinue the production of Deltox in Canada and to earn a 12 percent commission by making shipments direct from Oshkosh, Wisconsin, to the Canadian wholesalers.

QUESTIONS

1. Should Armstrong Cork Canada drop Deltox rugs, import them from Oshkosh, Wisconsin, or keep the product and revise its current marketing program?
2. If you decide to keep Deltox rugs, what changes would you recommend in the product, pricing, promotion and distribution to improve the profitability of the rugs?

Exhibit 1
Usage Patterrn for Deltox Rugs

Rooms	Percent of Purchasers Using Deltox in this Room
Game room	3
Porch	15
Bedroom	14
Nursery	3
Dining room	20
Living room	32
Sun room	6
Other rooms	7
Total	100

Exhibit 2
Profit and Loss Statements for the Deltox Operation

	Year							
	2 Four Months Sept. to Dec.		3		4		5 Nine Months to Sept. 30	
	$	%	$	%	$	%	$	%
Net sales	16,472	100.0	92,903	100.0	175,653	100.0	124,270	100.0
Variable cost of sales[a]	10,639	64.7	59,012	62.9	112,583	64.1	78,944	63.5
Variable cost variance[b]	16,150	—	18,250	—	23,766	—	12,289	—
Total variable cost of sales	26,789	162.7	77,262	83.2	136,349	77.6	91,233	73.4
GROSS MARGIN	(10,317)	(62.7)	15,641	16.8	39,304	22.4	33,037	26.6
Fixed manufacturing expense[c]	18,179	110.2	31,269	33.7	44,276	25.2	29,685	23.9
Selling expense[d]	20,431	123.0	20,507	22.1	37,026	21.1	23,741	19.1
Promotion expense	1,887	11.5	14,631	15.8	13,245	7.6	5,403	4.3
Administration expense[e]	—	—	8,786	9.5	7,614	4.3	8,605	6.9
Miscellaneous expense	—	—	7,810	8.4	17,580	10.0	1,107	0.9
Miscellaneous income	2,764	16.8	—	—	—	—	—	—
Commission income	13,110	79.7	2,689	2.9	—	—	—	—
NET PROFIT OR (LOSS)	($34,940)	(210.9)	($69,966)	(75.5)	(80,437)	(45.8)	(35,504)	(28.5)

[a] Based on standard costs for budgeted yearly volumes.
[b] Excess over standard costs. According to company executives, variances were primarily the result of production below budgeted volumes.
[c] Allocated to the Deltox operation in direct proportion to the percentage of total plant area it occupied.
[d] Eight percent of total selling expenses (allocated by management).
[e] Eight percent of total administrative expense (allocated by management).

Exhibit 3
Deltox Sales and Yardage

Year	Sales (Dollars)	Yards
1	36,000 (imported)	Not available
2	131,000 (imported)	Not available
	17,000 (produced in Canada)	Not available
	148,000	
3	93,000	75,000
4	176,000	159,000
5 (9 months)	124,000	120,000

Exhibit 4
Deltox Promotion Expense (Dollars)

	Year				(Budget)
	1	2	3	4	5
Catalogues and literature	430	539	3,100	4,791	5,000
Samples	280	1,348			
Dealer display promotion			4,896	2,969	
Advertising space and production			6,565		
Sales manuals				1,831	
Display units				3,654	
Miscellaneous			70		650
	710	1,887	14,631	13,245	5,650

Exhibit 5
Deltox Sales by Trade Classification, January-September

	Quebec	Ont.	Man.	Sask.	Alta.	B. C.	Maritimes
Cash sale[a]	12.6	6.6	9.2	5.8	11.3	6.4	1.0
Speciality store	23.7	11.7	—	—	2.0	12.9	—
Floor contractor	7.1	1.6	—	0.7	6.2	0.9	—
Furniture store	29.7	15.9	1.9	14.2	30.0	35.1	48.9
Department store	25.8	8.3	88.9	62.5	35.4	26.2	19.6
Hardware store	0.5	2.3	—	3.6	6.0	3.9	—
Building supply dealer	0.1	9.2	—	9.3	6.4	0.6	0.3
All other[b]	0.5	44.4	—	3.9	2.7	14.0	30.2

[a] Unclassified sales by wholesalers.
[b] Includes company sales to mail order firms.

Exhibit 6

Comparison of Deltox Sales by Districts

In order to compare the performance of the seven selling districts, the company used a formula of percentage of sales by the district over the percentage of buying power index as noted in *Sales Management* magazine.

Districts	Percent of Sales to Percent of B. P. I.
Montreal	201
Toronto	73
Winnipeg	3
Vancouver	57
Calgary	61
Moncton	58
Regina	28
	For an average of 100%

Eight
Pricing

Business thinking about pricing has been referred to as superstitious, fuzzy, and riddled with black magic.

Benson P. Shapiro

Efficient pricing of goods and services is often a critical factor in the successful operation of business organizations. Although the basic pricing ingredients are the same for all firms (costs, competition, demand, and profit), the optimum mix of these factors varies according to the nature of products, markets, and corporate objectives. Thus, the job for the manager is to develop and implement a pricing strategy that meets the needs of a particular company at a certain point in time.

For example, when a company is trying to break into a new industry, prices are often set low to build sales revenue rather than generate immediate profits. Established firms like DuPont, on the other hand, may emphasize high-margin specialty items and lower prices as markets expand. A common strategy among large companies (General Motors) is to set prices to generate a minimum return on invested capital. Other firms may stress low prices on basic products to build market share and keep competition at a minimum (Dow). Producers of some products (diamonds, crude oil) control such a high proportion of the supply that they can restrict output and price to maximize profits. Sometimes the demand for products is interrelated and a firm must consider how changes in the price of one item will affect the sales of other merchandise in the line. Also in times of shortages, price can be a useful device to ration limited supplies among customers.

These are only a few of the pricing strategies that will be discussed in detail later in the chapter. Since marketing managers are interested in practical guides for action, we will begin by reviewing several cost oriented pricing methods. These include the widely used markup, break-even, rate of return, variable cost, and peak-load pricing techniques. Next a simple, economic pricing model is introduced, followed by a discussion of price elasticity. New product pricing and competitive bid pricing are then examined and the chapter concludes with a consideration of environmental pricing factors.

PRACTICAL PRICING METHODS

Most businessmen prefer pricing procedures that are easy to administer and require only limited assumptions about demand. Perhaps the simplest technique is known as markup pricing.

343

Markup Pricing

With markup pricing, a fixed *dollar amount* is added to the cost of an item to yield a selling price. This amount is the markup designed to cover overhead expenses and produce a profit for the firm. Markups are usually expressed as a percentage of the cost or selling price of the item. Setting prices with cost markups usually involves multiplying the markup percentage times the cost of the item and then adding the result to the cost. This may be simplified by adding 100 to the markup percentage to create a cost multiplier. It is not unusual to find firms who calculate selling prices by informally multiplying cost by a factor of 2, 3, or 4.

Markups on selling price are more complicated because they cannot be multiplied directly times cost to give a price. With these markups, costs are divided by one minus the markup percentage to yield the selling price. From a practical standpoint, it makes little difference whether markups are based on cost or selling price, since the end result is the same no matter which is used.[1] Traditionally, resellers, such as wholesalers and retailers, have based markups on selling prices while manufacturers have tended to favor markups on cost.

An example of markup pricing in Table 8-1 shows how a manufacturer uses a multiplier of 1.8 to convert his factory cost of $2 into a selling price of $3.60 for a barbecue grill. The wholesaler and retailer divide their costs by one minus their markup percentages to produce selling prices. Note that although the manufacturer has the highest markup percentage ($1.60/3.60 or 44 percent on selling price), the retailer has the largest dollar margin ($3.00). This is a natural result of applying a similar markup to a larger cost and it is usually argued that the retailer needs a higher dollar margin because of the greater risks associated with this type of business.

Table 8-1

Using Markups to Set Factory, Wholesale, and Retail Selling Prices

Components of the Pricing Process	1975 Model Barbecue Grill (Dollars)	1976 Model Barbecue Grill (Dollars)
Factory cost (including direct labor, materials, and factory overhead)	2.00	2.20
Manufacturing margin (administrative overhead, marketing expenses, and profit)	1.60	1.76
Manufacturing selling price ($2.00 × 1.8)	3.60	3.96
Wholesale margin	.90	.99
Wholesale selling price [$3.60/(1 −20% MUSP)]	4.50	4.95
Retail margin	3.00	3.30
Retail selling price [$4.50/(1−40% MUSP)]	7.50	8.25

[1] For every cost markup, there is an equivalent markup on selling price. Since a smaller base is used, cost markups always exceed the corresponding markups on selling price. For example, a markup of 100 percent on cost is the same as a markup of 50 percent on selling price. Markups on cost and selling price may be equated by the use of the following formulas: $MUC = MUSP/(1—MUSP)$, $MUSP = MUC/(1 + MUC)$.

One problem with markup pricing is the tendency to magnify increases in costs. This is illustrated by the prices calculated for the 1976 model of the barbecue grill (Table 8-1). If the grill costs $.20 more to produce in 1976 and the same cost multiplier is used, the new factory selling price increases by $.36 even though costs rose only $.20. The extra $.16 margin could be kept as profit if marketing expenses, overhead, and sales volumes were kept at the same levels as 1975. Notice that a similar cost magnification occurs at the wholesale and retail levels so that the original $.20 increase results in a price of $.75 by the time it reaches the consumer.

An even more serious problem with markup pricing is the tendency to apply the same average markup percentage to broad classes of goods with little or no regard for possible differences in price sensitivity. Obviously, consumers are more concerned about the prices of some classes of goods than for others. This means a policy of using low margins on high demand items and larger margins for less popular merchandise could lead to greater total profits for the firm.

Kotler suggests that one reason markup pricing continues to be popular is that there is less uncertainty about costs than about demand.[2] By relying on costs, pricing is simplified and the seller does not need to make price adjustments as demand changes. Markup pricing is also flexible and fully compatible with actions of the firm designed to maximize profits. The size of the markups can be set to accomplish a variety of objectives and the inherent simplicity of the method makes it easy to pass pricing decisions on to other employees. Simplicity is important where pricing rules must be transmitted without error throughout large organizations spread over wide geographic areas. Markup pricing can also be a subtle way to reduce price competition. If all the firms in an industry or a particular area use the same markup percentage, their prices will resemble one another given a similarity in costs.

Break-Even Pricing

Break-even pricing shows how many units must be sold at selected prices to regain the funds invested in a product. A break-even chart prepared for the barbecue grill is shown in Figure 8-1. The diagram assumes that production and marketing of the grill involve annual fixed charges of $85,000 and the variable production costs for direct labor, materials, and factory overhead are $2.00 per unit. When the fixed and variable costs are combined, total costs intersect the revenue-price curves at points B_1, B_2, and B_3. These points show the volumes needed to recover full costs at factory prices of $3.00, $3.60, and $4.60. Profits are generated when volume exceeds the break-even points and losses occur when volume fails to reach the break-even levels.

Although a break-even diagram provides a useful *visual* representation, it lacks some of the detail that can be included in a tabular analysis. Table 8-2 calculates break-even volumes for six potential factory prices by dividing total fixed costs by the margin generated at each price. The table also shows the final prices the consumer would pay when the wholesale and retail margins are added to the manufacturer's selling prices. Note that price varies inversely with break-even volume and a price of $2.60 requires sales of about 141,000 units to break even, whereas a price of $5 gives a profit after only 28.4 thousand units have been sold.

Probably the most serious deficiency with break-even pricing is its inadequate treatment of *demand*. Obviously the relationship between the final retail price and the number of barbecue grills that will be purchased by consumers is crucial to the selection of the

[2]Philip Kotler, *Marketing Management: Analysis Planning and Control,* 2nd. ed., (Englewood Cliffs, New Jersey: Prentice Hall, Inc., 1972), p. 525.

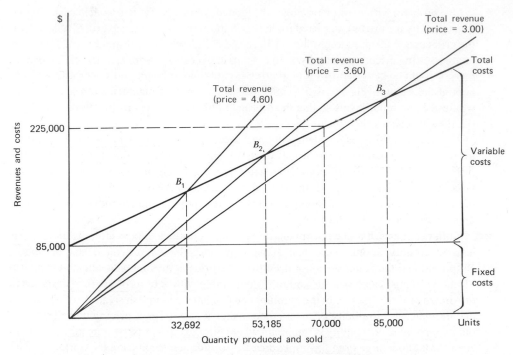

Figure 8-1 Multiple Break-Even Analysis for a Barbecue Grill.

optimum price. Break-even charts, however, usually show total revenue as a straight line implying that larger volumes can be sold without lowering prices (Figure 8-1). This is, of course, unrealistic and executives must consider which combination of price and break-even volume will lead to the most profits. Some of the factors influencing this decision are competitive offerings, previous pricing experience, and the special features of the barbecue grill. Ultimately, however, the decision must turn on the ability of the executive to estimate the number of units that will be sold at each possible price.

Table 8-2
Calculating Break-Even Volumes Using Margin Per Unit

Salesmen's salary and expenses						$25,000
Advertising and point of sale materials						40,000
Amortization of R & D expenses						5,000
Amortization of tooling expenses						5,000
Overhead expense allocation						10,000
Total						$85,000[a]
Retail price (Includes wholesale and retail margins)	$5.42	$6.25	$7.50	$8.33	$9.58	$10.42
Possible mfg. selling prices	2.60	3.00	3.60	4.00	4.60	5.00
Variable cost	−2.00	−2.00	−2.00	−2.00	−2.00	−2.00
Margin	$ .60	$1.00	$1.60	$2.00	$2.60	$ 3.00
Break-even volume in 1000's of units ($85,000/mfg's. margin)	141.7	85.0	53.2	42.5	32.7	28.3

[a]The fixed costs could be increased to include a profit so the break-even volumes would show the sales needed to return a planned profit.

Rate-of-Return Pricing

Pricing to achieve a planned rate of return on investment is a popular goal among large businesses. Lanzillotti, for example, found that nine out of twenty firms had a pricing policy designed to produce an after-tax return on investment of between 8 and 20 percent.[3] The key in this procedure is estimating demand and the utilization of facilities.

The methods used to set prices for individual products can be demonstrated by referring to the barbecue grill mentioned earlier. If plant capacity is assumed to be 100,000 units, and the firm expects to operate at 70 percent capacity, then it anticipates a demand for 70,000 units. Figure 8-1 suggests that production of 70,000 units involves total costs of $225,000 or about $3.21 per unit. The $3.21 represents the full cost to the firm of producing and marketing each barbecue grill. The next step is to add a profit margin to this cost so that the planned return on investment will be achieved. If the firm expects an after-tax return of 14 percent[4] on its $250,000 investment in barbecue grill inventories and facilities (0.14 ×$250,000 = $35,000), and the tax rate is 50 percent, then the price must be set to produce $70,000 in total profits. Since the company plans to sell 70,000 units, a factory selling price of $4.21 will generate the desired profit and return on investment. However, if competitors are charging $5.21, the firm could use this higher price and earn a 28 percent return of their investment.

The most serious deficiency with rate-of-return pricing is that sales estimates are used to derive a price even though the number of units sold is obviously a function of price. This rather detached view of demand implies that customers are *not very sensitive* to the prices charged for the product. While this may be true for large, dominant firms like General Motors and du Pont, it may not hold for smaller firms in more competitive industries. Another problem is that rate-of-return pricing can lead to wide fluctuations in profits because the amount earned is directly related to the accuracy of the sales estimate. For example, if the $4.21 price for the barbecue grill proves to be high and only 50,000 units are sold, the return on investment slumps to 5.1 percent. Thus, a 20 percent decline in volume results in a 64 percent reduction in return on investment.

Variable-Cost Pricing

Variable-cost pricing is based on the idea that the recovery of full costs is not always realistic or necessary for the profitable operation of business firms. Instead of using full costs as the lowest possible price, this system suggests that variable costs represent the minimum price that can be charged. For example, assume that the barbecue grill mentioned previously has been marketed successfully through normal wholesale-retail channels and a total of 70,000 units have been sold in the past year at a price of $4.21. This price covers full costs of $3.21 and allows the manufacturer a 14 percent after tax return on his investment of $250,000. The company is now approached by a large supermarket chain that wants to make a special purchase of 10,000 barbecue grills at $2.50 each. The buyer suggests that the grills carry the supermarket's label without the chrome trim and fancy wheels found on the regular model. To evaluate this proposal the company must know how much it will cost to produce the barbecue grills to meet the chain's specifications. If the design changes reduce variable costs to $1.50 per unit, the

[3]Robert F. Lanzillotti, "Pricing Objective in Large Firms," *American Economic Review,* Vol. 48, No. 5 (December 1958), p. 923. The nine firms included Alcoa, du Pont, Esso, General Electric, General Motors, International Harvester, Johns-Manville, Union Carbide, and U.S. Steel.

[4]Fourteen percent was the average target return on investment mentioned by the nine firms studied by Lanzillotti.

order for 10,000 grills from the supermarket chain would represent a potential contribution of $10,000.

The question that remains is under what circumstances can the firm accept the order for the 10,000 barbecue grills? Some would say that the order can *never* be approved since the price does not cover full costs. Others would point out that if the firm were to cut prices to the supermarket chain, other customers would demand equally low prices. This could lead to losses because there would be no way for the firm to recover the fixed development and marketing costs. While there is some truth in these remarks, the important point is that the full cost of manufacturing each barbecue grill is not constant but, in reality, is quite sensitive to changes in volume. This is shown in Figure 8-2 where unit costs decline as the fixed expenses are spread over a large volume. Assuming for the moment that variable costs are constant at $2 per unit, then 20,000 barbecue grills can be produced for $6.25 per unit and 70,000 for $3.21 per unit. If volume could be expanded further to 170,000 units, unit costs would decline to the $2.50 offered by the supermarket chain. This suggests that a very low price can cover full costs if volume expands sufficiently.

In the present situation, adding the 10,000 grills ordered by the supermarket chain to current production of 70,000 units lowers estimated fixed costs per unit to $1.06 ($85,000/80,000). When fixed costs are added to projected variable costs of $1.50 for the redesigned grill, total costs ($2.56) exceed the $2.50 offered by the chain. Since the order will return less than full costs, it is important to consider whether the two markets being served are really separate. Will sales through the supermarkets reduce sales through the regular dealers? If the supermarkets are in different geographic locations or service different income classes, then the additional business would begin to look more attractive. Acceptance of the order also depends on the availability of excess capacity and whether the firm's facilities could be used to manufacture other products more profitably. In addition, the firm must realize that the supermarket can probably find another supplier if the order is refused.

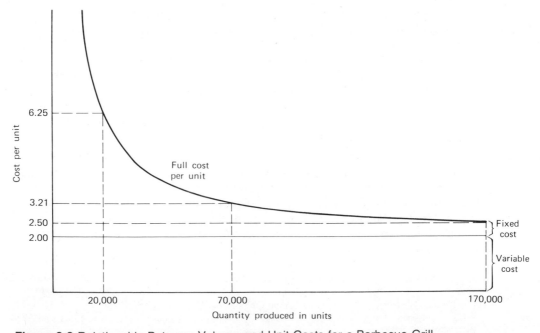

Figure 8-2 Relationship Between Volume and Unit Costs for a Barbecue Grill.

Another issue is whether the sale of 10,000 grills to the supermarket chain represents a violation of federal laws prohibiting price discrimination among similar types of buyers.[5] In this particular case, the manufacturer could claim that the redesigned grill is not the same "grade and quality" and the low price merely reflects the savings associated with building, selling, and delivering 10,000 units to one customer. Also since the barbecue grill industry is made up of many small firms, it is unlikely that the government could prove that the proposed sale would "lessen competition or tend to create a monopoly." Further, very few regular customers would want to buy 10,000 grills at one time and the low price can probably be justified as a quantity discount.

Variable-cost pricing is frequently encountered in situations where fixed costs make up a large proportion of total unit costs. The railroads and airlines are two industries with high fixed costs that have made effective use of the volume-generating aspects of variable-cost pricing. The rationale is that it is better to haul bulk commodities and special classes of travelers (i.e., wives, children, students) at low rates and make some contribution than to not have the business at all. Railroads typically face a declining unit-cost curve except when volume nears capacity and tracks and switching yards become congested. This means that more volume generally increases profits by reducing the average costs of hauling merchandise. The airlines have used variable-cost pricing when they set fares for excursions or special groups of customers. Variable-cost pricing is not a panacea for all products or for all firms, but it can lead to higher revenues and profits for the sophisticated firm who understands its potential and limitations.

Peak-Load Pricing

A special type of variable-cost pricing can be used when there are definite limits to the amount of goods and services a firm can provide and customer demand tends to vary over time. For example, the telephone company builds capacity to satisfy 97 percent of its callers during peak periods that occur during weekdays, but this means they have a lot of unused phone circuits at night and on weekends.[6] Peak-load pricing suggests that phone rates should be raised above average costs during high-demand periods and reduced toward variable costs during off-peak hours. This tends to shift price-sensitive customers to slack times and allows the phone company to operate with less total capacity. In addition, the very low off-peak rates may increase revenues by attracting some customers that normally do not use the phone for communication purposes.

Telephone companies have used peak-load pricing in setting rates for direct-dialed long-distance calls. The Bell system, for example, has advertised a three-minute coast-to-coast rate of $1.45 for weekdays from 8 A.M. to 5 P.M. However, if the call is placed from 5 P.M. to 11 P.M., the rate drops to $.85 and if the call is placed from 11 P.M. to 8 A.M. the rate is $.35 for the first minute and $.20 for each additional minute.[7] Another example of peak-load pricing occurs with golf courses that charge high greens fees on weekends when demand is high and lower rates during the week. Theaters also have fixed capacities and often charge lower prices during afternoon performances when demand is light. Peak-load pricing is occasionally used to smooth out consumer demand

---

[5]It is perfectly legal, however, to charge brokers, wholesalers, and retailers different prices because they perform different functions in the channel of distribution. The relevant law is the Robinson Patman Act, which is discussed in detail on pp. 368-369.

[6]See S. C. Littlechild, "Peak-Load Pricing of Telephone Calls," *Bell Journal of Economics & Management Science,* Vol. 1, No. 2 (Autumn 1970), pp. 191-210.

[7]Advertisement appeared in *Business Week* (July 2, 1973), np.

for electricity.[8] Some utilities charge a different rate in the summer than they do in the winter. Other utilities offer special low rates to factories that use electricity for smelting purposes if they operate at night and other off-peak demand periods.

The primary advantage of peak-load pricing is that it depresses peak demands and thereby reduces the total resources needed to fill customer wants. In addition, it stimulates off-peak consumption and allows more efficient utilization of existing facilities. Despite the tremendous economic advantages of peak-load pricing, it is only used to a limited extend in the U.S. economy. Most electricity is still sold at flat rates and when everyone turns on their air conditioners, we have a power shortage.[9] If power costs were doubled during peak periods, many customers would start adding more insulation to their buildings and begin installing more efficient cooling systems. Peak-load pricing makes good economic sense and hopefully we will see more widespread use of this method to set fares for bridges, tunnels, transportation, and other capital intensive facilities.

PRICING WITH KNOWN DEMAND

Let us assume that in the process of making price adjustments a vacuum-cleaner manufacturer learns the general shape of his demand function. This tells the company how many units they can expect to sell (Q) at alternative prices (P) (Figure 8-3). The basic relationship is negative where the quantity purchased increases as the price declines and the function can be represented by the equation:

$$Q = 4000 - 40P \tag{1}$$

This equation suggests that no vacuum cleaners will be sold when the price is $100 or more and when price is zero, demand will be 4000 units. Obviously, neither or these price alternatives is practical due to the lack of sales revenues.[10] The optimum price can be determined, however, by selecting a pricing goal and collecting additional cost data.

Profit Maximization

One pricing objective that might be used is to maximize short run profits. While many would argue that this goal is selfish, shortsighted, and unrealistic, it could be desirable if the product had a relatively short expected life cycle. Once a firm has decided to maximize profits, data on fixed and variable costs must be collected to help locate the optimum price. If fixed costs for tooling and overhead are estimated at $15,000 and variable costs for the vacuum cleaner are $20 per unit, then total cost (C) to the firm will be:

$$C = 15,000 + 20Q \tag{2}$$

---

[8]See Donald N. De Salva, "An Application of Peak-Load Pricing," *Journal of Business,* Vol. 42, No. 4 (October 1969) , pp. 458-476.

[9]The Wisconsin Public Service Commission recently made a step in the right direction by approving a new rate schedule for Madison, Wisconsin, in which residential, industrial, and commercial users pay more for blocks of electricity during the summer than during the winter. The new schedule was designed to curb peak usage of electricity during the summer for air conditioning and put the burden of costs on heavy users. The schedule allows the utility to charge up to 30 percent more in the summer for customers using over 1000 killowatt hours a month. [*The Wall Street Journal* (August 12, 1974) p. 10].

[10]In reality, as price approached zero the demand function would bend and the amount purchased would be considerably greater than the 4000 units assumed by the linear function.

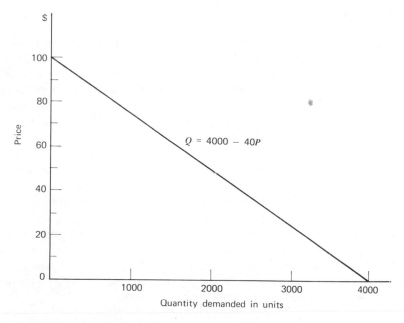

Figure 8-3 Demand Function for Vacuum Cleaner Manufacturer.

where Q is the number of units to be produced and sold. Since costs are subtracted from revenues to give profits, it is useful to have an equation that expresses total revenue *(R)* as a function of price *(P)*. This can be obtained by noting that revenue *(R)* is equal to price *(P)* times the quantity *(Q)* sold. Since equation 1 expressed quantity in terms of price, a revenue function can be obtained as follows:

$$R = PQ$$
$$R = P(4000 - 40P)$$
$$R = 4000P - 40P^2 \qquad (3)$$

Now that we have equations for demand, cost, and revenue, it is a simple matter to express profits *(K)* in terms of price.

$$K = R - C$$
$$K = (4000P - 40P^2) - (15{,}000 + 20Q)$$
$$K = 4000P - 40P^2 - 15{,}000 - 20(4000 - 40P)$$
$$K = -95{,}000 + 4{,}800P - 40P^2 \qquad (4)$$

This equation indicates that profits will hit a maximum of \$49,000 at a selling price of \$60 (Figure 8-4).[11] Short-run profit maximization thus leads to a situation where the company charges a fairly high price for the vacuum cleaner and restricts output to only 1600 units. While profit maximization may be a useful goal for some firms, it is by no means the only possibility to be considered.

[11]An exact solution can be obtained by noting that the slope of the profit curve is zero at the maximum point. Since the first derivative of the profit equation (4) is equal to the slope, the optimum price can be found as follows.

$$\frac{\delta K}{\delta P} = 4800 - 80P = 0$$

$$P = 60$$

Revenue Maximization

An alternative pricing objective that is available to our vacuum-cleaner manufacturer is to attempt to maximize revenue. Baumol argues that the objective of the typical oligopolist is "sales maximization subject to a minimum profit constraint."[12] He suggests that the pursuit of sales as a corporate goal is prompted by the growing separation of ownership from management, the salary systems used to reward executives, and the fear of loss of power associated with sales declines. Sales maximization appears to be widely followed in the business community and it seems desirable to examine the effects of this goal on our current pricing problem. When the price of the vacuum cleaner was set at $60 to maximize profits, sales revenues of $96,000 were generated (Figure 8-4). The sales curve indicates, however, the peak sales of $100,000 are produced at a price of $50.[13] At this price, volume increases to 2000 units and profits drop to $45,000. Thus, a $10 reduction in price increased revenues by 4.2 percent while reducing profits by 8.2 percent. This exchange of profits for revenue might be acceptable to branch managers who are evaluated on the basis of sales performance. Since it is difficult to measure demand, some managers may feel it is easier to maximize sales than the more abstract profit criteria. The lower prices associated with revenue maximization could also be used to push competitors out of a market.

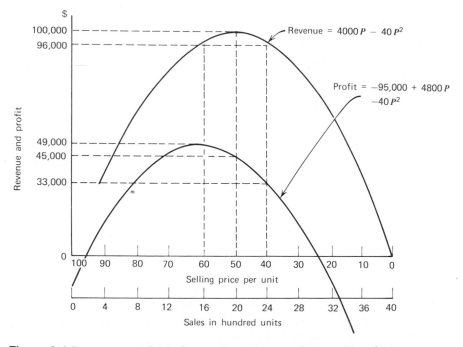

Figure 8-4 Revenue and Profit Curves for a Vacuum Cleaner Manufacturer.

[12]William J. Baumol, *Business Behavior, Value, and Growth,* Revised Ed. (New York: Harcourt, Brace and World, Inc., 1967), p. 49.

[13]A similar solution can be obtained by taking the derivative of the sales equation (3) and setting it equal to zero.

$$\frac{\delta R}{\delta P} = 4000 - 80P$$
$$P = 50$$

Unit Volume Maximization

A third pricing objective that is available to the vacuum-cleaner manufacturer is to maximize unit volume subject to a minimum profit constraint. Unit volume pricing sacrifices current profits and sales to gain supremacy in the number of units produced. If the vacuum-cleaner manufacturer wanted maximum volume and a profit of $33,000, then the optimum price would be $40 (Figure 8-4). In this case, a shift from a sales-maximizing price to a volume-maximizing price reduced revenues by 4.2 percent and profits by 26.7 percent. These declines are offset by a 20 percent increase in unit volume. Thus, the manager of the firm is being asked to trade substantial reductions in sales and profits for a boost in unit volume. This trade might be acceptable if the $40 price reduced competition without inciting the Justice Department to prosecute for antitrust violations. Lynn suggests maximum unit volume could be a desirable pricing goal where unit sales data and market share figures are made available to the public[14] (as in the case of automobiles). Under these circumstances the firm may be under great pressure to maintain its share of the total business regardless of the effects on sales and profits. This would be particularly true if distributors required a certain market share before they would stock the product. Low prices can also be an effective way to break into established markets and are frequently used on "leader" items to attract business to related lines of merchandise.

Most firms do not have complete data on the shape of their demand curves, but they usually have some information on customer sensitivity to selected price levels. The next section will show how price sensitivity can be estimated and used to price goods and services.

PRICE ELASTICITY

Consumers' price sensitivity can be measured by dividing percentage changes in the quantity sold by associated changes in price. This ratio is known as price elasticity and can be calculated with the formula:

$$e = \frac{\dfrac{\Delta q}{q}}{\dfrac{\Delta p}{p}}$$

where $\Delta q/q$ is the percentage change in quantity sold and $\Delta p/p$ is the percentage change in price.[15] Price elasticities are almost always negative with the quantity sold inversely proportionate to changes in price. When the quantity response is the same as the percentage change in price, elasticity is minus one and the revenues collected by the firm stay the same as prices are raised or lowered. When elasticity takes on smaller values ($e = -5$, say), total revenue increases as prices are reduced. In situations where elasticity is between zero and minus one, revenue increases as prices are raised. Although the relationship between price elasticity and revenue is quite precise, the firm must also understand the relationship between elasticity and profits.

[14]Robert A. Lynn, "Unit Volume as a Goal for Pricing," *Journal of Marketing,* Vol. 32 (October 1968), p. 36.

[15]Procedures that can be used to estimate price elasticity are discussed on pp. 356-357.

One theoretical argument[16] suggests that optimum profits occur when prices are set so that:

$$\text{Markup on cost} = -\frac{1}{1+e} \tag{5}$$

This expression suggests that the profit-maximizing markup is inversely related to the price elasticity of demand. This means that when price elasticity takes on values such as -6, the optimum markup on cost will be a low 20 percent. Alternatively with an elasticity of only -1.5, the profit-maximizing markup would be a robust 200 percent of cost. The general pricing rule that markup should vary inversely with the price elasticity of demand is widely used by businessmen in the real world. Retail executives with "great pricing skill" have been described as those who have the intuitive ability to accurately estimate price elasticities and vary markups accordingly.[17] While the profit maximizing markup formula (markup = $-1/1 + e$) appears to be quite useful, it does have some limitations. In addition to the obvious problems of estimating elasticities for a large number of products, average unit costs and elasticities must be stable over time and at different prices. These conditions usually apply to retail organizations, but they may not hold for other types of firms.

Elasticity and Costs

Although price elasticity is a great help in evaluating the impact of price changes on revenue, marketing executives must not overlook the influence of costs. The reason is simply that profits depend on both revenue and cost factors. When elasticity is less than minus one, it is frequently assumed that the firm can increase profits by lowering price. While revenue is sure to increase, the profitability of this action depends on the ratio of fixed to variable costs. For example, Table 8-3 shows an automobile manufacturer who is currently selling 100,000 cars per year at a factory price of $3,000 each. If unit costs are $2,700, then the automobile manufacturer will generate a total profit of $30 million for the year (Example A, Table 8-3). If the price of the cars is reduced $120 ($-4$ percent) and price elasticity[18] is realistically estimated at -1.5, then expected sales will increase to 106,000 units (-4 percent $\times -1.5 \times 100,000$). This means that more cars are sold at a lower price and total revenues will increase. However, since most of the costs are variable (80 percent),[19] the increase in production raises total variable costs by more than

---

[16]See Philip Kotler, *Marketing Mangement: Analysis, Planning and Control* (Englewood Cliffs, N.J.: Prentice-Hall, 1967), pp. 362-63; Lee E. Preston, *Profits, Competition and Rules of Thumb in Retail Food Pricing* (Berkeley: University of California, Institute of Business and Economic Research, 1963), pp. 6-8; and George Stigler, *The Theory of Price*, Rev. Ed. (New York: The Macmillan Co., 1952), p. 38. Equation 5 can be obtained by dividing the expression $MR = MC = AC = P(1+1/e)$ by $1+1/e$ to give $AC/(1+1/e) = P$ and then multiplying both sides by $1/AC$ to give $P/AC = 1/(1+1/e)$; multiplying both sides by e/e to yield $P/AC = e/(e+1)$ and subtracting AC/AC from both sides to give $(P\text{-}AC)/AC = -e/(e+1)-1$, substituting $(e+1)/(e+1)$ for -1 and combining terms to give $(P\text{-}AC)/AC = -1/(e+1)$.

[17]Bob R. Holdren, *The Structure of a Retail Market and the Market Behavior of Retail Units* (Englewood Cliffs, N.J.: Prentice-Hall, 1960), p. 72.

[18]Estimates of price elasticity for automobiles vary somewhat, but in most cases are less than 2. Griffin refers to an article by John Blair where price elasticity was said to range from 1.2 to 1.5. In another study by Hans Brems, *Product Equilibrium Under Monopolistic Competition* (Cambridge, Mass.: Harvard University Press, 1951), pp. 36-46, price elasticity was found to be 1.8.

[19]Fixed costs typically range from 15 to 20 percent of the total costs for heavy industries such as automobiles, steel, and aluminum. See Clare E. Griffin, "When Is Price Reduction Profitable," *Harvard Business Review*, Vol. 38, No. 5 (September-October 1960), pp. 125-32.

Table 8-3
Effects of a Price Reduction on the Profits of an Automobile Manufacturer When
Price Elasticity is −1.5

		A Before Price Reduction		B After 4 Percent Price Reduction	C After 4 Percent Price Reduction Variable Costs 20 Percent Total Costs
		(Millions)		(Millions)	(Millions)
Sales	($3000 × 100,000)	$300	($2880 × 106,000)	$305	$305
Variable costs	(0.8 ×$2700 × 100,000)	216	(0.8 × $2700	229	57
Fixed costs	(0.2 × $2700 × 100,000)	54 270	× 106,000)	54 283	216 273
Profit		$30		$22	$32
Selling price per unit		$3000		$2880	$2880
Average unit cost		2700		2670	2575

the growth in revenues and profits decline to about $22 million (example B). Thus, price elasticity would have to be less than −1.5 to make the price reduction profitable for the automobile manufacturer. In fact, an elasticity of −4 is needed just to maintain profits at their orginal level. When *fixed costs* represent a high proportion of total costs, increased volume can lead to sharp reductions in unit costs and increased profits. For example, assume that the variable costs shown in Table 8-3 represent only 20 percent of total costs (as they might in a railroad) and price elasticity remains at −1.5. Under these conditions a $120 price cut would actually increase the profits of the firm to $32 million (example C). This occurs because the decline in average costs associated with the increased volume exceeds the price reduction. Thus profits increase from the sale of more units (106,000) at a higher profit per unit ($305).

When price elasticity is close to minus one, there is generally little incentive to lower price and expand production unless variable costs can be reduced. The reason is that total variable costs will increase with added volume and profits will decline. A price increase may be desirable with a unitary price elasticity if variable costs can be held constant as volume declines. In situations where price elasticity is between zero and minus one, the natural tendency is to seek increased profits through increased prices. Although higher prices will reduce unit sales, the net result will be an increase in total revenue. An important factor in the amount of profit generated by these higher prices is the behavior of variable costs. If variable costs are constant as price rises, total variable costs will decline with the smaller production and profits will increase. The growth in profits results from the price increase and the decline in total variable costs. The greatest profits will accrue to products that have the highest proportion of variable costs that can be avoided as production declines. Similarly, products with high proportions of fixed costs have less to gain by raising prices and restricting output.

Measuring Price Elasticity

While it should be clear that a knowledge of price elasticities can improve pricing efficiency, the pragmatist will argue that marketing executives neither have this information nor the means to obtain it. The absence of hard data on price elasticities has been a serious problem for marketing executives, but it is becoming less of an issue with the growing sophistication of research techniques and personnel. For example, not long ago a letter to a professional journal complained that sales managers did not have real data on price elasticities. Russel Ackoff responded that management information systems can provide these data and he offered to name sales managers who had empirical price-elasticity information for their own products.[20] Most of the empirical estimates of price elasticity used by businessmen are obtained through market testing or by statistical analysis.

Historical relationships between price and the quantity sold are frequently analyzed to estimate price elasticities. One study of this type was done for a large manufacturer of synthetic fibers who wanted to know how rayon consumption was influenced by changes in prices and income.[21] Demand was assumed to follow the classical form:

$$Y = aX^b Z^c$$

where: Y = annual per capita rayon consumption in pounds
   X = real personal disposable income per capita
   Z = ratio of rayon fiber price to cotton fiber price
         and a, b, and c are coefficients to be estimated.

Twenty-five values for each variable were collected for the period 1928-1957 and least squares procedures were then employed to estimate the coefficients in the equation. The net result was the function:

$$Y = 10.12X^{.615} Z^{-1.15} \tag{6}$$

The coefficients (.615, −1.15) from the equation are elasticity estimates and as expected, income elasticity (.615) was positive and less than one. Thus, for every 1 percent increase in real income, there was a 0.6 percent increase in rayon consumption. The estimate of price elasticity was negative and close to 1 (−1.15) indicating a decline in the price of rayon relative to cotton was associated with a similar increase in the sales of rayon fiber. While useful estimates of price elasticity can be derived from a time series analysis of historical data, this procedure has the disadvantage that the elasticity estimates are averages for a period in the past and may not be representative of current or future market conditions.

Sometimes elasticity estimates can be obtained by studying variations in prices that exist across sales districts at a point in time. An example showing how cross-sectional analysis was used to derive a price elasticity for X-ray film is described in Chapter 11 (p. 531). In this particular case elasticity was found to be −2.6, suggesting that price was an important factor in the sale of X-ray film.

An alternative approach for the estimation of price elasticities is to systematically vary the price of the product and measure the corresponding changes in sales.[22] A variety of experimental procedures can be used to assess the impact of price changes including

[20]Letters to the editor, *Management Science,* Vol 14, No. 12 (August 1968), pp. B654, 656.

[21]Wroe Alderson and Paul E. Green, *Planning and Problem Solving in Marketing* (Homewood, Ill.: Richard D. Irwin, Inc., 1964), pp. 249-251.

[22]The firm must be careful in making these price changes to avoid violating the Robinson-Patman Act, which makes it illegal to discriminate among buyers of commodities of like grade and quality.

randomized block, Latin square, or factorial designs.[23] The objective of these methods is to isolate the relationship between price and sales from random elements. Experimental designs make it possible to control time and location factors while testing whether price changes have a significant effect on the quantity sold. For example, one of the authors obtained estimates of price elasticity for canned cherry sauce by rotating four prices across stores and time periods according to a Latin square design.[24] Significant increases in cherry sauce sales were obtained when the retail price was reduced from 26 to 34 percent below normal. The 26 percent price reduction increased sales by 128 percent suggesting a price elasticity of about −5. While revenues increased dramatically with lower prices, it is not clear whether a price reduction of this size would increase profits to the manufacturer. The ultimate desirability of lower prices for this or any other product depends on the ratio of fixed to variable costs and the resulting shape of the cost curves.

While experimental methods can provide fairly good estimates of price elasticity, they are more expensive and time consuming than other approaches. Survey and question-naire techniques have the advantage of simplicity and relatively low cost, but there is some doubt whether accurate price data can be obtained through direct questioning of consumers. Another approach is to bring consumers into a laboratory and expose them to different pricing situations. Subjects can be asked to compare an item to be priced with other merchandise or to engage in simulated shopping exercises. The problem with these shopping simulations is that subjects sometimes indicate higher price elasticities in the lab than they do in actual store purchases.[25]

Finally, it must be realized that there are situations where price elasticity is not constant over time. Advertising is often used to lower the price sensitivity of customers and if this goal is realized, elasticity becomes a function of the amount of advertising done by the firm. In situations where only a few firms produce a product, price elasticity may be related to the prices charged by other companies. There also are situations where changing prices alters the elasticity. For example, it has been argued that in the U.S. detergent market, raising prices makes many habitual consumers price sensitive, thus increasing price elasticity.[26] Thus, although the concept of elasticity and its implications for price policy are simple enough, it is important to realize that successful application of the concept requires careful and sophisticated study of the nature of the market for the product.

NEW PRODUCT PRICING

One of the most difficult problems that a marketing manager must resolve is setting prices for new products. These decisions are complicated by the frequent absence of adequate information on both demand and costs. Since new products have not been sold before, price elasticity cannot be estimated from an analysis of historical data. Also, the

---

[23]These are discussed in detail in Seymour Banks' *Experimentation in Marketing* (New York: McGraw-Hill, 1965), and in *Experimentation for Marketing Decisions* by Keith K. Cox and Ben M. Enis (Scranton, Pa.: International Textbook Co., 1969).

[24]Douglas J. Dalrymple and Donald L. Thompson, *Retailing: An Economic View* (New York: The Free Press, 1969), p. 206.

[25]Edgar Pessemier and Richard D. Teach found this to be true in a study reported in "Pricing Experiments, Scaling Consumer Preference and Predicting Purchase Behavior" in Raymond M. Hass, ed., *Science and Technology and Marketing* (Chicago: American Marketing Association, 1967), pp. 541-57.

[26]This argument is presented in Alfred A. Kuehn and Doyle L. Weiss "Marketing Analysis Training Exercise," *Behavioral Science,* Vol. 10, No. 1 (January 1965), pp. 51-67.

desire to keep competitors from learning about new products may prevent the firm from using test markets to obtain elasticity data. Even the simple expedient of copying your competitor's price is not a practical alternative for new products. Despite these problems, the marketing manager must find a price that will sell the product and still contribute to the profits of the firm. A common approach to new product pricing is to make an intuitive appraisal of the product and to apply either a skimming or penetration price strategy.[27]

Skimming Price

The concept of a skimming price was first proposed by Joel Dean in 1950 and it appears to be just as useful today as when it was first introduced. The basic idea is to set a relatively high initial price for the product and then to gradually reduce the price over time. This policy assumes that demand for the product is typical and somewhat inelastic. The situation is described by the downward sloping curve *DD* in Figure 8-5. The high initial price (P^1) is designed to skim off the segment of the market that is insensitive to price, and subsequent price reductions (P^2, P^3) broaden the market by tapping more elastic sectors of the market. The logic of skimming price strategy is supported by the observation that many new products have few technical substitutes and price is not as important as it is for more established products.

A skimming policy also has the advantage that it generates greater profits per unit than would be possible with lower prices. By charging a high initial price and then gradually lowering the price, the firm is able to obtain the maximum that each market segment is willing to pay for the product. These extra funds can be used to repay developmental costs or to finance expansion into large volume markets. Another advantage of a skimming price is that it helps to restrict sales at a time when the firm may be unable to keep up with customers' orders. A policy of slowly lowering prices to expand sales makes it easier for the firm to increase production capacity to meet the growing demand.

One of the strongest arguments for a skimming price policy is that it generally is the safest and most conservative approach available. By starting with a high price the firm can find out how much customers are willing to pay for the product while retaining the ability to lower price if competitive conditions make this necessary. If the firm should accidentally set a price that is too high, it can always be reduced, whereas a price that is too low may be difficult to raise.

The main disadvantage of a skimming price policy is that the high margins usually attract competitors into the field. This suggests that a skimming price is best used when the product has patent protection or there are other barriers to entry such as technical know-how or high capital requirements. For example, DuPont thought it had patent protection when it introduced its leather substitute Corfam at a high initial price. However, competition moved in fast with close substitutes and DuPont eventually lost $80 million on this product. The high price kept Corfam out of the volume markets that were needed to break-even.

A successful application of a skimming price strategy occurred with the introduction of electronic hand-held calculators in the early 1970s. When the sets were first introduced, retail prices were well over $300 and they were clearly designed for businessmen and other professionals. As competition increased, prices were gradually reduced to the point where some models now sell for less than $10. The price reductions opened up a vast market among the general population and the resulting economies of scale led to

---

[27]Joel Dean, "Pricing Policies for New Products," *Harvard Business Review,* Vol. 28 (November-December 1950), pp. 28-36; "Pricing a New Product," *The Controller* (April 1955), pp. 163-65.

further cuts. In this particular case, the price reductions were helped along by significant technological breakthroughs in the manufacture of the integrated circuits used in the calculators. By finding ways to improve the yield of good chips, the unit cost curve (or learning curve) dropped sharply with increased volume. Although price reductions are usually not as spectacular as they have been with the calculators, the general principle of broadening markets by gradually lowering prices holds for many lines of goods.

Penetration Price

A penetration price is an aggressively low price designed to open mass markets quickly. It is based on the assumption that demand for the product is highly elastic such as shown by the curve $D'D'$ in Figure 8-5. The implication is that sales will respond dramatically to relatively small changes in price. Penetration pricing also assumes that there is no elite market that can be exploited with high initial prices. Under these conditions, a high price (P^4) may actually result in zero sales (Figure 8-5). In addition, penetration pricing assumes that the high volume associated with the low introductory price (P^5, Q^5) will lead to significant savings in production costs. Indeed, penetration prices frequently require that a large volume be sold before profits can be produced.

Penetration pricing is a high-risk strategy that can lead to losses if sales do not live up to expectations. Another problem is the low margins suggest it will take longer to recoup development expenses than it would with a skimming price policy. Penetration pricing is frequently encountered in situations where there is a strong threat of potential competition. In this environment, penetration prices are designed to capture such a large share of the market that competitors will have a difficult time catching up. In addition, penetra-

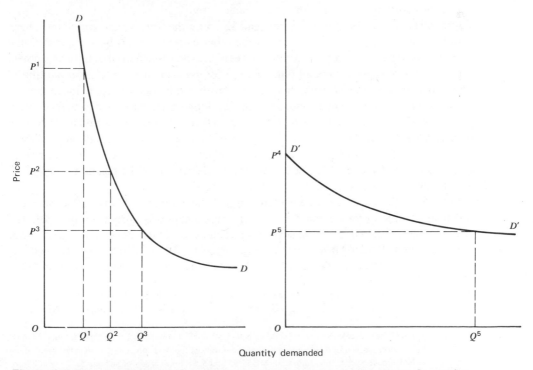

Figure 8-5 Demand Curves Assumed by Skimming and Penetration Price Strategies.

tion prices are set so low that competitors will be discouraged from entering the market by the lack of adequate profits. This strategy is especially effective when new firms must make substantial investments to bring out a competitive product. Penetration pricing can also be used in situations where research and development expenses are low and competition is strong. Under these circumstances, penetration pricing may be the only way for products (such as new beverage or cake mix flavors) to break into the market.

An example of effective penetration pricing was provided by the introduction of the first Mustang automobile in 1964. This new product was designed for the inexpensive sporty car market and could have been priced anywhere up to $3000. Instead of a skimming price policy, Ford brought the car out at a very aggressive price of $2368. At this price Ford was able to sell 400,000 Mustangs the first year and achieved a dominant market position that it maintained for the next four years. The low introductory price undoubetdly slowed the entry of General Motors, who did not bring out a competitive car until 1966. While it is obvious that a low price was not the only factor contributing to the success of the Mustang, it certainly helped to increase the potential market for this car.

Intermediate Pricing

While skimming and penetration pricing provide the basic alternatives for new products, they are only guides and cannot be applied in all situations. Under certain conditions, an intermediate price may be the best choice. The pricing policies used by the Polaroid Corporation for their first camera and film provide a classic example. The Polaroid camera was the first to provide the user with a finished print one minute after the picture was taken and the company enjoyed strong patent protection. The revolutionary character of the camera, the large potential market, and Polaroid's desire to recoup its development expenses all favored the use of a skimming price policy. Since the production costs were about $30 for the camera and $.50 for the film,[28] introductory skimming prices of $195 for the camera and $2.25 for the film at retail would have been entirely reasonable for the first year. At the other extreme, it has been estimated that Polaroid could have covered its promotional expenses and returned all of its development expenses in five years with retail prices of $65 for the camera and $1.22 for the film.[29] These low penetration prices do not include a profit and if adopted would mean that the project would not make money until after the development expenses had been recovered. A third possibility was to adopt a mixed strategy whereby the camera would be priced at a relatively low $65 with the idea of making a profit on the film at $2.25. Polaroid did not follow any of these strategies, but instead brought out the camera at a retail price of $89.75 and the film at $1.66. These prices were clearly above the penetration level yet well below the prices that could have been charged.

Polaroid's choice of intermediate prices can be partially attributed to the weak financial position of the company at the time the camera was introduced in 1949. The company had sustained losses for several years and was not in a position to wait three or four years for penetration prices to become profitable. Also, the firm was concerned that a high skimming price might have to be reduced during the first year, something they

---

[28]The actual costs of the camera and film are unknown, but were less than the $33.25 and $.57 figures reported in Milton P. Brown, Wilbur B. England and John B. Matthews, *Problems in Marketing* (New York: McGraw-Hill, 1961), p. 612.

[29]The calculation of these break-even prices is described in Milton P. Brown, Wilber B. England, and John B. Matthews, *Key to Problems in Marketing* (New York: McGraw-Hill 1961), pp. 164-5. Since the break-even prices were calculated with artificially high costs of $33.25 and $.57, retail prices of $65 and $1.22 would have actually recovered the development costs in less than five years.

wished to avoid. In addition, Polaroid wanted to keep the price of the camera under $100 where it would appeal to the larger amateur market. An unanswered question is whether an established camera company would have introduced the product at the same price.

More recently, Polaroid has made effective use of both skimming and penetration prices in the introduction of new products. For example, in 1969 Polaroid brought out its 360 model with an electronic flash at a high skimming price of $199.50 and in 1972 introduced the SX-70 model at $189. At the other end of the scale they introduced the zip camera at a very low penetration price of $13.95. These prices are obviously designed to expand sales in previously untapped sectors of their demand curve. The choice of an appropriate pricing strategy for new products thus appears to depend on the objectives of the firm as well as an appraisal of the competitive environment.

ENVIRONMENTAL PRICING FACTORS

Up to this point we have focused our attention on the immediate demand and cost factors that influence pricing activities in single product firms. There are, however, a number of other considerations that frequently influence pricing decisions. These include the effects of multiple product lines, distributor's margins, competitive reactions, and legal constraints imposed by governmental bodies. All of these factors tend to modify profit and revenue maximizing prices derived from an analysis of demand and cost data.

Product Line Pricing

When a firm has several items in its product line, prices must be set to maximize the sales or profits for a whole line of products. This can be difficult because margins vary and some items may have to be carried at a loss to round out a line or satisfy a particular class of customers. Also, some items are purchased simply because they are high priced. Status-conscious buyers often acquire expensive products to enhance their prestige among their peers. Cadillacs, for example, only cost General Motors a few hundred dollars more to build than Chevrolets, but they are priced $2000 higher to appeal to those who want distinctive transportation. Perfume, liquor, watches, and clothing are also sold at a variety of price levels so those who want to pay more for something different will have the opportunity to do so.

Products marketed by a single firm sometimes have interrelated costs and a price increase for one item may raise the costs of other products. A further complication is that the sales of one item may be influenced by the price charged for a second product in the line. For example, a price increase for product A might be associated with a rise in the sales of product B. This positive cross-price elasticity indicates that consumers considered the two items to be substitutes. A negative cross-price elasticity would indicate that the products were complementary and typically sold together.

Examples of cross-price elasticities estimated for a line of three consumer goods are shown in Table 8-4. The industry price elasticity for product one (-3.53) suggests that this new item was quite sensitive to price changes. The data also show that five of the six cross-price elasticities (CP_{ij}) were negative suggesting that the three products were complementary. Further analysis revealed that the three company brands were substitutes for competitive brands of related products. Thus, in this case company brands provided support for each other and competed with similar items sold by other firms.[30]

[30]David B. Montgomery and Glen L. Urban, *Management Science in Marketing* (Englewood Cliffs, N.J.: Prentice-Hall, 1969), pp. 173-74.

Table 8-4

Industry and Cross-Price Elasticities for Three Products

	Product One $j=1$	Product Two $j=2$	Product Three $j=3$
IP j[a]	−3.53	−1.58	−1.53
CP1 j[b]	—	− .28	.86
CP2 j	−1.33	—	− .55
CP3 j	− .22	− .32	—

[a]IP j stands for industry price elasticity for products one, two, and three.
[b]CPN j stands for cross-price elasticity between products one, two, and three. CPN $j < 0$ indicates complements.

Source. David B. Montgomery and Glen L. Urban, *Management Science in Marketing* (Englewood Cliffs, N.J. Prentice-Hall, 1969), p. 174. Reprinted by permission of Prentice-Hall.

The price elasticities from Table 8-4 were combined with cost data in a simulation to find the most profitable price level for each brand sold by the company. The simulation suggested that the company should take advantage of customer price sensitivities by lowering the price of brand one while raising the prices of brands two and three. Urban's success at measuring demand interrelationships suggests that managers no longer have to rely on rules of thumb for product line pricing.

Distribution Channel Pricing

The astute manager does more than just set factory prices for his products, he also adds a margin for distributors so he knows the planned selling price to the ultimate consumer. Total sales, after all, are influenced more by the final price the consumer pays than they are by abstract wholesale prices. The size of margins required by distributors usually increases with the complexity of the item and also depends on the type of product, the number and location of potential buyers, and the selling activities performed by the manufacturer. Small firms, with limited sales staffs, typically place greater reliance on the services of independent jobbers, wholesalers, and retailers and must allow fairly high margins to cover these activities. Large firms, on the other hand, may be able to operate their own wholesale and retail functions at lower margins than those required by independent distributors. As a general rule, the manufacturer must allow independent distributors at least as much margin as is available on similar items from other firms. Distributors are profit oriented and tend to push the products that make the most money. However, they usually gauge the profitability of an item by its margin and look unkindly at products that are supposed to generate profits through high sales and low markups.

New products frequently require extensive selling efforts on the part of distributors before they gain a respectable market position. One way for the manufacturer to obtain their cooperation is to offer higher margins than are available on other established products. Another problem with new products is that the margin needed for distributors may change as the product gains acceptance. For example, a firm may initially sell a new product directly to retailers in its immediate area to test consumer acceptance. If the product succeeds, wholesalers may be needed to expand distribution to other areas. It is important, therefore, that the manufacturer include a wholesale margin in his original retail price even if he does not plan to use wholesalers to introduce the product. If this is not done, the needed wholesale margin may have to be squeezed out of the manufacturer's profits, as it is often difficult to raise prices once a product is on the market.

Competitive Pricing

Most firms operate in a competitive environment and must consider the possible reactions of other companies when they set prices. This is less of a problem for the price leader who can use his dominant market position or low production costs to set prices to maximize profits. The typical firm, however, must devise a strategy that prevents competitive price changes from eroding his own sales and profits. One approach is to isolate your product from price competition through extensive advertising, the incorporation of special design features, or an emphasis on locational advantages. Certainly every marketing manager dreams of differentiating his product sufficiently to allow some pricing flexibility. If these tactics succeed, however, each product will vary in its susceptibility to price competition. This means that a single strategy will not work for everyone and each company must adapt to its own environment.

An example of a competitive pricing strategy employed by a large manufacturer is described in the flow diagram in Figure 8-6. The company sold a slightly differentiated product in an oligopolistic market. Price changes were initiated frequently by a few major firms and the several small private branders that make up the industry.[31] The basic policy of company X was to react to price changes instituted by other firms. The process begins in box 1 of Figure 8-6 with "Watch $Pwilt$," which means watch the wholesale (w) price (P) of the initiator (i) in each local (l) market at each time (t). If this price is the same as our price ($Pwxlt$), no action is taken. When the competitive price exceeds our price, it is followed if the district sales office (DSO) agrees (boxes 3, 4, and 5). If the district sales office does not want to raise the price, the decision maker (DM), who is the chief executive for the entire region, can raise the price if he thinks other competitors will raise theirs (Pwo, boxes 6 and 5). If the decision maker feels that the other major competitors will not raise their prices, a twenty-four hour waiting period is introduced (box 7). Price increases by major competitors that occur during this period are followed, otherwise no action is taken (return to box 1).

The procedure used by company X to respond to price cuts is somewhat more complex. When the market share of company X is smaller than that of the initiator, a price cut is more apt to be followed. Company X also attempts to prevent price cuts in local markets from spreading to nearby markets. A tendency for a price cut to lower prices in adjacent markets is called a "funnel" effect. The first response to a price cut is to check with the district sales office (box 8). If the district sales office is opposed to a price cut, a waiting period is introduced and the prices of the other major firms in the local market are observed for twenty-four to forty-eight hours (boxes 13 and 14). When the district sales office favors a price cut, the price is reduced if company X has a smaller share of the local market and if the quantity sold in the local market is greater than sales in the nearby market (boxes 9 and 10). In those situations where the nearby market is larger, company X will lower its price if its price in the local market exceeds its price in the nearby market (box 11) or if there is little chance that the price in the neaby market will decline (box 12).

This competitive pricing model was tested against thirty-one actual decisions made by company X and found to accurately represent their pricing procedures.[32] Also, the mean lag in responding to price increases was three days and only one day for price declines.

---

[31]The industry description and the procedures described in Figure 8-6 are similar to those encountered in pricing gasoline.

[32]J. A. Howard and W. M. Morgenroth, "Information Processing Model of Executive Decision," *Management Science,* Vol. 14, No. 7 (March 1968), pp. 416-28; a somewhat more detailed discussion of the alternative routes through the model is contained in W. M. Morgenroth, "A Method for Understanding Price Determinants," *Journal of Marketing Research,* Vol. 1, No. 3 (August 1964), pp. 17-26.

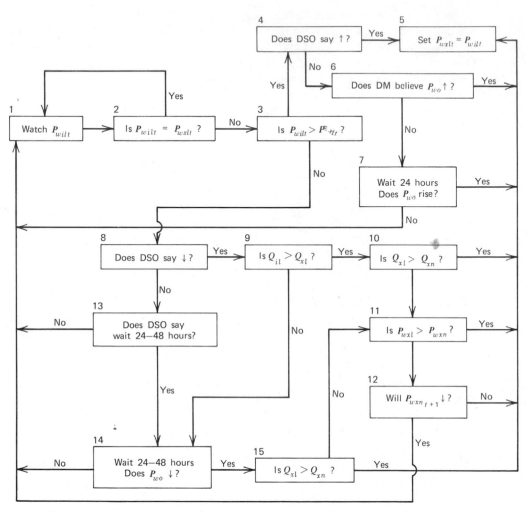

Symbols:

    P = Price

    w = Wholesale

    i = Initiator

    l = Local market wherein price change is being considered

    t = Time, at present

    x = Our company

  DSO = District sales office (distric sales manager)

    ↑ = Raise price

    ↓ = Drop price

  DM = Decision maker

    o = Other major competitors in local market

    Q = Quantity, i.e., sales volume in physical terms

    n = Nearby market with funnel influences

Figure 8-6 Model of a Competitive Pricing Process.
Source. John A. Howard and William M. Morgenroth, "Information Processing Model of Executive Decisions," *Management Science,* Vol. 14 (March 1968), p. 419. By permission of the publisher and authors.

This indicated that the company attempted to steal market share from those raising prices and tried to avoid the loss of market share when prices declined. The use of flow diagrams (Figure 8-6) in competitive pricing situations helps to simplify what may appear to be a complex decision process and makes it easier to modify the system to improve its efficiency. Once a workable model is created, simulation techniques can then be used to find optimum pricing strategies for each firm.

Competitive Bid Pricing

Competitive bidding is a specialized pricing procedure used in construction, industrial buying, and procurement by government agencies. The objective of the seller is to set prices low enough to get contracts and yet still generate an adequate profit. Since price is often a critical factor for the buyer, it is important to bid somewhat below your competitors. This means prices are set on the basis of what you expect competitors to bid, rather than on what the customer will pay or cost considerations. A number of models have been proposed to help executives produce better competitive bids. One model that has been used successfully at RCA utilizes information on buyer's preferences and the probable bids that will be submitted by competitors.[33] An example of some of the data needed is shown in Figure 8-7. This diagram shows the probability of winning a contract at a variety of differentials from the competitive price. The RCA model also requires that managers assign probabilities to all possible competitive bids. The probabilities of winning are then combined with the probability distribution of anticipated competitive bids to give an expected award probability (column 3, Table 8-5) that combines our expectations of how the buyer and our competitor will react.

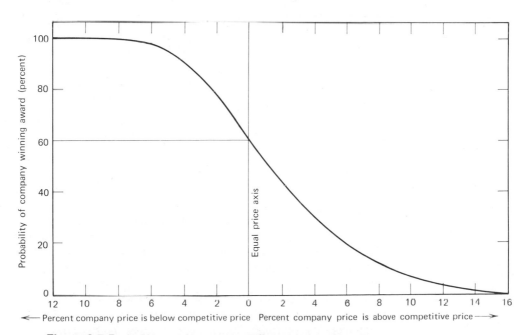

Figure 8-7 Probability of Success at Different Bid Differentials.
Source. Franz Edelman, "Art and Science of Competitive Bidding," *Harvard Business Review,* Vol. 43, No. 4 (July-August 1965), p. 56.

[33]Franz Edelman, "Art and Science of Competitive Bidding," *Harvard Business Review,* Vol. 43, No. 4 (July-August 1965), pp. 53-66.

Table 8-5

Summary of Bids, Probabilities, and Payoffs

Company Bid Prices (1)	Award Profit (2)	Expected Award Probability (3)	"Probability" Profit (4)
$44.00	$ 783,800	99.9%	$ 783,200
44.50	843,800	99.9	842,500
45.00	903,800	99.8	900,900
45.50	963,800	99.5	958,200
46.00	1,023,800	99.2	1,013,300
46.50	1,083,800	98.6	1,065,000
47.00	1,143,800	97.7	1,111,500
47.50	1,203,800	96.5	1,152,000
48.00	1,263,800	94.7	1,182,600
48.50	1,323,800	92.4	1,201,900
49.00	1,383,800	89.1	1,203,900
49.50	1,443,800	85.2	1,190,300
50.00	1,503,800	80.2	1,151,800
50.50	1,563,800	74.5	1,096,400
51.00	1,623,800	67.7	1,011,600
51.50	1,683,800	61.0	921,600
52.00	1,743,800	53.7	809,700
52.50	1,803,800	47.0	704,000
53.00	1,863,800	40.4	590,000
53.50	1,923,800	34.4	483,600
54.00	1,983,800	28.8	377,000
54.50	2,043,800	23.8	279,700
55.00	2,103,800	19.3	187,400

Source. Same as Figure 8-7 p. 56. Reproduced by permission.

Cost of failing to win contract:	$271,800.
At the optimum bid:	
Company price per unit	$48.81
Award profit	$1,361,600
Award probability	90.4%

The next step in the search for the optimum bid is to determine the award profits associated with each potential price (shown in column 2, Table 8-5). Award profits are calculated by multiplying the company bids by the number of units in the contract (120,000 in the current example) and subtracting the appropriate costs. One final item that must be considered is the dollar loss incurred if the firm fails to get the contract. Edelman suggests that the company described in Table 8-5 will lose $271,800 if the award is lost. This is *not* an opportunity cost but rather is contribution that will not be earned if the firm has to restrict its output due to the loss of the contract. Now the probability profit associated with each company price (column 4, Table 8-5) can be calculated using a marginal analysis where the expected gain is balanced against the expected cost. In the present example, a bid of $44 has a .99947 chance of generating a profit of $783,800 and a .00053 chance of losing $271,800.[34] Thus, the probability profit for the $44 bid is ($783,800 × .99947) minus ($271,800 × .00053) or

[34]Note that the expected award probabilities in column 3 of Table 8-5 have been rounded to three digits, but the probability profits shown in column 4 were calculated using five-digit probabilities.

$783,240.[35] Similar calculations for other bids gave the probability profits shown on the last column of Table 8-5. Note that the maximum profit occurs somewhere between a bid of $48.50 and $49. A search of all possible bids in this range reveals that the optimum bid in this example is $48.81 giving an expected profit of $1.36 million.

The efficiency of the RCA bidding model has been tested against traditional bidding procedures. In seven actual cases, bids were prepared in the normal manner while the same information was fed to the bidding model. The conventional method lost the contract in four cases, but all seven of the model bids were lower than the competition. In addition, the model bids were only 2 percent, on the average, under the lowest competitive bid. Thus, the use of the model would have resulted in a greater volume of business at a higher margin of profit than could have been obtained using the regular bidding process. This discussion suggests that bidding models can and in many cases should be used to improve pricing in competitive bid situations.

Legal Constraints[36]

Marketing managers should be aware that a number of attractive pricing strategies are illegal under various federal and state laws.[37] Unlawful activities include price fixing, price discrimination, deceptive pricing, and unfair pricing. Although price fixing is frequently used by international cartels to maximize profits, it is strictly illegal in the United States. The courts have consistently found that agreements among firms to set prices are per se violations of section 1 of the Sherman Act. This means that there is no defense on economic grounds and the government only has to prove that there was intent to fix prices to obtain a conviction. Almost all horizontal price agreements among competitors are illegal as well as many vertical arrangements between manufacturers and dealers.[38] Criminal penalties for those convicted of collusive price activity may include a maximum fine of $50,000 for each violation or a prison term of up to one year, or both. The government may also bring civil actions to stop collusive price agreements, force diversiture of subsidiaries, and even dissolve companies.

Perhaps the most serious penalty for price fixing is that injured customers may file a civil suit and collect triple damages. For example, in the famous electrical equipment case, twenty-nine firms were fined a total of $11 million, forty-four executives were fined $137,500 and seven executives were sent to prison for fixing prices and rigging bids.[39] However, these penalties were small compared to the hundreds of millions of dollars that were paid by the electrical companies to settle damage claims filed by customers. General Electric alone was reported to have paid $225 million in claims from 1961 to 1965.[40] Although the penalties in the great electrical conspiracy were spectacu-

[35]The $40 difference between the calculated value and the value shown in column 4 of Table 8-5 is due to rounding.

[36]A more detailed discussion of legal constraints on pricing can be found in A. D. Neale, *The Antitrust Laws of the United States* (Cambridge, England: University Press, 2nd ed., 1970).

[37]These include the Sherman Antitrust Act (1890), Federal Trade Commission Act (1914), The Clayton Act (1914). Robinson-Patman Act (1936), Miller-Tydings Act (1937), and various state laws such as the Illinois Antitrust Act (1965).

[38]Horizontal price fixing is legal when it is carried out under government sponsorship as in regional milk marketing orders, in regulated transportation industries, or in farm cooperatives.

[39]R. A. Smith , "Incredible Electrical Conspiracy," *Fortune,* Vol. 63 (April and May 1961), pp. 132-137+ and pp. 161-164+.

[40]"Antitrust," *Time* (September 10, 1965), p. 82.

lar, many price fixing cases are settled out of court.[41] Trade associations of gasoline dealers, for example, are frequently caught manipulating retail prices and allowed to sign consent decrees indicating they will stop the illegal pricing activity. In other situations, the government will permit firms caught fixing prices to plead no contest. This leaves the company liable for criminal penalties, but makes it more difficult for injured parties to collect damages because they must prove that the antitrust laws were violated. In light of the potential fines, jail terms, legal fees, damages, and loss of good will that can result from price fixing, there appears to be no valid justification for any firm to ever engage in this activity.

Price Discrimination. Price discrimination is an attractive pricing strategy that can boost volume and profits by taking advantage of differences in customer price sensitivities. Unfortunately there are legal constraints on price discrimination based on the Robinson-Patman Act that make it unlawful to discriminate in price among buyers of commodities of like grade and quality where the effect is to lessen competition or create a monopoly. The law was passed in the 1930s as the result of intense lobbying by the Retail Druggists' Association. Independent merchants wanted to protect themselves from price competition by making it illegal for manufacturers to offer better prices to chain buyers. The Robinson-Patman Act is a classic example of special interest legislation and probably has kept retail prices higher than they would have been without the law.

Interpretation of the Robinson-Patman Act by the courts has been rather confused.[42] This is due partly to the vagueness of the law and the number of legal defenses that are available. The Robinson-Patman Act specifically recognizes a cost defense that allows the seller to charge different prices based on variations in the cost of manufacturing, selling, or delivery. In addition, the law allows marketing managers to meet the equally low price of a competitor when the price differentials are temporary, localized, and defensive. It is also legal to discriminate in price when a product is sold for *different uses,* when *separate* markets are involved so there can be no injury to competition, and when sales take place at different points in time. Functional discounts offered to wholesalers and retailers may differ as long as all members of a group receive the same price and there is no injury to competition. Finally, all sales made in intrastate commerce are not covered by the federal legislation.

Despite the many defenses that may be used, companies have found it difficult to justify their behavior as legal price discrimination in a court of law. Even the cost defense, which would appear to be relatively easy to use, requires the maintenance of expensive and detailed records with no assurance that the government will accept the accounting methods used by the company. The confusion has been increased by the large number of different interpretations and rulings that have been made by both the Federal Trade Commission and the courts. Even judges are uncertain as to what constitutes a violation of the Robinson-Patman Act.[43] Under these circumstances it is no wonder that price competition has been discouraged and many firms rely on nonprice competitive techniques. Thus, while the antitrust laws encourage competition by prohibiting price

[41]Neale notes, for example, that 72 percent of the civil actions brought by the government in the period 1935-1955 were terminated by consent settlements, op. cit. p. 381.

[42]Detailed discussions of price discrimination and the Robinson-Patman Act are contained in Donald V. Harper's *Price Policy and Procedure* (New York: Harcourt, Brace & World, Inc., 1966), pp. 100-121 and Corwin D. Edwards, *The Price Discrimination Law: A Review of Experience* (Washington: Brookings Institution, 1959).

[43]In *United States vs. New York Great Atlantic and Pacific Tea Company, Inc.,* et. al., 67 F. Supp. 626, 677 (1946) a judge stated "I doubt if any judge would assert that he knows exactly what does or does not amount to a violation fo the Robinson-Patman Act in any and all instances."

fixing, the Robinson-Patman Act tends to protect *competitors* by restricting the firm's ability to vary prices. Fortunately for the businessman, most price discrimination goes undetected by the government and there is hope that some day this law (R-P Act) will be repealed. Until then, firms who wish to maximize profits by varying prices for different groups of customers, should be familiar with the rulings of the Federal Trade Commission and the courts regarding the current status of price discrimination.

Deceptive Pricing. Some unscrupulous marketing managers occasionally attempt to raise their profits by using deceptive pricing techniques. A typical procedure is to mark merchandise with an unusually high price and then claim that the lower selling price actually used represents a legitimate price reduction. Deceptive pricing works because many consumers are ignorant of actual price levels and are attracted by apparent bargains. The practice is usually employed at the retail level although manufacturers may contribute by premarking merchandise with unrealistically high prices. Deceptive pricing exploits the uninformed and cannot be defended on legal or ethical grounds. The Federal Trade Commission has attempted to control deceptive pricing by prosecuting violators and by publishing guides against deceptive prices. The guides list activities that are considered to be illegal and suggest that sellers not claim a price reduction unless it represents a saving from the usual retail price. Because of the vast number of products and firms involved, the Federal Trade Commission has to rely on voluntary compliance by businessmen and complaints by consumers and competing businesses to control deceptive pricing.

Where abuses have been particularly flagrant, Congress has responded with special legislation. For example, in 1958 Congress enacted the Automobile Information Disclosure Act requiring automobile manufacturers to preticket new automobiles. The objective was to prevent deceptive pricing by preventing dealers from "packing" or raising normal retail prices to allow for unrealistically large trade-in allowances. The law requires the manufacturer to post a price list on each car showing the suggested price of the automobile, additional equipment, and transportation charges. However, the Justice Department has attacked General Motors' posted window prices as being deceptive since the cars actually sell for several hundred dollars below the manufacturer's suggested prices. The passage of the Truth in Lending law (1969), has helped reduce the deceptive pricing of credit by requiring disclosure of credit charges and the true annual interest rates paid by buyers.

State Fair Trade and Unfair Sales Acts. Two other forms of state legislation that have influenced pricing decisions are the fair trade laws and the unfair sales acts. Fair trade, otherwise known as resale price maintenance, allowed manufacturers to make agreements with dealers to charge specific prices for their products. However, only a few states had enforceable fair trade laws and President Ford and members of Congress recently criticized the laws as a brake on the economy.[44] As a result legislation to repeal fair trade was recently passed by Congress. This means that vertical pricing agreements between manufacturers and dealers will be no longer enforceable.

About thirty-two states have "unfair sales" acts designed to prevent sales below cost.[45] The objective of these laws is to prevent large retailers from destroying their

---

[44]*Wall Street Journal* (Feb 14, 1975), p. 1.
[45]These states include Arizona, Arkansas, California, Colorado, Connecticut, Hawaii, Idaho, Kansas, Kentucky, Louisiana, Maine, Maryland, Massachusetts, Minnesota, Montana, Nebraska, New Hampshire, New Jersey, North Dakota, Oregon, Pennsylvania, Rhode Island, South Carolina, Tennessee, Texas, Utah, Virginia, Washington, West Virginia, Wisconsin, and Wyoming. See *CCH Trade Regulation Reports*, pp. 35,002- 35,008, 1970.

(smaller) competitors by selling at extemely low prices. Nineteen states specify minimum legal markups ranging from 4 percent in Pennsylvania to 12 percent in Arizona. Six percent is the most frequently specified retail markup and compares with a 2 percent minimum wholesale markup required in fourteen states. The primary tactic outlawed by unfair sales acts is pricing leader items below cost to build customer traffic. Most of the laws, however, do allow sale below cost when the objective is to meet the low price of a competitor or clear out perishable and seasonal merchandise. Enforcement of the unfair sales acts tends to be lax because state attorneys general do not prosecute unless they receive a complaint from an injured merchant. Some states have laws designed to prevent dealers from selling milk, cigarettes, and liquor below cost.[46] Unfair sales acts designed for specific items seem to be more effective than the general purpose laws. This may be due to more rigorous enforcement, vigilance by members of the trade, easier detection of violators, or the serious financial threat posed by the possible loss of licenses required to sell specific items, such as liquor.

Unit Pricing. In recent years consumer advocates have lobbied for the passage of state laws requiring stores to label merchandise with the cost per unit of measure in addition to the total price. For example, with unit pricing a consumer would know that a 6.75-ounce tube of toothpaste priced at 59¢ costs 8.7¢ per ounce. Because of the many brands and sizes of products carried in retail stores unit pricing would make it easier for the economy-minded consumer to identify the lowest cost items. Usually unit price labels are printed by a computer and are pasted on store shelves beneath each product. Unit pricing is widely used in grocery stores for meat, produce, and dairy items, but it is less often employed for other packaged merchandise.

When unit pricing was a hot issue in 1970 and 1971, several studies indicated that about one third of the shoppers were using unit price labels when they appeared in stores.[47] A more recent report revealed that less than 2 percent of shoppers were using the labels and it is possible that consumer interest has declined.[48] The cost to the retailer of installing a unit price system have been estimated to run between $800 and $1000 per store plus up to $1000 per store per year to keep the labels up to date. This amounts to less than $1/10$ of 1 percent of sales for large chains, but may amount to $4/10$ of 1 percent for smaller stores.[49] Because of the burden these costs place on small businesses, unit pricing laws in Connecticut, Massachusetts, Rhode Island, Vermont, New York City, and Seattle exempt smaller stores.

While it is clear that unit pricing offers benefits for shoppers, its impact on retailers and manufacturers is more obscure. If only one retailer in an area installed unit pricing, then he might be able to attract enough new customers to pay for the system. However, if all stores are required by law to use unit pricing, then total sales are apt to remain constant while costs increase. Unit pricing can raise retail profits when a significant portion of the merchandise is sold under the retailer's own labels. Under these conditions, unit pricing may shift consumers from higher priced national brands to the higher margin brands owned by the retailer. In addition, retailers who have installed unit pricing systems have found they produce tighter inventory control, better space management, and fewer

---

[46]Cigarette sales below cost are illegal in twenty-two states, milk in thirteen states, and liquor in five states, see *CCH Trade Regulation Reports,* pp. 10, 055, October, 1967, 35, 002-35, 008, 1970.

[47]James M. Carman, "A Summary of Empirical Research on Unit Pricing in Supermarkets," *Journal of Retailing,* Vol. 48, No. 4 (Winter 1972-73), pp. 63-71.

[48]Donald O. Schnuck, "Unit Pricing-Current Public Policy Issue," *Conceptual and Methodological Foundations of Marketing,* Thomas V. Greer, ed. (Chicago: American Marketing Association, Proceedings Education Conference, Series No. 35, 1974) p. 460.

[49]James M. Carman, op. cit., pp. 67-68.

price-making errors.[50] Another factor encouraging the growth of unit pricing is the gradual conversion of supermarkets to electronic-scanning check stands. These automated checkouts require printed shelf labels for all products and it is a simple matter to add unit prices to these labels. Thus, in spite of the costs and shopper apathy, supermarkets will probably continue to expand their use of unit pricing to show their support for the consumerism movement and to sell a little more store label merchandise.

Unit pricing does not appear to offer the national brand manufacturer anything but trouble. With unit pricing, shoppers can easily identify the most economical brands and sizes of products and national brands may lose volume to store labels. If the national brand manufacturer cuts prices to meet this threat, he is apt to reduce his profits. The national brand manufacturer could respond by taking on more private label customers himself, but this is typically a low-margin business. Perhaps the best response for the national manufacturer is to differentiate his product on the basis of quality or special features and then communicate these differences through advertising to the consumer.

Governmental Regulation of Prices

Prices that are set by governmental commissions are known as regulated prices. Normally price controls are reserved for "natural monopolies" such as the telephone, electrical, and natural gas industries where regulation is felt to be necessary to protect the interests of the consumers. Pricing in these industries consists of preparing documents for governmental commissions to explain why price increases and decreases are necessary. Since profits cannot exceed a fixed return on investment, pricing emphasizes revenue maximization rather than finding out how much customers are willing to pay. In recent years the federal government has adapted the principle of price regulation to help combat inflation. In 1971, for example, President Nixon froze all price increases[51] for a period of ninety days and then introduced a price commission to rule on what subsequent price increases should be allowed. These wage and price controls differed from the usual procedures because they applied to virtually all goods and services and lasted three years. The general price controls set maximum prices or percentage increases and businessmen were still free to boost sales by cutting prices.

Although regulated prices are often introduced with the noble objective of restraining inflation and monopoly power, they can lead to serious problems if they remain in force over extended periods of time. Considerable experience with price controls in other countries suggests that price controls are difficult to administer. One problem is that a small group of bureaucrats can never have enough information to set equitable prices and businessmen will quickly find ways to circumvent the controls. Perhaps the most obvious solution for the businessman is to stop selling products that price controls have made unprofitable. This could shorten product life cycles as businessmen emphasize new products where profit margins are higher. A less drastic response is to simply reduce the quality of products that are not producing adequate profits. Thus, while the government can set maximum prices for goods and services, they cannot guarantee that product quality will be maintained.

Perhaps the most serious problem with price freezes and controls is they can have disastrous effects on the supply of goods and services made available for sale. For example, the 1971 general price freeze began in August when the price of fuel oil for

---

[50]Kent B. Monroe and Peter J. LaPlaca, "What are the Benefits of Unit Pricing?" *Journal of Marketing*, Vol. 36 (July 1972), pp. 16-22.

[51]Price increases for raw agricultural commodities were not affected by the freeze.

heating was at a seasonal low and the price of gasoline was at a seasonal high. As a result, refineries found it profitable to produce large quantities of gasoline and shortages of fuel oil began to appear in the winter months.[52] Also, the government kept the price of natural gas so low in the 1950s and 1960s that producers cut back on their exploration for new reserves. Thus, while the low prices benefited customers, they also increased demand and helped reduce the supply of natural gas available for sale.

One of the most dramatic examples of supply problems caused by price regulation occured during President Nixon's sixty-day price freeze introduced in the spring of 1973. Because retail prices for chicken were fixed while feed costs were allowed to increase, farmers began to kill baby chicks rather than lose more money by raising them to maturity.[53] In addition, flour mills and food companies caught between rising costs of raw materials and fixed selling prices began to close down their factories. Thus, price controls that are designed to halt inflation lead to shortages and the call for more government action to ration diminishing supplies among buyers.

In addition to setting prices that are too low, government regulators sometimes set prices too high and restrict the demand for goods and services. A classic example occurred several years ago in the air travel market between Los Angeles and San Francisco. The large carriers, who operate under federal regulations, were charging $25 for one-way jet service between the two cities. PSA airlines came along with some used turboprops and installed a very competitive $11.20 one-way fare. PSA could charge this ridiculously low rate because they only flew within the state and were not subject to federal price regulations. The net result was a fantastic increase in the number of people who wanted to fly between the two cities and PSA was forced to add extra flights and buy more planes to keep up with the demand. The point of the story is that the air travel market between Los Angeles and San Francisco would never have developed as rapidly if the federal government had controlled the fares for all airlines flying between the two cities.

Pricing and Inflation

In periods of rapid inflation businessmen must pay careful attention to the pricing of their merchandise if they expect to maintain their normal profit margins. During the 1974 model year, for example, auto manufacturers had to raise car prices five or six times just to cover increases in labor and raw materials. Instead of the usual practice of projecting costs at the beginning of the year and setting a price for the next twelve months, the auto companies were forced into a game of catch up. Inflation places a premium on up-to-date cost figures and businessmen who have computerized information systems are in a better position to adjust prices to include inflationary changes.

Inflation can cause serious problems when companies decentralize pricing authority and allow field salesmen to shave posted prices to get orders. Under these conditions, salesmen do not have current cost figures and are apt to book a lot of unprofitable business. To control this problem many firms are centralizing pricing authority and forcing salesmen to check with headquarters before they depart from posted prices.[54] Since inflation raises the cost of working capital, the emphasis is on pricing to make a profit on current volume rather than pricing to maximize revenue.

Another effect of inflation is that firms become reluctant to quote prices on goods for

[52]"Nixon Lets Heating-Oil Imports Rise," *Louisville-Courier Journal* (January 18, 1973), p. A-4.
[53]"Food Shortages Loom as Firms, Farms Cut Output Under Phase 3½," *The Wall Street Journal* (June 28, 1973), p. 1.
[54]"Pricing Strategy in an Inflation Economy," *Business Week* (April 6, 1974), pp. 43-49.

future delivery. To protect the manufacturer on items with long lead times, customers are often asked to accept escalator clauses on their orders. For example, one-third of the industrial companies in a recent survey reported they are routinely using escalation clauses in their long-term contracts.[55] This means the buyer is quoted the current factory price and when the merchandise is shipped the price is raised according to the change in a standard wholesale price index. Some firms go even further and say that future prices will be determined on the date of delivery. Inflation thus distorts pricing relationships and increases uncertainty in an area of business that is already riddled with superstition and black magic.

Summary

Pricing is one of the basic components of the marketing mix and it is essential that marketing practioners understand the different pricing options that are available to the firm. If a company is fortunate enough to know demand, then it is fairly easy to set prices to maximize profits, revenues, or physical output of the firm. In the more typical case where demand data are scarce, the firm can set prices on the basis of costs. Perhaps the simplest approach is to use standard markup percentages to convert known costs into selling prices. Another technique divides costs into fixed and variable components and calculates the breakeven volumes associated with alternative prices. Cost data can also be manipulated to give prices that generate predetermined rates of return on the funds invested in the product. Where companies are operating at less than capacity, prices are sometimes set between variable and full costs to increase the contribution to the firm. Although cost-oriented pricing methods have a seductive quality, maximum profits are not likely to be obtained without some consideration of demand. In situations where firms face capacity limits and customer demand varies over time, peak-load pricing can lead to greater efficiency. This technique depresses peak demands for goods and services and encourages off-peak consumption, thus lowering capacity requirements and increasing utilization of facilities. Demand is often measured in terms of price elasticity and the firm must understand the effects of price changes when elasticity is less than, equal to, or greater than minus one. The ideal pricing system combines estimates of costs and price elasticity to obtain profit maximizing prices for the firm. Once a balance has been struck between cost and demand variables, the firm must temper its pricing decisions with data from the external environment. This means prices should not violate the numerous federal and state laws designed to protect competition and the consumer. It also means that unless the firm has a monopoly, it must consider the present and potential pricing activities of competitors. Knowledge of competitive pricing is particularly important where purchases are made on the basis of bids and price may be the deciding factor. Finally, the businessman should recognize his social responsibilities and avoid pricing techniques that tend to mislead or deceive the public.

Questions

1. If a retailer had product costs of $20 and he wished to make a 40 percent margin on his selling price, what selling price would he charge?
2. A refrigerator is produced at a cost of $200 to the manufacturer. On this cost is added

[5]*Business Week* (September 21, 1974), p. 109.

a margin of 35 percent and the refrigerator is shipped to an independent wholesaler. The wholesaler then adds a 20 percent margin based on his selling price. What would be the cost to the retailer? If the retailer then charged the consumer $675, what margin had he employed on his selling price? On his cost?

3. What is the break-even volume for a product with the following:

Fixed cost	$100,000
Variable cost/unit	$3.50
Selling price/unit	$4.00

   Is this type of analysis beneficial? Why or why not?

4. Two partners invest $40,000 to purchase a small production firm. If they make 20,000 units at a total cost of $30,000, what must their selling price be to return 14 percent on their investment? In larger firms, is cost data accurate?

5. Defend or criticize this statement: variable cost pricing below *full* cost is a short-run tactic inherently unprofitable.

6. A price decrease of $10 on a $200 television resulted in an increase in volume of 21,000 units. If the original volume was 300,000 units, what is the price elasticity of demand?

7. Given the price elasticity of demand in problem 6 and the following data, was the price decrease a wise move to increase profits?

Fixed cost	$21 million
Variable cost	$120/unit

8. What are some of the factors that must be considered when adopting a pricing approach for a new product?

9. Is product line pricing really of much concern to most manufacturers and marketers? Why or why not?

10. Do you feel legislation such as the Robinson-Patman Act is unhealthy for competition? Is the protection of the small retailer justifiable?

11. A price of $70 has an expected award probability of 95 percent on a desired contract for 10,000 units. If the cost of failing to win the contract is $100,000, what is the "probability" profit for this bid?

12. A federal price fixing case against five pharmaceutical companies revealed that tetracycline capsules costing 1.6¢ each were sold at retail for 51¢ and more each. Is this markup too high for a lifesaving drug? What factors should determine the markup for drug items? What markups for the manufacturer, wholesaler, and retailer would you recommend for a drug item with variable costs of 1.6¢ per capsule at the factory?

Case 8-1
E-Z-Tach Products Company[1]

In January, 1971, George Good and Howard Johnson, partners of the E-Z-Tach Products Company, were considering reentering the fishing sinker

[1]This case was prepared by Keith C. Good under the supervision of Professor Subhash Jain of the Univeristy of Dayton. Copyright © 1971 by the Department of Marketing, University of Dayton. Reproduced by permission.

market. The company withdrew from the market in 1960 and, since that time, inflation had caused the material and manufacturing costs to increase faster than the retail selling prices of sinkers. If the company were to reenter the market, they would have to decide what product lines to offer and how they should be marketed.

HISTORY OF THE COMPANY

The company was founded in 1951 at Miamisburg, Ohio, by George Good and Howard Johnson after they jointly designed the E-Z-Tach Sinker. Sinkers are weights attached to the fishing line that assist in casting the bait into the water and pulling the bait beneath the surface. Both partners were working full time for a large industrial company at the time they developed the E-Z-Tach Sinker and they devoted evenings and Saturdays to the company's operations. Manufacturing labor was primarily supplied by the owners and their families. At the peak of operations, however, six persons were employed.

Marketing activities were planned and executed by Mr. Good and Mr. Johnson with the occasional assistance of an advertising firm. The sinkers were first distributed by the owners to retail outlets located in the immediate area.

As volume increased, one wholesaler was used to distribute products in the eastern United States and a second in the state of Kentucky. The owners distributed products in Ohio on weekends. The sales achieved through the two wholesalers were not enough to support the expenses of the partners' growing families and they elected to continue in employment and slowly withdrew from the fishing sinker market in 1960.

In February, 1970, Mr. Good retired and he and Mr. Johnson were now considering reentry into the fishing sinker market. They felt that a partner working full time in the business could make it a successful operation. Since the E-Z Tach Sinker was the exclusive product of the company, and since its patent was to expire in the not-so-distant future, they considered this their last chance to become successful with their invention.

PRODUCT

The E-Z-Tach Sinker was unique and offered several advantages over all other sinkers. The main advantage was it could be assembled to the fishing line without tying any knots. This reduced assembly time and the line did not have to be cut to change the size of the sinker. Rerigging the line to change methods of fishing was also much faster and easier. Another advantage was the size of the weight could be changed by removing one part of the E-Z-Tach Sinker and replacing it with a different size weight. This provided flexibility for the fisherman using baits that required different amounts of weight. The changing of weights also required much less time than conventional sinkers.

The E-Z-Tach Sinker was composed of three parts as shown in Exhibit 1. The lead weight was manufactured with a threaded hole that accepted the screw. A noncorrosive brass screw was threaded on one end and had a square head on the other end that was undercut to accept the fishing line. The third part was a red plastic cap that was durable but soft enough to protect the line with a square hole that accepted the brass screw. To attach the E-Z-Tach Sinker to a fishing line, the user had to (a) place the line in the groove of the brass screw, (b) pull the plastic cap up over over the line, and (c) tighten the screw securely to the lead weight (Exhibit 1).

There were two lines of E-Z-Tach Sinkers. The major line was a set of seven sinkers packaged in a blue plastic box with a transparent lid. These sinkers came in various sizes ranging from one-tenth ounce to one ounce. Because of the interchangeability of weights, four caps and screws were provided in the box with seven weights. The plastic box had become popular with fishermen, for it could also be used for other tackle such as fish hooks. Twelve boxes of sinkers were packaged in a display carton for sale to the retailer.

E-Z Tach Sinkers were also sold separately. With bulk sales, a cap and screw were assembled to each weight and the merchandise was displayed in a refillable pastic box. The bulk product allowed the fisherman to purchase the size he used most frequently, instead of purchasing the entire set. Some retailers did not like the bulk sales because of the cost of handling low price items separately and the increased risk of shoplifting.

PRICING AND COSTS

The E-Z-Tach Sinkers were first introduced in 1952 and the retail price was established by using local test markets and comparisons with other products. The retail price was established at $.59 for a set of seven sinkers that was approximately 30 percent higher than the price of an equivalent number of conventional sinkers sold in bulk (no plastic box). Due to the desirable features of the E-Z Tach Sinkers, the market was expected to bear the higher selling price. The price to the retailers was $.337 per box, which provided them a margin of $.253 per box (43 percent of the selling price). A 40 percent profit margin was standard in the industry and the retailers were satisfied with the margin on E-Z Tach Sinkers.

After the E-Z-Tach Products Company withdrew from the market in 1960, the costs of manufacturing

Exhibit 1
E-Z Tach Promotional Literature

the sinkers rose approximately $.10 per set as shown in Exhibit 2. To offset the increased material and the labor costs, Mr. Good and Mr. Johnson were considering the following cost reductions:

1. Replace the twelve-cavity mold with a twenty-four cavity mold costing $1500 to reduce the cost of caps to $.0043 per cap.

2. Replace the brass screw with a nylon screw at the cost of $.012 per screw.

3. Replace the plastic box with a small heat-sealed plastic bag at a cost of $.001 per bag. This reduced bulk would allow eighteen bags to be packaged in the display carton.

4. Eliminate assembly of the cap, screw, and

weight at a savings of $.017 per set. This assembly would be required on bulk-sold sinkers, however.

Since the E-Z-Tach Sinkers were successful in 1960 priced 30 percent above competition, Mr. Good and Mr. Johnson felt that the current selling price could be adjusted accordingly. However, a recent market survey revealed that one competitor was presently packaging a set of ten various-size sinkers in a plastic bag at $.49. As a result, it was felt that the selling price of a set of E Z Tach Sinkers could not be raised above $.59. However, more flexibility existed with bulk sinkers and individual E-Z-Tach sinkers could be approximately 30 per cent above competition as shown in Exhibit 3.

In the case of bulk sales, each plastic refillable bulk box cost $.50 and would last approximately two years before having to be replaced. Based upon the average sales per retail store, the cost of the bulk trays amounted to $.0005 per sinker.

SINKER MARKET

Due to the small size of the E-Z-Tach Products Company, no extensive market research could be justified to determine the exact potential for the company's sinkers. However, Mr. Good recently obtained data on the fishing market from the public library and he felt that this would give some idea of the actual United States fishing sinker market.

Exhibit 4 shows the average annual expenditure of the sports fisherman in the United States. A sports fisherman was defined as a person over 12 years old who fished an average of three days a year. Sinkers would be classified as fishing equipment and the average fisherman spent $12.18 on these supplies in 1965. Based on these data and his fishing experience, Mr. Good estimated that each fisherman would use the equivalent of one box of E-Z-Tach Sinkers each year or seven sinkers. The reason for replacing sinkers was that they were usually lost when the fishing line was broken by a fish or an underwater obstruction.

The second piece of available information was the number of fishing licenses sold in the United States. Exhibit 5 presents the annual sales of fishing licenses from 1961 to 1970 in selected states and the total United States.

Using these market data, it was estimated that the annual market potential in the United States was in excess of 29,000,000 sets of seven sinkers. When the E-Z-Tach Products Company was previously operating, they had captured approximately 25 percent of the sinker market. Mr. Good estimated that in

five years, the company could have 10 percent of the total United States market. This would be accomplished by concentrating marketing efforts on high volume areas where 25 percent of the market could be obtained while spending little or no effort in other areas of the United States.

With this volume, the existing manufacturing facilities would be utilized at near full capacity. The required annual general and administrative expenses were estimated to be $12,000. The manufacturing equipment and tools currently in operating condition had been already written off the company's books. Mr. Good estimated that the cost to maintain the existing equipment would be $1000 per year and it would be equally distributed over six different pieces of equipment.

DISTRIBUTION

Because of the size of the E-Z-Tach Products Company and its limited line of products, Mr. Good did not believe that an E-Z-Tach Product Company sales force would be successful. To achieve market penetration and enough volume for a profitable operation, Mr. Good was considering the use of wholesalers of fishing tackle as the distribution channel.

Recent contacts with two wholesalers revealed they would require 12 percent of the retail selling price to handle the product. This was about the same as the charge in 1950s. At $.59 per box of sinkers, their charge would be approximately $.071 per box. Mr. Good felt that the price to the retailer would have to remain the same to produce dealer interest. One wholesaler expressed great interest in the E-Z-Tach Products Company's lines of sinkers.

QUESTIONS

1. Do you agree with Mr. Good's estimate of market potential and how will this influence the pricing decision?
2. What does a break-even analysis of costs suggest about selling prices?
3. Can the E-Z Tach Products Company afford $.071 per box for the wholesalers?
4. Which, if any, of the cost reductions should be implemented?
5. What prices should E-Z Tach Products Company set for consumers, retailers, and wholesalers?

Exhibit 2

Manufacturing Costs of E-Z-Tach Sinkers

Item	1955		1971	
	Unit Cost	Cost Per Set	Unit Cost	Cost Per Set
Cap	$.0050	$.0200	$.0075	$.0300
Screw	.0140	.0560	.0280	.1120
Weight	—	.0280	—	.0420
Plastic box	.0280	.0280	.0350	.0350
Display Carton (Holds 12 boxes)	.0700	.0058	.1000	.0083
Fabrication and assembly labor	.0049	.0342	.0074	.0517
Total cost per set		$.1720		$.2790

Source. Company records.

Exhibit 3

1971 Prices of E-Z-Tach Sinkers and Major Competitors

Product	Sinker Size	Selling Price	
		E-Z-Tach	Competitor
Set	Various	(Set of 7 in box) $.59	(Set of 10 in bag) $.49
Bulk	1 oz	$.16	$.12
	3/4 oz	$.13	$.10
	1/2 oz	$.10	$.08
	3/8 oz	2 for $.19	2 for $.15
	1/4 oz	2 for $.19	2 for $.15
	1/8 oz	$.07	$.05
	1/10 oz	$.06	$.05

Source. Company Records.

Exhibit 4

Annual Expenditures of Sport Fisherman
(Based on a sample of 18,000 Households)

	1960[a]	1965[b]
Boats and motors	$22.08	$30.00
General auxiliary equipment (tents, sleeping and cooking gear, clothes, etc.)	5.67	9.33
Fishing equipment	11.41	12.18
Total	$39.16	$51.51

[a]*Source. Statistical Abstract of the United States* (Washington, D.C.: United States Printing Office, 1962), p. 208.
[b]*Source. Statistical Abstract of the United States* (Washington, D.C.: United States Printing Office, 1968), p. 205.

Exhibit 5

Number of Fishing Licenses Sold in Selected States
(Thousands)

State	1961	1962	1963	1964	1965	1966	1967	1968	1969	1970
California	1,475	1,745	1,612	1,745	1,799	1,923	1,872	5,411	5,121	5,785
Indiana	709	754	726	747	727	689	617	652	696	721
Kentucky	328	316	321	347	362	388	414	440	461	476
Michigan	953	928	903	898	887	908	929	1,204	1,404	1,393
Minnesota	1,355	1,288	1,345	1,362	1,311	1,312	1,378	1,537	1,474	1,417
Missouri	657	691	654	701	665	704	763	1,244	1,273	1,328
Ohio	790	821	820	784	828	918	874	824	760	732
Tennessee	657	650	650	660	682	696	788	1,159	1,302	1,149
Texas	872	833	882	903	927	1,017	1,140	1,232	1,371	1,448
Wisconsin	1,080	1,060	1,049	1,017	1,097	1,052	1,128	1,144	1,122	1,246
Total U.S.	19.394	19,403	19,833	20,219	20,496	21,329	22,047	28,787	29,855	31,136

Source. Statistical Abstract of the United States (Washington, D.C.: United States Printing Office, 1963 through 1972).

Case 8-2
Aberdeen Electronics, Inc. [1]

The Aberdeen Electronics corporation was an industrial supplier of small electronic parts, switches, and subassemblies used by a wide variety of other manufacturing firms. The company prided itself on the quality of their products and their ability to manufacture to the precise specifications of their industrial customers. It was not unusual for the firm to design specific machinery, sometimes at considerable expense, in order to produce specialized parts for high-volume purchasers. The company "salesmen" were in reality highly salaried engineers who often acted as "troubleshooters" and were greatly respected by Aberdeen's customers.

One of Aberdeen's major customers was a producer of a varied line of electronic equipment and household appliances. This customer, Magnus Manufacturing, Inc., purchased a wide line of Aberdeen products. In the fall of 1971, Magnus had contracted with Aberdeen to purchase an intricate thermostatic switch to be used in conjunction with a government defense contract. The requested item, known as "Model K-50 subassembly," required

[1] This case was prepared by Barry J. Hersker, Professor of Marketing at Florida Atlanta University. Copyright © by Barry J. Hersker. Reproduced by permission.

that Aberdeen develop a specialized stamping machine and allied equipment that could not be readily used for any other purpose. Since the machinery in question required an investment of almost $250,000, including developmental costs, the decision to supply Model K-50 was not undertaken lightly.

At the time the decision was made, Magnus Manufacturing, based on their government contract, agreed to purchase "at least 10,000 units of K-50 yearly" at "a price not to exceed $16.00 per unit." This purchase agreement was to extend for a minimum of five years, from 1972 through 1976.

Aberdeen estimated that the cost of production of K-50, including depreciation on the specialized machinery, would approximate this price. That is, Aberdeen expected to "break even" at approximately $16.00 per unit. On the other hand, the Magnus account was believed to be so important that Aberdeen undertook to produce this item as a "service" to Magnus at $16.00

At the time of this decision, the possibility of selling additional quantities of Model K-50 to other users in an effort to increase its profitability was considered to be "rather remote." On the other hand, it was pointed out that the capacity to dramatically increase output would exist, and such potential increased production would not require any additional investment in machinery or tools. The President of Aberdeen, Mr. Alfred E. Maxwell, who personally entered into the decision, remarked at the time, "You know, the longer I am in this business, the more I am convinced that nothing really goes to waste. If you keep anything long enough, it will find a use and a market. The K-50 may surprise us in the long run."

After one year's production of Model K-50, Aberdeen found that Magnus' purchases were slightly higher than their original estimate; they purchased 12,000 units in 1972. Even at this volume, however, Aberdeen estimated that only $.49 profit was realized per unit at a selling price of $16.00 each. At one point management had considered increasing the price to Magnus, but this idea was rejected for two reasons: first, the original sales contract specifically limited the price to an amount "not to exceed $16.00," and second, Magnus threatened that they would revise their product and substitute another device for the assembly requiring Model K-50 if a price increase over $16.00 became necessary.

A few days after the matter appeared to have been settled, an executive from Magnus offered to "renegotiate" the original sales contract. He said that Magnus might be willing to increase the price paid for K-50 by 10 percent, if Aberdeen would remove the volume requirement. That is, Magnus might be induced to pay more for K-50, if Aberdeen would release them from their obligation to purchase 10,000 units yearly until 1976. The Aberdeen executives rejected this offer, stating in a closed meeting that their investment in this product was too great to risk any decline in volume, even at a higher price. The incident began to cause some uneasiness among the Aberdeen executives, especially when Magnus began to reduce their orders during the first six months of 1973. However, the total purchases of K-50 in 1973 were ultimately 8000 units at $16.00 each.

Early in 1974, when Aberdeen attempted to remind Magnus of their agreement under the contract in an effort to guarantee purchase of 10,000 units per year, the entire matter was again opened for rediscussion. Magnus claimed that they had indeed fulfilled their obligations under the contract since they purchased "an average of 10,000 units in the 1972 and 1973 two-year period." Furthermore, Magnus contended that certain defective parts were found in the K-50 device, which might necessitate that the contract be voided in its entirety. Aberdeen acknowledged that some defect had occurred in one shipment of the K-50 device in the fall of 1973, but pointed out that these units were replaced free of charge.

Magnus countered that the defects had proven very costly to them, since the devices had already been assembled into a finished product before the error was discovered. They estimated that their direct losses, associated with the defective units, exceeded the cost of the units themselves by $20,000. Aberdeen offered to allow Magnus a credit for $10,000 to reduce this loss to Magnus, but Magnus countered that they would not simply be willing to accept $10,000 as full payment in this instance.

They demanded that Aberdeen should (1) immediately reimburse Magnus for $20,000; (2) improve their quality control to insure that this problem would not reoccur; (3) reduce the price of the K-50 unit to $15.50 each; and (4) admit that the contract should be interpreted as 10,000 units *average* yearly over the entire period of 1972 through 1976.

After considerable negotiation and discussion, it was agreed that Aberdeen should meet all of these demands by Magnus. This decision was based in some degree on the ambiguity that existed in the requirements under the sales agreement of 1971, but of greater significance to the Aberdeen executives was their determination to maintain the loyal patronage of the Magnus Manufacturing Corporation. The volume of their other purchases was considerable and as the President, Mr. Maxwell, again pointed out, "The machinery and equipment currently used on Model K-50 cannot readily be used for other production. It cannot be permitted to remain idle. We'll just have to go along with Magnus in this instance."

Mr. Alfred Horn, Assistant to the President, pointed out that the new selling price was "dangerously close to actual cost." (Exhibit 1 presents the cost data at a volume of 10,000 units, as supplied to the Aberdeen management one week prior to the meeting by Mr. Fred Shaw, Comptroller of Aberdeen Electronics.)

"I have done my homework, Al," replied Mr. Maxwell, "but we are not in a strong position on this. It is my decision to sell an average of 10,000 units annually to Magnus at $15.50 until 1976. That is, unless you have a better solution, Al." Mr. Horn did not offer any reply.

The price cut to $15.50 per unit became effective February 1, 1974. Purchases of K-50 by Magnus totaled 5500 units in the six-months period ending June 1974. It appeared that relations with Magnus once again were quite cordial and the sale of K-50 was expected to reach 10,000 units by the end of 1974.

In June 1974 the purchasing director of Rigbee

Controls, who was not a previous customer of Aberdeen, contacted the firm about an unusual requirement for subassembly for a thermostatic switch to be used in aviation equipment. Rigbee had been referred to Aberdeen by Magnus and it was apparent that considerable executive friendships existed between the Magnus and Rigbee Corporations.

The Aberdeen engineers discovered that if Rigbee would make minor changes in their specifications for the thermostatic device, the Model K-50 subassembly would adequately fulfill their requirements.

Rigbee was pleased with the Aberdeen suggestion and did determine that Model K-50 could fulfill their requirements. They asked Aberdeen to quote a price in quantities of 15,000 units annually and assured Aberdeen that they could contract for delivery in these quantities for several years to come.

Aberdeen reconfirmed the fact that ample capacity existed to expand production of K-50 to 25,000 units per year. Their comptroller. Mr. Fred Shaw, also furnished revised cost information to the Aberdeen management which indicated that production costs would be lower at this increased volume. (Exhibit 2 presents the cost data supplied by Mr. Shaw for a volume of 25,000 units.) The management was pleased that the potential volume increase would permit Aberdeen to receive a profit estimated at $3.68 per unit, and it was decided to offer K-50 to Rigbee at $15.50 each.

Aberdeen notified Rigbee that they would supply them with Model K-50 at a price of $15.50 per unit. Rigbee responded that they could not use Model K-50 at any price higher than $11.50 per unit. It appeared that they would be better off to substitute another apparatus entirely if that price could not be met. Although Rigbee admitted that it was unlikely that they would ever be a large purchaser of Aberdeen products other than Model K-50, they nevertheless urged Arberdeen to lower the price. The Aberdeen engineering staff confirmed the fact that Rigbee could not afford K-50 at more than $11.50 and, furthermore, that Rigbee's needs were such they would probably never purchase any other items from Arberdeen. Furthermore, they also confirmed that Magnus would not use more than 10,000 of the K-50 units annually, no matter how low Aberdeen set the price of K-50.

At a meeting of the president and the vice-president of Aberdeen the renewed problem of K-50 production was again discussed at length. One vice-president said that maybe the Rigbee price would be acceptable, since increased volume lowered production costs enough to offset the small loss from the sale of K-50 to Magnus at $15.50. "You're not suggesting that we sell to Rigbee at $11.50 and to Magnus at $15.50, are you?" exclaimed Mr. Ernest Bennett, the Vice-President of the Sales Division. "This line of reasoning is out of the question. Rigbee and Magnus are friends. How would Magnus react if we charged them, our good customer, more than we charge Rigbee? This conduct is highly questionable on both a legal as well as an equitable basis!"

Mr. Maxwell interrupted the dispute, and asked the Vice-President of Sales for his specific suggestions on the matter.

"Well, let's look at it this way," Mr. Bennett continued. "K-50 has been an apparent loser since 1971. The reason? Sales volume was too low! Here we've got the chance to add 15,000 more units, and that's not all. I have reason to believe that we could sell still another 25,000 more units if this product were priced realistically!"

"What's this? I've never been told of such a potential," said Mr. Maxwell, with some surprise.

Mr. Bennett continued, "The specifications of K-50 are such that I believe they lend themselves to a wider range of industrial applications than we previously assumed. Five more of our current accounts would be willing to buy this item that would, I believe, push our volume to 50,000 units per year. This is, admittedly, our current productive capacity, but I feel sure we could reach this level within one year."

"Mr. Bennett, your job is to sell our products, so I assume you have reason to believe that the business is there," Mr. Maxwell interrupted, "but, although I have always felt K-50 was a good item, may I inquire why we have not exploited this market potential long ago?"

"Well, to hit a capacity volume of 50,000 units, we need to offer K-50 at a competitive price. If we can sell the item to all our customers for $10.00 each, I know this volume can be reached," Mr. Bennett responded.

"Pardon the interruption," broke in Mr. Horn, "wouldn't this mean we would suffer a loss of $5.51 per unit?"

"I have asked the Comptroller to bring the detailed cost data with him for capacity volume. While this is admittedly out of my area of responsibility, I do believe that the feasibility of my suggestion deserves your consideration," Mr. Bennett continued.

Mr. Fred Shaw, the Comptroller, was the next to speak. "Ernest, I'm sorry that I did not have time to go over this with you in greater detail before. It's true that we would have a declining cost situation present if we reached 25,000 or even the 50,000 capacity you described. But these savings are not as great as you evidently assumed. I have prepared a detailed cost schedule to make it easier for us to view the situation at capacity volume. This schedule presents our unit costs and charges at the 50,000 unit level of K-50 production.''

"Labor charges per unit are constant, since this is a machine operation and output varies directly with the time of the run. We can experience some economies on material by purchasing in larger quantities. Our yearly total material charges jump from $15,200 at 10,000 units to $37,000 at 25,000, saving $.04 per unit at 25,000 and $.04 more at the 50,000 unit levels. Similarly, plating charges are less in larger quantities. Our subcontractor will be able to plate the necessary components at half the price if we hit 50,000 units. But this only saves us $.05 per unit over what we pay now. And then, too, we must remember that capacity volume will require more frequent servicing. We'll lose some ground here—$.03, to be exact, between 25,000 and the double machine time required for 50,000 units of output. But of course, that is only an added expenditure of $1500.''

"You'll have to slow up, Mr. Shaw, I'm afraid this gray head can't absorb your calculations quite so quickly,'' Mr. Maxwell interrupted.

"I'm sorry, Mr. Maxwell—perhaps I'd better distribute the data. If we sell and produce K-50 at a capacity output, our costs per unit only fall to $10.56. I've itemized this in detail for you at Mr. Bennett's request on the cost sheet I've prepared for each of you.'' (At this point, Mr. Shaw distributed the cost data presented in Exhibit 3.)

"Perhaps I'd better summarize what Mr. Shaw appears reluctant to point out,'' interjected Mr. Horn. "He is saying that Mr. Bennett would have us lose $.56 on every item of K-50 we sell at this 50,000 volume! Or at least we would, in fact, lose $.32 per item, if we even sell to Rigbee and hit a total of 25,000 units!''

"But not if we average out—I say sell to Magnus at $15.50 and to Rigbee at $11.50!'' added another executive.

"That is out of the question!'' interrupted Mr. Bennett.

"Gentlemen, let's have a little order at this meeting,'' interjected Mr. Maxwell.

"Mr. Maxwell has the right idea—I say just sell only to Magnus as a favor at $15.50 and let the sleeping dogs lie,'' added Mr. Horn.

"That's does it; I'll not preside over a 'free for all!' And stop putting words in my mouth, Mr. Horn!'' angrily exclaimed Mr. Maxwell. "Ernest, we here at Aberdeen have an obligation to our stockholders as well as to our customers. It appears that perhaps I was the one who made all the decisions on the K-50 from the very beginning. So I'll make

this one, too. But first, I want to review all of the facts personally this evening. Gentlemen, I want all of you here in my office tomorrow at 9:00 A.M. sharp. This meeting is adjourned!''

QUESTIONS

1. Did Aberdeen handle the dispute with Magnus over contract volume, defective units, and the $.50 price reduction on the K-50 unit adequately?
2. Should Aberdeen sell the K-50 unit to Rigbee and/or Magnus? If so, what prices would you recommend? Why?

Exhibit 1
Cost Schedule Model K-50 Subassembly

Units costs at production volume of 10,000 units (dollars)		
Labor[a]	3.18	
Material[b]	1.52	
Plating[c]	.10	
Indirect charges[d]	.48	
Depreciation allowance[e]	4.00	
Overhead[f]	1.06	
Total factory production cost		10.34
Selling and administration charges[g]		5.17
Total costs per unit @10,000 units		15.51

[a]Combined man-hours of machine time directly allocated to each K-50 unit.

[b]Including some prefabricated parts and metal stock, with allowances for scrap value on waste residual stampings.

[c]Several components of K-50 are plated to increase resistance to corrosion. The subcontractor charges $.10 per unit at a volume of 10,000 units.

[d]Indirect charges include supplies, repairs, and routine maintenance on specialized equipment, electric power, etc., expressed on a per unit of output basis.

[e]Depreciation is straight line basis over the life of the Magnus contract less residual value, computed per unit of output.

[f]Allocation to cover fixed factory overhead burden, charged at the rate of 33.3 percent of direct labor.

[g]Allocation to cover selling and administrative expenses, charged at the rate of 50 percent of total factory production costs.

Exhibit 2
Estimated Cost Schedule
Model K-50 Subassembly

Unit costs at production volume of 25,000 units (dollars)		
Labor	3.18	
Material	1.48	
Plating	.08	
Indirect charges	.48	
Depreciation	1.60	
Overhead	1.06	
Total factory production cost per unit		7.88
Selling and administration charges		3.94
Total costs per unit @25,000 units		11.82

Exhibit 3
Cost Schedule Model K-50 Subassembly

Units costs at a capacity output of 50,000 units (dollars)		
Labor	3.18	
Material	1.44	
Plating	.05	
Indirect charges	.51	
Depreciation	.80	
Overhead	1.06	
Total factory production cost per unit		7.04
Selling and administration charges		3.52
Total costs per unit @ 50,000 units		10.56

Case 8-3
Geochron Laboratories, Inc.[1]

Mr. Robert Lemer, President of Geochron Laboratories, Inc. was developing a marketing plan to introduce a rock age-determination service to potential customers. Mr. Lemer believed that one of the most important questions facing Geochron was what price should be charged. Since no such service was currently available, there were few indications of what people might be willing to pay for age determinations or what affect different prices might have.

COMPANY BACKGROUND

Geochron Laboratories had been incorporated to operate a commercial geochronological laboratory. Initially, the company planned to concentrate on commercial determinations of the age of rock and mineral samples by potassium-argon isotope analysis. Geochron was in the process of raising funds to build and operate a laboratory and management anticipated that the company would be in full operation in six months.

[1]This case has been prepard by Philip McDonald of Northeastern University. Copyright © by Philip McDonald. Reproduced by permission.

POTASSIUM-ARGON AGE-DETERMINATION

Potassium-argon isotope analysis is a means of determining the geologic age of rock samples. Potassium 40 is a radioactive isotope and, over time, decays into argon 40, an inert gas. By studying the ratio of the argon isotope to the potassium isotope, it is possible to determine the age of rock or mineral samples in the age range of one million to five billion years.

Since potassium is a common ingredient of natural rock formations, potassium-argon age determinations are feasible for a wide range of rock types including micas, glauconites, amphiboles, and pyronenes.

Techniques for potassium-argon isotope analysis had been developed by academicians and nonprofit research organizations. While these techniques were not patentable, the equipment required to perform such analyses was expensive and analyses required a high degree of skill and professional competence.

Geochron management estimated that currently there were fewer than twenty laboratories possessing potassium-argon facilities in the United States and Canada. Most of these were owned and operated by universities or governmental departments. Four major oil companies were believed to operate their own age-determination laboratories. Geochron management believed that, in general, these facilities were inadequate to meet the needs of the sponsoring institutions. The lab operated by the Geological Survey of Canada, for example, was believed to limit permanent staff members to only one analysis per year.

Mr. Kruegar, Technical Director of Geochron, stated that none of these labortories would perform potassium-argon age determinations for geologists[2] not associated with the institution operating the labortory. Thus, it was impossible for most practicing geologists to obtain potassium-argon age determinations.

According to Mr. Kreuger, the primary uses of age determinations were in regional geological areas and in local petrological studies. The information provided by these age determinations[3] was used by academic geologists and governmental geological agencies to initiate or corroborate geological hypotheses, as a part of new investigating techniques and as an aid in the improvement of multi-dimensional geological appraisals.

Mr. Kruegar believed that the use of age determinations by mining and oil companies was limited by the newness of the techniques, the lack of commercial facilities, and a lack of research into practical applications. However, he felt in the future that age determinations would be valuable to mining and oil companies in their exploration and development work. He added that with the use of age determinations it would become possible to direct mine development or mineral exploration programs with more efficiency and less money than would otherwise be the case.

THE DEMAND FOR AGE DETERMINATIONS

While negotiations for funds were under way and work was begun on the construction of Geochron's laboratory, Mr. Lemer focused his attention on the development of plans for obtaining customers for the age-determination service.

Prior to the formation of the company, Mr. Lemer had conducted a market survey in an attempt to obtain some gauge of the potential demand for a potassium-argon age-determination service.[4] The survey consisted of a short mail questionnaire and a cover letter, which was sent to a sample of 500 geologists.[5] A copy of the questionnaire is shown in Exhibit 1.

Of the 210 respondents to the questionnaire, 41 percent indicated that they would utilize the proposed potassium-argon age-determination service at a price between $300 and $600 (Exhibit 2). This price range had been indicated by Mr. Lemer on the questionnaire, since he did not believe that potential customers would be able to assess their usage of the service without some reference to price. The specific range of $300 to $600 had been determined after a brief estimate of laboratory operating costs indicated that a minimum of 200 to 300 analyses per year would result in profitable operations.

The 87 questionnaire respondents who indicated that they would utilize the age-determination service estimated an average annual requirement of 2.5 determinations or a total of 225 per year (Exhibit 2).

While favorable responses to the questionnaire convinced Mr. Lemer that the demand for Geochron age-determination service would be above break-even, he was uncertain of the effect that a high or low price might have on demand. Many respondents, while indicating that they would use the service, had commented on the high cost.

While there was no established price for potasium-argon age-determinations, Mr. Lemer had heard that the University of Minnesota, which operated a potassium-argon labortory had, on at least two occasions, dated rock specimens for private individuals at $400 per sample. This price, however, was considered a "favor" both by the university and the geologists for whom the work had been done.

A related rock-aging technique, the carbon-14 radioactivity method, which was used for dating samples under 60,000 years of age was currently available commercially. Carbon-14 aging, which was a much simpler and less costly process than potassium-argon aging, had originally been priced at $800 per sample. As the market developed, the price

---

[2] The term geologist in used to include all professionals with a technical interest in age determinations (petrologists, mining and geological engineers, etc.)

[3] The number of age determinations for particular jobs varied substantially with the nature of the study being undertaken. In some instances, one or two analyses would be adequate; in others, or more age determinations were required.

[4] At that time, Mr. Lemer was a student at the Harvard Business School and his market survey was severely limited by time and financial restraints.

[5] Mr. Lemer estimated that there were about 50,000 graduate geologists in the United States and Canada. He believed that at least 5000 of them would be in a position to have funds available for such services as age determination.

had dropped gradually. Currently the price for a sample was generally about $200.

CAPITAL INVESTMENT AND OPERATING EXPENSES

To assist him in evaluating the effects of different levels of demand on profitability, Mr. Lemer requested that Mr. Altman, Geochron's treasurer, provide him with cost estimates for various levels of demand. Mr. Altman indicated that the minimum fixed-capital investment would be $90,500. This investment would equip a lab capable of handling up to 1000 samples a year. This estimate included $35,000 for a mass spectrometer, which could be used for an estimated 1500 analyses per year. Additional mass spectrometers could be purchased for $30,000. A variable capital investment of $825 for equipment would also be required for each 100 samples processed per year.

The average life of the equipment was estimated to be ten years. Exhibits 3 and 4 provide breakdowns of the fixed capital investment at different levels of activity.

Mr. Altman also provided estimates of the fixed and variable costs of operating the laboratory at different levels. These estimates are shown in Exhibits 5, 6 and 7. He cautioned that the estimates were rough and might vary upward or downward by as much as 25 percent.

Mr. Lemer believed that geologists would send samples to Geochron's lab for aging in the same manner that they would send a rock to an assay office for content analysis. Thus, he believed that Geochron's marketing effort should be directed toward informing potential customers of the availability of Geochron's rock aging service and convincing them that Geochron could perform accurate and reliable age determinations at a reasonable price.

Accordingly, a series of technical bulletins was planned. These bulletins, which would be written by Mr. Krueger, would cover technical questions of interest to geologists. They would also provide information on Geochron's rock-aging services and possibly suggest new applications for age determinations. The bulletins would be sent out on a more-or-less regular basis to a mailing of potential customers.

Geochron also employed one salesman, a geologist who had graduated from the Harvard School with Mr. Lemer. It was anticipated that much of his time would be spent visiting academic geologists and technical employees of oil and mining companies in an attempt to develop familiarity with Geochron's services throughout the geological profession. He was also expected to attend professional and trade conventions where he would discuss age determinations and provide literature on Geochron's age-determination service.

As a means of building trade familiarity with Geochron, Mr. Lemer planned to obtain promotional items to be distributed at conventions. Five thousand cloth rock-sample bags had been ordered. These bags would have Geochron's name printed on the outside and were expected to find continued use by field geologists.

A pocket-sized geological time scale was also to be distributed. It would present, in table form, the age ranges for common geologic structures as well as Geochron's address and the names of its technical director and salesman. A limited budget of no more than $1000 was also planned for advertising in trade journals.

QUESTIONS

1. What pricing alternatives are available to Geochron Laboratories?
2. Can the results of the survey be projected to a national market?
3. Given the cost and demand data provided in the case, what pricing schedule would you recommend to Geochron Laboratories?

Exhibit 1 Mail Questionnaire

Please Return to Geochron Laboratories
24 Blackstone Street
Cambridge, Massachusetts
Potassium-Argon Survey

This questionnaire is designed only to help us to determine your requirements. This is not a commitment on your part; we just want your best guesses. If you prefer to write us a note or letter rather than filling out this form, that would be equally helpful. You need not give your name unless you wish to.

1. Name _____.
   Address _____
   _____
   Specialty _____
   (Petrology, Sedimentation, etc.)

2. The exact cost per determination will depend very largely on the scale of operations that proves possible. We expect, however, that the charge will probably exceed $300, but will certainly be less than $600. Do you think you would utilize this service for potassium-argon age determinations?
   Yes_____ No_____ Probably _____
   As a rough estimate, how many determinations do you think you might require per year?_____.

3. Are there any other age-determination methods you would like to have available? Other uses of isotope analysis? Would you like us to provide a consulting service as well as the raw data?

4. Any additional comments, criticisms, or questions would be appreciated. Please use the reverse side if required.

Exhibit 2
Summary of Results of Mail Questionnaire

	Petrologists	Sedimentary and Oil Geologists	Geologists	Total
Questionnaires mailed	N/A	N/A	N/A	500
Questionnaires returned	46	40	124	210
Do you think you would utilize the service?				
Yes	31	20	36	87
No	15	20	88	123
Percent Yes (returns)	68	50	29	41
Percent Yes mailings	N/A	N/A	N/A	N/A
As a rough estimate, how many determinations do you think you might require per year?	79	51	95	225

Exhibit 3
Estimate of Fixed Capital Investment
(1000 Samples Per Year)

Mass spectrometer	$35,000
Vibrating reed	1,500
Electrical wiring	2,000
Air conditioner and dehumidifier	1,500
Water purifier	500
Binocular microscope	300
Petrographic microscope	1,000
Spectrophotometer	15,000
Gas outlets	500
Cooling, plumbing, acid-proof sink	2,500
Chemical glassware	1,000
Office equipment	2,000
Stationwagon	2,500
Sample preparation equipment	3,000
Electrical parts inventory	500
Organization expenses	2,500
Installation and contingencies	19,200
	$90,500

Exhibit 4
Estimate of Capital Investment at Different Volumes[a]

Annual Sample Volume	Fixed Capital Investment (Basic Lab Facilities)	Additional Mass Spectrometers	Variable Capital Investment	Total Capital Investment
0	90,500	—	0	90,500
1000	90,500	—	8,250	98,750
1600	90,500	30,000	13,200	133,700
2000	90,500	30,000	16,500	137,000
3200	90,500	60,000	26,500	177,000
4000	90,500	60,000	33,000	183,500
4800	90,500	90,000	39,500	220,000
5000	90,500	90,000	41,200	221,700

[a]Excludes working capital requirements.

Exhibit 5
Estimate of Fixed Operating Costs[a]

Selling and advertising expense	$ 9,600
Convention expense	2,500
Vehicle expense	3,000
Technical journals	500
Clerical expense	3,000
Administrative expense	30,000
	$50,600

[a]Excludes depreciation charges.

Exhibit 7
Estimate of Costs Directly Variable with Volume (Computed at 1000 Sample Volume)

Glass and electronic parts	$ 5,000
Liquid nitrogen	1,000
Chemicals	500
Utilities	3,500
Telephone	1,800
Equipment maintenance	2,000
Rent[a]	2,000
	$15,800

[a]Rent assumed fixed for each 1000-sample interval.

Exhibit 6
Estimate of Variable Operating Costs at Different Sample Volumes (Dollars)

Annual Sample Volume	Costs Directly Variable with Volume	Technicians				Taxes Other than Income	Total
		Argon Trains	K 40 Analysis	Argon Analysis	Sample Preparation		
0	2,000	6,000	6,000	6,500	4,500	8,900	33,900
1,000	15,800	6,000	6,000	6,500	4,500	9,900	48,700
1,599	25,300	6,000	6,000	6,500	4,500	14,000	62,300
1,600	25,300	6,000	12,000	6,500	4,500	14,000	68,300
1,999	31,600	6,000	12,000	6,500	4,500	14,700	75,300
2,000	31,600	12,000	12,000	6,500	9,000	14,700	85,800
3,199	50,600	12,000	12,000	6,500	9,000	19,800	109,900
3,200	50,600	12,000	18,000	6,500	9,000	19,800	115,900
3,999	63,100	12,000	18,000	6,500	9,000	21,400	130,000
4,000	63,100	18,000	18,000	6,500	13,500	21,400	140,500
4,799	76,000	18,000	18,000	6,500	13,500	24,000	156,000
4,800	76,000	18,000	24,000	6,500	13,500	24,000	162,000
5,000	76,000	18,000	24,000	6,500	13,500	25,500	166,500

Case 8-4
Sherwood Valley Logging[1]

The Sherwood Valley Logging Company was located in the town of Belmont Rapids at the head of Sherwood Valley on the western slope of the Cascade range in the Pacific Northwest. The company's Belmont Rapids office was managed by Mr. Thomas Watson, a forestry graduate from a prominent midwestern university. Mr. Watson had managed the Sherwood Valley Logging Company for the last ten years and had upheld his firm's reputation as a profitable timber buyer, logger, and road builder.

In early 1967 Sherwood Valley was faced with having to plan its raw materials acquisition schedule for the coming months. Mr. Watson was especially concerned this season because his chief timber cruiser, Bill James, had recently broken his leg on a skiing trip. Mr. Watson knew he could not look forward to his recovery for at least four months.

COMPANY BACKGROUND

Sherwood Valley Logging Company was founded by Mr. Watson's grandfather some sixty years ago. At that time the company's only assets were the timber it purchased. Over the years the firm expanded its operations so that by 1958 it owned a mill and several tracts of timberland. However, the mill was obsolete and the timber was somewhat depleted.

After his first year with the company Mr. Watson was able, in 1958, to foresee a trend toward increased demand for timber in conjunction with a decreased demand for milling operations. It was his contention that the company should specialize once again, as it had fifty years earlier, in timber purchasing. He also felt that the company could afford to set up an efficient logging operation that could compete with existing mills and independent loggers. In other words, Mr. Watson felt that Sherwood Valley could, through tight cost control, provide sawmills in his area with logs at a lower cost than the mills were providing themselves.

COMPANY OPERATIONS

By December 1966, following the course set in 1958, Sherwood Valley Logging Company had become the largest independent timber purchaser in the state. Annual timber requirements were about 100 million board feet (MMBM). In 1966 this volume was obtained from the following sources:

Private lands (company owned, on sustained yield)	12 MMBM
Privately owned timber (timberlands not owned by the company)	15 MMBM
USFS timber sales (total of six sales)	53 MMBM
BLM timber sales (total of three sales)	20 MMBM
	100 MMBM

Timber requirements in 1967 were expected to be similar to 1966 in regard to the volume of timber necessary to support Sherwood's current level of operations, but the mix was expected to change. Recently the company had sought to reduce the volume of logging done on a contract basis for other timber owners. This part of company operations had contributed very little to profits in 1966. Because of the increased competition from loggers specializing in contract logging, Mr. Watson hoped to reduce volume from this source to 10 MMBM or less in 1967. Since the volume coming from company-owned lands was somewhat fixed, the remaining volume would have to be made up by government sales.

Sherwood Valley attempted to keep an even balance between "cat"[2] and "hi-lead"[3] operations in order to give them greater flexibility in the scheduling of their equipment. Mr. Watson always attempted to buy several good winter jobs where he could keep a portion of his crew operating through the winter months. The company carried a large investment in road-building equipment and was primarily interested in sales that required a large amount of road construction. Mr. Watson believed that with the company's modern equipment, he

---

[1] This case is reproduced with the permission of its author, Dr. Stuart V. Rich, Professor of Marketing, and Director, Forest Industries Management Center, College of Business Administration, University of Oregon, Eugene, Oregon.

[2] A logging operation utilizing crawler tractors.

[3] A logging operation utilizing a cable system of logging. This system of logging is usually used on steep slopes where clear cutting of the stand is required.

could build road at a cost under the goverment allowances in some cases. Therefore, he was continually watching for sales that were well adapted to the company's equipment.

Mr. Watson had two right-hand men who assisted him in making timber and road cost appraisals. Bill James, a veteran timber cruiser, had worked for Sherwood Valley for many years. The company loggers had consistently cut close to Bill's estimate. This was a tremendous competitive advantages for the company, especially for Bureau of Land Mangement (BLM) sales where the timber was sold on a "cruise" basis. A "cruise" or lump-sum basis means that the purchaser pays a certain amount for the sale regardless of how much actual volume the sale contains. U.S. Forest Service (USFS) sales, on the other hand, are sold at a certain price per thousand board feet (MBM) for each species. The purchaser then pays this amount for the volume actually removed from the sale. Cruise refers to a statistical sample of a timber stand by volume and quality. Joe McAlpin was Mr. Watson's second right-hand man. Joe was a licensed logging engineer. Joe supervised the company's road contruction cost estimates on all the sales in which Mr. Watson was interested.

TIMBER BIDDING STRATEGY

Mr. Watson was a familiar figure at USFS and BLM timber sales. USFS sales featured open auction bidding and the buyers knew the outcome of each sale before the next parcel of timber was put on the block. Although he was not a consistently aggressive bidder, Mr. Watson was a strong competitor for sales in the Belmont Rapids drainage. Typically Mr. Watson was not interested in one third of the sales offered because of their low-volume, low-road-construction allowances, or because they represented sales in which the risk of a large loss was great but the probability of a good profit was small.

He was lukewarm on another third of the sales. Bill James would usually give these sales a 20 percent cruise and Joe McAlpin would walk the proposed road construction and come up with an estimated road-construction cost. Based upon Joe's and Bill's data, Mr. Watson would develop his bidding limit. On sales of this type, Mr. Watson limited his bidding to a price where he could make a 15 percent profit over his road-construction cost and a 10 percent on the appraised value of the timber. If time was pressing and Bill and Joe did not have time to study the sale, Mr. Watson would bid these sales to a maximum of 25 percent over the appraised price.

The final third of the government sales were the ones in which Mr. Watson developed the most interest. These sales were usually of large volume (greater than 6 MMBM) and fairly high road-construction allowances ($50,000+). Some of these would be low elevation, "hi-lead" logging operations with rocked roads that could be used for winter operations and were worth a premium bid just to keep the logging crews together and to keep the equipment busy. Occasionally a USFS sale was found at the higher altitudes in the drainage where Douglas fir was a minor species and where Bill's cruise was considerably below the USFS cruise for this species. High-elevation, old-growth Douglas fir is often defective and difficult to cruise. Bill had a lot of experience cruising this type of timber and in the past his cruises had proven to be quite accurate. In these cases Mr. Watson would bid very high on the Douglas fir but leave the off-species[4] at the appraised price. Mr. Watson's hope in this strategy was that the Douglas fir would underrun[5] the USFS cruise. Although he would pay a high price for the quantity of Douglas fir removed, he did not expect to remove the government cruise volume. (Since the sale is awarded to the bidder whose total bid, based on the government cruise, is the largest, this would have the effect of giving him a lower average purchase price on the off-species.)

Appraisal procedures on these "wanted" sales were quite detailed. Bill James would usually give these sales a 40 percent cruise and Joe McAlpin would make a detailed road-cost estimate. Mr. Watson would then take these data and, using current market prices for the logs, would develop a maximum paper bid. This bid would be computed in the following manner:

1. Compute the current market value of the logs.
2. Subtract the estimated road-construction costs.
3. Subtract estimated logging and slash-disposal costs.
4. Add the USFS road-construction and slash-disposal allowances.
5. Subtract 10 percent of the total logging and road-construction cost as an allowance for risk and profit. (This percentage, of course, might

[4]"Off-species" refers to those species within the sale that are usually not bid on, or that comprise a minor percent of the sale volume. In the Belmont Rapids region Douglas fir was most commonly the dominant species and hemlock, pine, noble fir, and cedar were off-species.

[5]Underrun is the amount by which the cruised volume exceeds the removed volume and is usually expressed in percent of the cruised volume. Overrun is the exact opposite.

vary as it represented Mr. Watson's evaluation of the risk inherent in a particular sale and also his profit desired from a particular sale.)

This final figure would then be the maximum amount that Mr. Watson could bid for the sale and still obtain a desirable return on logging and road-construction costs. Since the USFS road-construction and slash-disposal allowances were treated as a credit to the purchaser in the sale contract, Mr. Watson would first subract his estimated costs of road construction and slash disposal, and then add in the USFS allowance in order to adjust for any differences between the company's and the Forest Service's estimate. Sherwood Valley's competitors used a similar system for estimating their bid limits; however, the lumber and plywood mills usually calculated their realization values based on the final end product of the log.

COMPETITION

Competition had been increasing in the Belmont Rapids drainage for the last several years. Mr. Watson stated that there was a fairly close balance between the area's annual production capacity and the amount of timber sold by government agencies each year. Since the amount of timber placed up for sale each year by these agencies was controlled by their annual allowable cut, and since this volume was not expected to increase in the near future, any increase in production capacity in the local mills would likely increase competition. The entrance of bidders sponsored by exporters to the Japanese market had already affected competition in the area. Mr. Watson was quite concerned about reports that exports were expected to increase considerably over the next several years.

The Powers Corporation was Sherwood Valley's principal competitor in the Belmont Rapids drainage for sales that fell into Sherwood's "want" category. Powers was a well-established, large manufacturer of plywood, particle board, dimension lumber, and chips. Being a well-integrated mill, it possessed some cost advantages over the less sophisticated mills in the Belmont Rapids area. It could also fall back on its own timber if prices went too high on government sales. Powers was an especially aggressive bidder on sales that adjoined its timberland. This situation allowed Powers to haul to its mill on its own road network, and it could then use its off-highway trucks[6] to haul overloads, thus provid-

ing an additional cost advantage. Mr. Watson felt in this case it would be futile to bid against Powers, but he also realized, as did other bidders, that it was possible to "bid up a sale" before allowing Powers to win. This would tend to keep Power's cost structure more in line with the competiton. There were certain sociological norms within the industry, however, that restricted this practice. The feeling was that since everyone was competing for timber anyway, and since timber prices had climbed to almost unprofitable proportions, the "logical" company for the sale should be allowed to buy it with the implicit understanding that the favor would be returned. Mr. Watson expressed the feeling that on several occasions when a sale was a natural for Sherwood Valley, he had experienced in winning the sale a definite sense that the sale had been given to him. Because of this feeling, he had found himself reciprocating through restraint from bidding against companies he knew "had" to have a particular sale. Mr. Watson suggested that this sort of unspoken, implicit understanding was often responsible for keeping timber prices from being higher than they were.

CUSTOMERS

Sherwood Valley customers were primarily small to medium-sized sawmills, plus one large plywood plant. Mr. Watson felt that a good deal of the company's success rested on its ability to meet specific requirements in regards to log length and delivery times. He also felt that his pricing policy was fair during times of fluctuating log prices. Price agreements were generally made in one of two ways. The first, called "camp run," applied a straight or fixed price for all logs hauled off a sale or unit. The unit, a specified section within the timber sale, was the smallest lot size Mr. Watson liked to sell to any given customer. A contract was signed between the mill and Sherwood Valley for delivery of all logs (length and species specified) within the contract area at a set price, for example, $95/MBM, regardless of the actual grades logged.

Selling on a "graded" basis constituted 75 percent of the company's sales. Under this method of pricing, the mill pays for the logs it receives according to the species and grade of log. The price is prearranged and set under contract. Because of Sherwood Valley's good performance over the past

---

[6]Off-highway trucks are both overweight and overwidth for highway travel on public roads when loaded. For the timber owner with his own road system, this means a larger payload per trip with off-highway trucks. The cost saving, however, is not linear and depends on length of haul and quality of the haul road plus many other factors.

years, the company was often able to command a slightly higher price for its logs than the market would suggest.

BAYESIAN DECISION THEORY

The spring of 1967 saw Sherwood Valley in a rather comfortable financial position. However, to maintain that position it was necessary that the company be able to acquire additional timber sales at a price that would allow Sherwood to make a profit.

During the past winter Mr. Watson had enrolled at a nearby university in a night-school course concerned with formal planning techniques and their application to various business situations. The ideas of Bayesian decision theory[7] seemed to be very realistic to Mr. Watson, and he planned to adopt these ideas in his timber purchasing strategy in the hope that this would give him a more logical approach to bidding. The loss of Bill James for several months would impose an additional workload on Mr. Watson, and he hoped that these Bayesian techniques would alow him to utilize his information concerning future sales more efficiently.

Mr. Watson was on the regular mailing list for USFS and BLM timber sale notices. The BLM sales for the spring of 1967 consisted of fire salvage sales in a large area that had burned the previous summer. These sales were very restrictive in their harvesting schedules and therefore Mr. Watson was not interested in them. After examining the USFS sale data, Mr. Watson found eight proposed sales in the Belmont Rapids drainage that he felt deserved further field examination.

A closer look at these eight sales revealed three that fell into his "want" category. He was lukewarm on several of the other sales and felt that he would continue to apply his lukewarm bidding strategy to these sales. The three sales that Mr. Watson was interested in were Banion Butte, Cocho Valley, and Holmes Peak sales.

The Banion Butte sale was a 9 MMBM "hi-lead" operation with Douglas fir as the dominant species. Mr. Watson liked this sale because of the large timber volume, high road-construction allowance, and suitability for a late fall logging. This sale contained a high percentage of premium quality logs and

Mr. Watson expected that the Powers Corporation would be his principal competitor.

The Cocho Valley sale had a relatively low volume of timber, but it had a very high road-construction allowance. In addition, the haul to the expected buyer for the logs was very short. This sale was a "cat" show and covered a lot of acres for the sale volume. Mr. Watson wanted to pick up a "cat" operation to help utilize some of his logging cats,[8] and this sale would fit in well with his plans. The sale was composed primarily of low-quality Douglas fir, so Mr. Watson did not expect too much competition from the plywood mills.

The Holmes Peak sale was a high-altitude sale composed primarily of mountain hemlock. The sale included both "hi-lead" and tractor logging. The sale contract contained a special provision that required several of the units to be logged by rubber-tired tractors. Mr. Watson had recently leased such a tractor, and he felt this gave him a bidding advantage. This sale had another interesting feature. The Japanese were anxious to purchase so-called "white woods," such as hemlock and true fir, and these species commanded a premium price in the export market. Sherwood Valley had not as yet traded in this market, but Mr. Watson felt that the time was coming when he would have to sell to the Japanese if he wanted to remain competitive. This sale would allow him to "stockpile" logs suitable for this market and, therefore, would represent a chance for speculative gain.

Exhibit 1 shows a summary of pertinent data from the USFS prospectuses pertaining to these sales. Exhibit 2 shows the anticipated costs of logging these sales as estimated by Mr. Watson, and also Joe McAlpin's estimated road-construction costs. Exhibit 3 lists the latest market prices for each grade of each species.

Mr. Watson was also able to obtain from the USFS a study of 116 timber sales that showed the ratios of the winning bid price to the USFS appraised price. Although this information was two years old, Mr. Watson felt that it would still be relevant, since timber prices had been relatively steady over this time period. Mr. Watson then transformed this frequency distribution into an accumulated probability distribution of winning bid ratios. This table is shown in Exhibit 4.

Mr. Watson felt he "had" to win the Holmes Peak timber sale. He knew that bidding on this basis

---

[7]A thorough discussion of Bayesian decision theory may be found in Paul E. Green and Donald S. Tull, *Research for Marketing Decisions,* (Englewood Cliffs, N.J.: Prentice-Hall, 1975), Chs. 1 and 7.

Appendix A of this case contains an introduction to Bayesian decision theory.

[8]Logging cats are tractors that are rigged for logging operations as opposed to tractors rigged especially for road construction. In addition, tractors used for logging are generally smaller than those used for road construction.

was a dangerous practice, since it would be almost impossible to show a profit on the sale if he bid up to a bid-price ratio that would "guarantee" his winning the sale. In order to explore the profitability of this bidding approach versus several other bidding strategies, Mr. Watson formulated two bidding strategies for each sale. He would then use a Bayesian decision tree with subjective prior probabilities to determine the expected profitability resulting from each combination of strategies. His final decision would be to adopt the combination that would yield the highest expected profit. Mr. Watson wished to evaluate the following two bidding strategies for each sale:

1. *Actively bid on the sale.* Mr. Watson would bid to a bid-appraised price ratio that would give him a 10 percent profit margin on his logging and road construction costs.
2. *No profit bid.* Mr. Watson would use this approach to increase his chances of winning a sale. His goal using this strategy would be to continue to employ his crews and equipment thus reducing his losses. He would bid to a bid-appraised price ratio that would give him a zero percent profit margin on his logging and road-construction costs.

Mr. Watson knew that Sherwood Valley Logging Company would experience certain losses if it did not win either of the last two sales. Certain equipment already contracted for could be used only on these sales and could not be utilized if the firm won only the Banion Butte sale. However, some of the equipment could be shifted between the Holmes Peak sale and the Cocho Valley sale. In addition, Mr. Watson had made some commitments with mills that would require timber from Holmes Peak or Cocho Valley. Therefore, Mr. Watson identified costs associated with losing the last two sales. These costs are shown below:

1. Lose only Cocho Valley sale $15,000
2. Lose only Holmes Peak sale $30,000
3. Lose both sales $55,000

Mr. Watson would have to incorporate these losses into his decison making.

Since Mr. Watson felt that the third sale was a must, he wanted to consider an additional strategy. That is, if the firm lost both previous sales he wanted to consider bidding to limit his loss on the Holmes Peak sale to 5 percent of the road and logging costs. This was a desperate strategy but he wished to consider it along with the other two strategies. Possibly, he thought, it would be cheaper to take a 5 percent loss on the sale rather than take the $30,000 loss

from not employing his equipment and meeting his contracts (given he wins sale 2).

Mr. Watson wished to evaluate the strategies for each sale. He knew he must first compute the costs for each sale. The computed costs for the Cocho Valley and Holmes Creek sales, are shown in Exhibits 6 and 7. He expected to follow his normal bidding computation procedure for the other sale. Mr. Watson also constructed part of a decision tree (Exhibit 5), which he intended to use for his analysis.[9] He drew in the extreme branches and assumed the remaining branches would fit in between these extremes.

CONCLUSION

By mid-June Mr. Watson had completed most of his analysis on the three timber sales. Although he had not yet figured his costs on the Banion Butte sales, he had done so for the Cocho Valley and Holmes Peak sales (see Exhibits 6 and 7). These costs were based on the USFS timber sale data given in Exhibit 1, and on the Sherwood Valley Logging Company logging and road construction cost estimates shown in Exhibit 2. Mr. Watson had also inserted his profit and probability figures for sale 2. Since the USFS bidding session was scheduled for July 2, it was imperative that Mr. Watson figure his costs on the other two sales and complete his decision tree in order to know which of the alternative bidding strategies he should follow. He also wanted to evaluate this method of selecting bidding strategies and the implications of his solution.

QUESTIONS

1. Complete the cost-and-profit calculations for sale 1.
2. Calculate win-and-loss probabilities for sales 1 and 2 and complete the decision tree.
3. Based on expected value, what bidding strategy should Mr. Watson follow?
4. What is the probability that Sherwood Valley Logging Company will win all three sales following this strategy?
5. How will the subjective factors discussed in the case affect your final choice of bidding strategies?
6. How will winning or losing sale 1 and or sale 2 affect your bid on sale 3?
7. Should Mr. Watson consider bids at other prices than at 10 percent, 0 percent, and minus 5 percent profit?

[9] Appendix A explains the derivation of the values shown in Exhibit 5.

Exhibit 1
USFS Data for Sales 1, 2, and 3

Sale 1: Banion Butte

Species	Est. Vol in MBM	Min. Bid by Species (Per MBM)s	Est. grade recovery in Percent[a]							Min. Total Bid by Species
			1P	2P	3P	SP	1S	2S	3S	
Douglas Fir	6400	$34.11	—	1	32	7	—	51	9	$218,304
Western Hemlock	1600	22.77	—	—	—	—	—	72	28	36,432
Cedar	700	10.20	—	—	—	—	—	37	63	7,140
Pine	300	41.68	—	—	—	—	16	43	41	12,504
	9000									$274,380

USFS road-construction allowance[b] $74,660
USFS slash-disposal allowance[b]   6,000

Sale 2: Cocho Valley

Species	Est. Vol in MBM	Min. Bid by Species (Per MBM)	Est. Grade Recovery in Percent							Min. Total Bid by Species
			1P	2P	3P	SP	1S	2S	3S	
Douglas Fir	3650	$23.63	—	—	1	1	—	43	55	$86,249.50
Pine	100	31.53	—	—	—	—	—	49	51	3,153.00
	3750									$89,402.50

USFS road-construction allowance $71,060
USFS slash-disposal allowance   2,250

Sale 3: Holmes Peak

Species	Est. Vol in MBM	Min. bid by Species (Per MBM)	Est. Grade Recovery in Percent							Min. Total Bid by Species
			1P	2P	3P	SP	1S	2S	3S	
Mountain Hemlock	10,700	$16.68	—	—	—	—	—	67	33	$178,476.00
Pine	300	37.27	—	—	—	—	4	61	33	11,181.00[c]
Noble Fir	100	15.37	—	—	—	—	—	76	24	1,537.00[c]
	11,100									$191,194.00

USFS road-construction allowance $130,190
USFS slash-disposal allowance   6,500

[a] Log grades are, in descending order of value, 1, 2, and 3 peeler, 1, 2, and 3 sawlog. Peelers are most often cut into veneer for plywood while sawlogs are usually cut into lumber.
[b] These allowances are treated as a credit to the purchaser.
[c] Includes 2 percent grade 4S.

Exhibit 2
Sherwood Valley Cost Estimates for Sales 1, 2, and 3

Sale 1: Banion Butte

Estimated logging	Falling and bucking	$ 3.85/MBM
	Yarding and loading	12.50/MBM
	Transportation	10.00/MBM
	Overhead	1.50/MBM
	Slash disposal	.75/MBM
	Total	$28.60/MBM
Estimated road-construction cost	$71,000	

Sale 2: Cocho Valley

Estimated logging cost	Falling and bucking	$ 4.00/MBM
	Yarding and loading	12.50/MBM
	Transportation	8.50/MBM
	Overhead	1.50/MBM
	Slash disposal	1.50/MBM
	Total	$28.00/MBM
Estimated road-construction cost	$60,000	

Sale 3: Holmes Peak

Estimated logging cost	Falling and bucking	$ 3.75/MBM
	Yarding and loading	13.00/MBM
	Transportation	16.00/MBM
	Overhead	1.50/MBM
	Slash disposal	.50/MBM
	Total	$34.75/MBM
Estimated road-construction cost	$110,000	

Exhibit 3
Market Prices of Selected Species[a]

Species	Market Price ($/MBM)							
	1P	2P	3P	SP	1S	2S	3S	4S
Douglas fir	190	145	105	99	87	75	55	—
Western hemlock	—	—	—	—	85	65	55	—
Cedar	—	—	—	—	80	67	50	—
Pine	—	—	—	—	100	85	70	45
Noble fir	—	—	—	—	105	85	65	—
Mountain hemlock	—	—	—	—	85	65	55	—

[a] F.O.B. mill.
Source. USFS timber sale prospectus.

Exhibit 4

Frequency Distribution of Ratios of Winning Bids to Advertised Price, and Probability of Success[a]

Ratio of Winning Bid Price to Advertised Price	Frequency	Probability	Cumulative Probability
Less than 1.0	0	0	0
1.00 - 1.05	25	.2155	.2155
1.06 - 1.10	4	.0345	.2500
1.11 - 1.15	2	.0172	.2672
1.16 - 1.20	4	.0345	.3017
1.21 - 1.25	0	0	.3017
1.26 - 1.30	3	.0590	.3276
1.31 - 1.35	3	.0259	.3535
1.36 - 1.40	2	.0172	.3707
1.41 - 1.45	1	.0086	.3793
1.46 - 1.50	7	.0604	.4397
1.51 - 1.55	5	.0431	.4828
1.56 - 1.60	4	.0345	.5173
1.61 - 1.65	3	.0259	.5432
1.66 - 1.70	1	.0086	.5518
1.71 - 1.75	6	.0518	.6036
1.76 - 1.80	2	.0172	.6208
1.81 - 1.85	6	.0518	.6726
1.86 - 1.90	2	.0172	.6898
1.91 - 1.95	2	.0172	.7070
1.96 - 2.00	4	.0345	.7415
2.01 - 2.05	1	.0086	.7501
2.06 - 2.10	4	.0345	.7846
2.11 - 2.15	3	.0259	.8105
2.16 - 2.20	2	.0172	.8277
2.21 - 2.25	0	0	.8277
2.26 - 2.30	1	.0086	.8363
2.31 - 2.35	2	.0172	.8553
2.36 - 2.40	4	.0345	.8880
2.41 - 2.45	0	0	.8880
2.46 - 2.50	2	.0172	.9052
2.50 and over	11	.0948	1.0000

[a]This exhibit is from Table II in a paper by Richard W. Johnson and K. Dexter Cheney, "Application of a Mathematical Model to Bidding for United States Forest Service Timber, Some Practical Considerations," Forest Industries Management Center, University of Oregon (Eugene, Ore.: December 1964).

See also Norman Taylor, *A Bidding Model for Timber Purchasing,* monograph published by The Institute of Business and Economic Research (University of California: Berkeley, 1963).

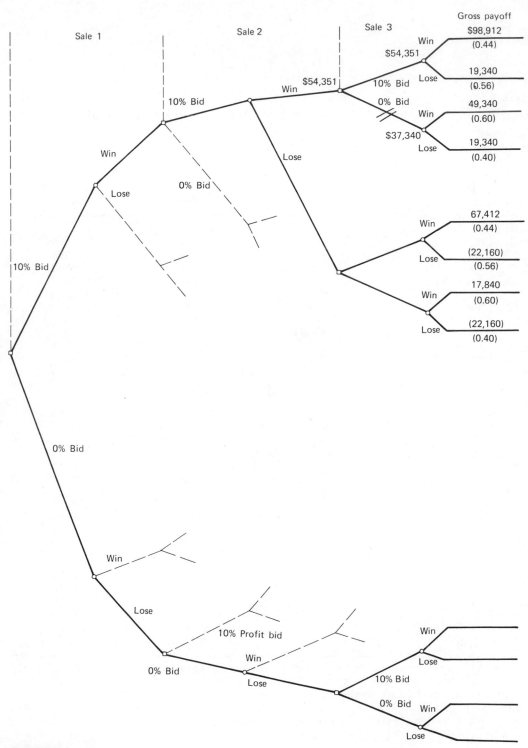

Exhibit 5
Bayesian Decision Tree

Exhibit 6
Calculation of Costs on Sale 2—Cocho Valley

Step 1: Compute current market value of logs.

Vol. by Species	×	%	of Grade	=	Vol. of Grade	× Selling Price	= Realization	Total by Species
D.F.3650		0.02	3P&SP		73.0	$102	7,446.00	
3650		0.43	2S		1569.5	75	117,712.50	
3650		0.55	3S		2007.5	55	110,412.50	
						Total for Douglas fir		$235,571.00
Pine 100		0.49	2S		49.0	85	4,165.00	
100		0.51	3S		51.0	70	3,570.00	
						Total for pine		$ 7,735.00
						Total market value of sale		$243.306.00

Step 2 & 3: subtract estimated road cost and logging cost.

$$
\begin{array}{r}
\$243.306 \\
-60,000 \\
3750\ \text{MBM} \times 28.00/\text{MBM} = \quad -105,000 \\
\hline
\$\ 78,306
\end{array}
$$

Step 4: add USFS road and slash-disposal allowances.

$$
\begin{array}{r}
+\ 71,060 \\
+\quad 2,250 \\
\hline
\$151,616
\end{array}
$$

Step 5: subtract 10% of road-construction cost and logging cost for profit and risk allowances.

$$
\begin{array}{r}
-\quad 6,000 \\
-\ 10,500 \\
\end{array}
$$

Maximum amount available for bidding $135,116
Bid to appraised price ratio at 10% profit
  $135,116/89,402 = 1.51 cumulative probability of winning sale = .4828
Bid to appraised price ratio at 0% profit
  $151,616/89,402 = 1.69 cumulative probability of winning sale = .5518

Exhibit 7
Calculation of Costs on Sale 3—Holmes Peak

Step 1: compute current market value of logs.

Vol. by Species	×	Percent	of Grade	=	Vol. of Grade	× Selling Price =	Realization	Total by Species
M.H.10,700		0.67	2S		7169	$65	$465,985	
10,700		0.33	3S		3531	55	194,205	
					Total for mountain hemlock			$660,190.00
Pine 300		0.04	1S		12	100	1,200	
300		0.61	2S		183	85	15,555	
300		0.33	3S		99	70	6,930	
300		0.02	4S		6	45	270	
					Total for pine			$ 23,955.00
N.F. 100		0.76	2S		76	85	6,460	
100		0.24	3S		24	65	1,560	
					Total for Noble fir			$ 8,020.00
					Total market value of sale			$692,165.00

Step 2 and 3: subtract estimated road cost and logging cost.

$$\begin{array}{r} \$692,165 \\ -110,000 \\ 11{,}100 \text{ MBM} \times 34.75/\text{MBM} = \quad -385,725 \\ \hline \$196,440 \end{array}$$

Step 4: add USFS road and slash-disposal allowances

$$\begin{array}{r} +130,190 \\ +\ \ 6,500 \\ \hline \$333,130 \end{array}$$

Step 5: subtract 10% of road-construction cost and logging cost for profit and risk

$$\begin{array}{r} -\ 11,000 \\ -\ 38,572 \\ \hline \end{array}$$
Maximum amount available for bidding $283,558

Bid to appraised price ratio at 10% profit
$283,558/191,194 = 1.48 cumulative probability of winning sale = .4397
Bid to appraised price ratio at 0% profit
$333,130/191,194 = 1.74 cumulative probability of winning sale = .6036
Bid to appraised price ratio at 10% loss
$382,702/191,194 = 2.00 cumulative probability of winning sale = .7415

Appendix A
Bayesian Analysis

Bayesian analysis is a method for evaluating alternative choices in the face of events with unknown outcomes. The technique is essentially a formal statement of human decision processes with some simplifying assumptions. The decision maker weights each value for an event by the probability of that event occurring. The value of an alternative is merely the sum of the weighted values for the events resulting from selecting that alternative. The procedure for specifying and solving simple Bayesian problems is set forth in the following paragraphs. This analysis utilizes the data and problems posed in the preceding case. The reader should note that we initially assume that the decision maker is indifferent to the trade-off between risk and the expected value of an alternative.

In reality, research has shown that the decision maker's utility functions for increasing profits are usually nonlinear. This means that businessmen typically become more conservative as the risk of a big loss increases. Thus under some conditions businessmen do not select the alternative with the highest expected value. Estimates of the risk preferences for Mr. Watson can be inferred from the case discussion.

When the evaluative criteria is the expected value of an alternative, the decision maker is indifferent to risk and selects that alternative with the highest expected value. The following steps are necessary to calculate expected values in this case:

1. *Identify the time horizon of the problem.* The expected value outcome is based on the value over a length of time in the future. Events beyond the time horizon are not included in the evaluation of the problem. This, therefore, sets the bounds of the problem for analysis.

2. *Construct a decision tree of the model.* This is a diagram of the decisions to be made in the order that they occur. The order only applies to when a decision must be made and not to the actual results of the decision. Exhibit 5 shows the upper and lower branches of a decision tree for Sherwood Valley Logging Company. Notice that each set of decision terminals (denoted by a square) is followed by two or more alternatives that the decision maker must decide on. Immediately after each decision branch is an event terminal (denoted by a circle.) These circles are followed by the possible outcomes of the uncertain event. For instance, the first decision terminal involves two possible bids for sale 1. Each bid is followed by two chance events—win the bid and lose the bid. This structure is continued until the entire problem is diagrammed. Some branches that obviously do not influence the outcome may be eliminated, thus simplifying the decision tree.

3. *Determine the partial cash flows for each branch.* These are the independent cash flows that would result if the particular branch were to occur. Again, the initial bid can be either the no profit bid or the 10 percent profit bid. Therefore, the partial cash flows for each branch are zero because no cost is encountered in making a bid. Now, suppose the 10 percent profit bid were successful, then the event branch "win" following that bid would be $32,840 (the profit resulting from a successful 10 percent profit bid on the Banion Butte sale. A similar profit is shown for Cocho Valley in Exhibit 6, step 5). The remaining partial cash flows are then determined in a like manner.

4. *Compute the gross payoff for each complete set of branches.* This is accomplished by adding together all the partial cash flows along a single set of branches from the start to the end of the tree. In Exhibit 5 the top branch can be identified as that of bidding the 10 percent profit bid on each sale and winning each sale. Adding up the partial cash flows along this route the payoff is $98,912 ($32,840 + $16,500 + $49,572). These flows are the sum of the profits for each sale. Calculation of the 10 percent profit for Cocho Valley is shown in Exhibit 6, step 5.

5. *Calculate the probabilities of the uncertain events.* This can be quickly accomplished by referring to Exhibit 4. The probability of a win outcome is calculated by taking the bid/appraised-price ratio for the respective bid and then comparing that ratio to column 4 of Exhibit 4. The chance of a win may be read directly from the right-hand column of the table. In Exhibit 5, probabilities are shown for sale 3, given that the firm won the previous two sales. A 10 percent profit bid on sale 3 would be the ratio 1.48 ($283,558/191,194). This can be found once the cost figures for the sales have

been computed. It is merely the bid/appraised-price ratio for the last sale. From Exhibit 4 this ratio would give an accumulated probability of .4397 or .44 thus the last win branch in Exhibit 5 shows a probability of .44. The remaining probabilities are computed using the same method.

6. *Compute the expected value of the decision branches.* This is accomplished in two steps. Starting with the gross payoff the problem is solved from right to left. First the weighted average of the decision terminal is computed by summing the weighted values of the chance events leading out of the decision branch. In Exhibit 5, the top branch considering sale 3 shows two payoffs for a 10 percent profit bid. The first payoff results from winning the bid ($98,912) while the next payoff ($19,340) results from losing the bid ($98,912-$49,572-$30,000). These payoffs are multiplied by their chances of occurring (.44 and .56 respectively) and then added together to get $54,351. This then, is the expected value of bidding a 10 percent profit bid given that the firm has won the two previous sales. The no-profit bid at the same level (sale 3) is then computed. Its value is $37,340. Second, the expected value of each decision branch leading from a single decision terminal is evaluated and the highest valued strategy is accepted. Again, in Exhibit 5 the profit bid expected value of $54,351 is selected over the other bid expected value of $37,340. Therefore, the no-profit bid at this stage need not be considered further and the expected value of the profit bid $54,351 is assigned to the decision terminal for that sale. The entire tree is then evaluated using an identical process.

Once the tree is completed the decision maker can then decide on what strategy to follow to maximize his expected profit. In this case the manager must decide which level to bid on the first sale and have alternative strategies ready for other sales once he knows the outcome of the first sale.

Bayesian analysis provides the decision maker with a rational method to systematically analyze complex problem situations. The manager can build the model and show possible outcomes while also explicitly stating the significant alternatives. He can also weight the possible outcomes of these alternatives using whatever information he has available. In most complex cases, the decision maker can see the path to maximum expected value, thus enabling him to make more rational decisions.

Nine

Distribution Management

It is well known what a middleman is; he is a man who bamboozles one party and plunders the other.

Benjamin Disraeli, 1845

Distribution management is concerned with selecting and locating middlemen to efficiently move products from factories to customers. The objective is to organize a system of transportation, storage, and communication that makes goods and services readily available to potential customers. The system must *minimize the cost* of storing and shipping merchandise while maintaining or *improving sales* to the ultimate user. Managers are thus faced with the dilemma of creating a distribution system that is both low in cost yet able to move the product to the customer when needed. This usually means that investments in improved distribution facilities must be balanced against the sales gains that may occur if customers receive faster delivery. The goal of this chapter is to explain the structure of channel alternatives and discuss methods that can be used to help businessmen make better distribution decisions.

WHY USE MIDDLEMEN?

One of the persistent myths in our society is the notion that you can eliminate the middleman and save a bundle on the distribution of goods and services. The truth is that you can eliminate the middleman as an institution, but the work of distribution still has to be performed. Students, for example, frequently organize cooperatives to save money by eliminating the retailer and his profit margin. They quickly find they need a location to stockpile goods and allow customers to pick up merchandise. In addition, they need someone to buy merchandise and transport it from wholesalers or manufacturers to the cooperative facility. They also need someone to contribute working capital, unpack and price the goods, collect the money, pay the bills, sweep the floor, and manage the operation. All of these cost money and unless the students are willing to contribute their time, they are not apt to reap the vast savings they expect. Thus, no matter how you organize the distibution channel, someone has to perform the work required to move the product from the factory to the customer. Over the years a number of specialized middlemen have emerged to perform the tasks of distribution and it is our objective to explain where, and when, and how they are used.

The most common argument employed to defend middlemen is that they help improve distribution efficiency. Sometimes it is difficult to see how the addition of another dealer with his attendant margins and delays can *raise* distribution efficiency. One way this efficiency can be demonstrated is with the channel diagrams shown in Figure 9-1. In part (*a*), the four manufacturers must make forty sales calls to contact the ten customers. However, when a middleman is added to the channel (*b*), the number of sales calls needed to contact wholesale and final customers is reduced to fourteen. Each manufacturer calls on the middleman and the middleman represents all of the manufacturers in contacting the customers. Thus, the addition of a distributor reduced the total amount of work to be done. Middlemen also provide manufacturers with a ready-made channel of distribution that is experienced in handling particular product lines. In additon, middlemen have established contacts with buyers and often have the special warehouse facilities and repair equipment needed for some items.

Sometimes middlemen are used even though they do not improve the efficiency of the distribution system. In Japan, for example, there are 1.5 million retail stores serviced by an elaborate multilevel system of 280,000 middlemen.[1] Most of the stores are small, buy frequently in small lots, expect credit, and pay their bills in cash. These conditions have fostered the growth of a maze of regional middlemen that inflate the cost of distributing merchandise.[2] However, when American firms have attempted to sell imported merchandise directly to department stores they have met considerable resistance. Many stores will not buy direct from manufacturers and insist that all purchases go through their regular wholesaler. The Japanese merchants will simply not risk creating a poor relationship with their major supplier of credit and merchandise over a single line of imported goods. Thus, until the Japanese retailers gain more power, American firms are almost forced to use a distribution system that employs too many middlemen.

DISTRIBUTION ALTERNATIVES

There are literally hundreds of ways goods and services can be distributed to customers. These range from direct bulk shipments in railcars or pipelines to the use of complex arrangements of brokers, wholesalers, and retailers. No *one* distribution system can

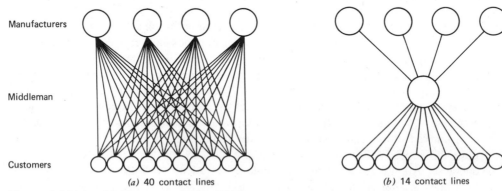

Manufacturers

Middleman

Customers

(*a*) 40 contact lines   (*b*) 14 contact lines

Figure 9-1 Using Middlemen to Raise Efficiency.

[1]Japan has about the same number of stores as in the United States but the United States has twice the population and twenty-five times the land area, "How Not to Do It: Cumbersome Japanese Distribution System Stumps U.S. Concerns," *Wall Street Journal* (March 2, 1972), p. 1, "Bending Japan's Barriers," *Time* (September 11, 1972), p. 71.

[2]*The Wall Street Journal* estimates that wholesale volume is five times retail volume in Japan compared to twice retail volume in the United States.

satisfy the needs of every business and many companies use several combinations of middlemen (each called a distribution channel) to reach different market segments. A paper mill, for example, may contact large users directly while smaller customers are serviced by independent wholesalers. Distribution systems not only vary across firms, but they also change over time. A channel that works well when a firm is small is apt to be inefficient when it grows larger and can handle some of the distribution functions with its own employees. Also, changes in customer needs and transportation methods can cause existing distribution methods to become obsolete. In addition, there is a trend toward *scrambled merchandising* where distributors carry much wider varieties of merchandise than they have in the past. Drug stores, for example, now routinely carry paint, motor oil, toys, and small appliances.

Another factor influencing the distribution alternatives utilized by businesses is the simple availability of various middlemen. A firm may decide that a particular type of wholesaler is ideal for a product line, but if the available companies are in the wrong location or handle competing merchandise then the firm may have to find another distribution channel. Manufacturers must also realize that middlemen are profit seeking organizations that take on and promote products for their own well being rather than that of the producer. This frequently means the manufacturer must offer middlemen special inducements to gain and keep their cooperation.

Direct Distribution

Some of the channel alternatives that are available for manufacturers are described in Figure 9-2. Perhaps the simplest channel is the direct sale of merchandise from the manufacturer to the consumer or industrial buyer. Although direct contact eliminates the need for middlemen, this method usually involves fairly high promotional expenses. Examples of merchandise distributed directly to consumers include the mail-order sale of books and records, factory outlets for baked goods, the sale of heavy machinery to industrial users, and the sale of some household items via door-to-door salesmen.[3] Each of these methods has some disadvantages that may restrict their use for certain products and firms. While mail-order works for standard items like records and flower seeds that can be described easily, it is less appropriate for appliances where delays in shipment, inability to examine the merchandise, and higher price levels may make the consumer more reluctant to buy. Factory outlets can also be an effective distribution method, but only a few customers live close enough to manufacturing plants to take advantage of these outlets. With door-to-door distribution, sales can increase only as fast as the number of salesmen, and it is very difficult to hire and retain good people for this type of work. Distribution channels for industrial goods tend to be simple and direct because there are relatively few buyers and they are concentrated geographically. Thus, if the volume of orders is sufficient, it can be more economical to sell industrial customers direct from the factory.

Adding Retailers to the Channel

One of the most popular methods employed to distribute goods and services is the manufacturer-retailer channel (Figure 9-2). Retailers perform a variety of useful func-

[3]Most door-to-door salesmen are not actually employed by the firms they represent and therefore these sales do not technically qualify as direct sales to the consumer. Avon, Fuller Brush, and Amway salesmen are really independent businessmen who buy and resell merchandise like other traditional retailers. Electrolux vacuum cleaner salesmen, on the other hand, are employees and these sales represent direct distribution from the manufacturer to the consumer.

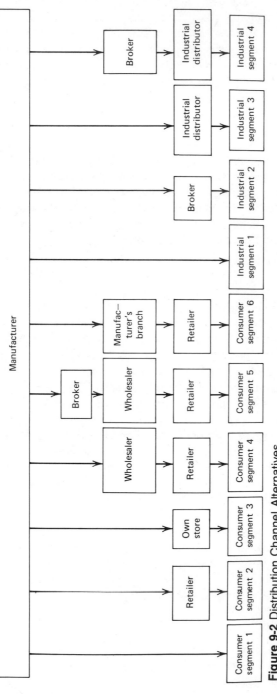

Figure 9-2 Distribution Channel Alternatives.

tions for the manufacturer, including the carrying of inventory, advertising, promotion, credit, delivery, and shopping convenience. The advantage of this channel of distribution to the manufacturer is that it is often more efficient to sell carloads to a few large retailers than single items to millions of consumers. The manufacturer-retailer channel is widely used in the distribution of food and is the dominant form of organization in the sale of clothing and automobiles. Industrial distributors (Figure 9-2) operate like retailers and buy industrial merchandise from manufacturers for resale to other companies. Retail stores and industrial distributors can, of course, be owned and operated by the manufacturer. When this occurs we have a vertically integrated system that can lead to substantial distribution economies.

Using Wholesalers

When products are sold in many different types of retail stores scattered all over the country, wholesalers may be needed to help transfer the merchandise from the manufacturer to retailers (Figure 9-2). Wholesalers are middlemen that buy in large volume and resell to retailers in case lots. They provide retailers with assortments of merchandise, backup stocks, credit, delivery, and promotional assistance. Manufacturers use wholesalers to get *intensive distribution* when they need maximum exposure for their products and direct contact with retailers is not justified because of low volume or lack of resources. For example, wholesalers are typically used to distribute beer to the many restaurants, hotels, taverns, liquor stores, supermarkets, drug stores, and corner groceries that sell this product in a given market area. Since specialized beer wholesalers carry several lines, they can perform the store contact work more efficiently than it could be done by delivery systems operated by individual brewers. Also, the beer wholesaler is apt to do a better job of promotion, inventory control, and stock rotation than would be available if the product were handled through general purpose wholesalers.

When to Use Brokers and Manufacturer's Reps?

While most people have heard of stock brokers and real estate brokers, relatively few understand why manufacturers use brokers to sell goods in a channel of distribution (Figure 9-2). Brokers and reps are specialized agent middlemen who neither own nor take possession of the merchandise they sell to wholesale or retail customers. They operate on commission in specified territories and sell under conditions where the manufacturer cannot handle the job himself. For example, small food packers with limited product lines often lack the resources to hire their own sales force. By using a broker the manufacturer avoids the high fixed costs associated with salesmen and branch facilities and gains the benefits of the contacts the broker has already established with the wholesale and retail trade. Large firms also use brokers to sell to wholesalers when they have an item that does not fit their regular distribution channels. Dow Chemical Company, for example, uses brokers to sell its line of auto care products to regional wholesalers who sell to retail organizations. Because of the relatively small volume generated by the motor additives and cleaners in this line, it is more profitable for Dow to use specialized brokers to handle this business than to hire their own salesmen.

Figure 9-2 also suggests that manufacturers can sell the same product through several channels of distribution to reach different market segments. A record manufacturer, for example, could establish a record club to sell records directly to consumers by mail. The same records would be available in department and discount stores. Smaller music shops, supermarkets, and drug stores could be contacted by specialized record wholesalers. Brokers might be used to sell to industrial markets and to distributors in overseas areas. Thus, for some products it may be more profitable to distribute products through several different channels. Distribution channels for industrial and consumer goods are rarely permanent and marketing executives must continually look for new procedures that will lower costs and improve service to customers.

Channel Ownership

Another factor that influences the selection of distribution alternatives is the issue of channel ownership. Manufacturers have the choice of selling their products through independent wholesalers and retailers or they can acquire facilities to perform these activities with their own employees. When a manufacturer extends this operation to the wholesale and retail level we have what is known as a *vertically integrated channel*. This method of distribution can improve efficiency by eliminating promotion and selling expenses that normally occur between the manufacturer and the wholesaler and the wholesaler and the retailer. With a completely integrated channel, the main job for marketing executives is building demand among the final buyers and coordinating the activities of the different units in the channel. The primary advantage of this system is that it gives the manufacturer maximum control over the selection of products sold in the channel, their prices, and the promotional activities designed to sell them to the final consumer. Examples of completely integrated distribution channels are provided by Sherwin-Williams who operates 2000 paint stores and Hart Schaffner Marx who owns more than 200 clothing stores.[4]

Although the completely integrated channel offers the manufacturer the most control over the distribution of his products, it also requires the greatest financial investment. Firms that do not have the resources or breadth of product line needed to operate their own retail units may decide there are advantages to factory operation of wholesale facilities. Factory-owned wholesalers have increased their share of total wholesale trade from 26.5 percent in 1939 to 34.2 percent in 1967.[5] This suggests that manufacturers have a growing interest in wholesaling and are willing to make the necessary commitments to expand operations of this type. Manufacturers' wholesale activities typically include the operation of sales offices and/or sales branches. A sales branch combines a physical product inventory with a group of sales representatives. Over the past forty years, sales branches have declined in importance and currently have about 14.6 percent of all wholesale trade. Sales offices, on the other hand, have grown from less than 10 percent of wholesale trade in 1939 to about 20 percent today. A sales office maintains a cadre of salesmen, but does not carry its own inventory of merchandise. The rapid growth of sales offices suggests that manufacturers need salesmen in the field, but are able to make deliveries to customers direct from factory or regional warehouses. This increased reliance on manufacturer's sales offices has probably been helped by improvements in transportation (such as air freight) and a judicious use of public warehouses.

The establishment of sales offices and sales branches gives the *manufacturer* greater control over inventories, promotions, and market coverage than is available from

[4]David T. Kollat, Roger D. Blackwell, and James F. Robeson, *Strategic Marketing* (New York: Holt, Rinehart and Winston, 1972), p. 289.

[5]Most of the increased volume was diverted from agents and brokers as the share obtained by traditional merchant wholesalers increased from 40.6 percent to 44.8 percent over the same period. See Louis P. Bucklin, *Competition and Evolution in the Distributive Trades* (Englewood Cliffs, N.J.: Prentice-Hall, Inc., 1972), p. 214.

independent wholesale organizations. Although many firms have deliberately moved into wholesaling, others have been forced to take over this function simply because they have been unable to find independent businessmen with the experience and financial resources needed to run this type of operation. Appliances and automobiles are two product categories where manufacturers have successfully absorbed the management of wholesale activities. For some firms, the costs of operating sales offices and branches have been more than offset by gains in revenue and profits produced by improving customer service.

Channel integration also occurs when *retailers* operate their own warehouse facilities. Retail control of wholesale functions is common in food, variety, discount, and department store chains. Sometimes independent retailers band together to run a wholesaling operation on a cooperative basis. Certified Grocers of California, for example, is a wholesaler that is owned and operated by a number of independent stores. These organizations tend to buy direct from manufacturers or brokers and often bypass traditional distribution channels.

Some of the food and department store chains have gone even further and operate their own factories. Sears is one of the most completely integrated of the general retailers and most merchandise is supplied by their own factories or is purchased under long-term contracts. For example, Sears buys tires from Armstrong Rubber (10 percent owned), clothing from Kellwood (16 percent owned), consumer electronics from Warwick (23 percent owned), appliances from Roper (47 percent owned), and plumbing fixtures from Universal Rundle (60 percent owned).[6] The purchase of merchandise in this manner means that the retailer assumes almost complete control over the branding, pricing, promotion, and distribution of these products.

Product Ownership

Distribution decisions are also affected by the systems employed to transfer title of the goods from the manufacturer to the customer. When a manufacturer sells merchandise outright to a middleman, he is, in effect, delegating control over the remaining distribution functions. If a manufacturer wants to retain control over these activities, he can keep title to the goods and sell on commission through agents and brokers. Another way to maintain influence in the distribution channel is to sell merchandise to middlemen on consignment. This allows the manufacturer to hold title to the goods, but gives the dealers possession so they can sell the items to the ultimate buyer. General Electric, for example, used this method for many years to sell light bulbs through retail stores. Since GE owned the bulbs, the stores were apt to carry a more complete line of the product and they were obliged to sell the bulbs at list price.[7]

Consignment selling can also be used as a way for a manufacturer to encourage dealers to carry his products. The manufacturer absorbs the full cost of carrying the inventory and the dealer pays for the goods as he sells them. For example, the Hanes Corp. used consignment selling to induce supermarkets and drugstores to handle its "L'eggs" brand of pantyhose.[8] A single display rack of the egg-shaped packages of pantyhose can generate $1300 a year in profit to the retailer since restocking and inventory control are performed by the manufacturer. Inventory carrying costs can present a severe financial

[6]*The Wall Street Journal* (August 7, 1973), p. 8 and *Forbes* (April 1972), p. 49.

[7]Pressure from the federal government eventually caused General Electric to discontinue the consignment selling of light bulbs.

[8]*Business Week* (March 25, 1972), pp. 96-100.

burden for dealers selling heavy industrial equipment and manufacturers sometimes ship goods for display. Perhaps the ultimate in distribution control is achieved by manufacturers who lease their products to customers. With this system the manufacturer assumes all the distribution functions plus the risks of delivering, installing, and servicing the merchandise.

Manufacturers planning a distribution system should realize that physical possession does not have to go hand in hand with ownership of the product. In fact, distribution efficiency often demands that the transfer of title be handled separately from the delivery of the product to the customer. For example, in Figure 9-3 one channel is used to physically move appliances from the factory to customers and a second channel is employed to transfer ownership of the product. In this particular case the manufacturer operates the sales branches, but inventories are only carried at the factory and regional warehouses. When the sales branch receives an order from a retailer, the appliances are shipped by company truck to public warehouses and held in the name of the retailer.

When a retailer makes a sale to a customer, a local delivery service picks up the item from the public warehouse and delivers it directly to the final consumer. The retailer can also arrange direct shipments from the manufacturer's regional stocks to the consumer for appliances that are not available from his own stock. The dotted line in Figure 9-3 show the communications networks used by the sales branches and retailers to control the physical movement of the appliances as they move through the distribution system.

The separation of physical possession from ownership allows the retailer to direct the movement of goods to customers without having to handle the items through his own facilities. Note that the physical transfer of the product to the consumer involved storage in three warehouses and deliveries by three different transportation services while the transfer of ownership was accomplished in just two steps (Figure 9-3). The separation of physical handling of the product from ownership also allows manufacturers to ship goods to markets even before they are sold. It is common practice, for example, to ship fruits

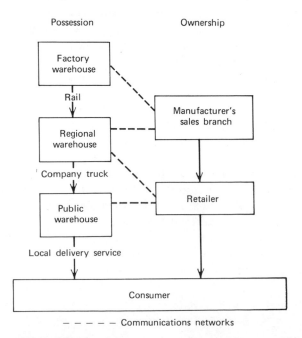

Figure 9-3 Possession Versus Ownership in Appliance Distribution.

and vegetables from the West Coast to eastern markets and arrange for the sale of the merchandise while it is in transit. Another way goods and services can be transferred to customers is through the use of franchised dealers.

Franchise Distribution

Franchising is a system of distribution where independent businessmen are given the right to sell products or services in exchange for a fee and/or agreements on buying and merchandising policies. The basic ingredient in franchising is a contract between a parent organization and a set of independent dealers specifying how the two will do business with each other. Franchising arrangements vary widely with regard to the assistance provided for the dealers and the types of goods and services distributed in this manner. The most popular franchising system is the *manufacturer-retailer* plan where the products of one or more manufacturers are sold to consumers through selected independent retailers. This method is used to distribute most of the gasoline and automobiles sold in the United States.[9] A second approach is the manufacturer-wholesaler franchise used by the soft drink industry. With this system the manufacturer of the soft drink syrups, such as Coca Cola or Pepsi, grants territorial franchises to independent bottlers who sell to the retail and institutional outlets in their areas. Thus the manufacturer ships only the high-value syrups and the bottler gets in under the "umbrella" of the manufacturer's national advertising program. Another type of franchising arrangement is the *wholesaler-retailer* plan encountered in the distribution of food. Here the organizing force is the wholesaler (such as IGA or Super Value) who recruits a group of independent retailers to buy through his organization. The retailer obtains centralized buying, group advertising, identifying brand names, and other merchandising help while the wholesaler gets an assured customer. The fastest growing segment of the franchising industry is the *service sponsor-retailer*. This category includes fast-food outlets such as McDonald's, auto and truck rental, motels, part-time help agencies, cleaning services, and equipment rental outlets. With service-sponsor organizations the emphasis is on providing the dealers with a set of proven operating procedures and national advertising support rather than merchandise for resale. Income for the parent firm with this type of arrangement comes from an initial franchising fee, markups on supplies sold to the dealers, and a percentage of dealer sales to cover advertising and other services.

Advantages of Franchising. The use of a franchised system of dealers to distribute goods and services has a number of advantages over complete channel ownership or reliance on the part-time efforts of independent wholesalers. Franchising offers the parent organizations a way to expand rapidly by utilizing the capital and managerial skills of local businessmen. McDonald's for example, requires its franchisees to come up with about $150,000 before they can open a restaurant.[10] This includes $10,000 for a license, $25,000 for a real estate fee, $60,000 for equipment, $15,000 for signs and $20,000 for landscaping, food inventory, and decorations. Given the magnitude of these investments, it is not surprising that franchised outlets sometimes generate higher sales than company-owned stores due to the personal interest of the owner-manager. Occasionally, franchising is used as a way of selling specialized equipment that is rejected by

---

[9] A small percentage of the auto dealers and gas stations are wholly owned and operated by manufacturers.

[10] Only about one half of the $150,000 must be in cash. The total investment is not excessive considering the average McDonald's outlet has annual revenues greater than $500,000. Quoted to the authors by J. Kenneth Props of the McDonald Corporation, and reported in *Time* (September 17, 1973), pp. 84-92.

conventional distribution channels. Chicken Delight, for example, was built around a unique $1500 cooker and Tastee Freez was organized as a way to sell a soft-ice-cream freezer.[11]

Franchising offers individual dealers the centralized purchasing and promotional skills of a large organization while retaining many of the advantages of a small business. The dealers enjoy the ownership of a business, get to hire and train their help, schedule local promotions, and manage their outlets, while the parent provides site selection, training, start-up assistance, new product development, and a proven package of operating techniques. In addition, the continuing supervision by the central organization helps keep the chance of dealer failure below levels encountered by independent merchants.[12]

Disadvantages of Franchising. Perhaps the most serious problem with franchising is the parent organization must give up some control over operating procedures, pricing, and promotion to the local dealers. This can lead to trouble if the local units are too independent and customers become confused about product and service standards. Only a few dirty motel rooms and skimpy hamburgers are needed to hurt the sales of other franchised units and depress the revenues of the parent organization. The local dealers, on the other hand, find that the controls needed to make a franchised system work often restrict their ability to innovate and make changes to meet local conditions.

The amount of control a parent organization can legally exert over franchised units is not clear, but recent court decisions have tended to increase the power of local dealers. Franchising organizations can no longer force local units to follow set pricing and merchandising guidelines or buy cookers, packing materials, mixes, or spices from company-owned suppliers.[13] Also, territorial restrictions that limit the freedom of franchised retailers as to where and to whom they may sell bicycles have been ruled illegal and similar provisions are being reviewed for other products.[14]

There are still a number of control procedures that can be used to help assure the success of a franchising organization. Locations are often critical and most oil companies and fast food restaurants buy the sites and lease them to the retail operator. In addition to location control, most franchising organizations require their dealers to follow prescribed accounting procedures and submit weekly or monthly operating reports. This allows the parent firm to make comparisons across dealers so that weaker units can be identified and suggestions made for corrective action. An important control device in service sponsor systems is the percentage of sales that dealers pay to the sponsoring organization. This provides income for the parent firm and allows them to engage in the advertising and supervisory programs necessary for growth. McDonald's hamburger stands, for example, pay a 3 percent royalty to the parent organization in addition to the initial franchising fee and 8.5 percent of sales for rent. If these controls are not sufficient, the parent organization can buy back units that are not performing up to company standards. Holiday Inns, for example, has brought back a number of franchised units to increase control and McDonald's has expanded company ownership to about 30 percent

[11]S. Michael Ingraham, *Management Control Potentials and Practices of Franchise Systems,* unpublished doctoral dissertation, (Los Angeles: University of California, Graduate School of Business Administration, 1963), p. 59.

[12]An executive of the International Franchise Association estimates that less than 10 percent of all franchisees fail, "Fortunes in Franchising," *Dun's Review,* Vol. 83 (April 1964), p. 82.

[13]See Milsen Company v. Southland Corp., CCH 73,774 (CA-7, December, 1971); Siegal v. Chicken Delight, CCH 73,703 (CA-9, September, 1971).

[14]United States v. Arnold, Schwinn and Co., Schwinn Cycle Distributors Assoc. CCH 72,480 (D.C. N. Ill., May, 1968).

of its retail units. Kentucky Fried Chicken claims to make more profit from 300 company owned stores than they do from 2100 franchised outlets.[15] Although the buy-back privilege can help maintain the growth of the parent organization, it obviously represents a direct and serious threat to the independent operators.

SELECTING DISTRIBUTION CHANNELS

The selection of middlemen for use in distribution channels should be made on the basis of *profit* considerations. This means the firm must balance the costs of employing different types of middlemen against the revenues generated by alternative distribution methods. The basic cost reductions offered by the inclusion of middlemen were illustrated in Figure 9-1. With a wholesaler in the channel, the manufacturer's sales and communication costs are reduced and it may be more profitable to let the wholesaler sell to the final customers. An example comparing the use of a direct sales force and a wholesaler has been developed by Artle and Berglund.[16]

Comparing Channel Costs

Artle and Berglund describe a situation where four items produced by different firms were supplied to ten retailers. The total costs of selling direct and using wholesalers were derived by adding up the costs incurred by each member of the channel. The example assumed that contracts between the manufacturers and the wholesaler were by phone and cost two dollars per order regardless of order size. This is somewhat unrealistic as most manufacturers would maintain some personal contact with the wholesaler to introduce new items and help schedule promotions.

Figure 9-4 shows that direct distribution involved total costs of $7590 per year compared to only $2120 when a wholesaler was used. Most of the difference was due to the increased number of calls and travel required by having each manufacturer call on every retailer. With direct selling a total of 2000 retail calls would be needed each year compared to only 500 calls with a wholesaler in the system.[17] Direct distribution also involved extra travel because the home base of the factory salesmen was assumed to be further from the retailers than the wholesale salesmen. Note that the introduction of a wholesaler greatly reduced the time retailers had to spend listening to salesmen. Since the efficiency of the retailer as well as the manufacturer was increased by adding a wholesaler, there was an added incentive to rely on this type of channel organization. When a second wholesaler was added to the example, the annual cost to sell the four items increased to $3610. Obviously too many wholesalers (as in Japan) could eat up the savings produced by having middlemen represent several manufacturers in contacts with retail customers.

This example has shown how selling costs and production economies influence the selection of distribution channels, but there are other factors that should be considered as well. Management must evaluate the cost and revenue generating aspects of order transmission procedures, transportation methods, and the techniques used to physically

[15]Charles G. Burck, "Franchising's Troubled Dream World," *Fortune* (March 1970), pp. 116-120.

[16]Roland Artle and Sture Berglund, "A Note on Manufacturer's Choice of Distribution Channels," *Management Science* (July 1959), pp. 460-71.

[17]Calculated by multiplying 4 manufacturers × 10 retailers × 50 calls per year = 2000 total calls. This compares to 1 wholesaler × 10 retailers × 50 calls per year = 500 total calls.

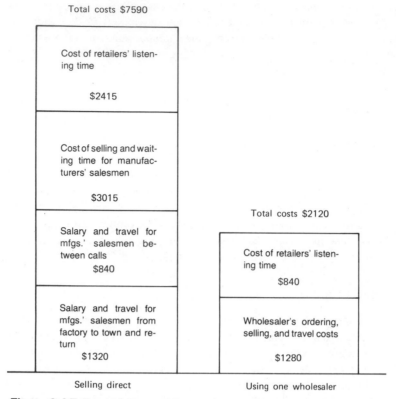

Total costs $7590

Cost of retailers' listening time

$2415

Cost of selling and waiting time for manufacturers' salesmen

$3015

Salary and travel for mfgs.' salesmen between calls
$840

Salary and travel for mfgs.' salesmen from factory to town and return
$1320

Selling direct

Total costs $2120

Cost of retailers' listening time

$840

Wholesaler's ordering, selling, and travel costs

$1280

Using one wholesaler

Figure 9-4 Estimated Costs of Selling the Output of Four Manufacturers to Ten Retailers.

Source. Adapted from data in Roland Artle and Sture Berglund, "A Note on Manufacturer's Choice of Distribution Channels," *Management Science* (July 1959), pp. 460-471.

handle the products. A detailed discussion of these issues is presented in the following example dealing with the distribution of frozen orange juice.[18]

Selecting Channels for Orange Juice

Frozen orange juice has many unique distribution problems because it is perishable and requires expensive storage and delivery facilities. Several years ago Minute Maid Corporation was considering reducing the number of independent wholesalers handling its juice from nineteen to six for the metropolitan New York market. The existing system was not giving the retailers frequent enough delivery and some wholesalers were using Minute Maid orange juice as a loss leader to promote the sale of their own brands of frozen foods. The price cutting by wholesalers led to wide differentials in retail prices and was eroding the quality image of the Minute Maid brand. Under the new plan, six of the better wholesalers would be given exclusive territories and the markup would be reduced from 15 percent to 10 percent of sales. The selected wholesalers would be required to establish a separate division where uniformed driver-salesmen would deliver Minute Maid products to retailers twice a week in special trucks. To help offset the lower margin available under the new plan, the wholesalers would only accept orders for full

---

[18]The complete case is described in Harry L. Hansen, *Marketing Text, Techniques, and Cases* (Homewood, Ill.: Richard D. Irwin, 1967), pp. 586-592.

cases of merchandise. This would eliminate the current practice of breaking packages to fill retailers' orders and would save the wholesalers an estimated 3 or 5 percent of sales. Minute Maid also planned to consign stocks to the wholesalers so they would not have to invest in an orange juice inventory.

The new distribution system was designed to increase Minute Maid's control over the sale of its orange juice without incurring the high fixed costs associated with company operated sales branches. Both of Minute Maid's major competitors, Snow Crop and Bird's Eye, had company-owned branches in the New York area. Minute Maid, however, had a more limited product line and was not in a position to finance its own branch operations. The key to the implementation of the new plan was obtaining the cooperation of six independent wholesalers. Although the six wholesalers would gain exclusive territories and greatly increased sales of Minute Maid orange juice, the cost of operating the delivery system would be substantial.

To help control dealer expenses, Minute Maid planned to buy forty-two delivery trucks and lease them to the six independent wholesalers. An estimate of the revenue and profits that could be derived by a wholesaler by operating a fleet of six or nine trucks is shown Table 9-1. This example assumes the number of customers and sales would be the

Table 9-1

Projected Weekly Operating Statement for One Minute Maid Wholesaler Using Three Different Sales Levels and Two Levels of Customer Service[a]

	Six Truck Operation			Nine-Truck Operation		
	I 25% Sales Decrease	II No Change in Sales	III 25% Sales Increase	IV 25% Sales Decrease	V No Change in Sales	VI 25% Sales Increase
Gross sales	$21,300	$28,400	$35,500	$21,300	$28,400	$35,500
Cost of goods sold	19,170	25,560	31,950	19,170	25,560	31,950
Gross margin	2,130	2,840	3,550	2,130	2,840	3,550
Expenses						
Trucks[b]	$656	$785	$875	$656	$785	$875
Dry ice	150	150	150	225	225	225
Driver-salesmen	480	480	480	720	720	720
Supervisors	275	275	275	412	412	412
Warehousemen	94	125	156	94	125	156
Clerical	52	70	88	88	105	123
Mgr. salary	75	100	125	125	150	175
Warehouse	338	450	562	338	450	562
	2,120	2,435	2,711	2,658	2,972	3,248
Profit before taxes	$ 10	$ 405	$ 839	($ 528)	($ 132)	$ 302

[a] This example assumes that the number of customers and sales volume would be the same for six and nine truck operations, but the nine-truck fleet would offer better service in terms of quicker delivery and more time per store visit.

[b] Since the trucks are leased, truck expense is assumed to be a linear function of miles traveled and is calculated at 23¢ per mile. Truck expense is the same for six and nine truck operations because the same numbers of customers are contacted.

Source. Prepared by John O. Summers from data presented in Harry L. Hansen, "Minute Maid Corporation," *Marketing-Text, Techniques, and Cases* (Homewood, Ill.: Richard D. Irwin, 1967), pp. 586-92.

same for different numbers of trucks, but the nine-truck fleet would offer customers better service. If all the present Minute Maid retailers were retained under the new distribution plan, then a six-truck wholesaler would make a small profit ($405 per week, Table 9-1). However, some retailers are likely to stay with their regular wholesalers and others will want the option of buying part cases. Thus, in the short run sales will probably decline and the wholesalers will do little more than cover expenses. Another problem with the Minute Maid proposal is that forty-two trucks making two visits per store per week only allows the driver-salesmen five minutes per call including travel. This suggests that the goal of increasing the number of visits to the retailers would not be achieved by the new distribution plan. The Minute Maid example indicates that the selection of distribution alternatives involves a series of trade-offs among the needs and objectives of the manufacturer, wholesaler, retailer, and the final consumer.

MANAGING THE CHANNEL

Control of distribution channels can be a serious problem for firms that rely on independent dealers to perform wholesale and retail functions. Independent distributors are in business to make money and are naturally interested in stocking and promoting items that increase their own profits. Manufacturers who sell through these dealers must design attractive products and marketing programs if they expect to gain the support of these entrepreneurs. A manufacturer's success with independent channel members also depends on his understanding of their strengths and weaknesses. The manufacturer must realize that his job extends through to the aftersale servicing of the final customer and his programs must be closely coordinated with those of his dealers. This means that a good communication network is essential to assure that information gets to the distributors and feedback on performance is quick and accurate. In addition, the manufacturer should realize that the dealers' problems are his own problems and cannot be ignored if he expects to maintain his market position. Finally, the manufacturer should reimburse his distributors for warranty work and other services he expects the dealer to provide to customers.

Dealers Incentives

A wide variety of incentives are available to help manufacturers build dealer enthusiasm. Some of the specific techniques that can be used are listed in Table 9-2. The most direct dealer incentives are price concessions granted for volume purchases, advertising support, and seasonal orders. Other more indirect methods for building dealer excitement include display materials, training programs, sales literature, and the hiring of in-store demonstrators. Perhaps the most enduring technique used to gain dealer cooperation involves the extension of credit. This may take the form of loans to finance inventories of display merchandise, loans for fixtures and equipment, or cash to finance customer purchases. Distribution incentive programs may also include plans to help dealers get new merchandise quickly and clear out old stock at the end of the selling season.

One of the most powerful methods used to stimulate dealer enthusiasm is to give distributors *exclusive* sales territories. This means that dealers benefit directly from sales promotion work in their territories and they do not have to share revenue gains with other companies. Although exclusive distribution is an excellent way to open up new territories, it can restrict the long-run growth potential of a manufacturer. This occurs when

Table 9-2

Techniques Used to Gain Dealer Cooperation

I. "Price" Concessions
   A. Discount structure

Trade (functional) discounts	Prepared freight
Quantity discounts	Seasonal discounts
Cash discounts	Mixed-carload privilege
Anticipation allowances	Drop-shipping privilege
Free goods	Trade deals
New product, display, and advertising allowances (without performance requirements)	

   B. Discount substitutes

Display materials	Advertising matrices
Premarked merchandise	Management consulting
Inventory control programs	services
Training programs	Merchandising programs
Shelf-stocking programs	Sales "spiffs"
Payment of sales personnel and demonstrator salaries	Technical assistance
	Catalogs and sales promotion
Promotional and advertising allowances (with performance requirements)	literature

II. Financial Assistance
   A. Conventional lending arrangements

Term loans	Accounts payable financing
Inventory floor plans	Lease and note guarantee
Notes payable financing	programs
Installment financing of fixtures and equipment	Accounts receivable financing

   B. Extended dating

E.O.M. dating	"Extra" dating
Seasonal dating	Postdating
R.O.G. dating	

III. Protective Provisions
   A. Price protection

Premarked merchandise	"Franchise" pricing
Agency agreements	

   B. Inventory protection

Consignment selling	Rebate programs
Memorandum selling	Reorder guarantees
Liberal returns allowances	Guaranteed support of sales events
Maintenance of "spot" stocks and fast delivery	

   C. Territorial protection
      Selective distribution
      Exclusive distribution

Source. Bert C. McGammon, Jr., "Perspectives for Distribution Programing" in *Vertical Marketing Systems,* Louis P. Bucklin, ed. (Glenview, Ill., Scott, Foresman & Co., 1970) pp. 36-37. Copyright © by Scott, Foresman & Co. Reprinted by permission of the publisher.

the market potential of an area grows faster than the capacity of one dealer to handle the business. For example, although auto manufacturers have historically relied on exclusive distribution they have begun to switch to a policy of *selective* distribution to gain better market coverage and encourage some healthy competition among their dealers. Selective distribution allows several of the better dealers in an area to handle a product, but avoids the high credit and selling expenses associated with more intensive distribution systems. Dealer cooperation is also influenced by the methods used to transport products from the factory to the customer.

Channel Conflict

Despite efforts by manufacturers to gain the cooperation of distributors, a great deal of conflict still exists in channels of distribution.[19] The underlying problem is that although channel members are often independent, they must work closely together to make the channel operate. This interdependence leads to both *cooperation* for survival and *conflict* because of different economic goals. Channel conflict seems to be most serious when there is an imbalance of power and there are differences in the ability of channel members to apply pressure on one another (i.e., large automobile, petroleum, and television manufacturers and small retail dealers.).

One study of the intensity of channel conflicts is summarized in Table 9-3. Most distribution conflicts grow out of the manufacturer's desire to maintain high production levels and the resulting pressure he places on dealers to increase sales volume. Manufacturers sometimes threaten dealers with franchise or lease cancellation if they fail to accept additional inventory, parts or engage in certain promotional activities. A second area of conflict is the absorption by one party of distributive functions previously performed by another. Examples include direct sales by manufacturers that bypass wholesalers or retailers, operation of factory owned retail outlets, and manufacturer control over local promotions. Conflicts can also develop over the proper role of wholesalers and retailers in the channel of distribution. Issues here include limits on sales territories and the size of functional discounts.

We believe that the best way to resolve channel conflicts is for the manufacturer and his distributors to work out their own solution, recognizing the divergent roles and economic goals of each party. This approach has the advantage that it avoids the bitterness and disruptions that often occur when disputes are left to the courts or to the passage of special legislation. For example, Chicken Delight found it was much more difficult to recruit investors for new franchises and harder to improve the sales of existing outlets after a group of disgruntled store owners sued the parent organization over operating procedures. Chicken Delight would have been much better off if they settled out-of-court with the dealers (like Kentucky Fried Chicken) and proceeded with the business of selling chicken.

Sometimes the size and power of the manufacturer is so vast that special legislation is required to resolve channel conflicts. In the past, for example, auto manufacturers took advantage of their dealers by forcing them to take unwanted parts and new cars. The National Automobile Dealers Association reacted to this threat of inventory forcing by obtaining the passage of a federal law that limited the right of manufacturers to cancel franchises (the Good Faith Act of 1956). Since independent channel members have been increasingly successful at defending their rights in court, some manufacturers may try to strengthen their position by raising the proportion of company owned distributors. Although a completely integrated distribution network minimizes channel conflict, most firms cannot afford this approach. Thus, for many companies the best solution may be to design special programs that recognize the unique problems (Table 9-3) and needs of all parties.

[19]Six good articles on channel conflicts are reproduced in Louis W. Stern, *Distribution Channels: Behavioral Dimensions* (New York: Houghton Mifflin Co., 1969), pp. 155-223.

Table 9-3
Distributive Conflicts in Nine Industries[a]

	Bypassing Wholesaler	Bypassing Retailer	Chain vs. Independents	Discounters vs. Traditionalist	Private vs. National Brands	Fair Trade	Retail or Wholesale Inventory Levels	Too Many Dealers	Price Discrimination or Discount Structure	Promotional Allowances	Service and Warranty	Franchise Cancellation	Pressure to Accept Parts and Accessories	Manufacturer Involvement in Store Management	Overall Intensity of Conflict	Intensity of Association Political Activities
Drug	VV	V	VV	VV	V	VV	X	.	V	X	*	*	*	X	VV	VV
Automobile	*	VV	*	V	*	X	VV	VV	V	V	V	V	V	VV	VV	VV
Petroleum	VV	V	*	V	VV	V	VV	V	VV	V	*	V	VV	VV	VV	VV
Food	VV	X	VV	V	VV	X	V	.	VV	V	*	*	*	V	VV	V
Electrical products	V	*	*	*	*	X	V	V	V	X	V	V	X	V	V	X
Television receivers	VV	V	*	VV	V	VV	VV	V	V	V	V	VV	X	V	VV	V
Pesticides	V	V	*	*	*	X	V	V	X	V	*	*	*	X	V	X
Liquor[b]	V	X	V	VV	VV	VV	X	*	V	X	*	*	*	X	VV	*
Farm equipment	V	VV	*	X	*	X	V	V	V	V	V	V	V	V	V	X

[a] VV Signifies intense conflict; V signifies moderate conflict; X signifies little or no conflict; * signifies not applicable to industry.

[b] Areas of conflict do not apply to seventeen states where distribution is state controlled.

Source. Henry Assael, "The Political Role of Trade Associations in Distributive Conflict Resolution," *Journal of Marketing*, Vol. 32 (April 1968), p. 23. Reprinted by permission of the American Marketing Association.

ORGANIZING PHYSICAL DISTRIBUTION

Once a firm has selected appropriate distribution channels, the next step is to design a physical handling system that will deliver merchandise to customers efficiently. This is a complex and recurring task because businessmen want to keep distribution *costs* as *low* as possible and at the same time *meet the customer's needs* for prompt delivery. These two goals frequently conflict and it is the job of the manager to find the best trade-off between a realistic level of customer service and reasonable expenditures on distribution.

Quite often distribution problems develop from a failure to adequately integrate manufacturing and distribution control systems. Signs of control failure include inventories that turn over less than six times per year and an inability to meet projected service levels. A distribution system audit may also be indicated if a company is experiencing high stock transfers among warehouses and the system is using a lot of premium freight.

The Costs of Distribution

At the present time the average manufacturer spends about 13 percent of every sales dollar on physical distribution.[20] Distribution costs include such things as transportation charges, fixed investments in facilities (such as stores and warehouses), and the cost of maintaining inventories in stores, warehouses, and in transit. Inventory carrying costs are made up of charges for capital, obsolescence, pilferage, taxes, and insurance. Other costs associated with operating a distribution system include the expenses of order processing, arranging for transportation, and tracing lost shipments. Operating costs also encompass charges for communication networks used to link salesmen, stores, warehouses, and factories plus any computers employed to process distribution data. Distribution costs typically vary directly with the level of customer service provided. Faster and more reliable delivery usually means more warehouses, more inventory, more expensive transportation methods, and higher costs.

Some distribution costs are more abstract and vary inversely with the level of customer service. These are the opportunity costs associated with failure to deliver goods to customers on time. If a store or warehouse cannot supply goods when they are needed, some customers will find other suppliers and the firm loses the current sale and probably some future business as well. The amount of lost business can be reduced by raising the level of reserve stocks, but this gain should be measured against increases in carrying costs. Since lost sales do not appear on any accounting records, they must be estimated if the firm expects to determine the best level of customer service to build into their distribution system.

Levels of Customer Service

Customer service has a variety of meanings depending on the industry and products under consideration. One definition centers on the amount of *time* from when a customer orders merchandise to the actual delivery of the items. For example, a firm might define customer service as delivery within a six-day order cycle. This could include one day for order transmission, two days for order processing and packing, and three days for shipping the merchandise to the customer. Sometimes *reliability* of service is more important to customers than pure speed of delivery.[21] Thus, buyers may not care whether

[20]Stephen B. Oresman and Charles D. Scudder, "A Remedy for Maldistribution," *Business Horizons* (June 1974), p. 61.
[21]Donald J. Bowersox, Edward W. Smykay, and Barnard J. LaLonde, *Physical Distribution Management* New York: The Macmillan Company, 1968), p. 115.

it takes six or eight days to get merchandise as long as the probability is 100 percent that the goods will arrive within ten days. A third dimension of customer service is related to the *in-stock* position of the firm. This shows the proportion of customers' orders that can be filled from existing finished goods inventories. For example, a firm might have a policy of filling 95 percent of incoming orders for high-volume items and 70 percent of incoming orders for low-volume merchandise.

The determination of optimum levels of customer service (however measured) is one of the most difficult tasks confronting physical distribution managers. Although there are a variety of sophisticated techniques for measuring and controlling distribution costs, the selection of service levels is often based on rules of thumb and seat-of-the-pants speculation.[22] The trouble is there are no easy ways to predict future sales of the firm. Will out-of-stock conditions result in the cancellation of current orders and the loss of future business or will customers accept delays and return to buy again in the future? The objective of our discussion is to show how customer service needs can be measured objectively and balanced against physical distribution costs. We have structured our review of the *customer service-distribution cost dilemma* around the problems of picking locations for retail stores and field warehouses.

HOW MANY WAREHOUSES ARE ENOUGH?

One of the most common problems in physical distribution is deciding on the number and location of field warehouses. The inclusion of branch warehouses in the channel of distribution is often defended in terms of reducing transportation costs. Bulk shipments are made from factories to branch warehouses by rail or truck and then smaller quantities are hauled from the branches to the customers by local delivery services. Thus most of the hauling is at car load (CL) rates rather than the more expensive less than car load (LCL) rates that would apply if all merchandise were shipped direct from factories to customers. This means that total transportation costs can often be reduced by adding branch warehouses to a distribution system. Having reserve stocks in branch warehouses may also speed up deliveries to customers and improve the reliability of a distribution system. Despite these advantages, the use of branch warehouses is not always the most efficient way to distribute merchandise.

An alternative to a branch warehouse system is to fill all customer orders from one centralized warehouse. This eliminates the fixed and variable costs of operating field facilities and allows tighter control over inventories and order-filling procedures. In addition, the total amount of inventory needed to provide a given level of customer service is less if the goods are held in one location. Random variation in customer demands are easier to fill from one large inventory than several small inventories spread over a number of warehouses. Direct distribution works best for products that are relatively light in weight compared to their value and for items where speed of delivery is more important than reliability of delivery. Repair parts, electronic equipment, bathing suits, and perishable drugs all share these characteristics and are often distributed using high-speed transportation methods (such as air freight). Let us now turn to some examples to see how business firms have solved the problem of "How Many Warehouses Are Enough?"

[22]"The Case for 90% Satisfaction," *Business Week* (January 14, 1961), pp. 82-85.

The Raytheon "Unimarket" System[23]

Perhaps the most famous example of a centralized distribution system was installed by Raytheon in 1960. Under their old system, Raytheon distributed electronic parts through six regional warehouses to 800 distributors. The distributors, in turn, sold to dealers or the final user. Because of rapid obsolescence and the high cost of the electronic parts, distributors tended to keep minimum inventories and relied on the $2 million in field stocks held at the six Raytheon warehouses. However, since Raytheon handled 3000 items, they could not afford to stock the regional warehouses with slow moving items. As a result, only 60 percent of the line was carried at the regional warehouses and about half of the customer requests had to be back-ordered from the main warehouse. This produced a low level of customer service and the normal order-cycle time was ten to twelve days. Orders to the main warehouse took as many as four days to be received through the mails, one to three days were consumed in order processing, and delivery took up to five days. Thus, Raytheon was spending $485,000 per year to operate a system of regional warehouses that gave poor service to customers.

Raytheon's problems were solved by eliminating the regional warehouses altogether and shipping orders by air freight from a single warehouse. Instead of relying on the mails to receive orders, Raytheon introduced a leased-wire communications network with six data-entry points scattered around the country. Distributors' orders were assembled at these points and sent to the warehouse where a computer checked inventories and printed up invoices.

Raytheon's decison to use air freight was based on an analysis of the time and costs of alternative transportation methods. Table 9-4 shows some typical cost data for two shipments from Raytheon's warehouse to New Orleans, Louisiana. Note that rail express had the lowest rate for the small shipment, and surface transportation (rail or truck) was the low-cost method for the heavier order. Although air freight was not the low-cost carrier, it offered Raytheon a way of reducing delivery time at a reasonable cost. Because of the minimum rate structure of air freight, Raytheon found that it was more economical to combine small shipments to some areas and break them at selected points for forwarding to individual customers. Air freight was used for most of the trip and then parcel post was employed to trans-ship to the final customer.

Table 9-4
Shipping Costs for Electronic Parts from Westwood, Massachusetts, to New Orleans, Louisiana

Carrier	20 lb.	220 lb	Time
Air freight[a]	$6.00	$35.20	1 day
Air express	10.05	110.57	1 day
Rail express	3.19	35.11	4-5 days
Surface	9.12	20.06	5-6 days

[a]Exclusive of pick-up and delivery charges.

Source. Boyd B. Barrick, "What 'Unimarket' Does for Raytheon," *Industrial Marketing* (February 1963), pp. 88. Copyright © 1963 by Advertising Publications, Inc., Chicago, Ill.

[23]Described by Boyd B. Barrick in "What 'Unimarket' Does for Raytheon," *Industrial Marketing* (February 1963), pp. 88.

The net result of Raytheon's decision to centralize reserve stock, introduce high-cost air freight, and establish a leased wire communication network, was a reduction in total distribution costs. Not only were total costs cut 17 percent under the new system, but order-cycle time was reduced to an average of two to three days. Thus, Raytheon was able to reduce distribution costs and improve customer service at the same time. Although Raytheon's solution to their distribution problems was successful, they did not attempt to measure sales lost under their old or new systems, and they did not find out what level of service was actually needed by their customers. This suggests they failed to optimize the distribution of electronic parts and further savings could be achieved by making additional refinements in their systems (more about this later).

Raytheon's spectacular success with centralized distribution was well publicized and other firms have been quick to adapt the ideas to their own particular situations. Burroughs, for example, was able to close eight regional warehouses and save hundreds of thousands of dollars in rent, personnel costs, taxes and inventory carrying costs by moving to centralized distribution.[24] More recently, Samsonite was able to close two regional warehouses as the result of reductions in air freight costs from Denver to several key market areas.[25] Savings on warehouse space, inventories, and safety stocks more than covered the increased cost of air delivery.

Despite the allure of air freight, many products cannot be shipped by premium transportation because the value of the items is low relative to their bulk and weight. Food products share these characteristics and manufacturers rely on field warehouse systems to get merchandise to customers quickly.

Selecting Warehouses for H. J. Heinz[26]

In 1960, Heinz was operating forty-three warehouses to supply 500 items to about 4000 distributors, chains, and institutional suppliers. The rapid growth of chain buying in the late 1950s had made it possible for Heinz to cut the number of branch warehouses in their system from sixty-eight in 1957 to forty-three without reducing distribution effectiveness. Heinz was concerned with finding out how many of the remaining warehouses could be eliminated without impairing customer service. Heinz had a policy of filling orders within four days, but more warehouses were located in large cities and many orders were filled in a day or two. Since large customers placed their orders weekly or biweekly, Heinz had more capacity in their distribution system than they really needed. Only the smaller customer who did not maintain significant inventories was using Heinz's quick delivery service.

Selecting additional branch warehouses for elimination was a complex task for Heinz because the branches served as mixing points to combine the output from nine processing plants. None of the factories produced all 500 items in the line, and each branch warehouse received merchandise from several different factories. Thus, when a branch was dropped, customers had to be reassigned to other warehouses and the output from the nine factories had to reallocated to the remaining warehouses. To help solve the problem,

[24]L. O. Browne, "Total Distribution in the Age of the Computer," *Marketing Logistics: Perspectives and Viewpoints,* Norton E. Marks and Robert M. Taylor, eds. (New York: Wiley, 1967), pp. 48-55.

[25]Samsonite Corporation Annual Report—1970, p. 11.

[26]Described in *H. J. Heinz Company Simulation* (Boston: Harvard Graduate School of Business Administration, ICH Case Number 9M78, 1963), 17 pages, with additional detail in an article "Simulation—Tool for Better Distribution" by Harvey N. Shycon and Richard B. Maffei, *Harvard Business Review,* Vol. 38, No. 6 (November-December, 1960), pp. 65-75.

Heinz hired a consultant who estimated the total distribution costs incurred by ten alternative warehouse systems. The ten plans were developed by a senior Heinz distribution analyst to test different numbers and locations of branch warehouses.

Basic data for the consultant's distribution analysis were derived from three months of customer demand figures from 1959 and 1960 plus a review of the operating costs for different warehouses. A computer program was prepared to estimate the total annual distribution costs associated with each of the ten warehouse systems. The computer was given the location of the warehouses in a particular plan and it assigned customers to warehouses to minimize delivery costs (usually the nearest warehouse). Next, the computer added up the volume purchased by the customers assigned to each warehouse. The volume estimates and the fixed costs for facilities were then used to calculate the total costs of operating a particular set of warehouses. A subroutine was employed to find the cheapest way to supply each set of the warehouses from the nine factories. Total costs of operating each system were obtained by adding up delivery costs, transportation from factories, and the fixed and variable costs of operating the warehouses.

The costs estimated for the ten configurations of branch warehouses considered by Heinz are shown in relative terms in Figure 9-5. Note that warehouse costs increased in almost linear fashion as more branches were added to the distribution system. Transportation costs, on the other hand, declined as branches were added to the system. This occurred because the volume of traffic moving at low carload rates increases with the number of warehouses. With only a few branch warehouses, most of the total volume is hauled long distances to customers at less than carload rates. As more warehouses are added to the system, the distance the goods are hauled at LCL rates declines. The lowest total cost of distribution occurred with twenty-seven warehouses (Figures 9-5), but the consultant did not recommend this number because Heinz would not be able to deliver within four days to some customers in the Midwest and Great Plains. The final recommendation was for thirty-two warehouses, which cost slightly more and allowed two warehouses in the New York City area. The simulation was not refined enough to tell whether one warehouse would be better than two to serve the New York market.

The Heinz warehouse study required the equivalent of five or six man-years to gather needed data plus a fee of $52,000 for the consultant to prepare and run the simulation program. However, the estimated annual savings of $217,000 produced by dropping eleven warehouses and relocating others greatly exceeded the out-of-pocket expenses of the study. Thus, it was possible for Heinz to maintain customer service at a predetermined level (four days delivery) while the number of warehouses was cut by 25 percent. The emphasis on cost reduction exhibited by the Heinz study is typical in distribution problems because it is easier to focus on measurable expenses than it is to find the optimum level of customer service. Since no attempt was made in the Heinz example to find out what level of customer service was actually needed in the Midwest and Plains areas, it is quite possible that six-day delivery would be adequate in these markets. If so, Heinz could eliminate five more warehouses and move to the minimum cost distribution network found in the simulation study.

Service Levels and the Number of Warehouses

In the Raytheon and Heinz examples the costs of transportation, information handling systems, facilities, and inventories were identified and added up for alternative numbers of warehouses. The next logical step is to estimate the costs of providing alternative levels of customer service for *each* distribution system being considered. This would make it easier for the manager to weight cost savings against the possible sales and

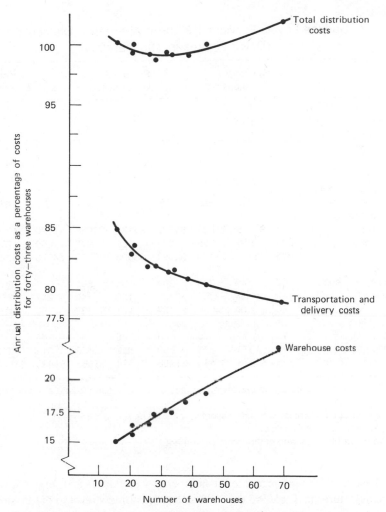

Figure 9-5 Estimated Distribution Costs for Alternative Numbers of Warehouses. *Source. H. J. Heintz Company Simulation* (Boston: Harvard Business School, ICH Case No. 9M78, 1963), p. 12, reproduced by permission.

competitive gains that might develop from improved service. Table 9-5 shows the costs of alternative service levels associated with three distribution systems. In this example, a boat manufacturer is considering a move from two regional warehouses to systems of eight and twenty field warehouses.

Note that as warehouses are added, the length of the order cycle declines and the percentage of orders delivered in less than six days increases dramatically (Table 9-5). Each of the three systems can be operated to fill 75, 85, or 95 percent of customer's demands by varying the size of the inventories carried at the branch warehouses. Facilities have been expanded slightly to provide room for the extra inventory needed for better service. The total annual costs of operating the three distribution systems include charges for transportation, amortization of facilities, inventory carrying costs, information networks, and the expenses of running the warehouses. Within each system, total costs increase as the proportion of orders filled from stock goes from 75 to 95 percent. Note that the greater investments in facilities and inventory required by the eight and twenty warehouse systems were partially offset by reductions in transportation costs.

Table 9-5
Costs and Service Levels Provided by Three Alternative Distribution Systems (Dollar Figures in Thousands)

	System 1 — 2 Warehouses			System 2 — 8 Warehouses			System 3 — 20 Warehouses		
Average order cycle time	8 days			5 days			3 days		
Percentage of orders delivered within 2 days	20			38			64		
6 days	55			80			95		
Percentage of orders filled from stock	75	85	95	75	85	95	75	85	95
Investment required									
Inventory	$ 510	$ 745	$1029	$1520	$2175	$2956	$3320	$4015	$4875
Facilities	325	359	395	871	920	976	1650	1708	1759
Total	$ 835	$1104	$1424	$2391	$3095	$3932	$4970	$5723	$6634
Annual costs									
Inventory expense[a]	102	149	206	304	435	591	664	803	975
Facilities[b]	49	54	59	131	138	146	247	256	264
Operations[c]	80	80	80	127	127	127	155	155	155
Information processing	20	20	20	35	35	35	40	40	40
Transportation[d]	1075	1075	1075	659	659	659	319	319	319
Total System Costs	$1326	$1378	$1440	$1256	$1394	$1558	$1425	$1573	$1753

[a] Carrying costs include taxes, depreciation, interest, and obsolescence and are caluculated as 20 percent of inventory value.
[b] Amortization of land, equipment, and buildings, plus taxes and insurance.
[c] Labor, supervision, and utilities.
[d] Inbound to warehouses and outbound to customers.

The best decision with regard to the number of warehouses and service levels for the boat manufacturer in Table 9-5 depends on how customers react to out-of-stock conditions and delays in delivery. If these factors are *not* important to customers, then the company should operate eight warehouses at a stocking level of 75 percent to give the lowest total distribution cost. On the other hand, if customers expect an 85 percent in-stock position, then the two-warehouse system is best. Note that system 2 is quite competitive with system 1 at the 85 percent stocking level and offers significant improvements in customer service for only $16,000 more per year. If fast delivery is more important to customers than the stocking level, then the twenty-warehouse system offers reasonable costs when it is operated at the 75 percent service level.

The final choice of distribution systems would, of course, be influenced by the size of the investments needed and alternative uses for the money within the firm. At the 85 percent service level, the eight warehouse system requires an additional investment of $2 million and the twenty warehouse system would require an extra $4.7 million. These are substantial sums of money and the distribution manager will have to build a strong case if he expects to gain approval ahead of requests for expenditures for advertising and manufacturing facilities.

Although the type of analysis presented in Table 9-5 is useful, it does not provide managers with the realistic data on lost sales and customers' service needs that are critical to making good distribution decisions. In the next section we will show how these factors can be measured and integrated in the distribution decision process.

Measuring and Controlling Customer Service[27]

Hutchinson and Stolle suggest that the successful management of customer service is based on a six-step procedure. The sequence of steps includes:
1. Define the elements of service.
2. Check customer views.
3. Design a service package.
4. Sell customers on service package.
5. Test the program.
6. Establish performance controls.

The first step involves the identification of the specific elements of customer service that are important for particular firms. These would normally include the order cycle time, reliability, and out-of-stock factors that have been discussed plus other elements such as minimum and maximum order sizes, consolidation privileges, and rush-order procedures that might be critical for certain types of products.

Business firms spend vast sums of money interviewing customers to determine attitude toward products, but very little research is done to find out how customers feel about distribution services. Step 2 of the Hutchinson-Stolle method employs survey research to find the additional elements of service that are important to customers. Would the customer like more or less frequent salesmen visits, improved ordering convenience via telephone or leased wire hookups, more shipping notices, or reorganized order forms? The survey also tries to find out how much customers would be willing to pay (either through larger orders or higher prices) for improved service. Finally, the customer survey solicits customers' evaluation of the service levels of competitors. This gives an indication of minimum service needs and points up areas where service can be used to gain competitive advantage.

Once real customer needs have been documented, this information can be combined with a traditional cost analysis to yield an optimum package of distribution services. Since the new programs may appear to reduce service through the closing of branches and the introduction of new procedures, it is usually desirable to make an effort to sell customers on the advantage of improved systems. In cases where sales increases are needed to justify a revised distribution system, a regional test of the program may be desirable. The final step in the Hutchinson-Stolle procedure is to set up quantitative performance standards to assure that new customer service programs are operated as intended.

An application of the six-step procedure can be illustrated by referring to a company that produced and distributed two completely different product lines. One line was sold in large quantities to institutional customers and the other was sold in small lots to 10,000 retail customers. Both product lines were handled through a network of twenty-five company owned branch warehouses. To find out how well this system compared to the services offered by independent wholesalers, the company interviewed 500 of their customers. They found that both classes of customers believed that the frequency of saleman's visits was a major service factor. The retail customers expressed satisfaction with three-to five day delivery service and complaints of out-of-stocks were rare. Although the retailers ranked the company first in delivery service, they felt that greater consistency of service was worth an extra day's delivery time and price concessions of 2 to 4 percent would induce retailers to accept double the service time. These results

[27]This section is based on the article "How to Manage Customer Service" by William M. Hutchinson and John F. Stolle, *Harvard Business Review,* Vol. 46, No. 6 (November-December 1968), pp. 85-96.

suggested that the present system of twenty-five warehouses was providing more service to retail customers than they actually required.

Service to institutional buyers, however, was found to be inadequate and the company was frequently out-of-stock and ranked second in terms of speed of delivery. Thus, although the twenty-five company branches were able to do a good job for the retail market, they did not have enough units to give the institutional buyers the one-day delivery that was required. Because of the differences in service required by the two classes of customers, the company decided to handle the retail accounts with company branches and to service the institutional buyers with inventories held in public warehouses. The total distribution costs associated with alternative numbers of branch and public warehouses are shown in Figure 9-6. Note that only ten of the twenty-five branch warehouses were needed to achieve minimum distribution costs for the retail market. In the institutional area, however, minimum distribution costs occurred with a system of forty public warehouses.

Next the company calculated the delivery times for each potential number of warehouses to see how many customers could be serviced in one, two, or three days. This revealed that service for the retailers declined slowly as the number of branches was reduced until a fourteen-branch network was achieved (Figure 9-7). After that, delivery service declined rapidly. With the institutional market, service improved dramatically as the number of warehouses was raised above twenty-five units and then leveled off at about forty-five units (Figure 9-7). The company balanced distribution costs (Figure 9-6) against delivery times (Figure 9-7) and decided to handle retail products through fourteen company branches and institutional products through thirty-five public warehouses. This resulted in a net improvement in service to 12 percent of the institutional buyers and an

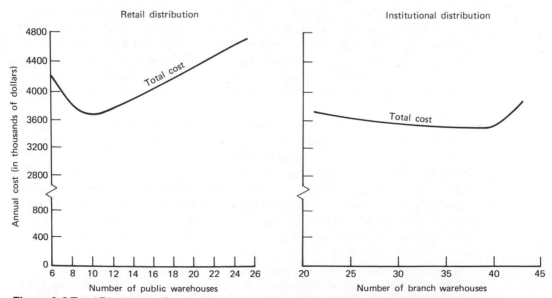

Figure 9-6 Total Distribution Cost for Varying Numbers of Branch and Public Warehouses. *Source.* William M. Hutchison and John F. Stolle, "How to Manage Customer Service," *Harvard Business Review,* Vol. 46, No. 6 (November-December 1968), p. 94, reproduced by permission.

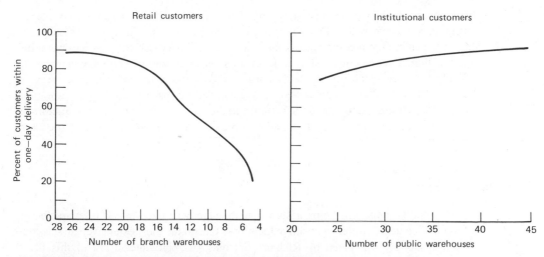

Figure 9-7 Service Levels for Different Branch Systems.
Source. William M. Hutchison and John F. Stolle, "How to Manage Customer Service,"
Harvard Business Review, Vol. 46, No. 6 (November-December 1968), p. 95.

increase in delivery time to 8.5 percent of all retail buyers. Since the survey showed delivery time was not critical to the retailers, increased sales calls were scheduled to offset this apparent loss in service. The overall result of the new distribution system was $1.3 million annual cost saving and the release of $2 millon in assets formally tied up in the branches.

This example has shown how customer service needs can be measured objectively and combined with traditional cost analyses to produce improved distribution networks. We now shift our attention to a second major distribution problem, that of finding locations for retail stores.

LOCATING RETAIL FACILITIES

Distribution managers attempt to locate retail outlets to maximize the sales and profit potential of the firm. The trick is to find convenient locations that attract customers from your competitors or untapped markets rather than simply drawing business away from existing company stores. Retail location studies are primarily concerned with forecasting and comparing the sales potential of alternative store sites in different towns and shopping areas.[28] Once a firm has selected a suitable geographical area, they often have

[28]Many locational studies are unpublished because of the natural reluctance of firms to reveal efficient location techniques to their competitors. Frequently theoretical approaches to retail location, such as Reilly's law, provide hints on trading areas, but do not give much help in picking sites. One form of Reilly's law [Paul D. Converse, "New Laws of Retail Gravitation," *Journal of Marketing* (October 1949), pp. 379-84] suggests: $DB = D_{ab}/1 + \sqrt{P_a/P_b}$ where DB is the distance from town B to the indifference point of the consumer, D_{ab} is the distance between towns A and B, P_a is the population of town A, P_b is the population of town B. The formula gives the break points for shoppers between pairs of cities based on population and distance, but does not consider other factors such as parking, income, travel time, and merchandise assortments, and it is hard to implement in urban areas that lack distinct population centers. Another model for locating shopping centers suggests that the probability of a consumer going to a particular center is a function of the size of the center, the travel time required to reach the center and a parameter that reflects the effects of travel time on types of shopping trips. See David L. Huff, *Determination of Intra-Urban Retail Trading Areas* (Division of Research, Graduate School of Business Administration, UCLA, 1962), 46 pages.

the problem of picking the best shopping center for their needs and then choosing a particular store site within that shopping center. Factors that influence decisions on shopping centers include the size of the trading areas, accessability, growth potential, and location of competitive stores. Decisions on sites within shopping centers are affected by more specific variables such as the cost and length of the lease, services provided by the landlord, number of square feet of selling space and its layout, amount of foot traffic past the location, and the distance to the parking lot. Site selection factors are often evaluated through the creation and interpretation of special maps and by the use of checklists.

Checklists for Store Location

The checklist approach helps assure that management looks at all relevant factors before making decisions on prospective locations. One of the most extensive site selection checklists has been prepared by Richard Nelson. An abbreviated form of this list is reproduced in Table 9-6. Each location factor on the list is evaluated for proposed sites and ratings of excellent, good, fair, or poor are assigned. The profiles that result highlight advantages and disadvantages and can be used to compare alternative store locations. Firms that employ checklists usually have fairly definite ideas about the minimum needs for each locational factor. For example, a company might restrict itself to sites that offered 100,000 square feet of selling space, a trading area of 75,000 persons, an average family income of $9000, 300,000 square feet of customer parking, and were within 100 miles of an exisiting company store. In this case the checklist is used as a screening device to focus management attention on the most likely locations.

The checklist approach to site selection can also be extended to build models to predict sales of new stores at proposed locations. Numerical values can be derived for checklist factors and then combined in an equation to explain variations in sales observed for existing retail units. Once a reliable equation is obtained, data for proposed sites can be fed into the equation to estimate the sales of new stores. For example, Rayco Manufacturing Company considered 300 locational factors in building an equation to explain variations in the sales of autombile seat covers among 150 franchised retail outlets.[29] The final equation they derived contained thirty-seven variables and was able to explain 92 percent of the variation in seat-cover sales. The two most important factors in the equation were the number of automotive outlets per family in each area and a scale that rated the effectiveness of the store operators. Rayco could evaluate the sales potential of prospective locations by collecting data on the thirty-seven variables for each proposed area and plugging them into the forecasting equation. Note that both the checklist and equation methods of site selection emphasize the gathering and analysis of standard demographic statistics. An alternative approach is to look at the spatial or geographical characteristics of prospective store placements.

Mapping Store Locations

The sales potential of new store locations often depends on accessibility, population, competition, and trading area boundaries. These factors are best interpreted through the

[29]Charles H. Dufton, *Rayco Manufacturing Company, Inc.; Pinpointing Store Locations by Electronic Computer,* Case 3M38, (Boston: Intercollegiate Case Clearing House, Harvard Graduate School of Business, 1958), 11 pages.

Table 9-6
Store Location Checklist

Location Factors

   I. Trading area potential
      A. Public utility connections (residential)
      B. Residential building permits issued
      C. School enrollment
      D. New bank accounts opened
      E. Advertising lineage in local newspapers
      F. Retail sales volume
      G. Sales tax receipts
      H. Employment—specific
      I. Employment—general
  II. Accessibility
      A. Public transportation (serving site)
      B. Private transportation (serving site)
      C. Parking facilities
      D. Long-range trends (transportation facilities)
 III. Growth potential
      A. Zoning pattern
      B. Zoning changes
      C. Zoning potential
      D. Utilities trend
      E. Vacant-land market (land zoned for residential use)
      F. Land-use pattern (in areas zoned for other than residential)
      G. Retail-business land-use trend
      H. Retail-building trend (building permits issued for new retail business construction)
      I. Retail-improvement trend (permits issued for remodeling, expansion, etc., in existing properties)
      J. Retail-location trend (changes in occupancy of retail-business locations)
      K. Income trend for average family unit
      L. Plant and equipment expenditure trend
      M. Payroll trend
 IV. Business interception
      A. Location pattern-competitive businesses between site and trade area
      B. Location pattern-competitive businesses between site and trade area (served by and sharing traffic arteries with site)
  V. Cumulative-attraction potential
      A. Neighboring business survey
 VI. Compatibility
      A. Compatibility factors
 VII. Competitive-hazard survey
      A. Competitve pattern—competitors within one mile of site (nonintercepting)
      B. Competitve pattern—potential competitive sites
VIII. Site economics
      A. Cost and return analysis
      B. Site efficiency
      C. Natural description
      D. Adjacent amenities (for both vacant-land and existing building sites)

use of special maps.[30] Prospective sites are usually evaluated for accessibility to make sure it is easy for customers to get to and leave the property. Accessibility is influenced by such things as distance, driving time, street configurations, and traffic lights. Figure 9-8 compares the traffic patterns observed for two store locations at shopping centers G

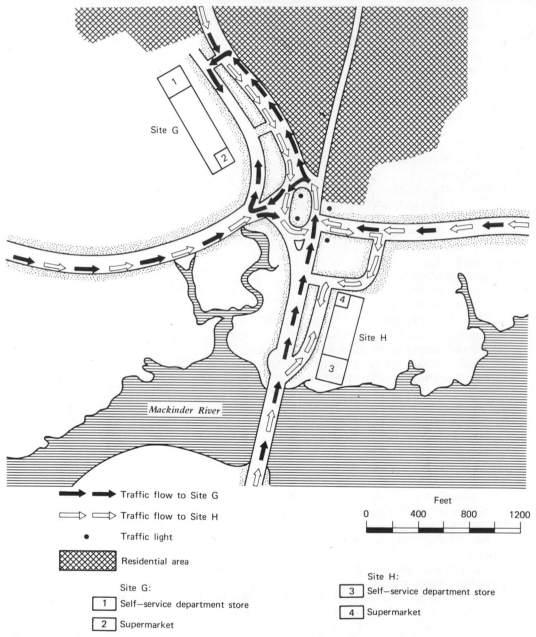

Figure 9-8 Comparing Traffic Patterns for Two Store Sites.
Source. Reprinted by special permission from Saul B. Cohen and William Applebaum, "Major Considerations in Evaluating a Store Site," *Guide to Store Location Research,* Curt Kornblau, ed. (Reading, Mass.: Addison-Wesley, 1968), pp. 86. © 1968. All rights reserved.

[30]The maps reproduced in Figures 9-8 and 9-9 are from a book considered to be the "Bible" of store location practice. Although the *Guide to Store Location Research* emphasizes supermarkets, it is the best single source of material on this subject.

and H. The traffic rotary is a major problem for center H because shoppers from the east cannot make a left turn into the center, but must go around the rotary first. As a result, center H only gets 40 percent of the customers coming into the area from the east and 30 percent of those from the northwest. Location H appears to be less desirable than G, but this would also depend on competition and the number of consumers located in the surrounding residential areas.

The size of the trading area for an individual store is influenced by street patterns and the location of competitors.[31] For example, Figure 9-9 shows the location of a sample of the present automobile customers of stores A, B, and C. A total of 1400 license plates was analyzed and 339 fell within the expected trading area of a new store to be located at L. Further analysis revealed that the three competitive markets only obtained 27 percent of the food business in the proposed store's trading area. In light of the limited competitive pressure, it was felt that the new store should be able to reach its sales objectives. A specific sales estimate for store L could be obtained by estimating the total number of persons residing in each of the concentric zones drawn around the proposed location. This information is readily available from published census figures. Next the firm would have to estimate per capita weekly purchases from each zone by referring to purchase data calculated for other existing stores in the chain. By multiplying the number of persons times the per capita purchases in each zone and summing, the firm would have an estimate of the total weekly sales of the new outlet. This would, of course, be deflated by any purchases lost from existing company stores due to the opening of the new unit.

Mapping By Computer

Trading area and market penetration maps for existing stores can also be developed with the aid of specialized computer programs.[32] The basic input needed for these programs is locational data for a sample of consumers plus information on the percentage of shopping trips made to stores and the amounts spent. The observations are spaced on a map of the area and an equation is developed to explain shopping trips and expenditures on the basis of grid coordinates. This equation is then used to calculate values for shopping trips and expenditures to fill in the rest of the space on the map where survey observations were not available.

When shopping trips are the dependent variable in the equation, the program prints numbers on the map that show the proportion of trips that are made to an individual store. These probabilities decline with distance and the break points are printed on the map as a series of concentric lines (Figure 9-10). Thus, for shoppers who live in the area between the fives and sixes, the probability is 50 percent that these consumers will visit the supermarket in question on a given shopping trip.

MacKay's computer programs can also construct trading area maps that show the proportion of the business of a store falling within a specified geographical area.

[31]A trading area is defined as a region that includes a specified percentage (usually 60 to 90 percent) of the customers or sales volume of an individual store. Trading area boundaries can be derived using data from license plate surveys of shoppers visiting different stores or from surveys of consumers selected at random from surrounding residential neighborhoods.

[32]The TAMPA (*T*rading *A*rea and *M*arket *P*enetration *A*nalysis) program described in this section was developed by David B. MacKay of Indiana University. See David B. MacKay, "Trading Area and Market Penetration Analysis," *Combined Proceedings* (Spring and Fall Conferences, American Marketing Association), 1973, pp. 367-372.

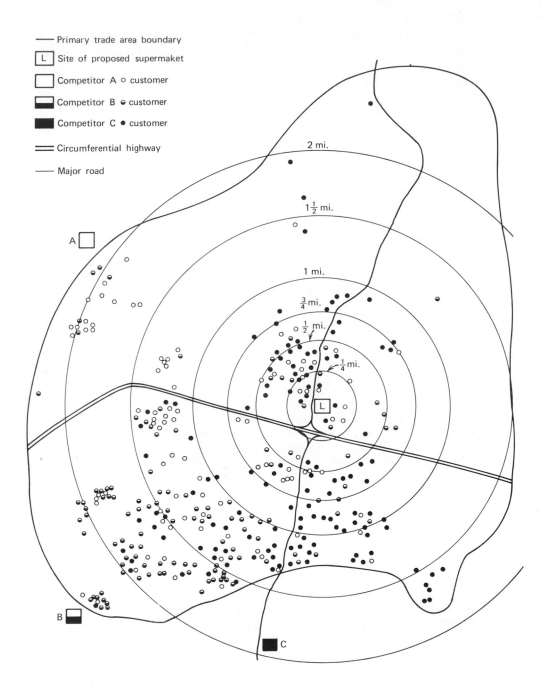

Figure 9-9 Using a License Plate Survey to Estimate Sales of a New Store.
Source. Same as Figure 9-8, p. 92.

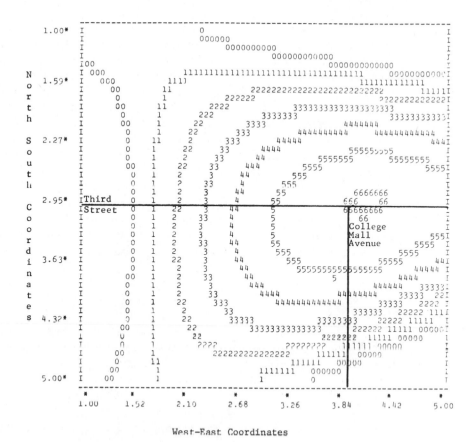

West-East Coordinates

Figure 9-10 Market Penetration Map for a Supermarket in Bloomington, Indiana.

Although the map shown in Figure 9-10 was developed for an existing store, the analysis can be extended to predict trading areas for prospective store locations. For example, MacKay has developed a model that predicts how consumers react to new stores and the output from this formula could be used to build trading area maps with the TAMPA program.[33]

Summary

This chapter has been concerned with selecting channels of distribution and designing systems to efficiently move goods and services to the point of final consumption. The firm must organize groups of brokers, distributors, wholesalers, sales branches, and retailers to meet the needs of customers without exceeding the resources available. Managers have the option of relying on the distribution efforts of independent middlemen, selecting franchised dealers, or owning and operating the channels themselves. This choice is influenced by the supply of independent distributors and the amount of money and sales volume the firm has to support their own distribution system. Once

[33]David MacKay, "A Microanalytic Approach to Store Location Analysis," *Journal of Marketing Research,* Vol. 9 (May 1972), pp. 134-40.

appropriate middlemen have been selected, managers must find ways to care for and nourish channel members to assure their continued cooperation and survival.

The second half of the chapter emphasized the physical handling aspects of distribution. Here the main issues are controlling costs while meeting the delivery and service requirements of customers. We believe the service needs of consumers should be determined through survey research and a package of centralized and field warehouses designed to meet these needs. Frequently decisions on the number and location of branch warehouses can be improved by using simulation techniques to evaluate alternative distribution networks. Distribution management is also concerned with retail store location. Here the objective is to select sites that maximize customer convenience and the potential sales volume of the retail organization. The most popular store location methods employ checklists and special maps that show street configurations and population densities. Sites for stores have also been picked using equations based on demographic statistics. Recently, site selection has been helped by the development of special computer programs that build trading area maps for existing and proposed store locations.

Questions

1. How can the addition of middlemen to a channel raise distribution efficiency?
2. Some consumer advocates have charged that distribution of goods and services is inefficient and leads to high prices for customers. Do you agree or disagree? Why?
3. Since there are so many different ways to distribute products to buyers, how does a manager decide on a channel or set of channels for a particular firm?
4. Under what conditions are consignment and franchised distribution most appropriate?
5. How can dealer incentive programs control channel conflict?
6. Why are vertically integrated channels more efficient than traditional wholesaler-retailer channels?
7. How is customer service measured and why is it important to marketing?
8. How do managers balance service costs against the need to minimize distribution expenses?
9. Under what conditions does centralized distribution work best?
10. Contrast the checklist and mapping approaches to retail store location problems.
11. Why do firms use branch warehouses and how do they decide on the location and number to employ?

Case 9-1
Yates Manufacturing Company[1]

The Yates Manufacturing Company produced a broad line of hand drills, large drilling machines, and air compressors. The major markets served by the company included mining, construction, stone quarries, and public utilities. In the past year, Yates sales reached $14 million. Of this amount, 55 percent represented new machinery; 30 percent, parts and services; and 15 percent, income from rental equipment.

Recently, Yate's controller, Mr. Atwater, had questioned the effectiveness of the company's distribution system. The company distributed its products through a company sales force and a network of mining and construction equipment distributors. Mr. Atwater felt that a large percentage of the company's distributors were underfinanced marginal operators. In his opinion, many of them maintained inadequate inventories and, as a consequence, did not provide the company adequate market coverage. Moreover, because the Yates line typically represented 5 percent of the distributor's total volume, the company was not receiving a reasonable amount of the distributor's sales effort. Mr. Atwater believed the product line had not kept pace with the competition and changing customer requirements. Company executives estimated that Yates had 10 percent of its market at the present time, as compared with 25 percent a decade earlier.

In Atwater's judgment, there were many instances where the company and distributor salesmen called on the same customer. It was his feeling that a well-trained distributor salesman would have no difficulty in closing a major sale without the assistance of a Yates salesman.

At present, the Yates sales force consisted of forty salesmen and ten district managers operating out of ten offices located throughout the United States. District managers devoted approximately 75 percent of their time to selling. The Yates salemen were paid a salary plus bonus; salaries ranged from $600 to $800 per month, while bonuses ranged from ½ to 2 percent of net sales, depending on the product sold. The average total compensation of the company's salesmen was $9400. District managers received a salary plus bonus, with total compensation ranging between $15,000 and $19,000 a year. Total field

sales costs including travel, branch office expense, demonstrators, and field service personnel were estimated to be approximately 9 percent of net sales, while total selling costs averaged 17 percent of sales. The breakdown of selling costs was as follows:

Field sales expenses	
Salesmen's salaries	$ 376,000
District manager's salaries	170,000
Travel expense	250,000
Branch office rental and personnel	450,000
Total field sales expenses	$1,246,000
Advertising and sales promotion	$ 210,000
General marketing overhead	
(included headquarter personnel,	
customer service, government office,	
engineering assistance)	924,000
Total selling costs	$2,386,000

The company's district offices maintained a $20,000 to $40,000 inventory of parts and equipment. On the average, 60 percent of their inventory investment was in parts and 40 percent in equipment. Although both parts and repair service were important factors in the sale of mining and construction equipment, the district offices performed no repair work. Construction companies, mines, and stone quarries placed a high premium on "overnight" parts and maintenance service. They also wanted immediate job site delivery of equipment. These customer requirements placed substantial inventory burdens on manufacturers and their distributors.

To service this market, the Yates Company had 102 mining and construction equipment distributors located throughout the United States. Each of these distributors sold products ranging from small hand tools to major earth-moving equipment. On the average, distributors employed five salesmen and maintained a $5000 to $10,000 inventory of Yates parts and equipment. Distributor salesmen were compensated on a straight commission basis. Distributorships had been opened by the Yates Company salesmen and most of the training of distributor salesmen had been done by the Yates sales force. Six distributors accounted for 60 percent of the Yates total distributor sales volume. Distributors to the metal mining industry received a 15 percent discount. All others received a 20 percent discount from list prices. A major activity of the distributors

[1]From *Marketing Management* by Kenneth R. Davis, 3rd ed., copyright © 1972 by The Ronald Press Company, New York. Reproduced by permission.

was reselling used equipment, a function not performed by Yate's district offices.

Recently, the Yates Company established two new distributors that they referred to as subsidiary distributors. These subsidiary distributors were financed by the company and were closely controlled. This experiment had been introduced by the Yates Company's new marketing manager, Mr. Harworth. He believed that 50 percent of the company's present distributors were not doing an adequate job. It was his opinion that a new network of subsidiary distributors would correct this situation. Mr. Harworth felt that some of the company's present salesmen might well be established in these subsidiary distributors through the financial aid of the Yates Company. Under his plan, the distributor who had built sufficient volume at the end of four or five years would have the option of purchasing his distributorship from Yates. At the same time, he believed that the key to a successful distribution system was a successful mining and construction equipment salesman. If the company could develop more effective salesmen, the distributors could get the kind of training they needed.

In setting up these two subsidiaries, the availability of portable air compressor rental business had been a major consideration. Both subsidiaries had been located in markets where a large number of portable air compressors were being rented, and the servicing and replacement of this equipment alone would provide the subsidiary distributor a reasonable income. It was estimated that a potential rental market of fifty portables would provide adequate support. Because the subsidiary distributors had provided only 25 percent of the total required investment, Yates maintained close financial control of their operation. Both distributors were required to submit monthly and weekly projections of their future cash needs. Yates checked these projections and removed any excess cash in the distributor's account. Mr. Harworth was satisfied with the performance of the two distributors. In their first year of operation, 55 percent of their income was derived from rentals and 45 percent from sales of Yates products and service.

Although the experiment of subsidiary distributors seemed to be working satisfactorily, several questions still remained. One question was the need for the Yates sales force to have direct customer contact. If the company set up a company-controlled subsidiary distributor system, this contact might be limited. One alternative was to maintain the company's own district offices in major distributive centers and use subsidiary distributors in marginal areas. At present, the company was still uncertain as

to the cost of setting up, maintaining and operating subsidiary distributorships and consequently was uncertain as to what discount structure should be used. For the current experiment, the distributors were getting a 30 percent discount on the sale of portable compressors and 25 percent on drills. Mr. Harworth advocated the subsidiary distributor experiment, but he felt it was only an interim step to setting up strong independent distributors.

Shortly after Yates set up its two subsidiary distributors, Mr. Atwater visited the McGraw Diesel Company. McGraw sold over $300 million of its products through a network of company-financed, company-trained, and company-controlled distributors. Atwater learned that McGraw felt that if a distributor invested his own funds, he would put forth a maximum effort. They also felt that the dealer would be more highly motivated if he had the option to purchase full ownership of his distributorship. At present, McGraw distributors were required to have a minimum of two salesmen and two servicemen, a warehouseman and a business manager. The minimum investment for a McGraw distributorship was $500,000. McGraw would provide up to 75 percent of this amount.

McGraw distributors received extensive training in sales, repair work, inventory control, cost accounting, and finance. All distributors were required to submit weekly audit reports. McGraw management audited these reports carefully, and if a distributor's reports indicated possible problem areas, a company adviser was sent to the distributor to work with him in solving the problem. McGraw's policy was to maintain complete control over the distributors in which it still had funds invested.

Recently there had been a tendency to rent and lease certain types of equipment that Yates sold. Reasons for this trend was underfinancing on the part of many construction and mining companies, short-term needs for a particular piece of equipment, and a desire on the part of some customers to expense rather than capitalize their equipment requirements. The majority of Yate's distributors were unable to finance rental or leasing operations. However, if they were to remain competitive, they had to engage in this type of business. Thus, Yates found itself absorbing a major portion of their distributors' financing requirements.

When Yates financed distributor rental and leasing activities, the distributor received title to the equipment involved. This arrangement raised legal as well as financial problems. Customers often required rental and lease contracts that contained a "purchase option price." A purchase option price indicated what it would cost to purchase a piece of equipment in succeeding months as the price declined. This type of contract was, in effect, a conditional sales contract and jeopardized Yate's legal right to the equipment. If one of the company's underfinanced marginal distributors was forced into bankruptcy, Yates would not have title to the equipment the distributor was currently renting or leasing. This had forced Yates into several complicated legal arrangements in order to protect their investments in equipment being leased or rented by distributors.

A further problem was the price at which Yates equipment was sold. The true market price of mining and construction equipment was the product of several factors, the least of which was apparently the list price. Prices were determined by the importance of the customer, the competitive situation at the time of the sale, the repair and parts business to be generated by the sale, the amount of service that would be necessary, and the number of calls that would be required. Yates priced its equipment to yield an average gross margin of 30 percent. However, competitive pressures and the importance of particular customers often forced them to sell substantially below list prices. Recently, a No. 125 portable air compressor with a list price of $5700 had been sold for $3500. Yate's distributors contacted the company whenever they were under competitive price pressure. If Yates considered a particular sale important, it would lower the price to the dealer in order to assure him a reasonable margin. The major responsibility for this pricing activity was centered in the company's product analysts. Product analysts were acutely aware that the Yates Company was a minor factor in the industry. Currently, the Rath Company was the industry leader, with 40 percent of the market share. The number two firm in the industry was Williams with 25 percent, and an additional 30 percent was divided equally among Yates and two other firms.

Credit was used as an extension of the company's pricing policy. Although industry-wide terms were net 30 days, credit was frequently extended for 60 to 90 days and sometimes even longer. Yates extended credit for more than 90 days to the majority of its distributors. Contracts frequently had clauses in their sales arrangements that allowed them to hold back payment until they had been paid for a construction job.

Any shift to a company-controlled distributor system would have to take into account particular characteristics of the company's market. Exhibits 1 and 2 indicate the company's present sales by market. Mr. Harworth had made a survey of Yate's mining market and believed that the market was much more concentrated than the company currently

recognized. In 1964, he found that there were 122 underground mines and 97 open pit mines in the United States. Sixty-three percent of all the iron ore mined in the United States came from Minnesota; 15 percent from Michigan. Twenty-four lead and zinc mines accounted for 91 percent of the country's production of these two metals. Four companies supplied 71 percent of the country's copper ore; the next ten largest companies supplied an additional 26 percent. Geographically, Arizona produced 55 percent of the copper; Utah, 17 percent; Michigan, Montana, Nevada, and New Mexico, 7 percent.

At some point, Mr. Harworth believed the company should consider developing a small highly qualified sales force to call on a few key customers. He believed that a few top-grade salesmen could call on 300 to 400 major accounts. These salesmen would sell only new equipment, while distributors would perform the maintenance and service function as well as selling used equipment. Mr. Harworth noted that while the company had seven major product lines, they essentially were dealing in drilling and excavation problems. Viewed this way, four distinct markets were:

1. *Rock excavation*–40,000 contractors but only 5000 dealing in rock excavation and of these only a few were major customers.
2. *Mining*–47 companies do 90 percent of the mining.
3. *Commercial crushed stone*–300 plants out of 3000 did 31 percent of the business. Some of these plants were chain operators.
4. *Small contractors, plumbers, utilities*–large numbers and widely scattered geographically.

QUESTIONS

1. What portion of Yates' sales is presently handled by distributors? How much does it cost to sell through distributors? What are the advantages and disadvantages of keeping the present distribution channel?
2. What is to be gained and lost by moving to more direct selling through subsidiary distributors? Will direct selling reduce price cutting?
3. Would a key account sales force to supplement the distributors help solve Yates' problems?
4. What should be the role of the forty company salesmen and the ten district sales offices? Are the company's salesmen presently organized and managed efficiently?
5. What changes and sequence of steps do you recommend to help improve Yates' distribution efficiency?

Exhibit 1
Yates Company Sales by Product Line and Market Segment (In Thousands)

Product Line	Construction			Mining			Stone Quarries			Utilities			Total Division Sales
	Division Sales	Sold Direct	Sold by Distributor	Division Sales	Sold Direct	Sold by Distributor	Division Sales	Sold Direct	Sold by Distributor	Division Sales	Sold Direct	Sold by Distributor	
Rock drills	$3010	$ 753	$2257	$ 430	$ 387	$ 43	$ 645	$ 65	$ 580	$ 215	—	$215	$4,300
Blast drills	80	72	8	320	288	32	400	360	40	—	—	—	800
Core drills	360	180	180	360	180	180	90	45	45	90	45	45	900
T.C. bits	1935	—	1935	430	—	430	1935	—	1935	—	45	—	4300
Portables	2470	235	2235	190	95	95	380	19	361	760	38	722	3800
Hoists	100	100	—	90	90	—	—	—	—	—	—	—	190
Totals	$7955	$1340	$6615	$1820	$1040	$ 780	$3450	$ 489	$2961	$1065	$83	$982	$14,290
Percent of total sales	55.7			12.7			24.1			7.5			100

Exhibit 2
Percentage Analysis by Product Line and Market Segment, of Yates Company Sales

Product Line	Construction			Mining			Stone Quarries			Utilities		
	Percent Division Sales	Percent Sold Direct	Percent Sold by Distributor	Percent Division Sales	Percent Sold Direct	Percent Sold by Distributor	Percent Division Sales	Percent Sold Direct	Percent Sold by Distributor	Percent Division Sales	Percent Sold Direct	Percent Sold by Distributor
Rock drills	70	25[a]	75	10	90	10	15	10	90	5	—	100
Blast drills	10	90	10	40	90	10	50	90	10	—	90	10
Core drills	40	50	50	40	50	50	10	50	50	10	50	50[b]
T.C. bits	45	—	100	10	—	100	45	—	100	—	—	—
Portables	65	5	95	5	5	95	10	5	95	20	5	95
Hoists	10	100	—	90	100	—	—	—	—	—	—	—

[a] Direct to national contractors.
[b] All core drills sold through distributors are sold to the export market.

Case 9-2
Hoosier Meat Packers[1]

The Hoosier Meat Packing Company served parts of central Indiana and western Ohio with high quality beef and other meat products. The company operated six meat packing plants as shown in Exhibit 1. During the past two years, demand in the sales districts served by the Bloomington and Richmond plants had increased rapidly due to new contracts with regional food chains. This development made it necessary to consider building a new meat-packing plant. Benjamin Dover, Manager of Customer Service, was asked by the Executive Vice-President to prepare a report outlining the anticipated effect of the proposed new facility on the company's distribution system by July 1, 1972.

PROPOSED FACILITY

Hoosier Meat Packers had designed their proposed new facility to have a daily capacity of 800 hundredweight (CWT). The facilities engineers estimated that a plant of this size would cost approximately $1,922,000, fully equipped. This figure was considered a good estimate as it was very close to the published national average of $2400 per hundredweight of daily capacity for plants with at least 500 CWT daily capacity. Plants with daily capacity of less than 2000 CWT daily capacity could be constructed and equipped in ten to twelve months. The added capacity was considered necessary in view of the forecasted increases in demand shown in Exhibit 2.

Hoosier Meat Packers sold its output at an average delivered price of $25.20 per CWT. Delivered prices were about the same on similar quantities throughout the Hoosier marketing area. Average daily sales (300 days per year) from each plant to important market areas are shown in Exhibit 2.

THE COLUMBUS LOCATION

Two possible plant locations were under consideration. The Eastern Region sales manager (Anderson, Marion, and Richmond districts) expressed his

belief that the new plant should be located in Columbus, Indiana. He pointed out that Columbus was a rapidly growing market area. Indeed, it was expected that the Columbus market would double in the next five years. This jump could be compared to a 10 percent increase in other markets (except Indianapolis). Establishing the plant in Columbus would insure rapid delivery of products to the local stores. Furthermore, transport costs from Columbus to the Eastern Region would also be much less than if the plant were located elsewhere, making the region more profitable.

The sales manager also reminded Ben of the company's long-standing policy of insuring freshness of the product to maintain the quality image of the "Hoosier" label. For Hoosier, this policy meant that all plants *must* be within two hours travel time of the markets they served. As a matter of fact, the company's president did not think it was good business to serve a market from a plant that was more than one hour's travel time. Ben had argued about the costs of this policy, but had difficulty showing the real impact of relaxing the two-hour maximum. Normal transit time between existing and proposed plant locations and markets are shown in Exhibit 3.

THE BEDFORD LOCATION

The production manager had suggested his home town of Bedford as an alternative location for the new facility. He noted that production costs at Bedford would be $18.30 per CWT while at Columbus the costs would be $19.50 per CWT. He explained that these lower costs were primarily due to the low wage scale prevailing in Bedford. Expected closings of several general manufacturing plants in the area would tend to keep wages steady for the immediate future. Moreover, a small meat plant had recently been closed in Mitchell, a few miles south of Bedford.

Varying costs of labor, animal stock, and operations affected the total cost of preparing a standard mixture of case, knife, and saw-ready meat products at each of the locations. This average cost for each of the present plants is shown in Exhibit 4 along with the daily capacity at each location. The full line of the company's meat products was produced at each

[1]Case prepared by Daniel W. DeHayes, Jr. of Indiana University for instructional purposes. Copyright © 1972 by Daniel W. DeHayes, Jr. Reproduced by permission.

Indiana   Ohio

⊘ Packing plant and
major market

△ Major market, no plant

– – – – Marketing territory
boundary

Exhibit 1
Maps of Plants and Marketing Territories

of the six locations to minimize confusion and eliminate cross hauling.

The production chief also pointed out that part of
the reason to consider a new facility was the age and
inefficiency of the Bloomington plant. The
Bloomington facility had the highest cost for production of any of the six existing plants. The Bedford
location was closer to Bloomington than Columbus
and would be able to supply the Bloomington and
Bedford demand at a lower overall cost per unit.

DISTRIBUTION AND CUSTOMER SERVICE

Hoosier owned and operated a fleet of refrigerated
delivery trucks to help assure product freshness and
control distribution costs. Dover was charged with
the responsibility of minimizing transportation costs
from plants to market areas while meeting customer
service standards. Working within the production
limitations of the company, he had achieved the

transport costs shown in Exhibit 5. This exhibit also shows delivery costs between the proposed facility locations and all market areas.

After reviewing the situation, Dover decided to call for outside help from a "management science" consulting firm in Bloomington. He asked them to perform a quick analysis of the problem and submit a report in several days. As a guide to their work, Dover asked the following questions:

1. Is it possible to relocate the present output from the six plants among the existing markets to reduce cost?
2. Will the addition of a new plant reduce costs with current demand? Future demand? When?

3. With a two-hour maximum delivery time, which of the two new plants will give Hoosier Meat Products the lowest costs?
4. If the two-hour maximum delivery time were relaxed, how would this influence: (1) the present allocation of output to markets? (2) the decision to build a new plant and its probably location?
5. What is the cost of meeting a one-hour constraint on delivery time? What is the cost of reducing delivery time to forty-five minutes?
6. What is the overall affect of the new facility on distribution costs? What other factors should be considered before making a final decision on adding a new plant?

Exhibit 2

Current Average and Five-Year Forecasted Demand Pattern

Major Market	Origin Plant	1972 Daily Quantity (CWT)	1977 Daily Quantity (CWT)
Lafayette	Lafayette	350	400
Marion	Marion	550	610
Anderson	Anderson	700	770
Muncie	Anderson	400	440
New Castle	Anderson	1200	1320
Indianapolis	Indianapolis	1450	1570
Columbus	Bloomington	650	1300
Bloomington	Bloomington	100	110
Bedford	Bloomington	100	110
Richmond	Richmond	450	500
Dayton	Richmond	100	110
		6050	7240

Exhibit 3

Average Travel Times (One Way) Between Plants and Markets (In Hours)

	Meat Plants							
Markets	Lafayette	Marion	Anderson	Indianapolis	Richmond	Bloomington	Columbus[a]	Bedford[a]
Lafayette	0.50	2.25	2.50	1.75	3.50	2.75	2.75	3.50
Marion	2.00	0.50	1.00	1.75	2.50	3.00	3.00	4.00
Anderson	2.25	1.00	0.50	1.50	1.75	2.75	3.00	3.00
Muncie	2.75	1.00	0.75	1.75	1.00	3.00	2.25	3.00
New Castle	3.00	1.50	0.75	1.50	0.75	2.75	2.25	3.50
Indianapolis	1.75	2.00	1.50	0.50	1.50	1.50	1.50	2.00
Columbus	3.00	2.50	2.25	1.50	2.50	1.00	0.50	1.50
Bloomington	2.75	3.00	2.50	1.50	3.00	0.50	1.00	0.75
Bedford	3.50	4.00	3.00	2.00	3.50	0.75	1.50	0.50
Richmond	3.50	2.50	1.50	1.50	0.50	3.00	2.50	3.50
Dayton	4.50	3.75	3.00	2.75	1.25	4.00	3.00	4.50

[a] Possible sites for plants.

Exhibit 4
Standard Production Costs and Capacities At Hoosier Meat Packers Plants

Location	Standard Production Cost (Per CWT)	Daily Production Capacity (In CWT)[a]
Lafayette	$20.90	500
Marion	18.90	800
Anderson	18.30	2500
Indianapolis	18.70	2000
Richmond	19.80	600
Bloomington	23.30	1000
Total		7400

[a]Current market value of each plant was roughly estimated at $240 per unit of daily capacity (CWT). New plants could be constructed in multiples of hundredweight (100 CWT).

Exhibit 5
Estimated Delivery Costs Between Plants and Market Areas[a]

	Meat Plants							
Markets	Lafayette	Marion	Anderson	Indianapolis	Richmond	Bloomington	Columbus[b]	Bedford[b]
Lafayette	$2.10	$4.10	$3.20	$3.75	$4.10	$4.30	$4.00	$5.20
Marion	4.30	1.60	2.50	4.05	3.00	4.60	4.00	5.50
Anderson	3.20	2.65	1.40	2.50	2.50	4.10	3.20	5.00
Muncie	3.20	2.65	1.75	4.00	2.20	4.30	3.50	5.50
New Castle	3.40	3.75	1.90	3.50	2.00	4.25	3.20	5.50
Indianapolis	3.45	4.00	2.25	1.50	2.55	3.30	2.80	3.70
Columbus	4.30	4.30	3.30	2.40	3.00	2.80	2.00	3.20
Bloomington	4.70	5.00	4.00	2.65	4.00	2.00	2.60	2.60
Bedford	5.20	5.60	5.25	3.00	4.50	2.55	2.90	2.00
Richmond	4.60	4.10	2.90	3.00	1.10	4.50	3.80	5.60
Dayton	5.30	5.25	4.00	4.25	2.00	5.50	5.00	6.70

[a]Delivery costs are influenced primarily by the distance of the market area from the plant and the distance between deliveries in the market area.

[b]Proposed plant sites.

Case 9-3
Webb's Markets[1]

Over the past sixteen years, Bill Webb had risen from manager of a nationally owned supermarket to president and majority stockholder of Webb's Markets. Webb's was a small but profitable chain of three supermarkets in the southwestern suburbs of Chicago, an area dominated by a few national chains. The success of Webb's Markets was due to their skillful merchandising that (as Bill Webb liked to say) came from "knowing the customers best." A comparison of Webb's performance to that of the industry (Exhibit 1) attests to Bill Webb's skill as a supermarket operator.

In August 1972, Bill Webb had to decide whether Webb's Markets should expand once more. The decision was precipitated by George Merlin, a real estate developer and promoter who had known Bill Webb for several years. Merlin had been holding some land in the north end of Tinley Park, a community in the southwest corner of Cook County. He had recently acquired a ninety-day option on an adjoining piece of land. By combining the two areas, he expected to have an excellent location for a neighborhood shopping center.

To understand Merlin's optimism, one had only to look at the recent history of Tinley Park. The preliminary census estimate of Tinley Park's population was 12,253. This represented a growth rate of over 90 percent since the last census. In addition, Tinley Park's retailers attracted two to three thousand families who lived in the rural areas to the south and west of the community. Most of the families who lived north and east of Tinley Park shopped at the larger suburbs near Chicago.

The expected growth in the 1970s was even greater than that of the 1960s. For years Tinley Park had been just another rural community between Chicago and Joliet. The northwestern suburbs of Chicago had developed very rapidly because they had excellent transportation, including what some thought was the best rail service in the country. The southwestern suburbs had poor commuter service and no direct highways to Chicago. This had recently changed with the completion of Interstate 80 and would improve further when Interstate 57 was completed. Direct access to the South Side and heart of Chicago would be available and driving time to the Loop would be halved to thirty to forty minutes.

Bill Webb had thought before of locating a store in Tinley Park. He did not have any stores there but did have one in Homewood that was about seven miles east of Tinley Park. He had gone as far as to speak to his food distributor about building a store in Tinley Park. The distributor had sent a real estate specialist to look over the town. A "number 2" recommendation had been given in the report, which meant that a new store would probably go but its success was by no means guaranteed. The distributor had mentioned that the best available site (B) for a free-standing store was on an undeveloped piece of commercial land on Oak Park Avenue between 178th and 179th streets (see Exhibit 2). He thought that an investor could be found to build the supermarket in return for a twenty-five year 1½ percent lease.

The development proposed by George Merlin (A) was also on Oak Park Avenue but about two and one-half miles north of the location suggested by the distributor (Exhibit 2). For the past month Mr. Merlin had been trying to find if there was enough interest on the part of local merchants to develop a neighborhood shopping center (see Exhibit 3). The center he had in mind would have fourteen stores with one primary anchor store and two other major stores.

The ability of the proposed center to attract merchants would depend on the tenants Merlin could get for units F, G, and H. Merlin was almost certain that Walgreens would lease unit G. Unit F, the other major store, would probably be leased to either a furniture or limited line variety store. Before making a formal proposal to these stores, he wanted to have a commitment for the anchor store (unit H) and it was for this reason that he had come to see Bill Webb.

The proposed shopping center was very attractive to Webb. Merlin had developed a center in nearby Flossmoor that, despite its unimaginative design, had proven to be very successful. He also liked the dimensions of the proposed supermarket and this was the size he had discussed with his distributor for the south side of Tinley Park. The three stores he presently owned averaged 21,000 square feet and grossed around $184,000 per week. A store of 25,000-30,000 square feet could handle a volume of $100,000 and yet break even at a relatively low sales volume.

Unfortunately, there were also some reservations about the proposed center. Competition was more

[1]Case prepared by David MacKay of Indiana University. Reproduced by permission.

intense at the north end of town than at the south end. Two supermarkets, both belonging to established national chains, Jewel and National Tea, were right in the middle of several recently developed housing tracts. The proposed center was about one-half mile north of this residential area. In addition, several small stores had located around the National supermarket to form a little shopping center (the only one in town). Webb estimated that the Jewel store, which was fairly old and in need of remodeling, did about $35,000 a week and the nearby National, which was a spacious, attractive store, did about $50,000 a week. There were other factors, however, in its favor. The north end of town had two thirds of Tinley Park's sales potential and many customers seemed to be going outside of town to shop. The Jewel store was poorly run and had a crowded, dirty appearance. National was just the opposite in appearance, but its prices were high and its trading stamps were losing their appeal. The South Side had just one store, an independent named Motto's, which averaged about $35,000 per week.

Webb's Markets had a loyal following in the towns where they operated. This was largely due to the way the stores were merchandised. Webb's had never given trading stamps and was known as an aggressive price competitor. His policy had been to meet the competition's grocery prices and undercut their produce prices. Produce typically accounted for 7 to 8 percent of sales but it was almost ten percent in Webb's markets. Bill Webb's gross margin on produce was only 5 percent below the 35 percent margin of the other supermarkets, but he bought as much of his produce as he could directly from local farmers. As a result, the prices on Webb's locally grown produce averaged 20 percent under their competiton. In the last ten years a dependable, high quality distribution system for produce had been built up.

Another aspect of his merchandising policy that had proved to be very profitable was his inclusion of such nonfood goods as health and beauty aids, softgoods, housewares, and school and photo supplies. The percentage of shelf space given to nonfood and general merchandise items was the same in Webb's Markets as it was in most supermarkets, but a modest discounting policy had increased turnover to the point where nonfood items accounted for almost 20 percent of gross profits. At present, none of his primary competition discounted nonfood items.

There were several sources of secondary information that Bill Webb used to decide whether he should enter Tinley Park. The Census of Business had esti-

mated the food store sales in Tinley Park to be $6,429,000 and the just-released Nielsen survey of the grocery industry had stated that the average household in the East Central portion of the United States spent about $24.00 a week on grocery purchases.[2] Bill Webb knew from his own experience, however, that this figure varied widely across geographic areas. An informal sample he had conducted in one of his stores last year had shown an average estimated total food store expenditure of $34.49 that to him, indicated that his stores drew more of the heavy shoppers.

In addition to the Census Bureau and Nielsen Co. data, several extensive studies of chain store operations and customer shopping patterns had been published by the trade press. These were useful, but Bill Webb thought that he needed some more specific information on the shopping patterns of Tinley Park. Webb felt that the three alternatives open to him were (1) agree to join George Merlin's shopping center at location A, (2) build on the undeveloped commercial land at location B on the south side, or (3) stay out of Tinley Park altogether. To help in this decision he commissioned George Wendell, a partner in a suburban marketing research agency, to study the Tinley Park shopping patterns. A summary of Wendall's findings is provided in Exhibit 4.

While Webb was pondering what to do, George Merlin called to see if he had made up his mind. Merlin said that he needed a decision within the week if he was to take the option on the north side land. George Merlin also indicated that if Webb joined the center, he could arrange a percentage lease for 1.25 percent. This would reduce the financing Bill Webb needed for fixtures and inventory to about $450,000. If he made a decision to build now, he would probably be in operation by September 1973.

QUESTIONS

1. How successful will Webb's merchandising policies be in Tinley Park?
2. Is Tinley Park big enough for another supermarket?
3. How will the proposed center (A) and its tenants influence the sales of a new Webb's Market located at the northside location?
4. Should Webb's Markets located in Tinley Park? If so, where?

[2]U.S. Bureau of the Census, *United States Census of Business, Retail Trade Statistics*
A. C. Nielsen Co., *36th Annual Nielsen Review of Retail Grocery Trends,* Chicago, 1970.

Exhibit 1
Operating Expense Breakdown

	Webb's Markets (Percent)	Chain Store Composite[a] (Percent)
Sales	100.0	100.0
Cost of sales	80.4	78.5
Gross margin	19.6	21.5
Payroll	8.0	10.5
Supplies	0.8	0.9
Services	1.1	1.3
Promotion	1.8	1.5
Insurance	0.5	0.5
Taxes and licenses (other than income)	0.6	0.9
Depreciation and amortization	0.9	0.8
Repairs	0.3	0.5
Rentals	2.0	1.7
Interest expense	0.9	0.7
Miscellaneous expenditures	0.6	1.6
Total costs and expenses	17.5	20.9
Gross operating profit	2.1	0.6
Other income	0.5	1.4
Net profit before tax	2.6	2.0
Income tax	1.3	1.0
Net profit after tax	1.3	1.0
Net profit after tax/net worth	10.4	9.7

[a]Covers entire chain operation (store and warehouse).

Source. Cornell University, *Operating Results of Food Chains, 1970-1971.*

Exhibit 2
Tinley Park, Illinois

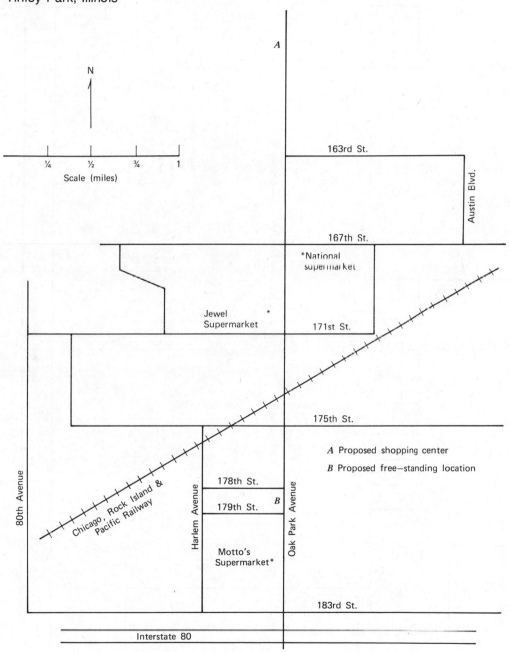

Exhibit 3
Proposed Shopping Center

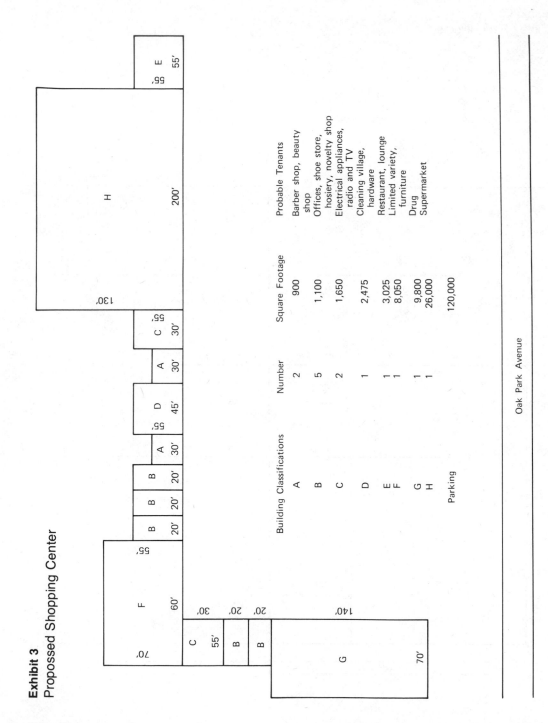

Building Classifications	Number	Square Footage	Probable Tenants
A	2	900	Barber shop, beauty shop
B	5	1,100	Offices, shoe store, hosiery, novelty shop
C	2	1,650	Electrical appliances, radio and TV
D	1	2,475	Cleaning village, hardware
E	1	3,025	Restaurant, lounge
F	1	8,050	Limited variety, furniture
G	1	9,800	Drug
H	1	26,000	Supermarket
Parking		120,000	

Oak Park Avenue

Exhibit 4
Shopping Patterns in Tinley Park

by George Wendell

Introduction
   The objective of this study is to describe the shopping patterns of customers in Tinley Park, Illinois. In particular, the study looks at the shopping patterns generated by residents of Tinley Park on shopping trips that include at least one stop at a supermarket.

Data Collection
   Most of the information in this report comes from a mail questionnaire that was sent to 20 percent of the 3000 households in Tinley Park. The household's response rate was a little over 50 percent. Additional information was obtained through informal talks with the merchants in Tinley Park and a survey of local business conditions.

Summary of Findings
   1. *Mobility* is the most outstanding characteristic of Tinley Park shoppers. All of the families interviewed had at least one car and there was an average of 2.5 cars per family. This high degree of mobility is due to the above average income in Tinley Park and to the lack of *public transportation.* Mobility affects both the distance traveled to supermarkets and the number of stops made on shopping trips.
   2. *Distance traveled* while on shopping trips to supermarkets is much greater than was expected. The modal distance traveled while on a shopping trip to a supermarket was two to three miles, but over 6 percent of the families go over ten miles, and over a third go more than three miles. This is in contrast to the industry rule of thumb that the trip to the supermarket is invariably under two miles.
   3. *Stops made* while on shopping trips to a supermarket are also greater than was anticipated. The average number of stops was 2.7 with over 25 percent of the population making four or more stops. Previous research has usually assumed that supermarket shopping trips were one-stop trips. Table 1 shows the joint distribution of shopping trips by distance and number of stops. On multiple-stop trips, the supermarket was usually the last stop.
   4. *Shopping trip frequencies* vary significantly from day to day though the number of stops made per trip is relatively stable. Stores in Tinley Park are open seven days a week but almost 45 percent of the shopping is done on Friday and Saturday. Many of the trips in the earlier parts of the week are "filler" trips with major purchases being reserved for the Friday and Saturday trips. Table 2 shows the joint distribution of shopping trips by day of the week and number of stops.
   5. *Where stops are made* is as important, or more important, than the distributions of shopping trips and trip stops. For every one hundred shopping trips made by Tinley Park residents to supermarkets, 273 establishments were visited. One hundred of these were "primary" supermarkets. The remaining 173 stops covered a wide range of stores. Most of these stores were "convenience" good stores. Table 3 gives a breakdown of these establishments by type. Note that 116 supermarkets are visited on every 100 shopping trips. This implies that a significant portion of the shoppers in Tinley Park hit several supermarkets on one trip. When this information is combined with the high shopper mobility shown in Table 1, the implication is that store loyality is relatively weak.
   6. *Supermarket patronage* by Tinley Park residents is given in Table 4. The three major supermarkets in town attract most of the traffic, but almost 14 percent goes to other stores. These stores are primarily supermarkets in other suburbs. Very few purchases are made at smaller grocery stores.
   7. *Dollars spent per customer* were found to be a function of several variables. From the information collected in the mail questionnaire, a regression analysis was undertaken to explain the amount of money spent at a supermarket. Independent variables included the following:

(a) Socioeconomic variables.
        Number of children at home.
        Family income.
(b) Shopping history variables.
        Average number of weekly purchases over $5.00.
        Average number of days elapsed between shopping trips to supermarkets.
        Percentage of supermarket purchases at Jewel.
        Percentage of supermarket purchases at Motto's.
        Sex of household's primary food shopper (0 = female, 1 = male).

(c) Variables relating to the shopping trip on which the purchase was made.
    Mode of transportation (0 = other, 1 = drove)
    Accompanied by spouse (0 = no, 1 = yes)
    Accompanied by children (0 = no, 1 = yes)
    Accompanied by friend (0 = no, 1 = yes)
    Previous stop at another supermarket (0 = no, 1 = yes)
    Previous stop was at a gas station (0 = no, 1 = yes)
  Results of the regression analysis are summarized in Table 5.

Table 1
Percentage Distribution of Shopping Trips by Distance and the Number of Stops[a]

Number of Stops	0-1	1-2	2-3	3-4	4-5	5-6	6-7	7-8	8-9	9-10	10-19	Total[b]
One	4.2	12.6	11.6	—	—	—	—	—	—	—	—	28.4
Two	6.3	4.2	10.5	4.2	1.1	2.1	—	—	—	—	2.2	30.5
Three	—	4.2	5.3	2.1	—	2.1	—	—	—	—	1.1	15.8
Four	—	2.1	1.1	1.1	2.1	1.1	1.1	—	1.1	1.1	—	10.5
Five	—	—	3.2	1.1	1.1	—	—	—	—	—	1.1	6.3
Six	—	—	—	1.1	1.1	3.2	—	—	—	—	3.3	8.4
Total	10.5	23.2	31.6	9.5	5.3	8.4	1.1		1.1	1.1	6.6	100.0

[a]0.0 entries are omitted for clarity.
[b]Some respondents traveled over 19 miles and were not recorded in this table. These omissions account for the differences between this total column and the one in Table 2.

Table 2
Percentage Distribution of Shopping Trips by Day of The Week and Number of Stops

Number of Stops	Sunday	Monday	Tuesday	Wednesday	Thursday	Friday	Saturday	Total
One	2.9	5.7	2.9	0.0	1.9	6.7	5.7	25.7
Two	2.9	5.7	5.7	2.9	1.9	5.7	7.6	32.4
Three	0.0	2.9	2.9	1.0	1.0	3.8	3.8	15.2
Four	0.0	1.9	1.9	0.0	3.8	0.0	3.8	11.4
Five	1.0	0.0	1.0	1.9	1.0	1.9	1.0	7.6
Six	0.0	1.0	1.9	0.0	0.0	1.9	2.9	7.6
Total	6.7	17.1	16.2	5.7	9.5	20.0	24.8	100.0

Table 3
Mean Number of Stops Made at Ten Establishment Types for Every One Hundred Supermarket Shopping Trips

Establishment Type	Number of Stops
Supermarkets[a]	16.2
Variety stores	24.4
Gasoline stations	16.2
Drug stores	21.8
Cleaning and laundry	11.2
Other food stores	12.2
Friend's home	14.2
Other establishments	38.6
Post office	5.9
Financial institutions	12.7
Total	173.4

[a]Refers to those supermarkets that were frequented only on trips where another supermarket was also frequented.

Table 4
Percentage of Consumer Stops by Store

Store	Percent of Stops
Jewel	31.6
Motto's	21.9
National	32.6
Others	13.9

Table 5
Regression Equation Developed to Predict Amount Spent on Last Supermarket Stop

Independent Variables	Coefficient	Std. Error
(constant)	(−4.97)	
Children at home between 6 and 14	2.40	.63
Children at home 15 and over	2.11	.89
Family income level (000)	.67	.18
Average number of food purchases over $5.00	2.14	.69
Average days elasped between trips	2.70	.47
Percentage of purchases at Jewell	−1.91	.77
Percentage of purchases at Motto's	−1.96	.68
Sex of primary shopper	−4.36	3.06
Mode of transportation	6.37	3.48
Went to supermarket with spouse	4.76	1.86
Went to supermarket with children	3.13	1.61
Went to supermarket with friend	−1.87	2.19
Supermarket frequented previously	−5.21	2.32
Gas station frequented previously	−4.13	2.79

$R = 0.64$ $N = 288$

Ten

Advertising

If you think advertising doesn't pay—we understand there are 25 mountains in Colorado higher than Pike's Peak. Can you name one?

The American Salesman

The role of advertising in the marketing mix of an individual company depends on the type of product, the nature of its market, the competitive situation, and on numerous other factors. Wide variations in marketing variables lead to important differences between industries and companies in the magnitude of advertising expenditures, the objectives that advertising is intended to achieve, and results.[1] Some of this diversity is shown in the advertising expenditures of twenty-five national advertisers presented in Table 10-1.

The focus of this chapter is on the management of advertising activities and the evaluation of advertising effectiveness. Advertising is but one aspect of the marketing communications of a firm. Decisions about advertising must take into account its interrelationships with other marketing communications such as personal selling and product sampling. The sequence of decisions involved in developing marketing communications as well as the associated data-gathering steps are diagrammed in Figure 10-1.

The chapter begins with an appraisal of the opportunity for advertising. Given a realistic assessment of what advertising can accomplish, advertising objectives and goals are discussed. Then the message component of creative strategy is stressed. Next, alternative methods of budgeting are reviewed within the context of the stated goals. A consideration of the problem of selecting media in the face of a budget constraint follows. The measurement of the sales results of the campaign is the final aspect of advertising management considered. An appraisal of the benefits and costs of advertising to society completes the chapter.

THE OPPORTUNITY FOR ADVERTISING

Prior to setting budgets and other advertising planning, the manager must ask himself whether he should do any advertising.[2] His appraisal of the opportunity for advertising

---

[1] Robert D. Buzzell, "The Role of Advertising in the Marketing Mix" *Marketing Science Institute Special Report* (Cambridge: October 1971).

[2] The Hershey chocolate bar, for example, has become a leading product in the United States on the basis of extensive distribution gained through the use of salesmen and not as the result of consumer advertising. Cook Inc., a leader in cardiovascular catheters, also uses no advertising and relies entirely on personal selling, a catalogue, and exhibits at trade shows.

Table 10-1

Advertising Expenditures of Selected National Advertisers, 1973

	Total Advertising Expenditures (Millions)	Advertising as a Per-cent of Sales	Percentage Distribution of Advertising Expenditures [a]								
			News paper	Gen. Mag.	Farm Pub.	Bus. Pub.	Spot TV	Net. TV	Spot Radio	Net. Radio	Out-door
Proctor & Gamble	310	6.3	0.7	4.3	—	0.4	39.2	55.3	0.1	—	—
Sears	215[b]	1.7	0.7	19.9	—	—	21.8	37.1	20.2	0.2	0.1
General Foods	180	8.1	4.6	8.6	—	0.2	37.2	48.0	1.2	0.1	0.1
General Motors	158	0.4	21.8	19.5	0.5	2.7	12.8	30.4	10.0	1.2	1.1
Bristol-Myers	132	12.7	1.2	14.7	—	6.0	16.8	56.6	3.9	0.7	0.1
U.S. Government	99	—	20.4	51.6	—	—	1.2	—	—	—	26.8
A.T. & T.	95	0.4	7.6	22.0	—	4.4	25.6	29.0	8.3	1.1	2.0
R.J. Reynolds	85	2.6	43.5	29.8	0.3	0.2	1.9	9.1	0.1	—	15.1
RCA	80	1.9	25.4	30.6	—	4.5	11.5	25.6	2.0	—	0.5
Heublein	78	5.9	8.3	12.0	—	0.8	44.3	22.2	6.0	—	6.4
Gillette	75	7.0	0.8	6.6	—	0.2	18.5	70.7	2.8	0.4	—
Goodyear	73	1.6	—	12.0	1.8	6.6	29.6	48.2	0.4	0.7	0.7
DuPont	55	1.5	1.9	24.3	2.2	19.0	4.3	45.5	2.1	0.7	—
S.C. Johnson	50	18.4	1.1	6.2	—	—	9.9	81.8	0.3	0.8	—
McDonald's	46	3.1	0.1	2.7	—	—	53.6	36.6	4.7	—	2.3
Kellogg	45	5.4	4.6	4.4	—	0.4	22.3	65.8	1.3	1.3	—
Anheuser-Busch	37	2.5	1.3	1.2	—	1.4	27.7	31.4	35.2	—	1.8
Revlon	35	6.9	0.4	34.9	—	0.6	6.4	56.0	1.6	—	0.1
Exxon	28	0.1	5.9	10.1	—	—	26.8	41.4	12.9	—	2.8
Wrigley	28	12.1	11.0	2.1	0.5	—	64.9	5.5	13.9	2.4	0.2
American Express	28	1.5	20.1	20.5	—	1.2	16.5	34.5	7.2	—	—
Seven-Up	27	18.6	1.2	1.0	—	0.3	68.5	7.0	11.6	0.6	9.8
Polaroid	25	3.5	13.5	28.6	—	3.7	5.1	46.8	1.9	—	0.4
American Airlines	22	1.5	39.5	10.8	—	2.8	24.7	2.2	16.4	—	3.6
Mattel	18	6.4	0.5	6.2	—	—	35.3	57.9	—	—	0.1

[a] Based on measured media except for newspaper estimates.
[b] Sears spends about $250 million on local promotions that are not included in total.

Source. Reprinted with permission from the August 26, 1974 issue of *Advertising Age.* Copyright © 1974 by Crain Communications, Inc.

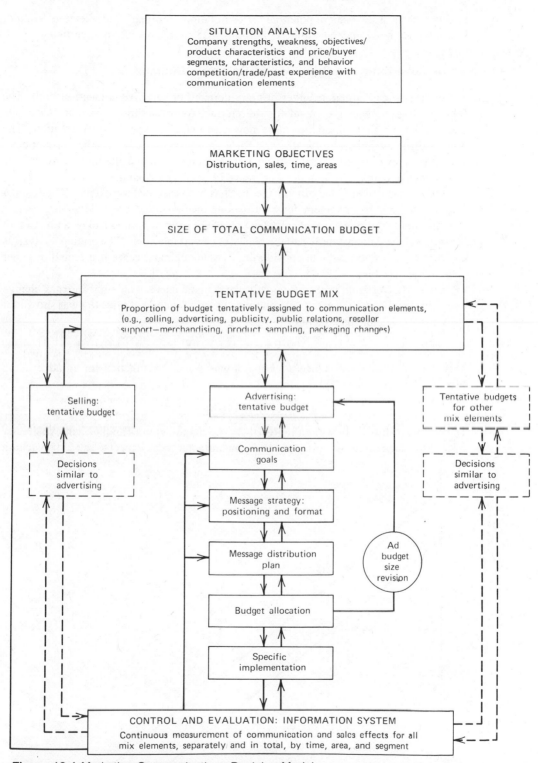

Figure 10-1 Marketing Communications Decision Model.
Source. Reprinted from Michael L. Ray, *"A Decision Sequence Analysis of Developments in Marketing Communications," Journal of Marketing*, Vol. 37 (January 1973) p. 31.
Published by the American Marketing Association.

begins with an assessment of potential for stimulation of primary and selective demand. The manager must understand the conditions that are conducive to advertising.

The Effects of Advertising on Primary and Selective Demand

Advertising can stimulate either primary demand or selective demand or both. The first involves increasing demand for the product category through raising per capita consumption or through adding more new customers than are lost by attrition. The second involves increasing the demand for a particular brand within the product category. Often the competitive activity generated when each brand attempts to increase its own selective demand results in an increase in primary demand.

Thus far, the demand curve facing the firm has been assumed to be fixed. Recall that a price cut resulted in movement downward along the demand curve and increased sales. Whether or not this new level of sales led to higher profits was shown to be a function of the shape of the demand curve and the behavior of variable costs. The pricing analysis is incomplete, however, without considering how the demand curve is affected by other managerial variables.

Increased advertising expenditures shift the demand curve to the right and may change its shape. Previously, the expected unit sales (Q) as a function of price (P) was shown for the vacuum cleaner manufacturer to be

$$Q(0) = 4000 - 40P \qquad (1)$$

This demand function assumed advertising was zero. The function for an advertising expenditure (A) of $10,000 is:

$$Q(10,000) = 4800 - 40P \qquad (2)$$

The resulting shift is shown in Figure 10-2. The manufacturer can thus achieve greater sales at the same price. At a price of $60 the manufacturer can expect to sell 2400 vacuum

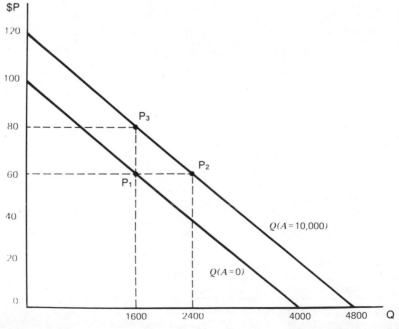

Figure 10-2 Demand Functions Faced by Vacuum Cleaner Manufacturer.

cleaners instead of 1600. In the diagram, this is indicated by a movement from point P_1 to point P_2. Alternatively, the manufacturer can obtain a higher price at the current volume. With increased advertising the manufacturer can raise his price from \$60 to \$80 and still sell 1600 units. This is shown as movement from point P_1 to point P_3.

The demand curve for vacuum cleaners is assumed to be linear. However, it would be more realistic to assume that it is curvilinear. Furthermore, increased advertising expenditures are likely to reduce the price sensitivity of buyers; that is, the price coefficient would be smaller.

Criteria for Effective Advertising

The ease of increasing selective and primary demand by advertising varies across product categories and brands. In order to assess opportunities for advertising, the manager must understand which factors contribute to the variation.[3] Four factors that seem most important are (1) the trend in primary demand is favorable, (2) product differentiation is marked, (3) hidden qualities of the product are important to the consumer, and (4) funds for advertising are available.

The social and environmental factors that underlie the basic trends in product demand are often more important than the amount of advertising expenditures. Advertising might accelerate an expansion in demand that would have occurred without advertising or, correspondingly, might retard an adverse trend. However, a reversal of a trend by advertising alone is most unlikely. When demand is expanding there are frequently opportunities for selective advertising appeals.

These selective appeals are more effective if the product has unique attributes. Product differentiation facilitates the establishment of brand preference. This preference enables the product to have a larger gross margin than might have been possible with an undifferentiated product. In turn, a larger gross margin provides more funds for advertising. However, the firm must have sufficient resources to make an impression on the consumer, and high advertising costs are a barrier to entry into some markets.

Not all attributes of a product are obvious from an external inspection by the consumer during a shopping trip. Some qualities of the product such as durability are hidden. If these qualities are important, then the consumer tends to rely on advertising for his information. There is also a trend toward interpreting advertising claims as implicit product warranties by the courts.[4]

ADVERTISING OBJECTIVES AND GOALS

The primary objective of a firm under most conditions is profit. Consequently, the manager should select the advertising alternative that generates the highest present value for long-term profits. Nonprofit organizations focus on net benefits rather than profits.

The advertising objectives for a product will depend on the stage of the life cycle that the product is in. New product advertising makes the customer aware of the existence of the new product, forces distribution of the new brand, and provides the customer with

[3]This section is based on Neil H. Borden, *The Economic Effects of Advertising* (Chicago: Richard D. Irwin, 1944), pp. 162-168, 422-438.

[4]Charles W. Walton, "Effect of Advertising on Product Liability," *Industrial Marketing,* Vol. 57 (August 1972), pp. 56-59.

a reason for buying the product.[5] Established product advertising is aimed at maintaining the product's market position.

The task of advertising is also a function of the product category. For more expensive products such as cars and appliances, the decision process of the buyer is deliberate and occurs over a comparatively long time horizon. Buyers usually would be able to identify various brands even when labels are removed. In contrast, many package goods such as soaps and detergents are almost physically identical. Furthermore, these products are often of low interest to buyers. Consequently, manufacturers of these products seek to achieve top-of-mind awareness among buyers. Ideally, they attempt to associate their brand name with the generic product category. An example would be Kleenex and facial tissue.[6]

The fundamental purpose of advertising is to increase demand for the product. Demand can be enlarged by increasing the number of customers and/or by increasing the usage rate among current customers. More customers come from converting customers from competing brands, holding current customers by developing brand loyalty, and from expanding the total market for the product class. Greater usage comes from reminding customers to use the brand and from telling them about new uses. Another purpose of advertising is aimed at middlemen in the distribution channel. This advertising seeks to encourage the wholesaler and retailer to stock and promote our brand.[7]

Advertising objectives should be coordinated with the objectives set for the other managerical decision variables. For instance, advertising can be used to solicit sales leads. Salesmen can then reach these prospects. In cases where the product is too complex to explain in an ad, advertising might be used to sell the salesman rather than the product. Culligan doubled its sales of water conditioners in five years by preselling its salesmen through its slogan "Hey Culligan Man!"[8]

Sometimes advertising objectives are described as "demand pull" or as "demand push" advertising. Pull advertising is designed to sell the final user of the product so he will go to the distributor and ask for the product and in effect pull the merchandise through the channel of distribution. Most brand name advertising falls into this category (Timken bearings, Haggar slacks). Push advertising, on the other hand, is directed at brokers and distributors and is intended to presell the dealers on the merits of the product. It is more common to use push advertising with industrial products and stress direct mail, trade journals, and display materials rather than broadcast media.

Defining Advertising Goals

Advertisers should specify their advertising objectives and subsequently measure the results. The idea is to measure performance in terms of achievement of a quantitative statement of performance. A goal for a new brand might be attain 80 percent brand identity within six months after introduction. This provides a benchmark against which to measure accomplishment. Whenever possible advertising performance should be measured in terms of sales because of the simple accounting equation that relates sales to profits.

[5]Leonard J. Parsons, "An Econometric Analysis of Advertising, Retail Availability, and Sales of a New Brand," *Management Science,* Vol. 20 (February 1974), pp. 938-947.

[6]Leo Bogart, *Strategy in Advertising* (New York: Harcourt, Brace & World, 1967), pp. 61-62.

[7]Kenneth A. Longman, *Advertising* (New York: Harcourt Brace Jovanovich, 1971), pp. 120-133.

[8]"How to Get Salesmen Through the Doorway" in Otto Kleppner and Irving Settel (eds.), *Exploring Advertising* (Englewood Cliffs, N.J.: Prentice-Hall, 1970), pp. 67-69.

There are two situations in which sales cannot be used. The first occurs when the effects of advertising cannot be isolated from the effects of other elements in the marketing mix. The second occurs when the effects of current advertising cannot be isolated from the effects of past advertising. In these situations, sometimes changes in a buyer's knowledge or attitude can be used as a proxy for changes in purchase behavior.

Therefore, when advertising goals can not be expressed in terms of sales, they must be defined in terms of the intervening variables linking advertising to sales. The rationale for this approach can be found in the hypothesis of a hierarchy of effects.

The Hierarchy of Effects. The hierarchy of effects hypothesis states that advertising guides the consumer through a sequence of steps that culminates in purchase. Consumers can be classified into seven groups. The first group contains potential purchasers who are *unaware* of the existence of the product. The second group contains consumers who are merely *aware* of the product's existence. The third group contains consumers who possess *knowledge* of the product and its benefits. The fourth group contains consumers who *like* the product. The fifth group are those who have developed a *preference* for the product over all other possibilities. The sixth group contains consumers who are *convinced* that they should buy the product. The final group contains consumers who *purchase* the product.[9]

The role of advertising in moving consumers from one group to another will tend to vary. A panel survey can provide the data necessary to assess the economic value of causing consumers to change groups. For instance, some data gathered on an automobile that General Motors developed for the youth market illustrates the relative worth of prospects. In Table 10-2, we see that probabilities of visiting a dealer and of buying increase markedly as a prospect progresses through the purchase process.

Acceptance of this theory means that immediate sales results do not have to be the major criterion for measuring advertising effectiveness. Simply measuring the consumer's progress through the intermediate steps may provide a better indicator of the long-term effects of advertising.

DAGMAR. (Defining Advertising Goals, Measuring Advertising Results) assumes that the hierarchy-of-effects theory works in the real world.[10] Most mass merchandisers

Table 10-2
Step in Purchase Process and Propensity to Buy

| | Percent of | Probability of | |
Step	Sample	Visiting Dealer	Buying
Brand is first choice	5	.840	.560
Will consider brand	7	.620	.220
Will not consider brand	8	.400	.090
Aware of brand	14	.240	.050
Not aware of brand	66	.015	.004
	100		

Source. Adapted from Gail Smith, "How GM Measures Ad Effectiveness," *Printer's Ink* (May 14, 1965), p. 24. Copyright 1965 by *Printers Ink.*

[9]Robert J. Lavidge and Gary A. Steiner, "A Model for Predictive Measurement of Advertising Effectiveness," *Journal of Marketing,* Vol. 25 (October 1961), pp. 59-62.

[10]Russell Colley, *Defining Advertising Goals for Measured Advertising Results* (New York: Association of National Advertisers, 1961); Harry D. Wolfe, James K. Brown, and Clark Thompson, *Measuring Advertising Results,* Studies in Business Policy No. 102 (New York: National Industrial Conference Board, 1962); Stewart Henderson Britt, "Are So-called Successful Advertising Campaigns Really Successful?" *Journal of Advertising Research,* Vol. 9 (June 1969), pp. 3-9.

of frequently purchased, low-cost products prefer to measure the sales effects of advertising directly. Nonetheless, other firms such as General Motors have adopted DAGMAR.

General Motors develops advertising goals from research findings.[11] In the case of the car developed for the youth market, GM compared the attitudes and perceptions of those who would consider buying their car with those who would not. They found, as shown in Table 10-3, that the most significant difference between these groups occurred in their opinions about the car's trade-in value. Therefore, GM established the improvement of the rating on trade-in value as the advertising objective.

The target market was defined as all-male heads of new car owning households. The goals were to be in effect for the model year. The rating on the initial survey of 59 percent provided a benchmark. At the end of the model year, this rating had been raised to 75 percent. The fact that the car had, in actuality, the highest trade-in value in its price class made this accomplishment easier.

Another industry where DAGMAR might be successfully implemented is the oil industry where advertising is a relatively unimportant ingredient in the marketing mix (see Table 10-1). Research in this case has shown a high correlation between objectivity in managing advertising dollars and corporate success across nine major oil companies.

Qualifications.   Several attempts have been made to evaluate the hierarchy of effects hypothesis. For example, one study found a strong relationship between awareness and market share. However, higher levels of advertising activity failed to strengthen the awareness-purchase relationship. This study was able to show that higher awareness coexists with higher purchasing rate, but was unable to confirm that awareness tends to

Table 10-3

Attitude Profiles of Prospective Buyers of a Brand of Automobile

Attribute	Would Consider[a]	Would Not Consider[a]	Difference
Smooth riding	91	86	5
Styling	89	76	13
Overall comfort	87	81	6
Handling	86	83	3
Spacious interior	85	85	0
Luxurious interior	85	79	6
Quality of workmanship	83	80	3
Advanced engineering	83	77	6
Prestige	82	73	9
Value for the money	79	76	3
Trade-in value	77	59	18
Cost of maintenance	67	63	4
Gas economy	58	58	0

[a]Based on a scale of 1 to 100.

Source. Adapted from Gail Smith, "How GM Measures Ad Effectiveness," *Printer's Ink* (May 14, 1965), p. 27. Copyright 1965 by *Printers Ink.*

[11]Gail Smith, "How GM Measures Ad Effectiveness," *Printer's Ink* (May 14, 1965), pp. 19-29.

[12]Donald C. Marschner, "DAGMAR Revisited—Eight Years Later," *Journal of Advertising Research,* Vol. II (April 1971), pp. 27-33.

precede or even contribute to the rate of purchase.[13] Other research has shown that intervening variables in the purchasing process are important factors in explaining variance in aggregate behavior. The value of particular intervening variables varies by product class and by brand. Support was found for the proposition that changes in attitude are more closely related to purchase than are changes in awareness. The findings also suggest that attitudes predict market share better than market share predicts attitudes. This result leads to the tentative conclusion that attitude change precedes rather than follows a behavior change.[14] However, research has also shown that in some cases the influence of advertising goes from awareness directly to behavior, by-passing attitude.[15]

The nature of the attitude-behavior relationship and the hierarchy of effects controversy remain unresolved. One reason is inadequate measurement of the concepts. Certainly measurement validation is necessary before testing. Otherwise, unsatisfactory test results could be the result of the quality of the theory or the quality of the measures or both. Advertising strategy should probably focus on the components of attitude as well as on some overall measure of attitude.[16]

Advertising Process Model. A model that describes how the components of attitude might be influenced by advertising and other communications is shown in Figure 10-3. Note that when individuals are exposed to ads with relevant product attributes, the attitude formation function operates to increase the probability of exposure to additional advertising or moves the customer towards product purchase. The process of attitude formation is also influenced by product experience, personal needs, shopping, competitive ads, and by comments from friends.

Several advertising strategies have been suggested for implementation by marketing managers using a simplified version of the advertising process model.[17] These include:

1. Influence the choice criteria that govern product class selection.
2. Change the relevances of a product attribute (create a new salient attribute).
3. Change the ideal amount of an attribute that a brand should possess.
4. Change the perceived amount of an attribute held by the firm's brand.
5. Change the perceived amount of an attribute held by competitor's brands.

Note that these strategies do not attempt to change the degree of uncertainty about the perceived amount of an attribute.

The first strategy attempts to stimulate primary demand by modifying the individual's motivation and choice criteria. Usually, this involves accelerating an environmental trend, such as the use of margarine instead of butter. The second strategy can take several forms. Sometimes an existing attribute can be made more prominent. At one time, all appliance manufacturers had wheels as an optional feature for their refrigerators, so the

[13]Kristian S. Palda, "The Hypothesis of a Hierarchy of Effects: A Partial Evaluation," *Journal of Marketing Research,* Vol. 3 (February 1966), pp. 13-24.

[14]Henry Assael and George S. Day, "Attitudes and Awareness as Predictors of Market Share," *Journal of Advertising Research,* Vol. 8 (December 1968), pp. 3-10.

[15]David A. Aaker and George S. Day, "A Recursive Model of Communication Processes" in David A. Aaker (ed.), *Multivariate Analysis in Marketing: Theory and Applications* (Belmont, Calif.: Wadsworth, 1971) pp. 101-114.

[16]The components of attitude were discussed in the sections on "Attitude Structure" and "Building an Attitude Index" in Chapter Five, "Buyer Behavior."

[17]This section is taken from Harper W. Boyd, Jr., Michael L. Ray, and Edward Strong, "An Attitudinal Framework for Advertising Strategy," *Journal of Marketing,* Vol. 36 (April 1972), pp. 27-33.

The importance of considering alternative attitude structures and composition rules is discussed in Peter Wright, "Use of Consumer Judgement Models in Promotion Planning," *Journal of Marketing,* Vol. 37 (October 1973), pp. 27-33.

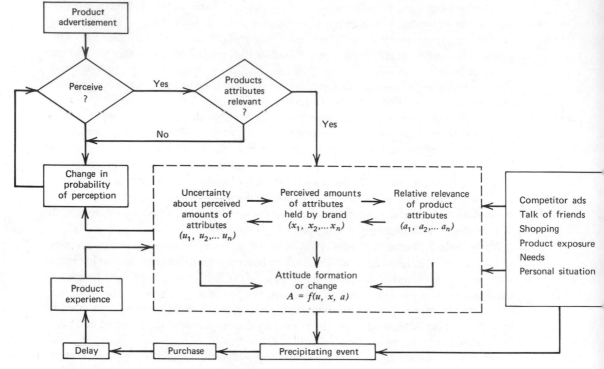

Figure 10-3 Advertising Process Model.

homemaker could move the appliance in order to clean under it, but none of the firms advertised this feature. One company with a history of noninnovation decided to advertise this attribute. After the campaign, image studies revealed that the consumer viewed the firm as innovative! Sometimes a new attribute is added to extend the life of a mature product. The ready-to-eat cereal product class has had several major modifications, including the introduction of presweetened and adult nutritional cereals.

The remaining three strategies involve positioning the firm's brand relative to ideal and competing brands by moving the ideal toward its own brand position (strategy three), by moving its brand toward the ideal (strategy four), or by moving competitive brands away from the ideal (strategy five). An example of this last strategy is a china ad that reads "Royal Doulton, the china of Stratford-on-Trent, England versus Lenox, the china of Pomona, N.J." Thus, Royal Doulton is repositioning Lenox china, a brand that many consumers believed was imported. This advertisement resulted in a 6 percent gain in market share for Royal Doulton.

The Goal-Setting Process

We will now consider the goal-setting process for determining advertising objectives in a hypothetical firm with invested capital of $100 million.[18] The board of directors of the company might adopt the corporate goal to earn 10 percent on invested capital. This implies profits should be $10 million. Next the corporate profit goal must be translated

[18]This section is from L. W. Jacobs, "Advertising Objectives: Proper Setting and Use," unpublished doctoral dissertation, Ohio State University 1966.

into a marketing goal. Assume marketing believes the profit goal can be achieved if company sales are $40 million. Once a sales level has been set, the funds available for advertising can be found by subtracting production costs, overhead costs, and the profit goal from the potential revenue. If the costs other than direct advertising costs total $25 million, then $5 million is available for reaching the advertising goal. Suppose the advertising manager thinks that a 60 percent level of awareness is necessary to reach the sales goal. Then 100 million impressions, costing $5 million, will be required to obtain this level of awareness in the relevant market.

This goal-setting process involves a hierarchy: profitability, sales, communication, and there must be agreement among these goals. In the example, the advertising manager felt that an advertising expenditure of $5 million was necessary to achieve the sales goal, while the marketing manager felt that given the sales goal, $5 million would be available for advertising. Suppose, however, that the available funds had been less than the amount required. In this case, the goals would have to be revised so that they were consistent. In order to establish meaningful goals, there must be useful relationships between variables, such as impressions and awareness. Understanding of the nature of these relations may be intuitive. The crucial step in the hierarchical procedure is the choice of the first number from which lower goals are based. This raises the question of whether the initial goal will maximize the profits of the firm.

The only way to answer this question is by clearly stating the intuitive model of the system. The relationships can be specified by management judgments and verified by empirical evidence. The relationships for this example are drawn in Figure 10-4. The 0

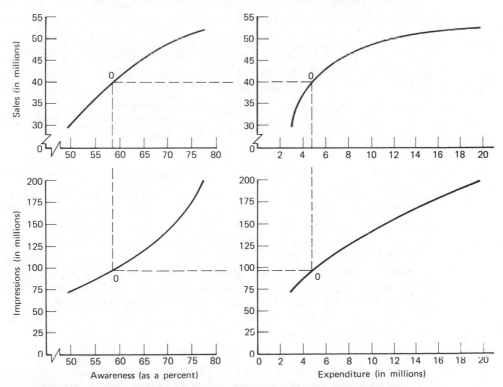

Figure 10-4 Four Quadrant Analysis of Profit-expenditure Relationships.
Source. L. W. Jacobs, "Advertising Objectives: Proper Setting and Use," unpublished doctoral dissertation, Ohio State University, 1966, p. 108.

points coincide with our original goals for sales and profits.[19]

The original goals were associated with a profit of $10 million, but were the original goals optimal? By examining the relationship between sales and cost as well as the relationships shown in Figure 10-4, the connection between advertising expenditures and profits can be found. The maximum profit is actually $17.2 million. This optimum position requires advertising expenditures of $7.8 million to produce sales of $46.7 million. Thus goal setters who test just one number often forego potential profits. This approach assumes, of course, that advertising content is immaterial.

MESSAGE CONTENT

Creative strategy contributes to the effectiveness of advertising campaigns. Previous chapters on "Segmentation" and "Buyer Behavior" have indicated the importance of message content in building creative strategies. The purpose of this section is to provide further illustrations of the role of message content. Coverage of the design and presentation of creative advertisements is left to more specialized texts.

Positioning

Creative strategy can be used to help position a product in the marketplace. Product names, for example, can affect the impact of advertising expenditures. Try to identify "Airline X" in the following list of leading airline advertisers in 1967:

United	$24,123,000
Airline X	21,700,000
Pan American	19,800,000
TWA	15,800,000
American	15,720,000
Braniff	10,000,000

Surprisingly, the name of "Airline X" is Eastern. The data suggest Eastern spends more on advertising than other lines with higher revenues and more extensive route systems. Although Eastern flies to cities such as St. Louis and Acapulco, its regional name suggests that it only flies along the East Coast. Thus, the more money Eastern spends on advertising, the more people think that it is impossible to get there from here.[20]

Another example showing how names affect market positions is suggested by Stolichnaya vodka ($8 per 80 proof fifth) now being imported from Russia. Stolichnaya may have difficulty establishing itself as the only genuine Russian vodka in the United States because surveys show Americans believe that Smirnoff ($5 per 80 proof fifth) and other U.S. brands are Russian. The names of the U.S. brands often are or sound Russian and serve to position the brands favorably.

[19]See Robert S. Weinberg, "Multiple Factor Break-Even Analysis: The Application of Operations-Research Techniques to a Basic Problem of Management Planning and Control," *Operations Research*, Vol. 4 (April 1956), pp. 152-186.

[20]Jack Trout, "Positioning Is a Game People Play in Today's Me-too Market Place," *Industrial Marketing*, Vol. 54 (June 1969), p. 53.

Segmentation

Many firms make different appeals to different market segments. An obvious example is a multinational company which practices geographical market segmentation. Datsun asks people in Southeast Asia, Africa, and the Middle East to buy its car as a first car. In the United States, Australia, and Canada where there is a demand for larger cars, Datsun asks people to buy its car as a second car. In large car markets Datsun conducts separate sales campaigns for students, housewives and leisure groups.[21]

THE ADVERTISING BUDGET

Marketing managers need sound methods for setting advertising appropriations. The efficiency of these procedures often depends on the ability of the firm to measure the effectiveness of advertising. Available techniques include the subjective approach, the fixed guidelines approach, the task approach, or the normative approach. Selection among these methods depends on the extent to which returns from advertising can be identified.[22] The normative approach has the most substance and will be given the most attention in our discussion.

The Subjective Approach

The subjective method sets budgets on the basis of executive judgment and experience. The executive generally has the task of allocating a fixed budget between advertising and other marketing costs. When direct customer contact is viewed as the most important element in the marketing mix, advertising needs are often subordinated. Also when a firm is under pressure to lower costs, advertising is usually cut because of the absence of hard data to support the need for promotion.

The Fixed Guidelines Approach

A fixed guidelines approach involves setting the advertising budget in terms of a percentage of sales, a fixed sum per unit, or competitively with other firms. Many companies determine their budget as a percent of the sales volume forecasted or anticipated for the period that the advertising budget will cover. This percentage often remains the same over a period of years. A variant of the percentage of sales method sets the budget as a fixed sum per unit. In this approach the appropriation for advertising is determined by multiplying the projected unit sales volume by a certain number of dollars per unit. The method is used primarily for consumer durables. When applied to convenience goods, the method is called the case-rate method.

The Task Approach

The task approach involves setting objectives, then determining the appropriation necessary to attain them. Firms using this approach begin by setting specific and measurable objectives for their advertising. We have already covered this approach in

[21]Yoshinori Ikeda, "Nissan Motors' Overseas Marketing," *Management Japan,* Vol. 2 (1969), pp. 21-26.
[22]Albert W. Frey, *How Many Dollars for Advertising* (New York: The Ronald Press, 1955); David L. Hurwood, "How Companies Set Advertising Budgets," *How Much to Spend for Advertising,* Malcolm A. McNiven (ed.) (New York: Association of National Advertisers, 1969), pp. 11-22.

some detail in the section of "Advertising Objectives and Goals." The Texasgulf company provides a useful case history.

Texasgulf supplies phosphoric acid to fertilizer manufacturers.[23] Before advertising began, Texasgulf had a market share of about 5 percent, and about six large customers accounted for most of the sales. A short-term advertising goal was set to increase the awareness of Texasgulf's superior phosphoric acids by 10 percent in a one-year period.

The campaign that was employed centered on the fact that Texasgulf acid products had less impurities than those of the competition and had a distinctive green color. The acid products were always referred to as being "clean and green," and the overall campaign theme was "Texasgulf has changed things."

A before and after research study found the following: (1) An increase from 15.3 percent to 35.1 percent in the number of respondents who recognized that Texasgulf made a clear, green acid. (2) An increase from 3.6 to 16.3 percent in the number of respondents who associated Texasgulf with the theme "(Blank) has changed things." (3) An increase from 9.4 percent to 24.3 percent in the number of respondents who thought that Texasgulf made an "above-average" acid. The results clearly indicate that the advertising campaign met the objectives that were set.

The Normative Approach

The normative approach involves finding the *optimal* advertising budget with respect to the goals that have been established. In contrast to the task approach, the normative approach uses sales rather than one of the intermediate variables of the hierarchy of effects hypothesis. Sales are useful in setting budgets because they are a prerequisite for profit maximization. The specific normative approach chosen depends on the presence or absence of carryover effects. If there is no carryover effect, then we need only to maximize short-run profits.

Carryover occurs when current marketing expenditures influence sales in future periods. Two types of carryover effects can be distinguished. The delayed response effect comes about when there is a delay between the advertisement and the resulting purchase. The customer holdover effect comes about when the advertisement influences a sequence of purchases.[24] Carryover is represented in the advertising response function by the use of lagged variables.[25]

The specific procedure for finding the optimal budget also depends on the availability of historical data to derive the response function that relates the elements of the marketing mix to sales. New products require Bayesian methods or field experimentation to find optimal budgets. Established products can make use of mathematical models. The Bayesian method is one way of budgeting in the absence of historical data.[26] For an example, see Problem 1 in Chapter Two, "Decision Making in Marketing."

The Controlled Field Experiment.   An example of a controlled field experi-

---

[23]Charles S. Bryk and Robert Davis, "Ads Work, Texasgulf Proves in Positioning Campaign for Acids," *Industrial Marketing,* Vol. 58 (August 1973), pp. 56-62.

[24]Philip Kotler, *Marketing Decision Making: A Model Building Approach* (New York: Holt, Rinehart and Winston, 1968).

[25]The term distributed lags describes a phenomenon in which the total effect of advertising is not felt in the same period that it occurred, but is distributed over time. A special case of distributed lags occurs when the effect of each independent variable decays to zero at a constant rate.

[26]Ben M. Enis "Bayesian Approach to Ad Budgets," *Journal of Advertising Research,* Vol. 12 (February 1972), p. 16.

ment[27] is DuPont's evaluation of its advertising for Teflon coatings for cookware. DuPont was following a pull strategy in which they hoped that advertising could create sufficient consumer demand so that cookware manufacturers would be forced to coat the inside of their utensils with Teflon. Advertising was varied in selected markets to determine the best level of Teflon advertising expenditures between zero and $1 million. The results are shown in Table 10-4. There appeared to be threshold effect where $½ million had little impact, but $1 million gave significantly greater sales. The million-dollar expenditure was known to be profitable, but not necessarily the most profitable level. Another experiment was conducted in which much higher levels were tested. This second experiment permitted DuPont to set the advertising level so that the marginal profit from the sale of Telfon was just greater than zero.[28]

The Mathematical Model. Historical data can be used to estimate the unknown parameters of a mathematical model of an advertising response function. Once estimation is complete, the optimal position can be achieved by solving the model using calculus or mathematical programming. An illustration is provided by the vacuum cleaner manufacturer described in the pricing chapter.

The quantity of vacuum cleaners demanded is a function of price and advertising. The relationship can be represented by the equation:[29]

$$Q = 4000 + 0.14A - .000006A^2 - 40P \qquad (3)$$

This equation presumes that the sales response to advertising as well as price is known. This particular equation also reflects diminishing returns to advertising. That is, each additional dollar of advertising generates less additional sales than the preceding dollar of advertising.[30]

Table 10-4
Winter Results in Units/1000 Households

		Fall Advertising		
		None	$500,000	$1,000,000
	None	25	26	32
Winter Advertising	$500,000	29	29	35
	$1,000,000	49	53	70

Source. Malcolm A. McNiven, "Choosing the Most Profitable Level of Advertising: A Case Study" in Malcolm McNiven, ed., *How Much To Spend for Advertising* (New York: Association of National Advertisers, 1969), pp. 90-96.

[27]Jack B. Haskins, *How to Evaluate Mass Communications: The Controlled Field Experiment* (New York: Advertising Research Foundation, 1968), and Keith K. Cox and Ben M. Enis, *Experimentation for Marketing Decisions* (Scranton: International Textbook, 1969).
[28]Malcolm A. McNiven, "Choosing the Most Profitable Level of Advertising: A Case Study," in Malcolm A. McNiven (ed.), *How Much to Spend on Advertising* (New York: Association of National Advertisers, 1969), pp. 90-96.
[29]A more common functional expression for this type of equation is a multiplicative model that is linear in logarithm form. See equation 6 in Chapter Eight.
[30]Economists are interested in the opposite phenomenon. See Julian L. Simon, "Are There Economies of Scale in Advertising?" *Journal of Advertising Research,* Vol. 5 (June 1965), pp. 15-20.

The total revenue and total cost functions and consequently the profit equation can be expressed in terms of the sales response function. According to the profit equation, profits will hit a maximum of $75,000 at a selling price of $70 and an advertising level of $10,000 (Figure 10-5). If we did not advertise, we would give up a profit of $26,000 ($75,000 − $49,000). By advertising we not only can charge $10 more for each vacuum cleaner, but we can sell 400 more vacuum cleaners.

More complex models of sales response to advertising can be optimized through mathematical programming. In one case, the market mechanism for several brands of a product sold predominantly in supermarkets was represented by a four-equation, dynamic model. The optimization problem was multiperiod in character. Sales and profit in a single period depended not only on the advertising for that period but also on advertising in previous periods. Moreover, since the system involved simultaneous dependencies, the advertising and sales of all competitive brands influenced and were influenced by sales and advertising for an individual brand. Nonlinear programming techniques were applied to calculate the optimal decision strategy. The calculation showed that the firm was significantly overspending for some brands while significantly underspending for others.[31]

These methods for determining the best budget can still result in overspending on advertising. Unusual amounts of free publicity and/or word-of-mouth communication

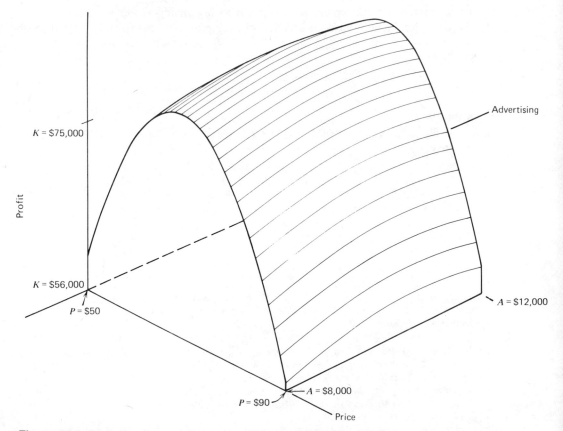

Figure 10-5 Profit Function for a Vacuum Cleaner Manufacturer.

[31]Leonard J. Parsons and Frank M. Bass, "Optimal Advertising-Expenditure Implications of a Simultaneous-Equation Regression Analysis," *Operations Research*, Vol. 19 (May-June 1971), pp. 822-831.

can reduce the needed expenditures. In retrospect, Ford spent too much on its promotion for the introduction of the first Mustang. Extensive free publicity included simultaneous cover stories by *Time* and *Newsweek* and reception of the Tiffany Award for Excellence in American Design.

MEDIA SELECTION

The objective in media planning is to select the set of television shows, radio programs, magazines, newspapers, and other media vehicles that will maximize profits within a given budget. Quantitative models have been developed to help structure and evaluate media and audience data. These models require the specification of media weights that reflect the difference in suitability of the various media vehicles. Development of computer media models are predicated on an understanding of the appropriateness of media vehicles and on a knowledge of how media are matched with markets.

Media Vehicle Appropriateness

Media vehicles are not passive conductors of messages and can often influence the effectiveness of the message. Factors that determine the appropriateness of media vehicles include editorial climate, product fit, technical capabilities, competitive advertising strategy, target population receptiveness, and the product distribution system.[32]

A vehicle has an image and personality that can add or detract from a message. *Sunset* is regarded as an expert source and *Vogue* as a prestige source. The relative value will depend on the campaign objectives (awareness versus attitude change versus image creation), the target segment, the campaign tactics (image versus reason-why advertising), and the product.

Media are believed to work in different ways.[33] At each stage in the purchase process, one medium may be superior to another. Relative to television commercials, print advertisements are less able to command attention, are more able to arouse personal involvement, and are more likely to cause conscious, discrete attitude change.

The consumer can pay *no* attention to a print advertisement or deliberately expose himself to one. He does the latter when he is seeking information for decision making. The consumer can concentrate longer on an advertising theme and thereby make more personal connections with it. This means he can become more personally involved in print advertisements for products that possess intrinsic interest. Since attention is voluntary, the consumer is more likely to be consciously influenced. Attitude change under conditions of high involvement occurs through the process of dissonance resolution.

Even when a customer does not notice a commercial while watching TV, he usually listens to it. His involvement is low and he is unaware that his attitudes are slowly being modified by the onslaught of repeated exposure to the message.[34] His attitudes may change more rapidly later when the source of the message is forgotten. This phenomenon

---

[32]Qualitative factors that influence media selection are discussed in Dennis H. Gensch, "Media Factors: A Review Article," *Journal of Marketing Research,* Vol. 7 (May 1970), pp. 216-225.

[33]This section is based on J. Nolan, "Combined Media Campaigns" in *Ten Years of Advertising Media Research* (London: The Thomson Organization, 1972), pp. 321-349. See also J. Douglas McConnell, "Do Media Vary in Effectiveness?" *Journal of Advertising Research,* Vol. 10 (October 1970), pp. 19-22.

[34]Herbert E. Krugman, "The Impact of Television Advertising: Learning Without Involvement," *Public Opinion Quarterly,* Vol. 29 (February 1965), pp. 349-356.

is called the sleeper effect.[35] When the consumer ultimately faces a purchasing situation, these shifts in attitude move to a more conscious level.

These differences suggest that print and television advertising may be used most effectively in combination. One may be more suitable than the other for a particular step in the intermediate process. Thus, the manager needs to match the media with his goals. Next, he must match the media with his target audience.

Matching Media with Markets

Advertisers like to choose media whose audience characteristics are closest to the profile of market characteristics of their consumers.[36] Characteristics by which the target population may be identified include demographic, psychographic, and purchase behavior variables. These characteristics can be weighted in proportion to their importance. Managers also need methods to help them select media that show the best combination of cost and exposure value.

Cost-Per-Thousand

One method used to select media is to compare the cost-per-thousand persons reached by different vehicles. For example, a four-color one page ad in *Reader's Digest* costs $61,765 and circulation in the United States is 17,750,000, so the cost-per-thousand circulation is $3.48. By comparison, *Newsweek* has a lower four-color rate of $26,680, but the circulation is only 2,878,000, so the cost-per-thousand is $9.26. Cost-per-thousand figures for all appropriate magazines can be compared and the magazines with the lowest cost-per-thousand would be chosen for use in the advertising campaign.[37]

The main problem with cost-per-thousand is that circulation figures do not include all persons exposed to the ads and may not be a good measure of the number of people who are in the market for the product. This deficiency can be overcome by gathering additional data on media readership and making appropriate adjustments. For example, *Reader's Digest* reports a total audience of 42 million readers and *Newsweek* has 13.9 million, so their costs-per-thousand readers for a four-color page are fairly close at $1.47 and $1.90. Further adjustments can be made to the denominator of the cost-per-thousand ratio for products that appeal to special market segments. Thus a cost-per-thousand for women readers could be developed to compare alternative vehicles for products that are sold only to women.

Although cost-per-thousand calculations are helpful for finding the best vehicle buys within a particular medium, the technique is not appropriate for making comparisons across media. Differences in the form and presentation of ads are so vast among radio, TV, newspapers and direct mail that cost-per-thousand comparisons are just not meaningful. In addition, restrictions on the distribution or patronage patterns of the advertiser may limit the portion of a media audience that is useful.

A retailer, for example, can buy a quarter page in the *Chicago Tribune* during the week for about $1500. Circulation of this paper is 700,000, so the cost-per-thousand is a low

[35]S. Johns, J. Lannon, and M. R. C. Lovell, "The Theory of Sleeper Effect: A Discussion,"in *Ten Years of Advertising Media Research* (London: The Thomson Organization, 1972), pp. 141-159.

[36]Jack Z. Sissors, "Matching Media with Markets," *Journal of Advertising Research*, Vol. 11 (October 1971), pp. 39-43.

[37]Cost, circulation, and other media data are published monthly by Standard Rate and Data Service Inc. The numbers used in the Examples are from *Consumer Magazine and Farm Publication Rates and Data* (October 27, 1973), pp. 158-163.

$2.14. An alternative approach might be to employ a direct mail campaign where the cost-per-thousand would run between $150 and $200 for a letter, postage, brochure and mailing list. If the choice of an advertising medium is based simply on cost-per-thousand, then the newspaper is obviously the better buy. However, retailers typically draw their customers from a restricted market area and the *Tribune* may provide a lot of waste circulation. This means a dry cleaning store may be better off to spend $1500 sending direct mail literature to 10,000 consumers in his immediate area than taking a chance that an ad in the *Tribune* will reach his customers. When ads are placed in more than one media or vehicle, audience duplication must be taken into account.

Duplication

Duplication in advertising occurs because some of the individuals exposed to your ad in one vechicle will also see the ad in a second vehicle. For example, suppose magazine A has an audience of 300,000 and magazine B has an audience of 200,000. If 100,000 of these people subscribe to both magazines, then the unduplicated audience is only 400,000. This suggests that the more media vehicles you buy, the greater the chance for duplication and the more likely you are to have diminishing returns to advertising.

Research[38] has shown that the effects of duplication of the reach of an advertising program can be estimated using the formula:

$$C = \left(\frac{1}{1 + KD/A}\right) A \tag{4}$$

where C = total reach or number of persons exposed one or more times during the campaign

K = a constant, estimated[39] to range from 1.125 to 1.5

D = sum of the duplicated readership for all pairs of media in the set

A = total number of persons in the audiences of media in the set

To use the formula, a manager must have data on the pairwise duplication between media vehicles he is planning to use and be able to estimate K from the available materials (i.e., regression techniques). The Agostini formula (4) has been shown to give accurate projections of the reach of advertising schedules involving multiple insertions in several media.[40]

Reach Versus Frequency

The total impact of an advertising campaign can be measured by counting the number of exposures that result from *reaching* different people and multiplying by the average *frequency* of ad exposure per person. Thus we have:

Total exposures = reach × frequency

This implies that high total exposure can be obtained by reaching a large number of people with a few ads or by exposing a small number of potential buyers to many ads. The problem for the manager is to decide what combination of advertising reach and frequency is best for a particular product at a point in time.

---

[38]J. M. Agostini, "How to Estimate Unduplicated Audiences," *Journal of Advertising Research,* Vol. 1, No. 3 (March 1961), 11-14.

[39]H. J. Claycamp and C. W. McClelland, "Estimating Reach and the Magic of K," *Journal of Advertising Research,* Vol. 8, No. 2 (June 1968), pp. 44-51

[40]Pierre Hofmans, "Measuring the Cumulative Net Coverage of Any Combination of Media," *Journal of Advertising Research,* Vol. 3, No. 3 (August 1966), pp. 269-278.

When an advertiser has a message that has to be heard only once, he employs a media schedule that maximizes reach. The idea is to have every exposure appeal to a different potential buyer. Most of the retail advertising that we see emphasizing special sales and prices falls in this category. Also many of the direct mail promotions used for book and record clubs are designed to make a sale on the first impression and reach is crucial to their success. In addition, reach can be important when introducing new products to the market-place. This is especially true when cents-off coupons are offered to encourage trial and the firm wants each potential buyer to get only one coupon.

Alternatively, some advertisers must repeat ads frequently to get the attention of the buyer and bring about attitude changes that precede purchase. In these situations, the emphasis is on the number of exposures per person rather than the reach of the campaign. This approach is based on research that shows that recall of ads and purchase intentions increase with the number of exposures per person.[41] For example, magazines often use a planned series of four or five direct mail ads to convince people to renew their subscriptions. Repetition in advertising is also used to keep the name of the product in the mind of the buyer so that when a purchase is planned the company's brand will be remembered. This is particularly important for frequently purchased consumer goods such as cigarettes where brand loyalty is low. Reminder ads can also be used to promote the sale of products and services that are bought infrequently. Funeral homes, insurance agents, and car dealers all employ repetition in their advertising to build a favorable image so they will be considered when the buyer is ready to make a purchase.

Because of differences in products and market conditions, it is probably foolish to generalize about the optimum combination of reach and frequency for an advertising campaign. However, managers usually have better data on the reach of media vehicles than they have on duplication and the effects of repetition on sales. This suggests that media selection will often emphasize reach with a more subjective adjustment made for frequency.

Computer Media Models

Traditional procedures for media selection that rely on judgment and experience are suspect because of their inability to consider the very large number of possible combinations of vehicles. Computer models that help in making better media decisions are currently being developed. However, the original media models were used by advertising agencies more as promotional gimmicks than as tools to aid actual decision making.

There are two major groups of models. In the first group, enough assumptions are made so that the best media schedule can be found. This schedule is optimal only if the underlying assumptions are true. Optimizing models generally include some type of mathematical programming: linear, dynamic, integer, or nonlinear. In the second group, less restrictive assumptions are made so that it is unknown whether the best media schedule examined is optimal or not. Nonoptimizing models involve heuristic problem solving and simulation.[42]

Batten, Barton, Durstine, and Osborne (BBD&O), a major advertising agency, announced in the early 1960s that it had a linear programming model available for its clients. Linear programming is a mathematical technique for allocating some scarce

---

[41]Michael L. Ray and Alan G. Sawyer, "Repetition in Media Models: A Laboratory Technique," *Journal of Marketing Research,* Vol. 8 (February 1971), pp. 20-29.

[42]This section is based on Dennis Gensch, *Advertising Planning* (Amsterdam: Elsevier Scientific Publishing Company, 1973).

resource such as time, money, or materials among several alternative uses under constrained conditions. This allocation is done in such a way that some stated criterion called an objective function attains its maximum value within the constraints. One scarce resource is the total amount of money available for advertising. The alternatives are different combinations of the various media vehicles. The objective function usually measures the effectiveness of the media schedule in terms of total exposure.[43] An example illustrating the use of linear programming in media selection is given in the Appendix.

Linear programming solutions to media allocation problems must be viewed as a first approximization. There are three major weaknesses to this approach. One is that the objective function is unlikely to be linear. We do not believe that repeat exposures have equal effects.[44] Another is that media costs are not constant. Discounts exist for multiple time or space purchases.[45] The last weakness, and perhaps the most important one, is the failure to take into account audience duplication. These problems have led to the use of more advanced programming techniques and heuristic methods.

Heuristic models are based on the actual decision rules used by media planners. These rules have evolved through experience and have been found to work satisfactorily. They do not guarantee that they will produce the best solution. One of the first heuristic models was developed by British European Airways (BEA).

More recent heuristic models include POMSIS and MEDIAC.[46] POMSIS and MEDIAC are designed for industrial and consumer markets respectively. MEDIAC incorporates information on market segments, sales potentials, exposure probabilities, media costs, forgetting, seasonality, individual response to exposures, and vehicle exposure values. MEDIAC has been implemented on a time-share computer that permits the user to obtain immediate on-line access.

THE MEASUREMENT OF ADVERTISING EFFECTIVENESS

The ability of a firm to measure the effectiveness of its advertising is crucial to developing more efficient advertisements, to determining the optimal level of expenditures, and to allocating available funds to media. As soon as the relationship between advertising pressure and effectiveness is known, a firm can calculate the optimal advertising budget size, can compare various media (intermedia optimization), and select vehicles within the same medium (intramedia optimization).

The importance of measuring the effectiveness of advertising can be illustrated by some case histories:

1. An advertiser had a great story. Twenty percent more of those who remembered it bought. Then the campaign was changed and now only 10 percent more buy. But the advertiser did not realize this because an appropriate measurement was lacking.

---

[43]Frank M. Bass and Ronald T. Lonsdale, "An Exploration of Linear Programming in Media Selection," *Journal of Marketing Research*, Vol. 3 (May 1966), pp. 179-188.

[44]Michael L. Ray, Alan G. Sawyer, and Edward C. Strong, "Frequency Effects Revisited," *Journal of Advertising Research*, Vol. 11 (February 1971) pp. 14-20.

[45]Robert S. Kaplan and Allan D. Shocker, "Discount Effects on Media Plans," *Journal of Advertising Research*, Vol. 11 (June 1971), pp. 37-43.

[46]David Aaker, "A Probabilistic Approach to Media Selection," *Journal of Advertising Research*, Vol. 8 (September 1968), pp. 46-54; John D. C. Little and Leonard M. Lodish, "A Media Planning Calculus," *Operations Research*, Vol. 17 (January-February 1969), pp. 1-35.

2. An advertiser, spending $4 million a year, had a story with enormous pull. Yet this story was hidden in a small box in the advertising. Knowledge of this fact would enable the advertiser to make copy changes.

3. An advertiser was spending $7 million a year, but the campaign had no usage pull. People who did not remember the advertising bought just as much as those who did remember it.

4. A beer manufacturer spent $10 million a year advertising one dominant, memorable picture theme. Unfortunately, the picture repels consumers. Those who remember the theme drink less of this beer than those who do not remember it.[47]

These cases suggest that one cannot make advertising decisions on intuition alone.

The four most commonly used measures of advertising effectiveness are changes in sales, number of inquiries received, increases in knowledge of the product, and attitude changes. While the intermediate measures of effectiveness can provide helpful insights, sales is the primary criterion used to evaluate advertising results.

The analysis of the influence of advertising on the sales of a product or service is a complex undertaking. The difficulties involved in measuring the influences of advertising may be separated into three major categories: (1) the problem of isolating the effects of advertising from the many other variables that influence sales; (2) the problem of measuring the quantity of advertising, taking into account the fact that advertising dollar expenditures reflect alternative choices of media, psychological appeals and copy; and (3) the problem of identifying the relationship that reflects the influence of advertising upon sales—the so-called identification problem.

The methods available for measuring advertising elasticities are the same as those already discussed for measuring price elasticities. Controlled field experiments have had some limited success and they are expensive. These market tests seem to be most useful for new products when historical data is unavailable. Econometric methods are a more popular approach for the study of advertising effects for existing products.

Econometric Methods

Econometric models have been constructed that permit (1) the isolation of the effects of advertising from those of other factors; (2) the characterizations of carryover and feedback effects, nonlinearities, simultaneous interactions, the intrinsic relative effectiveness of advertising, and the impact of different campaigns; (3) comparison of various media; and (4) prediction of the behavior of competitive advertising and sales as well as the behavior of brand advertising and sales.[48] The most important recent innovation in this area has been the trend toward simultaneous equation regression models.

Single equation models are suspect in this analysis because they assume a unidirec-

[47]Rosser Reeves, "Reality in Advertising" in Otto Kleppner and Irving Settel (eds.), *Exploring Advertising* (Englewood Cliffs, N.J.: Prentice-Hall, 1970), pp. 126-127.

[48]Taken as a whole, the following five articles contain most of these features: Seymour Banks, "Some Correlates of Coffee and Cleanser Brand Shares," *Jouranl of Advertising Research,* Vol. 1 (June 1961), pp. 22-28; Kristian S. Palda, *The Measurement of Cumulative Advertising Effects* (Englewood Cliffs N.J.: Prentice-Hall, 1964); Jean-Jacques Lambin, "Is Gasoline Advertising Justified?" Paper No. 6-1270, Center of Socio-Economic Studies in Advertising and Marketing, University of Louvain, 1970; Alfred A. Kuehn, Timothy W. McGuire, and Doyle L. Weiss, "Measuring the Effectiveness of Advertising," *Proceedings* (Chicago: American Marketing Association Fall Conference 1966), pp. 185-194; Frank M. Bass and Leonard J. Parsons, "Simultaneous-Equation Regression Analysis of Sales and Advertising" in Ralph L. Day and Leonard J. Parsons (eds.), *Marketing Models: Quantitative Applications* (Scranton, Intext, 1971), pp. 364-391.

tional flow of influence. Although sales is a function of advertising expenditure, advertising is also a function of sales. Frequently the demand for a product shifts while the firm's advertising budgeting practices remain rigid. Under these conditions, advertising budgets that are set as a fixed percentage of sales or in relation to the size of markets will increase with demand. Although it may seem that larger ad budgets produce higher sales, in reality advertising is just reacting to changes in volume. Thus what appears to be a demand curve showing the relationship between advertisng and sales, is merely a trace of the advertising budget line.[49] In econometrics, this is known as the identification problem. Processes that involve multiple relationships must be represented by a system of equations.

Data Bases

Attainment of empirical results that have practical value requires good input data. The marketing information system of the firm should provide the necessary figures. Most of the data can be obtained from longitudinal panels and/or store audits as well as the available internal records. Some manipulation of the decision variables may be necessary to insure that the variability in these factors is great enough for drawing policy implications. That is, since any model is only applicable over the range of data upon which it is based, that range should be large. This manipulation need not be synonymous with a controlled field experiment, but it could be. The data base is an integral part of econometric model building.

ADVERTISING AND SOCIETY

Thus far, advertising has been considered from a managerial viewpoint. The manager must also be aware of economic and social viewpoints. These viewpoints provide the rationale for the control of advertising by either government or industry self-regulation.

Economic Concerns

Four major economic concerns have been identified: (1) advertising is an unnecessary business cost and raises prices unnecessarily; (2) advertising encourages costly, yet unimportant product differentiation; (3) advertising is too often merely competitive—attempting to induce consumers to cease buying one brand and start buying another that is practically identical in value—and ties up resources that could be put to better use; and (4) advertising enables some manufacturers to have an undesirable, monopolistic influence on supply and prices.[50]

Advertising will normally have a favorable effect on unit manufacturing and distribution costs. When advertising permits economies of scale in manufacturing operations, unit manufacturing costs will be lower. When advertising is more efficient than other elements of the marketing mix (i.e., sales calls), when advertising lowers the sales costs of channel members, or when advertising results in economies of scale in distribution organizations, then unit distribution costs will be lower.

---

[49]An example of a leading advertising agency that made this error is provided in Alfred A. Kuehn and Albert C. Rohloff, "Fitting Models to Aggregate Data," *Journal of Advertising Research,* Vol. 7 (March 1967), pp. 43-47.
[50]Albert Wesley Frey and Jean C. Halterman, *Advertising* (New York: Ronald Press, 1970), p. 513.

Prices are determined primarily by supply and demand factors. However, unit manufacturing, distribution, and other costs along with minimum profit requirements create a floor below which prices cannot fall. If advertising causes lower costs, then it can lead to lower prices.[51] For example, the advertising of eyeglasses and eye examinations is controlled in many states. A comparison of prices in states with a complete prohibition on advertising with prices in states without such a prohibition reveals that prices are higher in states that prohibit advertising. In the case of eyeglasses, prices were from 25 to more than 100 percent higher.[52]

The most important public policy issue centers on the relationship between advertising, economic concentration, and monopoly power. The argument is made that large firms use advertising expenditures to establish in the consumers' minds that there are differences among products. These perceived differences are the foundation on which preferences and brand loyalty are formed. Existing advertisers have a consumer franchise that new entrants into the market find difficult to overcome. Furthermore, this consumer franchise generates funds for more advertising. Thus, advertising is a major barrier to entry for new firms. In this situation when new competitors are limited and weaker existing firms are driven out of the market, economic concentration results. Economic concentration means market power. This power permits the firms to charge higher prices while foregoing product improvements and, consequently, to achieve higher profits. However, the argument remains only conjecture. Empirical research has failed to conclusively prove or disprove the existence of the asserted causal relationships.

Social Concerns

Six major social concerns have been identified: (1) advertising persuades people to do things they otherwise would not do; (2) advertising takes unfair advantage of consumers by conveying false and misleading information; (3) advertising is frequently in bad taste; (4) advertising fosters a materialistic attitude throughout society with the resultant neglect of more important values; (5) advertising lowers the moral and ethical standards in society; and (6) advertising exploits the relative lack of sophistication of children.[53]

Obviously advertising and other marketing communications are *attempts* at persuasion. This should not concern anyone since the right to advocate one's position is an essential element of a free society. Fair and truthful advertising will not cause anyone to purchase a product or service that they do not want. Certainly, it cannot cause anyone to purchase such a product the second time and national advertisers have a self-interest in building customer satisfaction. It should be clear that the cost of making only one sale per prospect through advertising is prohibitive. Advertising is only profitable when prospects make repeat purchases.

Moreover, both wants and standards of taste are learned.[54] The distinctions between wants and needs and between good and bad taste are a function of many factors including general culture, education, social pressure, and advertising. No group should presume that their evaluation is the only correct one.

The effect of advertising on values and life styles is very difficult to assess.[55]

[51]Robert L. Steiner, "Does Advertising Lower Consumer Prices?" *Journal of Marketing,* Vol. 37 (October 1973), pp. 19-26.

[52]Lee Benham, "The Effect of Advertising on the Price of Eyeglasses," working paper, May 18, 1972.

[53]Michael Pearch, Scott M. Cunningham, and Avon Miller, *Appraising the Economic and Social Effects of Advertising* (Cambridge: Marketing Science Institute, 1971,) p. 4.1.

[54]Harry G. Johnson, "The Consumer and Madison Avenue, " *Current Economic Comment,* Vol. 22 (August 1960), pp. 3-10.

[55]John G. Myers, *Social Issues in Advertising* (New York: A.A.A.A. Education Foundation, 1971).

Judgments about what a consumer ought to prefer or ought to select is a question of ethics. This is an area in which individual differences are important. Beyond this, it is unclear how one can separate the effects of advertising from those of the broader socioeconomic system of which it is an integral part.

Advertising should provide truthful information to aid buyer decision making. The Federal Trade Commission (FTC) acts to insure the truthfulness of marketing communications. Most businessmen support the principal of substantiation of advertising claims advocated by the FTC. They do not support the principle that charges of deceptive advertising can be made solely on the capacity of the advertisement to mislead. Instead these charges should be made on demonstration of the intent of the advertiser to mislead or of an occurrence of someone, in fact, being mislead. Furthermore, a degree of puffery is considered acceptable by the public.[56]

Summary

Under the appropriate conditions, advertising can assume an important role in the marketing mix. Advertising planning begins with the determination of objectives and goals. The optimal advertising budget with respect to these goals can be obtained using normative methods. When the effectiveness of advertising can be measured, analytic solutions are achieved using calculus or mathematical programming. Given the budget, the best set of media vehicles must be chosen. Computer media models are available to assist in this planning. Econometric and experimental methods can be used to measure the effectiveness of advertising. This result is then used in making the next budgeting decision. In addition, the advertiser must be sensitive to the bounds of public tolerance.

Appendix
Linear Programming Media Selection

Assume that the product manager of a new consumer product has an advertising budget of $500,000. His company has already made commitments for time or space in three media vehicles: The Monday Night Movie, *TV Guide,* and *Reader's Digest.* Available to him are twenty-six minutes of television time and four pages in each of the magazines. The manager does not want to spend more than 40 percent of his budget on magazines. Media data from his advertising agency are available on the costs and expected exposures (in this example, the data is hypothetical):

	Cost	Expected Exposures
Monday Night Movie, 60 seconds	$30,000	40,000
TV Guide, 4-color page	20,000	80,000
Reader's Digest, 4-color page	40,000	80,000

The manager can now formulate his problem in linear programming terms as shown in Figure 10-6.

[56]Michael Pearch, Scott M. Cunningham, and Avon Miller, *Appraising the Economic and Social Effects of Advertising* (Cambridge: Marketing Science Institute, 1971), pp. 4.21-4.29. Also see Tom Dillon, "What is Deceptive Advertising?" *Journal of Advertising Research,* Vol. 13 (October 1973), pp. 9-12.

Maximize: Total Exposures = $40{,}000 \begin{bmatrix} \text{Minutes in Monday} \\ \text{Night Movie} \end{bmatrix} + 80{,}000 \begin{bmatrix} \text{Pages in} \\ \textit{TV Guide} \end{bmatrix} + 80{,}000 \begin{bmatrix} \text{Pages in} \\ \textit{Readers Digest} \end{bmatrix}$

Subject to:

$\$30{,}000 \begin{bmatrix} \text{Minutes in Monday} \\ \text{Night Movie} \end{bmatrix} + \$20{,}000 \begin{bmatrix} \text{Pages in} \\ \textit{TV Guide} \end{bmatrix} + \$40{,}000 \begin{bmatrix} \text{Pages in} \\ \textit{Readers Digest} \end{bmatrix} \leq \$500{,}000$

$\begin{bmatrix} \text{Minutes in Monday} \\ \text{Night Movie} \end{bmatrix} \leq 26$

$\begin{bmatrix} \text{Pages in} \\ \textit{TV Guide} \end{bmatrix} \leq 4$

$\begin{bmatrix} \text{Pages in} \\ \textit{Readers Digest} \end{bmatrix} \leq 4$

$\$20{,}000 \begin{bmatrix} \text{Minutes in Monday} \\ \text{Night Movie} \end{bmatrix} + \$40{,}000 \begin{bmatrix} \text{Pages in} \\ \textit{TV Guide} \end{bmatrix} \leq \$200{,}000$

$\begin{bmatrix} \text{Minutes in Monday} \\ \text{Night Movie} \end{bmatrix} \geq 0$

$\begin{bmatrix} \text{Pages in} \\ \textit{TV Guide} \end{bmatrix} \geq 0$

$\begin{bmatrix} \text{Pages in} \\ \textit{Readers Digest} \end{bmatrix} \geq 0$

Figure 10-6 Linear Programming Formulation.

The various combinations of insertions in the three media which satisfy the constraints can be viewed as the feasible region shown in Figure 10-7. The optimal solution occurs at one of the corner points of the feasible region. Thus, we need only to evaluate the objective function at each of the ten corners and choose the one which generates the greatest value. Examination of all the points is tedious and inefficient, especially for complex allocation problems. The simplex method is a procedure for doing an efficient search of the corner points.[1] This method is the foundation for the computer results shown in Figure 10-8. Starting from the origin, the optimum is reached in four steps. The best schedule consists of ten minutes in the Monday Night Movie, four pages in *TV Guide* and three pages in *Reader's Digest*. This schedule provides 960,000 exposures. Note in Figure 10-7 that the optimum occurs at the point that the hyperplane of the objective function first touches the feasible region from above.

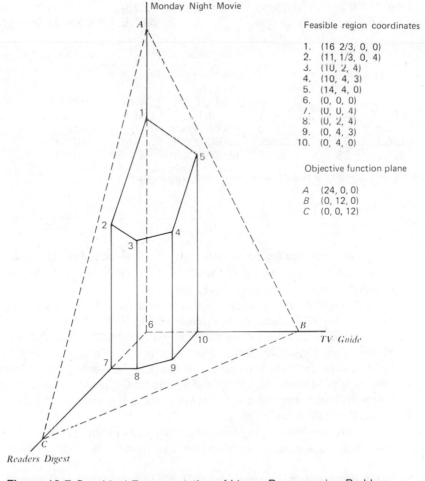

Figure 10-7 Graphical Representation of Linear Programming Problem.

[1] This method is explained in texts on mathematical programming. One reference is Harvey M. Wagner, *Principles of Operations Research* (Englewood Cliffs; New Jersey; Prentice Hall, 1969).

```
EXECUTOR. MPS/360
SOLUTION (OPTIMAL)
TIME = 0.15 MINS. ITERATION NUMBER = 3

   ...NAME...        ...ACTIVITY...   DEFINED AS
   FUNCTIONAL        960000.00000     OBJECT
   RESTRAINTS                         B


EXECUTOR. MPS-360


SECTION 1 - ROWS
```

NUM-BER	ROW	AT	ACTIVITY	SLACK ACTIVITY	LOWER LIMIT	UPPER LIMIT	DUAL ACTIVITY
1	OBJECT	BS	960000.00000	960000.00000-	NONE	NONE	1.00000
2	BUDGET	UL	500000.00000	.	NONE	500000.00000	1.33333-
3	MOVLIMIT	BS	10.00000	16.00000	NONE	26.00000	.
4	TVGLIMIT	UL	4.00000	.	NONE	4.00000	40000.00000-
5	RDLIMIT	BS	3.00000	1.00000	NONE	4.00000	.
6	MAGLIMIT	UL	200000.00000	.	NONE	200000.00000	.66667-

```
EXECUTOR. MPS/360

SECTION 2 - COLUMNS
```

NUM-BER	COLUMN	AT	ACTIVITY	INPUT COST	LOWER LIMIT	UPPER LIMIT	REDUCED COST
7	MONMOVIE	BS	10.00000	40000.00000	.	NONE	.
8	TVGUIDE	BS	4.00000	80000.00000	.	NONE	.
9	RDIGEST	BS	3.00000	80000.00000	.	NONE	.

Figure 10-8 Sample printout from linear programming program.

Questions

1. Assess the opportunities for advertising for each of the following products in terms of the four criteria given in the text: room air conditioners, toothpaste, garbage disposals, corporate common stock, fresh milk.

2. Exxon, Wrigley, and American Express have about the same advertising expenditures, yet their sales are vastly different (Table 10-1). Why is this?

3. One television commercial for the Yellow Pages features Lou Brock, a baseball player, in his florist shop. Brock says "As long as my business keeps blooming, I'll keep advertising." Do you agree with Brock's philosophy about advertising?

4. Use calculus to show that the optimal profits for the vacuum cleaner manufacturer discussed in the text (equation (3)) will occur when advertising expenditures are $10,000 and the price of the product is $70.

5. Advertising models are imperfect representations of the real world. Under what conditions does it make sense to find the optimal advertising implications of a model?

6. Lever Brothers test marketed Phase III, a deodorant soap, in Pittsburgh. Seventy percent of the advertising budget was allocated to spot TV. This resulted in nine to twelve announcements a week during the daytime and fringe time. In addition, eleven full-page magazine ads were run in the regional editions of *Life, Look,*

McCall's, Ladies' Home Journal, Reader's Digest, Family Circle, and Better Homes and Gardens.

In the precampaign survey, only 1 percent of the women said they had heard of Phase III and correctly identified it. After three weeks this figure rose to 30 percent after five weeks, 39 percent, and after 13 weeks, 45 percent.

On the basis of this information, what recommendations would you make to management concerning Phase III's going national? What additional information would you like to have?

7. Coca-Cola's Coke dominates the soft drink industry. Information on sales and advertising of Coke is given in Table 10-5. In 1969, Seven-Up had sales of 237 million cases and advertising expenditures of $12.5 million. Recommend a media strategy for Seven-Up.

8. Annual data on Camel cigarettes are given in Table 10-6. In which stage of the product life cycle is Camel? Estimate the advertising and price elasticities for Camel. What recommendations do you have for Camel?

9. To what extent must advertising be compatible with the value system of the country? Which criticisms of advertising are independent of criticisms of this value system? Which are not?

10. Is advertising that lauds the competitive differentiation among brands that are substantially alike economically wasteful? How would refrigerators, canned soups, and tires fare under your reasoning?

11. Quaker Oats offered to consumers, as a premium, a shaker for making perfect pancakes. A large TV advertising campaign offered the shaker to consumers for 75¢ with the purchase of Aunt Jemima pancake mix and/or Aunt Jemima pancake syrup. After the campaign began and a substantial number of product packages carrying information about the offer had been placed on the market, Quaker Oats found that despite assurances from the supplier, the shaker leaked.

What actions should Quaker Oats take?

12. Recently toilet paper sales soared in response to unfounded rumors about a shortage. Soon the shelves of the consumer were full. How should a marketer change his promotion and advertising in light of pantry inventories of ten weeks supply instead of the usual two-weeks supply?

Table 10-5
Coke

Year	Sales (Million Cases)	Total Advertising (Million Dollars)	Spot TV (Million Dollars)	Network TV (Million Dollars)	Radio (Million Dollars)	Magazines (Million Dollars)	Newspapers (Million Dollars)	Outdoor (Million Dollars)
1969	1390	24.546	9.498	2.244	7.377	2.899	1.313	1.349
1968	1250	28.435	12.862	3.453	7.203	2.603	1.191	1.123
1967	1065	29.560	14.371	2.727	7.100	3.761	0.824	1.190
1966	975	31.434	14.742	2.145	7.171	3.813	0.934	2.335

Table 10-6
Camel Cigarettes

Year	Sales (Billions)	Advertising (Millions)	Consumer Price Index Nonfilter Tip Cigarettes (1967 = 100)
1972	29.9	6.659	134.8
1971	31.6	6.968	127.9
1970	32.9	9.470	122.4
1969	35.3	9.366	112.7
1968	40.1	10.732	106.9
1967	44.9	12.678	100.0
1966	48.1	10.413	96.0
1965	49.1	7.478	91.1
1964	52.5	8.813	86.6
1963	63.0	8.568	83.9
1962	66.0	9.164	80.5
1961	67.0	9.189	79.7
1960	66.5	9.665	78.9
1959	63.5	9.367	76.3
1958	62.5	6.991	73.1
1957	66.0	6.580	70.7
1956	72.5	9.117	68.7
1955	77.0	7,872	67.1
1954	84.0	13.701	66.9
1953	99.0	14.866	66.0

Case 10-1
Revere Sugar Refinery[1]

The Revere Sugar Refining Company, a subsidiary of United Fruit Company, produced a full line of bulk and packaged sugar that was distributed throughout New England and the northern portion of New York State. The larger portion of the refinery's output was sold to industrial users and the balance was sold through wholesalers or directly to the retail trade. In mid-1965 executives of the company were reviewing the promotional program for Revere Sugar.

[1]This case was prepared by John R. Jenkins under the supervision of Derek A. Newton of the Harvard Graduate School of Business Administration. The case was made possible by the cooperation of the Revere Sugar Refining Company and its advertising agency. Copyright © 1967 by John R. Jenkins. Reproduced by permission.

INDUSTRY BACKGROUND

The bulk of cane-sugar refining was conducted by fourteen companies that handled about two thirds of the finished sugar sold. The American Sugar Refining Company, with five plants, had approximately 22 percent of the total U.S. productive capacity. The National Sugar Refining Company had approximately 16 percent of the total. The California and Hawaiian Sugar Refining Corporation Ltd., with one plant, had 7 percent. The other eleven major companies had 21 percent of the sugar market. One of the major problems of the sugar industry was excess capacity; refiners typically operated at only 60 percent of maximum volume.

THE MARKETING OF SUGAR

The sugar industry sold its products to the consumer market via retailers and to industrial firms. In 1963 the industry delivered about 43 percent of its production to the retail trade. Of this volume, 5.1 billion pounds were sold through wholesalers and 2.5 billion pounds were sold directly to the large food chains. The remaining 10.0 billion pounds of sugar were delivered to industrial buyers. The industrial market for sugar had been growing at a faster rate than the consumer market, due to the consumers increasing their per capita purchases of convenience foods. During the thirty-year period before 1964, total sugar consumption had risen almost proportionally to the increase in population. Annual per capita consumption in 1963 was approximately 99 pounds.

Because of freight rates and the competition of small inland cane and beet sugar refineries, no brand of sugar had attained national distribution in the United States. The American Sugar Refining Company, by far the largest in the industry, came closest to distributing nationally. It reportedly sold its sugar in all states east and in five states west of the Mississippi.

ADVERTISING BY INDIVIDUAL REFINERS

Traditionally sugar refiners had placed little emphasis on advertising. "Soft pedaling" of such promotion reflected two distinct factors: (1) the lack of discernible differences among various brands of sugar, and (2) the narrow gross margin available to sugar refiners. Promotional programs employed by three large firms are described below.

The American Sugar Refining Company

With its introduction of packaged sugar in 1912, the American Sugar Refining Company intiated a campaign of magazine advertising to develop consumer demand for its "Domino" brand of packaged sugar. The firm discontinued use of magazines in the mid 1920s and subsequently confined its principal promotion efforts to newspapers. In 1953, to combat the growing concern of consumers over the high calorific property of sugar and its possible relationship to problems of obesity, the American Sugar Refining Company once again used magazines in addition to its normal newspaper schedule. American's advertising during the period, was directed toward telling the consumer:

1. That a teaspoon of sugar contained only 18 calories "less fattening than many . . . diet foods."
2. That sugar had quick energy value.
3. That sugar had important nutritional value.

During the latter part of the 1950s while continuing to use newspapers, American increased further its advertising schedule in women's magazines, and also used farm publications between 1958 and 1963. Domino sugar packages and some of the American Refining Company's advertisements featured self-liquidating premium offers. For example in 1964, the firm offered "parchment" reproductions of famous documents such as the Declaration of Independence.

The National Sugar Refining Company

The National Sugar Refining Company had used a variety of media to promote its "Jack Frost" brand over the years. During the decade from 1929 to 1939 this firm, although smaller than American Refining, actually spent more for newspaper advertising—an average of $254,000 per year versus an average of $116,000 for American. After World War II, with the exception of the year 1950, National's expenditures generally were less than those of American. Newspaper advertising was used extensively, but after 1950 such outlays were trimmed sharply as being "too costly." Subsequently, most of National's advertising appropriation was spent on car cards and outdoor displays for which expenditures were not reported.

In 1955, National Sugar indicated that it was going to place more emphasis on industrial sales, since the trend was toward more prepared or ready-to-eat foods. During the late 1950s, however, the company's newspaper advertising continued to tell the housewife how to make food taste better with sugar. In 1962, National began to advertise in consumer magazines.

The Imperial Sugar Company

The Imperial Sugar Company which operated one cane sugar refinery in Sugarland, Texas, has used advertising for many years to meet aggressive competition in its local market. Rival firms included the California and Hawaiian Sugar Refining Company, The

American Sugar Refining Company, distributors of off-shore refined cane, and occasionally some Louisiana refineries.

Imperial commenced its promotional campaign during the 1930s, reportedly setting aside 2¢ cents per 100 pounds of sugar to provide an annual budget of about $80,000 for newspaper advertising of its packaged sugar. The underlying theme of the company's campaign was: "What Texas makes, makes Texas." This exploitation of "Imperial" sugar as a local product was said to have given it an "edge" over competitive brands of sugar in Texas.

The executives of the Revere Company, however, felt that in appealing to local pride the Imperial Sugar Company was not actually selling its product on its own merits, and that any success the campaign attained was chiefly because of Imperial's unusual local situation. A consumer advertising program conducted by Imperial in the 1950s was believed by some observers to have been quite effective. The company discontinued its newspaper campaign in 1959, however.

Exhibit 1 lists published advertising expenditures for selected sugar refiners during the eight-year period from 1956-1963, inclusive.

THE REVERE MARKETING PROGRAM

Revere Sugar Refinery's market was limited by freight costs to New England and a portion of Northern New York State which extended as far as the Pennsylvania border. Revere held roughly 55 percent of the New England market, although the share varied somewhat by area. American Sugar's Domino brand held the remainder. There was no other significant competitor in the region.

It was estimated that between 75 and 90 percent of all retail outlets in New England carried two brands of sugar. Only 5 to 10 percent of all stores insisted on carrying only one brand. In New England, chain store organizations that stocked only one brand of sugar per store typically purchased both Revere and Domino sugar, but stocked their individual stores with whichever brand could be transported to the store with minimum cartage expense. Chain and wholesale buyers appeared to be realistic about the homogeneous nature of sugar.

THE REVERE ADVERTISING PROGRAM: 1957-1960

Before 1957 Revere had had no major experience with consumer advertising. Revere executives were convinced that advertising helped Domino create some degree of brand preference in New England. There was sales evidence, for example, that in some areas of New England Domino was gaining business, most noticeably in the higher-margin one-pound package and novelty sugars. Revere salesmen also reported spotty sales resistance to Revere sugar by the trade, and some retailer and jobber pressure for Revere to undertake an advertising campaign. In the three years before 1957 Domino stepped up its advertising effort to include radio and television spots in addition to representation in national magazines.

In 1957 Revere executives, impressed by the example of Domino advertising, decided to undertake a consumer promotion campaign. Although they acknowledged that "sugar is sugar," executives believed that they could develop consumer recognition and acceptance of Revere so that a consumer, when faced with the choice of Revere or Domino, would be motivated to select Revere. It was also believed that the campaign would have favorable effects on the trade.

After consultation with their advertising agency, Revere executives decided that the most beneficial first step would be to redesign the Revere one-pound cardboard packages. The new package design contained color illustrations of food that was associated with the kind of sugar contained in the carton. The new packages were introduced to consumers during the Easter season in 1957 with a six-week newspaper advertising campaign. In addition, Revere participated for thirteen weeks in the spring in a New England homemaker's radio show.

At the conclusion of the six-week introductory campaign, Revere began a sustaining newspaper advertising campaign that continued until 1960. Because it was difficult to find anything meaningful to say about sugar, the advertising agency determined that an unusual approach was necessary to attract reader attention on a continued basis. The agency therefore created the Revere horse, "Sugar," which appeared in Revere advertisements giving hints to housewives on good food buys, and providing recipes. The Revere advertisements were usually three columns by 7 inches or two columns by 10 inches, and appeared in morning and evening newspapers in twenty-eight New England and Northern New York cities. The advertisements appeared weekly in the larger cities and two or three times a month in smaller cities.

Revere's advertising agency presented the promotional campaign to the Revere salesmen, giving them instructions on how to promote the campaign to jobbers and retailers. Salesmen were given a three-page presentation booklet to use when explaining the new advertising program to the trade. The booklet contained copies of advertisements, a media schedule, and information on what the campaign was designed to do. No point of purchase material was issued since executives believed that, because of the nature of the product, stores would not accept display material for sugar.

Both Revere executives and the agency executive for the Revere account believed that the campaign that began in 1957 had enjoyed a considerable degree of success. Revere salesmen indicated that the trade had reacted favorably to the Revere campaigns. It was noted that since the beginning of the campaign the Revere sales decline had been arrested and the company was now maintaining its share of northeastern sugar industry sales, which were increasing by 3 to 4 percent per year. Two wholesale distributors were persuaded in 1957, for the first time, as a result of the advertising campaign, to stock Revere one-pound packages. Several years later they were continuing to order the small packages in sizable quantities.

THE REVERE ADVERTISING PROGRAM: 1961 1965

Revere's advertising agency acccount executive in discussing the company's advertising strategy during the years from 1961 to 1965, emphasized the problem of differentiation between different brands of sugar. He summarized Revere's overall marketing objectives during the 1961-1965 period as follows:

1. Stimulating Primary Demand

   As a member of the Sugar Association, Inc., Revere played an important part in that group's campaign to stimulate primary demand for sugar. A 1965 example of a Sugar Association advertisement that ran in *Life, Good Housekeeping, Ladies' Home Journal* and *Parents' Magazine* is shown in Exhibit 2.

2. Increasing sales volume of Revere Sugar.

   (a) Building and maintaining the customer list.

   Advertising copy was designed to keep the Revere name before the general public. This not only helped maintain the loyalty of exsiting Revere customers, but also made Revere name more familiar to consumers who were currently purchasing another brand of sugar.

   In addition, Revere made use of self-liquidating premiums to maintain existing

brand loyalty and attract new customers. In 1964 and 1965, for example, individual handcrafted aluminum bowls imported from Italy were offered to the public for $1.00 plus a Revere boxtop.

In 1965 Revere was running an annual "Sugar Sweepstakes" contest in which a large number of prizes were offered to the public. Three complete kitchens were offered as first prizes.

Consumers were encouraged to enter the contest by returning the boxtop from a one-pound Revere package. The Sweepstakes contest was advertised via four-color, full-page advertisements in the New England editions of *Life, Look, Ladies' Home Journal, McCall's* and the *Saturday Evening Post,* and by 20-second television commercials in four leading New England markets. A magazine advertisement announcing the contest is shown in Exhibit 3.

   (b) Increasing per capita consumption.

   Revere sought to increase per capita consumption among both old and new customers by educating the public in new and different ways of using sugar. Recipes were featured not only on Revere packages, but also via four-color, full page advertisements in consumer magazines. For example, some Revere advertisements showed housewives different ways of using sugar to heighten the flavor of other ingredients in popular recipes (see Exhibit 4).

3. Maintaining and increasing distribution.

   On a regular basis the Revere Company was able to maintain its distribution in spite of the unfavorable market conditions[2] by making its clear to the trade that Revere brand name was being kept in front of the public through consumer advertising. Not only were wholesalers and retailers (who were, of course, themselves also consumers) exposed to Revere consumer advertisements in consumer magazines, but they were also shown copies of these advertisements by the Revere sales force. In addition, retailers were also invited to participate in the contest via black-and-white, one page advertise-

---

[2]In the 1963 Annual Report of the United Fruit Company included the statement: "Revere's total sales reached an all-time high in 1963."

ments appearing in two New England grocery publications (see Exhibit 5).

Exhibit 6 gives details of the 1965 Revere Sugar advertising campaign. The sweepstakes and recipe advertisements in consumer magazines are both identified. The regular 20-second TV commercials featured ways in which sugar could improve the flavor of certain dishes. These were supplemented by "Sweepstakes" commercials.

QUESTIONS

1. Is the Revere advertising program well designed to build demand for sugar and the Revere brand in particular?
2. What changes would you recommend to improve the Revere program?
3. What procedures would you recommend to help Revere evaluate the success of its advertising expenditures?

Exhibit 1

Published Advertising Expenditures of Selected Sugar Manufacturers ($000)

Year	American				National			California and Hawaiian				
	Consumer Magazines[a]	Farm Papers[a]	News-papers[b]	Total	Consumer Magazines[a]	News-papers[b]	Total	Consumer Magazines[a]	News-papers[b]	Total	Savanah[b]	Imperial[b]
1963	197	16	97	310	47	110	157	192	28	220	35	—
1962	448	47	191	686	92	28	120	36	96	132	66	—
1961	292	29	291	612	—	56	56	—	455	455	66	—
1960	203	14	218	485	—	66	66	—	357	357	109	30
1959	286	27	229	542	—	113	113	70	157	227	81	25
1958	126	9	243	378	—	145	145	—	114	114	72	33
1957	66	—	453	519	—	107	107	—	44	44	73	33
1956	106	—	364	470	—	107	107	—	159	159	75	37

[a]National advertising investments (Leading National Advertisers, Inc.).
[b]Expenditures of national advertisers in newspapers (American Newspaper Association, Inc.).

487

Exhibit 2

Mary got to school early for Student
Council. Her team won in gym.
After play rehearsal, she'll Watusi
with the gang.
She needs sugar in her life.
For energy.
She needs energyless,
artificially sweetened
foods and beverages
like a turtle needs a seat belt.
Sugar swings. Serve some.

Sugar's got what it takes

...18 calories per teaspoon and it's all energy

Note to Mothers:

Exhaustion may be dangerous—especially to
children who haven't learned to avoid it by
pacing themselves. Exhaustion opens the door
a little wider to the bugs and ailments that are
always lying in wait. Sugar puts back energy
fast—offsets exhaustion. Synthetic sweeteners
put back nothing. Energy is the first requirement of life. Play safe with your young ones—
make sure they get sugar every day.

Sugar Information, Inc.

For sweetness with energy, get beet or cane sugar.

This advertisement appears in *Good Housekeeping, Ladies' Home Journal, Parents' Magazine,* May 1965, and *Life Magazine,* May 7, 1965.

(Printed in U.S.A.)

Exhibit 3

Win the kitchen of your dreams — in

REVERE SUGAR'S SWEET DREAMS SWEEPSTAKES

Never won anything before? Best reason in the world for entering this sweepstakes. You see, the odds are in your favor. We're advertising only to people in the New England Area. So be a *winner* for once. Enter now . . . and as often as you wish!

GRAND 3 PRIZES

OF COMPLETE KITCHENS
(installation not included)

Time-saving TAPPAN RANGE with hood, completely automatic, beautifully styled and designed for carefree cooking.

Spacious TAPPAN REFRIGERATOR-FREEZER, automatic defrosting even in the freezer compartment! . . . and room for all the food a growing family needs, and more.

TAPPAN REVERSA-JET DISHWASHER, the quick, modern answer to your most tiresome household chore.

Gleaming TAPPAN STAINLESS STEEL SINK, built for a lifetime of hard-working good looks . . . can't chip, stain, or rust.

A sparkling kitchen floor of STYLON VB Ceramic Tile—the floor that takes care of itself.

. . . or one of nearly 600 other valuable prizes!

8 Homelite 1965 Yard Trac Riding Power Mowers — A powerful 5-horse-power motor and 26" rotary mower

15 Linde Star Pins — Heart-shaped in 14K gold, with diamonds and a pear-shaped Linde Star

15 Tappan Reversa-Jet Dishwashers — Exclusive scrubbing water action guarantees clean dishes. A real time saver

35 Hoover Dial-A-Matic Vacuum Cleaners — First 2-in-1 action cleaner. Beats, as it sweeps, as it cleans

40 Bell & Howell Canonet Cameras — Fully automatic exposure system, F 1.9 lens, built-in self-timer and rangefinder

85 Helbros Watches for Men or Women — Wafer-thin, self-winding, water-proof, shock-resistant, 17 life-time jewels, unbreakable mainspring

110 Toastmaster Hair Dryers — Fast, quiet, portable, controlled heat, 10' cord, large plastic hood

110 Toastmaster Imperial Toasters — Bread lowers automatically. Chrome-satin finish — black Bakelite handles

150 Ronson Can-Do Openers — Mixes drinks; whips; mashes potatoes; sharpens knives

OFFICIAL RULES

No purchase required to enter.

Here's all you do. On an official entry blank or plain piece of paper, hand-print your name and address and the name of the store where you shop for Revere Sugar. Mail each entry separately to Revere Sugar Sweepstakes, Box #582, New York, N. Y. 10046

Enter as often as you wish but each entry must be accompanied by a box top from any of the 1 pound packages of Revere Sugar or a 3" x 5" piece of paper on which you have hand printed "Revere Sugar" in plain block letters. Entries must be post-marked by July 20, 1965, and received by July 30, 1965.

Winners will be selected in random drawings conducted by D. L. Blair Corporation, an independent judging organization. Its decision with respect to all phases of the sweepstakes will be final. Everyone living in areas where Revere Sugar is sold in retail stores is eligible except employees, and their families, of Revere Sugar refinery, their advertising agency, and the D. L. Blair Corporation. Offer void where prohibited by law.

REVERE SUGAR SWEEPSTAKES
Box #582
New York, N. Y. 10046

I have enclosed a REVERE Sugar 1 lb. box top or a 3" x 5" piece of plain paper on which I have printed "REVERE SUGAR".

Name_____

Address_____

City_____ State_____ Zip_____

Grocer's Name_____ Address_____

Exhibit 4

Put new excitement in your recipes with "...the flavor rouser"

REVERE Sugar heightens the flavor of other ingredients in main-course meat dishes, vegetables, soups and stews. Hidden flavors you never knew were there come to life with "the flavor rouser" — REVERE Sugar. It's the surprise ingredient that smart New England cooks have been using for nearly 100 years to add gourmet glamour to their favorite dishes.

CRÈME BRÛLÉE BANANE

Prepare 1 package of vanilla pudding mix according to package directions but use only 1⅔ cups of milk. Cool the mixture and add 1 teaspoon of rum extract and fold in 1 cup of heavy cream whipped. Pour into casserole dish. Mix together ½ cup of Revere Light Golden Brown Sugar and 2 teaspoons of cinnamon and sprinkle over top of pudding. Set casserole in pan of ice cubes and place about 6 inches from broiler. Broil 5 minutes or until sugar is melted. Slice 4 bananas into dessert dishes and spoon the sauce over the top. Makes 6 servings.

MEAT BALLS AND SAUERKRAUT

Mix together 2 pounds of ground cooked meat, 3 tablespoons of chopped onion, 2 cups of cold cooked cereal, 1 teaspoon of salt, ¼ teaspoon black pepper, 1 unbeaten egg and a generous pinch of celery salt. Shape into small balls and brown in cooking oil or bacon fat in a skillet. Be sure all sides are browned. Pour a number 2 can of sauerkraut over the meat balls and add ⅓ cup of firmly packed Revere Old Fashioned Dark Brown Sugar, ¼ cup of vinegar and ¼ cup of water. Cover and simmer about 30 minutes until meat balls are thoroughly cooked. Serves 6.

PINEAPPLE GLAZED CARROTS

Wash and scrape 2 pounds of carrots and cut cross-wise into pieces about 2 inches long. Place in a large saucepan and add about 2 cups of boiling water and 1 teaspoon of salt. Bring to a boil, then cover and simmer over a low flame for 15 to 20 minutes. Drain off all water. Add to carrots one 8½ ounce can of crushed pineapple, drained, and ½ cup of firmly packed Revere Old Fashioned Dark Brown Sugar. Stir continuously over a high flame until carrots are glazed, being careful not to break carrots while stirring. Serves 4 to 6.

There's a type for every cooking and table need.

* Granulated
* Light Golden Brown
* Instant Superfine
* Confectioners 10X
* Old Fashioned Dark Brown
* Tablets

If you're on a salt-free diet, try a little sugar in vegetables. You'll be surprised how good it makes them taste.

REVERE SUGAR
...the flavor rouser

REVERE SUGAR REFINERY, Boston, Mass. . . . Subsidiary of United Fruit Company

R2

Exhibit 5

Exhibit 6
Revere Sugar Refinery 1965 Media Schedule

A. *Magazines* (New England editions) *Full Pages: Four-Color*		No. of Readers
April	Life	2,632,000
May	McCall's	1,742,910
May 28[a]	Life	2,632,000
June[a]	Ladies' Home Journal	1,120,000
June 5[a]	Saturday Evening Post	1,885,500
June 25[a]	Life	2,632,000
June 29[a]	Look	2,005,000
July[a]	McCall's	1,742,910
September	McCall's	1,742,910
October	Ladies' Home Journal	1,120,000
	Total number of readers	19,255,230

B. *Television*
60-second and 20-second announcements in four New England markets:

1. *March 21–October 1 (including "Sweepstakes" period May 24 - July 16).*
   26 announcements per week

2. *May 24–July 16 ("Sweepstakes" period).*
   An additional 14 announcements per week

[a] Sweepstakes advertising.

Source. Company records.

Case 10-2
Lafontaine Potteries[1]

Founded in 1908, Lafontaine Potteries, Ltd. is Quebec's leading manufacturer of glazed and unglazed giftware. In addition, it has contracted with a local firm to manufacture wrought iron ware that it assembles with its pottery line. There are approximately 100 product items in each of the company's two product lines. Some of these items are:

1. Glazed and unglazed giftware: cups and saucers, tea and cofee pots, mugs and steins, ash trays, planters, tidbit servers, barbecue sets of plates and mugs, fancy flower pots, casseroles, wall plaques, rustic TV dinnerware sets, vases and "Habitant" dinnerware sets.
2. Wrought iron ware: Wrought iron is matched up with the company's pottery items to make smok-

ers, planters, casserole and coffee warmers, cocktail and barbecue sets, and umbrella stands.

Of the company's $4,000,000 sales volume, approximately 65 percent is realized in pottery items. The major portion of Lafontaine's line of products is low-priced and is merchandised primarily in variety stores, department stores, and in independent retail gift shops. Thirty percent of the firm's sales is made through large retail chains. The province of Quebec accounts for 40 percent of the company's total sales and 30 percent comes from Ontario.

The wrought iron giftware products are all tagged "Made in Quebec by Lafontaine, Montreal" and provide the biggest profit margin to the company. Lafontaine relies primarily on personal selling to market these goods to chains, department stores and independent retailers.

The wrought iron giftware has been given some consumer advertising in recent years, mainly as the

[1]Case prepared by Isaiah A. Litvak and Peter M. Banting of McMaster University. Reprinted from *Canadian Cases in Marketing* by I. A. Litvak and P. M. Banting. Reprinted by permission of McGraw-Hill Ryerson, Ltd.

result of pressure from the chain and department stores who handle it. It was only reluctantly that Mr. Guy Lafontaine, the firm's President, agreed to enter limited cooperative advertising with these outlets. He insisted that the retail ads included the line "a Lafontaine Pottery product." But Mr. Lafontaine still feels that no one sees the company name on these ads, that they are of greater benefit to the retail store, and that his firm's share of this cooperative advertising is for the better part "money down the drain."

Guy is more favorably inclined towards specialty advertising to members of the trade through sales promotion novelties such as imprinted rulers, ball point pens, calenders and the like. For the large volume buyers his salesmen call on, he occasionally offers a Lafontaine Pottery promotional Zippo View-Lighter, crystal paper weight, or other prestige sales promotion novelties. Twice a year he issues a black-and-white catalogue and price list, which is circulated to all Lafontaine's customers.

During the past six months, Lafontaine's Ontario sales manager, Maritime salesmen, and D. C. representative have all sent reports to Mr. Lafontaine that competing manufacturers are beginning to advertise their little-known brands, particularly if they are made in Canada. Many of these products are been given distinctly Canadian brand names, such as Maple Leaf, Beaver, Three Rivers, Fleur de Lis, and so on. Futhermore, these manufacturers are advertising their private brands very heavily. The Lafontaine sales force reports that this advertising has been effective, for they are finding it more difficult to sell their products, and their customers frequently are saying, "your products aren't as well known as some of our other suppliers."

Despite his personal feelings about the value of the advertising, Guy called a conference with the executive officers of the company, explained the situation, and as a group they decided to allocate about $60,000 to advertising. Upon careful discussion of the various media approaches and their associated costs, they concluded that no member of the executive group knew enough about advertising to determine and allocate the funds for the most effective advertising mix. In fact, they were shocked to discover how much a simple advertising program would cost. To avoid making errors, they thought it best to bring in an advertising agency that would plan a promotional strategy for Lafontaine Potteries, Ltd. Guy remarked, "After all, the advertising agencies are allowed a 15 percent discount by the various media that we as manufacturer cannot take advantage of; therefore, it won't cost us a cent to use the expert services of an advertising agency."

QUESTIONS

1. What copy themes should be emphasized in the Lafontaine advertising campaign?
2. Is the $60,000 proposed for Lafontaine's advertising program the right amount to achieve their objectives?
3. What criteria should be used to select media (TV, magazines) and particular vehicles within each media for the Lafontaine campaign?
4. What consideration should be given to the geographical needs of the market place?
5. Prepare a detailed budget for the Lafontaine Potteries advertising campaign. Include a time schedule for insertions.

Exhibit 1
Newspaper Rates

Montreal:	*LaPress* (published in French) Circulation: 212,707	Full page:	(2480 lines)	$3100
Montreal:	*Star* Circulation: 194,939	Full page:	(2488 lines)	$1866
Toronto:	*Globe and Mail* (morning paper) Circulation: 238,478	Full page:	(2772 lines)	$3742
Toronto:	*Star* Circulation: 363,852	Full page:	(2772 lines)	$4158

Exhibit 2
Television Rates

Toronto: *CBLT*—divides its program times into priorities as follows:

Class "AA"   6-7 P.M. Sunday, 7-11 P.M. daily
Class "A"   5-6 P.M. Sunday, 6-7 P.M. weekdays, 11-11:30 P.M. daily
Class "B"   4-5 P.M. Sunday, 5-6 P.M. weekdays
             11:30-midnight Sunday-Thursday, 11:30 P.M.
             12:30 A.M. Friday and Saturday
Class "C"   Sign-on to 4 P.M. Sunday, sign-on to 5 P.M.
             Saturday, 12 midnight to sign-off Friday
             and Saturday
Class "D"   Sign-on to 5 P.M. Monday-Friday

Time	AA	A	B	C	D
60 seconds	$386	$297	$206	$150	$100
30 seconds	356	260	181	131	88
20 seconds	327	223	155	113	75
10 seconds	223	149	103	75	50

Montreal: *CFTM* (French language television station)

Time	AA	A	B	C	D
60 seconds	$495	$325	$275	$200	$100
20 seconds	380	260	220	160	80
10 seconds	240	165	140	100	50

Exhibit 4
Consumer Magazines

Magazine	Published	Circu-lation	Four-Color Page	Monotone		
				Page	Half Page	Quarter Page
Maclean's Magazine	25th of month	615,138	$6835	$4830	$2560	$1330
Le Magazine Maclean (French)	25th of month	171,996	2180	1535	815	420
S W Magazine	every Saturday	671,515	3000	2625	1335	670
Time Canada	weekly	359,579	5095	3395		
TV Guide Toronto-Lake Ontario	every Wednesday	429,800		900	495	270
TV Guide Montreal-St. Lawrence	every Wednesday	166,640		250	138	76
TV Guide Western-B.C.	every Wednesday	82,615		150	83	46
Chatelaine, English ed.	last week of month	921,665	7560	5900	3070	1565
Chatelaine, French ed.	last week of month	250,090	2300	1795	930	475

Exhibit 3

Trade Magazines[a]

Magazine	Published	Circ- ulation	Monotone		
			Page Rate	Half Page	Quarter Page
Volume Retail Merchandising	Every third Friday	7,139	$450	$270	$160
Home Goods Retailing	Every other Monday	14,079	788	392	210
Hardware/Housewares Trades	15th of month	12,869	385	215	127
Product News	Bimonthly	10,466	440	225	146
Furniture and Furnish- ings Magazine	Monthly	8,461	320	180	115
Gift Buyer	25th of month	4,507	276	153	81
Hardware Merchan- dising (English)	Monthly	9,458	780	429	241
Le Quincaillier (French)	Monthly	4,169	780	429	241

[a]Each publication provides trade distribution and geographic distribution figures. For example, *Volume Retail Merchandising* shows:

Trade Distribution

Chain store head office exec. and admin. personnel	809
Chain store branch, asst. and dept. mgrs. and buyers	2302
Large ind. dept. and variety notion, novelty and small- wares stores; exec. and managerial personnel, buyers, dept. mgrs., etc.	2548
Wholesalers, jobbers and distributors	1051
Gen. mgrs., mgrs.; premium supply houses, shopping plazas, college book stores	146
Manufacturers	253
Misc.: assns., trade commissioners, serv's to trade libraries	34

Geographical Breakdown

Nfld.	93	Que.	1739	Alta. and N.W.T.	539
P.E.I.	28	Ont.	2963	B.C. and Yukon	659
N.S.	254	Man.	342	U.S.A.	2
N.B.	198	Sask.	320	B.C'wealth	6

Exhibit 5
Outdoor Advertising

Toronto subway station displays: $24.65 per 62″ × 48″ board per month

Toronto subway car interior displays: $2347.75 for one 20″ × 28″ card in each of 334 units for three months

Exterior bus boards: $21.65 per 21″ × 88″ side panel board per month

Montreal billboards: $3378 per 42 billboards per month
$9103 per 112 billboards per month

Theater film advertisements of one-minute duration:
Indoor:	120 Ontario theaters:	$ 4,248.50 per week
	281 Quebec theaters:	11,811.50 per week
Drive-ins:	91 Ontario theaters:	$ 5,371.00 per week
	9 Toronto theaters:	1,030,00 per week

Exhibit 6
Direct Mail Advertising

	Cost per 1000
Mailing list of homeowners	$ 30
Envelope, letter, two-color brochure, 50¢-off coupon[a]	150
Bulk postage	40
Total	$220

[a]Does not include cost to redeem coupons since this expense is usually charged to promotional budget. Redemption rate will probably run from 1 to 5 percent plus 4¢ per coupon handling charge.

Case 10-3
Erie Paper Company[1]

"We must decide how we can best use the $70,000 proposed in the 1970 budget for advertising to the converting industries," said Mr. Edward Graham, Director of Advertising for the Erie Paper Company. Mr. Graham was discussing the firm's converting industries advertising program with his assistant, Mr. Gerald Ridder.

Mr. Graham had received a report from the firm's

[1]From *Marketing of Forest Products* by Stuart U. Rich. Copyright © 1970 by McGraw-Hill, Inc. Used with permission of McGraw-Hill Book Company.

Marketing Research Department concerning advertising in the three major converting industries of business forms, envelopes, and greeting cards. The report included data on trade journal and business periodicals advertising and some additional categories of nonpersonal promotion commonly used in the converting industries. Nonpersonal promotion included all forms of promotion except personal selling. The report classified all forms of nonpersonal communication used to promote a product or a firm as promotional communication.

Mr. Graham advised Mr. Ridder that his task would be to analyze the report data and make recommendations for the promotion program. Mr. Ridder had to select the most significant data from the report and then determine what the results would mean to the firm. Since it was already the middle of August 1969, he knew that he must complete his analysis soon.

COMPANY BACKGROUND

Erie Paper Company was formed in the early 1900s as a producer of printing papers for magazine and book publishers. A series of rapid expansions soon elevated the company to a leading position in the pulp and paper industry. The firm was headquartered in Pennsylvania and had mills located there, in other parts of the Northeastern United States, in the Southeastern United States, and in Ontario, Canada.

Company sales in 1955 were approximately $150,000,000 and had reached nearly $720,000,000 by 1968. The firm anticipated highly accelerated growth within the industry and within the company during the 1970's. Future company growth plans, therefore, called for the production of new converting paper grades. The firm was currently working on several lines of converting papers to supplement its existing lines.

The company's product line included wood pulp, newsprint, kraft papers, printing and fine papers, paperboard and packaging materials, and converting papers. The last category accounted for almost 14 percent of the firm's 1968 sales, a proportion that had remained nearly constant since the early 1950s. The company categorized its converting papers by industry into business forms, envelopes, and greeting cards. Gross sales of business forms in 1960 amounted to $39,000,000 while envelopes totaled $17,000,000 and greeting cards were $19,000,000. These figures steadily increased so that by 1968 business form sales were $50,000,000, envelope sales were $25,000,000, and greeting card sales totaled $25,000,000. The firm's management, although pleased with past sales performance, was concerned that production capacity for converting grades exceeded sales in 1968. Management felt that an examination of the firm's and of the industry's growth rates might indicate where Erie's promotional effort should be concentrated.

Erie Paper Company had a large technically trained and highly regarded sales force. Although it sold converting papers throughout North America, its sales were concentrated in the northeastern United States, where most of the paper converters were located. Generally the firm tried to sell these papers direct from its mills through its own sales force. Approximately 95 percent of its paper for business forms and 80 percent of its paper for envelopes was sold through its own sales force, while only 55 percent of its paper for greeting cards was sold in this manner. The remainder of the company's converting papers were sold through paper merchants, although their role in paper distribution had been steadily decreasing in recent years. This distribution pattern was typical of the converting industries.

THE CONVERTING INDUSTRIES

The major grades of paper sold to the converting industries (business forms, envelopes, and greeting cards) were relatively standardized among the larger manufacturers. Converters generally considered one mill's paper substitutable for another mill's paper. A few specialty paper grades existed, such as carbonless copy papers, which exhibit some product differentiation. However, once a mill marketed a unique paper, other mills would soon copy it.

Mills attempted to develop some degree of product differentiation by offering various combinations of quality and service. Although price was a predominant factor in paper procurement, mills had very limited pricing flexibility. Industry demand for converting papers was a derived demand and tended to be somewhat inelastic to price decreases. In addition, mills could ordinarily successfully pass on a price increase only when demand conditions were strong and the industry was operating near capacity.

Growth rates varied considerably among the converting industries. The business forms industry had experienced the most rapid continuous expansion among the three industries by achieving an annual growth rate of 11 percent between 1960 and 1966. The envelope industry and the greeting card industry had each grown at an annual rate of 6 percent during the same period. The high growth rate of the business forms industry was expected to continue due to a constant increase in the use of continuous forms or computer data sheets. Growth rates for the envelope and greeting card industries were expected to generally keep pace with the growth in the Gross National Product, or approximately 6 percent per year. The value of total industry shipments grew considerably from 1958 to 1966 as shown on the next page.

Industry structure varied as to economic and geographic concentration. The structure of the greeting card industry was the most concentrated of the three converting industries, with the five largest companies accounting for 60 to 70 percent of total industry sales. Although once dominated by many

Industry	Shipments by Year	
	1958	1966
Business forms	$374,000,000	$794,000,000
Envelopes	272,000,000	446,000,000
Greeting cards	292,000,000	460,000,000

Source. U.S. Department of Commerce, *1958 Census of Manufacturers* and *Annual Census of Manufacturers, 1966.*

small firms, the industry had witnessed a steady decline in the number of these firms in recent years. Business forms appeared to show an opposite tendency. While the top ten firms sold 60 percent of the industry's papers, their relative position had been deteriorating. Many new, smaller firms were entering the industry and reducing the concentration ratio. The envelope industry was the least concentrated with the top four firms achieving only 30 percent of the industry's sales. The industry was characterized by numerous small, family-owned and operated firms, and was expected to continue this pattern for the immediate future.

Generally the converting industries were geographically concentrated in the Northeastern United States, although some firms had begun to expand in the West. This geographic concentration allowed paper mills to rely heavily on personal selling to move and promote their papers.

ERIE'S PROMOTIONAL EXPERIENCE

Erie Paper Company relied on its sales force to promote its papers, as was typical in the converting industries. On a sales call salesmen were expected to visit the purchasing manager first, even though their purpose was to see top management, the production manager, or the sales manager. They often left paper sample books or product literature with the purchasing managers and mailed product literature to top management, production mangers, and sales mangers. Although the Erie sales force was considered slightly larger than the industry average, salesmen felt they could not call often enough on purchasing managers and top management. Some salesmen had complained, also, that when they were able to call on top management, production managers, or sales managers, these individuals often indicated that they had not received some of the product literature that had been left with purchasing managers by salesmen on routine sales calls. In addition, product literature mailed directly to top managers was sometimes discarded by their secretaries.

During each of the past several years Erie had allocated $70,000 for advertising and $50,000 for product literature and sample books to provide its products to the converting industries. These funds were equally divided among the three converting industries. The company had determined that some of its competitors were spending around one-tenth of one percent of their sales on promotional communications.

Marketing personnel had observed several buying situations that were common throughout the industry. One situation was the purchase of a new product from a new supplier or a regular supplier. Another situation, which was the most common, was the purchase of a currently used product from any one of several regular suppliers. The third situation, the purchase of a currently used paper from a new supplier, arose only when the converter became dissatisfied with an existing regular supplier. Erie had discovered that once a converter acquired regular suppliers the relationship tended to be long lasting.

MARKETING RESEARCH SURVEY

The marketing research project had been divided into a presurvey phase and a survey phase. The research department designed a questionnaire that they tested through personal interviews with converter personnel during the preliminary survey phase. They discovered that the buying process could be divided into four phases, as hypothesized by Robinson, Faris and Wind.[2] These phases are described as follows:

1. Consideration phase: What grade of paper will perform satisfactorily for the purpose intended?
2. Acceptance phase: Which suppliers are acceptable?
3. Selection phase: Which suppliers will receive a particular order?
4. Evaluation phase: Will a given supplier be retained or dropped?

The preliminary survey indicated that decisions were usually made by different personnel in each phase of the paper buying process. During the consideration phase, production, sales, and purchasing personnel participated most in the decision-making process. In the acceptance phase and the evaluation phase, top management made the buying decision with the assistance of purchasing personnel. During

[2]Patrick J. Robinson, Charles W. Faris, and Yoram Wind, *Industrial Buying and Creative Marketing*, (Boston, Mass.: Allyn and Bacon, Inc., 1967), pp. 11-38.

the selection phase the purchasing manager made the decision alone.

The researchers also determined that certain technically informed persons could be found in each firm who were consulted by the decision makers. These individuals were usually management personnel, although the specific individuals varied in different firms, and their opinions were well respected by decision makers.

The final questionnaire was completed and sent out by mail after the preliminary survey had been completed. Questionnaires were sent to buying influentials who were randomly selected from lists in trade directories. A summary of the respondents is shown in Exhibit 1. The exhibit shows only the usable responses received that amounted to about half the number of questionnaires mailed. Questions were asked concerning who made the buying decision, who influenced the decision, what sources of information were consulted, and what publications were read. Exhibit 1 shows that 3 percent of the respondents were creative art directors all of whom were found in the greeting card industry.

The results of the mail survey were tabulated in a number of exhibits. Exhibit 2 illustrates the forms of promotional communication consulted by buying influentials, or those persons who influence the purchasing decision, during each phase of the buying process except the selection phase. Purchasing managers usually made the buying decision during the selection phase based on mill-run schedules rather than information from promotional communication. The exhibit classifies the answers of buying influentials according to the buying phase or phases in which they are heavily involved. For example, product literature was consulted during the consideration phase by 43 percent of the purchasing managers responding to the survey. In the acceptance phase, some buying influentials did not consult promotional communication. Instead, they relied soley on personal communication for information. The exhibit shows that 38 percent of top management indicated that they did not consult promotional communication during the evaluation phase.

Exhibit 3 shows the relative frequency with which buying influentials were exposed to different forms of promotional communication. Of all the purchasing managers who responded to the survey, 50 percent indicated that they were exposed to product literature once a week or less while 50 percent stated that they were exposed to it more than once a week.

Exhibits 4 and 5 present the sources of information through which paper mills introduce new papers to each converting industry and to each buying influential. Exhibit 4 discloses that 78 percent of the

respondents in the business forms industry relied on mill respresentatives for some information about new papers. Exhibit 5 similarly shows that 86 percent of top management respondents referred to mill representatives for information about new papers. The survey also disclosed that the introduction of new papers by mills was ventured during the consideration phase of the paper buying process.

Exhibit 6 indicates those periodicals that buying influentials stated they favored. In the business forms industry, 27 percent of the respondents mentioned that they favored *Business Week* as a source of information.

Exhibits 7 and 8 give some data for each mentioned periodical as to circulation, advertising rates, and readership. Mr. Ridder planned to use these exhibits as a basis for determining the allocation of funds among the different magazines. The exhibits give advertising rates for full page ads and one-sixth page ads in black and white. For instance, if Mr. Ridder decided to place thirteen ads in *Business Week* during the year each full page ad would cost $7050 while each one-sixth page ad would cost $1290.

Finally, Exhibit 9 gives the recommendations of the respondents as to what action paper mills should take on each form of promotional communication. Of all the respondents who returned the questionnaire, 58 percent stated that more paper seminars should be held by paper manufacturers, while 40 percent recommended no change should be made and only 2 percent recommended a reduction. Mr. Ridder thought that this exhibit gave some interesting information but he wondered how much weight he should give it.

CONCLUSION

Mr. Ridder knew that he must soon present his recommendations to Mr. Graham. Mr. Graham had asked him several key questions that he had to answer. First, he had to determine the objectives of the promotional mix. These, he knew, should reflect the relationship of promotion to the overall sales program. Second, should the firm advertise and, if it should, is $70,000 sufficient? Third, how should the $70,000 be allocated among the various publications? Fourth, to whom should the promotional effort be directed? Finally, how should new papers be introduced?

He felt that each form of promotional communication should be evaluated to determine how it could best fit into the firm's promotional program. Mr. Ridder knew that he must also analyze each converting industry and each phase of the buying process to see how the promotional effort could best be applied. Erie's future growth in the converting industries rested heavily upon Mr. Ridder's recommendations. Therefore, these recommendations had to be complete and well justified.

QUESTIONS

1. What is the role of research in planning an advertising program?

2. Do you feel the marketing research conducted by the Erie Company provided the data needed to plan the 1970 promotional program?

3. Assume you have Mr. Ridder's job and prepare a promotional program for 1970. Specify expenditures for each of the three converting industries for advertising, product literature, and sample books, allocate funds to media, select specific publications, and suggest ways to introduce new papers to the converting industry.

Exhibit 1

Questionnaire Respondents by Converting Industry and Job Position (Percent)

Converting Industry	Top Management	Purchasing Managers	Production Managers	Sales Managers	Creative Art Dir.	Total
Business forms	13	13	6	5	0	37
Envelopes	16	6	9	8	0	39
Greeting cards	11	6	1	3	3	24
Total	40	25	16	16	3	100
(Number of respondents)	(77)	(51)	(32)	(32)	(5)	(197)

Exhibit 2

Forms of Promotional Communication Consulted by Buying Influentials

	Percentage of Responses by Phase of Paper Buying Process and Job Position						
	Consideration				Acceptance	Evaluation	
Form Mentioned	Purchasing Managers	Production Managers	Sales Managers	Top Management	Top Management	Top Management	Purchasing Managers
Product literature	43	41	47	36	27	20	28
Journal ads	43	19	50	29	5	6	5
Sample books	40	15	47	36	34	20	33
Journal articles	34	33	50	28	19	12	13
Magazine ads	28	30	27	25	2	4	8
None	—	—	—	—	13	38	13
Total	a	a	a	a	100	100	100
(Number of respondents)	(47)	(27)	(30)	(59)	(59)	(59)	(47)

aTotal exceeds 100 percent because of multiple responses.

Exhibit 3

Relative Exposure to Promotional Communication Among Buying Influentials[a]

Form of Promotional Communication	Buying Influential	Percentage Exposed	
		Once a Week or More	Less Than Once a Week
Ads in business or news publications	Purchasing	51	49
	Top mgmt.	33	67
	Sales	34	66
	Production	33	67
Product literature	Purchasing	50	50
	Top mgmt.	21	79
	Sales	23	77
	Production	31	69
Advertisements in trade journals	Purchasing	46	54
	Top mgmt.	22	78
	Sales	28	72
	Production	26	74
Articles in trade journals	Purchasing	34	66
	Top mgmt.	25	75
	Sales	28	72
	Production	30	70
Paper sample books	Purchasing	39	61
	Top mgmt.	12	88
	Sales	13	87
	Production	0	100

[a]Based on responses from 41 purchasing managers, 68 top management personnel, 27 production managers, and 32 sales managers.

Exhibit 4

Forms of Promotional Communication Through Which Mills Introduce New Papers to Converting Industries (Percent)

Forms of Promotional Communication	Converting Industry		
	Business Forms	Envelope	Greeting Cards
Mill representative	78	93	83
Paper merchant salesman	52	30	78
Product literature	38	45	39
Paper sample books	28	32	59
Ads in trade journals	45	34	20
Ads in business magazines	38	18	22
Articles in trade journals	41	37	17
Conversations with persons in			
Own firm	36	32	20
Other firms	25	32	17
Trade shows	20	11	17
Total	a	a	a
(Number of respondents)	(64)	(71)	(41)

[a] Total exceeds 100 percent because of multiple responses.

Exhibit 5

Forms of Promotional Communication Through Which Mills Introduce New Papers to Buying Influentials

Form of Promotional Communication Mention	Percentage of Responses by Job Title				
	Top Management	Purchasing Managers	Production Managers	Sales Managers	Creative Art Directors
Mill respresentatives	86	100	82	63	100
Paper merchant salesmen	44	66	33	43	100
Product literature	36	43	41	47	67
Paper sample books	36	40	15	47	100
Ads in trade journals	29	43	19	50	33
Ads in business magazines	25	28	30	27	—
Articles in trade journals	28	34	33	50	—
Conversations with persons in					
Own firm	23	21	33	60	33
Other firms	29	21	26	30	—
Trade shows	13	19	15	7	—
Total	a	a	a	a	a
(Number of respondents)	(69)	(47)	(27)	(30)	(3)

[a] Total exceeds 100 percent because of multiple responses.

Exhibit 6

Publications Favored by Buying Influentials by Converting Industry

Publication	Percent Respondents Favoring Publication by Industry		
	Business Forms	Envelope	Greeting Cards
Business Week	27	—	24
Wall Street Journal	20	32	15
Time	15	—	12
Newsweek	—	14	—
U.S. News & World Report	—	13	—
Business Forms Reporter	18	—	—
Paper Trade Journal	18	—	—
Graphic Arts Monthly	12	—	16
Paper, Film, & Foil Converter	—	56	—
Modern Converter	—	26	16
Greeting Card Magazine	—	—	24
Total	a	a	a
(Number of respondents)	(64)	(71)	(41)

[a] Total exceeds 100 percent because of multiple responses.

Exhibit 7

Sample Advertising Rates, Circulation Data, and Readership Data in General Business Publications

Publication	Circulation	Ad Size	Ad Rates[c] ($ Per Ad)		Frequency of Publication
			1 Time/Yr.	13 Times/Yr.	
Business Week[a]	630,000	1 pg.	$ 7,620	$ 7,050	Weekly
		1/6 pg.	1,300	1,290	
Wall Street Journal[a]	1,151,536	1 pg.	17,617	15,460	Weekly days
		1/6 pg.	2,202	2,202	
Time[b]	3,982,780	1 pg.	22,000	21,120	Weekly
		1/6 pg.	8,030	7,710	
U.S. News[b]	1,739,356	1 pg.	10,268	9,855	Biweekly
		1/6 pg.	3,703	3,556	
Newsweek[b]	2,367,104	1 pg.	13,340	12,805	Weekly
		1/6 pg.	4,815	4,620	

[a]Standard Rate and Data Service, *Business Publication Rates and Data* (Chicago: McGraw-Hill Company, June 24, 1969). (Rates effective June 1969.)
[b]Standard Rate and Data Service, *Consumer Magazine and Farm Publication Rates and Data* (Chicago: McGraw-Hill Company, June 27, 1969). (Rates effective June 1969.)
[c]Rates are given for black-and-white advertisements only.

Exhibit 8

Sample Advertising Rates Circulation Data, and Readership Data in Trade Publications

Publication	Circ.	Ad Size	Ad Rates ($ per Ad)[a] Times/Year						Publication Frequency
			1	3	6	7	12	13	
Business Forms Reporter	6,900	1 pg.	600	—	480	—	400	—	Monthly
		1/6 pg.	175	—	120	—	100	—	
Paper Trade Journal	12,901	1 pg.	640	—	—	560	—	480	Weekly
		1/6 pg.	240	—	—	210	—	170	
Graphic Arts Monthly[b]	64,517	1 pg.	1200	1125	1050	—	960	—	Monthly
		1/6 pg.	325	305	285	—	260	—	
Paper, Film, Foil Conv.	17,843	1 pg.	695	—	610	—	545	—	Monthly
		1/6 pg.	195	—	170	—	155	—	
Modern Conventor	14,871	1 pg.	690	—	610	—	545	—	Monthly
		1/6 pg.	190	—	170	—	150	—	
Greeting Card Magazine	7,067	1 pg.	375	325	287	—	250	—	Monthly
		1/6 pg.	97	85	75	—	65	—	

[a]Rates are given for black-and-white advertisements only.
[b]Effective August 1, 1969.

Source. Standard Rate and Data Service, *Business Publication Rates and Data* (Chicago: McGraw-Hill Company, June 24, 1969). (Rates effective June 1969.)

Exhibit 9

Forms of Promotional Communication Recommended by Converters[a].

Format Promotional Communication	Percentage of Respondents Recommending		
	Increased	Left Unchanged	Decreased
Paper seminar and schools	58	40	2
Product literature distributed by mill reps	48	48	4
Mill tours	44	55	1
Calls by mill reps	35	64	1
Trade journal articles	37	59	4
Product literature sent by mail	42	42	16
Paper sample books	36	54	10
Trade show exhibits	14	67	19
Trade journal ads	6	77	17
Business magazine ads	8	70	22
Entertainment	4	58	38

[a]Based on 173 respondents.

Case 10-4
New Brunswick Travel Bureau[1]

Mr. W. P. Kilfoil of the New Brunswick Travel Bureau was reviewing his advertising expenditures for the past year and was attempting to outline an advertising plan for the coming year. He wondered whether the results of previous advertising justified a higher budget, how the budget should be distributed among various media, what particular newspapers, magazines, and other publications should be used, and what overall theme, if any, should be created.

New Brunswick is one of the four so-called "Atlantic" Provinces situated on the Eastern seaboard of Canada. Two of the other provinces, Newfoundland and Prince Edward Island are islands. The remaining province, Nova Scotia, is southeast of New Brunswick and almost completely surrounded by water (the term "Maritime" refers to New Brunswick, Nova Scotia, and Prince Edward Island). Exhibit 1 shows the geographic relationship of these provinces to each other and to some U.S. and Canadian cities.

The tourist industry is one of the major industries in New Brunswick. It is estimated that over 1.5 million tourists visit the province each year spending about $50,000,000. The provincial population is about 600,000. By studying the tourist registration

[1]Case prepared by W. J. Redding and A. Doyle of the University of New Brunswick. Reproduced by permission.

books in the province's tourist information centers, Mr. Kilfoil knew that almost all of the U.S. tourists visiting the province came from the Eastern states. In addition, almost all of the Canadian tourists came from Quebec and Ontario. Very few tourists came from abroad.

The main function of the New Brunswick Travel Bureau is to get more people to visit the province and to encourage these people to stay as long as possible. The current budget for the Bureau was approximately $521,000 allocated as follows: advertising, $180,000; literature, $150,000; salaries, $100,000; tourist development in municipalities, $30,000; photographic and art work, $15,000; tourist information centers, $6000; and miscellaneous, $40,000 including signs and maintenance of picnic sites.

The Bureau conducted its own annual advertising campaign from March to June each year. This campaign was supplemented by an extensive federal government campaign together with an Atlantic Provinces campaign, and a Maritime area cooperative campaign. The total federal campaign expenditure was about $1.7 million, part of this was spent to promote Canada as an entity, and part to promote specific regions. All expenditures were in U.S. publications. One part of this federal campaign was the Atlantic Provinces' campaign amounting to $300,000. The Maritime cooperative campaign

Exhibit 1

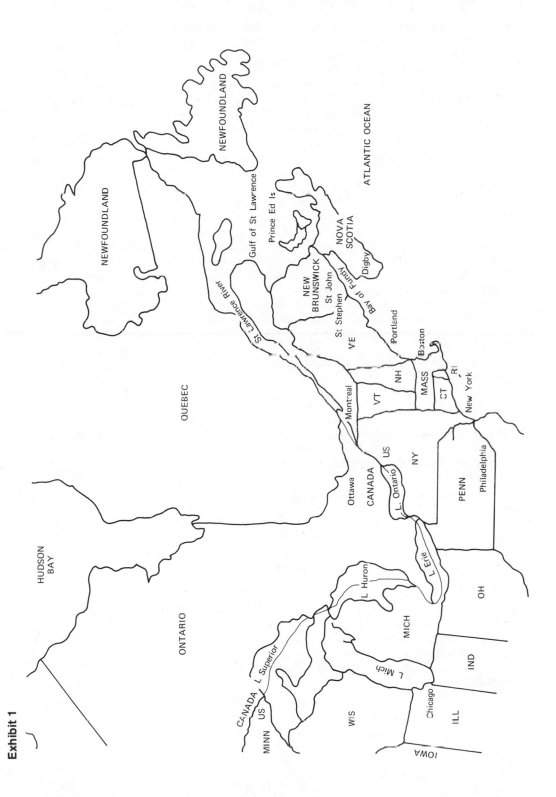

promoted the region in Canadian newspapers and magazines. Currently the provincial contributions were New Brunswick, $20,000; Nova Scotia, $20,000; Prince Edward Island, $10,000.

The budget for the federal and regional campaigns had been decided on and were not part of Mr. Kilfoil's responsibility. Thus, Mr. Kilfoil was only concerned with optimizing the New Brunswick Tourist Bureau advertising expenditures for the next year. Exhibit 2 shows the amounts spent on various media by the New Brunswick Travel Bureau in recent years. Exhibit 3 shows the tourist promotion expenditure for all four "Atlantic" provinces including the printed literature budget but excluding the small amounts spent on billboards. The exhibit also shows how the media budget was distributed between U.S. and Canadian media.

The standard method of evaluating the suitability of any particular newspaper or magazine was to calculate the cost per inquiry. This was obtained by dividing the total seasonal expenditure in any medium by the number of requests for information received through advertisements in that medium. Every printed advertisement carried a coded reply coupon. In the past year approximately 102,000 inquires were received. Exhibits 4, 5, and 6 give cost figures and other information for all print media used in the last year. Mr. Kilfoil felt that the cost per inquiry figure was the only effective method of objectively evaluating the suitability of the media. In contrast to the variety of different magazines and newspapers used in the New Brunswick campaign, Prince Edward Island used only fourteen publications.

A recent experiment with television was considered a success by the tourist bureau's advertising agency. One-minute spot advertisements of various New Brunswick scenes were shown on a Toronto station during the early evening. The spot ran twice weekly for thirteen weeks beginning in March. The announcements attracted an average of forty responses a week during the period.

In addition to evaluating the suitability of specific media, the Bureau estimated the total volume of tourist traffic and the total expenditure of tourists. Most bureaus used car counts at entry points to estimate total traffic. This total car entry figure was multiplied by an estimated car occupancy figure which in turn was multiplied by an estimated average expenditure per person per day. The resulting figure was seen as a "good approximation."

To collect information on cars entering New Brunswick, the Travel Bureau maintained ten checkpoints around the province. These points were manned from dawn to dusk, seven days a week, from June to September inclusive. Staff consisted of two men working on shift. These men were often small farmers, lumbermen, fishermen, or alert old-age pensioners. Three of the ten points were on the north shore of the province and counted cars entering New Brunswick from other parts of Canada. One point was at Aulac on the New Brunswick-Nova Scotia boundary. The other six points were at six major entry points on the New Brunswick border with the state of Maine. In addition to figures obtained in this way, the Bureau also used figures published by other organizations such as the U.S. customs report of all U.S. cars through the thirty customs points bordering New Brunswick. In addition ferry transportation figures were used for cars entering New Brunswick from Nova Scotia via the Digby ferry and from Prince Edward Island. Mr. Kilfoil felt that these figures combined to give a good indication of tourist traffic. Except for informal reports from a variety of sources these figures were the only measure of tourist traffic used. Exhibit 7 gives figures for all car counts used to estimate the value of tourist traffic.

QUESTIONS

1. How useful is the car entry data in evaluating the advertising program of the new Brunswick Travel Bureau?
2. Do you agree with Mr. Kilfoil that cost per inquiry was the only effective method of evaluating the suitability of the media?
3. Prepare an advertising program for the New Brunswick Travel Bureau for the coming year. Indicate the size of the budget, media allocations, specific newspapers and magazines to be used.
4. What copy themes would you recommend to promote travel to New Brunswick?

Exhibit 2
NBTB Advertising Expenditures

	Year			
	5	6	7	Current
United States				
Magazines	33,000	83,000	96,000	81,000
Newspapers	64,000	25,000	11,000	15,000
Bulletin boards	2,000	2,000	2,000	2,000
Canada				
Magazines	18,000	14,000	26,000	43,000
Newspapers	18,000	14,000	26,000	13,000
Television	—	—	—	6,000
United States and Canada				
Mechanical production	11,000	11,000	13,000	15,000
Other	4,000	4,000	5,000	5,000
Total	$150,000	$153,000	$179,000	$180,000

Exhibit 3
Tourist Promotion Expenditures

Newfoundland (Population 468,000)
        Advertising   Nil
        Printed literature $38,000
Prince Edward Island (Population 105,000)
        Magazines $23,000   52% United States   48% Canada
        Newspapers   3,000
        Printed literature   65,000
Nova Scotia (Population 730,000)
        Magazines $138,000   69% United States   31% Canada
        Newspapers   70,000
        Printed literature   118,000
New Brunswick (Population 608,000)
        Magazines $124,000   61% United States   39% Canada
        Newspapers   28,000
        Television   6,000
        Printed literature   150,000

Exhibit 4
NBTB Canadian Newspaper Advertising

Publication	Circ.	Purchased Space (Lines)	Cost	Free (Lines)	Value	Inq.	C/I
LeSoleil (Fr.) Quebec	132,000	2000	$ 900.00	—	$ —	706	$1.26
Montreal (Eng.) *Star*	190,541	2000	1,300.00	3206	2,083.90	515	2.57
LeDevoir (Fr.) Montreal	38,133	2000	400.00	—	—	197	10.15
La Presse (Fr.) Montreal	284,429	2000	2,000.00	70	70.00	929	2.04
Gazette (Eng.) Montreal	124,686	2000	800.00	2212	884.80	191	4.18
Citizen Ottawa	72,093	2000	510.00	2576	256.88	248	2.05
Journal Ottawa	70,000	2000	480.00	1848	443.52	218	2.20
Globe & Mail Toronto	232,255	2000	2,000.00	700	700.00	507	3.94
Toronto Star	344,845	2000	2,400.00	574	68.80	703	3.41
Telegram Toronto	288,176	2000	2,200.00	1708	1,878.80	577	3.81
Spectator Hamilton	108,511	2000	760.00	980	372.40	303	2.50
Free Press London	109,614	2000	720.00	1499	539.64	319	2.25

Exhibit 5

NBTB U.S. Newspaper Advertising Summary

Publication	Circ.	Purchased Space (Lines)	Cost	Free (Lines)	Value	Inq.	C/I
Boston Herald	298,604	925	$693.75	714	$ 714.00	299	$2.32
Boston Globe	431,274	935	935.00	1206	1,206.00	428	2.18
Boston Advertiser	452,425	900	765.00	700	560.00	487	1.57
Boston C.S. Monitor	172,229	900	837.00	700	651.00	174	4.81
Springfield Repub.	112,352	900	315.00	896	313.60	67	4.70
Hartford Times	130,000	900	306.00	84	28.56	90	3.40
Hartford Courant	153,611	900	360.00	98	34.30	253	1.42
Providence Journal	191,274	900	567.00	714	428.40	147	3.85
Albany T. Union	119,614	925	379.25	154	69.30	124	3.05
Buffalo C. Express	305,367	900	720.00	1652	1,321.60	271	2.65
New York Times	1,371,939	935	1,916.75	1148	2,238.60	2019	.94
New York Mirror	1,200,036	555	721.50	1050	1,260.00	466	1.54
New York World Telegram	477,595	925	1,137.75	924	1,136.52	133	8.55
Rochester Democrat	314,832	900	495.00	658	361.90	161	3.07
Syracuse Herald	202,376	900	594.00	252	163.80	178	3.33
Philadelphia Inq.	1,041,740	900	1,305.00	198	350.36	583	2.23
Pittsburgh Post	377,938	540	577.80	180	192.60	116	4.98
Pittsburgh Press	575,446	360	450.00	—	—	—	—
Newark News	392,215	900	647.50	490	294.00	232	2.79
Cleveland Plain Dealer	510,406	925	962.00	490	465.50	291	3.30
Wilmington Jour.	108,379	900	378.00	428	180.76	74	5.10
Pennsylvania Motorist	145,000	420	168.00	—	—	4	42.00

Exhibit 6

NBTB Magazine Advertising

Publication[a]	Circ.	Purchased Space (Lines)	Cost	Free (Lines)	Value	Inq.	C/I
Saturday Evening Post	1,854,000	1p-4c	$12,020.44	—	—	1392	$8.63
Holiday	944,126	2p-4c Jr	16,480.00	—	—	3384	4.86
National Geographic	2,500,000	1p-4c	13,380.00	—	—	2287	5.87
Field & Stream	1,089,000	2-2/3p BW	6,490.00	—	—	3478	1.86
Sports Afield	1,082,000	2-2/3p BS	5,680.00	—	—	2022	2.80
Time	930,000	2p-4c	18,780.00	—	—	1779	10.55
Saturday Review	220,000	2p-4c	6,440.00	—	—	159	40.50
Popular Boating	140,000	1p-BW	1,210.00	—	—	113	10.70
MacLeans (E)	301.900	3p-4c Jr	8,197.89	—	—	2802	2.92
MacLeans (F)	101,605	2p-4c Jr	2,030.00	—	—	2104	.96
Readers Digest (E)	510,587	2p-4c	8,272.00	—	—	2617	1.42
Readers Digest (F)	125,000	2p-4c		—	—	3187	
Le Samedie	80,142	3p-4c Jr	2,280.00	—	—	579	3.93
Chatelaine	478,047	3p-4c Jr	11,740.17	—	—	3411	3.44
Revue Moderne	125,000	3p-4c Jr	3,555.00	—	—	1687	2.10
Revue Pop.	111,066	2p-4c Jr	2,460.00	—	—	835	2.95
Canadian Homes	83,967	2p-4c Jr	3,598.00	—	—	587	6.12
Rod & Gun	36,000	2-2/3p BW	766.00	990	$1386.00	148	5.17

[a]In as many magazines as possible regional (Eastern United States and Canada) advertising space was purchased. Thus circulation figures do not always show total circulation.

Exhibit 7

Summary of Tourist Car Entries Into New Brunswick
(June, July, August, and September)

				Year				
	1	2	3	4	5	6	7	Current
Canadian cars through three north shore points	—	42,607	43,120	52,595	46,778	52,185	56,392	60,502
U.S. cars through three north shore points	—	24,831	20,097	20,878	23,150	25,208	23,042	23,015
Total cars through three north shore points	59,656	67,438	63,217	73,473	69,928	77,393	79,434	83,517
Canadian cars through Aulac	—	—	67,806	80,960	77,032	77,100	77,023	98,764
U.S. cars through Aulac	—	—	22,244	26,595	23,839	24,725	27,644	30,076
Total cars through Aulac	—	—	90,050	107,555	100,871	101,825	104,667	128,840
Canadian cars through 6 customs ports	—	—	—	39,935	41,866	56,218	54,445	47,251
U.S. cars through *all* custom ports	99,367	104,011	101,711	104,079	120,348	140,588	188,260	201,388[a]
Total cars entering via Digby ferry	—	—	4,239	4,205	4,030	4,254	4,130	3,841
Total cars entering via P.E.I. ferry	—	—	35,022	39,286	35,502	39,137	45,493	45,425
Total Canadian cars (all sources except two ferries)	—	—	—	183,490	165,676	185,503	187,860	206,517
Total U.S. cars (all sources except two ferries)	—	—	—	151,522	167,337	190,521	238,946	254,429
Grand total cars, all sources				379,175	372,545	419,415	476,427	510,212

[a]These figures not comparable with previous years due to a change in procedure of recording entries at border points.

Case 10-5
Atlas Copco Ltd.[1]

In late 1966 Atlas Copco (Great Britain), Ltd. completed a concentrated advertising campaign in Scotland. The latter part of this program had consisted of an intensive two-stage television promotion of their line of industrial equipment. These efforts marked the first time an industrial products manufacturer had used television advertising in Scotland to any significant extent.

THE COMPANY

Atlas Copco had its origins in 1873, when an engineering firm called AB Atlas was formed in Sweden to manufacture railway equipment, boilers and bridges. By 1900 the company had begun to investigate possibilities for the application of compressed air as a source of power to industry, and shortly thereafter production of pneumatic equipment began in earnest. The product line of Atlas continued to change, consisting in 1948 of a line of marine diesel engines in addition to an extensive range of compressed air equipment. Following a major breakthrough in rock drilling technique immediately after World War II, Atlas management decided to restrict the product range in order to concentrate all its resources on the continued development and marketing of the compressed air equipment line. This decision marked the beginning of a period of rapid growth for the company that, by 1965, was recognized as the world's largest firm specializing solely in the design, development and manufacture of compressed air equipment, with 119 subsidiaries spanning the globe.

The Atlas Copco product line in 1965 was divided into three main groups:

1. *Mining division.* A variety of heavy and light rockdrills, drill steels, loaders, winches and grinders.
2. *Construction division.* Portable compressors, concrete breakers and hand-held rock drills.
3. *Industrial division.* Stationary compressors, industrial tools, hoists, garage compressors and paint-finishing equipment.

[1]Copyright © 1967 by l'Institut pour l'Etude des Méthodes de Direction de l'Enterprise (IMEDE), Lausanne, Switzerland. Reproduced by permission.

A selection of Atlas Copco industrial air tools is shown in Exhibit 1.

UNITED KINGDOM MARKET

"Our main objectives and strategy in Great Britain as everywhere else, have been ruled by local environmental conditions," said Mr. Peter Wallenbert, Managing Director of Atlas Copco in the United Kingdom. "Since very little rock work is done nowadays in Britain, being confined to the highly specialized coal mining industry and some quarry and roadwork, our main marketing emphasis has been toward construction and, above all, general industry."

The British company, founded in 1919 as Atlas Diesel, Ltd., had evolved in the same way as the parent company. Since portable compressors and contractors' tools had been manufactured by the British organization for some twenty years, management felt this product sector had advantages from a marketing point of view. Increased effort in the four years up to 1966 had enabled Atlas Copco to secure a 15 percent share of the market for compressed air construction equipment. The total market was estimated to be about £6.5 million annually.

"However," continued Mr. Wallenberg, "by far the biggest single area of potential in the United Kingdom is represented by the industrial uses of compressed air. The total number of registered manufacturing industries in Great Britain is in excess of 50,000. Consequently, our prime objective has become to break into industry. As our company's product offering includes everything from the smallest to the largest air compressor, hand tools that are operated by air and spraying equipment as well, this is really a gigantic task.

"Our strategy has been first to identify the biggest users of our type of equipment, then to hit them as hard and consistently as we can, and in between, to go anywhere and everywhere. This is how we started about four years ago—nowadays we are perhaps a little bit more sophisticated. In terms of competitive advantages in the industrial product field, we claim better economy of operation in the compressor range (lower power consumption in relation to output) and better quality (lower spares and service requirements) in our range of tools. Considerable evidence

Exhibit 1
Selected Atlas Copco Industrial Air Tools

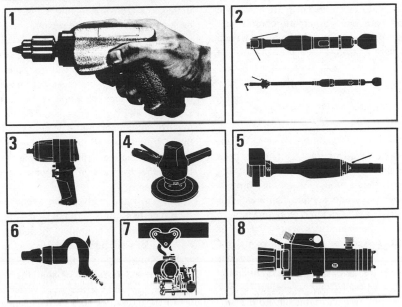

ADVANCED-DESIGN AIR TOOLS

LBB 33 H26 Hand Drills. Range includes ergonomic-design 2 lb/½ hp high-efficiency tools. Grinders, tappers, screwdrivers in this series utilize interchangeable spares.

SV 18 & 21K Rammers. Perfectly balanced tools for all foundry applications, concrete vibration, backfill tamping and ramming furnace refractories.

LMS 24 Impact Wrench. Advanced design impact mechanism comprises only five parts including rotor. Features: high power/weight ratio, correct torque.

LSS 52 Surface Grinder. High capacity tools – with patented speed governor – for all metal cleaning, grinding, cutting, sanding, wire brushing.

LSR 52 Straight Grinder. New 5-vane motor gives optimum power. Special governor ensures constant speed for all metal grinding jobs.

RRC 31 Chipping Hammer – delivers 2700 blows per minute. Perfect control from smooth starting to full power. Available with round or hexagon nozzle.

MT 605K Air Hoist – ultra sensitive control response from creep to full lift speed. Completely safe. Units range from ½ to 10 tons lifting capacity.

ECCO 40A Automatic high capacity, entirely air operated. Special short, large diameter air ducts prevent pressure loss in gun.

of the reliability of these claims exists from sophisticated, large users all over the world. In addition to specific product advantages, we believe our inventory policy has given us marked advantages with regard to after-sales servicing of our products. On the other hand, it is fair to say that our prices are somewhat higher than the average for the industry.

COMPETITION

"As Atlas Copco has a wider range of compressed air products than any other single manufacturer in the business, it follows that we are faced with considerable competition, not only from other larger firms in the industry, but also from a number of smaller speciality manufacturers," continued Mr. Wallenberg.

"In the industrial products field we can distinguish four main product categories: stationary compressors, garage compressors, industrial tools and finishing equipment. In each of these subdivisions we have not only the British-owned competitor, but also a large number of the major US manufacturers who produce this equipment in their own plants in Britain. Hence, there are some 150 competitors in the two compressor categories, and about 20 in each of the two tool and finishing equipment areas.

"The geographical distribution of these competitors is such that whatever area we operate in, there is at least one major competitor's plant locally—usually more than one. Consequently competition tends to be fierce, in particular since many of the most powerful participants complement their own sales force with local dealers who have a tendency to exert a strong price pressure on the market."

THE ADVERTISING PROGRAM

"To simplify the administration of our U.K. operations," said Mr. Wallenberg, "Britain has been divided into eight sales areas, each equipped during the last few years with a modern warehouse providing ample inventories and service facilities. Our company underwent considerable reorganization in order to provide these facilities, not the least of which involved a revitalizing and training of men for the area sales forces. Once we had settled our strategy of concentrating our resources on breaking into industry on a broad front, we began to look carefully at our promotional problems and the promotional tools available to us.

"Our immediate discovery was that a market such as the British one required tremendous resources if it were to be tackled all at once. There was no doubt that the media were there; the real questions that remained were, which media would be most suitable to our needs and could we find enough funds to make a national impact? The technical press seemed the most logical choice for both advertising and public relations, as this is the traditional way of promoting industrial goods. The conventional argument was that to sell such goods, plant engineers and other members of the enginering fraternity were the people who had to be converted.

"For us to embark on such a program would mean that we would be approaching the entire nation simultaneously, and that we would have to rely on the overriding power of the engineering world alone for our success. Furthermore, by concentrating on the technical press, of which there are vast numbers competing for the attention of each engineer, we would have to advertise very heavily to create any impact amongest the welter of advertising carried by these publications.

"Neither of these aspects seemed to us to be the criteria that could be applied to our industry. In the first place, we knew we could not expect to be equally well prepared everywhere in the country with a new form of organization, largely composed of new people. In addition, we felt that, in the unlikely event that a nationwide success did materialize, at the existing stage of our company's development, we could be ruined. Second, our experience from selling this kind of commodity to these kinds of customers told us that our salesmen, to be successful, needed the recognition of a far wider spectrum of industrial employees than engineers alone. The guard on the gate, the receptionist, the secretary in the engineer's office, the maintenance foreman, and often the president himself as well as the chairman and other members of the Board of Directors, all played a role in the decision as to what make of equipment should be purchased at any given time. We felt that all these people would be biased toward associating with a name that was familiar to them rather than with one of which they had never heard.

"As a result, our advertising agency suggested we should perhaps think about the local daily press that, in their opinion, would meet the requirements. We, on our side, were more strongly convinced that television would supply the only true answer to our problem. It seemed to us that the only possible common medium for the great variety of individuals, male and female, which we needed to indoctrinate or familiarize with our name was TV. In Rhodesia, some years earlier, we had successfully used this medium, although the market requirements and conditions were somewhat different from those currently prevailing in Britain.

"The fight between ourselves and the agency was bitter. There were countless arguments put up against TV such as 'no top executive ever watches it,' 'it has never been done for capital goods before,' and 'look at the expense.' The struggle ended in a draw. One thing, however, was certain: we could not afford nationwide mass media advertising. Thus we decided to concentrate our efforts initially on one area that was ready to exploit publicity and where there was a particularly strong industrial potential and excellent regional mass media facilities. The area we chose was Scotland.

"We didn't, of course, forget the rest of the country, covering the balance with a blanket of editorial activities, local and national exhibitions and advertising in a nucleus of specific technical journals (Exhibit 2). In Scotland, we decided on a minimum two-year promotional program. With its history of vast hydroelectric schemes involving much tunneling and road construction, our image in Scotland was one of a well-known supplier of equipment to civil engineering companies. Industry, as such, had never heard of us. Our target was to create an industrial image for Atlas Copco in the fast-growing industrial development area—and this would require

Exhibit 2
Sample Trade Journal Ad for Air Compressors

A NEW COMPRESSOR CLOCKS IN-
IT WILL BE INSTALLED AND WORKING BY LUNCHTIME!

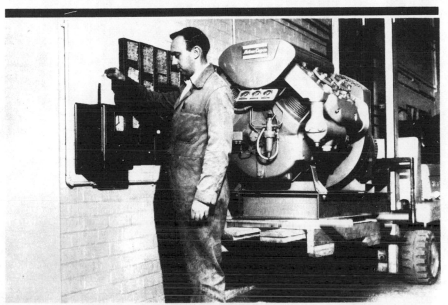

BT AIR COMPRESSORS NEED NO FOUNDATIONS...

that's why they virtually eliminate installation *time and costs*. These continuous-duty power units are dynamically-balanced to give vibration-free running. Simply set them down on any good floor, connect up and put them to work. They're available with output capacities of 141, 212 and 282 cfm at 100 psi

BT single-acting, two-stage compressors feature many built-in advantages: 100% air cooling to bypass all

water problems—costs, summer shortages, frost hazards, scale formation; new-concept over-square design to pack more power in less space—and give longer working life; optional automatic regulating systems to give minimum running costs.

The BT Series completes the Atlas Copco range of fully air-cooled compressors for industry—from 1 cfm to 1088 cfm.

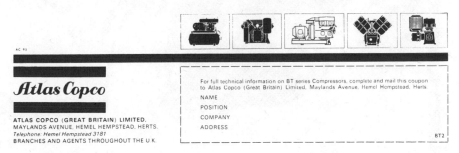

AC 93

Atlas Copco

ATLAS COPCO (GREAT BRITAIN) LIMITED,
MAYLANDS AVENUE, HEMEL HEMPSTEAD, HERTS.
Telephone: Hemel Hempstead 3181
BRANCHES AND AGENTS THROUGHOUT THE U.K.

For full technical information on BT series Compressors, complete and mail this coupon
to Atlas Copco (Great Britain) Limited, Maylands Avenue, Hemel Hempstead, Herts

NAME

POSITION

COMPANY

ADDRESS

BT2

---

time to achieve. Our program began in Janurary 1965 with a series of advertisements that specifically promoted Atlas Copco industrial air tools and equipment to industry. In all these cases the advertising copy was linked by a common theme of 'Atlas Copco puts the pressure on' (Exhibit 3).

"Atlas Copco first used the Scottish daily press in order to localize the campaign. Three major advertisements were placed in *The Scotsman*, the *Glasgow Herald*, the *Edinburgh Evening News and Despatch*, and the *Glasgow Evening Times*. Each advertisement covered half a page and featured the following subjects:

Exhibit 3.
Sample Newspaper Ad for Industrial Air Tools

Atlas Copco

PUTS THE
PRESSURE ON
PRESSURE ON
PRESSURE ON
PRESSURE ON

PACKS MORE AIR POWER INTO INDUSTRY

Atlas Copco puts the benefits of advanced compressed air technology in the hands of industry. Superb 'vital line' handtools, ergonomically designed for optimum grip, weight and balance—for greater productivity with less fatigue. Spray guns to give finest finish—faster. High-capacity grinders with unique speeds control. Powerful chipping hammers delivering up to 3,500 blows per minute. Drills that whip to production speed in 1/10th second! Screwdrivers that spin screws home at a touch. Rotary and percussive tools for every application. Each with that vital design feature to keep operator output at peak level—SAFELY.

New-concept compressors pump out more air power, take up less floor space, keep power costs down. The 'over-square' design—extra short stroke large diameter piston—minimises wear on piston rings and cylinder walls to increase dependability and working life. Atlas Copco provide everything necessary to compress air into power and put it to work—PROFITABLY.

ATLAS COPCO (GREAT BRITAIN) LIMITED, 591 Nitshill Rd., Glasgow S.W.3. Tel: Barrhead 2347. 14, Albany St., Edinburgh 1. Tel: Waverley 1918. HEAD OFFICE & WORKS: MAYLANDS AVENUE, HEMEL HEMPSTEAD, HERTS.

1. Atlas Copco's sales and service representation throughout Scotland.
2. The application and range of industrial products.
3. The application and range of construction equipment.

"The advertisements appeared throughout January to May 1965, and were backed up by company demonstration vans that were also announced in the press wherever they went. The campaign ended with an exhibition held exclusively by Atlas Copco on the outskirts of Edinburgh.

"During the same period, a wide range of product films were shown in individual companies. In addition, public relations activities were concentrated almost entirely to this area of Scotland for the duration of the program.

"To top it all off," said Mr. Wallenberg, "we bought one entire eight-page supplement to *The Scotsman* on October 13, giving a comprehensive picture of Atlas Copco's activities in Scotland, Great Britain, and internationally. It was the first time such a supplement has been issued in Scotland for a single customer. Miniature copies of the insert were taken and distributed widely throughout the area.

"In assessing the situation at the end of the first year, there appeared to be no dramatic climb in sales (Exhibit 4). Such a result was not unexpected since the campaign had been intended merely to create a more favorable selling climate for the sales force.

Indeed, the salesmen were full of enthusiasm while exploiting the promotion to the utmost and finding an increasing awareness of their company. The total cost of phase one, the Scottish campaign, amounted to £22,000.

"The coverage of Scottish Television fits neatly over Scotland's central industrial area, and in January 1966 television spearheaded the second phase of the campaign. We concentrated a large number of 45-second spots between January and April to create maximum impact and memorability. This was followed by a further burst in September and October. In all cases, these commercials featured a cartoon approach and in addition they contained the central theme of 'Atlas Copco puts the pressure on' (Exhibit 5).

"In order to exploit our Scottish Television debut to the utmost, we held two receptions at the TV studios in Glasgow, where we entertained not only large numbers of existing and potential customers, but also many of the foremost civic leaders in Scotland. After a speech of welcome and a live TV interview with our Scottish manager, we showed the commercial and one of our industrial films. The interest shown was very gratifying and the several hundred guests proved excellent ambassadors during the months to come, taking with them quantities of literature and souvenir brochures.

"During the second year, and overlapping the television advertising, was a background of press

Exhibit 4

Selected Monthly Sales for Market Area Covered by Advertising Campaign

	Industrial Tools		Industrial Compressors Over 1 m³/m		Total Sales[a]	
	£ 1965	£ 1966	£ 1965	£ 1966	£ 1965	£ 1966
January	1,465	1,925	375	3,500	9,000	14,000
February	2,400	1,975	6,060	8,500	20,500	32,000
March	1,400	3,850	3,250	4,125	24,750	36,750
April	4,200	3,800	—	6,125	28,250	19,000
May	2,550	3,600	9,375	3,300	34,000	32,100
June	16,720	3,150	5,875	8,375	54,500	58,000
July	3,500	2,800	3,250	4,625	25,000	20,000
August	1,250	1,850	3,125	2,375	27,750	9,500
September	2,975	1,875	7,400	8,600	39,000	26,750
October	2,700	3,175	5,125	2,875	42,250	17,000
November	1,850	2,575	2,150	9,625	15,575	34,400
December	2,500	11,700	2,250	5,150	31,200	35,100
Total	43,510	42,275	48,235	67,175	351,775	334,600

[a]Total sales exceed the sum of the columns due to inclusion of other products.

Exhibit 5.
Storyboard for Television Commercial

THE COMMERCIAL

The 24 frames above form the storyboard – the first visual conception of a television commercial. Object of this commercial: to associate the Atlas Copco namestyle with compressed air technology. To achieve this, the namestyle undergoes a series of animated metamorphoses symbolizing the compression of air into power – and the tools that in turn translate this power into productivity. Punctuating the animation are brief film sequences showing the tools in action. And running throughout this 45-second commercial is a specially composed theme on which is superimposed the actual sounds of the tools and the rich accents of the Scots commentator.

from conception to transmission

Visualizer and writer discuss the storyboard with the publicity manager.

The graphic artist puts his drawings under a special animation camera.

A film unit shoots the live-action sequences on the factory floor.

At the recording studio the music, effects and voice are precisely timed to the film.

Finally the commercial is beamed out by STV to make another 'first' for Atlas Copco.

advertising and considerable editorial support in the area. In contrast to the first local press advertising campaign, this later series included a number of advertisements with an institutional message presenting compressed air as a powerful and advantageous source of energy to industry rather than specifically promoting Atlas Copco air tools and equipment. The newspaper campaign ran from January through April, 1966 and included half page and 4″ x 10″ ads in Scottish dailies. In addition, a campaign of trade press advertising was conducted from March through December 1966 in the *Scotland* and *Scottish Public Services* journals. The total cost of the second phase of the Scottish campaign, including production of the commercial, was £23,000.

"I should make a few comments regarding our sales performance during and immediately following the television campaigns," concluded Mr. Wallenberg. "First, you must keep in mind that it is not at all unusual for two years to elapse between the moment an industrial salesman makes first contact with a company and the time when he actually writes up a firm order. Consequently, it is conceivable that if the TV campaign successfully achieved its objective of opening the door for our salesmen, the effect on sales may not be felt for two years."

Since the use of Scottish TV advertising was the first such venture by an industrial concern, Atlas Copco was anxious to appraise the ressults of this campaign. In October 1965 Atlas Copco hired Marketing Economics, Ltd. to assess the effectiveness of the TV campaign to be conducted in Scotland in early 1966. The results of the study are summarized in Tables 1-9 in Appendix A.

QUESTIONS

1. What is the rationale for advertising in a capital goods firm like Atlas Copco?
2. To whom should the campaign be directed? Why?
3. Was the ad copy ("Atlas Copco Puts the Pressure On") shown in Exhibits 2, 3, and 5 appropriate for the campaign?
4. Was the selection of the advertising media and scheduling of the campaign over a two year period suitable?
5. What do the sales results (Exhibit 4) suggest about the results of the campaign?
6. What did the recall study (Appendix A) reveal about the impact of Scottish TV advertising?
7. Was the campaign worth the cost and would you recommend the same approach be used in other areas?

Appendix A
Table 1
Recall of Atlas Copco

	Interviewed			
	Before	Campaign %	After	Campaign %
Number of people interviewed	320	100	312	100
Number who had heard of Atlas Copco	31	10	154	49
Number who had not heard of Atlas Copco	289	90	158	51

Table 2
Knowledge of Atlas Copco Products

	Interviewed		
	Before	Campaign	After	Campaign %
Number who had heard of Atlas Copco	31		154	100
Number who said Atlas Copco make				
Tools (unspecified)	—		82	53
Compressed air tools	—		37	24
Compressors	—		4	3
Other wrong answers	10		18	12
Don't know	21		40	26

Table 3
Knowledge of Desoutter Products

	Interviewed			
	Before	Campaign	After	Campaign
Number who had heard of Desoutter		32		27
Number who said Desoutter make				
Pneumatic tools		—		2
Power tools		—		2
Tools (unspecified)		—		8
Other wrong snswers		3		2
Don't know/can't remember		29		13

Table 4
Knowledge of Holman Products

	Interviewed		
	Before	Campaign	After Campaign
Number who had heard of Holman	25		25
Number who said Holman make			
Tools (unspecified)	1		1
Compressed air tools	1		—
Compressors	—		1
Other wrong answers	5		6
Don't know/can't remember	18		17

Table 5
Knowledge of Pressed Steel Products

	Interviewed			
	Before	Campaign	After	Campaign
		%		%
Number who had heard of Pressed Steel	226	100	199	100
Number who said Pressed Steel make				
Car bodies	71	31	65	33
Refrigerators	7	3	5	3
Steel (unspecified)	22	10	16	8
Other wrong answers	17	8	16	8
Don't know/can't remember	109	48	97	49

Table 6
Knowledge of Black & Decker Products

	Interviewed	
	Before Campaign	After Campaign
Number who had heard of Black & Decker	270	253
Number who said Black & Decker make		
Do-it-yourself tools	41	30
Power tools	32	25
Tools (unspecified)	119	104
Other wrong answers	—	1
Don't know/can't remember	78	93

Table 7
Recall of Atlas Copco Advertising

	Interviewed		
	Before Campaign	After Campaign	%
Number of people who had heard of Atlas Copco	31	154	100
Number who said they had seen advertisements for Atlas Copco	7	154	100
Medium			
Newspaper	1	12	8
Magazine	1	5	3
Television	1	149	97
Poster	1	5	3
Don't know	3	4	3
Number who had seen T.V. advertisements for Atlas Copco		154	100
Number who described the advertisements as saying			
Showed tools working (unspecified)		56	36
Showed tools drilling		18	12
Showed tools digging up roads		3	2
Showed tools grinding		6	4
"Atlas Copco puts power to work for the world"		31	20
Don't know		50	33

Table 8
Characteristics of Respondents

	Interviewed			
	Before	Campaign	After	Campaign
		%		%
All respondents	320	100	312	100
Sex Male	150	47	142	46
Female	170	53	170	54
Age 16-24	49	15	47	15
25-34	55	17	51	16
35-44	62	19	61	20
45-54	65	20	60	19
55-64	41	13	43	14
65 +	48	15	50	16
Class AB	37	12	38	12
C	179	56	179	57
D	104	32	95	30
TV BBC only	—	—	3	1
BBC/ITV	311	97	296	95
No TV	9	3	13	4
Paid job Yes	191	60	98	63
No	129	40	114	37

Table 9
Advertising, Product, and Company Image: Ratios of 25 Respondents

Atlas Copco is	
A go-ahead company OR an old-fashioned company	25:0
A new company OR an old company	2:1
A large company OR a small company	2:1
An English company OR an overseas company	4:1
An international company OR a national company	3:2
Atlas Copco products are	
Modern products OR not very modern products	24:1
Expensive products OR not expensive products	2:1
A wide range of products OR a narrow range of products	24:1
Efficient products OR not very efficient products	25:0
Atlas Copco's advertisements are	
Interesting OR not interesting	3:1
Informative OR not informative	4:1
Right length OR not right length	5:1
Too noisy OR not too noisy	5:1
Effective OR not effective	7:1
Particularly liked OR particulary disliked parts of ads	4:1

Eleven
Sales Management

Everyone lives by selling something.
Robert Louis Stevenson

This chapter is concerned with raising the efficiency of the salesmen and saleswomen employed by business organizations. Sales personnel are the front line troops in the battle for customers' orders and their direct contact with clients represents a vital channel of communication for the firm. Since personal selling accounts for 55 percent of the marketing expenses of American industry[1] (versus 36 percent for advertising and 9 percent for other promotional materials), the effective management of these resources can increase business productivity and earnings.

THE SALES MANAGEMENT TASK

Successful sales management requires close attention to a variety of tasks described in the flow diagram in Figure 11-1. As might be expected, the first job is to define the overall role that personal selling will play in the total marketing program of the firm. The importance of personal selling varies with the size and resources of the organization and the length of the distribution channel employed to reach the final industrial or consumer buyer. In some door-to-door companies,[2] for example, personal selling dominates the marketing programs almost to the exclusion of other forms of promotion. At the other extreme, book clubs and mail order firms rely entirely on advertising and employ no field salesmen at all. Other companies with limited resources, restricted product lines, and specialized merchandise reap greater profits by hiring independent agents to sell their products. The vast majority of businesses, however, employ a blend of advertising and personal selling to stimulate the purchase of their products. Although the ideal combination of these ingredients varies among firms, salesmen are generally more important in the sale of industrial goods where products are complex and often require special tailoring to meet the needs of the customer. Consumer goods, on the other hand, are often presold with massive advertising campaigns and salesmen are primarily order takers who keep dealers in-stock and help with promotions and displays.
Advertising and personal selling can be substituted for one another and a theoretical

---

[1]Patrick J. Robinson and Bent Stidsen, *Personal Selling in a Modern Perspective* (Boston: Allyn and Bacon, Inc., 1967), p. 14.
[2]Examples include such firms as Electrolux, Avon, and Fuller Brush.

523

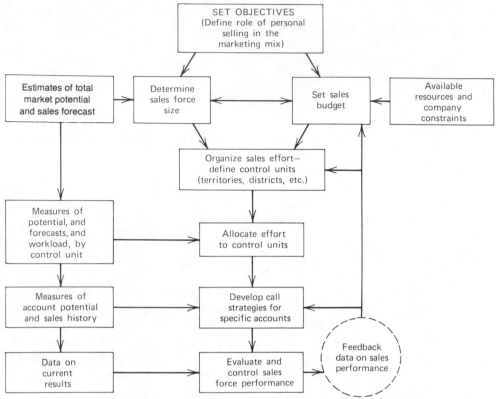

Figure 11-1 The Sales Management Program.
Source. David B. Montgomery and Fredrick E. Webster, Jr. "Application of Operations Research to Personal Selling Strategy," *Journal of Marketing,* Vol. 32, No. 1 (January 1968), p. 54. Reprinted by permission of the American Marketing Association.

argument showing how they interact is given in Figure 11-2. The curves on the chart are equal-sales contours for one firm that show how alternative levels of sales can be attained with different combinations of advertising and personal selling. The budget lines show the minimum expenditure that is needed to reach each level of sales. For example, the most economical way to reach sales of $600,000 is to spend amount (A) on advertising and (B) hours on personal selling. However, if amount (A) is the absolute limit on the amount spent on advertising, then the only way the firm can reach sales of $700,000 is to spend (C) hours on personal selling. Since this point (A,C) does not fall on the minimum budget line for this level of sales, it represents an uneconomic combination of advertising and personal selling. Obviously the most difficult problem implementing this approach is estimating realistic values for the equal-sales curves for a particular firm. Perhaps the most practical benefit of Figure 11-2 is the idea that a given sales level can be attained with different combinations of advertising and personal selling. This suggests that the final decision on mixing these two demand stimulants depends on competitive conditions and the needs of the individual product.

Sales Budgets and Territories

Once the importance of personal selling has been determined, the next step is to derive a sales budget and to calculate the size of the sales force needed to accomplish the

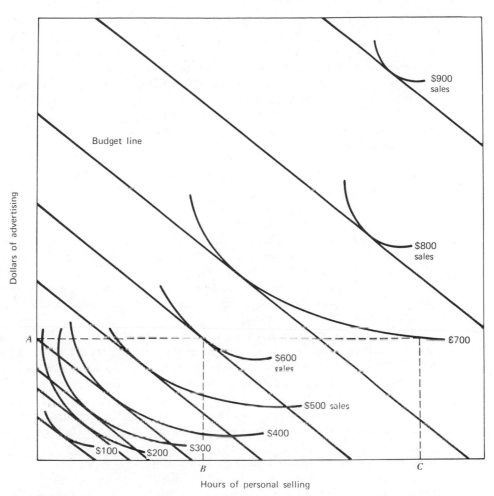

Figure 11-2 Optimum Combinations of Advertising and Personal Selling to Reach Alternative Sales Goals.
Source. Harry Allison, "Framework for Marketing Strategy," *California Management Review* (Fall 1961), p. 84. Reprinted by permission of the Regents of the University of California.

objectives of the firm. Decisions on numbers of salesmen and budgets are interrelated and a choice on one factor should not automatically determine values for the other. For example, the sales budget could be set on the basis of available resources and then the size of the sales force derived by dividing the budget by the average cost of a salesman. An alternative approach would be to set the budget on the basis of the number of potential customers and the corresponding number of salesmen needed to cover the expected work load. Neither method is apt to lead to profit maximization, however, because they do not consider cost and revenue factors simultaneously. Specific approaches to the problems posed by budgets and the number of salesmen will be discussed in greater detail in a later section.[3]

After the overall dimensions of the sales program have been hammered out, the next job is to design equitable sales territories and assign personnel to specific jobs. Territories are usually organized around geographic areas (states or counties), products, or

---

[3]See p. 530.

customer groupings. While it is unlikely that any two territories can be exactly alike, sales force morale and efficiency are improved when territories are balanced in terms of numbers of existing accounts, sales potential, and work load. Decisions must also be made with regard to call frequencies and the portion of the salesman's time to be devoted to soliciting new customers, pushing particular products, traveling, and writing reports. In addition, the sales organization must design a compensation program that motivates the salesman to achieve the sales objectives. The ability of a salesman to cover his territory will also be enhanced if the firm plans the sequence and routes to be used in contacting customers.

Evaluating Sales Performance

The final step in the sales management task involves monitoring the performance of the sales organization that has been created. This means that management must design an information system to assemble data on current sales operations and set appropriate standards for control purposes. The idea is to gather the kind of data (such as the amount of business lost to competitors) that can help correct deficiencies in the sales organization. Two key sources of control information are the call reports prepared by individual salesmen and the invoices describing each transaction. Call reports, for example, can be used to tell whether the sales force is making the desired number of calls to the desired mix of customers. The sales invoices can be processed to show historic and current volume by territories, individual salesman, customers, products, and product lines. Other reports can be prepared to compare actual sales performance against the planned figures and to highlight sales expenses incurred in specific territories or districts. Selling expense data can also be combined with price and margin figures to show the contribution profits generated by individual products or salesmen. The primary objective of the evaluation phase of the sales management program is to identify problem areas and to devise methods for improving the operation of the sales force.

Although the generalized sales management model described in Figure 11-1 does not cover all aspects of sales force administration, it does highlight the main topic areas that will be discussed in this chapter.

THE ROLE OF PERSONAL SELLING

Personal selling plays an important role in the communication process in most firms. Salesmen are expected to (1) disseminate factual information to customers, (2) present persuasive arguments to convert nonbuyers into buyers, (3) provide service, and (4) transmit market information back to the firm. As a dispenser of information, salesmen tell customers about product availability, delivery times, prices, discounts, technical specifications, warranties, and repair services. The persuasive role is frequently associated with personal selling and it focuses on winning the confidence of the buyer, overcoming objections, and marshaling data to show how the product or service fills the needs of the customer. Service work performed by salesmen is designed to help the customer solve problems related to the products sold by the firm. This includes activities such as expediting orders, obtaining repair parts, setting up displays, stocking shelves, taking inventories, and training dealer personnel. It is not unusual for equipment salesmen, for example, to help customers rearrange machinery and personnel to improve efficiency. Since salesmen are in constant touch with customers, they are in a good position to feed vital market information back to the firm. Some of the more useful data gathered by salesmen include information on competitive price changes, new product opportunities, orders secured by competitors, repair problems, and future product requirements.

When products are in short supply, the role of the salesman is less concerned with finding new business and more focused on keeping present customers happy. This means explaining the need for allocation systems based on past purchases, keeping buyers informed on the status of their orders, finding substitute materials in more abundant supply, and even sending customers to competitors with products to sell when customer shortages become critical. The strategy in the short run is to keep as many of the best customers supplied as possible so that they can be retained as customers when shortages ease.

Recruiting and Selecting Salesmen

New salesmen cost over $10,000 to recruit, train, and supervise during their first year and sales managers have the job of getting the best return they can from these expenditures. Job requirements for salesmen, however, vary widely depending on the type of product, customer, and travel requirements and there are few hard-and-fast rules on recruiting and selecting sales personnel. In the absence of good decision rules, some companies use a checklist approach. McMurry, for example, suggests that successful salemen tend to be energetic, self-confident, hungry for money and status, habitual hard workers, persistent, and competitive.[4] The problem for the salesmanager is where to find such "supermen" and how to screen out candidates that lack the physical and mental toughness that may be necessary to succeed in sales work. The process is particularly difficult in industrial selling where dollar sales tend to be large, customer relations are often critical, and the wrong man can destroy in a few minutes business contacts that have taken years to establish. In more routine selling jobs, on the other hand, (door-to-door, retail deliverymen, and insurance agents) turnover is so high that it doesn't pay to spend much money on recruiting and training. Here the best policy is to place the candidates on the job as quickly as possible and let the "sink or swim" philosophy identify the trainees with the most potential.

Sources of new salesmen vary with the job to be performed, but young trainees are often recruited from schools and colleges, employment agencies, and from among present employees. Experienced salesmen, on the other hand, are more apt to come from newspaper ads, recommendations by business associates, and employment agencies. There are no formulas guaranteed to match job requirements with the available candidates. The usual procedure is to have the applicant fill out an application blank, go though an interview, have references checked, credit checked, complete aptitude or psychological tests, and a physical exam. All of these steps are designed to weed out the applicants that do not have the physical or mental qualifications to perform the job. For example, it may be just as important to eliminate persons that score too high on aptitude tests if the sales job is menial as it is to eliminate candidates that cannot add and subtract from clerical jobs. Psychological tests are sometimes employed to try to weed out alcoholic and other high-risk candidates before they have a chance to embarrass the company. However, standardized tests have the disadvantage that applicants sometimes fake their answers to improve their chances of being hired. This problem can be partially

---

[4]Robert N. McMurry and James S. Arnold, *How to Build a Dynamic Sales Organization* (New York: McGraw-Hill, 1968).

handled by having only experienced personnel interview candidates and evaluate test results. Another approach used by some firms is to send candidates out with a regular salesman to see how they react to actual field selling conditions. In one insurance company, candidates selected after exposure to actual field selling conditions were much more successful than salesmen selected by other methods.[5]

Often the key step in hiring new employees is identifying the most important characteristics of the selling job and matching these with the characteristics of your most successful salemen. If these factors can be pinned down in terms of age, education, drive, empathy, experience, material possessions, and other personality factors, then it will be considerably easier to recruit replacements. Unfortunately it is rarely this simple because rigorous screening devices often eliminate good candidates and looser criteria are apt to bring in candidates that later have to be fired. Some turnover is desirable and exit interviews are one way to find methods to improve the selection and training of new salesmen. In addition, persons who fail in a sales role may be able to perform in a superior fashion in another capacity.

Types of Selling

The different tasks perfomed by salesmen are often classified according to the type of customer contact that is involved in the sale.[6] *Trade Selling* occurs when manufacturers and wholesalers call on retailers to try to improve the distribution of their products. This includes working with dealers on promotions, displays, inventory, and new items. The accent is on "selling through" the dealers rather than "selling to" final customers. *Missionary Selling* tries to increase sales by encouraging customers to purchase products from company dealers. These salesmen are in effect "selling for" the dealers. The medical detailman who calls on doctors for pharmaceutical companies is a good example. *Technical Selling* seeks to build sales by providing advice and counsel to the final users of the product or service. The primary role of the technical salesman is to identify and analyze customer problems and show how his products or services can provide solutions. *New Business Selling* attempts to open new accounts by converting total strangers into customers. This kind of selling is often described as "cold calling" and is used by door-to-door organizations and in the sale of insurance.

Types of Sales Organizations

Sales organizations are set up to supervise and motivate the field sales force as well as to provide staff support for estimating potentials and planning programs. In the sales organization described in Figure 11-3, two staff positions have been included to help the general sales manager with recruiting, training, and the analysis of sales reports.

Field salesmen are typically organized around geographic control units. Each salesman is given an area and these are grouped into districts and regions headed by sales managers (Figure 11-3). Within each geographic area salemen may be organized on a *territory, customer,* or *product* basis. When a territory orientation is used, salesmen sell all products to all customers in their territories (Figure 11-3, region 1). With a customer orientation, salemen sell all products to select groups of customers (region 2). If a company has a very large product line and different types of selling are needed for

---

[5]*Precontract Selection and Training: A Study in One Company* (Hartford, Conn.: Life Insurance Agency Management Assoc., 1957, Research Report 1957-2).

[6]This section is based on Derek A. Newton's article "Get the Most Out of Your Sales Force," *Harvard Business Review,* Vol. 47 (September-October 1969), pp. 130-143.

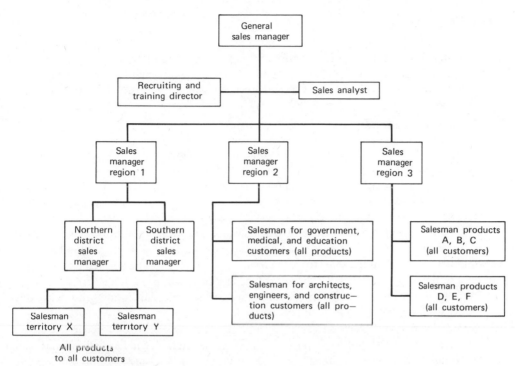

Figure 11-3 Sales Organization Using Territory, Customer, and Product Orientations.

separate items, it may be desirable to employ special salesmen to handle various product groups (Figure 11-3, region 3).

There is a great deal of controversy whether a territory, product, or customer-oriented sales force is best for business organizations. All three systems have been used successfully and some firms switch back and forth depending on the needs of the times. Xerox, for example, was able to cut turnover among their salemen by one third by moving from geographic sales territories to a customer orientation.[7] With product-focused salesmen it is not unusual for customers to be called on in the morning by a salesman selling products A, B, and C and then in the afternoon by a second saleman from the same company selling products D, E, and F. These presentations are rarely coordinated and may compete for the same buyer's time and the budget he has to spend. In addition, the duplication of coverage greatly increases the travel expenses of the sales organization. Thus during hard times it is easy to see why a sales manager might want to switch from a product to a territory orientation in an effort to save money.

On the other hand, a geographic-oriented sales force sacrifices product knowledge on the part of the salesman and this may be a key factor in building sales in a multiproduct firm. This is one reason, for example, that Hewlett-Packard recently moved away from an area approach. Since geographic-oriented salesmen have more products to sell, they are usually given extra training and smaller territories. Sometimes it is possible for companies with broad product lines to assign a single salesman to each large customer on a full-time basis. Because of the problems of keeping up to date on a wide product line, area sales forces must be provided with more support by technical salesmen, engineers, and laboratory personnel. Although these backup systems are essential, they are apt to operate slowly and give competing product and customer oriented salemen an advantage.

[7]"The Two Faces of Xerox," *Fortune* (September 1974), p. 119.

HOW MANY SALEMEN?

Although it is probably impossible to optimize the size of the sales force without considering variation in territories, salesmen, routing, and compensation plans; a rough idea of the personnel needed can be obtained by looking at costs and the number of customers.

Two Traditional Approaches

The size of the sales force is often a compromise between what the firm can afford and the total number of people needed to call on all existing and potential customers.[8] An example of the "what can I afford" approach is provided by Harry Bullock.[9] He suggests that a firm with $20 million in annual volume might be able to allocate 5 percent for field sales or about $1 million per year. If supervisory expenses ran about 20 percent of selling costs, the firm would have $800,000 to hire salesmen. Assuming salesmen cost $20,000 per year for salary and expenses, the company could afford to acquire a total of forty fieldmen. The size of the sales force is thus a direct function of the amount budgeted for field selling. This approach has the advantage that costs will be in line with current sales from the beginning and the company does not have to wait until future growth in sales reduces selling expense ratios to acceptable levels.

The "work load" method of determining the size of the sales force is based on decisions with regard to the frequency and length of calls needed to sell existing and potential customers. An estimate of the total number of salesmen required using this approach can be made with the formula:

$$\text{Number of salesmen} = \frac{\left[\begin{array}{c}\text{Number of}\\\text{existing}\\\text{customers}\end{array} + \begin{array}{c}\text{Number of}\\\text{potential}\\\text{customers}\end{array}\right] \times \begin{array}{c}\text{Ideal}\\\text{frequency}\\\text{of calls}\end{array} \times \begin{array}{c}\text{Length}\\\text{of}\\\text{calls}\end{array}}{\text{Selling time available from one salesman}}$$

For example, if a firm had 2500 existing customers and 500 potential clients to be called on five times per year for 2 hours (including travel time) and available selling time per salesman was 1500 hours,[10] the size of the sales force would be:

$$\text{Number of salesmen} = \frac{(2500 + 500) \times (5) \times (2)}{1500} = 20$$

This estimate of twenty salesmen is based on the assumption that the desired frequency and length of calls are the same for all customers. If it is decided that these should vary according to the size and type of customer, then the formula can be modified accordingly. The success of the system is clearly dependent on the ability of management to estimate the ideal number and length of calls to make on each buyer. Perhaps the biggest weakness with the "work load" approach to sales force size is the failure to consider the costs and profits associated with different numbers of salemen. An alternative approach considers what happens to sales and profits over time as existing territories are divided to make way for more salesmen.

[8] See Figure 11-1 and the discussion on p. 524.

[9] Harry L. Bullock, "Basic Factors in Sales Territory Design," *Allocating Field Sales Resources* (New York: The Conference Board, Experiences in Marketing Management, No. 23, 1970), p. 9.

[10] The figure of 1500 hours of available selling time per salesmen has been used by the Celanese Corporation to realign sales territories, M. A. Brice, "The Art of Dividing Sales Territories," *Duns Review,* Vol. 89 (May 1967), p. 93.

Marginal Sales Productivity

Typically, decisions on the optimum size of the sales force are made when companies already have salesmen in the field. This means that the sales manager must know what will happen to the volume of existing salesmen as new employees are added. In addition, it is desirable to know whether current efforts to solicit customers are sufficiently profitable to warrant further expansion of the sales force. The profitability of new accounts can be determined by analyzing the cost and gross margins associated with such business. For example, a firm might find that it takes 5000 prospect calls to generate $1 million of new sales over a one-year period. If the cost of an average sales call is $50,[11] then the new business was obtained at a direct expense of $250,000. Assuming that the cost-of-goods sold was 65 percent, then the new business generated $350,000 of margin the first year. Since the potential margin exceeds the selling costs by $100,000 in this case, the firm would be advised to look further at the possibility of hiring additional salesmen.

Equating Marginal Profits with Costs. Experience has shown that as companies add salesmen, the increase in new business typically is smaller with each new employee. The idea is to add salesmen until the gross profit on new business is equal to the costs of deploying another man. Since the new business associated with the additional manpower varies over time and among salesmen, firms must monitor sales activities closely to see whether they are approaching the point of diminishing returns. For example, one company systematically recorded the amount of new business obtained when salesmen were added or removed from sales territories.[12] This made it possible to construct an index showing how new business reacted to changes in the number of salesmen (Figure 11-4).

In the case where one territory is divided in half, the number of salesmen increase by a factor of 2.0 and Figure 11-4 indicates that the anticipated new business ratio would be about 1.4 for the company supplying the data. This means that placing two men in a territory resulted in 40 percent more new business than was generated by a single salesman. The firm is now in a position to compare the gross margin produced by this sales increment with the costs associated with adding another salesman.

A Cross-Sectional Approach. Marginal responses to sales effort can also be estimated from cross-sectional data. Lambert, for example used differences in the number of salesmen assigned to twenty-six districts to explain variations in X-ray film sales.[13] X-ray film was an ideal product for this analysis because it was purchased frequently and the absence of advertising support made the salesman a vital link in promoting the sale of the product. Lambert's sales response function included price and product mix variables[14] and took the form:

$$SV_i = 409,220,750 \ S_i{}^{.785} \ PM_i{}^{1.170} \ P_i{}^{-2.645} \tag{1}$$

where SV_i is sales volume of X-ray film in district i, S_i is the number of salesmen, PM_i is the percentage of company volume in each area derived from X-ray film, and P_i is the selling price index. This sales response function managed to explain 91 percent of the

[11]Includes salary, bonus, and travel plus allocations for increases in overhead, handling, and shipping associated with the added volume.

[12]S. E. Heymann, "Determining the Optimum Size of the Sales Force," *Marketing Research in Action* (New York: The Conference Board, Studies in Business Policy, No. 84, 1957), pp. 82-84.

[13]Zarrel V. Lambert, *Setting the Size for the Sales Force* (University Park, Pa.: Center for Research of the College of Business Administration, The Pennsylvania State University, 1968).

[14]Lambert also collected data on sales potentials, but this factor did not help explain sales variations among districts and was dropped from the analysis.

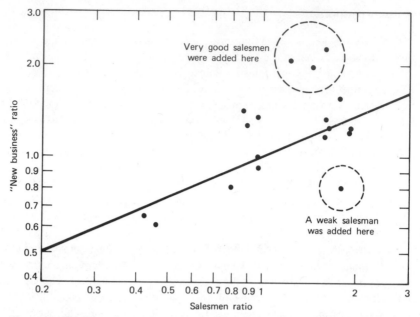

Figure 11-4 Relationship Between Additional Salesmen and New Business.
Source. S. E. Heymann, "Determining the Optimum Size of the Sales Force," *Marketing Research In Action* (New York: The Conference Board, Studies in Business Policy, No. 84, 1957), p. 83.

variation in X-ray film sales among the twenty-six sales districts. The coefficient for the S_i factor (+.785) suggests that sales were directly related to the number of salesmen in a district and that changes in the number of salesmen resulted in less than proportional changes in X-ray film sales. Lambert's data thus supports the popular notion of diminishing returns to added sales efforts.[15]

In addition, the coefficient for the product mix factor (PM_i) was positive and greater than one (+1.170) indicating increasing returns for this variable. The coefficient of the price variable (P_i) was negative and quite small (−2.645). This suggests that price cuts were a powerful weapon that could employed by the salesmen to boost the sales of X-ray film in a particular district.

To estimate the aggregate affects of changes in the number of X-ray film salesmen on gross profits, Lambert combined his sales response function with cost and margin data to give an equation showing the estimated change in gross profit. As long as the expected change in profit was greater than zero, contribution profits would be increased by adding salesmen. When Lambert applied this equation to the X-ray film sales districts, he found that twenty-nine additional salesmen could be profitably employed in nine of the districts.[16] If the new salesmen were as productive as the old, then gross profits would increase by $295,000, plus the profits from the other products that the new salesmen would be selling for the firm.

Lambert's approach is appealing, yet there are obviously some risks. For example, it is unlikely that the sales response coefficient (+.785)would remain constant as twenty-nine salesmen were added to nine sales districts. Other factors that could cause trouble

[15]In contrast, Heymann's results suggested less than proportional but linear returns to sales efforts.
[16]Zarrel V. Lambert, *Setting the Size for the Sales Force*, p. 33.

for Lambert's model include variation in the size and number of customers per district and the fact that selling ability is not the same for all members of the sales force.

A second example of a marginal approach to optimising the size of the sales force has been proposed by Lucas, Weinberg, and Clowes.[17] They studied the relationship between the sales of a clothing manufacturer and the independent variables sales potential and the number of counties in each sales territory. One linear equation they developed took the form:

$$\text{Sales} = 680 + .003 \text{ Potential} - 6.97 \text{ Number of counties} \qquad (2)$$

$$R^2 = .30 \text{ N} = 129$$

This equation says (quite logically) that sales increased with the potential in the territory and declined as the territory grew in size. Assuming that territories with equal potential and equal workload can be created, then it is possible to combine such a sales response function with cost and margin data to find the number of salesmen that maximizes profits. Because of the real differences that exist among territories and salesmen, the results of this approach are probably best interpreted as showing whether the sales force should be expanded or contracted rather than as a precise solution to be implemented without question.

Despite the handicaps of these two examples, the marginal approach does represent a positive step toward optimizing the size of the sales force. Beyond the problem of size is the issue of the proper design of sales territories.

DESIGNING EFFICIENT SALES TERRITORIES

One of the most critical jobs performed by the sales manager is dividing the available market area into equitable and efficient sales territories. Sales territories are usually constructed from groups of present and potential customers and assigned to individual salesmen to help assure adequate customer contact, minimize selling costs, and simplify control. Territory design is a never-ending task because customers, products, and salesmen change regularly and territory boundaries must be adjusted to the new conditions. Given the frequency of decisions on territory dimensions, businessmen need standardized routines for designing efficient sales territories. Unfortunately, these have not been developed and the majority of companies still design territories with trial-and-error techniques. Despite the scarcity of operating models, there appears to be agreement on the basic approaches to territory design.

The Buildup Method

The most popular technique employed to create sales territories is known as the buildup method. Standard geographic control units, such as counties, are selected and combined into territories for individual salesmen. Other commonly used geographic units are states, census districts, Zip code areas, and census tracts. Control units must be small enough to allow flexability in setting boundaries, yet not so tiny that the geographic areas lose their identity. States, for example, are often too large for effective combination

---

[17]Henry C. Lucas, Jr., Charles B. Weinberg, and Kenneth W. Clowes. "Sales Response as a Function of Territorial Potential and Sales Representative Workload," *Journal of Marketing Research,* Vol. 12 (August, 1975, pp. 298-305.

into sales territories and census tracts may be unnecessarily small. The selection of appropriate control units for individual companies depends on the availability of data on population, sales, and prospective customers in each of the areas. This information is readily available for political units, and these areas have the advantage of clearly defined boundaries.

Allocation Criteria. A number of criteria may be employed to guide the combination of standard geographic control units into viable sale territories. These include the obvious quantitative factors of existing volume, population, and future potential, plus the more subtle qualitative factors such as the ability and preferences of the salesmen. Management also needs some guiding principle to set priorities and simplify the process of grouping control units into territories. One possible rule would be to give the largest accounts to the salesmen with the most seniority. Despite the widespread use of this approach, a more equitable solution would be to divide up the total market to minimize differences in the number of present customers per territory and in the amount of sales potential per territory. Not only is the principle of "equal opportunity" more acceptable to the American way of life, but it could lead to better morale and greater productivity among the sales force. Salesmen should have the opportunity to earn an adequate living and equality among territories can help make this possible. In addition, similar territories make it easier for the sales manager to identify and reward outstanding performance. If territories are essentially the same, differences in productivity can be attributed to individual effort.

Although "equal opportunity" sales territories appear desirable, they are not universally accepted by American business. One study of eighty firms showed that the top third of the territories produced 55 percent of the sales in consumer goods companies and 65 percent of the sales in industrial firms.[18] These results suggest either it is difficult to make territories equal or that firms emphasize other factors when they divide up market areas.[19] Obviously many companies could stand a realignment of their sales territories to promote a spirit of fair play among the sales force and reduce the element of chance in territory assignments.

Combining Control Units. The actual process of creating sales territories is reasonably simple once a company has decided on a standard geographic control unit and a set of allocating principles. For example, marginal analysis[20] might suggest that a firm should employ ten salesmen in a particular region. Assume further that the firm decided to use counties as a control unit and wanted territories that were equivalent in terms of number of customers. The first step in building territories for this company would be to obtain a map showing all the counties in the region and to label each area with the number of customers. Next ten geographic locations would be picked to serve as starting points for building the sales territories. These points could be selected arbitrarily by the sales manager and are often cities that appear desirable as home bases for the salesmen. Once the starting locations are chosen, territories are constructed by simply adding and subtracting adjacent counties until all the counties are assigned and the number of customers is the same for all territories. Hopefully potential customers will be evenly dispersed across the region and territories based on current sales will also be equivalent in terms of potential. When potential customers do not follow the same locational patterns

---

[18]Harry D. Wolfe and Gerald Albaum, "Inequality in Products, Orders, Customers, Salesmen, and Sales Territories," *Journal of Business,* Vol. 35, No. 3 (July 1962), p. 300.

[19]Other factors that might be used would include short-run profits, preferences of the salesmen and sales managers, historic patterns, and a reluctance to disturb existing buyer-seller relationships.

[20]Discussed on p. 531.

as present buyers, the dimensions of the territories can be adjusted so that the salesmen will have the same opportunities to develop future as well as present income.

The Work-Load Approach

An alternative to the buildup method of designing sales territories is Talley's work-load approach.[21] This procedure creates territories that are equivalent in terms of the work to be performed by salesmen rather than territories that have equal sales potential. The key step in Talley's method is determining the optimum call frequencies for particular classes of customers. For example, in one case present and potential customers were grouped into volume classes and "theoretical call frequencies" were assigned on the basis of discussions held at a sales meeting.[22] Present and potential customers were then located geographically and the number of firms in each volume class were multiplied by the theoretical call frequencies to give a total of number of planned calls for each county. Next the counties were grouped together to create territories that required about 750 sales calls per year.[23] Although this method balances the number of calls among the salesmen, territories are not apt to be equal in terms of current volume or sales potential. These inequities could lead to serious morale problems if the income of the salesmen depended on commissions paid on territory sales. Thus the work-load approach to territory design would seem to be best employed when salesmen are on salary and are not compared on the basis of volume. Since the buildup and work-load methods both create territories by combining geographic areas according to a set of rules, computers can be employed to speed the search for the most efficient territory boundaries.

Designing Territories by Computer

The use of computer models to help managers design sales territories evolved from efforts to create legislative districts that satisfied the Supreme Court's "one man—one vote" rule. Since politicians frequently disagree on redistricting plans, some states have turned to nonpartisan computer programs to provide solutions that are acceptable to both the courts and the political bosses.[24] The programs are designed to construct compact, contiguous districts, of equal population. This tends to reduce gerrymandering,[25] increase the communality of interest of the voters in the districts, and to make it easier for representatives to visit their constituency. These principles seem equally relevant in the business world and legislative computer routines have been successfully adapted to solve sales territory design problems.

Computer Flow Charts. The basic dimensions of one computer approach to territory design are revealed in the flow chart shown in Figure 11-5. Input data for the program includes the coordinates of the centers of all geographic areas (i.e., counties,

[21]Walter J. Talley, Jr., "How to Design Sales Territories," *Journal of Marketing,* Vol. 25, No. 3 (January 1961), pp. 7-13.

[22]The actual number of calls per year recommended by the sales executives were 1, 3, 9, 10, 14, or 20 depending on the sales volume of the customer.

[23]A consideration of nonselling time devoted to travel, meetings, and vacations suggested that the average salesman in this firm could make 750 calls per year.

[24]Sidney W. Hess, "Realigning Districts by Computer," *Wharton Quarterly* (Spring 1969), pp. 25-30. See also S. W. Hess, J. B. Weaver, H. J. Siegfeldt, J. N. Whelan, and P. A. Zitlau, "Nonpartisan Political Redistricting by Computer," *Operations Research,* Vol. 13 (1965), pp. 998-1008.

[25]Gerrymandering is designing districts for political gain. Its counterpart in the business world would be the creation of districts that favored particular salesmen or managers.

census tracts) that are to be combined into territories. The program also needs information on the specific control activity that will be used to guide the combination of the geographic units. In the legislative version of the program[26] this is simply the population of each geographic area. Population can also be used as a guide in designing sales territories when everyone is a prospect for the product, such as in the case of encyclopedias. When the number of buyers is less than the total population, the control activity can be an actual customer count, some measure of work load, or the current or potential sales volume in each area. Finally the computer must be provided with estimates of the ideal number and location of the trial territory centers.

Up to this point the computer program closely resembles the "build up" method described earlier.[27] However, instead of a trial and error approach to the combination of geographic areas, the computer utilizes the transportation method to group areas into territories. The computer assigns areas to emphasize compactness and equalize the

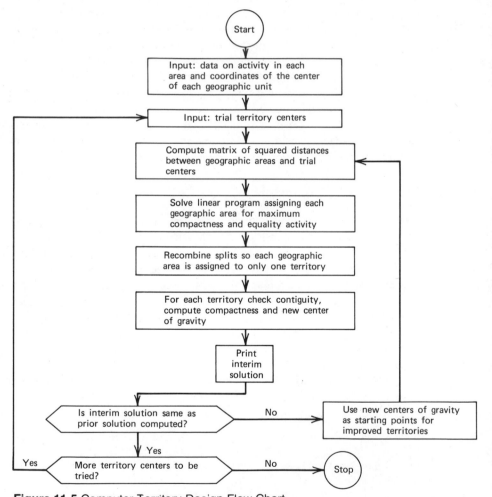

Figure 11-5 Computer Territory Design Flow Chart.
Source. Sidney W. Hess, "Realigning Districts by Computer" *Wharton Quarterly* (Spring 1969), p. 27. Copyright © 1969 by the Trustees of the University of Pennsylvania.

[26]Copies of the 3,000 card legislative program may be purchased from Ketron Inc., 256 East Swedesford Rd., Wayne, Pa.
[27]See pp. 533-534.

activity factor. The measure of compactness employed by the computer is the moment of inertia. This is simply the sum of the squares of the distances from the areas to the trial territory centers, weighted by the amount of activity in each area. In symbols the relationship is:

$$M = \sum_{i=1}^{m} \sum_{j=1}^{n} A_j \, d^2_{ij} \tag{3}$$

where M is the moment of inertia for a whole sales district, A_j is the size of the activity in the jth area, d^2_{ij} is the squared distance from area j to trial territory center i, m is the number of trial centers and n is the number of areas to be combined. The smaller the moment of inertia the greater the compactness of the territories that make up a sales district.

In its zeal to combine areas to minimize the moment of inertia and equalize activity, the program sometimes splits areas into pieces. These splits must be recombined and assigned to one territory (see flow chart, Figure 11-5) because demographic data are not available for fractions of areas. Next the program checks to be sure the areas assigned to territories have some contact with one another. This is simplified if the computer has a "touch list" that shows which areas share a common border. Once the program is satisfied that the territories are made up of contiguous areas, it calculates the location of a new center of gravity for each territory. These new centers become starting points to repeat the process of allocating areas to territories.

Legislative Districting. An example showing how the computer has been employed to design legislative districts is presented in Figure 11-6. Part (*a*) of the diagram gives the boundaries of the census areas that are to be grouped into six legislative districts. The initial trial centers for these six legislative districts are shown in part (*b*) of the figure. When the computer program grouped the census units around these centers, it obtained the legislative districts described in part (*c*) of Figure 11-6. This solution allowed considerable variation in population and one district had about 5 percent less people than the average. After the computer calculated new population centers of gravity, the program realigned the census areas to give the districts shown in part (*d*) (Figure 11-6). These revised legislative districts were more compact and almost equivalent in terms of population. Although the population deviation and moment of inertia declined significantly for the second computer districting plan, further attempts to improve the districts were not successful (Figure 11-6, *e*).

Some Business Examples. In addition to the applications in legislative districting, the computer program has been successfully used to build territories for pharmaceutical salesmen, typewriter repairmen, and salesmen who call on supermarkets. The CIBA Pharmaceutical Company, for example, employed the program to realign territory boundaries for 400 detailmen grouped into 40 sales districts.[28] The company first selected three districts to test the computer technique and then expanded the program to revise all of their sales districts. The activity measure used to balance the territories was the number of physicians in seven specialties. Geographical regions combined into territories included several thousand Zip code areas and counties.

Three revised territory plans were prepared for each CIBA sales district and the

---

[28]Sidney W. Hess and Stuart A. Samuels. "Experiences With a Sales Districting Model: Criteria and Implementation, *Management Science*, Vol. 18, No. 4 (December 1971, Part II), pp. 50-52.

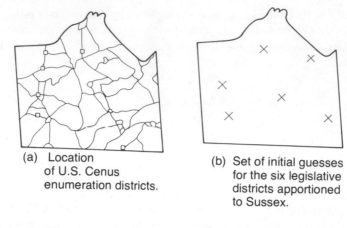

(a) Location
     of U.S. Cenus
     enumeration districts.

(b) Set of initial guesses
     for the six legislative
     districts apportioned
     to Sussex.

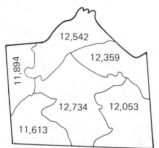

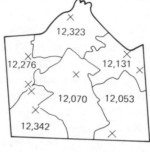

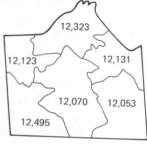

(c) First assignment of population
     to legislative districts
     based on guessed centers
     Maximum deviation: 5%,
     moment of inertia: 143,774.

(d) Second trial: improved
     assignment based on
     actual centers of first
     assignment (X's indicate
     towns of over 1000 population)
     Maximum deviation: 1%,
     moment to inertia: 133,923.

(e) Third trial: slightly
     worse results
     Maximum deviation: 2%,
     momen of inertia: 133,992.
     (Fourth trail—no
     further change.)

Figure 11-6 Legislative Districting by Computer: in Sussex County, Delaware.
Source. James B. Weaver and Sidney W. Hess, "A Procedure for Nonpartisan Districting:
Development of Computer Techniques." Reprinted by the Yale Law Journal Company and
Fred B. Rothmand Company from *The Yale Law Journal,* Vol. 73, p. 298.

average maximum variation achieved in the number of doctors per territory was only 5.7
percent. One of the new plans for each district used the current salesman's home as a trial
center. To help assure acceptance of the revised territories, district managers were free to
reject all plans and ask for additional computer plans (none did), make their own changes
to one of the prepared plans (some did), or accept one of the plans without changes (most
did). The managers were generally pleased with the computer territories and felt the
solutions were imaginative, realistic, and at the same time relieved them of a major
clerical burden.

ALLOCATING SELLING EFFORT

Once sales territories have been designed, the sales manager must decide how to
employ the sales force to cover different customers and product lines. The primary

objective of these efforts is to assign salesmen so that total revenue or gross profit will be maximized. This has become more difficult in recent years because the cost of an average industrial sales call has gone up to about $70.[29] The ideal solution would be to devise a model that considered the cost and revenue aspects of allocating sales resources across all possible territory, customer, and product dimensions. Unfortunately, a general solution is not available and firms must resolve each selling allocation separately. This section will review several methods that have been employed to help deploy salesmen to customers, products, and across time.

Allocations to Customers

One of the most difficult sales force allocation decisions is how much selling time to devote to different customers. For example, a rule-of-thumb approach led one company to devote one third of its salesmen's time to present customers or known prospects, one third to door-to-door canvassing to locate new prospects, and one third to responding to unsolicited customers requests.[30] When the company ran a market survey they found that 3500 existing customers accounted for 85 percent of total market sales. This suggested that one third of the salesmen's time devoted to prospecting was wasted and the time would be better spent with present customers. Also the time allocated to following up on requests from unknown prospects was not very productive and this work could be better handled by mail. In addition the survey revealed that over 88 percent of the customers concentrated more than half of their purchases with a single supplier. This suggested that the firm should attempt to become the favored supplier for known customers rather than concentrating sales efforts on obtaining individual jobs as in the past. The salesforce allocation problem thus reduced to finding out how much time salesmen should devote to persuading customers to concentrate their purchases and how much time to spend on keeping customers that already concentrate their purchases.

Call Frequency and Sales Response. An experiment to measure the relationship between call frequency and sales led to the construction of the response curves shown in Figure 11-7. These curves demonstrate the association that was found between salesmen's contact hours per month and the probability that a customer exposed to a certain amount of sales effort would respond with a substantial increase in purchases. After the customer was converted, the holding curve provided an estimate of the probability that a customer's business would not decrease significantly with a given level of sales contacts. The firm wanted to obtain the maximum number of conversions per hour of selling effort and this occurs where a line from the origin is just tangent to the conversion curve. Thus the recommended number of contact hours would be ten per month with a corresponding conversion probability of 20 percent. To pick an optimum value of the holding factor, the firm used a marginal approach. They wanted a level of holding effort such that a small increment in selling time would prevent the loss of the same number of customers as if the additional time had been devoted to converting customers. Although a precise solution could not be obtained from the data in Figure 11-7, the firm estimated that about two hours per month of holding effort and a 5 percent lapse rate was about right.

Even though the firm determined the appropriate number of hours of selling effort for converting and holding customers, they still had to decide on the number of accounts of each type to assign to each salesman. In this particular case, the company estimated that

[29]"Toward Higher Margins and Less Variety," *Business Week* (September 14, 1974), p. 99.
[30]Arthur A. Brown, Frank T. Hulswit, and John D. Kettelle, "A Study of Sales Operations," *Operations Research*, Vol. 4 (June 1956), pp. 296-308.

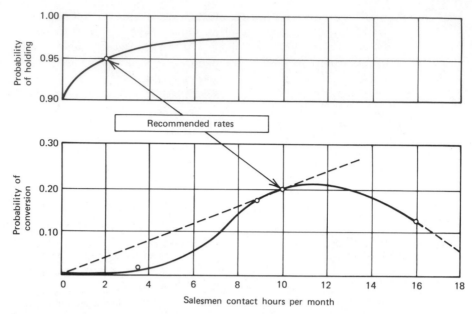

Figure 11-7 Estimated Customer Responses to Alternative Sales Efforts.
Source. Arthur A. Brown, Frank T. Hulswit, and John D. Kettelle, "A Study of Sales Operations," *Operations Research,* Vol. 4 (June 1956), p. 303.

about 110 hours per month were available for customer contact by each salesman after allowances were made for travel, report writing, and meetings. Thus if C was the planned number of customers in a salesman's conversion group and H was the number in the holding group, the ideal allocation would occur when $10C + 2H = 110$. Since the firm wanted the number of customers lost and the number converted to be equal at the margin, the following condition must also hold: $0.20C = 0.05H$. This gives two equations and two unknowns that can be solved to show that the optimum allocation was twenty-five hold customers and six conversion customers for each salesman.

The allocation of selling time to hold and conversion customers appears reasonable, but success depends on several key assumptions. First the equating of hold and conversion probabilities (Figure 11-7) assumes that the customers gained and lost are similar in sales volume and profitability for the firm making the calls. The model also assumes that accounts that are allowed to lapse have the same conversion probability as someone who has never bought from the company. Further, the analysis assumes that the total number of salesmen employed by the firm is fixed. Although none of these assumptions are likely to hold in the real world, the call frequencies suggested by the analysis are probably an improvement over the informal guidelines used previously.

CALLPLAN.   An interactive computerized approach to the problem of allocating selling time to customers has been proposed by Leonard Lodish.[31] This program is designed to help salesmen consider alternative call policies by improving the processing of the salesman's information. CALLPLAN is self-instructing and salesmen can work with the model at remote computer terminals using simple conversational language.

An example of the input data supplied by a Pennwalt Corporation salesman to help allocate 25 percent of his time to an industrial product is shown in Table 11-1. The

[31]Leonard M. Lodish, "CALLPLAN: An Interactive Salesman's Call Planning System," *Management Science,* Vol. 18, No. 4, Part II (December 1971), pp. 25-40.

Table 11-1
Input Data for CALLPLAN—A Sales Call Planning Model

Type 1 to enter data for a new problem.
2 To use data saved from a previous terminal session.
3 To recover from a session where input was aborted.
4 To list file names or erase files.
5 To end this session.
>1
Type a title for this problem.
>Williams territory
How many clients?
>14
How many prospects?
>2
Into how many (limit 15) geographical areas do you wish to divide the territory?
>4
Unit of time (e.g., hours, ½ hrs., etc.) for specifying call length?
>½ hrs.
Length (e.g., 1 month, 3 months, 6 months, etc.) of effort period?
>3 Months
Length of response period?
>1 Year
Total number (limit 1000) of ½ hrs. available for selling + travel time in 3 months?
>251
Upper limit (maximum of 15) on number of calls to consider making on any account during 3 months?
>13
Type names of each geographic area under its Id number.
   1
>NJER
   2
>NYC

   .
   .
   .

Type names of each client under its Id number.
   1
>BALFOR
   2
>CHEMPRO
   .
   .
   .

Type name of each prospect under its Id number.
   15
>BRDNG
   16
>MARLOW
Do any of these accounts represent classes of accounts rather than individual accounts?
>No
Do you wish to use adjustment factors that vary by account?
(The user wanted to maximize unadjusted sales)
>No

Type the constant adjustment factor.
>1
On the line following each listed account, type the following three numbers separated by spaces:
1. The Id No. of the accts. geographic area.
2. The ½ hrs. per call for each account assuming you are in its geographic area.
3. The number of calls presently being made in an average period of 3 months.
BALFOR
>4 2 8
CHEMPRO
>1 3 6

On the line following each client type 5 estimates separated by spaces:
1. Anticipated sales during 1 year if no calls are made.
2. Sales during 1 year if ½ the present no. of calls (rounded up) are made during 3 months.
3. Sales if present level of calls is continued.
4. Sales if present call level is increased by 50 percent (rounded up).
5. Sales if saturation calls are made.
(Note well—if either zero or one call is presently being made during 3 months, then type instead the estimated sales if 0, 1, 2, 3, and saturation calls are made.)
BALFOR (Sales are in hundreds of dollars)
>0 50 80 90 100
CHEMPRO
>0 14 23 26 27

For each of these prospects, type on the first line following the name probabilities of conversion to a client during 1 year if zero, ½ the present call level, the present call level, the present level +50 percent and if saturation calls are made in an average period of 3 months (the previous exception applies for present call levels of zero or one).
On the second line type the sales anticipated during 1 year if the prospect is converted.
BRDNG
>0 .1 .2 .25 .26
>3
MARLOW
>0 .1 .2 .25 .26
>12
On the line following each of these areas, type separated by spaces:
1. The number of ½ hrs. per average trip.
2. The cost per trip.
NJER
>6 0
NYC
>6 0

Type 1 to save the current data
2 To change data
3 To print the current data
4 To obtain an optimal call frequency policy
5 To end this terminal session
>4

Source. Leonard M. Lodish, "CALLPLAN: An Interactive Salesman's Call Planning System," *Management Science,* Vol. 18, No. 4, Part II (December 1971) pp. 32-34.

symbol > in the left margin indicates information supplied by the salesman and the rest of the comments were typed by the computer. First the program asks for the number of clients and prospects and then calls for identifying names. The salesman must also specify the number of areas to be used in the analysis, the length of the call, the maximum calls per account, and the total available selling time. Next the program asks about the present number and length of calls for each account.

Perhaps the key inputs for the model are the estimates of how individual customers and prospects will respond to different call frequencies. The salesman must indicate the sales that will result if no calls are made, one half the present calls are made, the present level of calls is continued, 50 percent more calls are scheduled, and a saturation level of calls are made. He also must estimate the probabilities of converting prospects into customers with different call frequencies. CALLPLAN then fits curves to these data points and prints out the expected sales for all feasible call frequencies. To help make geographic recommendations on the number of sales calls, the computer asks for the current amount of time and cost of trips to each sales area.

Some of the output provided by CALLPLAN is shown in Table 11-2. Allocations of sales calls to individual customers are made by the program so that the sum of the revenue

Table 11-2
Optimal Account Call Frequency Policies

Account	Optimal Calls In Average Three Months Period	Expected Sales In One Year	Present Policy	Expected Sales Using Present Policy
Balfor	7	75	8	79
Chempro	3	14	6	22
Chemplst	10	195	3	171
Dilctx	5	15	4	8
Emerson	0	0	1	0
Ethlyn	6	64	4	52
F/C	5	37	5	37
M-I	0	0	1	2
Micro	0	0	4	2
Polyfin	1	5	3	8
Slctro	5	36	3	18
Severna	9	59	6	38
Surf	0	0	3	2
Tri-Pt	5	72	3	36
Brdng	0	0	1	0
Marlow	0	0	1	1
Total	56	572	56	475

Source. Lodish, *Management Science*, p. 36.

produced by the sales response functions is maximized. Note that in this case shifting calls from smaller customers to larger buyers such as Chemplst, Ethlyn, Slctro, Severna, and Tri-Pt raised expected sales by $97,000. Thus it appears that sales efficiency was improved without raising the total number of calls.

CALLPLAN is best suited to repetitive selling situations where the amount of time spent with the client is important in determining the size of the order. Experience with CALLPLAN suggests that the model call frequencies can increase expected sales by 5 to 25 percent over results achieved by the intuititve allocations used by salesmen. Not only have salesmen been able to make better allocations of their selling time, but the direct costs are only $80 per salesman for computer time sharing services during each planning session.

Allocations to Products

In multiproduct firms, it is often impossible for salesmen to promote all items in each and every time period. Since the size of the sales force is usually fixed on the short run, the firm must find a way to divide the limited selling time among its products so that profits on the total line are maximized. A typical solution to this problem is for the product managers to bargain for selling time with the executives who control the sales force. While this approach may produce an acceptable compromise, there is no reason to believe that it leads to the optimum allocation of resources for the firm.

One model that has been successfully employed to solve the product allocation problem is based on response functions developed by product managers that show how products respond to additional sales efforts.[32] Separate response functions are prepared for each product in the line and then combined to estimate total gross profits over the planning horizon. The next step is to allocate sales efforts to products by means of a special computer program. The program begins with a trial allocation supplied by the sales manager and then calulates the incremental profits associated with different levels of sales efforts. The available selling time is then allocated to products using the marginal response rates that have been determined.

A comparison of sales allocations made using the computer model and allocations based on rules-of-thumb is shown in Table 11-3. The example is based on calls made to physicians and some products received full coverage (C), some half (H), some quarter (Q), and some products were not mentioned at all (N). Note that the allocations of selling time for the managers (I) and the model (M) were very similar for six of the nine products (numbers 1, 2, 3, 5, 7, and 8). However, for the remaining products the model solution differed sharply from the recommendations of the managers. The computer model suggested that total expected profits would be increased by $129,000 ($112 + $176 − $159) if selling efforts were shifted from product 4 to products 6 and 9. This meant that the expected overall increase in profitability for the first four periods ($86,000) was over three times the cost of developing the model.[33]

---

[32]David B. Montgomery, Alvin J. Silk, and Carlos E. Zaragoza, "A Multiple-Product Sales Force Allocation Model," *Management Science,* Vol. 18, Number 4, Part II (December 1971) pp. 3-24.

[33]The model is relatively inexpensive to use and the allocation heuristic employed to solve the problem in Table 11-3 required only 15 seconds of 360/67 time.

Table 11-3
Comparing Management and Model-Based Allocations of Salesmen's Time to Ethical Drug Products

	Products																	
	1		2		3		4		5		6		7		8		9	
Period	I[a]	M	I	M	I	M	I	M	I	M	I	M	I	M	I	M	I	M
1	Q	Q	H	N	H	C	N	N	H	N	Q	Q	H	Q	N	N	N	N
2	H	Q	Q	Q	H	Q	N	N	Q	Q	Q	C	Q	Q	N	N	N	Q
3	H	H	Q	Q	Q	Q	H	N	Q	Q	H	Q	Q	C	N	N	N	Q
4	H	H	Q	Q	Q	Q	H	N	Q	Q	H	H	Q	H	N	N	N	Q
5	H	H	Q	Q	Q	Q	H	N	Q	Q	H	H	Q	Q	N	N	N	H
6	H	H	Q	Q	H	Q	Q	N	Q	N	H	C	Q	Q	N	N	N	Q
7	H	H	Q	Q	Q	Q	H	N	Q	Q	H	H	Q	Q	N	N	N	Q
8	H	H	Q	N	Q	H	H	N	Q	Q	H	H	Q	Q	N	N	N	H
Total profit in thousands of dollars	1559	1552	906	905	918	925	622	463	1623	1632	4192	4304	511	523	650	650	1179	1355
Model profit less manager's profit in thousands of dollars	−7		−1		+7		−159		−1		+112		+12		0		+176	

[a] I denoted managers' Initial plan, M denotes the model's allocation, C × complete coverage of physicians in salesman's territory, H = half coverage, Q = quarter coverage and N = no coverage.

Source: David B. Montgomery, Alvin J. Silk, and Carlos E. Zaragoza, "A Multiple-Product Sales Force Allocation Model," Management Science, Vol. 18, Number 4, Part II (December 1971), p. 16.

SCHEDULING AND ROUTING SALESMEN

After a salesman has decided on the customers and prospects he wants to visit during a particular time period, he still has the problem of selecting a sequence of calls that will minimize travel time or expense. Careful scheduling can produce substantial benefits and one firm has reported that an analysis of driving patterns reduced the travel mileage of salesmen by 15,000 miles per year and allowed each salesman to make eight more calls per week.[34] Techniques used to schedule and route salesmen have received considerable attention from management scientists and the issue has become known as the "traveling salesman problem." The dilemma is usually stated as a search for a route through the territory that visits each customer and returns to the starting point with a minimum expenditure of time or money. Traveling salesman problems are difficult to solve because there are $(n-1)!$ possible routes to be considered (where n is the number of customers).

A variety of techniques have been employed to search for the best routes for salesmen including linear programming, integer programming, nonlinear programming, heuristic programming, and branch and bound methods.[35] While a discussion of these procedures is beyond the scope of this book, they all appear to give good solutions. Unfortunately, the constraint imposed by these solutions that the salesman must visit every account during the period is rather unrealistic. Differences in the size of accounts may suggest more than one visit to some customers while smaller accounts may be skipped entirely on a particular sales trip. To allow for these possibilities, the problem would have to be solved for every subset of customers, something that is unrealistic in terms of computer time. An alternative approach that modifies the traveling salesman solution[36] to allow for customer differences has been proposed by Cloonan.[37]

Cloonan looks at sales force scheduling in terms of planning individual sales tours. A sales tour is a set of customers to be called on by the salesman during a single trip away from his home base. Although a tour may include a whole territory it usually represents a group of calls that can be handled in five or ten days. This allows the salesman to spend every weekend or every other weekend at home rather than having to stay on the road until the whole territory is covered. The search for the ideal sales tour can start with a traveling salesman solution that shows the optimum sequence of calls for a whole territory.

A flow diagram showing how customer differences can affect the selection of accounts for sales tours is shown in Figure 11-8. The procedure begins with the salesman at location X facing the decision of whether to go to the customer at Y (the first call on the traveling salesman solution) or to go directly to the customer at Z (the second customer on the territory solution). This choice is made by comparing the value of the customer with the costs of the time and travel involved in going from the present location (X) to the customer under consideration (Y) then to the next account (Z) as opposed to the cost of going directly from X to Z. Customer value is measured on a relative basis rather than in dollars of potential sales or profits. When the value/cost ratio of the customer under

[34]Reported by Spencer S. Meilstrup of the Diamond Crystal Salt Corporation in *Allocating Field Sales Resources* (New York: The Conference Board, Experiences in Marketing Management, No. 23, 1970).

[35]See David M. Montgomery and Glen L. Urban, *Management Science in Marketing,* (Englewood Cliffs, N.J.: Prentice-Hall, Inc., 1969), p. 282 for specific references.

[36]The route that visits each customer and returns to the starting point at a minimum of time or expense.

[37]James B. Cloonan, "An Analysis of Sales Tours," *Proceedings of the Fourth International Conference on Operational Research,* David B. Hertz and Jacques Melese, eds. (New York: Wiley, 1966), pp. 284-292.

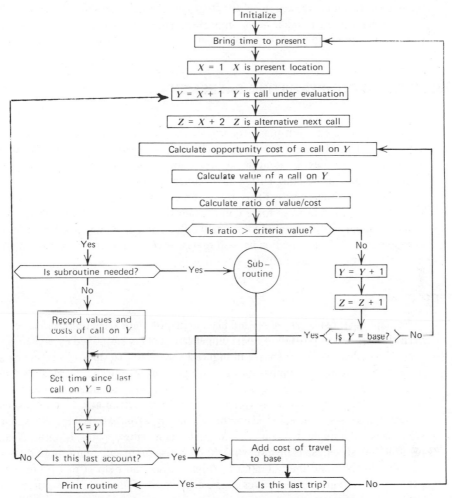

Figure 11-8 Planning Sales Tours Using Value and Cost Criteria.
Source. James B. Cloonan, "An Analysis of Sales Tours," *Proceedings of the Fourth International Conference on Operational Research,* David B. Hertz and Jacques Melese, eds. (New York: Wiley, 1966), p. 288.

consideration (Y) exceeds a critical level[38] the account is included on the sales tour, otherwise the program goes on to evaluate the next stop on the optimum territory route. If an account is included on a sales tour after several customers have been skipped, a subroutine is used to reevaluate the dropped accounts in terms of known future destinations.

Weekly sales tours of twelve customers were compared using the heuristic and two other methods. The results revealed that the simple expedient of dividing the sales tour into groups of adjacent accounts was clearly inferior to the other methods. The use of judgment to select accounts from size classifications (A, B, C) closely resembles real world methods and was found to operate at 80 to 90 percent of the optimum value determined by an exhaustive simulation run. The value/cost heuristic had an efficiency of

[38]The critical level of the value/cost ratio is set so the salesman will select just enough accounts to use the available time.

96 percent. Cloonan's research on sales tour planning indicates that a systematic analysis of customer value can make some improvements on the rules-of-thumb that are often used to schedule calls and route salesmen.

MOTIVATING AND COMPENSATING SALESMEN

Creating compensation plans for salesmen is an art rather than a science because differences in products and customers make it necessary to tailor programs to the needs of individual companies. In addition, compensation plans are constantly being revised to reflect changes in the competitive environment and it is difficult to compare the efficiency of salary plans across firms or over time. Although there are few universal truths that can be applied to sales force compensation, research has shown that sales performance is more closely related to the method of compensation than it is to the level of compensation.[39] In this section we will review several of the more popular methods that have been employed to motivate salesmen.

Cash Incentives

Perhaps the most common reward used to inspire field sales representatives is simply cash. Preferences for different cash compensation plans employed by 665 consumer and individual sales forces are shown in Figure 11-9. Note that only 11 percent of the plans are based on straight commission or "100 percent incentive."[40] Most of these plans provide for a draw against commissions to give the salesman a minimum income regardless of variations in sales volume. The primary advantage of commission plans is that selling costs are variable and companies only pay for performance. Straight commission is a popular method of compensating salesmen in the apparel, furniture, leather, and printing industries. Salesmen on straight commission usually earn more than salesmen on other plans[41] and the potential for high wages can help attract professional sales personnel. Even greater incentives can be achieved by following Townsend's suggestion that commission rates should increase with the amount sold.[42] This means that the first $100,000 of sales might carry a commission of 5 percent and the second $100,000 a rate of 7 percent and so on. Townsend believes commission rates should *not* be lowered when a salesman earns a fortune because this information will stimulate the rest of the salesforce into a frenzy of activity. Despite the benefits that have been mentioned, commission salesmen are usually more difficult to control and are less likely to work together to make joint sales.

Sometimes companies use a negative commission system to control salesmen's activities. Under this plan commissions are subtracted from the salesman's compensation when customers are lost to competitors. At Xerox, for example, when a copying machine lease is terminated by a customer the salesman assigned to that account loses the original commission paid when the machine was placed.[43] This occurs regardless of

[39]Derek A. Newton, "Getting the Most Out of Your Sales Force," *Harvard Business Review*, Vol. 47 (September-October 1969), p. 132.

[40]Commission rates for salesmen range from 5 to 10 percent of sales or more depending on the type of product and industry.

[41]See *Compensating Field Sales Representatives* (New York: National Industrial Conference Board, Studies in Personal Policy, No. 202, 1966), p. 41.

[42]Robert Townsend, *Up the Organization* (New York: Alfred A. Knopf, 1970), pp. 166.

[43]"The Two Faces of Xerox," *Fortune* (September 1974) pp. 119-120.

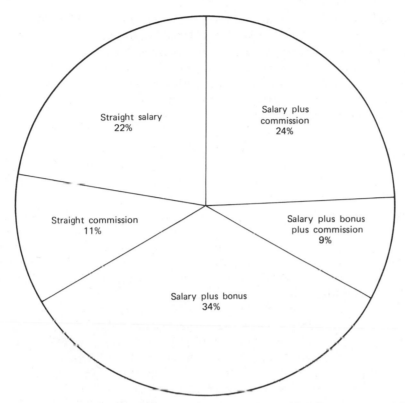

Figure 11-9 Compensation Plans Employed by 665 Consumer and Industrial Sales Forces.
Source. Adapted from Tables 9 and 10 appearing in *Compensating Field Sales Representatives* (New York: National Industrial Conference Board, Studies in Personnel Policy, No. 202, 1966), pp. 19 and 21.

whether the same salesman is handling the account. Thus the salesman is under a great deal of pressure to keep present customers happy as well as to place new machines.

An alternative to the commission approach is the straight salary system where compensation is a fixed amount for each period. This method gives management more control over the salesmen's time and is useful in missionary work and situations where considerable effort is needed to make a sale. Straight salary is popular in the aerospace, petroleum, and chemical industries and Figure 11-9 suggests that 22 percent of the sales forces surveyed used this approach. Salary compensation plans are common in industrial selling where service and engineering skills are more important than having salesmen press for an immediate order. Straight salary plans do not, however, provide much incentive for extra effort and about all a salesman can look forward to is the chance for a raise at the end of the year. The combination of a regular monthly wage and no cash incentives means that management must exercise very close control over salesmen's activities if maximum efficiency is to be achieved.

Salary Plus Incentives. The most popular sales compensation system employed by American business combines a base salary with a cash incentive. Over two thirds of the sales force reported in Figure 11-9 used this approach and 83 percent of a group of firms changing their compensation plans from 1955 to 1965 switched to salary incentive programs.[44] The cash incentives used in these plans usually takes the form of a sales

[44]*Incentive Plans for Salesmen* (New York: National Industrial Conference Board, Studies in Personnel Policy, No. 217, 1970), p. 3.

commission or a bonus. Where commissions are used, the rate may stay the same for the entire range of sales volume (2 percent of all bookings, for example) or it may increase or decrease with sales volume. A common practice is to offer a higher commission rate on sales that exceed some predetermined quota. Commission rates frequently vary by product classes so that sales managers can push items that are new, in excess supply, or carry high margins. Some firms tie commission rates directly to item profitability and others vary rates according to the type or size of customers.

Bonus payments are more loosely tied to volume and are usually drawn from a pool of funds based on the overall sales or profitability of the firm. Qualification of salesmen for bonus payments depends on whether the salesman exceeds his sales quota. Volumes achieved above the quota are converted into points or shares which are used to divide up the bonus pool. Other factors employed to set bonus payments include managerial evaluations, sales expense control, and the number of new accounts. A recent study of 100 bonus plans revealed that about half of the programs calculated bonus points on the basis of sales achieved in certain product categories.[45] This is an attempt to focus the attention of the salemen on new, surplus, or high margin products. Apparently it is more difficult to tie bonus payments directly to profitability and only 18 of the 100 plans made profits on sales a key performance factor.

One of the crucial issues with salary plus incentive programs is how much of the total payment should be salary and how much should be incentive. A study of 367 plans by The Conference Board revealed that a typical bonus payment was 12 percent of total wages and the proportion of incentive pay increased to about 35 percent for the salary plus commission and the salary plus commission plus bonus plans.[46] In another study of 1029 sales executives, Newton found that the highest productivity in trade selling occurred when 60 percent of compensation was paid as fixed salary.[47] For missionary, technical, and new business selling Newton found that 80 percent fixed salary was best.

Despite the growing use of incentive payments, there are many firms that limit the total amount of money that salesman can make under these programs. From a marketing point of view it would seem foolish to place a ceiling on incentive pay, but apparently some companies are more concerned with controlling expenses than in maximizing sales.

Optimizing Commission Rates.   The main objective in creating sales compensating programs is to devise a system that encourages salesmen to maximize the profits of the firm. Unfortunately this is not easy to do and salesmen are very clever at manipulating salary plans to maximize their own wages. For example, it has been shown that when incentive payments are based on a percentage of the sales of each product, it is unlikely that the salesmen will sell the mix of products that will lead to the most profits.[48] Since salesmen do not have data on production costs and economies of scale, they will simply look at the incentive rates and emphasize the items that are easy to sell and carry the highest commissions.

An alternative approach that can help improve the profits of the firm is to set commission rates as a percentage of the gross margin available on each product.[49] Weinberg has shown that when salesmen have control over price, a commission system

[45]*Incentive Plans for Salesmen,* op. cit., p. 42.

[46]*Compensating Field Sales Representatives,* op. cit., p. 28.

[47]Derek A. Newton, "Getting the Most Out of Your Sales Force," p. 135.

[48]Otto A. Davis and John U. Farley, "Quotas, Commissions and the Economics of the Sales Force," Robert L. King, ed., *Marketing and the Science of Planning* (Chicago: American Marketing Association, 1968), p. 77.

[49]See Ralph L. Day and Peter D. Bennett, "Should Salesmen's Compensation be Geared to Profits?" *Journal of Marketing* (October 1962), pp. 6-10.

based on gross margins will lead to optimal profits for the firm.[50] The reason is the company and the salesman share the same pool of money (realized gross margin) so that both are interested in maximizing this amount. It is common practice, for example, to pay retail automobile salesmen a percentage of the gross margin produced on each sale so they will bargain with customers to obtain the highest possible profit for themselves and the dealer.

A third possibility is to let management set individual sales quotas on each product so that the total sales force sells the amount that minimizes the average cost of production. The problem with this approach is that salesmen tend to be underutilized and the firm will have to hire more help than it needs.

A quota-setting procedure recommended by Davis and Farley overcomes some of these problems by utilizing a system of bargaining between the salesmen and central management. First the firm gives the salesmen a set of commission rates and asks them how much they expect to sell of each item. The company then reviews the plans of the sales force and adjusts the commission rates up or down to encourage a more desirable mix of sales. The new rates are resubmitted to the salesmen and the process continues until the quotas planned by the salesmen agree with the amounts the company wants to sell to maximize profits. While this approach is conceptually appealing, it has not worked very well in the real world. For example, one company allowed some salesmen to reduce their quotas on a hard-to-sell product in exchange for larger total quotas.[51] They expected that this increased flexibility would allow the salesmen to increase their earnings and make more money for the firm. Unfortunately, the control group with high quotas on the difficult product had significantly greater total sales than the men with the flexible quotas. These results suggest that more research is needed to determine how salesmen respond to alternative reward systems.

Noncash Incentives

There is a vast array of noncash incentives that can be used to motivate salesmen to work harder. These include such obvious techniques as sales meetings, honor awards, and recognition plus more subtle methods designed to stimulate salesmen by influencing members of their families. Noncash incentives are employed by all sales organizations and the dollar value of these incentives has been estimated to exceed $225 million.[52] One of the most common noncash incentives is to give a salesman a car and allow him to use it for personal as well as business travel. Some firms expand on this theme by offering more expensive cars to salesmen who stay with the company for a prescribed number of years. Another standard approach is to award merchandise or vacation trips to winners of sales contests. For example, the Kirby division of Scott & Felzer Company recently took thirty of their top vacuum cleaner distributors and their wives on a five-day, all-expense-paid junket to Hawaii.[53] These excursions are usually a mixture of work sessions and sightseeing so the participants can avoid reporting the trip as taxable income.

[50]Charles B. Weinberg, "An Optimal Commission Plan for Salesmen's Control Over Price," *Management Science*, Vol. 21, No. 8 (April, 1975) pp. 937-943.

[51]Leon Winer, "The Effect of Product Sales Quotas on Sales Force Productivity," *Journal of Marketing Research*, Vol. 10, No. 2 (May 1973), pp. 180-183.

[52]*Incentives for Salesmen* (New York: The Conference Board, Experiences in Marketing Management, No. 14, 1967), p. 92.

[53]"Expense-Paid Junket Beats Mere Money As a Sales Incentive," *Wall Street Journal* (June 25, 1973), p. 1.

A study completed in 1967 revealed that three quarters of the firms contacted were using sales contests and 76 percent of these reported excellent or good results with these incentive programs.[54] Contests are appealing because the prizes can be purchased at wholesale so they represent greater values to the salesmen than the equivalent amount of cash. A recent Dictaphone sales contest, for example, awarded fifty-two prizes including a speedboat or a vacation, a mink stole, twenty-five television sets, and twenty-five wristwatches.[55] This contest was organized in the form of a lottery so everyone had a chance to win and salesmen were awarded tickets in proportion to how well they exceeded their sales quotas. Other noncash incentives that can be used to stimulate salesmen include free life insurance, college educations for children, and stock option plans. Noncash incentives work best when they are tied to short-run sales performance and are viewed by the salesmen as special awards outside of the regular salary system.

EVALUATING SALES PERFORMANCE

The evaluation of sales performance is an incredibly complex task because salesmen and territories are all different and field representatives normally spend most of their time away from their supervisors. In addition, salesmen perform a vast array of jobs and the diversified nature of their work has spawned a host of control measures that can be used to monitor their activities. A further complication is that salesmen are not above manipulating the reward system to increase their own salaries rather than maximizing the profits of the firm. Thus it becomes the task of the sales manager to design a performance evaluation system that properly balances all dimensions of the salesman's job. One place to start this review is with the activities of individual fieldmen.

Measuring Individual Performance

The basic information used to evaluate sales performance is derived from the call reports, expense accounts, and merchandise orders that are prepared by the salesman as he travels through his territory. Research has shown that sales performance is directly influenced by the effectiveness of the system used to gather this information. Companies that required their salesmen to send in regular reports, for example, achieved higher sales levels in a study reported by Newton.[56] Although reports prepared by salesmen are vital for control purposes, turnover[57] is apt to increase if salesmen spend excessive time writing reports.

The data collected from salesmen are compared with planned performance figures and cost data to help gauge the progress of the sales organization. Some of the specific factors that can be employed to judge individual salesmen are shown in Table 11-4. In this

[54]Albert Haring and Malcolm L. Morris, *Contests, Prizes, Awards for Sales Motivation* (New York: Sales and Marketing Executives-International, 1968), p. 9.

[55]Note that the mink stole is intended for the salesman's wife and the speedboat, vacation, and the television sets could be enjoyed by the whole family. This choice of prizes is obviously designed to enlist the help of the family members to make sure the salesman does everything possible to win the contest. It is quite possible, however, that prizes for sales contests designed to exploit family relationships could lead to discontent. A pet food company, for example, once ran a sales contest where the prizes were vacation trips for the wives. After all, don't wives have to stay home to work and brood about the fun their husbands have on business trips and conventions? In this case the husband was left at home to work and brood about the fun his wife was having.

[56]Derek A. Newton, "Getting the Most Out of Your Sales Force," p. 132.

[57]Turnover is the number of salesmen who quit or are discharged divided by the average size of the sales force during the period.

Table 11-4
Rankings of Salesmen on Ten Performance Factors

Salesmen	Dollar Sales	Direct Selling Cost Percent	Gross Margin Dollars	Gross Margin Percent	Net Dollar Margin	Overhead Allotment	Dollar Profit	New Accounts	Least Acts. Lost	Sales to Potential	Total of Ranks
Ford	1	3	5	5	5	2	5	1	4	5	36
Bell	2	4	2	3	4	5	4	4	3	4	30
Shaw	3	5	4	3	4	5	2	2	1	3	28
Mann	4	1	3	4	3	3	1	5	5	2	31
Gold	5	2	1	2	2	4	3	3	2	1	25

Source. Adapted from an article by Richard I. Levin, "Who's on First?" *Sales Management* (July 17, 1964), pp. 53-56.

example, five salesmen employed by a firm are ranked on ten different criteria. If the firm is primarily concerned with sales volume and new accounts, then Ford was the best salesman. Bell, on the other hand, produced the highest gross margin percentage and net dollar margin while Shaw had the lowest overhead allotment and lost the smallest number of accounts. The fourth ranked salesman in terms of sales volume also did poorly on the number of new accounts and accounts lost, but Mann produced the highest dollar profit and the lowest selling expense. Perhaps the biggest sleeper among the five salesmen was Gold, who despite low sales did the best on gross margin dollars and sales in relation to potential. In general, performance of the five salesmen varied widely across the ten factors and each man ranked first on two criteria and last on at least one factor. If all of the criteria are considered equal in importance, then the ranks shown in Table 11-4 can be added across to give a measure of overall performance.[58] This procedure shows that Bell, Shaw, and Mann had total performance scores close to the expected value of 30 points, while Ford and Gold were enough different to warrant special attention. Note that although Ford had the highest sales volume, he actually had the worst overall record while Gold was doing an excellent job despite low sales volume. This example was contrived, but it does show that sales performance is directly related to the factors used in the evaluation process and the weights assigned to the criteria.

Since differences in sales territories distort comparisons across groups of salesmen, it may be more useful to evaluate salesmen on an individual basis. This can be done by designing reports that show how each salesman achieves his own planned sales goals. An example of a personal sales analysis prepared for R.M. Jones has been reproduced in Figure 11-10. This Sales Planning and Achievement report (SPA) is both a record of accomplishments and a planning guide to help the salesman do a better job of budgeting his time. Note that Jones' customers are listed in the left-hand column and a summary for all accounts is shown across the bottom. Although only a single page is shown in Figure 11-10, the report would be as long as needed to cover all the salesman's clients. The information included in the report shows the factors the company considers to be the most important in evaluating sales performance. Perhaps the most startling dimension to the report is the absence of any data on planned or actual sales levels. While these data are no doubt available somewhere, this report emphasizes the gross profit on sales for the past year, and the coming year on both a three-month and year-to-date basis. Expense control is a standard entry on sales evaluation forms and the SPA report shows planned versus actual figures for each customer.

The inclusion of small-order reduction in Figure 11-10 as a control factor is unique and would probably be important to only a limited number of firms. In this particular case the company wanted to reduce orders under $20 because they tended to be unprofitable. Product line balancing is another criterion that is included in the SPA report shown in Figure 11-10. The proportion of sales achieved in each of six product categories is reported and HI and LO signals are placed next to entries that depart from expected norms. One final dimension is a weighted performance index shown at the bottom of the report. This overall measure is compiled from the scores achieved on gross profits, expense control, small-order reduction, product mix, and is adjusted by the supervisor to reflect any special performance by the salesmen. The sales planning and achievement report appears to be a useful document to help improve the supervision of individual salesmen, but there are some questions to be answered. One problem is that elaborate

---

[58]This assumes, of course, that ranking is a good procedure for showing the relative position of each salesman on the various factors. Ranking actually does not measure up to this standard but is used here for simplicity.

SALESMAN: R.M. JONES

ACHIEVEMENT SECTION

ACCOUNT NUMBER		GROSS PROFIT ($M) — INDUSTRIAL PRODUCTS: 1964 ACTUAL	1965 POTENTIAL	1965 ACTUAL	PERCENT OF 1965 POTENTIAL	CONSUMER PRODUCTS: 1964 ACTUAL	1965 POTENTIAL	1965 ACTUAL	PERCENT OF 1965 POTENTIAL	COMPOSITE PERCENT OF 1965 POTENTIAL	CONTROLLABLE EXPENSES (Percent of Sales)*: ACTUAL	GOAL	% OF GOAL	SMALL-ORDER REDUCTION (Percent of Sales)**: ACTUAL	GOAL	% OF GOAL
18	THREE-MONTH AVERAGE	$10.3	$ 18.2	$ 10.3	57%	$ 7.0	$ 7.3	$ 5.1	70%	61%	35%	25%	72%	28%	20%	72%
	YEAR-TO-DATE AVERAGE	7.8	13.5	10.2	76	6.9	6.4	5.0	78	81						
4	THREE-MONTH AVERAGE	12.4	17.8	17.0	86			None		86	21	18	87	30	18	60
	YEAR-TO-DATE AVERAGE	11.3	18.6	14.1	76					76						
7	THREE-MONTH AVERAGE	10.3	13.3	12.5	94	7.9	10.4	8.7	84	89	19	20	105	10	12	118
	YEAR-TO-DATE AVERAGE	8.8	10.1	11.4	113	7.4	9.2	7.6	83	99						
9	THREE-MONTH AVERAGE			None		36.1	36.7	33.4	91	91	29	28	98	14	16	110
	YEAR-TO-DATE AVERAGE					29.3	29.3	27.7	95	95						
22	THREE-MONTH AVERAGE	18.6	16.9	24.1	143	8.0	8.8	8.0	91	125	20	22	108	22	15	70
	YEAR-TO-DATE AVERAGE	19.5	16.2	19.7	122	6.7	7.3	7.1	97	114						
TOTAL	THREE-MONTH AVERAGE	$88.1	$111.8	$100.1	[illegible]	$122.1	$138.4	$134.1	97%	95%	24	[illegible]	93%	18	15	84%
	YEAR-TO-DATE AVERAGE	[illegible]	92.1	[illegible]	[illegible]	[illegible]	[illegible]	[illegible]	[illegible]	101						

CONTROL SECTION / PLANNING SECTION

ACCOUNT NUMBER	PRODUCT LINE MIX — PRODUCT GROUPS (as a % of total): A	B	C	D	E	F	ACCOUNT TIME — JULY HOURS: PLAN	ACTUAL	ADJUSTED STANDARD HOURS	ACTION PLAN FOR AUGUST: ACTIVITIES TO ACCOMPLISH	PLANNED HOURS
18	22%	17% LO	13%	12%	20% HI	16% LO	18	19½	22	Put trading stamps in. Extend hours on Fridays. Educate manager in using "E-Z Expense Control" system. Replace displays for Product F.	24
4	50 HI	40 LO	10	–	–	–	14	15	21	Check condition of Product B inventories. Set up special sale if in poor condition. Survey possibilities of adding consumer line (check potential major buyers)	20
7	26	28	20 HI	0 LO	10	16	12	14¾	15	Compliment on good performance, esp. small-order reduction. Check D inventories and displays. Help interview for new sales clerk	16
9	–	–	–	80 HI	9	11 LO	10	8½	14	Compliment on small-order performance. Check F inventories and displays. Set up C displays (new). Follow up on "E-Z" system usage.	12
22	12 LO	25	33 HI	10	12 HI	8 LO	8	6½	6	Discuss small-order costs and encourage larger orders. Stress value of balanced-line selling and try for order of A and F.	8
TOTAL	20	26	11	13	15 HI	15 LO	121	130	127	Repeat upcoming F promotions with all accounts.	127

WEIGHTED PERCENTAGE PERFORMANCE (Unadjusted) 96.3%
SUPERVISOR ADJUSTMENT† (Indicate reason below) .... + 2.0
98.3% ← WEIGHTED PERCENTAGE PERFORMANCE (adjusted)

† Explanation of adjustment, if any:
Jones has done exceptional job in reducing turnover and training new outlet managers in his territory.

* Based on percentage of sales targets, which are converted to dollar expense targets according to actual sales. "% of goal" is the dollar target divided by actual expenses.
** Based on territorywide [illegible] target percentage of goal for orders under $20. Goal number of small orders is divided by actual number of small orders to get percentage of goal.

Figure 11-10 Salesman Planning and Achievement Report.
Source. Jon R. Katzenbach and R. R. Champion, "Linking Top-Level Planning to Salesman Performance," *Business Horizons,* Vol. 9, No. 3 (Fall, 1966) p. 95.

control forms (like Figure 11-10) are expensive to prepare and the firm must decide how much they can afford to pay for such detailed information.

Using Models for Evaluation

Up to this point we have evaluated the performance of a salesman primarily in terms of his success on individual control factors. Another approach is to build a model that shows the sales manager the relative importance of a variety of factors. One model of this type explained the sales observed in twenty-five territories using eight performance variables.[59] The equation took the form:

$$\text{Unit sales} = f\left(\begin{array}{l}\text{Number of accounts, industry potential,}\\ \text{workload, salesman effort, sales experience,}\\ \text{sales change in market share, market share,}\\ \text{and company advertising}\end{array}\right)$$

[59]David W. Cravens, Robert B. Woodruff, and Joe C. Stamper, "An Analytical Approach for Evaluating Sales Territory Performance," *Journal of Marketing,* Vol. 36 (January 1972), pp. 31-37.

Industry potential was measured by industry sales, workload was based on the volume of purchases per account and the geographical concentration of accounts, sales effort on an evaluation by sales managers, and sales experience was simply the length of employment with the company.

The relative importance of the eight performance variables is shown in Table 11-5. Note that most of the variation in sales among the twenty-five territories was explained by the number of accounts and potential as measured by current industry sales. Individual effort of the salesman, on the other hand, accounted for only 1 percent of the variation in sales and length of employment and advertising were not significant at all.

Interestingly the relationships observed between sales and number of accounts and sales and workload were both positive. This is contrary to expectations as logic would suggest that with equal potential per territory, the salesman with the smaller area and fewer customers would sell more than the salesman with a large number of widely scattered accounts. Thus we would expect the relation between sales and potential to be positive (as it is) and the relation between sales and workload to be negative. The positive effect of workload in this case may be due to high intercorrelations among the independent variables or to the small number of salesmen included in the study (25).

The low impact of individual sales effort in this case is suspicious and suggests that the product was easy to sell and the salesmen were functioning primarily as order takers. It is also possible that the sales manager's evaluations were inaccurate. If the results shown in Table 11-5 are representative, then the sales manager should restructure the salesmen's job to stress the more creative side of the selling task. This could take the form of more emphasis on opening new accounts, installing an automatic reorder system for replacing customers' regular stock, more emphasis on pushing new items, and additional attention on helping customers with product utilization and promotional problems. The model also suggests that increasing the work load and obtaining more accurate estimates of territorial potential would help improve sales performance. Although these recommendations are only meaningful for the company supplying the data, the method can be employed by other firms to help improve sales force evaluation procedures.

Table 11-5
Explaining Sales in Twenty-Five Territories With Eight Performance Factors

Variable	Percent of Sales Explained
Number of accounts	.57
Industry potential	.07
Company market share change	.05
Workload per account	.02
Performance of salesman	.01
Company market share	Insignificant
Length of employment of salesman	Insignificant
Company advertising expenditures	Insignificant

Source. David W. Cravens, Robert B. Woodruff, and Joe C. Stamper, "An Analytical Approach for Evaluating Sales Territory Performance," *Journal of Marketing,* Vol. 36 (January 1972) p. 35. Reprinted by permission of the American Marketing Association.

Summary

This chapter has examined the components of the sales management task as they are performed in modern business organizations. Selling is basically a personal encounter between the salesman and his customer and the firm must understand how this relationship works. If salesmen with certain characteristics are more successful than others then it may pay to select or train fieldmen to fill these needs. The optimum size of the salesforce is hard to pin down unless figures are available showing how revenues respond to different numbers of salesmen. If these data can be obtained, then salesmen should be added until the marginal profit from an additional salesman is equal to the marginal cost of adding another man. In the absence of sales response data, the firm can set the size of the sales force on the basis of what they can afford or the work load that needs to be performed. The creation of equitable territories for salesmen is important for building morale and improving the efficiency of the sales organization. Sales territories are usually created by combining geographic areas and the computer has proven to be a great help in speeding up this tedious and recurring task. Once sales territories have been created, the sales manager must decide how to deploy the sales force to cover different customers and products lines. Improved allocations of selling time have been achieved by studying responses to alternative call strategies and employing models that help direct efforts to the most productive products or customers. In addition, the careful scheduling and routing of salesmen through their territories can reduce expenses and increase the number of calls that can be made by the sales force. Salesmen also must be rewarded for their services and the design of compensation plans is one of the most creative jobs performed by sales managers. The idea is to mix up a blend of salary, bonuses, commissions, and noncash incentives that stimulates the salesmen to work hard and maximizes the profits of the firm at the same time. The final sales management task is to evaluate the sales performance that has been achieved. This requires decisions on what factors measure success and the subsequent inclusion of these criteria in a sales reporting system that is both easy to use and economical to operate.

Questions

1. Sales organizations can be set up on either a customer, product, or geographic orientation. Describe situations where each system would lead to optimum results.

2. How important is it for territories to have equal sales potential and equal workloads?

3. What information does the sales manager need to decide whether to increase or decrease the number of fieldmen under his control?

4. How should a company split the marketing budget between advertising and personal selling expenditures?

5. Under what conditions should sales compensation plans emphasize commissions, salary, bonus, recognition awards, contests, or fringe benefits?

6. Since customer density varies widely, how can a sales manager create territories with equal work loads?

7. How many different sales reports does a sales manager need?

8. What are the key factors that determine whether models can be used successfully to allocate sales efforts across customers and products.

9. What criteria are most important in evaluating sales performance? Do the weights attached to these factors change over time and across districts?

10. Efficient scheduling and routing of salesmen can lead to significant economies. What techniques are available to help solve these problems and why have sales managers been able to increase their utilization of these techniques in recent years?

11. You have recently moved from a field sales position to a new job as sales analyst for a competitor of your old employer. The new job pays 25 percent more and all relocation expenses were paid by the new company. At a cocktail party during a sales meeting the general sales manager begins to ask you detailed questions about the wages, costs, price discounts, and customers of your former employer. What should you do?

12. Jones Inc. a manufacturer of industrial equipment, was trying to help their salesmen allocate their time more efficiently to individual accounts. They developed a multiple regression equation to show the relationship between current selling time allocations and customer potential and current sales to customers for their 100 man salesforce. The equation took the form:

$$T = .95 + .005P + .01S$$

where T is the percentage of a salesmen's total time spent with a specific account, .95 is the amount of time to be spent on any account regardless of size, P is the account's potential in thousands of dollars, and S is current sales to the account in thousands. Thus if an account had a potential volume of $500,000 and current sales of $200,000, the salesman would devote 5.45 percent of his time to this customer $[.95 + (.005 \times 500) + (.01 \times 200)]$. All company salesmen were paid on commission. Do you think this is a good way for company salesmen to allocate their time? Under what conditions would the formula work best? When would it be of little value?

Case 11-1
Dovinsher Drug Company[1]

Dovinsher Drug Company hired David Lear as a salesman near the end of 1967. All indications were that Lear was well qualified for the position, and Bob Heller, the sales manager, anticipated that Lear would become one of the firm's more productive salesmen.

David Lear applied on November 28, 1967 for a position with Dovinsher Drug Company at the suggestion of a pharmacist friend who was employed at the Boynton Pharmacy, one of Dovinsher's customers. On his application, Lear gave the following as his reason for desiring to work for Dovinsher:

Having learned through Cliff Wilson of Boynton Pharmacy that Dovinsher Drug Company was seeking a representative for the Haywood area, I immediately began a personal investigation and found that Dovinsher Drug was a progressive organization and, by virtue of its marketing and

research on hormone products, was a leader in its field.

With my experience in the service as a medical corpsman, coupled with the four-year premedical program in college and part-time as an industrial first-aid attendant, I feel convinced that I can succeed in medical sales.

By virtue of the aforementioned, and with the desire and temperament for meeting and conversing with people, I feel that I can be of use to myself and for the betterment of the organization.

Lear sent his application to the home office of Dovinsher; from there it was forwarded to Sam Foythner, who at the time was manager of the Haywood district. Foythner hired Lear after interviewing him once, pending a favorable retail credit report and a successful physical examination, both of which he (Foythner) instituted.

The following is a letter from Sam Foythner (district manager) to Bob Heller (sales manager), dated December 10, 1967:

Mr. David Lear is being employed by us on December 13. He is being hired as a replacement for Rudy Flemer after the first of the year.

We are not enclosing the file on Mr. Lear at this time, since it and his processing have not been completed. So far we have only his application and the investigational report from Retail Credit. Seemingly premature action is being taken to employ him because (a) of the action taken in Mr. Flemer's case, outlined in yesterday's correspondence, (b) Mr. Lear is unemployed, and (c) any other arrangements would have delayed our employing him until at least the second week in January, one month hence. Reference inquiries have been sent to previous employers, and his character references listed on his application. A physical has been scheduled for his first day of employment and training here. He has been given to understand that his permanency in Dovinsher employment is contingent upon our receiving favorable reports from these sources.

Mr. Lear will begin his employment on December 13 with training under Mr. Dunhill's supervision (new district manager to replace Foythner about January 1, 1968). He should be on open expense until December 20, receiving fixed expense for the last one third of the month. His starting salary is to be $550 per month. He has his own car, a 1965 Plymouth, which he intends to use on his territorial assignment with Dovinsher. Mr. Dunhill, I believe, can and will take care of all the supplies and equipment needed for Mr. Lear to start on territory. He has most of it here, and it will be supplemented by that taken over from Mr. Flemer.

Briefly, Mr. Lear is thirty-four years of age, married, and has one child less than two years of age. He is a nice-looking, neat-appearing, dark-complexioned individual (Slavic descent) with black hair, brown eyes, height 5 feet 9 inches, and weight 160 pounds. His wife, too, seen during my interview, is a dark, very attractive, sensible woman, age about twenty-five. Mr. Lear has completed pre-med at Haywood University and was a pharmacist's mate in the Navy for three years. His background includes primarily four years as a chemist in customer service for Frampton Corporation. His only selling came from part-time work while attending school.

Mr. Lear's outside activities included:
  Sports: basketball
  Editor: high school newspaper
  President: Slavic Youth Organization
  Reading preferences: *Business Week, Chemical Week, Factory Management, Selling*
  Mr. Lear's application and employment file should be completed within a few days. It will be sent to you at that time along with your file

copy and the original, signed Letter of Employment.

The following are replies to letters sent by Foythner to references given by Lear:

Dear Mr. Foythner:
I have known Dave Lear since he was a child. He is honest, trustworthy, and very intelligent. I can recommend him without qualification whatsoever.
  (signed) F. Gayton
    Municipal Judge
    City of Riverville

Dear Mr. Foythner:
It is a pleasure to recommend Mr. David Lear for a position on your staff.
I have known Mr. Lear and his family for several years and have always found them to be honest and stable members of the community. His appearance and way of presenting himself should make him a good addition to your group.

I have known many of the representatives of the Dovinsher Drug Company, and I feel confident he will be a successful member of the detail sales staff.
  (signed) Sincerely yours,
    Flavius P. Golus, M.D.

The following information was received from Lear's former employer, Frampton Corporation, on a form sent by Dovinsher:

Date of employment: 6/30/63-9/8/67
Reason for termination: Own volition
Position held: Chemist
Would you rehire: No
Quality of work: Good
Quantity of work: Good
Attitude: Fair
Attendance: Excellent

The following remark was added: "Lear left because he wanted to do sales work and we had no opening in that department."

The following Retail Credit report was received December 11, 1967:

Sales ability and qualifications: Average
Scope of investigation: During the investigation of Mr. David Lear, the field investigator talked to a personal friend who has known him all during his lifetime, a present residential neighbor who has known him two years, a former employee who knew him four years, and also another employer with whom he worked for two months.

Summary of employment: David Lear was employed with the Frampton Corporation, a firm engaged in plating equipment manufacturing from 6/30/63 to 9/8/67. He was a chemist in their customers' service laboratory. He was on their training program and was doing very well until he became impatient, as he wanted to go into their sales field and they did not have an opening for him at this time. He had some customer contact work in which he would go out and help customers with their problems. He was a very competent worker and needed very little supervision. He left of his own accord for a position where he would be doing sales work. He is eligible for rehire.

Applicant was employed in the personnel department of the Valley Forge Iron Works, a large steel manufacturer from 11/18/56 to 1/15/57 when he returned from the service, prior to going to college. His record was clear with this firm.

The following report was received from Life Extension on Lear's physical examination: Class 1—fit for any type of employment.

Memo from Foythner (district manager) to Thomas (division manager) concerning Dave Lear's personnel file, dated January 3, 1968:

Attached is the file on our recently employed representative for the Haywood area, Mr. Dave Lear. Mr. Lear's file was held in our pending file for completion; however, it appears that no more letters of reference are forthcoming. Should we receive additional references, we shall forward them to you immediately.

Memo from Thomas to Personnel Division:

Mr. Foythner has employed Mr. Dave Lear for Territory 109, formerly covered by Mr. Flemer. His effective date of employment was December 13, 1967, with a starting salary of $9600 per year. The file on Mr. Lear is attached.

Memo to Thomas from Lear concerning car depreciation fund (a fund built up monthly to cover depreciation of salesmen's cars; normally held by Dovinsher until a new car was purchased), dated January 15, 1968:

It is respectfully requested that the car depreciation fund for January and February be sent directly to me. Thank you.

Memo to Dunhill (district manager) from Thomas (division manager), dated January 18, 1968:

I believe you will recall from our telephone conversation that Mr. Lear is having a considerable amount of doctor bills due to the pernicious vomiting of his four-month-old baby. He will use this money for medical payments. I suggest we give it to him for these two months only.

Memo from Thomas to Kraft (controller) concerning auto reserve—Mr. Lear, dated February 7, 1968:

This is an unusual request; however, it was approved in a conversation with Mr. Dunhill. Apparently Mr. Lear has incurred some bills through illness in his family and requests his entire auto reserve at this time. He would like to have his January deposit, and, in addition, send him the deduction for February. If an amount must be kept on deposit to keep the account current, please indicate this on the check stub.

Memo from Dunhill (district manager) to Burke (training director) concerning Dave Lear's attendance at training class, March 15, 1968; memo dated February 4, 1968:

Dave Lear and I worked together this past week for a couple of days. I believe he is ready for the training class despite the short time he has been on territory. But . . .

Dave has a family problem that may not clear up before the training class and could seriously interfere with his doing as good a job as he might. He has a four-month-old daughter who has been vomiting perniciously since birth. They have spent a lot of medical time and money on the child and a definite diagnosis still has not been reached. I know he loses a lot of sleep at nights walking with the baby. Inasmuch as this is their firstborn, you could expect a number of telephone calls to Haywood while he is in training. There could be a possibility that he might be called home if surgery is indicated.

Dave has any number of times asked when he would be allowed to go in to our home office for training. If, on the basis of the above personal information, you would like to delay his training until the next class, the additional "field seasoning" would not hurt him a bit.

Memo from Frobisher (insurance manager) to Lear, dated March 4, 1968:

Request you complete and return the attached Automobile Insurance Agreement, which should have been submitted when you were first employed.

On March 15, Lear entered the training class, which met at the Dovinsher home office for one week out of each month.

Memo from Dunhill (district manager) to Lear concerning transfer of Sales Control Unit, dated April 8, 1968:

Dave, I just received final approval from Mr. Thomas for you to take over Territories 111-112, effective April 1, 1968, as you requested.

Needless to tell you these are key territories in our district, and it is not the usual thing to entrust two territories to a relatively new man. However, the showing you have made with Dovinsher in the relatively short time you've been with us, makes me believe that you will do a job in those territories and that two of them are not too much.

That's on the plus side of the ledger. Against making the switch was the change itself. By that I mean we've shifted men so frequently in the Haywood area in the past year that our accounts no doubt must wonder what we are doing. I'm sure you'll be able to satisfy any questions that may come up as the result of this switch in territories.

As you can appreciate, this change will no doubt make a lot of extra work for not a few people in our home office. The best way you and I can justify this change is to have your and my objective met with at least 100 percent. Can you do it? I know you can or I wouldn't have passed along your request. Now it's up to you to prove I was right in requesting the change from Home Office.

I've asked Bud Gingold to have his territory records ready to pass on to you; would you make arrangements with him to pick up this material at the earliest possible date? You already know which syndicated accounts you will be covering from my previous memo.

If there are any questions you'd like to go over, I'll be in Haywood during the week of April 25, staying at the Blakeston. How was the training class, Dave? I'll be interested to hear your impressions on that.

Memo from Thomas (division manager) to Lear, dated April 13, 1968:

To date we have not received your monthly summary for March. In order for you to be reimbursed for your expenses, it is necessary for us to have this report. Would you please forward it as soon as possible.

Memo from Lear to Thomas, dated May 9, 1968:

It was called to my attention that I had not submitted any copies of prescription blanks. I misplaced the bulletin pertaining to this matter and overlooked mailing them in.

This is wholly my fault and I am sorry this had to happen. I do not expect nor anticipate any credit for these Rx blanks. However, to show that I have obtained some, I am remitting these 21 blanks.

Memo from Dunhill to Thomas, dated May 12, 1968, concerning actual expenses and budget variances:

Thank you for the above report. I have gone over the report quite thoroughly and believe the biggest single headache as far as expenses go are samples. I'm about 40 percent over my allotment.[2] The rest of the report doesn't look too bad for me. Attached are some figures that will be of interest to you and that I shall use at the District meeting (names hidden, of course).

It is quite evident from this breakdown that certain Haywood District representatives need education in the use of samples. Rest assured this will be taken care of in the immediate future. I have attempted to cut sample requests of the entire district to put myself more into line with my budget and naturally have had some objections from the men.

In the future may I be sent all sample requests from Mr. Lear and Mr. Gingold, whether they be the regular requests or requests for physicians on physician request forms.

Memo from Dunhill to Thomas, dated June 4, 1968:

I'll be looking for you on the 16th.

If you have no objections, I wish you would work with Lear on the 17th instead of Raymonds. Will you notify the man of your intention to work with him?

Memo from Frobisher (insurance manager) to Lear, dated June 22, 1968:

Second Request

I have been advised that you are using your personally owned automobile for Dovinsher business. You are undoubtedly aware that it is our policy to cover all of our representatives under our Master Automobile Insurance Policy and we pay 50 percent of the liability premium.

Please complete the attached insurance agreement and, if you desire the additional optional coverages, please check off the desired coverages. If you are currently carrying insurance, please cancel your policy and advise the

---

[2] Salesmen were allotted a certain number of samples per month. This limitation was necessary because of the high cost of drug samples.

date of cancellation so that I can make our effective date concurrent. If you have not been carrying insurance, you have been covered under our policy ever since you joined our company, beginning December 19, 1967.

Upon receipt of the completed attached form, I will be in communication with you concerning the premium payment, which is accomplished through monthly salary deductions. If you have any questions concerning this insurance, please do not hesitate to call upon me.

Memo from Frobisher to Dunhill (district manager), dated July 8, 1968:

Last December 15th we were formally advised through channels that Mr. Lear had been employed by us and was using his personally owned automobile for Dovinsher business. When I did not receive a completed Automobile Insurance Agreement we wrote to him on March 4th requesting that he complete the necessary form, which we enclosed. For some reason he did not answer my memo so I wrote again to him on June 22nd, a copy of which is attached.

I cannot understand why Mr. Lear will not complete the form or at least drop a note in connection with the matter.

Therefore, I will appreciate your discussing this matter with him the next time you see him and see what you can do about getting the form completed. As you know, it is our firm policy that all representatives must be insured under our Master Policy and that we pay 50 percent of the premium. Furthermore, it would be mighty embarrassing if he became involved in a serious accident and we had not had an opportunity to register his automobile with the insurance company.

Your cooperation in handling this matter will be sincerely appreciated.

Memo from Dunhill to Lear, dated July 16, 1968:
As you have requested, you will be covering only Territory 111 sometime after the 15th of August. George O'Brien will be covering Territory 112 after we are able to train a man around that time for Territory 110 on the East Side. I would appreciate your arranging to transfer to Mr. O'Brien your records on Territory 112 at such time as the assignments are announced as firm.

The transfer of an up-to-date and neat route book to a new man is always an indication of the working habits of a representative. I know the material you transfer to Mr. O'Brien will be in the best possible arrangement you can make it, Dave.

Memo from Dunhill to Lear, dated July 30, 1968:

Dave, you remember when I called you a couple of weeks ago, I asked if you had submitted a route list for the month of July? I mentioned I had not received a photostat of it from the office so perhaps it had become misplaced, and asked if you would send me a copy of it. I have not as yet recieved it and of course the need has passed with the end of July. Now I find I have everyone's route list for August except yours. You remember these are due in the Home Office before the 15th of the month preceding the month for which they are made out. Would you please submit your route lists through the month of October to our Home Office as soon as possible?

Memo from Burke (training director) to Lear, dated August 5, 1968:

You did an excellent job in the final March Training Class Examination, Dave, with a score of 96 in sales and 94 in the medical section, ranking you fifth in both instances in your class.

We are attaching your papers, which I am sure you will like to look over and keep in your files as an excellent review.

We enjoyed having you here in the Home Office, and I am looking forward to seeing you in the Haywood area.

Memo from Lear to Professional Service Department, dated August 25, 1968:

I have been informed by our family doctor that he wishes to place my mother on Articol for bronchial asthma. She will be using (3) three tablets per day. As her need is decreased I will inform you. May I have the Articol tablets sent to my address.

Memo from Lear to Thomas (division manager), dated August 25, 1968:

I wonder if you can help me? I am desirous of purchasing a new home. Before I can do same, I must have certain information relayed for approval of a G I. loan. I need an employment verification letter in triplicate, addressed to "Whom it may concern," including the following information:

(a) Type of work—including qualifications, such as degree required, technical background, etc.
(b) Base rate—this should include also bonuses, expenses, etc.
(c) Earnings thus far.
(d) Length of employment.

Any other information that would be conducive toward an approval of a loan will be appreciated. Thanking you, I remain,

The above memo was forwarded to the Personnel Division for preparation of "To whom it may concern" letter, which was sent to Lear on August 30.

Memo from Dunhill (district manager) to Lear, dated August 29, 1968:

Once again, Dave, I have everyone's route list for September except yours. Since I have not received the route lists requested exactly a month ago, I would like to ask you for the third time, will you please make these out and submit them to the Home Office for duplication.

Excerpt from Dunhill's monthly report for August, 1968:

Lear's operation has not been the best, and a personal interview with facts and figures was held. It is hoped this will increase his activities to what they can be.

Excerpt from Dunhill's monthly report for September:

Lear, who also appears to be delinquent in his activities, was interviewed for the third time, and suggestions were made as to how he could improve his operations.

Memo from Dunhill to Thomas (division manager), dated November 8, 1968:

As previously mentioned to you in our phone conversations, the above named man (Lear) has been leaving home late in the morning and coming home early in the afternoons. Lear's call activities have been discussed with him on previous occasions. They quickly increased and have been running consistently at about seven per day. One day, while in his neighborhood about 4:30 P.M., I drove by his house to find him home (October 21). The following Monday (October 24) he left for work at 10:50 A.M. and got home at 3:30 P.M. On October 25, he left home for work at 10:30 A.M. and made only two calls (Alpha Pharmacy and Hayes Drug Company) before noon—two places, incidentally, that are reputed to be purchasers of samples and whom Mr. Gingold (who was formerly with us) had reportedly sold samples to. I had lunch with Lear on this date, saying nothing about "accidentally" meeting him in the Hayes Drug Company.

In checking the daily report of activities with the physicians on whom he called, the following is presented. Using the excuse of a supposedly misplaced catalogue, I personally called on the physicians shown below on November 6:
Lear admitted to me today that he has been faking reports because, as he put it. "A lot of others do it also." He also admitted leaving late in the mornings for work and coming home early. He gave as his reason "the amount of Saturday work" he has been doing. When asked why he did not submit reports for Saturday work, he had no answer.

Lear, almost from the first day he was hired (approximately one year ago), has been extremely difficult to supervise. He asked for and received a transfer from Territory 109, for which he was hired, to his present one, Territory 111 because it would be closer to home for him, and I thought this would improve his attitude and work

Physician's Name	Date Reported Called On	Comments of M.D.
Dr. M. J. Hubinger	October 24	Did not see Lear. Someone left literature.
Dr. Henry Swift	October 24	Could have seen, doesn't remember him, though.
Dr. G. A. Read	October 24	Physician's day off.
Dr. George Lerch	October 24	Physician saw Lear.
Dr. E. S. Trueheart	October 24	Physician did not see, never in office in daytime.
Dr. L. E. Zeman	October 24	Saw Lear.
Dr. Laura L. Young	October 24	M.D. does not remember seeing him nor a detail on Articol.
Dr. Albert H. Campbell	October 21	M.D. said man left literature but hasn't seen Dovinsher man personally in long time.
Dr. J. M. Gillespie	October 21	M.D. did see him.
Dr. K. H. Packard	October 21	M.D. says he was too busy to see man who called; hasn't been detailed on Articol in months.
Dr. Ray A. Chandler	October 28	M.D. doesn't remember seeing Lear, but could have.
Dr. John R. Banach	October 28	M.D. saw Lear.
Dr. Fred La Mar	October 28	M.D. says he probably saw him, doesn't remember.
Dr. Thomas R. Koontz	October 28	M.D. saw him.

activities. On three separate occasions Mr. Lear and I had discussions on how to improve his operation from planning a day's work on paper the evening before (three requests for this alone) to answering Home Office correspondence without repeated requests (see July 8, 1968, memo from Mr. Frobisher) to sending in route lists, Daily Report of Activities, etc. The last time I talked with Mr. Lear, he came to my home and we talked in the room I use for an office for nearly three hours. At that time he outlined those things on which he would begin to work and improve himself. Attached is my copy of this list (attachment A), along with notes made on items to talk to him about (attachment B). Of these, his sample requests have been less, due to my editing; nothing else has been accomplished.

Lear has been unable to adjust himself to writing orders in drug stores despite demonstrations and personal counseling (he only sold three deals in two accounts).

Lear is bitter and may be vindictive about our conversations today. He was extremely difficult to talk with.

ATTACHMENT A
List Prepared by Lear of Things He Would Work On to Improve Himself: September 28, 1968

1. Supply information on activities to district manager and home office.
2. Maintain route book in good condition and up to date.
3. Report daily activities.
4. Read sales manual from cover to cover.
5. Call activities—increase M.D. calls.
6. Attention to correspondence—promptness.
7. Take sales course.
8. Watch gripes.
9. Sampling.

ATTACHMENT B

List Prepared by Dunhill of Things About Which to Talk to Lear

Does he think company and I have been fair with him?
Been with company over six months.
Wants salary raise—conversation sometime back.
No real evidence of efforts.
Remind him of initial training—did little or no studying.
Attitude since then—surly to me and to home office; uncooperative.
Itinerary requests—three of them.
Doesn't appear that he is trying to cooperate with company and do things the way they outline them.
Belittles company in light of entertaining done by previous employer.
Conferences: hotel room, district sales meeting; at his home, August 3, 1968. Noted little change if any; typically is wanting to keep all of Hanford (large drug chain) purchases for self; suggest he try to be a little more cooperative.
Making out outline for next day's work—three requests.
Daily call average: first six months, 4 M.D.'s; first three months, 3.5 M.D.'s; second three months, 6.0 M.D.'s
Samples: six physicians per day for twenty working days, 120 samples per month. Huge requests—more than anyone else in district.
Fatzler Drug letter: What did he do about it?
Route book: up to date—not on inspection.
Relations with accounts: i.e., direct account call with him where there were two owners—irritating accounts.

QUESTIONS

1. What mistakes were made during the selection and training of the new detailman David Lear?
2. What is Lear doing with all the samples?
3. What action should be taken by Dovinsher with respect to Lear? By whom?
4. Could this situation have been prevented? How?

Case 11-2
Servel Office Supply Company[1]

The Servel Office Company manufactured a wide line of office cements, pastes, artists' supplies, stamp pads, ink, ink eradicators, crayons, tempera paints, marking pencils, and ink solvents. During the past four years sales had increased from $1,504,881 to $2,359,337. In December, the president received the final income statement for the company's fiscal year ending November 30. He was extremely disappointed in the net income figure of $23,595 (Exhibit 1). The president immediately began an analysis of the company's plans for the following year.

Servel, which had originally specialized in the ink business, was an old and well-established company. With the decline in the sale of conventional writing ink as the result of the ball-point pen, it had expanded into other lines of office supplies. The policy of adding new products was successful, and the fastest-growing items in Servel's line were water-color paints, rubber cement, stamp pads and stamp-pad inks.

The Servel sales force consisted of twenty salesmen, five manufacturers' representatives, and a promotion man. Sales were made directly to large retail stationers and to wholesale office supply companies. Many customers were both wholesalers and retailers. Institutional and industrial customers were not sold direct; they generally bought from retail stationers. One salesman handled the major chains and the balance of the sales force worked specific territories. The same salesman who handled the chain-store business was also responsible for export sales, which were a growing factor accounting for about 6 percent of the company's current sales.

One manufacturer's representative covered the state of Washington, another Oregon, and a third northern California. These were supervised by the salesman in that territory. Another representative covered Colorado, New Mexico, and Arizona, but he was dropped recently because his volume was too small. The fifth manufacturer's representative covered almost all the rest of the United States. Salesmen from these representatives competed with Servel's own salesmen. Management felt, however, that this competition was good because it forced Servel's salesmen to be more aggressive and it was one way to raise the firm's sales volume quickly.

The president believed that aggressive selling in all territories had resulted in sales growth but that it had also been responsible for higher selling costs, thus reducing net income. Salesmen had been placed in new territories where there was no established volume. The firm had to support these men until they developed the market to a profitable level. Such investments could not be capitalized, however, and had to be carried as expenses. He had the controller prepare a study of the sales potential for the company's products by areas. This study (Table 1) substantiated his belief that more effort had to be expended to develop areas in which Servel's present sales were relatively low.

Exhibit 1
Servel Office Supply Income Statement

Net sales	$2,359,337	100.0%
Costs of sales	1,403,805	59.5
Gross margin	955,532	40.5
Commercial expenses		
Shipping and delivery	224,137	9.5
Selling expense	408,165	17.3
Administrative	198,184	8.4
Advertising & promotion	101,451	4.3
Total expenses	931,937	39.5
Net operating income	23,595	1.0

Servel sales had always been low in New York City, for example. This city had been part of two larger territories, but in the previous year Clark and Woodbury, were assigned to New York City alone. One of these men, Woodbury, was to concentrate on industrial accounts to be sold directly—a new procedure for Servel. Strand and Stevenson were also new salesmen who were given new territories in which to build up Servel's volume.

In checking selling costs in some of the new areas, the president found that selling costs ran as high as 24 percent of net sales. In the more established territories covered by experienced salesmen, the costs of selling averaged 13 percent (see Table 2). The company did not have a uniform sales compensation plan, but believed that the ideal plan would be straight commission and hoped that ultimately all salesmen could be compensated on this basis.

Table 1
Office Supply Potential and Servel Sales

Salesmen	Territory	Share of U.S. Potential	Annual Servel Sales	Share of Servel Sales
		%	$	%
Payne	New England and part of New York	5.4	130,943	7.1
Clark	Part of New York City	4.1	45,641	2.5
Woodbury	Part of New York City	4.1	63,793	3.4
Dillion	Parts of New York, Pennsylvania, W. Virginia, and Maryland	6.4	52,681	2.8
Strand	Delaware, New Jersey, and parts of Pennsylvania and New York	6.7	70,344	3.8
Adams	Virginia, District of Columbia, Tennessee, Kentucky, and parts of W. Virginia, Maryland, and Indiana	6.5	125,915	6.8
Pospisil	N. Carolina, S. Carolina, Georgia, and Florida	6.9	125,840	6.8
Berwick	Ohio	5.7	80,631	4.4
Stevenson	Alabama, Mississippi, Louisiana, and Arkansas	4.7	50,037	2.7
Thomas	Southern Michigan and parts of Indiana	4.3	64,655	3.5
MacRae	N. Dakota, S. Dakota, and parts of Minnesota, Wisconsin, and Michigan	3.7	104,547	5.6
Herbert	Parts of Minnesota, Wisconsin, and parts of Chicago	4.4	81,751	4.4
Finia	Northern Illinois and northwest Indiana	4.7	167,043	9.1
Ragsdale	Part of Chicago	4.0	251,761	13.6
Henderson	Missouri and Iowa	4.8	110,079	5.9
Lewis	Kansas, Nebraska, Oklahoma, Wyoming, Colorado, New Mexico	4.8	69,937	3.7
Miller	Texas	5.6	97,604	5.3
Hinit	Washington, Oregon, Northern California, Montana, Idaho and Northern Nevada	7.4	74,852	4.0
Dashiell	Southern Nevada, Arizona and Southern California	5.8	84,948	4.6
	Total Territories	100.0	1,853,002	100.0
Strother	Chain stores and export		420,550	
Naismith	Promotion man		3,964	
Five manufacturers' representatives			78,126	
House sales[a]			3,695	
	Total sales		2,359,337	

[a] Sales made by major officers of the company.

Table 2
Servel Sales and Selling Expenses by Territory

Salesman	Sales	Salary and/or Commission	Expenses[a]	Total Selling Cost as of Sales (Percent)	Method of Compensation
Payne	$130,943	$13,094	$3,000	12.3	$250 monthly expense allowance plus 10% of net sales
Clark	45,641	8,645	1,000	21.1	Reimbursed expenses and salary
Woodbury	63,793	15,000	1,500	24.3	Car, reimbursed expenses, and salary
Dillion	52,681	6,720	2,400	17.3	$200 monthly expense allowance plus 12% of net sales[b]
Strand	70,344	8,400	5,500	18.3	Car, reimbursed expenses, and salary
Adams	125,915	12,592	3,000	12.4	$250 monthly expense allowance plus 10% of net sales
Pospisil	125,840	12,584	3,000	12.4	$250 monthly expense allowance plus 10% of net sales
Berwick	80,631	8,063	2,400	13.0	$200 monthly expense allowance plus 10% of net sales[a]
Stevenson	50,037	6,000	5,000	22.0	Car, reimbursed expenses, and salary
Thomas	64,655	9,600	5,000	22.6	Car, reimbursed expenses, and salary
MacRae	104,547	10,454	2,400	12.3	$200 monthly expense allowance plus 10% of net sales
Herbert	81,751	8,200	4,100	15.0	Reimbursed expenses and salary
Finan	167,043	12,000	2,800	8.8	Car reimbursed expenses, and salary
Ragsdale	251,761	15,500	3,200	7.4	Car, reimbursed expenses, and salary
Henderson	110,079	11,008	3,000	12.7	$250 monthly expense allowance plus 10% of net sales
Lewis	69,937	8,392	3,000	16.3	$250 monthly expense allowance plus 12% of net sales
Miller	97,604	8,088	5,000	13.4	Car, reimbursed expenses, and salary
Hinit	74,852	9,600	5,600	20.3	Car, reimbursed expenses, and salary
Dashiell	84,948	11,000	4,300	18.0	Car, reimbursed expenses, and salary
Strother	420,550	28,000	5,800	8.0	Reimbursed expenses and salary
Naismith	3,964	10,000[c]	4,300[b]	360.7[c]	Car, reimbursed expenses, and salary
Five mfr.'s reps.	78,126	8,472	—	10.8	See footnote[d]
House sales	3,695	—	18,000[e]	487.0[e]	
Totals	$2,359,337	$241,412[e]	$93,300[f]	487.0[e]	

[a]Rounded to nearest $100 because final expense reports were not in.
[b]Commission rate was 13 percent part of year.
[c]Naismith was the company promotion man. While his salary and expenses were properly chargeable to selling expenses in the broadest sense, they could not be compared directly with his own sales, since he spent only a small part of his time in face-to-face selling.
[d]Three representatives were paid commissions of 10 percent; one got 15 percent; and one had a sliding scale of 5 percent on all sales over $10,000.
[e]House sales were made by company officers, whose salaries and expenses were not directly chargeable as selling expense. Travel expenses of $18,000 were not all properly allocated to selling.
[f]The difference between total selling expenses shown here and the total in the operating statement is made up of the sales managers salary and expenses and office sales expenses.

Sales forecasts were prepared by three independent procedures. First, each salesman was instructed to submit a realistic estimate of his next year's sales, broken down by fifteen major product groups. This estimate was to reflect current trends in the salesman's territory.

The second sales projection was based on a separate estimate for each of the 150 items handled by the company. The president, controller, and sales manager worked on this forecast. In making this projection the historical record was first considered and then modified by knowledge of industry conditions with respect to the specific item. Long-term trends in demand and competitive conditions were considered. For example, heavy sales promotions in the previous year or price cutting that resulted in the dumping of unusually large supplies on the market were factors that would affect sales in the following year.

The third sales projection was made at a round-table discussion among the president, sales manager, controller, and several of the older, more experienced salesmen. At this conference, sales were forecast for each of the fifteen product groups. Each group was considered as a unit, and dollar volume was estimated for the coming year from data on past sales, current trends, economic conditions, and any other information possessed by the salesmen.

The three sales forecasts for each of the fifteen products groups were then considered and a "best" forecast selected. For example, the forecasts for tempera paints were $290,000, $300,000, and

Exhibit 2

Forecast of Sales and Selling Costs by Salesman

Salesman	Forecast Sales	Forecast Selling Costs	
		Salary and/or Commission	Expenses
Payne	$130,000	$13,000	$3,000
Clark	75,000	11,000	2,500
Woodbury	70,000	16,000	2,500
Dillion	a	a	a
Strand	74,000	8,000	5,500
Adams	135,000	13,000	3,000
Pospisil	135,000	13,500	3,000
Berwick[b]	130,000	9,000	2,400
Stevenson	65,000	6,000	4,200
Thomas	80,000	9,600	4,000
MacRae	108,000	10,800	2,400
Herbert	80,000	8,700	4,000
Finan	182,500	13,000	3,000
Ragsdale	263,000	16,500	3,800
Henderson	125,000	12,500	3,000
Lewis[c]	90,000	9,900	2,400
Miller	90,000	9,000	5,000
Hinit	85,000	10,000	5,600
Dashiell	95,000	11,500	4,000
Strother	450,000	36,000	6,600
Naismith	d	10,000	4,500
Four mfr.'s reps.[e]	75,000	7,500	—
House sales[f]	5,000	b	12,000
Total	$2,542,500	$254,500	$86,400
Less cash discounts	42,500		
Net sales	$2,500,000		

[a] Dillion resigned. His territory was divided between Clark and Berwick.

[b] Berwick's compensation plan was changed, when he got part of Dillion's old territory, to a monthly expense allowance of $200 and a $9000 salary.

[c] Compensation rate changed to $200 monthly expense allowance and 11 percent commission on net sales.

[d] It was planned that Naismith would devote all his time to promotion.

[e] One manufacturer's representative who had covered Colorado, New Mexico, and Arizona was dropped.

[f] House sales would be made by company officers whose salaries could not be charged directly to sales.

$327,000. Since this was a growing product line, the highest estimate was chosen. The total of the group forecasts was $2,500,000. This total was then broken down by salesmen on the basis of their forecasts and past performances (see Exhibit 2).

Next the controller was instructed to prepare an expense budget based upon this level of sales (Exhibit 2). All other items of expense were also estimated and a forecast income and expense statement prepared (Exhibit 3).

The president considered these budgets adequate to appraise whether to develop some territories at a high sales cost. Another use for the budgets developed when the president had to decide whether or not to take part in a $38,000 promotional program that had been presented to the company. This program had not been included in the present budget. The program involved a special dealer promotion on paste and the awarding of prizes, including a number of English bicycles to leading salesmen and dealers.

The president planned to present it at a sales meeting in order to get the reaction of the entire sales force.

QUESTIONS

1. Are Servel's present sales territories equitable and efficient?
2. Should Servel continue to employ the five manufacturers representatives to compete directly with its own salesmen?
3. Would you recommend any changes in Servel's sales compensation and expense plan?
4. Does Servel need to prepare three independent sales forecasts? Why or why not?
5. What value does Servel's projected sales budget (Exhibits 2 and 3) have as a planning and control device?
6. Should Servel participate in the $38,000 promotional campaign? Why or why not?

Exhibit 3

Projected Annual Operating Statements at Three Sales Levels

Net sales	$2,359,000	100.0%	$2,500,000	100.0%	$2,600,000	100.0%
Cost of sales	1,389,000	58.9	1,473,300	58.9	1,531,400	58.9
Gross margin	970,00	41.1	1,026,700	41.1	1,068,600	41.1
Shipping and delivery—variable	188,700	8.0	199,800	8.0	208,000	8.0
Shipping and delivery—fixed	39,600	1.7	39,600	1.6	39,600	1.5
Total shipping and delivery	228,300	9.7	239,400	9.6	247,600	9.5
Selling expense—variable[a]	99,100	4.2	104,700	4.2	109,200	4.2
Selling expense—fixed[b]	316,300	13.4	316,300	12.7	316,300	12.2
Total selling expense	415,400	17.6	421,000	16.9	425,500	16.4
Administrative expense	209,000	8.9	209,000	8.4	209,000	8.0
Advertising and promotion	96,000	4.1	96,000	3.8	96,000	3.7
Total expenses	948,700	40.2	965,400	38.7	978,100	37.6
Projected net profit	21,300	0.9	61,300	2.4	90,500	3.5

[a]Variable selling expenses included commissions only.
[b]Fixed selling expenses included salesmen's salaries of five sales clerical people, sales meeting expenses, and miscellaneous other selling expenses.

Case 11-3
Warrenton Furniture Company[1]

"It's pretty obvious that the S & S territory won't be much better than last year, at least according to the goals we set up. We've been talking about taking action for some time—I guess now is the time." Bill

[1]Case prepared by Neil H. Borden, Jr. of the University of Virginia. Copyright © 1967, Colgate Darden Graduate School of Business Administration, University of Virginia. Reproduced by permission.

Goodman, Western Regional Sales Manager for Warrenton Furniture, was looking at the estimated 1966 sales for the S & S Company, Warrenton's exclusive representative in five western states. The figures indicated that the territory would wind up the year with an approximate 12 percent sales gain over 1965, but reach only 60 percent of its 1966 sales quota. Bill wondered if he would be justified at this point in recommending to Emmett Gleason, Warrenton's Vice-President of Sales, that S & S be notified that their services be terminated as soon as replacements were found. Although such a move had been discussed in the past, Bill knew that considerable study and deliberation would precede any final decision.

WARRENTON FURNITURE COMPANY

Warrenton Furniture, with 1965 sales of slightly over $20 million, was an old and respected member of the furniture industry. The company had enjoyed a substantial growth record since the middle 1950s, almost doubling its size in that time. Growth in the last few years had taxed production facilities despite expansions in plant capacity. Control of the firm was in the hands of the founding Hadley family who continued in active management. Crandell Hadley, a grandson of the company founder, served as President and his brother, Preston Hadley, was Vice-President in charge of manufacturing.

For many years Warrenton produced only casegoods and occasional furniture. Recently, however, an upholstered plant had been acquired in an attempt to broaden product representation at the retail level. Although the upholstered operation was going as well as projected, it accounted for only 9.6 percent of Warrenton's 1965 sales. The 1965 sales in other categories were as follows:

Casegoods	56.3 percent
Occasional	27.2 percent
Cabinets (elec. appliance)	6.9 percent

Warrenton produced highly styled furniture that sold in the higher-price categories. Designs were intended to reflect the latest developments in national and international fashion. Because the company stressed newness and sophistication in its design, the product line, while quite broad in the number of patterns offered, experienced fairly rapid obsolescence.

SALES ORGANIZATION

Emmett Gleason, Warrenton's Vice-President of Sales, had been with the company over forty years, having started as a factory worker early in his youth. Most of Mr. Gleason's experience was in sales and sales management; for a period he had acted as one of the company's sales representatives. Reporting to Mr. Gleason were three regional sales managers (including Bill Goodman, the Western regional sales manager), the advertising manager, and the sales administration manager.

Warrenton achieved national distribution through sales representatives in seventeen sales territories. Most of the representatives served Warrenton exclusively; many were partnerships and a number of the representatives employed additional salesmen. Mr. Gleason was proud of the fact that most of the representatives had been with the company for many years; in fact, within the past ten years only two territories had changed hands. Many of the older representatives had sons in their businesses. Mr. Gleason attributed the low sales-representative turnover to the close personal control he and his regional sales managers exercised over the representatives, the excellence of the product line, the growth of the company, and the opportunity for above average compensation.

The sales representatives received formal letters from the sales managers every quarter appraising them of their performance against quota and discussing general performance and problems in their respective territories. Another quarterly report—the quarterly cumulative order analysis—summarized territory sales by pattern in sales and as a percent of quota. Weekly the representatives received a "sales percentage of quota" report that listed, in rank order, the seventeen territories and their percentage attainment of quota by major product category for the week prior and the year to date. This report also summarized the overall company performance against quota. Representatives also received a constant flow of memoranda covering such things as price changes, specials, stock status, closeouts, new salesmen, advertising news, and so forth.

Beginning in 1966 sales representatives were required to submit a one-page monthly report to sales management covering such items as general area business conditions, news of competition, dealer news, service comments, product comments, design comments, and so forth. These reports were designed to keep management abreast of developments in the field.

Quotas were assigned to each sales territory. These quotas were intended to be realistic measures of what sales level should be attained in a given territory. Sales representatives were assigned these quotas as an attainable goal to work for and were made aware that management was measuring their performance in good part by their achievements against quota. Territory quotas were assigned for casegoods, occasional, upholstery, and total volume, and were expressed as percentages of the overall company sales goals and in dollars. The dollar figures were given for the total year and as a weekly amount. For instance, a representative's quota was expressed as follows:

1966 Quota—G. T. Haverford

	Percent of Company Sales	Weekly	Total Year
Casegoods	5.88	$17,197	$ 790,272
Occasional	5.88	7,327	381,024
Upholstery	5.88	2,714	141,120
Total	5.88	$25,238	$1,312,416

Casegoods and occasional quotas were always an equal percentage of the national total. In the above illustration, upholstery was also equal to casegoods and occasional but only because the territory involved was located in the mid-Atlantic states. Because of the bulk shipping and local competitive problems of upholstery quota burden (relative to casegoods); mid-Atlantic quotas were equal, and western lighter.

Much of the preliminary work on the quotas was done by Melvin Harris, the sales and advertising assistant who had the responsibility for doing much of the sales statistical work. The regional sales managers added their analyses and recommendations to his work and the final decisions were made by Mr. Gleason. The increase in dollar volume projected for the company as a whole were short range corporate goals set by Mr. Crandell Hadley and the Board of Directors. These overall volume goals had been set in the aggregate (by major product group) by projecting company sales trends tempered by general and furniture industry economic forecasts, and by determining specific company growth and profit objectives for each major product group. These goals were reviewed and revised annually.

Specific territory quotas were derived by examining, for each territory, past sales performance, buying power indices, and management objectives for the territory. In setting the quotas the objective was to approach the buying power index (percentage) as closely as practical since this was thought of as the sales share Warrenton should get from each territory. Management believed, however, that this sales potential index had to be tempered by past performance and particular problems in the territory and

thus most territory quotas and buying power indexes for territories usually did not vary by more than one percentage point. Variances on smaller areas such as a state wide basis were more pronounced, however. Warrenton currently employed the Buying Power Index for Household Furniture issued in 1964 by the Southern Furniture Manufacturers' Association. On occasion this index was checked against the estimates of the National Association of Furniture Manufacturers. See Exhibit 1 for 1965 sales by state compared to SFMA and NAFM Buying power indexes.

STAFFORD AND SPROUSE (S & S)

Stafford and Sprouse, a partnership, represented Warrenton in Minnesota, Wisconsin, Iowa, North and South Dakota, and the eastern portion of Nebraska. The men, who were close personal friends as well as partners, lived in Minneapolis.

Campbell Stafford had grown up within sight of the Warrenton plant. Although his family had been able to supply very little in the way of economic advantages he did well in his schooling, made a wide circle of friends (including many in the Gleason and Hadley families), and succeeded in graduating from a good college. Prior to World War II he was assistant principal and a teacher in a local high school. During the war he served over four years as an Army officer. Upon discharge from the military Stafford returned briefly to teaching, but soon sought employment with Warrenton as a sales representative. He was assigned to the Minnesota territory (which had just become open) where Emmett Gleason spent several weeks "breaking him in." Stafford, who was 56, was married and had one grown daughter who was in college. Mr. Gleason described "Cam" (as Stafford was known) as "a good man, a true Christian gentleman, a true friend, a very likable man who tells a good story."

Floyd Sprouse, also in his fifties, joined Stafford in 1953. Sprouse had a background in furniture sales and had been a friend of Stafford's for some time. Mr. Gleason thought of Sprouse as "a gentleman, a fine family man with no vices."

S & S sales, as a percent of overall company retail volume, had been dropping since 1961. Although

	1965	Percent of Quota	1964	Percent of Quota	1963	Percent of Quota
Overall	604,505	61	545,622	52	467,262	55
Casegoods	333,832	54	287,242	46	277,095	56
Occasional	190,693	58	200,460	60	158,659	60
Upholstery	79,980	99	57,920	69	31,508	48

the territory volume had increased from a ten-year low of $467,262 in 1963 to $604,505 in 1965, the peak in sales occurred in 1959 at a level of $746,611. See Exhibit 2 for S & S territory sales and percent of Warrenton volume, 1956-1965.

The territory had repeatedly fallen short of its assigned quotas although there had been some improvement since 1963. The table on page 571 summarizes quota experience 1963 through 1965.

Cam Stafford and Floyd Sprouse had often stated to sales management that they weren't happy with results in their territory. They complained, however, that much of the problem could be ascribed to some poor product quality experienced in the early 1960s (and even before) and product design that for many years just "wasn't right" for the territory. It was their opinion that quality and design were showing improvement but building a territory in face of a "tarnished image" was a slow and difficult task. They did not think that quotas based largely on "theoretical" sales potentials were particularly relevant to their situation. Both men were extremely cooperative, however, and continually pledged to make every effort to reach their assigned goals.

Over the past several years sales management had taken great pains to set quotas for the S & S territory that, in their opinion, would be fair to the men yet reflect the potential of the area. Quota experience for 1965 and the assigned 1966 quota were as follows:

	SFMA BPI	1965 Quota	1965 Sales	1966 Quota
Minnesota	1.8	1.50	1.1	1.45
Wisconsin	2.2	1.84	1.1	1.78
Iowa	1.5	1.25	0.8	1.22
N. & S. Dak.	0.6	0.50	0.05	0.48
Nebraska	0.4	0.33	0.2	0.32
	6.5	5.42	3.25	5.25

BILL GOODMAN'S REVIEW

Bill Goodman had received some preliminary figures on 1966 sales that indicated to him that the S & S territory would show an increase of approximately 12 percent over 1965 but reach only 60 percent of quota. In light of this performance Bill decided to review his 1966 file on the S & S territory.

The first item in the file was the 1965 year end review and 1966 quota setting letter from Mr. Gleason to Cam Stafford and Floyd Sprouse. This annual "December letter" expressed disappointment with the fact that the 1965 quota had not been realized and stressed the importance of meeting quotas in 1966. (See Exhibit 3, December 1965 letter to S & S.)

In late January Bill Goodman had visited the Minnesota territory. Upon returning (somewhat discouraged, as he remembered it) he had a conference with Crandell Hadley and Emmett Gleason at which the

Hearst/SFMA Trading Area	1965 Sales Vol.	SFMA BPI	1965 Vol. Percent of Co.	1965 Vol. as Percent of S & S Territory	BPI as Percent of S & S Territory
Duluth/Superior	$ 15,717	0.220	0.084	2.61	3.38
Fergus Falls	3,083	0.044	0.016	.51	0.68
Mankato	20,928	0.086	0.112	3.46	1.32
Rochester	6,770	0.052	0.036	1.12	0.80
St. Cloud	8,584	0.061	0.046	1.42	0.94
Madison	21,097	0.217	0.113	3.49	3.34
Lincoln	12,030	0.126	0.064	1.99	1.94
Total Territory	$604,505	6.500	3.250	—	—

Total number of active accounts in territory: 177

	1965 Active Accounts	Number of Potential Accounts Per Credit Guide
Duluth/Superior	2	51
Fergus Falls	1	14
Mankato	4	19
Rochester	3	23
St. Cloud	2	18
Madison	4	43
Lincoln	3	37

Exhibit 1

Furniture Order Comparison By State

State	Percent Warrenton 1965 Sales	SFMA Buying Power Index[a]	NAFM—Estimates of Buying Power
New York	14.9	11.4	10.1
California	13.1	11.4	12.6
Illinois	7.6	6.5	5.1
Michigan	6.9	4.7	4.0
Ohio	6.8	5.9	5.4
New Jersey	6.4	4.0	3.5
Pennsylvania	5.4	6.4	6.4
Florida	4.0	2.2	3.5
Texas	3.4	4.7	5.1
Massachusetts	2.7	3.2	2.9
Missouri	2.4	2.5	2.5
Indiana	2.4	2.8	2.6
Georgia	2.3	1.4	2.0
Virginia	2.2	1.6	2.2
D.C.	1.8	0.6	0.8
Maryland	1.8	1.9	1.7
Connecticut	1.6	1.7	1.4
Louisiana	1.5	1.3	1.6
Alabama	1.4	1.1	1.7
Colorado	1.3	1.0	0.9
Minnesota	1.1	1.8	1.7
Wisconsin	1.1	2.2	1.7
Iowa	0.8	1.5	1.3
North Carolina	0.8	1.7	2.6
Tennessee	0.8	1.5	2.1
Arizona	0.6	0.6	0.8
Kentucky	0.6	1.0	1.3
Nebraska	0.5	0.8	0.7
Utah	0.5	0.5	0.5
Kansas	0.4	1.0	0.9
Oklahoma	0.4	0.9	1.4
West Virginia	0.4	0.9	0.8
South Carolina	0.4	0.7	1.2
Mississippi	0.3	0.6	0.7
Washington	0.2	1.7	1.6
Rhode Island	0.2	0.5	0.5
Delaware	0.2	0.3	0.3
New Mexico	0.1	0.4	0.4
Arkansas	0.1	0.5	0.7
Oregon	0.1	1.0	0.7
Nevada	0.1	0.3	0.2
Maine	0.1	0.4	0.3
Idaho	0.1	0.3	0.3
New Hampshire	0.1	0.4	0.2
Wyoming	0.1	0.2	0.2
Montana	0.04	0.4	0.2
North Dakota	0.03	0.3	0.2
South Dakota	0.02	0.3	0.2
Alaska	0.00	0.1	0.1
Hawaii	0.00	0.4	0.1
Vermont	0.00	0.2	0.1

[a]The SFMA Buying Power Index estimated the percentage of total U.S. furniture sales for each area.

Exhibit 2

S & S Territory Sales

Year	S & S Sales Volume	Percent of Warrenton Retail Volume[a]
1956	$540,185	4.21
1957	661,780	5.29
1958	636,016	5.49
1959	746,611	5.30
1960	647,474	4.61
1961	608,042	4.79
1962	486,794	4.19
1963	467,262	3.58
1964	545,622	3.30
1965	604,505	3.25

[a]"Retail" volume excluded cabinet sales that were handled by the home office exclusively.

Exhibit 3

December 1965—Letter to S & S

December 20, 1965
Messrs. Campbell Stafford and Floyd Sprouse

Dear Cam and Floyd:

Your year end figures show $604,505—61 percent Overall, $333,832—54 percent Casegoods, $190,693—58 percent Occasional, and $79,980—99 percent Upholstery. Attached is a sheet showing your quota for 1966. Your overall percentage of quota compares with the factory average of 97 percent and we know that you are very unhappy with these figures and realize that they must be brought up. This year's figures do represent an 11 percent increase over 1964, however.

We would like to once again impress on you the importance of meeting your quota in each of the three product categories. Our production facilities are set up so that we must produce a mix of products within certain limits. For example, if, at a given time, we are selling more casegoods than we can produce, the slack cannot be taken up on the upholstery lines. Therefore, the problem is not solved if we sell heavily in one product category at the expense of another. This is not to say that you balance between product groups. Our quotas are set fairly with the location of your territory and all other pertinent factors in mind. Therefore, there is no excuse for a salesman having wide divergences in his percent to quota in the three product categories. With this in mind, we think you can see that you must concentrate more on casegoods and occasional but remembering your upholstery business must be at quota also.

You have read Crandell Hadley's letter concerning the plans and goals for our company. These goals are reasonable, no one year's increase being more than the increment this past year has shown over 1964. And these goals will have to be met by whatever means necessary.

Cam, as we have discussed, the line is the best it has been in the past several years and of course you have several good patterns going for you. We know that both of you are pushing hard, and we want to help in any way possible in traveling with you or making plans with you.

We naturally are not satisfied with your volume, and neither are you since of course your income certainly is not what it should be. We think it would be a good idea to point toward a six-months review at the end of May and see how the line has developed in your territory, and see how much your sales have developed and see what can be done to make them even higher.

You, naturally, are a very important part in the goals Crandell has set, and must start making your plans—short term and long term—accordingly. If your overall assigned percentage remains the same your territory will have to produce $1,203,000 in 1967 and $1,325,000 in 1968. There is no question but what your territory will need, and can support, an additional man. Both of you have mentioned this to us, and we know you are ready to put on an additional man as business develops.

We hope to be introducing a key account program in each territory during the next few months. This will consist of a list of top accounts that we are selling with goals set for how much we want to sell them and a list of top accounts that we aren't selling with periodical reviews dealing with progress made in opening these accounts.

We will be wanting to know more about your distribution than in the past. We expect to help you move in this respect not only in the field, but by design and better quality which better stores require. This distribution profile of course, is closely connected with the above-mentioned key accounts program. We need to sell more of so-called A & B accounts and certainly overall distribution is affected.

Another program to be initiated is a better communication system between you in the field and the Sales Department. The reporting forms you will receive are self-explanatory. We need more information from you on quality, design, and many facets of this business to help do the job that must be done. This we are asking for monthly.

We want you to call on any one of us here in Sales to help at any time on any problem. Aside from your requests, each of us expect to travel your territory at least once during this year to counsel with you, and help you with these various programs.

We want to wish you the best of luck, and hope 1966 is the best year ever for you.

Sincerely,

Emmett Gleason & Bill Goodman

Stafford and Sprouse 1966 Quota

	Percent	Per Week	Total Year	
Casegoods	5.39	$12,504	$	650,187
Occasional	5.39	6,262		325,625
Upholstery	4.72	2,266		117,868
	5.25	$21,032		$1,093,680

territory problems were outlined and the possibility of a change in representatives discussed. Exhibit 4 is a memorandum "for the files" summarizing the conference.

At the end of the first quarter the territory had shown a 15 percent sales increase over corresponding performance for 1965, but most of the gain was in casegoods. Only one of the major accounts mentioned in the Goodman memorandum had purchased. Exhibit 5 is the first quarter's review letter to S & S.

The rate of sales gain in the territory slipped in the second quarter and the net overall gain for the first half was 11 percent. Exhibit 6 is the first half-year review letter to Stafford and Sprouse.

Over the course of the year Bill Goodman had asked Melvin Harris, the sales and advertising assistant, to do some analysis on the S & S territory. Melvin made an analysis of selected S & S territory areas, summarized in the table on page 572.

Melvin pointed out that the figures showed that some areas were doing very much better relative to others. Further research into the differences among areas revealed that the areas doing poorly had fewer active accounts relative to the areas that were making a better showing. From this sales penetration and account analysis Melvin concluded that (1) the fairly good sales performance in certain of the areas argued against the contention that the design of the line was

not good for the territory, and (2) greater exposure through more accounts was the key to progress in the territory.

After the close of the first half year Melvin did some additional analysis on the territory. In a memorandum to Bill Goodman, Melvin pointed out that the territory was yielding about half its buying power potential. Melvin also reminded Bill of a territory goal of 75 percent of quota that had been discussed back in December 1965 when 1966 quota letters were being discussed. Bill knew that Mr. Gleason did not set down this goal in his December letter to Cam and Floyd on 1966 quotas. See the Exhibit 7 memorandum on S & S First-Half Performance.

QUESTIONS

1. Is the SFMA Buying Power Index a good guide for creating sales quotas for Warrenton Furniture Co.?
2. Why has the S & S territory consistently failed to reach its sales quota?
3. What sales goals should Warrenton set for the S & S territory for the second half of 1966?
4. What can Warrenton's marketing executives do to help improve sales in the S & S territory?
5. Should S & S be given an ultimatum to increase sales or be replaced by new sales representatives?
6. Will the appointment of new representatives lead to increased sales in the S & S territory?

Exhibit 4
Summary of Conference

February 10, 1966

Memo

To: Crandell Hadley
      Emmett Gleason

From: Bill Goodman

Subject: S & S

It is suggested that I put some things on paper during our conference this morning concerning the S & S territory. As you know, I have just returned from a week in Minneapolis, St. Paul, Milwaukee, Davenport, Omaha, and places in between. I want to say at the outset that Cam Stafford and Floyd Sprouse are very well received and liked by their dealers. I think their working habits are equally as good. These are two positive statements that I want to make.

Our main problems, and ones that must be overcome, lie in the cities of Milwaukee and Omaha. Being successful in these two cities means the difference in being successful or unsuccessful in the entire territory, assuming the rest of the territory is producing satisfactorily.

In Milwaukee you have four tremendous stores that dominate the business. As of now we have one pattern on the floor of one of these stores. In a city such as Omaha with 550,000 people, you have equally large stores. We do not have a single pattern in any of these stores. Our only account in Omaha is Helperts and Sons, a somewhat rundown showroom. Anyone of these large class accounts could give us a minimum of $80,000 a year if they were successful with only two or three of our patterns. For example, North Star Furniture is running one group and two suites from Smith Furniture Company, and gave them $50,000 during the month of December.

I had a lot of conversation with each of these accounts, promising them the utmost in cooperation from the factory etc. I think we have an excellent chance this April with about five of them. This remains to be seen.

At any rate this is what we have to watch at the April market. If we do not open some of these accounts, then there is no direction to go but to make a change in the territory.

I was asked during the conference about the attitude of Cam and Floyd. They both feel that the line is the best they have had in years, but here again a good line is useless unless you have it on the floors of major stores that I've mentioned. They both realize that the biggest problem is Milwaukee and Omaha and, of course, their reasoning has been bad quality and bad design on the patterns these stores have had. For instance, Futuro in both Stevens Bros. and Brown's Cathedral in Goldbaum's. Sam Goldbaum made the statement to me that the only successful pattern he had had from Warrenton was Winchester years ago, and that patterns he has tried since then have been flops. He even mentioned the fact that Fred Stevens asked him when he bought Cathedral, why, since he had never been successful with Warrenton merchandise. Sam's answer was that he liked to do business with the Warrenton Furniture Company and with Cam Stafford and Floyd Sprouse. But, we know that we had these patterns and the same quality in other territories. The Minneapolis area is the strongest area of the territory. The Wisconsin and Dakota areas are very weak.

Cam and Floyd both are willing to do anything at all. They want to put an additional man on as quickly as possible. They definitely would not fight us taking Iowa and their part of Nebraska if it would help. Cam mentioned to me that they both wanted so much to make the territory go, but certainly if we wanted to make a change it would be all right with them. It seems that Cam was offered another line about a year ago and Floyd as recently as three months ago. Cam said that there would be more income from either of these other jobs than they are now making from Warrenton. I concur with Emmett's statement during the conference that if we do make a change it would possibly be hard to get top men. Cam and Floyd both are well known over the territory, and I'm sure anyone we talk to would wonder why Cam and Floyd could not make a go of it.

We have definitely made the decision to have a meeting after the April market, and if some of these stores have not bought, then there is no other course but to make a change.

Exhibit 5
First Quarter Review Letter S & S Territory

March 28, 1966

Messrs. Campbell Stafford & Floyd Sprouse

Dear Cam and Floyd:

Your sales figures at the end of the first quarter of 1966 are as follows:

	1966	Percent of Quota	Percent change over 1965
Overall	$159,951	58.5	+ 15.2
Casegoods	103,404	63.0	+ 40.7
Occasional	38,610	46.2	− 2.1
Upholstery	17,937	58.5	− 28.5

As you know, we must have an overall increase of around 12 percent this year to meet our quotas and fulfill our objectives. And, of course, this increase must be spread over the three product groups as the quota was set. Overall you show an increase of around 15 percent, and your casegoods picture is looking much better than a year ago. However, in occasional you are showing a decrease over a bad 1965 and a 28 percent decrease in upholstery, which last year was your strongest product category. It seems that you will have to concentrate more on upholstery. Are there any specific reasons why your upholstery would be off this much? Cam and Floyd, as I have discussed with both of you, I hope we are getting ready to break through in your territory to some good figures. I think our main problem is to get into the ten stores in Milwaukee and Omaha, which we visited the last time I was with you. This certainly could solve the problem, and I am anxious to see how we make out with these people at the coming market. I am happy that we have already sold Accent to Tannenbaum's. In a letter in December we menioned the fact that we wanted to point toward a six-months review at the end of May. Of course, we will talk about this even more at our individual conferences at the upcoming sales meeting. At that time we will want to discuss your thinking about an additional man, and I know that both of you are willing to do this as soon as advisable.

The key account program mentioned to you at the end of the year is very definitely under development. We will have a discussion on this with you during the meeting. You will be a very important part of this program, and much information will be needed from you.

I am sending in a separate letter the new field-report communication form mentioned in December. You will see this is fully explained. We expect this to play a big part in improving quality design, and other facets of our business.

I am sending your quarterly cumulative order analysis. You should study this carefully as to your sales on patterns relative to factory sales. Emphasis should be put on the patterns doing well factorywise, but not in your territory. Are you getting your part of shipments out of the patterns we cut most?

All of us here in sales are still available to help at any time on any problem. I have been in your territory during this quarter, but certainly am willing to come back anytime I can be of help.

With kindest regards,

Sincerely,

Bill Goodman

Exhibit 6
First-Half Review S & S Territory

June 16, 1966

Messrs. Campbell Stafford & Floyd Sprouse

Dear Cam and Floyd:

Sales figures at the end of the first half of 1966 are as follows:

	1966	Percent of Quota	Percent change Over 1965	Factory of Change
Overall	322,636	59	+10.6	+11
Casegoods	200,155	61	+25.4	+11
Occasional	82,406	50	+ 4.8	+ 8
Upholstery	40,075	68	−19.1	+15

You know of the overall increase of 12 percent that we must have this year. We are a bit behind as of now. But, we made tremendous gains during April and May and are continuing to do so. It has been emphatically stressed many times that the increase has to be spread over the three-product categories equally. It is of utmost importance that you be near quota in each product category. You show the same overall increase as the factory, but yet you are only 59 percent of quota. It seems you have stengthened your occasional and upholstery somewhat since the end of the first quarter and have gone down some on casegoods. As you know, we had all hoped that the April market and the weeks thereafter would give you a big increase and push your percentage toward quota closer. We guess the main problem is still the eight or ten stores in Milwaukee and Omaha that we aren't selling. We understand you have sold Tannenbaum's, Merriman's, and Modern House of these stores. Are there any of the others?

In our letter of December 24th we pointed toward a six-months review at the end of May. I think we should get together in Chicago for a meeting. We made plans at the end of last year and submitted them to management as far as manpower was concerned. We feel that your territory needs another man, and you have said that you are ready to put this man on just as soon as possible. We had hoped that sales would be up to the point where a new man could be put on and therefore start increasing business. Our production department is and will continue to be ahead of its production goals set at the beginning of the year, and this product will, of course, have to be sold. On the other hand, our sales plans for additional coverage are behind at this point, but will have to be met by December 1st.

We are still doing work on the key account program and field communication form. This key account program requires a lot of thought and it will probably be the rest of the year in development. Several contacts will have to be made with you before a program can be finalized. We should have the field communication form out to you during this next quarter.

We want to point out again the fact that we're being backed 100 percent by our customer service department. Our service is getting better and better each day, and this improvement is in every phase of customer service. During the April sales meeting our remarks were that with our increased effort in customer service we must have more cooperation from the men in the field.

All of us here in sales are still available to help at any time on any problem. Give any of us a call if you need us.

With kindest regards.

Sincerely,

Emmett Gleason
Bill Goodman

Exhibit 7

Memorandum on S & S First-Half Performance

Memo to: Bill Goodman and Emmett Gleason

From: Melvin Harris

Re: Stafford and Sprouse Territory

Some recent figures on the S & S territory:

By State

	First Half 1965			First Half 1966		
	Sales	Co. Percent	BPI Percent	Sales	Co. Percent	Percent Sales Change
Minnesota	$101,101	1.1	1.8	$128,141	1.29	+26
Wisconsin	95,636	1.1	2.2	102,331	1.02	+ 7
Iowa	71,488	0.8	1.5	64,340	0.64	−10
N. & S. Dakota	4,359	0.05	0.6	4,402	0.04	—
Nebraska	18,017	0.2	0.4	23,422	0.23	+30
	$290, 601	3.25	6.5	$322,636	3.22	+11

By Product Category

	First Half 1965		First Half 1066		
	Sales	Percent of Quota	Sales	Percent of Quota	Percent Sales Change
Casegoods	$160,124	51	$200,155	61	+25
Occasional	79,236	48	82,406	50	+ 4
Upholstery	51,241	127	40,075	68	−19
	$290,601	60	$322,155	59	+11

If I remember correctly, a goal of 75 percent of quota was originally set for S & S to meet by midyear but was not included in their December year end letter. They have not come near it and are actually under where they were at this time last year in terms of percent of quota.

They do have an 11 percent increase in sales over last year that equals the company's increase. But they will never get their sales-to-quota figure up unless they exceed the company sales increase.

Breaking it down geographically, most of the increase has come from Minnesota. Iowa is substantially under what it was last year; Wisconsin is up very slightly; and Nebraska shows a good percentage increase. However, none of the states improved enough to change the percent to total company sales and the ter-

ritory still stands at about 50 percent of BPI.

Breaking it down by product category, almost the entire increase is in casegoods. Upholstery figures for 1966 are far below comparable 1965 figures.

It is obvious that S & S will not reach 75 percent of quota for 1966. They would have to be 107% of quota for the rest of the year to average 75 percent for the entire year.

My understanding is that we are to review their performance at year end to determine what will be done about the territory. It seems to me that if they are on the firing line, we should set territorial goals for us to use as yardsticks on reckoning day and that they should be informed of the goals in all fairness to them.

Twelve
Marketing Programming

It is a capital mistake to theorize before one has data.
Sir Arthur Conan Doyle

Up to this point each element of the marketing mix has been discussed as a separate problem area and we now want to bring the factors together under the banner of marketing programming. We view marketing programming as an integrative process where information is collected and used to plan and control marketing operations. The basic theme of this chapter is coordinating the implementation of the marketing activities of the firm.

OPTIMIZING THE MARKETING MIX

The main objective of marketing programming is to put together a set of marketing strategies that will achieve the goals of the firm. This means assembling an *ideal mix* of products, prices, personal selling, advertising, promotion, and distribution networks for a particular company. Obviously finding the best combination of marketing strategies is not easy because of nonlinear relationships between sales and marketing mix variables, interactions among the factors, the largely unknown character of competitive responses, and the sometimes fickle nature of the customer. The process is also complicated by changes in general business conditions and modifications in the legal environment made by regulatory agencies and the courts. If these conditions are not bad enough, the manager is asked to find a marketing mix that generates adequate profits in the short run and contributes to long-run goals of the firm such as growth and stability.

In light of the complex nature of marketing activities, it would be useful to have some mathematical programming routines to help find the optimum marketing mix for individual firms. Unfortunately mathematical techniques are rarely employed by businessmen to search for the ideal mix because of the nonlinear and interactive relationships that are found among marketing variables. One rather imaginative solution to the marketing mix problem that overcomes some of these issues used seven years of monthly beer sales from a midwestern brewery.[1] First a series of log regressions[2] were run to predict sales using combinations of eleven independent variables. This

[1] V. Balachandran and Dennis H. Gensch, "Solving the 'Marketing Mix' Problem Using Geometric Programming," *Management Science,* Vol. 21, No. 2 (October 1974), pp. 160-171.
[2] A regression equation where logarithms of the dependent and independent variables are used to get estimates of the elasticities of the predictor variables. Thus an equation of the form: sales $= aX^b_1 X^c_2 \ldots$ is reduced to the linear form: log sales $= \log a + b \log X_1 + c \log X_2$, etc.

helped to show the important relations among the variables and provided estimates of the impact of the various factors.

Next the best of the variables were combined into an equation. The equation included such things as price, advertising, package appeal, population, income, percent distribution, sales compensation, and was able to explain 72 percent of the variation in beer sales in one area. After setting some realistic constraints on the marketing variables in the equation, a special form of nonlinear programming[3] was employed to find values of the marketing variables that maximized beer sales for the firm. This analysis suggested that sales could be increased if part of the advertising budget was reallocated to improve beer quality, packaging, and personal selling. Thus the executives of a major brewery changed their advertising budget to improve their marketing mix as the result of the application of a mathematical optimization procedure.

In a more typical situation, the selection of an optimum marketing mix is made on an *intuitive* basis by product managers who are responsible for one or two brands within an individual line. By specializing in only a few items brand managers are able to learn enough about how their products respond to marketing mix variables to be able to build workable marketing programs. Whether a particular program leads to optimum results, however, depends on the skills of the product manager and on the quantity and quality of the information that he has to work with. Once an acceptable marketing program has been created, the next step is to see that it is implemented properly and then monitored in subsequent time periods to see that planned objectives are met.

The complex task of marketing programming can sometimes be helped along by utilizing procedures that simulate conditions in the real world. First, data are collected on the basic marketing elements employed by the firm and their interrelations. Then models are developed to show how marketing factors react in a business environment. Finally, the models are used to test the probable impact of different combinations of marketing variables. We will discuss several applications of simulation to show how this technique can assist managers in their strategic planning and in finding the elusive optimum marketing mix.

SIMULATION AND THE MARKETING MIX

Simulation is the use of a model to replicate the operation of a real system over time.[4] Marketing simulations, for example, feed price, promotion, advertising, and distribution values into a model to estimate the sales volumes or market shares that products might have at the end of a time period. The main advantage of marketing mix simulations is they allow the manager to bring together and study the interaction of several marketing variables all at once. In addition, the manager can test various combinations of marketing factors without having to spend the money or take the risks associated with making changes in the real world.

A classic example showing how simulation is used by managers is described by Little

[3]In this case geometric programming was used to find the optimum marketing mix. Although this procedure is too complex for discussion here, interested readers may want to refer to R. J. Duffin, E. L. Peterson, and C. Zener, *Geometric Programming–Theory and Application* (New York: Wiley, 1967). An example of an application of linear programming to optimize the allocation of advertising across media is discussed in an appendix to Chapter Ten.

[4]Randall L. Schultz and Edward M. Sullivan, "Developments in Simulation in Social and Administrative Science," Harold Guetzkow, Philip Kotler, and Randall L. Schultz, eds., *Simulation in Social and Administrative Science* (Englewood Cliffs, N.J.: Prentice-Hall, 1972), p. 4.

for an oil refinery where mathematical programming has been employed for many years.[5]

INTERVIEWER: "Do you make regular mathematical programming runs for scheduling the refinery?"

ANALYST: "Oh yes."

INTERVIEWER: "Do you implement the results?"

ANALYST: "Oh no!"

INTERVIEWER: "Well, that seems odd. If you don't implement the results, perhaps you should stop making the runs?"

ANALYST: "No, No. We wouldn't want to do that!"

INTERVIEWER: "Why not?"

ANALYST: "Well, what happens is something like this: I make several computer runs and take them to the plant manager. He is responsible for this whole multimillion dollar plumber's paradise. The plant manager looks at the runs, thinks about them for a while and then sends me back to make a few more with conditions changed in various ways. I do this and bring them back in. He looks at them and probably sends me back to make more runs. And so forth."

INTERVIEWER: "How long does this keep up?"

ANALYST: "I would say it continues until, finally, the plant manager screws up enough courage to make a decision."

Simulation, thus, encourages manager-model interaction to improve understanding of the business environment and help make better decisions. When the manager does not agree with the simulation results, the input data can be reexamined and tests run to see how sensitive the results are to changes in parameters. This process of interacting with a model allows managers to learn more about their problems without giving control to the computer.

For example, Crown Zellerbach has developed a computer model that helps allocate paper production to the most profitable markets.[6] The model recently matched company products with potential customers and recommended that Crown Zellerbach ship 20,000 tons of industrial papers overseas. However, when the model recommended shifting a large tonnage of toilet tissue to foreign markets, the vice president in charge overruled the model because of its lack of sensitivity to the needs of domestic customers. Businessmen must be careful when they shift items in short supply to overseas markets that they do not trigger customer boycotts of their other products or bring about the imposition of governmental export controls.

A Brand Manager Simulation

The operation of a marketing mix simulation can be shown by referring to a model that predicts market shares from data on advertising expenditures, media coverage, prices,

[5]John D. C. Little, "Models and Managers: The Concept of a Decision Calculus," *Management Science,* Vol. 16, No. 8 (April 1970), p. 468.

[6]"Shaking Up Crown Zellerbach's Line," *Business Week* (January 5, 1974), p. 52-53.

promotions, and packaging.[7] The model was developed for use by brand managers because they control most elements of the marketing mix and are experienced in gathering data and making judgments on their products. Brand managers provide the basic inputs for the model with a series of projections on the relationships between sales and other variables. The simulation asks the brand manager to estimate market share during a period when there is no advertising (min), then the market share associated with a 50 percent increase in advertising, the ceiling market share (max) that can be achieved by saturation levels of advertising, and finally, the amount of advertising required to maintain the current share. An equation can be fitted to these points to give:

$$\text{Share} = \text{min} + \frac{(\text{max}-\text{min}) \, (\text{adv})^\gamma}{\delta + (\text{adv})^\gamma}$$

where the γ and δ parameters are determined by the data fed into the program. Little adjusts the impact of the advertising expenditures in the model (adv) by using index numbers that reflect media coverage and the quality of ad copy. He also adjusts the market share estimates with a composite index to show the effects of nonadvertising factors such as price, promotions, packaging, and competitive activities.

A summary of the input data needed for the marketing mix simulation is shown for a product called GROOVY in Figure 12-1. The thirty-seven items of information requested by the program are shown first and the manager's responses appear after the colons. Note that the indexes for seasonality, nonadvertising effects, media efficiency, and copy effectiveness must be given for each period of the planning horizon. The results produced by running the marketing mix simulation with these data are presented in Figure 12-2. The output indicates that GROOVY's market share will increase from 1.868 to 2.009 percent in the fourth quarter while dollars of contribution will peak in the third quarter. Advertising efficiency in each quarter is shown as the SLOPE factor at the bottom of Figure 12-2. A positive SLOPE indicates advertising is profitable in that period and a negative value indicates it is unprofitable. Thus, the SLOPE observed for GROOVY in the fourth quarter (—0.379), suggests that another run of the simulation with a lower fourth-quarter ad budget would raise the projected contribution.

Little's simulation has been used successfully by brand managers to help set budgets and to test reallocations of advertising funds during quarterly reviews of marketing plans. The primary advantage of the model is that it shows how advertising and other marketing variables interact to build profits for the firm. A somewhat more complex marketing simulation has been developed by Claycamp and Amstutz for the drug industry.[8]

Simulating the Prescription Drug Market

The drug simulation was designed for a pharmaceutical manufacturer who wanted to learn more about the impact of alternative marketing programs. The firm was particu-

[7]John D. C. Little, "Models and Managers: The Concept of a Decision Calculus," pp. 471-481.

[8]Henry J. Claycamp and Arnold E. Amstutz, "Simulation Techniques in the Analysis of Marketing Strategy," *Applications of the Sciences in Marketing Management,* Frank M. Bass, Charles W. King and Edgar A. Pessemier, eds. (New York: Wiley, 1968), pp. 113-150.

```
/GROOVY-70/

 1 BRAND NAME:  GROOVY
 2 NO. PERIODS: 4.000
 3 PER. LENGTH: QUARTER
 4 FIRST PER.:  1ST Q 70
 5 AREA: US
      REFERENCE PER.-BRAND
 7 INIT. SHARE (% OF UNITS): 1.860
 8 MAINT. ADV (DOL./PER.): .486M
 9 MIN. SHARE AT END: 1.770
10 MAX SHARE AT END: 2.250
11 END SHARE WITH +50% ADV: 1.950
12 LONG RUN MIN SHARE: .000
14 MEDIA EFFCY: 1.000
15 COPY EFFECT: 1.000
16 SALES UNIT: HOGSHEADS
17 CONTRIBUTION (DOL./UNIT): .680
18 BRAND PRICE (DOL./UNIT): 1.812
      OTHER BRAND DATA
19 STARTING SHARE: 1.860
      REFERENCE PER. - PROD. CLASS
21 PROD. CLASS NAME: TREACLE
22 INIT. CLASS SALES RATE (UNITS/PER.): 290M
29 CLASS PRICE (DOL./UNIT): 1.880
   TIME VARIATIONS
   PERIOD                        1        2        3        4
30 CLASS SALES INDEX:          .943    1.012    1.065     .939

31 NON-ADV EFFECT INDEX:      1.000    1.050     .980    1.000

32 MEDIA EFFCY:               1.000    1.000    1.000    1.000

33 COPY EFFECT:               1.000    1.000    1.000    1.000

34 CONTRIBUTION (DOL./UNIT):   .650     .680     .680     .680

35 BRAND PRICE (DOL./UNIT):   1.812    1.812    1.812    1.812

36 CLASS PRICE (DOL./UNIT):   1.880    1.880    1.880    1.880

37 BRAND ADV (DOL./PER.):      .486M    .606M    .876M    .414M
```

Figure 12-1 Input Data File for a Multiperiod Marketing-mix Simulation.
Source. John D. C. Little, "Models and Managers: The Concept of a Decision Calculus,"
Management Science, Vol. 16 (April 1970), p. B-478.

larly concerned with evaluating segmentation strategies and checking the progress of
new products after they had been introduced. The manufacturer also wanted a system
that would measure the effectiveness of salesmen and other promotional methods.

The basic structure of the prescription drug market is described in the flow diagram in
Figure 12-3. Starting in the upper left-hand corner, the company sends information (I) to
wholesalers, pharmacies, hospitals, and doctors using a variety of methods. These
include personal calls by salesmen (detailmen), journal advertising, free samples, and
direct mail promotions. This information is used by doctors to help prescribe a course of

```
1 SAVE DATA
2 PRINT DATA
3 CHANGE DATA
4 OUTPUT
5 RESTART
ANS = (4)

1 STANDARD OUTPUT
2 EXCLUDE SPECIFIED LINES
3 INCLUDE SPECIFIED LINES ONLY
ANS = (1)

1 CALCULATE CURRENT CASE
2 SEARCH
3 FINISHED
ANS = (1)
```

1	OUTPUT FOR	GROOVY			
2	PERIOD LENGTH:	QUARTER			
3	STARTING PERIOD:	1ST Q 70			
4	AREA:	US			
5	SALES UNIT:	HOGSHEADS			
6	DATA FROM FILE:	/GROOVY-70/			
8	PERIOD	1	2	3	4
9	MARKET SHARE: (% OF UNITS)	1.868	1.999	2.002	2.009
10	PROD. CLASS SALES(UNITS/PER)	273M	293M	309M	278M
11	PROD. CLASS SALES(DOL/PER)	514M	552M	581M	523M
12	BRAND SALES (UNITS/PER)	5.89M	5.87M	6.18M	5.59M
13	BRAND SALES (DOL/PER)	9.22M	10.6M	11.2M	10.1M
14	CONTRIBUTION (DOL/PER)	3.46M	3.99M	4.20M	3.80M
15	BRAND ADV (DOL/PER)	.486M	.606M	.876M	.414M
16	CONT. AFTER ADV(DOL/PER)	2.97M	3.38M	3.33M	3.39M
17	CUMULATIVE CONT. AFTER ADV	2.97M	6.36M	9.69M	13.1M
23	SLOPE	1.634	1.169	.228	-.379

Figure 12-2 Sample Output for the GROOVY Simulation.
Source. Same as Figure 12.1, p. B-479.

treatment (Rx) for patients who exhibit particular symptoms. The patients place orders (0) at the pharmacy for drugs that cause reorders to flow to the wholesaler and the manufacturer. Physical distribution of drug products (P) is handled through wholesalers who sell to hospitals, pharmacies, and to doctors.

The goal of the drug simulation was to predict how doctors would react to different sources of product information. The model included a set of hypothetical doctors who were exposed to marketing communications and then asked to treat a variety of patient illnesses. The reactions of the doctors were based on data from weekly audits of prescriptions, quarterly reports from doctors on patient treatment, direct mail promotions and salesmen's calls, and other studies designed to determine doctors' attitudes, experience, and knowledge. Each simulated doctor was given a memory that kept track of illnesses that could be treated with each drug plus a record of how well the drugs had

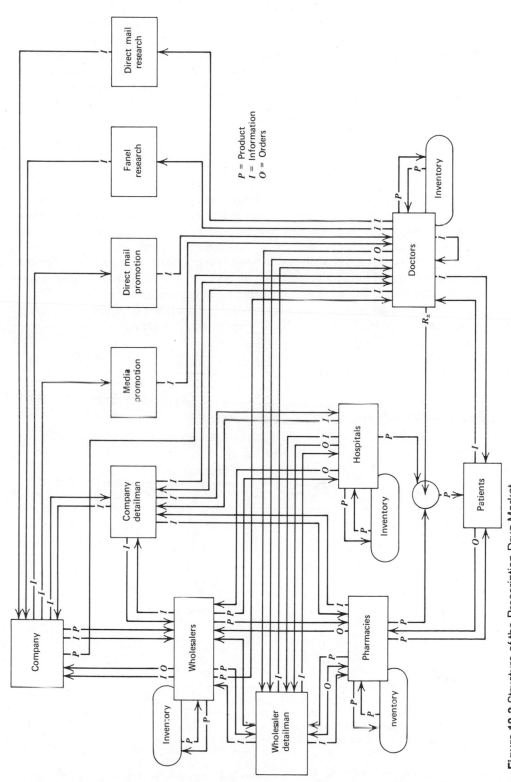

Figure 12-3 Structure of the Prescription Drug Market.
Source. Henry J. Claycamp and Arnold E. Amstutz, "Simulation Techniques in the Analysis of Marketing Strategy," in Frank M. Bass, et. al (eds.); *Application of the Sciences in Marketing Management* (New York: John Wiley, 1968), p. 128.

performed in the past. During each week of the simulation, the model determined the probability that a given doctor would be exposed to journal advertising, direct mail pieces, or a salesman, and the doctor's memory was updated to include portions of these communications. Exposure to presentations at conventions and word-of-mouth messages from other doctors were handled in a similar manner. Once a doctor's memory file was updated, he was exposed to patients from an artificial patient population and asked to decide what drugs (if any) to prescribe. Patients that were not cured with the first treatment, returned in the future and the doctor's memory was adjusted to note the success or failure of any drugs prescribed.

The output of the drug simulation was a stack of prescriptions written by the pool of hypothetical doctors. These were converted to a time series showing market shares for each brand in a product class. A test of the accuracy of the drug simulation was run using the promotional activities and market conditions that existed in 1961. The market shares estimated by the model for ten brands in one product class are shown in Table 12-1 along with the actual shares achieved at the end of the year. Note that the average error was less than one percent indicating the simulation was successful in replicating the operation of the prescription drug market. Once a simulation is able to duplicate the past, the obvious next step is to load in some proposed values for price, promotion, and advertising and try to predict the future. The company sponsoring the drug simulation was pleased with the operation of their model and one executive said that, "Even if there are . . . errors in prediction, it is worth the expense because of the way it makes people think."[9]

Table 12-1

Accuracy of the Prescription Drug Simulation

Product	Year-End Market Share (Percent)		Difference (Magnitude) Percent
	Simulated	Actual	
1	15.0	16.1	−1.1
2	9.1	8.7	+0.4
3	9.3	9.0	+0.3
4	3.2	2.8	+0.4
5	—	—	—
6	27.6	28.8	−1.2
7	13.0	12.7	+0.3
8	13.9	14.4	−0.5
9	5.9	5.5	+0.4
10	2.5	2.0	+0.5
	99.5	100.0	5.1

Source. Arnold E. Amstutz, "Development, Validation, and Implementation of Computerized Microanalytic Simulations of Market Behavior" in *Simulation in Social and Administrative Science,* Harold Guetzkow, Philip Kotler, and Randall L. Schultz, eds., (Englewood Cliffs, N.J.: Prentice-Hall, © 1972), p. 570. Reprinted by permission of Prentice-Hall.

[9]Henry J. Claycamp and Arnold E. Amstutz, "Simulation Techniques in the Analysis of Marketing Strategy," p. 149.

Using Marketing Simulations

Both of the examples that have been discussed suggest that marketing mix simulations can help evaluate the impact of alternative marketing programs. Simulation gives brand managers a captive test market that will hopefully show the effects of strategies without spending a great deal of money or revealing plans to competitors. Another advantage is that marketing simulations are tailor made and managers can include variables that are important to particular industries. Schultz, for example, used the number of airline flights offered between two cities in a model to help predict shares of an air travel market.[10] In another study, distribution effectiveness (number of service stations) was used in a simulation to forecast market shares for gasoline producers.[11]

In situations where firms need decisions in a hurry, have limited funds, or lack computer expertise, they may be better off with traditional "seat of-the-pants" marketing programming procedures. Experience has shown that simulations can cost from $10,000 to over $200,000 and often take a year or more to become fully developed and tested.[12] A more serious problem with simulation is that it does not automatically lead to optimum solutions. Each simulation run is a single experiment conducted with a given set of conditions. Thus, a large number of computer runs are often needed to find the best combination of price, promotion, advertising, and distribution variables for a particular firm. Despite this handicap, Weitz suggests that "analytical models that yield optimum solutions can frequently be developed as a result of simulation studies.[13]

Much of the time needed to build successful marketing simulations is spent gathering data.[14] This is particulary true when simulations are used to forecast market positions and managers must make subjective judgments about competitive reactions and the stability of parameters. Obviously marketing simulations are easier to develop and use when a firm already has a well-organized marketing information system.

To summarize our discussion, simulation can help managers build better marketing programs by employing models that replicate the operation of real world systems. Simulation is not a "cure-all," but one of several tools that are available to simplify complex marketing problems. The main applications of simulation in marketing have been to (1) help develop alternative marketing strategies, (2) provide inexpensive test markets to evaluate strategies, and (3) help control the implementation of marketing programs.

MARKETING CONTROL

The success of marketing plans frequently depends on the level of execution that is achieved by the salesmen, dealers, and advertising agencies who implement programs in the real world. Business firms must have a system of control that quickly points out

[10]Randall L. Schultz, "Market Measurement and Planning With a Simultaneous-Equation Model," *Journal of Marketing Research,* Vol. 8, No. 2 (May 1971), pp. 153-164.

[11]Jean-Jacques Lambin, "A Computer On-Line Marketing Mix Model," *Journal of Marketing Research,* Vol. 9, No. 2 (May 1972), pp. 119-126.

[12]Henry J. Claycamp and Arnold E. Amstutz, "Simulation Techniques in the Analysis of Marketing Strategy," p. 118.

[13]Harold Weitz, "The Promise of Simulation in Marketing," *Journal of Marketing,* Vol. 31, No. 3 (July 1967), p. 30.

[14]John D. C. Little, "Models and Managers: The Concept of a Decision Calculus," p. 483.

execution errors and helps managers take corrective action. An important first step is to decide what factors will best explain the success or failure of an individual marketing program. Depending on business conditions, a firm might emphasize market share, dollar volume, unit sales, dollar profit, or return on investment. Marketing control is basically a set of procedures that allows managers to compare the results of marketing plans with predetermined standards so that corrective action can be taken to assure that objectives are met. Effective control requires a marketing information system that gathers data on market conditions and places it in the hands of executives who can make adjustments in plans and operating procedures.

Marketing control is a logical extension of the planning model (Figure 1-3) first presented in Chapter 1. A flow diagram that highlights the basic elements of the marketing control process is presented in Figure 12-4. The first few steps involve planning and are usually performed on an annual basis. Objectives are adopted; price, promotion, advertising, and distribution strategies selected; and then performance standards are set for sales quotas, selling expenses, and other control variables. Next, the marketing program is implemented over a period of time and periodic measurements are taken to record the reactions of customers and competitors. The basic aim of the control process is to see whether the predetermined performance standards are being met. If they are, the successful results are fed back to the starting point and used to set the objectives for the next planning period (Figure 12-4).

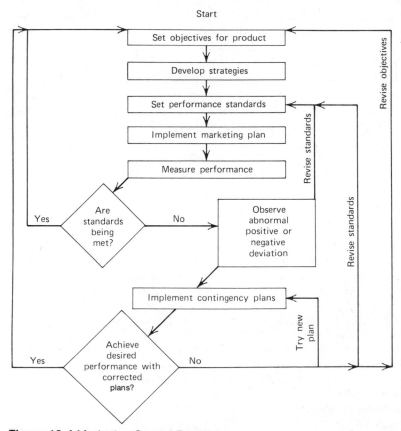

Figure 12-4 Marketing Control Process.

When significant deviations from performance standards are observed, the manager has the choice of changing the standards or implementing contingency plans that attempt to correct the problem (Figure 12-4). For example, suppose a new product expected to attain a 3 percent market share after six months actually grabbed 10 percent of the market. This suggests the original estimate was low and the manager should probably raise the annual forecast to 8 percent or more so that production, advertising, and distribution efforts can be adjusted to reflect realized demand.

In the more typical situation where sales fail to reach desired levels, managers can try a variety of short-run strategies to get the product back on target. These may take the form of "cents-off" coupons, new advertising themes or media, deals for retailers, changes in ad schedules, increased advertising, contests for salesmen, or simple changes in packaging or product specifications. If these tonics fail to do the job, the manager may have to revise the standards or objectives for the next planning period (Figure 12-4). In addition, managers can initiate special market research studies to find out why products do not reach long-run sales goals. These efforts may result in entirely new products, major changes in existing items, new channels, realignments in selling efforts, or a decision to drop the offending products entirely.

Setting Standards

Performance standards are planned achievement levels for selected marketing variables that the firm expects to attain at stated intervals throughout the year. Managers do not have time to watch all dimensions of the marketing plan and they must pick out the most important performance factors to be monitored on a regular basis. In addition to traditional sales and contribution profit goals, most firms set standards for selling and advertising expenses. These are often expressed as a percentage of sales to simplify comparisons with past performance and the experience of other firms in the industry. For example, a company could measure the efficiency of its sales organization by setting a standard of 10 percent of revenue to cover branch office overhead, salaries of salesmen and sales managers, travel, commissions, bonuses, and customer entertainment. Other marketing factors that can be used for control purposes include:

1. Turnover rate of salesmen.
2. Percentage of goods returned.
3. Warranty and service expense.
4. Distribution cost per unit.
5. Months of inventory in dealer's hands.
6. Sales calls per day.
7. Average order and delivery time.
8. Advertising costs per unit sold.
9. Markdowns as a percent of sales.
10. Sales as a percent of quota.

Most firms employ several marketing variables to control their operations because reliance on a single rule can be dangerous. For example, the authors are familiar with a San Francisco department store that got into trouble by setting rigid standards for markdowns as a percent of sales. The managers easily met the standards by failing to cut prices and clear out leftovers at the end of each selling season. This caused the departments to accumulate a lot of old, unsalable merchandise and eventually the store went out of business. Thus, it was not enough to just control the markdown percentage, the managers also had to worry about the age of their stock and maintaining an inventory of merchandise to meet customers' needs.

Another example of the problems created by misguided control occurred in a Russian plate glass factory where the key performance factor was the number of square meters of glass produced each year. In this case, the manager met production standards by simply reducing the thickness of the glass. Thus, although the manager exceeded his production quota, the glass was too weak to be transported and breakage increased drastically. Both examples suggest that a combination of interrelated control factors are often needed to make sure overall objectives are achieved.

Measuring Performance

Marketing information systems provide the basic data used by control systems to compare planned performance with real world results. Managers rely on a variety of special MIS reports to point out deviations between standards and actual operations so corrective action can be taken. One way managers can be alerted to problems is through the use of control charts. Figure 12-5 shows a chart used to monitor selling expenses over time. Although the planned level of expenses was 15 percent, random events caused this ratio to vary between 13 and 17 percent of sales. If selling expenses fell within this range in 90 out of 100 periods, then corrective action would not be needed. Only when expenses fell outside the normal range would the manager be alerted to the possibility of a selling expense problem. The application of a "management by exception" policy saves executive time and is quite popular in the business world.

When expenses fall outside control limits, the manager must decide whether it is just a chance event or evidence of a real change. For example, the low expense ratio in period 3 (Figure 12-5) appears to be just random variation and probably can be ignored. However, the two high values observed in periods 12 and 14 suggest an unfavorable trend and should be investigated. Other types of graphic control devices that can be used to monitor marketing programs include Gantt charts, PERT diagrams, histograms, and flow charts.[15]

Another way managers keep track of marketing programs is through the use of special cost and profit reports. These reports help companies identify the most profitable products, customers, channels, and sales territories so marketing efforts can be adjusted to increase efficiency. For example, Table 12-2 compares the profits and related selling time derived for eleven products produced by one company. Two of the items (K + L) were unprofitable and a further analysis revealed that revenues did exceed variable costs for these products. Thus, in the short run, there was little incentive to drop K and L until more profitable replacements could be found. The table also indicated that selling efforts were not allocated across products according to profit potentials. Two low-profit items (G + L) were receiving undue attention and one high-profit item (B) received too-little selling effort. These results persuaded the company to try an experiment where the selling emphasis for products B and L was exactly reversed. The net effect was a dramatic increase in the profits of B and achievement of a break-even position for product L.

In another example where cost and profit reports were used to measure marketing performance, a manufacturer found that the high cost of serving small accounts reduced the profitability of two distribution channels (Table 12-3). This prompted the company to discontinue channel D and eliminate the small customers from channel C. When selling pressure was increased on the remaining accounts, profits doubled within a year.

[15]Earl P. Strong and Robert D. Smith, *Management Control Models* (New York: Holt, Rinehart and Winston, 1968), pp. 85-117.

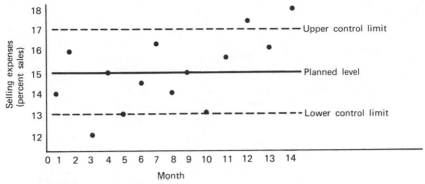

Figure 12-5 Control Chart for Monitoring Deviations from Plans.

Sometimes an analysis will reveal wide differences in profitability across territories (Table 12-4). In this case, action was taken to drop unprofitable products from territories H, I, J, and K and shift selling and advertising efforts to the more profitable areas. As a result, the four territories became profitable and total profits of the company increased substantially.

Although most of our examples of performance measurement have focused on problem situations, marketing control systems should also encourage managers to search for new business. It is not enough just to protect existing markets and managers must be constantly alert so they can find and exploit new opportunities to expand sales for the firm. Opportunity is a difficult concept to measure, however, and control systems may have to settle for alternative factors such as percentage of sales from new products, number of new customers, and new markets entered. These factors are more subjective than traditional criteria, but they do emphasize manager initiative and the future earnings of the company.

Table 12-2

Comparing Profit Contribution and Selling Time by Product

Item	Percent Total Dollar Marketing Profit Contribution	Percent Total Selling Time
Total, all products	100.0	100.0
Profitable products		
A	49.2	19.6
B	15.8	3.8
C	15.8	13.7
D	11.8	5.2
E	7.8	4.6
F	4.8	3.0
G	4.5	15.7
H	3.4	3.7
I	1.4	4.5
Subtotal	114.5	73.8
Unprofitable products		
K	− 5.7	8.8
L	− 8.8	17.4
Subtotals	− 14.5	26.2

Table 12-3

Comparing Sales, Costs, and Profit Margins by Channels of Distribution

	Before Changes in Channels			
Channels of Distribution	Sales	Variable Costs[a]	Profit Margin	Sales
A	$ 750,000	$ 400,000	$350,000	47%
B	250,000	100,000	150,000	60
C	300,000	300,000		
D	200,000	250,000	−50,000	−25[b]
Total	$1,500,000	$1,050,000	$450,000	30
Less: nonvariable expense			300,000	
Net profit			$150,000	10%

	After Changes in Channels			
Channels of Distribution	Sales	Variable Costs	Profit Margin	Sales
A	$ 825,000	$415,000	$410,000	50%
B	315,000	130,000	185,000	59
C	120,000	110,000	10,000	8
Total	$1,260,000	$655,000	$605,000	48
Less: nonvariable expense			310,000	
Net profit			295,000	23%

[a]Production plus distribution costs.
[b]Loss.

Source. Charles H. Sevin, *Marketing Productivity Analysis* (New York: McGraw-Hill Book Co., 1965), pp. 61-77. Used with the permission of McGraw-Hill Book Co.

Table 12-4

Comparing Profit Contribution by Sales Territories

Territory	Percent of Total Dollar Marketing Profit Contribution
Total	100.0
A	48.4
B	33.8
C	11.4
D	8.2
E	2.8
F	1.3
G	0.7
Subtotal	106.6
H	−0.6
I	−0.8
J	−1.3
K	−3.9
Subtotal	−6.6

Source. Same as Table 12-3.

Control Conflict

Sometimes marketing performance standards employed by one division of a firm conflict with the standards emphasized in other areas. This is often true in vertically integrated companies where profit centers are operated at different levels within the firm. For example, grocery chains frequently have a manufacturing division to produce baked goods and a retail division to sell the merchandise to consumers. With this separation, it is not difficult for the profit objectives pursued by the bakery to get out of phase with the sales and gross margin goals employed by the retail division.[16] The potential conflict between the two divisions can be explained by referring to the control loops in Figure 12-6.

The first loop shows how the manufacturing division responds when profits are not up to standards. In order to build volume, the factory may start to overship to the retail stores and lower transfer prices. Unfortunately, the overshipments may require increased retail reductions to clear out the excess goods and lead to reduced orders by the retail division. In addition, the lower transfer prices may not be passed on to consumers, but absorbed by the retail division to maintain its gross margins.

The second and third control loops (Figure 12-6) show how the sales and margin standards of the retail division interact with each other and with the activities of the bakery division. If sales are below expectations, the retail division responds by lowering prices, ordering more merchandise, and offering more specials. This raises sales, but also tends to depress retail margins. Failure to meet gross margin goals generates pressure to raise prices, reduce the number of specials, and order more carefully.

The overall impact of conflicting performance standards within and between divisions of the grocery chain was estimated by means of a simulation. The results indicated the company was able to achieve a rate of growth in excess of its competitors despite conflicts in performance standards. However, the rate of expansion was below the potential that could have been achieved if the two divisions had cooperated more fully in their marketing activities. The moral of the story is that firms must understand how managers *react to controls* if they expect to set standards that will achieve corporate objectives.

One of the essential ingredients needed in the creation and control of marketing programs is information. Marketing managers must know the results of past programs, be aware of changing consumer needs, and keep close tabs on competitive activities. Many firms are providing their executives with these types of data through the use of marketing information systems.[17]

MARKETING INFORMATION SYSTEMS

The basic characteristics of marketing information systems (MIS) have been aptly described as:

"A structured, interacting complex of persons, machines and procedures designed

[16]Edward B. Roberts, Dan I. Abrams, and Henry B. Weil, "A Systems Study of Policy Formulation in a Vertically Integrated Firm" *Management Science,* Vol. 15 (August 1968), pp. 674-694.

[17]The utilization of marketing information systems is described by Louis E. Boone and David L. Kurtz in "Marketing Information Systems: Current Status in American Industry," *Marketing in Motion-Relevance in Marketing,* Fred C. Alvine, ed. (Chicago: American Marketing Association, Combined Proceedings, 1971), pp. 163-167 and Arnold E. Amstutz in "Market-Oriented Management Systems: The Current Status," *Journal of Marketing Research,* Vol. 6, No. 4 (November 1969), pp. 481-496.

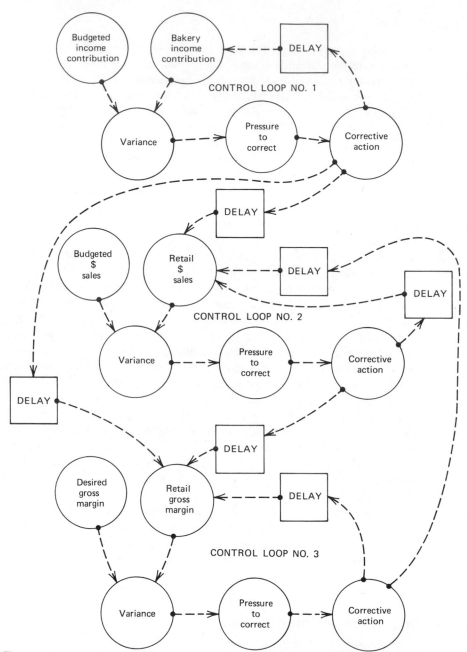

Figure 12-6 Controlling the Manufacture and Sale of Baked Goods in a Grocery Chain.

Source. Edward B. Roberts, Dan I. Abrams, and Henry B. Weil, "A Systems Study of Policy Formulation in a Vertically Integrated Firm," *Management Science,* Vol. 14 (August 1968), p. B-684.

to generate an orderly flow of pertinent information, collected from both intra- and extra-firms sources, for use as the basis for decision-making."[18]

This suggests that marketing information systems are specially designed procedures for gathering and distributing data to managers.

[18]Samuel V. Smith, Richard H. Brien, and James E. Stafford, *Readings in Marketing Information Systems* (Boston: Houghton Mifflin Co., 1968), p. 7.

MIS differ from traditional marketing research activities because information systems operate continuously and draw on data from both internal and external sources. Marketing research on the other hand, is more specialized and emphasizes the collection of external data to solve individual problems. Although marketing research departments supply a lot of data for MIS, the development and control of these systems is typically given to other managers who are supported by programmers and information specialists.

The growing interest in the systematic collection and analysis of marketing data is prompted in part by expansion in the size of firms and the isolation of decision makers from the realities of the marketplace. The quest for timely information is also encouraged by the growth in the numbers of items marketed by firms and declines in the length of the product life cycle.[19] Perhaps the most important reason for the development of MIS is the increased availability of computers that allow vast quantities of marketing data to be processed quickly at relatively low cost.

The implementation of efficient MIS offers businessmen a variety of benefits such as more detailed marketing reports and quicker recognition of trends. In addition, information systems combine and compare scattered pieces of data and allow managers to selectively retrieve the facts they need. MIS also make it possible to collect new types of data and reduce the likelihood that important marketing information will be suppressed.

Building Marketing Information Systems

The basic components of a marketing information system are a data bank, a set of analytical tools, and a communications network. An example showing how managers interact with these components is given in Figure 12-7. Notice that MIS allow managers to retrieve selected historical figures from data files, process raw data with standard statistical programs, and test alternative strategies against complex planning models. Executives may also call on MIS to generate a variety of routine and special reports to help them in their day-to-day decision making. Thus MIS can be used both for planning marketing activities and then later to help control the programs after they have been implemented.

The types of information collected and stored in MIS data banks often depends on the models and simulations (discussed earlier) employed by the firm to build and assess marketing activities. Companies that use complex decision procedures will naturally need more and better data than firms that rely on simple statistical analysis of past figures. Data banks draw most of their historical records from internal sales figures, call reports, and from external publications put out by research firms and governmental agencies (Figure 12-7). Another type of data that can be useful is a record of past decisions and the assumptions employed to make these decisions. This information allows managers to compare expected results with real world events to learn more about their decision environment.

A key factor in building data banks is determining the amount of detail or the level of aggregation that should be employed. Amstutz says:

> "At the heart of every successful information system is a disaggregated data file—a file in which information is maintained in detailed time sequence as it is generated. As new inputs are received they are maintained along with existing data rather than replacing or being combined with existing information.[20]

[19]Conrad Berenson, "Marketing Information Systems," *Journal of Marketing,* Vol. 33, No. 4 (October 1969), p. 17.

[20]Arnold E. Amstutz, "The Marketing Executive and Management Information Systems," *Science, Technology & Marketing,* Raymond M. Haas, ed. (Chicago: American Marketing Association, 1966 Fall Proceedings), p. 76.

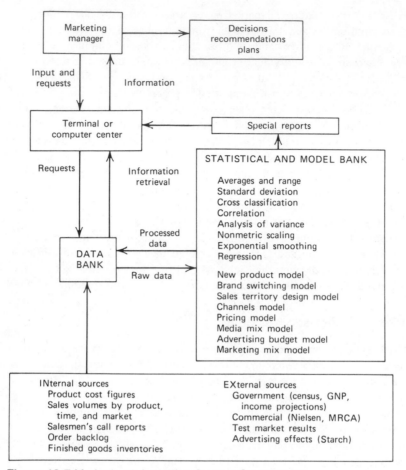

Figure 12-7 Marketing Information System Components.

This means that information is stored in its most basic form rather than in summary categories. For example, a disaggregated customer file would contain the consumer's name, location, and demographic characteristics plus a chronological record of all transactions. This not only makes it easy to reconstruct past purchasing relationships, it allows the manager more flexibility in combining and comparing pieces of data. In addition, disaggregated data files allow the system to be changed without costly reorganization of the data bank.

Once needed data files have been accumulated, a variety of analytical tools can be employed to process and summarize the information (Figure 12-7). These include simple statistical programs for means, standard deviations, cross tabulations, and more sophisticated programs that study correlations among data. These programs also allow relationships and decision alternatives to be evaluated by means of statistical tests. Computer models can also be used to help managers answer the various "what if" questions that arise when businessmen build marketing programs and try to solve problems after plans have been implemented. Alternative advertising schedules, for example, are frequently run through simulation models to find which media mix gives the best customer exposure. Longman describes a new product model that is used to evaluate the impact of alternative package sizes, coupon schedules, and promotions on the sales of newly introduced items.[21] This program has proved to be so valuable that it is often run over 400 times in a single month.

Desirable MIS Features

The creation of a good MIS requires more than just a computerized data bank and the designer must adapt his system to the special needs of the business environment.[22] For example, marketing information systems should be able to reduce masses of data to a form that can be easily read by businessmen. Although MIS are often sold on the basis of providing more and better data, Ackoff suggests that most managers already suffer from an overabundance of *irrelevant* information.[23] He cites one example where executives received a daily 600 page stock report that could not possibly be read by the managers. This implies that MIS should be designed to filter and condense data as well as to assemble information.

MIS should also include procedures so users will not accidently erase data or modify basic programs. In addition, systems should be designed to prevent access by unauthorized employees or competitors. This can usually be accomplished by having persons requesting data identify themselves by means of passwords or special access codes.

Another axiom of good MIS design is flexibility so that programs can be upgraded as conditions change. Successful information systems usually start simply and evolve into more sophisticated programs as managers become familiar with procedures and demand more complex reports.[24] Often it is easier to build and integrate several subsystems than to construct a total information system all at once.

Perhaps the most critical factor in the development of successful MIS is gaining the *cooperation* of the managers who will make use of the system.[25] Marketing executives must be encouraged to specify the types of information they will need from the system and the form in which it should be presented. This means the managers must understand the intricacies of their own decision processes and the control procedures employed by the firm. If executives help build a marketing information system, they are more apt to know how the system works and are more likely to use it to make decisions.

Cost Versus Value of MIS

Information systems range in cost from a few thousand dollars to several million dollars for complex systems with real time capabilities.[26] General Mills, for example, provides its executives with daily sales reports and Schenley's system allows executives to retrieve sales and inventory figures for all products within seconds on video display

---

[21]Kenneth A. Longman, "The Question-Asking Machine," *Management Science*, Vol. 14, No. 8 (April 1968), p. 524.

[22]Some of the pitfalls to be avoided are described by Joel N. Axelrod in his article "14 Rules for Building An MIS." *Journal of Advertising Research*, Vol. 10, No. 3 (June 1970), pp. 3-11.

[23]Russell L. Ackoff, "Management Misinformation Systems," *Management Science*, Vol. 14, No. 4 (December 1967), p. 147.

[24]See Lawrence D. Gibson et al., "An Evolutionary Approach to Marketing Information Systems," *Journal of Marketing*, Vol. 37 (April 1973), pp. 2-6.

[25]For a good discussion of the problems of building MIS see Donald F. Cox and Robert E. Good, "How to Build a Marketing Information System." *Harvard Business Review*, Vol. 45 (May-June 1967), pp. 145-154.

[26]Boone and Kurtz reviewed 66 MIS and found 21 percent cost less than $50,000, 50 percent between $50,000 and $500,000, 14 percent between $500,000 and $1 million, and 15 percent over $1 million, op. cit., p. 167.

desk consoles and printers.[27] While these systems are spectacular, it is unlikely that either their speed or expense can be justified on the basis of cost reductions. MIS are usually defended on the grounds of helping marketing managers make *better decisions*. As one executive said "The test of the new system is not data cost but data value." The proof of data value is no longer found in the reduction of administrative personnel, but in the profitable utilization of increasing numbers of highly qualified middle management people.[28] Although statements like this may satisfy the comptroller, they do not tell the firm how to balance its need for information against the costs of retrieval systems. Given the uncertainties in measuring the value of MIS, perhaps the best approach is to start small and add increments of data and equipment as they can be justified for specific decision problems.

A Simple Example

The types of data provided by marketing information systems can be illustrated by referring to a program developed by Amstutz for a small firm selling a new product in a new market.[29] The company could not afford extensive market research and was forced to gather information on their customers as they introduced the product. Media advertising was the primary promotional tool employed by the firm to generate initial orders and requests for information. Customers could buy direct from the factory or through distributor-retailer channels. The key inputs for the marketing information system were inquiries from consumers and warranty card data. The requests from consumers provided a basic list of prospects and allowed the firm to make additional mailings to persons who did not buy within a specified period. Requests for information were also used to evaluate the performance of different advertising media. Warranty cards gave demographic data on customers and made it possible to link purchases to original requests for information.

In addition to providing timely sales figures, Amstutz's system generated a variety of special reports shown in Tables 12-5 through 12-9. The Channel Analysis Report, for example, gave a summary of unit and dollar sales for individual outlets. The system also estimated the gross margins earned by dealers and projected inventory positions from warranty card returns. Sales invoices were analyzed to give the breakdown of product sales by customer type shown in Table 12-6. An example of the demographic data that can be derived from warranty cards is given in Table 12-7. This table showed the manager what age segments were currently being reached by the company's products.

One of the most useful reports prepared by Amstutz's program was a media analysis based on customer inquiries and sales traced through warranty cards (Table 12-8). This report shows how thirty-five media tried by the company in 1961 compared on a cost-per-inquiry and cost-per-sale basis. The media are ranked according to increasing cost per sale and the publications with zero sales and others at the bottom of the list would be candidates for elimination from subsequent advertising programs. Table 12-9 shows that the average advertising cost per sale was $17 and the inquiry to sale ratio was about 12:1. This means that additional mailings would be profitable as long as 1 out of every 200 prospects contacted bought the product. The main advantage of Amstutz's information

---

[27]Philip Kotler, *Marketing Management Analysis, Planning and Control,* (Englewood Cliffs, N.J.: Prentice-Hall, 2nd ed., 1972), p. 299.

[28]Terrance Hanold, President of the Pillsbury Company, quoted by Harry Stern in "Management Information System—What Is It and Why," *Management Science,* Vol. 17, No. 2 (October 1970), p. 120.

[29]Arnold E. Amstutz, "A Basic Marketing Information System—A Case Study in the Economical Use of Computerized Management Information Systems," *The Marketing Concept in Action,* Robert M. Kaplan, ed., (Chicago: American Marketing Association, June 1964 Proceedings), pp. 373-392.

Table 12-5
Channel Analysis Report, Dates Covered—1/1/62 Through 6/31/62

	Class—Electronic Supply		
Total Sales For Period	Units	Dollars	Est. Inventory Units
Product 1	158	9,756.50	32
Product 2	26	2,619.50	8
Product 3	12	72.00	—
Product 4	19	304.00	25
Total sales to this channel		12,752.00	
Estimated channel gross margin		6,883.00	

Source. Arnold E. Amstutz, "A Basic Marketing Information System—A Case Study in the Economical Use of Computerized Management Information Systems," *The Marketing Concept in Action,* Robert M. Kaplan, ed., (Chicago: American Marketing Association, June 1964 Proceedings), pp. 386, 387. Reprinted by permission of the American Marketing Association.

Table 12-6
Percentage Breakdown of Direct Sales by Customer,
Period Covered—5/1/62 Through 5/31/62

	Consumer	Secondary	Colleges	Business	Government	Foreign
Product 1	48.0	18.0	8.0	9.0	7.0	10.0
Product 2	14.0	30.0	22.0	24.0	9.0	1.0
Product 3	51.0	6.0	10.0	18.0	3.0	12.0
Product 4	12.0	0.0	9.0	3.0	3.0	73.0

Source. Same as Table 12-5.

Table 12-7
Analysis of Warranty Cards Returned, 1/1/62 Through 5/31/62

	Product 1	
Age	Units	Percent
15-18	129	16.9
19-25	72	9.4
26-35	78	10.2
36-45	246	32.2
46-	239	31.2

Source. Same as Table 12-5.

system was it gave the company timely marketing data at a monthly operating cost of only $2000. A more complex system under development at the Singer Company is discussed in the next section.

Table 12-8
MEDIA ANALYSIS—COST PER SALE (Dollars)
Dates Covered—9/1/61 Through 1/1/62
Report Date—1/7/62
Media Cut-Off Date—12/5/61

Medium	Inquiries	Media Cost	Cost Per Inquiry	Orders	Cost Per Sale
Science News Letter-1	310.00	430.00	1.39	93.00	4.62
Scientific American-2	1244.00	2310.00	1.86	213.00	10.85
New York Times-2	2940.00	3090.00	1.05	213.00	14.51
New York Times-3	2092.00	1989.00	.95	136.00	14.63
Science News Letter-2	155.00	430.00	2.77	29.00	14.83
New York Times-1	2057.00	3090.00	1.50	191.00	16.18
Pop. Electronics-3	2873.00	1640.00	.57	97.00	16.91
Wall St. Journal-1	255.00	880.00	3.45	50.00	17.60
Pop. Electronics-1	1167.00	1640.00	1.41	91.00	18.02
Electronics III.	316.00	825.00	2.61	36.00	22.92
Electronic World	1337.00	1495.00	1.12	55.00	27.18
Wall St. Journal-2	98.00	608.00	6.20	22.00	27.64
Popular Science-1	1874.00	3445.00	1.84	123.00	28.01
Scientific American-1	496.00	2310.00	4.66	77.00	30.00
El. Design News	289.00	350.00	1.21	11.00	31.82
Science News Letter-3	126.00	430.00	3.41	13.00	33.08
Science News Letter-4	65.00	430.00	6.62	13.00	33.08
Popular Science-2	2220.00	3445.00	1.55	104.00	33.13
Pop. Electronics-2	1112.00	1640.00	1.47	48.00	34.17
Automation	166.00	500.00	3.01	13.00	38.46
Mathematics Teacher	95.00	250.00	2.63	6.00	41.67
Science News Letter-5	17.00	90.00	5.29	2.00	45.00
Industrial Research	90.00	410.00	4.56	9.00	45.56
Electronics Products	26.00	285.00	10.96	4.00	71.25
Datamation	445.00	460.00	1.03	6.00	76.67
New York Times-4	25.00	164.00	6.56	2.00	82.00
Science World	396.00	1350.00	3.41	16.00	84.38
Wall St. Journal-3	125.00	385.00	3.08	4.00	96.25
Science	17.00	230.00	13.53	2.00	115.00
Pop. Electronics-4	758.00	1640.00	2.16	11.00	149.09
Business Week	93.00	835.00	8.98	4.00	208.75
Business Automation	71.00	360.00	5.07	0.0	∞
Electronic News	92.00	330.00	3.59	0.0	∞
Radio Electronics	36.00	340.00	9.44	0.0	∞
Saturday Review	61.00	777.00	12.74	0.0	∞

Source. Amstutz, "A Basic Marketing information Systems", p. 390.

Table 12-9

Advertising Cost Analysis

Dates covered—9/1/61 through 1/1/62
Media excluded—C/I greater than $30.00
Average cost per inquiry = $ 1.41
Average cost per sale = $17.00
Inquiry—sale ratio based on one mailing = 12.05
Average inquiry processing costs for 12.05 mailings = $3.62
Average total marketing cost per sale = $20.62
Break-even analysis on addition mailings—conversion = 0.005000

Source. Amstutz, "A Basic Marketing Information System," p. 391.

MIS At Singer

The Singer information system is designed to link factories, warehouses, and retail outlets with twenty-five field marketing organizations.[30] The basic dimensions of the system are described in Figure 12-8. When the system is complete, Singer's centralized computer will collect daily sales data from point-of-sale terminals in each store, check warehouse inventories, ship merchandise to stores as needed, and replenish warehouse stocks by scheduling production at the factories. The system will also provide the field sales agencies with daily sales reports and direct access to the central data bank for any additional data they may need.

Singer developed their system through a series of planned evolutionary steps. These involved such things as centralizing accounting functions, simplifying reporting forms, upgrading equipment, and designing point-of-sale terminals. The company was careful to solicit the help of the field managers and made sure they approved of the system before moving on to the next phase of development. Singer planned to pay for the new information system out of cost reductions and they were able to increase sales and keep accounting and EDP charges constant during the first four stages of the MIS developmental process.

THE COSMOS Experiment

Not all marketing information systems have been as successful as the Singer and Amstutz examples we have discussed. For a number of years the National Association of Food Chains has been promoting the COSMOS system to help improve merchandising data available to grocery stores.[31] This system calculates a direct product profit for each item by subtracting store, warehouse, and delivery costs from gross margins (described in Table 7-1, p. 315). The system keeps track of sales rates and makes recommendations on what items to stock, prices, and facings to be employed in each store to optimize profits. COSMOS is operational and is currently being used by eight firms.[32] Unfortunately, it appears that the high cost of installing the system ($30,000 to $85,000) and the trouble and cost of updating basic data on package sizes, prices, facings, and handling costs at the store level have prevented the system from being adopted by more firms.

[30]"Some Day I'm Going to Have a Little Black Box on My Desk," *Sales Management* (May 1, 1967), p. 33, p. 35.
[31]COSMOS stands for Computer Optimization and Simulation Modeling for Operating Supermarkets, see *COSMOS Progress and Prognosis* (Washington, D.C.: National Assoc. of Food Chains, July, 1973).
[32]King Soopers, P&C, Winn-Dixie, Oshawa, Stop and Shop, Brocton, and Smith's. The NAFC claims that the cost of installing the COSMOS system in these organizations was returned during the first year of operation.

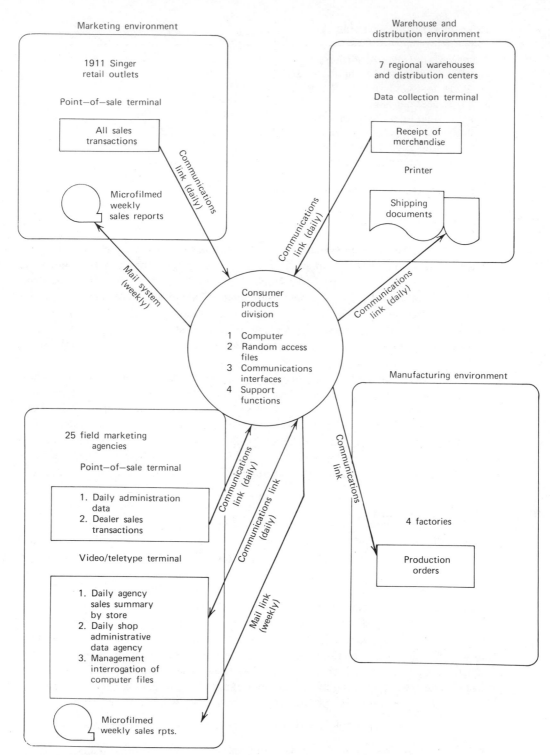

Figure 12-8 Singer's Proposed Information System.
Source. "Some Day I'm Going to Have a Little Black Box on My Desk," *Sales Management* (May 1, 1967), p. 34. Copyright 1967. Reprinted by permission.

Although COSMOS was developed and initially tested at Jewel, this company is no longer using the system.

The inability of some retailers to provide cheap data for the COSMOS system may be partially remedied by the recent adoption of electronic point-of-sale terminals by many retail stores. These machines collect data on each sale by reading information off merchandise, tickets, and credit cards with optical scanners and store it in minicomputers for later transfer to central processing units. J. C. Penny, for example, has ordered 17,000 NCR terminals in addition to 10,000 Singer data terminals for use in its stores.[33] The growth in the use of point-of-sale terminals and the COSMOS experience suggests that progress in developing marketing information systems depends not only on the invention of new methods of analysis, but also on the creation of low-cost procedures to gather input data.

One of the principal benefits derived from introducing marketing information systems is an increase in the availability of timely and detailed market data. However, if this information is not put to good use, the system may not pay its way. Progressive firms have taken the improved data from MIS and have made greater use of models that simulate the impact of alternative marketing programs on their own competitive environment. The output of these models can then be employed to plan marketing programs and control their implementation in the real world. Thus one of the great benefits of MIS is that it allows managers to learn more about their business environment and may enhance the long-run performance of the firm.

THE MARKETING AUDIT

Marketing programming is not complete unless it includes periodic reviews of the entire marketing efforts of the firm.[34] These reviews, called marketing audits, are designed to point out the strength and weaknesses of the marketing objectives, organization, personnel, and operating procedures employed by companies. The idea is to appraise the overall condition of the marketing program so the firm can capitalize on its strengths and improve areas that are weak.

Areas To Be Audited

The marketing audit is not concerned with measuring past performance, but looks to the future to see how well the resources of the firm are being used to exploit market opportunities. The auditor first looks at marketing objectives to make sure they are sufficiently broad so the firm doesn't get trapped with an obsolete product line. For example, an abrasives company would be advised to state their objective as improved sales of metal polishing and removal services rather than just as sales of grinding wheels. This approach allows the company to offer a variety of ways to solve customers' problems without restricting themselves to the sale of a single product.

The audit should also include an appraisal of the structure of the marketing organization. Does the chief marketing officer have enough power to control all relevant

---

[33]Note that the point-of-sale terminals Singer developed to provide data for its own information system are now being successfully marketed to other firms. *Wall Street Journal* (January 9, 1974), p. 3.

[34]The best single reference on marketing audits is a collection of papers published by the American Management Association under the title *Analyzing and Improving Marketing Performance*, Management Report No. 32, 1959.

marketing functions? Are the channels of communication open among sales, advertising, promotion, and product development executives? Do the managers of each marketing function have the skills, training, and experience needed to successfully perform their jobs? Should new product development be handled by a committee, venture teams, or a separate department? These represent only a few of the many questions that need to be asked to evaluate the organizational arrangements used to structure marketing activities.

In addition, marketing audits must evaluate the procedures that are used by the firm to implement marketing programs. This means the auditor considers how well the product line meets the needs of the perceived market segments. In addition, the auditor reviews the coverage of the sales territories and checks the speed of delivery provided by the warehouse and transportation network. Auditors should also talk to dealers and customers to find out how they view the marketing operations of the firm. One thing auditors look for in judging operating efficiency is balance across elements of the marketing program. It would be foolish, for example, to spend lavishly on a trade promotion unless salesmen were available to make follow-up calls. In another case, an auditor found a large portion of a pharmaceutical manufacturer's ad budget devoted to billboards. This is an unusual way to promote prescription drugs and does not agree with the typical procedures described earlier in Figure 12-3. The selection of billboards as an advertising medium had been made years before and it had become such a "sacred cow" that no one in the company questioned its efficiency. Fortunately, the auditor convinced the company to drop billboard advertising in one area and sales remained constant. Thus, in this case, a single operational change saved the manufacturer more than enough to pay for the marketing audit.

Implementing the Audit

Marketing audits should be conducted in healthy firms as well as in those that are sick. Audits can help fine tune successful programs in addition to identifying problem areas in companies with declining markets and low profits. To achieve the maximum benefit from a marketing audit, it is probably best to hire someone from outside the company to direct the investigation. Outside consultants are apt to be more objective and can devote full time to the project. In addition, consultants often have a breadth of experience that allows them to see problems with current practices and recommend improvements.[35] Marketing audits operate from a different perspective than typical short-run control procedures. Where marketing control asks, "Are we doing things right?," the marketing audit goes beyond and asks, "Are we doing the right things?"[36]

Summary

We have shown how marketing information systems collect and process the basic knowledge needed to plan and control marketing operations. The computer files of information systems are continuously updated so managers will have the figures required to make decisions on products, prices, promotion, and distribution channels. Information systems also analyze marketing data and prepare special reports that highlight

[35]Richard D. Crisp, "Auditing the Functional Elements of a Marketing Operation," *Analyzing and Improving Marketing Performance* (New York: American Management Association, Management Report No. 32, 1959) p. 44.

[36]David T. Kollat, Roger D. Blackwell and James F. Roberson, *Strategic Marketing* (New York: Holt, Rinehart and Winston, Inc., 1972), p. 500.

salesforce productivity, realign territories, measure price elasticity, and calculate marginal responses to advertising.

The success of marketing programs in the real world frequently depends on how well the various elements of the marketing mix work together. Enlightened managers are now able to pretest the interactions of marketing variables by running examples through special business simulations. These simulations are developed from data supplied by marketing information systems and from subjective inputs provided by executives. The advantage of these simulations is they allow the manager to test combinations of marketing factors without spending the money or taking the risks associated with making changes in an actual competitive environment.

Simulations can also be used to help control the implementation of marketing programs. The basic control process is a check for differences between desired performance standards and actual results. When negative deviations occur, simulation can be employed to find out what has gone wrong with the marketing plans and help develop new strategies. The primary data used to highlight problem areas is provided by control charts and special profit reports prepared by the marketing information system.

In addition to monitoring current operations, marketing managers must prepare themselves for the future. This means that marketing programs should be audited periodically to make sure the firm has the right products, personnel, and channels of distribution to fill customer needs and meet the challenges offered by competitors.

Questions

1. What procedures do product managers use to put together an optimum marketing mix?
2. What contributions can simulation make to help produce managers in their marketing programming?
3. Since simulation does not seek out the best marketing mix, how does the manager know whether he has the right combination of marketing variables?
4. What factors have prevented more widespread usage of simulation in marketing?
5. How do marketing information systems differ from marketing research?
6. At what point should a deviation from planned objectives prompt executives to make adjustments in their marketing programs?
7. Do marketing performance standards vary among firms and if so why?
8. What are the basic ingredients of a successful marketing information system?
9. Experience has shown that marketing information systems are often expensive to install. How can this cost be justified to the stockholders?
10. The media analysis shown in Table 12-8 calculated an advertising cost per sale. Where did the MIS get the data needed to make this calculation?
11. Why should businessmen spend money on marketing audits?

Case 12-1
Gem Frocks, Inc.[1]

Arthur Greenspan of Gem Frocks, Inc. was considering a proposal from Eugene Miller to extend a recently installed marketing information system to encompass several new types of sales reports. According to Miller, the new reports would permit more effective management of the sales force, and would more than justify the time and expense of field and home office personnel in gathering the requisite information and preparing the reports. Ultimately Miller envisioned even further expansion of the marketing information system so that it would be a total "sales information system."

THE COMPANY

Gem Frocks was a small family-run firm with annual sales of about $10 million (see Exhibit 1 for organizational chart). Gem manufactured thirty groups of coordinated sportswear per year that were offered in seven seasonal lines. The number of items in a group ran into the hundreds because there were 9 to 100 styles, one to five colors, and five to eight sizes. Exhibit 2 shows the order form for the Irish Mist group.

The groups were sold to 2000 active accounts. A sales executive said that if the company sold 7500 accounts actively it would have essentially complete coverage of its potential market. It made 65 percent of its sales to traditional department stores, 30 percent to specialty shops, and 5 percent to chain discount department stores.

PRODUCTION

The Gem Frocks' sample department made garments from designers sketches that were then modeled for a top management committee. Samples of the best items were made for the sales force and for developing patterns. From the early orders, decisions were made to produce quantities of some items in excess of orders on hand, to discontinue others, and on still others to await specific orders. It took approximately one to six weeks for fabric delivery

(depending on availability), and from five to six weeks for production.

FIELD SALESMEN

Gem Frocks employed twenty-one field salesmen and all but seven were exclusive with the company. The seven non-exclusive salesmen were located in the Midwest where Gem's volume was low. (See Exhibit 3 for a map of sales territories.)

Nineteen of the twenty-one field salesmen were paid a commission of 6 percent of net sales. The remaining two most recently hired salesmen received a salary plus a commission for exceeding budget. The company could control salesmen by adjusting territory sizes and varying the amount of cooperation from the home office concerning mailings and publicity. Perhaps the most effective method of control consisted of varying the amount of service extended to customers of particular salesmen. It was within the company's discretion to ascertain which salesmen's accounts obtained rapid delivery of reorders of fast-selling merchandise.

Management hoped that a better sales-information system would help improve the control process. The salary-plus-commission plan under which the two newest salesmen worked was an experiment to ascertain if more control could be exercised over the salesmen if their income depended not only on booking orders, but also on cooperating with the plans of the home office. The idea was to relate the base salary partly to cooperation with office plans. Success to date was hard to determine.[2]

The company communicated with the salesmen through a weekly memo that reviewed current trade data and included notices on the addition or the discontinuance of items. Regional sales meetings were held before each major selling season (spring and fall). A national sales meeting was held annually for primarily social and morale purposes. In addition, the president and vice-president traveled around the country before the beginning of each major selling season visiting salesmen and larger customers.

---

[1]This case was prepared by Stanley A. Tractenberg. Copyright (c) by Stanley A. Tractenberg. Reproduced by permission.

[2]Few experienced salesmen wished to work under such a compensation plan. Furthermore, management had been disappointed with the production of inexperienced salesmen in this field.

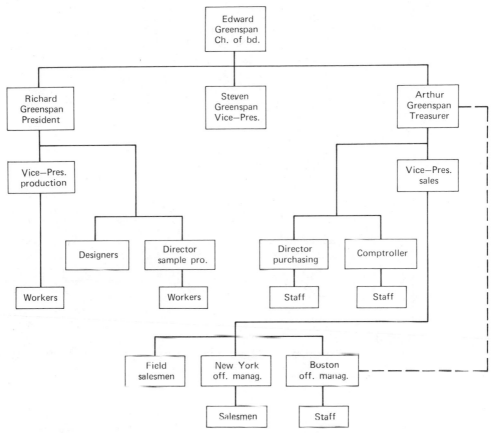

Exhibit 1

Partial Organization Chart (As visualized by case writer—no formal chart existed.)

Salesmen were requested to file activity reports on their visit to each account (Exhibit 4). These reports were intended to keep management up to date on the activities of the salesmen. Currently, only three field salesmen regularly filed the reports. Two were the men on salary plus commission and one was a regular field salesman. Seven salaried salesmen were permanently attached to the New York sales office and showroom to service customers who visited the New York office when field salesmen were traveling their territories.

A company executive noted that plans were under consideration to place regional sales managers over all of the salesmen in the field. The managers would supervise and control the sales force to increase sales, to break into new markets, and to introduce new product lines. They would be responsible for the hiring and training of salesmen and in the opinion of management offered potential for better control over the sales force. While several of the salesmen had shown great managerial potential, the company had not committed itself to selecting managers from the sales force.

NEED FOR THE SALES INFORMATION SYSTEM

Eugene Miller suggested that the systematic collection of sales information would provide management with a better basis for controlling salesmen and making marketing decisions. Miller explained why improved control of salesmen was needed in the following terms.

"Apparel salesmen have traditionally acted as 'agents' rather than as employees of the manufacturers. Since a majority of firms have not been able to generate sufficient volume to support their own sales force, salesmen in the industry have generally been encouraged to represent more than

IRISH MIST

				Bill/To: Account No.	Ship To: Account No.	Mark For Account No.	ORDER DATE	CUST. ORDER NO.	DEPT. NO.

STYLE	PRICE	PCS.	COST	DESCRIPTION	A.R.P.	SEAMIST — GREN	ROSEMIST — RED	LILACMIST — LILA
5400	11.75			EMBROIDERED JACKET	20.00			
5401	10.75			PORTRAIT COLLAR JACKET	18.00			
5410	6.75			SLIM SKIRT	12.00			
5411	7.75			A-LINE SKIMMER SKIRT	13.00			
5412	7.75			A-LINE GORED POCKET SKIRT	13.00			
5405	7.75			EMBR. EMPIRE OVERBLOUSE	13.00			
5406	7.75			EMBR. SCOOP NECK O'BLSE.	13.00			
5407	6.00			COWL BOW OVERBLOUSE	10.00			
5408	6.75			PETAL COLLAR OVERBLOUSE	12.00			
5410	6.75			SLIM SKIRT	12.00			
5411	7.75			A-LINE SKIMMER SKIRT	13.00			
5412	7.75			A-LINE GORED POCKET SKIRT	13.00			
5415	11.75			EMBROIDERED SHIFT	20.00			
5416	10.75			SCALLOP COLLAR SHIFT	18.00			
5420	4.75			FLORAL PRINT BOW BLOUSE	8.00			
5425	4.75			CREPE SHAWL COLLAR BLOUSE	8.00			
5426	4.75			CREPE BOW BLOUSE	8.00			

Exhibit 2

Order Form Showing Retail and Manufacturer Prices for Items in a Group

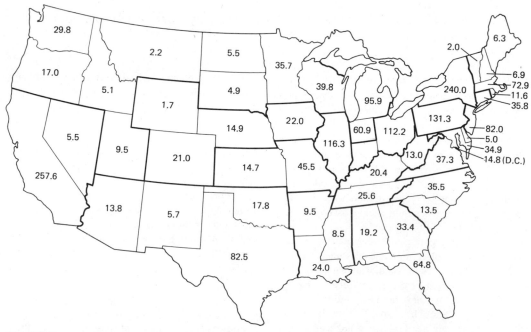

Exhibit 3

Gem Frocks' Sales Territories and Retail Sales of Women's Sportwear for All
Companies (millions of $) *Source.* Company records and the Bureau of the Census.

DATE 4-1		ACCOUNT ACTIVITY REPORT		SALESMAN MIKE ANDERSON 020

ACCOUNT NAME	THE HOUSE OF TEE	BUYER	MR. BERNARD TORTORICK
STREET ADDRESS	305 STATE STREET	MDSE. MGR.	
CITY AND STATE	NEW LONDON, CONN.	ADV. MGR.	

ORDER RECEIVED ☐	SUMMER ☐	MID–SUMMER ☐	FALL ☐	TRANS–ITIONAL ☐	HOLIDAY ☐	MID–WINTER ☐	TOTAL UNITS _____ $ _____

WHERE SHOWED LINE		STATUS OF ORDER		TYPE OF STORE		CLASSIFICATION		SPECIAL INSTRUCTIONS
IN STORE	✓	MAILING ORDER		DEPARTMENT		EXCLUSIVE		
SAMPLE ROOM		PROMISED LATER		SPECIALTY	✓	MEDIUM		
N.Y. SHOW ROOM		WON'T BUY NOW	✓	CHAIN OR BRANCH	✓	POPULAR		
MARKET SHOW		NO INTEREST		DEPARTMENT		ADVERTISING		
PHONE	✓	BUYER OUT				NO ADVERTISING		

MAILING LIST INFORMATION								
PROSPECT ☐	NEW ACCOUNT ☐	OLD ACCOUNT ☑	PREVIOUSLY REPORTED ☐	CORRECT LIST ☐	NO MAIL ☐	REMOVE FROM LIST ☐

CUSTOMER REACTIONS AND COMMENTS

THIS ACCOUNT HAD TRIED THE LINE WITH FAIRLY GOOD DEPTH AND WAS NOT TOO SUCCESSFUL WITH IT- CLAIMED WE'RE TO MISSY - SUGGEST A LETTER EXPLAINING THE NEW CONCEPT IN LOOK OF THE BIG 'R'

Exhibit 4

Salesman's Account Activity Report Requesting The Boston Office to Write to an Inactive Account

one manufacturer. Feelings of independence are also fostered by the commission system since the salesmen's incomes have been directly dependent on their own efforts.

"As apparel firms have grown, the larger firms have tended to employ salesmen on an exclusive basis in those territories where a salesman could support himself on the offerings of one manufacturer. Even though these salesmen represent one firm exclusively, many of them still view themselves as relatively independent agents and tend to resent bookkeeping chores imposed by the manufacturer that do not obviously benefit the salesman. Indeed some manufacturers have been somewhat at the mercy of their exclusive salesmen. Many of the salesmen have taken great care to reveal as little information as possible about their customers and their relationship with the customers. Thus, if a good salesman decided to move to another manufacturer, he frequently takes the customers' loyalty with him and the manufacturer cannot retain many of his accounts.

"Until we acquired the computer we were not able to compile enough information about a specific salesman to know in what direction we should try to move him. If we can get this system working, we should be able to obtain a reading of how well a salesman is doing relative to the potential of his territory. With this information we can then make some changes in his territory size or take other steps to bring him into line."

Prior to the arrival of the computer, two reports were prepared twice a year and one on a weekly basis. One showed sales for each salesman listed by account and the second showed sales of individual items within each group. The third showed total bookings per week for each salesman. This report was felt by management to be the most important. These reports required the half-time services of three clerks earning $85 per week.

Sales Information System Proposal

Miller's proposal (see below) suggested that a file be constructed for each salesman. From a summary "recap" sheet prepared weekly for each salesman management would, according to Miller, be able to "evaluate each salesman without becoming burdened with excessive details. Each recap sheet would, however, be derived from several more detailed reports that management could use to evaluate any particular salesman in depth."

Memo to: Arthur Greenspan, Treasurer
From: Eugene Miller, Boston Staff
Subject: Integrated Use of Marketing Information for Better Sales Control

A file will be made up for each salesman.
It will contain the latest copy of each report.
It will be prefaced with a weekly recap analysis of his productivity (on a standardized form).
(See Exhibit 5.)
All decisions regarding this man and his territory can be made on the basis of the information in his field.

Recap Analysis

A. From the weekly booking report (Exhibit 6)
   1. Compare net dollar sales this year with last year and list percentage difference.
   2. Compare origin of sales—road versus N.Y. office in percentage.
   3. Compare actual sales this year with budget and list percentage difference.
   4. Analyze which groups are strong or weak for him.
   5. Compare 1, 2, 3 and 4 against last week.
   6. Comment on above: for example,
      Does salesman know how to sell all groups?
      Is there a territory problem with specific groups?
      Is too much business written in the N.Y. office?
      How does he stand against company averages?
      Is next two weeks' sales last year reasonable for this year?

B. From the sales distribution report (by trading area).[3] (See Exhibit 8.)
   1. Compare net sales against "area potential guide."
      Is he obtaining volume where potential is?
      Is he traveling correct areas (analyze field activity reports)?
      Comment further.
   2. Check into specific trading areas.

Compare this year with last year by account.
Where does problem lie?
Is executive help needed for specific accounts?
Comment further.

C. From field activity reports (filled out by salesmen after each call). (Exhibit 4)
   1. Total Number of accounts called on:
      (a) Current accounts (bought within the last year from Gem Frocks).
      (b) Inactive accounts (formerly bought from Gem Frocks).
      (c) Prospects (never bought from Gem Frocks).
   2. Number of times line showed.
   3. Number of accounts sold.
      (a) Number mailing in orders.
      (b) Number took order form from.
   4. Number of groups sold to all accounts?
      Analysis on above, for example:
      (a) Is he covering enough accounts?
          If not—why? Poor planning?
          Lack of appointments?
      (b) Is he adequately servicing current and inactive accounts?
      (c) How effective is he showing the line?
          (Number of times showed line divided by number of calls made)
      (d) How effective is he in closing the sale?
          (Number of accounts sold divided by number of times showed line.)
      (e) How effective is he in taking orders with him?
          (Number of orders taken with him divided by number of accounts sold.)
      (f) Is he placing enough groups with our accounts?
          (Number of groups sold divided by number of accounts sold.)

D. From volume distribution report[4]
   1. In what volume categories are his accounts?
   2. Is there a trend in moving his accounts up into the next higher volume category?
   3. How many accounts from last year are unsold this year?
   4. How many new accounts has he opened?
   5. How many old-current accounts has he maintained last year to this year?

E. From the weekly shipping report by salesman[4]

---

[3] A trading area was comprised of several cities.

[4] Not yet programmed for computer.

WK. ENDG.

	LAST WEEK—ACTUAL			THIS WEEK—ACTUAL			ORIGIN	
	L.Y.	T.Y.	% DIFF.	L.Y.	T.Y.	% DIFF.	ROAD	NYO
SEASON—A								
SEASON—B								
A								
B								

	LAST WEEK			THIS WEEK			LAST YEAR
	ACTUAL	BUDGET	% DIFF.	ACTUAL	BUDGET	% DIFF.	NEXT 2 WKS.
WEEK—A							
WEEK—B							
A							
B							

ACTIVITY THIS WEEK	TOTAL ACCTS. CALLED ON	CURRENT	PROPOSED	NO. TIMES SHOWED LINE	EFF.	NO. ACCTS. SOLD	EFF.	MAIL ORD.	TOOK ORD.	FFF.	TOTAL NO. ACCTS. SOLD STD.

ACTIVITY THIS WEEK	NO. CAPS COND.	EFF.	CUM. FIGS.	L.Y. SOLD T.Y. UNSOLD	NEW ACCTS. OPENED	OLD CURR. ACCTS. MAINT.	VOL CATEGORIES			
							0—1000	1—5000	5—10,000	10,000

SHIPPED	ORDERS CANC. NO. OF FIGS.	% SHIPPED	BACKLOG	

GROUPS	CUM. ACTUAL SALES	CUM. BUDGET	% DIFF.	TRADING AREAS NAME	NO.	NET SALES	AREA POTENTIAL (GUIDE)	% OF POTENT
1.								
2.								
3.								
4.								
5.								
6.								
7.								
8.								
9.								

Exhibit 5.
Draft of Proposed Recap Sheet

1. Percentage unjustified cancellations to gross bookings.
2. Percentage shipped to gross bookings—less unit cancellations.
3. Backlog this year.

F. From linear programming study of territories (under discussion: not yet approved)
   1. Optimum route sheet for each territory.
   2. Compare travel of salesman with optimum.

COMPONENTS OF SYSTEM

Although parts of Miller's system were still in the proposal stage, three reports that could contribute to the system had already been programmed for the computer and were available to management on a weekly basis. The first of these, the salesman's weekly booking report (Exhibit 6), was a weekly tabulation of bookings by each salesman for each merchandise group presented on a "this-year" versus "last-year" basis. The second report was a weekly sales distribution report by city (Exhibit 7), which was a tabulation of sales to individual stores within a specific city for each salesman. It showed sales of each merchandise group for the year-to-date, last year's sales of the comparable group, and last year's sales for the period corresponding to the forthcoming two weeks. The third report, the salesman's credit limit report, (Exhibit 8) was a listing of current credit limits for each store in a salesman's territory.

Much of the additional information needed for the proposed sales information system would be obtained from an analysis of the activity reports made out by each salesman after he called on an account. In addition, territory potentials would be developed by staff personnel in the Boston office from published statistical sources and lists of stores in each town.

Miller indicated that complete implementation of the system would take about one year. If the complete system was not adopted, the present sales information reports would still be quite useful in making decisions concerning the sales force.

COST OF THE PROPOSED SYSTEM

The three reports that were currently being prepared (Exhibits 6, 7 and 8) required intracompany charges of $6000 for computer time each year that included the charge for the services of the computer operator. This figure excluded the time needed to prepare the necessary input data in the form of punched cards or tapes. Miller believed these input charges were not appropriately chargeable to the sales reports since the same data were used also for other purposes.

The programs used to prepare the three existing reports were constantly being modified to make them more efficient. The programmer was paid $12,000 a year and Miller estimated that it would take 40 percent of the programmer's time for a year to complete the programming of the current proposal. Miller anticipated that the routine processing of the additional portions of the proposal would involve intracompany charges of $3500 a year in computer and operator charges.

Even with these additional reports total usage of the computer would still be less than 40 hours per week. Under the present contract Gem Frocks was obligated to pay for a minimum of 40 hours of computer time per week. Within the next two or three years, however, use of the computer was expected to exceed 40 hours per week and at that time additional expense would be incurred both for machine time and operators.

In evaluating the proposal Arthur Greenspan was concerned about the positive or negative effect the system would have on the salesmen, whether management could make effective use of the information developed, and whether the system adequately prepared the company for future changes in the apparel field. Specifically he wondered if all of the reports were necessary or if other reports might be more useful to management.

THE SALES MEETING

In preparation for the Fall selling season, several of the salesmen had come to New York to confer with the executives of the company. Participants were Eugene Miller; Jerry Katz, the New York sales office manager; Jack Samet, a New England salesman on salary plus commission; and Arnold Barysh, a midwestern salesman on commission. After discussing the best way to sell the new groups, the conversation drifted to the filing of reports by the salesmen:

ARNOLD BARYSH: "Gene, I keep receiving your request for all different types of forms to be filled out. I'm a busy man with a big territory to cover, so I don't have time to fill out additional paperwork. Between my records and the order blanks, I do enough pencil pushing. If I could see some constructive use for the reports, maybe I might feel differently but I just don't have the time.''

EUGENE MILLER: "Arnie, I know you're busy. But a couple of minutes after each account is all that is needed to fill in an activity report. It provides different information than the order blank. Under the present system, our information is about the successful order, not the reasons for firms not buying.

ARNOLD BARYSH· "I have all the useful information in my notebooks. As long as I know who to see and not to see, the company has nothing to worry about. Instead of worrying about my reports, why don't you help me get some additions to the line that would really sell in my territory.''

JERRY KATZ: "Arnie, your problems are no different than anybody else's. If we listened to everyone of you salesmen, we would be carrying twice the number of items and still have the same sales. It's like the budget, accept it—don't question it.''

ARNOLD BARYSH· "The worst thing are those damn budgets. You boys keep sending me your figures on what you think I should sell. You sit back in your easy chairs, both you and Gene, having never had to travel hundreds of miles a week and never been on commission, and tell me that I'm not booking enough business. I get these figures with no explanation and every time I try to pin you down you hem and haw.''

JERRY KATZ: "You can always protest if you think Boston is unfair. I noticed that you and Jack haven't picked up your weekly reports.''

ARNOLD BARYSH: "Save yourself the money. My records are in shape. I don't know why I need a computer to tell me what I sold this year or last.''

JACK SAMET: "I have been with the firm for four months so the report isn't worth anything to me. After all, the comparable figures were set by another salesman. Besides, I keep all my information on cards in black books, which I follow for a route.''

EUGENE MILLER: "Jack, how long do you spend each night bringing these cards up to date?''

JACK SAMET: "To tell the truth, I have been getting a little lax. With my two youngsters running around, nothing gets done. After they're asleep, I do the reports in front of the TV. That drags my report and the activity reports out to three instead of one hour.''

JERRY KATZ: "I can sympathize with you. I spend anywhere up to three hours daily reviewing all the figures by territory and by line. In that way, I can spot trends to keep you men informed and tell you where to place your emphasis in selling. These reports may be an adjunct to the operations but they're the Bible as far as I'm concerned.''

ARNOLD BARYSH: "If you didn't review each individual salesman, it wouldn't take that long. Why do you keep up with all of the statistics? That's our responsibility. Our personal records, like Jack's, have all the information on one sheet that we need. There's no need to wade through the reports every week; instead you should allow the computer to do something more useful like bookkeeping.''

EUGENE MILLER: "The computer was purchased for both bookkeeping and marketing reports. The computer and the reports are here to stay.''

QUESTIONS

1. How equitable and efficient are the present sales territories?
2. Should Gem Frocks hire additional regional sales managers? If so, how many should be hired, where should they be located, and what jobs should they perform?
3. How much will the proposed marketing information system cost and who will benefit most from the information?
4. What can be done to encourage the salesmen to send in the data needed to operate the information system?
5. Does the proposed system generate the types of information needed to manage Gem Frocks now and in the future?
6. Should Gem Frocks adopt the proposed information system?

Exhibit 6

Salesman's Weekly Booking Report

WINSTON (0)	T/YR GROUPS (1)	L/YR (2)	T/YR GWB (3)	T/YR NWB (4)	T/YR NCC (5)	T/YR NET BOOKINGS (6)	L/YR BOOKINGS (7)	PCT. DIFFERENCE (8)	DOL. DIFFERENCE (9)	L/YR N/T/W (10)	T/YR NO. OF ACCTS. (11)	L/YR (12)	PCT. N/Y (13)	PCT. ROAD (14)	BDGT (15)	DOL. DIFFERENCE (16)	PCT. DIFFERENCE (17)
	CACS					1, 2					6						
	CRET	MOHR			7	20, 0	102, 8	80-%	82, 8-	11, 1	30		73%	26%		24, 7-	55-%
	CRES			2	1, 1			See numbers ( ) above					23%	76%	44, 7		
	TWEE				5	1											
	TWES																
	HEAH																
	HEAS																
	DTOH	DTFT	2	2	2, 0	2											
	DTMS		3	3	9	2											
	P&PT		3	3		1											
	P&TS		4	4		1											
	CROC				1, 5	3											
	PEAK			2	2, 9	1											
		BLSE			11, 6	19											
	TFAL		1, 4	1, 0													
	SETS																
	VELV	VELV	4, 0	4, 0													
	KNIT	LACE	1, 0	1, 0													
	SHIFT																
		BJER															
		GOLD															

0. Name of Salesman

   Name of this year's group

   Name of last year's group

1. T/YR GRP:
2. L/YR GRP:
3. T/YR GWB: This year's gross weekly bookings in 000's of $
4. T/YR NWB: This year's net weekly bookings in 000's of $
5. T/YR NCC: This year's net cumulative cancellations in 000's of $
6. T/YR NCB: This year's net cumulative bookings in 000's of $
7. L/YR NCB: Last year's net cumulative bookings in 000's of $
8. PCT. DIFF: Percent difference between 6 and 7
9. DOL. DIFF: Dollar difference between 6 and 7 in 000's of $
10. L/YR NTW: Last year's cumulative business at the end of the next two weeks in 000's of $
11. T/YR NOAC: This year's number of accounts sold. (Total of accounts buying each group add to more than the total of accounts sold because store buying four groups will appear four times, but only once in the total season figure)
12. L/YR NOAC: Last year's number of accounts sold. (This information not available for last year yet)
13. PCT/N/Y: Percent of business booked in the N.Y. office
14. PCT/ROAD: Percent of business booked on the road. (Total does not necessarily add to 100% because of orders originating from store)
15. BDGT: Budget for group in 000's of $
16. DOL. DIFF: Dollar difference between budget and this year net cumulative bookings in 000's of $ (Column 6)
17. PCT. DIFF: Percent difference between budget and this year net cumulative bookings

Exhibit 7

Salesman's Weekly Sales Distribution Report by City

RODENBORN

(0) CITY (1) / STATE ACCT. (2) / NAME (3)	GROUP (4)	LAST Y/T/D (5)	GROUP (6)	CUR Y/T/D (7)	DOL. DIFF (8)	PCT. DIFF (9)	LST. YR. NEXT 2 WKS (10)
	* BLAZ	428	* MEAN	239	189-	45-%	*
	*	918	* TFAL	931	13	1 %	*
MUSCATINE IOWA 26060 GLASS SMART SHOP	*		* TSPG	1,996			*
	* NOHR		* CACK	348			* 444
	* REGN		* CRET	533			* 346
	* BLAZ		* HEAH	418			* 495
	*		* PEAK	231			*
	*		* TFAL	1,638	1,630	%	* 1,385
SIDNEY IOWA 51600 PAULYS	*		* SPG	1,006			*
	*		* MIC	186			*
	*		* TTRM	448			*
	*		* BSIC	88			*
	*		* CACK	224			*
	*		* CRET	408			*
	*		* THEE	118			*
	*		* HEAH	37			*
	*		* PEAK	124			*
	*		* TFAL	969	969	%	*
WASH- INGTON IOWA 45295 A MCGANNON	* NOHR		*				*
	* REGN	See numbers	* TSFG	891			*
	* BLAZ	( ) above					*
***TOTALS TRADING AREA	*	0,370					*
AMES IOWA 66100 TOWN & CAMPUS	* PROP	208					*
	* REGN	38C					*
	* BLAZ	90					*
	*	1,078					*

0 Name of salesman
1 City/State: Location of store
2 Acct: Reference number of store
3 Store
4 Name: Name of last year's group
5 Last Y/T/D: Last year-to-date sales
6 Group: Name of current year's group
7 Current Y/T/D: Current year-to-date sales
8 Dol. Diff: Dollar difference between 5 and 7
9 Pct. Diff: Percent difference between 5 and 7
10. Lst. Yr. Next 2 Wks: Last year's sales for next two weeks

Exhibit 8
Salesman's Credit Limit Report

ACCT. (1)	SLM (2)	T/A (3)	NAME (4)	STREET (5)	CITY (6)	STATE	CR. LIMIT (7)
67520	365	589	UHLMANS	HIGH & LONG ST	TROY	OHIO	00250
67610	365	589	UNION CO		COLUMBUS	OHIO	00200
67830	365	586	V & V STORES INC	3054 MADISON ROAD	CINCINNATI	OHIO	00035
68391	365	586	VICKIS	342 LUDLOW AVENUE	CINCINNATI	OHIO	00025
68450	365	607	VICTORIA MODES	6420 MARKET ST	YOUNGSTOWN	OHIO	
68550	365	586	VILLAGE SHOP	CHERRY GROVE PLAZA	CINCINNATI	OHIO	00030
68390	365	581	VIS FASHIONS	COLLEGE PLAZA	ALLIANCE	OHIO	00025
27905	365	586	W A GUENTHERS & CO	910 E MC MILLAN	CINCINNATI	OHIO	00060
69338	365	588	WALKERS	1621 NORTH			
69540	365	589	WALZS STYLE SHOP	856 HAMILTON			
70450	365	603	WESTGATE LION STORE	SECOR & CEI			
70931	365	586	WILLENBRINGS	5849 HAMILTON			

See numbers ( ) above

1. Acct: Reference number of store
2. SLM: Salesman's number
3. T/A: Trading area
4. Name: Store
5. Street: Address of store
6. City/State: Location of store
7. Cr. Limit: Credit limit in tens of dollars

Case 12-2
Hahn, Inc. (A)[1]

As a young man, Lloyd Hahn observed that there was a serious weed problem in the cornfields near his home. Chemical spraying seemed to be the best solution, but the available sprayers were high-pressure units designed for spraying orchards. In 1948, he developed a workable low-pressure tank sprayer that could be attached to the back of a tractor and used for spraying the weeds in and between rows of corn. A few years later, he developed a larger machine called the Quick-Spray to fill the farmer's need for a high-clearance, self-propelled sprayer that could straddle the rows after the crop's growth prevented the use of tractor-mounted spraying equipment (Exhibit 1).

The Quick-Spray, the pioneer sprayer of its type, built an excellent record of performance, and by 1958, was considered the best brand in the field. "We sold more of this type of sprayer than all our competition put together," says Lloyd Hahn. However, the company held no patents and faced growing competition from other manufacturers. In 1959, the Double-O line of garden tillers was acquired by Hahn for $50,000. While Hahn, Inc. faced numerous competitors in the garden tiller field, company officials were confident that this part of the firm's business would grow steadily.

[1]Case prepared by Robert L. Taylor of the United States Air Force Academy and James Utterback of Harvard University. Data made available through the courtesy of Hahn, Inc. Reproduced by permission.

At first, parts for sprayers and tillers were purchased from other firms. Gradually, the company acquired its own facilities for manufacturing, and in 1962 purchased an abandoned automobile manufacturing plant for slightly over $325,000. The new plant gave Hahn over 600,000 square feet of floor space, more than enough for current and projected operations.

PRODUCT DEVELOPMENT

Up until 1961, Hahn's product line included sprayers, tillers, and a limited line of agricultural chemicals. To expand the line, Lloyd Hahn designed three prototype low-profile machines for crops not requiring the high-clearance of the Quick-Spray. Development costs exceeded $50,000 and still, the idea would not work. Lloyd Hahn could not spend the time needed to make the necessary changes and so, the idea was scrapped. At about the same time, Lloyd Hahn noted that the recently acquired garden tillers did not meet the needs of the market. He completely redesigned the tiller and it soon became an important profit maker for the company.

By 1960 the lawn-and-garden equipment industry was in a period of flux, with many of the major firms moving to fill out their lines in an aggressive attempt to gain distribution leverage. These conditions prompted the Buckeye Products Company to ap-

Exhibit 1
Hahn Quick-Spray

proach Hahn with an offer to buy out Hahn's tiller line. Though it lagged in the development of new types of mowing equipment, Buckeye was well known for its quality mowers. Hahn decided not to sell, but later in the year a representative from Buckeye's parent company indicated they wanted to move out of the consumer goods field and were looking for a buyer for their mower products. They argued that the Buckeye mowers would be a natural complement to Hahn's tiller and would fill out their line. The main question was whether Hahn could raise the $1.2 million needed (four times Hahn's net worth). A deal was finally made involving a nominal cash payment for the manufacturing equipment, with the balance due over the next year and a half as the finished-goods inventory was sold off. There would be no drain on working capital so long as Hahn could dispose of the inventory at full market prices. Also, it was felt that the company would be able to use the manufacturing equipment in other ways even if the mower business did not work out. The purchase gave Hahn a trained sales force and distribution network in the "lawn care" business.

The Buckeye purchase required a rapid selloff of the finished-goods inventory, but Buckeye distributors and outlets became frightened that the mower line would be dropped and sales fell sharply. As the units piled up at the Hahn plant, Lloyd Hahn realized that he would have to sell them at a loss. He also found some engineering flaws in the mower and began to redesign the product. He worked for nearly 18 months perfecting the mower with the end-result being an exceptionally well-designed, high-quality machine called the Klip-EZ.

At the request of a number of distributors and in order to stay abreast of competition, a snow blower was planned for introduction in 1962. Lloyd Hahn saw this as a profitable item as well as a way to reduce the seasonality of production.

Hahn continued the agricultural chemical operations until 1962 when the materials and equipment were sold because of Hahn's growing need for capital. By the end of 1962, Hahn's product line included four high-quality products: agricultural sprayers, lawn mowers, garden tillers, and snow blowers. Feeling that quality should be placed above price, Hahn made service and guarantees integral parts of his products. Exhibit 2 details the product line as it existed in late 1962.

PLANNING AND BUDGETING

In 1962, Hahn started an accumulated forecast. Housing starts gave the company a good idea of the overall consumer demand for mowers (Exhibit 3). Hahn salesmen also were asked to forecast the number of sales for their area, but Lloyd Hahn was always sure to temper these estimates as he thought prudent. Similarly, the farm spray distribution centers were asked to define the projected sales of sprayers, but again, Hahn, his brother, and the sales manager, feeling that the distributors were always on the optimistic side, made the final estimate. Estimates were made by product and model; no field research was conducted. Some of the leading indicators important to their estimates are contained in Exhibit 3 through 6. At the sales meeting in 1962, the salesmen and distributors were asked not only to forecast for the year ahead, but they also previewed the market for the next five years as well. From that estimate, Lloyd Hahn and his top staff projected a five-year forecast of sales and profits.

CHANNELS OF DISTRIBUTION

All Hahn products were marketed through a network of wholesale distributors and retail dealers. The sprayers were sold through forty distributors, the tillers and mowers through twenty-three specialty distributors and twelve independent hardware distributors. Each wholesale distributor had an exclusive arrangement to sell within a prescribed market area. The various distributors sold to approximately 7500 retail dealers. The sprayers were carried by farm implement stores and farm chemical dealers—the latter called spray centers. A very small number of dealers handled the complete line of Hahn products. Separate sales forces were used by each division.

Little private brand work was done by Hahn. Also, Hahn did not sell to discount houses. The fear was expressed that if the firm's products were used in discount or loss-leader operations, consumer loyalty and the reputation based on quality would be lost, while distributor and dealer discontent would be increased.

Several distribution channel problems were reported and discussed at the 1962 board meeting. A few of the distributors had appeared to be doing business with a large proportion of weak dealers. The suggestion was made that a series of specifications for dealers be drawn up, agreed on, and enforced. Then if a dealer failed to abide by requirements for a full line, minimum stock, and nondiscount pricing, it could be replaced promptly with a stronger outlet. The company's counsel cautioned the board to go slow with this recommendation, pointing out that it presented many legal problems.

Exhibit 2
1962 Price List for All Lines

	List Price
Sprayer Division	
Basic quick-spray unit	$2100.00
Sprayer attachments and accessories	
Fender guards (set)	450.00
All-angle boom	625.00
Flexible arm	875.00
Other accessories P.O.R.	
Mo-Til Division	
Deluxe reel-type mowers	
18″ 2 hp, B&S engine, Easy Spin recoil	134.95
20″ 2 hp, B&S engine, Easy Spin recoil	144.95
20″ same as above with five blades	169.95
21″ 2.5 hp, B&S engine, Easy Spin recoil	189.95
25″ 3 hp, Tecumseh engine	399.95
Klip-EZ rotary mowers	
20″ 2.5 hp, B&S engine, hand propelled	89.95
22″ 3 hp, Tecumseh engine, hand propelled	119.95
22″ 3.5 hp, Tecumseh engine, self-propelled	149.95
Rotary tillers	
20″ 3 hp, nonreverse	129.95
24″ 3 hp, power reverse	144.95
24″ 4 hp, power reverse	159.95
Buckeye rider	
6 hp, Tecumseh engine, impulse starter	380.00
6 hp, Tecumseh engine, electric starter	450.00
Attachments and accessories	
24″ rotary mower	79.95
36″ rotary mower	79.95
34″ reel mower	129.95
26″ snow plow	49.95

Exhibit 3
Indicators of Demand for Mowers

	1950	1955	1957	1958	1959	1960	1961	1962
Mower Related Data								
New housing starts (millions)	—	—	873	975	1,095	1,009	989	994
Family personal income $/yr.	4,969	—	6,992	—	7,453	7,660	7,782	—
Power Lawn Mower Sales								
Sales (in thousands)	1,080	2,570	—	—	—	3,800	3,500	4,000
Value (in millions)	100	237	—	—	—	285	254	280
Commercial Mower Data								
Number of golf courses	4,931	5,218	—	—	—	6,385	—	7,895
Municipal park acreage	301,492	323,049	—	—	—	362,935	—	—

Exhibit 4

Indicators of Demand for Sprayers

	1959	1960	1961	1962	1963	1964[a]	1965[a]	1966[a]
Farm equipment expenditures (in millions)	1,376	1,483	1,480	1,475	—	—	—	—
Price index—farm items	101	101	101	103	—	—	—	—
Adjusted farm equip. exp. (in millions)	1,361	1,470	1,465	1,430	—	—	—	—
Farm acreage, 1 million acres	1,183	1,177	1,170	1,161	1,153	1,150	1,140	1,135
Corn acreage, 1000 acres	72,091	71,649	58,499	56,609	60,549	57,290	55,330	59,930
Cotton acreage, 1000 acres	15,090	15,309	15,634	15,569	14,210	14,060	13,610	9,550
Tobacco acreage, 1000 acres	1,152	1,142	1,174	1,225	1,176	1,080	980	970
Acreage treated by aircraft, 1000 acres	50,891	51,987	54,978	64,828	—	—	—	—

[a] Projected figures.

Source. U.S. Bureau of the Census, *Statistical Abstract of the United States* (Washington, D.C., Vols. 1962-1963).

Exhibit 5

Usage of Preemergent and Postemergent Space

1000's of Acres	Preemergent			Postemergent		
Treated	1959	1962	Percent Change	1959	1962	Percent Change
Corn	2235	6,382	186	17,816	18,920	6
Cotton	1001	3,365	236	553	2,068	274
All crops	4038	15,402	282	48,885	55,265	1
Percent harvested acres treated						
Corn	2.7	9.8	263	21.8	24.0	33
Cotton	6.6	21.6	228	3.7	13.3	254
All crops	40.3	41.1	2	43.7	44.3	1

Source. Agricultural Research Survey, U.S. Department of Agriculture, ARS 34-23-1 August 1965, "A Survey of Extent and Cost of Weed Control and Specific Weed Problems."

Exhibit 6

Production of Farm Sprayers and Dusters

Year	Number Produced	Value ($000's)
1958	88,057	38,500
1959	96,536	42,000
1960	73,657	41,000
1961	52,455	37,000
1962	60,094	41,000
1963	70,344	43,000
1964[a]	73,000	43,000
1965[a]	72,000	47,000
1966[a]	71,000	52,000
1967[a]	66,000	53,000

[a] Projected figures.

One of the local members of the board called attention to the fact that local discount houses were selling a great many power mowers, and even one of the local food chains was displaying a full line of mowers in its supermarket. In both cases there was heavy emphasis on price. He was wondering how widespread this practice might become, and what it would mean for the present distributor-dealer organization.

PRICING

In the early days, Lloyd Hahn set prices by adding a premium to the Sears catalogue price. The initial price was then tested in selected markets and adjustments made until a final list price was selected. In 1962 the company approached the pricing problem in the following manner:

1. First, a sales forecast was made of the quantity that would be sold in a given period.
2. The direct costs of material and labor were added to an estimate of indirect factors costs per unit. Then a share of administrative expense, production engineering expense, and selling expense were added to give the standard total cost. A "reasonable" profit for the company was added to give a first approximation of the company's price.
3. This price was tested by adding the normal markup of the distributor and the dealer to give a suggested retail price.
4. The retail price was then compared against the prices of competitors (Exhibits 7).

The price was considered acceptable if it was not more than $10 higher than competition. If the price was higher, the entire situation was examined to decide whether or not the product should be sold, or whether the design could be modified to reduce the cost. The company was reluctant to have a suggested retail price that narrowed the margin of the dealers and distributors. They believed success in selling the product rested with the willingness of the dealers to carry the complete line and their confidence in the quality of the product. Lloyd Hahn said, "If the dealer will carry it and believe in it, he can sell it when a customer comes in. A little difference in price is not going to stop sales."

Many dealers and distributors were chronically short of working capital and they attempted to place orders and accept deliveries immediately prior to their seasonal needs. This placed strong seasonal demands on Hahn's working capital, factory operations, and made it difficult to operate at full capacity

the year around. The company followed a strategy of early order discounts and preseason discounts that were intended to help spread factory orders and cash flow throughout the year (Exhibits 8 and 9). Distributors were not compelled to grant the discounts suggested by Hahn, but customarily did so.

PROMOTION AND ADVERTISING

Hahn engaged in some consumer advertising, but its major promotional thrust was targeted at its distributors and dealers.

Sprayer Advertising.

The sprayer program was divided into national consumer advertising and local cooperative advertising. An attempt was made to select media that reached the major corn growers and cotton producers in the Corn Belt and the South. The *Farm Journal* was used, for example, to reach the vast corngrowing regions of the Midwest. Space in the *Prairie Farmer* was intended to strengthen the coverage in the important Indiana-Illinois market. Added coverage in other areas of the Corn Belt was achieved through cooperative advertising programs with distributors. The farm market in the cotton states was reached through *Farm & Ranch, Delta Farm Press,* and *Farmer Stockman.* These media reached over a million cotton and tobacco farmers in twenty southern states. A cooperative advertising plan that offered dealers up to 2 percent of total Hahn purchases was made available to dealers. This advertising was coordinated with the advertising in the national, regional, and state farm papers.

Mower and Tiller Advertising.

The market for mowers and tillers included the homeowner, the farmer with sizable tilling needs, and the owners of commercial properties that have acreage in lawn space. National consumer advertising was used to reach part of this market. During March, April, and May, a series of two-color advertisements of tillers, reel-type and rotary mowers, and Buckeye riding mowers would appear in issues of *Flower Grower, Flower and Garden,* and *Popular Gardening.* This program would make twenty million advertising impressions. An additional two million lawn and garden enthusiasts would be reached through advertising in *House Beautiful* and *House and Garden.*

Hahn also had an active program of trade advertising. Dealers were a vital link in the distribution channel and it was imperative that they think well of

Exhibit 7

Selected Price Comparisons

Model	Sears Price[a]	Hahn Price[b]
20″ 3 hp, deluxe rotary-type mower— hand powered	$ 86.88	$ 89.95
22″ 3.5 hp, deluxe rotary type mower— hand powered	143.50	149.95
22″ 3 hp, rotary tiller—no power reverse	114.95	129.95
26″ 4 hp, rotary tiller—with power reverse	159.95	159.95
6 hp, deluxe tractor—recoil starter	385.00	380.00

[a] From Sears and Roebuck *General Catalogue* for 1963 (published in 1962).
[b] From Hahn, Inc. Price Sheet for 1962-1963.

Exhibit 8

Sales Program to Distributor

Trade discount
    Units and accessories: 40%
Early order discounts
    Order received prior to or on November 1:   5%
    Order received prior to or on December 1:   4%
    Order received prior to or on January 1:   3%
    Delivery must be taken prior to February 15 to receive the benefit of the early order discount.
    All orders must be firm and noncancellable and cannot be changed in quantity to receive the benefit
    of any of the early order discounts.
Preseason cash discount
    If paid by October 10:   6.5%
    If paid by November 10:   5.5%
    If paid by December 10:   4.5%
    If paid by January 10:   4.0%
    If paid by February 10:   3.5%
    If paid by March 10:   3.0%
    If paid by April 10:   2.5%
    If paid by May 10:   2.0%
    Orders placed after January 1 will receive regular 2%, 10, net 30 terms. All past-due invoices will be
    charged 1% per month carrying charge.

Exhibit 9
Distributor-to-Dealer Sales Program

Discounts

1 to 5 units:	25% and 5% early order
6 to 11 units:	25% and 6% early order
12 to 24 units:	25% and 7% early order
25 to 49 units:	25% and 8% early order
Over 50 units:	25% and 10% early order

General terms of sale
   Dealer must place order prior to November 1 for quantity early order discount.
   Delivery must be taken prior to March 1.
   Quantities apply to units only.
Preseason cash discount

Invoice paid by November 1:	6.5%
Invoice paid by December 1:	5.5%
Invoice paid by January 1:	4.5%
Invoice paid by February 1:	3.5%
Invoice paid by March 1:	3.0%

   Recorders receive regular 2% 10-day, net 30 terms and all past-due invoices will be charged 1% per month carrying charges.
Service parts discount
   25% nonstocking dealer
   40% authorized service station

---

the Hahn line. Thus, in 1962 plans called for 53 insertions in the following trade publications:

Modern Garden Center	Lawn Equipment Journal
Home and Garden Supply Merchandiser	Hardware Age
Flower Garden Merchandiser	Hardware Retailer
Lawn and Garden Dealer Guide Directory	Southern Hardware

The ads ran in these media during the period from January to early spring and again from September through November. A cooperative advertising plan that provided for expenditures up to 3 percent of dealer purchases was also available.

Sprayer promotion included three-color metal road signs that were made available to dealers at nominal cost. Brochures and catalogues were also used to describe applicators and accessories. Direct-mail handouts could be obtained by sprayer distributors for use at meetings, shows, fairs, and other similar gatherings.

Mower and tiller dealers received a catalogue of Buckeye products and a complete sales-promotion kit. Three types of signs could be obtained. They were designed for display at the point of sale over counters and cash registers, in windows, on the walls of retail stores, and on store fronts.

Advertising and Promotion Expenditures.

Because close relationships with distributors and dealers were considered of paramount importance, the company placed a high priority on sales-promotion efforts. To some extent, the amount for advertising and promotion was a residual; it was set on the basis of "how much was left to spend in a total budget that must keep costs down to where prices can be competitive." The 1962 breakdown for advertising and sales promotion in percent for the two divisions was:

	Sales Promotion	Advertising	
Sprayer Division	10	15	
Mo-Til Division	25	50	
Total	35	65	100

The 1962 promotion and advertising budget amounted to 4.5 percent of anticipated net sales. An advertising agency assisted the company in deciding how the advertising budget was to be spent. The agency also performed what little research was done on circulation and cost of different media.

A sales force of sixteen men called on distributors in 1962. The sales force was divided into two broad groups with five in the sprayer division and eleven in the mower division. Each salesman was assigned a territory and a quota. Compensation was on a commission basis. Total selling expense (advertising, sales promotion, and personal selling) amounted to nearly 10 percent of sales in 1962.

THE FUTURE

The tremendous growth and expansion of the period preceding 1962 had enveloped Hahn in a wave of optimism. Sales had increased sevenfold, a division had been added, another product line had been introduced, and a new plant had been purchased.

At the end of 1962, Lloyd Hahn appeared confident about the six years ahead. The sprayer had finally been designed to the point where he felt it was the best on the market. The development of preemergence chemicals did not bother him since he felt that the Quick-Spray could be used for low clearance application with ease—thus serving two purposes.

With regard to mowers, a housing boom was projected. The Hahn high-quality line would allow

the young homeowner to "move up" to the Klip-EZ or perhaps even a riding mower. Tillers and snow blowers were also projected for growth and with the new plant, Mr. Hahn felt that his company would be able to grow with the increased demand.

QUESTIONS

1. Is the product development program at Hahn well organized and producing the type of new items needed for growth?
2. Will the forecasting variables considered by Hahn (Exhibits 3, 4, 5, 6) and the methods employed by the company lead to accurate sales forecasts?
3. Should Hahn sell its Mo-Til products under private labels to large retailers and discount stores?
4. Are the pricing procedures and discounts described in Exhibits 2, 7, 8, and 9 a reasonable approach for Hahn Incorporated?
5. Evaluate the budget and media allocations used for advertising and promotion.
6. What changes in the marketing programs of Hahn, Inc. are suggested by the financial data presented in Exhibit 10?

Exhibit 10
Departmental Statement of Operating Profit Before Administrative Expenses, Year Ended September 30, 1962

	Mo-Til Division	Sprayer Division	Total
Sales	$5,579,760	$2,339,259	$7,919,017
Less: sales discounts	138,934	142,003	280,936
Net sales	$5,440,845	$2,197,256	$7,638,081
Cost of goods sold			
Beginning inventory	1,431,915	302,226	1,734,141
Materials and freight	4,716,274	1,243,114	5,959,388
Direct labor	257,301	138,258	395,559
Manufacturing expenses	604,906	246,181	851,087
Research and development costs	97,375	39,373	136,748
Less: ending inventory	2,453,065	429,745	2,882,810
	$4,654,706	$1,539,407	$6,194,113
Gross Profit on Sales	786,120	657,849	1,443,969
Marketing Expenses[a]	509,611	260,142	769,753
Operating profit before administrative expenses	$ 276,509	$ 397,707	$ 674,216

[a] For a detailed accounting of marketing expenditures, see Schedule A.

Schedule A
Statement of Marketing Expenses

Item	Mo-Til Division	Sprayer Division	Parts and Service[a]	Total
Salaries and wages	$95,046,66	$78,304.10	$65,789.42	$239,140.18
Commissions and subcontract labor	75,171.60	9,033.01	4,149.75	88,354.36
Advertising	103,537.39	53,584.20	—	157,121.59
Auto and truck expense	24,966.44	20,069.70	143.71	45,179.85
Collection expense	274.88	415.09	2.00	691.97
Depreciation	—	—	189.33	189.33
Dues and subscriptions	673.50	763.71	—	1,437.21
Employees' group insurance	—	—	—	—
Employees' welfare	77.74	—	25.00	102.74
Freight, express, and postage	5,157.14	1,286,04	341.92	6,785.10
Insurance	5,269,78	3,043.62	1,362.30	9,675.70
Professional fees	—	—	—	—
Rearrangement expense	—	—	53.00	53.00
Rent, storage, and leases	28.74	—	8,238.32	8,267.06
Repairs and maintenance	—	—	210.48	210.48
Sales promotion	59,059.99	23,512.30	—	82,572.29
Scrap and rework	230.26	515.23	97.43	842.92
Shipping supplies	—	—	942.42	942.42
Small tools	—	—	122.89	122.89
Supplies	7,366.12	3,966.76	6,170.02	17,502.90
Taxes—Indiana gross income	1,588.92	2,244.05	435.42	4,268.39
Taxes—payroll	4,138.49	2,829,56	3,249.73	10,217.78
Taxes—local property	—	—	1,120.00	1,120.00
Telephone and telegraph	7,583.77	7,298,35	364.50	15,246.62
Travel	41,715.44	33,844.45	2,902.07	78,461.96
Utilities	—	—	1,200.00	1,200.00
Warranty expenses	—	—	46.62	46.62
	$431,886.86	$240,710.17	$97,156.33	$769,753.36

[a] Before allocation to divisions.

Case 12-3
Hahn, Inc. (B)[1]

Optimistic projections made for Hahn, Inc. for the 1963-1968 period did not hold true. Although Hahn achieved its five-year forecast of sales in less than three years, profits fell below expectations. Demand for sprayers declined and Hahn was unable to develop a suitable alternative for that line. The most important events that occurred during this period are shown in Exhibit 1.

[1] Case prepared by Robert L. Taylor of the United States Air Force Academy and James Utterback of Harvard University. Data made available through the courtesy of Hahn, Inc. Reproduced by permission.

MO-TIL DIVISION

In 1966, Mo-Til sales began to advance rapidly. Market coverage was expanded and the home and garden centers were serviced by Hahn salesmen as well as independent distributors.

Lloyd and Helen Hahn sensed that one of the trends in mowers was the "steel deck" line, some of which retailed for less than $50. Mr. Hahn did not feel the investment in automated equipment needed for such a product would be worthwhile, particularly when the margin for such a mower would be less than 1 percent. Further, he did not want to tarnish the quality image that Hahn now enjoyed. No serious consideration was given to a proposal that a private brand mower be developed.

Distributors began to clamor for a garden tractor. Although Hahn had a tractor, it was more for institutional use and not adaptable for residential purposes. Both dealers and distributors wanted to compete with the Wheelhorse and Cub Cadet while offering a complete home-and-garden line of power equipment. Hahn introduced a garden tractor, but by 1968 it had made little impact in the marketplace. Sales of tillers and snow blowers were steadily increasing yet they still accounted for only a minor portion of the Mo-Til Division Sales.

SPRAYER DIVISION

After a sales peak in 1966, sprayer sales began to decline. This decline coincided with the increased use of preemergence chemical fertilizers. These materials, used primarily on small weeds and grasses, were sprayed on the ground before the crop "emerged" through the ground. Many farmers were reluctant to buy a Quick-Spray unit at a cost of $3600 when a fifty-gallon drum mounted behind a tractor could be used to dispense preemergent chemicals. To compound the problem, the acreage planted in cotton sharply declined during the 1967-1968 period.

To counter the sprayer situation, Lloyd Hahn developed a new four-wheel drive sprayer with a greater than three-crop flexibility. Fifty machines were sold, but the new model proved to be a mechanical failure. All of the units were repurchased and the project was written off after nearly $200,000 had been lost. At the same time, Hahn consigned a number of Quick-Spray units to a large farm implement company to be sold under their brand name. However, very few units were sold and the arrangement was quickly terminated.

In 1965, Hahn bought a small Midwest fertilizer equipment firm to get in on the liquid fertilizer boom. After three years of operation and a deterioration price structure in the fertilizer industry, the company had lost nearly $400,000 on this venture.

FINANCE

Hahn was unable to confine short-term capital needs to the local banks and over half of the capital needs had to be met from the Commercial Credit Corporation where Hahn paid 12 percent, or 5 percent more than the bank rate. The debt-to-equity ratios of Hahn and it's competitors are shown in Exhibit 3. Hahn Inc. experienced its best year in 1966 with profits of $350,000 on sales of $10 million. Nevertheless, Lloyd Hahn was perplexed by the low profits and felt that more capital would be needed to sustain the firm's growth. He saw three possible alternatives: he could slow the growth of the company and consolidate the substantial gains already made; he could raise funds privately to continue the present rate of growth; or, he could seek to merge with another firm that had funds available. The venture capital firm that had made an investment in Hahn recommended that Hahn consider a merger because of the high cost of borrowed funds.

MARKETING

Marketing activities remained much the same for the Sprayer Division while the Mo-Til Division continued to expand. Mower sales were very strong in the Northeast as well as in Pennsylvania, Ohio, Indiana, and Illinois, but weak in the South and Southwest. Mr. Hahn believed this to be the result of competition from cheaper models.

Since Mr. Hahn felt that sprayers had a greater potential for profit, research and engineering were concentrated on the sprayer line after the development of Klip-EZ. Hahn did not want the Sprayer Division to fall by the wayside because it had given the company its start. Looking back, Mr. Hahn felt that more money should have been spent developing a replacement for the Quick-Spray and in extending the mower line.

THE FUTURE

Late in 1968 Hahn was approached by a small conglomerate who offered to buy the company and continue operations by providing engineering assistance and a strong capital base. Lloyd Hahn was concerned about his company's cash position and perplexed by the recent downturn in profits. The book value of Hahn stock was $140 per share and Lloyd Hahn felt the offer of nearly 50 percent more than book value was favorable. He would be retained as the manager of the Hahn Division and would have complete responsibility for its operations.

Lloyd Hahn felt the offer might represent a chance for the expansion in profits that he had been striving

Exhibit 1
Key Decisions and Events for Hahn, Inc., 1948-1968

(The asterisk denotes an environmental factor or event affecting Hahn operations.)

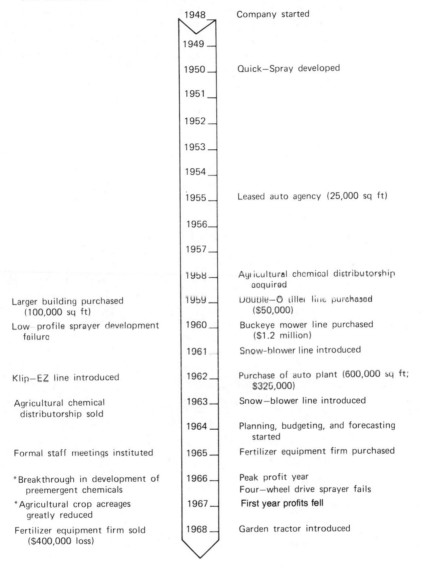

1948	Company started
1949	
1950	Quick—Spray developed
1951	
1952	
1953	
1954	
1955	Leased auto agency (25,000 sq ft)
1956	
1957	
1958	Agricultural chemical distributorship acquired
Larger building purchased (100,000 sq ft) — 1959	Double—O tiller line purchased ($50,000)
Low—profile sprayer development failure — 1960	Buckeye mower line purchased ($1.2 million)
1961	Snow-blower line introduced
Klip—EZ line introduced — 1962	Purchase of auto plant (600,000 sq ft; $325,000)
Agricultural chemical distributorship sold — 1963	Snow—blower line introduced
1964	Planning, budgeting, and forecasting started
Formal staff meetings instituted — 1965	Fertilizer equipment firm purchased
*Breakthrough in development of preemergent chemicals — 1966	Peak profit year / Four—wheel drive sprayer fails
*Agricultural crop acreages greatly reduced — 1967	First year profits fell
Fertilizer equipment firm sold ($400,000 loss) — 1968	Garden tractor introduced

for. On the other hand, he had never worked for anyone else in his life. He felt a merger might snuff out the pioneering spirit that had brought the company to its present position. Lloyd Hahn pondered the offer and promised a decision before the end of the year.

COMPUTER SIMULATION

The marketing practices of a young, growing company have been highlighted and the financial results have been reported. The reader is now given the opportunity to analyze some of the critical decisions made by Lloyd Hahn during the period 1963-1968 using a business simulation. Much can be learned by attempting alternative strategies in a computer simulation that closely approximates the environment in which Hahn, Inc. operated. There is no "correct" solution, but there are strategies that will result in a much different profit and financial picture for the company. Thus, the reasons for a particular strategy will be as important as the strategy itself.

Examples of the planning and forecasting tools necessary in decision-making were presented in the earlier Hahn, Inc. discussion. Hahn, Inc. is a real company, and additional data may be drawn from library sources to test alternative decisions against the same environment faced by Mr. Hahn. The thoroughness and accuracy of any supplemental information will be reflected in the simulation results.

Exhibit 2

Statement of Financial Condition on September 30, 1968

ASSETS	
Current assets	
Cash on hand and on deposit—includes, advances, prepaid expenses, and cash value of life insurance	$ 566,724
Accounts receivable less provision for uncollectable accounts and includes contracts receivable and notes receivable	2,466,616
Inventories	5,450,732
Fixed assets net of depreciation	
Land	
Leasehold improvement	
Marketing and equipment	
Office equipment	
Automotive equipment	1,700,432
Total assets	$10,184,504
LIABILITIES AND STOCKHOLDER'S EQUITY	
Current liabilities	
Notes payable—secured and unsecured and includes contracts payable	4,117,518
Accounts payable includes accruals of payroll, interest, rent, and taxes	1,349,832
Long-term liabilities	2,113,016
Stockholder's equity	
Stock	1,056,650
Retained earnings	1,547,488
Total	$10,184,504

Exhibit 2

Departmental Statement of Operating Profit, Year Ended September 30, 1968

	Mo-Til Division	Sprayer Division	Total
Sales	$13,065,150	$4,110,717	$17,175,867
Less: sales discounts	360,049	131,860	491,909
Net sales	$12,705,101	$3,978,857	$16,683,958
Cost of goods sold			
Beginning inventory	4,306,102	1,874,384	6,180,486
Materials and freight	7,481,891	2,098,807	9,580,698
Direct labor	637,567	284,737	922,304
Manufacturing expenses	1,568,765	787,682	2,356,447
Research and development	202,705	236,512	439,217
Less: ending inventory	3,491,542	1,959,190	5,450,732
	$10,705,488	$3,322,932	$14,028,420
Gross profit on sales	1,999,613	655,925	2,655,538
Marketing expenditures	880,479	527,090	1,407,569
Operating profit before administrative expenses	1,119,134	128,835	1,247,969

Consolidated Statements of Operating Profit

	1963	1964	1965	1966	1967
Sales	$8,165,030	$7,348,810	$8,868,023	$10,690,581	$13,185,352
Less: sales discount	313,721	323,606	356,232	442,580	389,465
Net sales	$7,851,309	$7,025,204	$8,511,791	$10,248,001	$12,795,887
Cost of goods sold					
Beginning inventory	2,882,811	3,356,989	2,691,706	3,044,371	4,185,929
Materials and freight	5,134,724	3,543,056	5,279,063	6,855,918	9,172,694
Direct labor	390,921	302,868	415,384	523,838	828,840
Manufacturing expenses	951,359	877,338	1,045,427	1,293,937	1,868,614
Research and development	188,554	174,940	174,959	256,807	333,659
Less: ending inventory	3,356,989	2,691,705	3,044,371	4,185,929	6,180,486
	$6,191,382	$5,563,486	$6,562,168	$7,788,942	$10,209,250
Gross profit on sales	1,659,927	1,461,718	1,949,623	2,459,059	2,586,637
Marketing expenditures	873,322	783,519	958,765	1,162,384	1,358,935
Operating profit before administrative expenses	786,605	678,199	990,858	1,296,675	1,277,702

Exhibit 3

Debt-to-Equity Ratios for Hahn and Several Competitors

Company	1963	1964	1965	1966	1967	1968
Hahn	4.39	2.36	2.86	2.98	4.00	2.90
Southern	2.04	1.33	.77	.58	.39	.38
Jacobsen	—	—	—	.84	1.04	—
Toro	—	—	—	.41	.36	.33

Author Index

Subject Index

Case Index